PRAISE FOR *APPLIED CONSUMER PSYCHOLOGY*

"Harvey's **Applied Consumer Psychology** is a must-read for anyone looking to understand how psychology shapes the way we buy, choose and behave. Packed with engaging real-world examples, it breaks down the key concepts of consumer psychology in a way that's both clear and relatable. Beyond its six foundational chapters, ten insightful applied chapters equip the reader with the tools needed to make informed, evidence-based decisions in real consumer contexts. This book is an invaluable guide for anyone seeking practical advice on consumer psychology challenges."
Prof Dr Rainer Greifeneder, Professor of Social Psychology, University of Basel, Switzerland

"Discover why certain ads stick, why BOGO deals are irresistible and why some stores make you buy everything. This book reveals the hidden psychology behind successful marketing and how to ethically influence consumer choices through better branding, pricing and customer experiences."
Prof Dr Michael Schulte-Mecklenbeck, Professor of Research Methods and Decision Science, University of Bern, Switzerland

"**Applied Consumer Psychology** masterfully bridges the gap between rigorous psychological science and practical marketing application. Harvey has created an exceptionally comprehensive yet accessible guide that spans everything from fundamental attention and perception principles to cutting-edge insights on digital behaviour and pricing psychology. What sets this book apart is its rare combination of scientific depth and readability, making complex psychological concepts immediately clear, compelling and actionable for marketers. This is an indispensable resource for anyone seeking to understand the psychological drivers behind consumer behaviour and translate that knowledge into effective marketing strategies."
Prof Matt Johnson, Professor of Consumer Psychology, Hult International Business School

"Harvey has developed an impressive platform bridging the art and science of consumer psychology. This is a one-stop theoretical and practical take on the inner psyche of consumers and how and why they behave the way they do."
Dr Mansur Khamitov, Professor of Marketing, Kelley School of Business, Indiana University, USA

"**Applied Consumer Psychology** is a must-read for anyone serious about marketing. Harvey masterfully blends clear, accessible explanations of psychological principles with compelling real-world examples and practical applications. Whether you're a student, professional or simply curious about what drives consumer behaviour, this book delivers insights that are both engaging and actionable."
Prof Joe Devlin, Professor of Cognitive Neuroscience and Vice Dean for Innovation and Enterprise, University College London, UK

"A must-read for students who want to see how consumer psychology can be applied directly to real marketing problems. Unlike many textbooks that remain abstract or get lost in theory, this book takes a problem-first approach, offering clear and practical insights. Its accessible structure and interactive experiments make complex ideas easy to grasp, while still being rooted in the latest research. It is exactly the kind of applied, student-friendly guide needed for modern teaching and learning."
Dr Jan Breitsohl, Senior Lecturer in Marketing, University of Glasgow, UK

"In an age where data-driven insights are everywhere, **Applied Consumer Psychology** reminds us of the human mind at the heart of consumption. It's an invaluable guide for students, researchers and executives who want to turn psychological knowledge into competitive advantage."
Prof Bart F. Norré, Associate Professor of Neuromarketing, School of Management Fribourg, University of Applied Sciences and Arts of Western Switzerland

"Plenty of people including me have written books on this subject. What Harvey has now produced is the encyclopaedia!"
Rorry Sutherland, Vice Chairman of Ogilvy UK and author of *Alchemy*

"Harvey has created the definitive bridge between psychological science and marketing practice. This is the comprehensive playbook every marketer needs to understand not just what works, but why it works. It's a great book that should be on any serious marketer's shelf."
Roger Dooley, author of *Brainfluence* and *Friction*

"Most of what drives our choices happens below the surface. Harvey unpacks a wide range of hidden cues and biases that shape buying decisions – and shows, with practical examples, how brands can put them to work effectively."
Richard Shotton, author of *The Choice Factory* and *The Illusion of Choice*

"Fabulous! Well-written, well-researched and well-resourced, this should have a permanent place on every marketer's bookshelf."
Phil Barden, author of *Decoded: The Science Behind Why We Buy*

"This book should be required reading for every marketer. It's the reference guide I wish I had when I started out a decade ago, packed with behavioural science that explains what makes great marketing. It's the one playbook you'll always keep within arm's reach."
Phill Agnew, podcast host of *Nudge*

"**Applied Consumer Psychology** distils decades of behavioural science into practical, evidence-based insights that marketers can apply immediately. Harvey's engaging writing, real-world examples and clear frameworks make this essential reading for anyone who wants to understand and influence how consumers think and act. Entertaining, informative and immediately useful – once you start exploring how real science transforms marketing, you won't want to put this book down."
MichaelAaron Flicker, 9× CEO and Founder of XenoPsi Ventures, and co-author of *Hacking the Human Mind*

Applied Consumer Psychology

How to use psychological insights in marketing

Gareth J Harvey

Publisher's note
Every possible effort has been made to ensure that the information contained in this book is accurate at the time of going to press, and the publishers and author cannot accept responsibility for any errors or omissions, however caused. No responsibility for loss or damage occasioned to any person acting, or refraining from action, as a result of the material in this publication can be accepted by the editor, the publisher or the author.

First published in Great Britain and the United States in 2025 by Kogan Page Limited

All rights reserved. No part of this publication may be reproduced, stored in a retrieval system or transmitted in any form or by any means - including electronic, mechanical, photocopying, recording or by any artificial intelligence (AI) or machine learning system - without the prior written permission of the publisher. Unauthorized use, including the use of text or images to train AI models, is strictly prohibited and may result in legal action.

Kogan Page
Kogan Page Ltd, 2nd Floor, 45 Gee Street, London EC1V 3RS, United Kingdom
Kogan Page Inc, 8 W 38th Street, Suite 902, New York, NY 10018, USA
www.koganpage.com

EU Representative (GPSR)
Authorised Rep Compliance Ltd, Ground Floor, 71 Baggot Street Lower, Dublin D02 P593, Ireland
www.arccompliance.com

Kogan Page books are printed on paper from sustainable forests.

© Gareth J Harvey, 2025

The moral rights of the author have been asserted in accordance with the Copyright, Designs and Patents Act 1988.

ISBNs
Hardback   978 1 3986 2083 4
Paperback   978 1 3986 2079 7
Ebook   978 1 3986 2082 7

British Library Cataloguing-in-Publication Data
A CIP record for this book is available from the British Library.

Library of Congress Control Number
2025044551

Typeset by Integra Software Services, Pondicherry
Print production managed by Jellyfish
Printed and bound by CPI Group (UK) Ltd, Croydon CR0 4YY

To paraphrase a famous advert, you never forget a good teacher

Mum and Dad,

*James Intriligator, Brian Jones,
Mr (Darren) Gelder & Mr (Dave) Harbertson*

For Eileen Jones

CONTENTS

List of figures and tables xv
About the author xvii
Walkthrough of textbook features and online resources xviii

PART ONE Consumer psychology: Theoretical essentials

1 **An introduction to consumer psychology** 3
What is this consumer psychology thing? 3
So, what does a consumer psychologist study? 5
How will this book work? 6
References 7

2 **Attention and perception** 8
What is attention? 8
Advertising and attention 11
Subliminal advertising 13
Perception 14
Forming perceptions: Little clues that matter 15
Expectations and advertising 20
Closing thoughts 22
References 24

3 **The psychology of motivation** 29
What is motivation? 29
Maslow's Hierarchy of Needs 30
Self-Determination Theory 32
Implementation intentions 36
When to motivate 37
The Cobra Effect: When marketing interventions backfire 38
Motivation and sustainable behaviour change 40
Closing thoughts 42
Suggestions for further reading 44
References 44

4 The psychology of personality 49
Personality: A new approach to segmentation 49
Freudian marketing 50
Measuring personality: Myers-Briggs 52
Personality and the Big 5 53
Using personality in marketing 55
Putting personality-based messaging into action 56
Personality and retail behaviour 57
Why isn't personality used more in marketing? 58
Personality and conspicuous consumption 60
Closing thoughts 61
Suggestions for further reading 63
References 63

5 The role of learning and memory in marketing 68
Introduction 68
Learning 69
Cognitive learning 77
Memory 78
Closing thoughts 89
Suggestions for further reading 91
References 91

PART TWO Consumer psychology in action

6 The psychology of copywriting: Words that sell 101
Finding the right words 101
Abstract vs concrete language 103
Prospect theory: Gains, losses and risk 106
What marketers can learn from TV gameshows 108
Message framing and healthcare 108
Message framing: In practice 110
The power of a story 110
Making sense of numbers 112
How to apologize 115
Dealing with shoppers who haven't paid 117
Closing thoughts 119
Suggestions for further reading 120
References 120

7 The psychology of branding 124
What is a brand? 124
Building a brand: It's all about associations 126
Does a brand need to be unique? 127
Building brands 128
Sonic branding 134
Brand personality 135
Brand myths 138
Brand rituals 139
Branding and social norms 140
Measuring brand strength 142
Closing thoughts 145
Suggestions for further reading 147
References 147

8 The psychology of advertising 153
Introduction 153
Does advertising change behaviour? 154
Am I watching the programme or the adverts? 155
Advertising and branding 158
Reactance theory 168
The risk of advertising avoidance 170
Closing thoughts 171
Suggestions for further reading 172
References 173

9 The psychology of social media: Likes, shares and sales 180
Social media: Democratizing marketing? 180
The development of influencer marketing 181
Does social media work? 182
Building a following 182
Implementing influencer marketing strategies 185
Crafting a winning post 189
Getting your timing right 190
Being open: What happens when you label a post as an ad 191
Closing thoughts 192
Suggestions for further reading 193
References 193

10 The psychology of pricing 197

Introduction 197
Paying is painful 197
Framing: It's a question of how you look at it 198
Comparative pricing 201
Asymmetrical dominance (the decoy effect) 202
The compromise effect 203
Charm pricing: It's all in the nines 204
Expectation effects 206
Services and price 208
Precise pricing 209
Pricing: It's all a matter of timing 211
Anchoring 212
Closing thoughts 214
Suggestions for further reading 216
References 216

11 The psychology of price promotion and competitions 222

Introduction: How do shoppers react to special offers? 222
Price discounts 223
Free gifts 229
Loyalty schemes and discounts 230
Communicating value 232
Promotional limits: Is there too much of a good thing? 233
Paradox of choice and promotions 234
The long-term implications of promotions 235
Cracking the code: Why context matters 236
Ending deals 237
Competitions 239
Closing thoughts 241
References 243

12 Psychology in the aisles: Psychological influences in the shopping environment 249

Designing the perfect bricks-and-mortar store 249
Decompression zone: Getting you into the mood to buy 252
Is there too much of a good thing? 253
Store layout and shopping time 254
The contagion effect 255
Shelf help: Displaying products 256

Buying something new 258
Are all shoppers the same? 259
Impulse purchases 260
The importance of touch 262
The shopping trolley: The 'greatest salesman' around 263
Olfactory cues: The smell of success 265
The power of music 269
Let there be light 273
Closing thoughts 274
Suggestions for further reading 277
References 277

13 The psychology of online shopping 287
A new approach to retail 287
How do people read a webpage? 287
Navigating online shops 290
Recommendations, defaults and online shopping 292
Scarcity appeals 295
Recommendations, testimonials and reviews 297
How to take product photos that sell 299
The last step: Check-out 303
Closing thoughts 304
Suggestions for further reading 306
References 306

14 The psychology of packaging 312
Introduction 312
Visual salience and customer attention 312
Bringing products to life: The power of photography 319
Inferences: Decoding what isn't said 321
Secondary packaging 324
Closing thoughts 326
Suggestions for further reading 328
References 328

15 The science of persuasion 333
Introduction 333
The elaboration likelihood model 333
Rational persuasion 335
Negotiations 342

Experts in persuasion 346
Peripheral routes to persuasion 348
Closing thoughts 353
Suggestions for further reading 355
References 355

16 Market research: A psychological approach 362
Introduction 362
What makes a good research project? 362
Secondary data: Letting other people do the work for you 369
Primary research: Collecting your own data 371
Closing thoughts 392
Suggestions for further reading 394
References 394

Index 399

LIST OF FIGURES AND TABLES

Figures

Figure 5.1 A visual representation of Richard Atkinson and Richard Shiffrin's multi-store model of memory 79

Figure 5.2 An example of the Ebbinghaus forgetting curve showing how quickly people forget information over time if they don't actively try to retain this information 87

Figure 8.1 An example of the three different newspapers given to participants in Shapiro, MacInnis, & Heckler (1997) experiment. In each case participants were only asked to read Column B each time 156

Figure 10.1 An example of two price tags, the left-hand label makes the prices feel more expensive, whereas the label on the right makes the product feel cheaper 200

Figure 10.2 An example of a company using the decoy effect to make their more expensive product feel like a better purchase 203

Figure 10.3 An example of two labels. One is written in a clear and easy-to-read font, whereas the other is written in a more complex font. As shoppers' brains need to work harder to process this information, they perceive the product as more expensive 211

Figure 11.1 An example of two price discounts 225

Figure 11.2 An example of percentage discounts 225

Figure 15.1 A graphical representation of the Elaboration Likelihood Model as developed by Petty and Cacioppo (1986) 334

Figure 16.1 A recreation of the four different types of labels used in Pierre Dubois' 2021 study 367

Figure 16.2 Example stimuli used in Solomon Asch's 1956 social conformity experiment 373

Figure 16.3 Sampling error estimates for various sample sizes drawn from a population of 70,000,000, calculated using both a 95% and 99% confidence intervals 378

Tables

Table 4.1 The typical behaviours shown by people who score high or low on each personality trait 54

Table 4.2 An example of the types of advertising appeals that work best for different personality types, based on research by Hirsch et al 57

Table 5.1 The four different techniques that can be used to influence behaviour from an operant conditioning perspective 74

Table 6.1	A selection of English words of Anglo-Saxon origin paired alongside the equivalent English words of French origin 102
Table 6.2	Two different messages that can be used to encourage people to take a calcium supplement. One option uses a gain frame, whereas the other uses a loss frame 109
Table 7.1	Examples of renamed food products 127
Table 8.1	Two different approaches to promoting a razor. One using the central route to persuasion, whereas one uses the peripheral route to persuasion 157
Table 8.2	The stimuli used in Shotton, Treharne, & Burnett's 2020 study 164
Table 10.1	Results of the experiment 214
Table 12.1	Average spend per minute in a US supermarket, based on time spent in-store (adapted from data from Sorensen, 2009) 255
Table 16.1	Example of the different attributes that could be used in a conjoint analysis 381

ABOUT THE AUTHOR

Gareth J Harvey
Chartered Psychologist, Visiting Professor and Consumer Psychologist

Gareth Harvey is a chartered psychologist, whose career bridges the worlds of academia and industry. As a former professor of consumer psychology, he spent over a decade researching and leading programmes at universities in Genève, Paris, and North Wales. At Bangor University, he was the programme director for their MSc in Consumer Psychology and at Haute école de gestion de Genève he led the BSc in Marketing Science and Analytics. He later transitioned into the industry, working as Director of Consumer Psychology at Decide, the UK's longest established creative agency, shaping campaigns for household names including Proctor & Gamble, Dr Oetker and Cadbury. Today, he brings his expertise to Severn Trent, working in partnership with Nectar, the UK's largest loyalty programme.

WALKTHROUGH OF TEXTBOOK FEATURES AND ONLINE RESOURCES

Learning objectives

A bulleted list at the beginning of each chapter summarizes what you can expect to learn, to help you track your progress.

LEARNING OBJECTIVES

- Understand how concept of motivation has developed over time.
- Apply principles of motivational psychology to develop effective marketing campaigns.
- Analyse how businesses apply principles of gamification to create engaging products.

Real-world examples ('Psych in action')

A range of examples illustrate how key ideas and theories are operating in practice to help you place the concepts discussed in real-life context.

REAL-WORLD EXAMPLE: PSYCH IN ACTION

Strava is an online running app where runners can make a public declaration about how much they intend to run each week or month. Once someone has made a public commitment, they're more motivated to maintain the behaviour as they feel like they need to maintain a consistent and positive self-image. Each time you go for a run, your time, distance and heart rate is shared amongst followers, which again motivates users to run more. Friends can 'give kudos', virtual rewards, which again helps to motivate them to run more. Over time, runners tend to change their behaviour, mimicking the behaviour of the people who provide them with the most kudos.

Exercises

Questions and activities throughout the text encourage you to reflect on what you have learnt and to apply your knowledge and skills in practice.

> **GIVE IT A GO**
>
> Want to see how SDT applies to you? Complete the Intrinsic Motivation Inventory, which is one of the standard tools to measure intrinsic motivation and self-regulation and has been used in numerous laboratory experiments.
>
>

Key learning points

Key learning points at the end of each chapter summarize the main themes of the chapter and act as a useful revision tool.

> **KEY LEARNING POINTS**
>
> - Although Maslow's Hierarchy of Needs is one of the most commonly used models to discuss human motivation, most psychologists do not consider it a valid model due to its lack of empirical evidence.

- Currently the dominant model used by psychologists to measure human motivation is Self-Determination Theory. The three core components are autonomy, competence and relatedness.
- Intrinsic motivation (engaging in behaviour for its own enjoyment) is more powerful than extrinsic motivation (behaviour driven by external rewards like praise or money).
- Offering extrinsic rewards can undermine intrinsic motivation, leading to reduced long-term engagement in the target behaviour.

Putting theory into practice

In each chapter, reflective questions will encourage you to reflect critically on what you have read and reinforce what you have learnt.

PUTTING THEORY INTO PRACTICE

1. Imagine you are developing a new phone app to help people train their dog. How could you incorporate principles of both gamification and Self-Determination Theory (SDT) to encourage users to continue using the app?
2. If a government health initiative offered to financially reward unfit people for completing the 'couch to 5K' (a fitness plan where people aim to run 20–30 minutes, three times a week, and then after nine weeks they aim to complete a 5km run), from a Self-Determination Theory perspective, what are the potential risks when the scheme ends?
3. Consider the apps that you use most on your phone. What principles of motivational psychology do they use to encourage you to keep using these apps?

Further reading

The further reading sections provide additional key readings in the area to help you further develop your skills and understanding.

SUGGESTIONS FOR FURTHER READING

Reeve, J. (2024). Understanding motivation and emotion: 8th Edition. John Wiley & Sons.

References

Detailed references provide quick and easy access to the research and underpinning sources behind the chapter.

Online resources

This book includes online resources for lecturers and students comprising:

- lecturer PowerPoint slides
- multiple choice questions
- interactive experiments

These resources can be accessed through the Kogan Page website: www.koganpage.com/ACP

PART ONE
Consumer psychology: Theoretical essentials

1 | An introduction to consumer psychology

LEARNING OBJECTIVES

- Understand the differences between consumer psychology and neuromarketing.

What is this consumer psychology thing?

Twenty years ago, if you asked most marketers if they knew what consumer psychology was, they could probably guess what it meant, but were unlikely to know much about it. Today things are very different. After the prominent role that behavioural science played in influencing governments' responses to the Covid-19 pandemic, most marketers are now aware that small tweaks to a campaign can dramatically change its effectiveness. For example, when a charity asks for a *gift* rather than a *donation*, the average donation size is 29% more.[1] In a restaurant, guests tend to spend 10% more if the menu is listed in descending price order rather than ascending order, i.e. the most expensive items are listed first and the cheapest items last,[2] and online adverts have a higher click-through rate if the model is looking directly at the call to action.[3] By understanding the psychology that underpins human behaviour, marketers can optimize their work before launching, saving both time and money.

As a discipline, consumer psychology differs to most other areas of psychology which focus on a specific mental process (e.g. cognitive psychology, abnormal psychology etc.). Instead, consumer psychology is an applied domain that shamelessly borrows insights from all aspects of psychology and applies them to tackle marketing challenges. For example, to create an effective advertisement, a consumer psychologist might draw on insights from cognitive psychology to ensure your advert captures attention. To ensure your advert is memorable, they would review the literature exploring 'learning & memory'. But ultimately, an advert is (or should be) all about persuasion. And here again, consumer psychologists should be familiar with the research into decision-making. In each case, psychologists are able to improve a firm's marketing activity by understanding the psychological factors that drive consumer behaviour.

Is there a difference between consumer psychology and neuromarketing?

Unfortunately, there is still a lot of confusion as to what consumer psychology is, and terms such as neuromarketing, consumer neuroscience and consumer psychology are frequently used interchangeably. While they are closely related, they have different meanings. To appreciate the differences between neuromarketing and consumer psychology, we need to first appreciate the difference between neuroscience and psychology. At the simplest level, psychology is the study of the mind, whereas neuroscience is the study of the brain. While this appears to be semantics, when you dig a little deeper, the differences become important. Psychology is the study of human behaviour and all the mental and cognitive processes that lead to behaviour, meaning that psychologists study topics such as thoughts, feelings, desires and decision-making.[4]

In contrast, neuroscience focuses on the biological and chemical processes in our brain and nervous system. Neuroscientists are less interested in human behaviour and are more interested in understanding how the human brain works at a fundamental level. To answer these questions, they rely on tools such as electroencephalogram, functional magnetic resonance imaging, magnetoencephalography or transcranial magnetic stimulation.

Therefore, consumer psychology is the study of the cognitive and mental process involved when an individual or group selects, purchases, uses or disposes of a product, service, idea or experience,[5] and neuromarketing is the application of neuroscience methods to analyse and understand human behaviour related to markets and marketing exchanges.[6] While neuromarketing typically focuses on neural processes, this does not mean its insights aren't useful for practising marketers.

A good example of this in action is the study by Michael Koenigs and Daniel Tranel. They were able to show that patients who had damage to the ventromedial prefrontal cortex (a region of the brain critically involved in emotion, emotional regulation and decision-making) are immune to the Pepsi-paradox (the idea that most people prefer the taste of Pepsi in a blind taste test, but when they know which drink they're drinking, they claim to prefer Coca-Cola). This provides clear evidence of the role of emotions in developing a successful brand,[7] which should change how marketers go about creating their brands.

In order to try to avoid confusion, some academics and marketers have started to use the term 'behavioural science' instead of consumer psychology or neuromarketing. Rather than focusing on the differences between related disciplines, behavioural science is an all-encompassing term that brings all of the disciplines under one name. Technically, behavioural science is 'the systematic study of human behaviour and strategies to intentionally and verifiably change it, leveraging psychological insights and experimental methods from a variety of disciplines, including (but not limited to) behavioural economics, psychology, cognitive science, decision science, sociology and neuroscience'.[8]

Although behavioural science is a multidisciplinary term that includes consumer psychology, this book avoids using it. Behavioural science covers a wide range of disciplines from consumer psychology to public policy and even organizational behaviour. While some of the principles discussed in the book will be relevant to public policy and organizational psychology, most are not. Using the term behavioural science can lead to confusion. Instead, we'll use the term consumer psychology as it is a more relatable and practicable term for those working in marketing. A consumer psychologist will always be a behavioural scientist, but a behavioural scientist will not necessarily be a consumer psychologist.

So, what does a consumer psychologist study?

At first, this seems like a simple question: marketing and how shoppers choose what to buy. But if you reread the definition, you'll see that the field is much broader than that. Consumer psychologists are not just interested in influencing what products people purchase. They're also interested in how consumers use these products and what happens when they're no longer needed. This means that you can find consumer psychologists working in areas like healthcare, exploring how to improve patient adherence to medication, or even recycling, where they're trying to encourage consumers to dispose of a product in a specific way once they've finished with it (maybe recycling it or returning it to the manufacturer so it can be upcycled).

Similarly, it is not just physical products or services that consumer psychologists are interested in. They also work with clients who are interested in promoting specific ideas or even people. You will find consumer psychologists advising political parties on how to influence voting behaviour, helping barristers frame arguments to be more persuasive or even working across government departments, encouraging behaviour change (such as working towards the Net Zero target or encouraging people to exercise more).

That said, the majority of consumer psychologists still work in the more traditional realm of marketing. As a result, this book will primarily focus on the challenges faced in that context, although there will be a range of other examples to demonstrate the depth of work undertaken in this field.

How will this book work?

Book structure

This book is divided into two sections: 'Theoretical essentials' and 'Consumer psychology in action'. The first section aims to provide readers with a clear grounding in the key psychological principles that influence how consumers behave. The second half explores the specific practical problems marketers are confronted with every day; from packaging and advertising to store design and copywriting. If a marketer is faced with a specific problem, such as designing a new online shop, they can just focus on the specific chapters.

Online experiments

Consumer psychology depends on psychologists designing and running complex experiments to systematically investigate cause-and-effect relationships between different variables in a controlled way. While reading about an experiment is helpful, it is a lot easier to understand how the study works if you can experience it first-hand. Consequently, in each chapter, exercises allow you to take part in many of the experiments described in that chapter. These experiments are hosted using Gorilla Experimental Platform, and it is completely free to participate in each experiment as many times as you like. If you'd like to modify any experiment so that it can be customized to fit your needs, each experiment is free to download and completely customizable. There is a small fee for collecting participant data, unless your university or company already has a subscription.

> **PUTTING THEORY INTO PRACTICE**
>
> 1 Find five different research articles that provide marketers with tangible insights. Would these articles be best described as consumer psychology, neuromarketing or behavioural science?
>
> 2 Come up with your own definition for 'consumer psychology', 'neuromarketing' and 'behavioural science'.
>
> 3 Find five job adverts looking to recruit a 'behavioural scientist'. If you were asked to create an alternative job title for the role, what would you choose?

References

1. Wang, P. X., Wang, Y., & Jiang, Y. (2022). Gift or donation? Increase the effectiveness of charitable solicitation through framing charitable giving as a gift. *Journal of Marketing*, 87(1). https://doi.org/10.1177/00222429221081506 (archived at https://perma.cc/LG6K-7AFM)
2. Huff, S. C. (2021). Money on the table: Increasing revenue through menu order. *Journal of Digital & Social Media Marketing*, 9(3), 275–283.
3. Adil, S., Lacoste-Badie, S., & Droulers, O. (2018). Face presence and gaze direction in print advertisements: How they influence consumer responses—an eye-tracking study. *Journal of Advertising Research*, 58(4), 443–455.
4. Colman, A. M. (2001). *A dictionary of psychology*. Oxford University Press.
5. Solomon M. (2004). *Encyclopaedia of applied psychology: Volume 1*. Elsevier
6. Babiloni, F. (2012). Consumer neuroscience: A new area of study for biomedical engineers. *IEEE Pulse*, 3(3), 21–23. doi: https://doi.org/10.1109/MPUL.2012.2189166 (archived at https://perma.cc/Q2UC-83ZG)
7. Koenigs, M. & Tranel, D. (2008). Prefrontal cortex damage abolishes brand-cued changes in cola preference. *Social Cognitive and Affective Neuroscience*, 3(1), 1–6, https://doi.org/10.1093/scan/nsm032 (archived at https://perma.cc/4VCD-LQHA)
8. The global association of applied behavioural scientists (2020) Constitution for the global association of applied behavioural scientists. https://gaabs.org (archived at https://perma.cc/9GDH-63KZ)

2 | Attention and perception

LEARNING OBJECTIVES

- Understand the difference between top-down and bottom-up attention.
- Critique the different techniques that brands can use to capture shoppers' attention.
- Analyse how brands can use multi-sensory cues to shape consumers' perception of their products.

What is attention?

Marketers face a constant challenge trying to capture customers' attention, whether it is crafting an advert so that it stands out from the clutter, designing packaging so that it can capture shoppers' attention or crafting copy that people notice on your webpage. And this is not just a theoretical problem. Research indicates that only 16% of advertising is noticed, recalled and, most importantly, correctly attributed to the right brand.[1]

This has become such a challenge that some scholars now argue that we are living in the attention economy. Human attention is a scarce commodity as we only have so much of it. While this may sound like the latest buzzword, neuroscience does provide limited support for it. It is estimated that we are exposed to roughly 11 million bits of information every second, however, our brain is only capable of processing about 50 bits of information a second. And if we are forced to engage our cognitive process, such as trying to remember a shopping list, our performance deteriorates to just 5–9 bits of information.[2] But there are some caveats. Firstly, the human brain is not a computer, and we can't make direct comparisons to memory. Secondly, these numbers are just estimates and not based on experimental data.

Top-down attention

So, what is attention? It's the psychological process where we decide which stimuli to focus on (at the expense of other stimuli), so that it becomes clear and vivid in our mind.[3] While this may sound like a simple process, the psychology behind it is complex. To explain how attention works, psychologists typically break attention down into (at least) two different categories: bottom-up or exogenous attention, and top-down or endogenous attention. Top-down attention is what occurs when people deliberately choose to focus on a particular stimulus. For example, when you decide to sit down and watch the television, you are paying top-down attention to the television. This behaviour is characterized by three elements. It is *controlled*, meaning that it does not happen automatically but was a conscious decision, *slow*, as it occurs after a build-up and it is *volitional*, requiring a deliberate focusing of your mind.[4] A clear example of this occurs if you are having a conversation at a noisy party. There could be music playing, lots of other people having conversations and yet you are able to focus on just the one conversation you're having.[5]

Apart from being slower, the other disadvantage associated with top-down attention is the fact that it can cause people to not notice a visually salient stimuli if they are looking for something else; what is known as inattentional blindness or perceptual blindness. Possibly the most famous example of this is an experiment conducted by Daniel Simons and Christopher Chabris. They asked participants to watch a video featuring two teams playing basketball, one wearing black and the other white. Participants were asked to count the number of passes the team in white made. While virtually everybody correctly counted the number of passes made, with participants' attention focusing on the ball, it meant they were completely unaware of a moonwalking gorilla that appeared in the middle of the video.[6] Even experts at spotting unusual features are susceptible to this effect. When Trafton Drew's team created a second variation in an x-ray to see if it contained an abnormally long nodule, 83% of radiologists did not see a gorilla superimposed onto the x-ray, even though it was 48 times larger than the nodule they were looking for.[7] In a retail context, shoppers specifically looking for one brand are unlikely to notice the other brands competing for their attention.

REAL-WORLD EXAMPLE: PSYCH IN ACTION

Inattentional blindness can explain why the most common type of motorbike crash is one where a car pulls out in front of a motorcycle at a junction, even though the motorbike has right of way. It's not that the car driver didn't look, but that they were looking expecting to see another car or lorry. As they weren't expecting to see a motorcycle, they looked straight through it, and pulled out.[8] Consequently, some motorbike safety groups encourage parents to teach their young children to count motorbikes on car rides. This way, they are inadvertently training them to spot motorbikes.

Bottom-up attention: How to attract attention

When something instinctively captures our attention, like a product in visually striking packaging on a supermarket shelf, this is an example of bottom-up attention. This type of attention is characterized by three key traits: it is *automatic*, happening beyond our conscious control; it is *fast*, with our attention being drawn immediately; and it is *non-volitional*, requiring no conscious effort or willpower.

In practice, marketers are more interested in understanding bottom-up attention. They want to know how they can involuntarily capture shoppers' attention when they're browsing a supermarket or watching ads when streaming. Luckily there are a number of rules that can help predict where shoppers will look.

In a supermarket context, the products that shoppers first look at are the most visually salient, the ones that have the brightest packaging or the ones where the packaging contrasts with the environment. When Milica Milosavljevic and her team showed participants 105 different products, she discovered, using eye-tracking technology, that a product's most visually salient features can predict where people will look with 85% accuracy.[9] This is because our brains prioritize high-contrast information, and hence we spend more time looking at them.

From a commercial perspective, this is highly valuable, as the products that people look at first are often the ones most likely to be purchased. However, when our working memory is engaged (a process that temporarily holds limited information to help us make immediate decisions), such as when trying to decide what to buy, this effect is magnified, making us even more drawn to visually striking products. The key takeaway is that the longer a customer looks at a product or the more times we look at a product, the more likely we are to buy it.[10]

A related concept to visual saliency is the idea of novelty. If we see something that is novel, it is likely to capture our attention, even if we are not consciously aware of it.[11] From an evolutionary perspective, there is a good argument for this behaviour. If our ancestors stumbled across something novel in their environment, they needed to quickly pay attention to it and determine if it was a threat or not. Or to put it another way, they needed to decide whether to approach or avoid it.

> **SHOULD MARKETERS CARE ABOUT EVOLUTIONARY PSYCHOLOGY?**
>
> While evolutionary arguments make logical sense, they are notoriously hard to prove. A trait may be present in most humans, and while researchers can create a plausible story (hypothesis) for why it evolved, it is almost impossible to create an experiment to test. However, the fact that this is a trait we are born with gives credence to this theory as even babies as young as two months old spend more time

looking at novel stimuli. When researchers showed babies photos of people's faces, some of which were novel and others they had seen ten times, the babies spent significantly longer looking at the new faces.[12]

Advertising and attention

Using contrast to attract attention is not only restricted to packaging but also works just as well when it comes to advertising, regardless of the medium being used. When Douglas Olsen played participants four sets of radio adverts – these were (a) no background music playing throughout the advert, (b) background music playing throughout the advert, (c) background music playing only during the first piece of information, and (d) background music only – he discovered that only 10% of listeners remembered the call to action when background music was played all the way through the advert. Things were slightly better if the advert featured no music, with 21% of listeners remembering the call to action. But the most effective way to use background music was when it was played all the way throughout the advert, except when the call to action was made at the end. This time, 65% of listeners could remember the information.[13] Listeners realized that something was different and ended up paying more attention to that part of the advert.

Some advertisers think they can overcome the attention challenge by producing a highly creative advert. Unfortunately, the evidence suggests that creativity alone is not enough. It is true that people are most likely to remember the more creative adverts, but this is only true for advertisements that pass an attentional threshold. In order for the advert to be memorable, it needs to first hook our attention so that we notice its creativity.[14] Fail to overcome this threshold and the advert is likely to fail.

The usual goal of advertising is to increase sales of the target product, normally by increasing brand awareness and giving shoppers a reason to believe in the product or brand. But it also unexpectedly changes what products shoppers notice in store. While it's almost impossible to measure the exact influence an advertising campaign or the packaging has on consumer attention, as there are just so many extraneous variables, it hasn't stopped researchers trying. Over a series of eye-tracking experiments, a team led by Ralf van der Lans created a mathematical model that estimates how much influence the packaging and adverts have over what we look at when shopping. This revealed that advertising contributes one-third of our in-store attention and in-store marketing (primarily packaging) explains two-thirds of where shoppers look.[15]

Theoretically, this makes sense. If we repeatedly pay attention to one product (for example, by being exposed to it via an advert), it significantly increases the likelihood that we will purchase this brand when we need to make subsequent choices.[16] We are inadvertently training ourselves to pay attention to that brand at the expense of competing brands. However, the reverse is also true. If we are constantly exposed to an advert which we find annoying, our brain trains itself to ignore that advert and, more worryingly, the brand.[17] Consequently, when we go shopping and start browsing the shelves, we are less likely to notice the advertised brand, which has become known as the *distractor devaluation effect*.

This goes to show that although marketers spend more time focusing on exogenous attention, endogenous attention is still important. And this is where advertising comes in. By running marketing campaigns, brands hope to generate top-of-the-mind recall. They are aiming to be the first brand you think of when you think of that product category. If they achieve this, it has some dramatic implications for attention. As described by Johnson and Ghuman, consumers who are looking for a particular product on a shelf, those using endogenous attention, have a degree of immunity to the visual saliency bias.[18] Under these circumstances, the brand with the most visually salient packaging is not going to be the one that jumps out on the shelf. Instead, it is the brand that the consumer is looking for. When consumers are just browsing, visual saliency predicts where consumers look with 85% accuracy, however, if they are looking for a specific product, this drops to just 40%.

This would suggest the only way to achieve top-of-the-mind recall is to advertise a lot. But new research has shown that exposure to just one advert is enough to influence what customers look at in-store. As part of an eye-tracking experiment, researchers asked participants to go into a store and purchase paint to decorate their living room. But before going into the store, the researchers needed to calibrate the eye-tracking glasses (or that's what they told the participants). To do this, they asked the participants to watch a series of 15-second adverts, one of which was for a paint brand. The results showed that the participants who had been shown the advert for the paint brand spent significantly more time looking at that brand of paint on the shelf. Even more remarkably, this translated directly to sales. In the control condition, where participants saw unrelated ads, 78% of participants purchased the target brand. However, amongst those who saw an ad for the target brand, 91% purchased the target paint. At the end of the experiment, researchers asked the participants to explain why they chose to purchase the brand they did. Everybody came up with reasons, and while a few remembered that they had previously seen an advert for the brand, nobody thought it influenced their purchase decision.[19]

Subliminal advertising

When talking about consumer psychology, there is one topic that is likely to get the public excited: subliminal advertising, which is the idea that messages are hidden in adverts or television programmes below our threshold of sensation which influence our behaviour (or brainwash our behaviour in a way we have no control over).

This idea stems from an experiment conducted by James Vicary in 1957. While watching a film at the cinema, Vicary claimed that every five seconds he flashed the words 'Drink Coca-Cola' and 'Eat Popcorn' for 1/3,000 of a second. Flashing these words so quickly is below the rate at which humans can consciously perceive a stimulus, and as such, nobody noticed the text. But despite not being able to read the words, sales of popcorn increased by 18.1% and Coca-Cola sold 57.7% more.[20] The study was never reported in any scientific journal, but the results gained notoriety amongst the general public (partly because rather than being an academic researcher, Vicary worked in PR) and the effect of subliminal advertising has subsequently been discussed in numerous bestselling books.[21] There was such a public outcry that subliminal advertising became illegal in both Britain and Australia, and in the US, a judge ruled that it constitutes an invasion of privacy.[22]

But there is one catch. The study never happened! The whole thing was a hoax designed to create publicity to promote a failing marketing firm.[23] Over the years, numerous researchers have attempted to recreate the study, but there is no evidence that it works.[24] That is until 2006, when Johan Karremans, Wolfgang Stroebe and Jasper Claus were able to recreate the effect, albeit under very strict laboratory conditions, with a number of prerequisites. Participants were asked to complete an attention task, and while completing it, the words 'Lipton Ice' (a brand of iced tea) flashed on-screen for 23ms. None of the participants in the study noticed the words, but it increased the likelihood that participants chose to drink Lipton iced tea compared to mineral water after the experiment.[25] However, this was only true for participants who were already thirsty and participants who knew and liked the primed brand. When one of the researchers tried to replicate the finding in an actual theatre (albeit for a radio show rather than a journal), once again the effect failed to materialize,[26] suggesting that subliminal advertising has no impact on viewers' behaviour.

When talking about subliminal advertising, people don't just think about flashing stimuli quickly on screen, they also think about hiding words or symbols in a design. For example, the Amazon logo featuring an arrow point from A to Z, or Skittles hiding the word 'sex' in an advert.[27] But psychologists do not consider this subliminal advertising. The fact that we can read the word sex, even if we do not notice it at first, means that it is supraliminal – it is above our level of conscious threshold. If you can see it, it is not subliminal! Regardless of what we call it, does it work in attracting attention or increasing sales? Once again, there is no evidence that it has any impact on behaviour.

Perception

Our senses provide our brains with an electrical signal from our different sense organs: our eyes, ears, nose, mouth and skin. But it is up to our brain to translate these signals and ascribe a meaning to them, a process known as perception. Everything we sense is an elaborate illusion created in our brains. However, when our brain is creating a world for us to experience, it does not treat all of our senses equally. It prioritizes our strongest senses, which are vision followed by hearing, with taste being the weakest.[28] This chapter will explore the role of touch, taste and vision in depth, whereas the impact of aromas and sound is explored within Chapter 12, discussing atmospherics.

Bottom-up and top-down processing

If our brain processes information it receives from our senses directly with no interpretation, this is called bottom-up processing. However, as the brain constantly receives thousands of bits of information every second, it is unable to systematically analyse all this information. Instead, it uses shortcuts to help us make sense of the world. Rather than relying on bottom-up processing and only perceiving what our senses tell us is out there, our brain uses contextual cues to spot patterns based on our prior experiences and predicts what it expects to sense. This is known as top-down processing and while it may not be perfect, it's quicker and uses less energy. But it does mean marketers can change how shoppers perceive their products as top-down processing has a greater role in influencing how people perceive the world. Context, expectations, emotions and attention all affect how we perceive the world, even if this contradicts what our senses are telling us.[29]

Imagine you have a phobia of snakes and, on holiday in Australia, you are walking through a forest and spot a snake blocking your path. Once your friends have stopped laughing at you, they point out that it is just a stick. You were expecting to see a snake in the forest, your brain interprets anything that looks vaguely like a snake as a snake. While this may seem like a design flaw, the evolutionary explanation makes sense. If one of our distant ancestors mistook a stick for a snake, there was no cost to them. However, if they looked at the snake and failed to identify it as a snake, the results could have been fatal. And over tens of thousands of years, early homo erectus and subsequently homo sapiens, who were better at identifying patterns and predicting the future, were more likely to survive and pass this trait on to their descendants.

While the snake is an extreme example, there are numerous examples of top-down processing in everyday life. When proofreading a document, it is often challenging to spot any typos because our brain reads the words we expect to see. This highlights one of our brain's greatest abilities: to predict how we are going to feel in the future and change our behaviour accordingly. If you are thirsty and you drink a large glass of water, almost immediately you no longer feel thirsty. But this is an example of our brain predicting how we expect to feel. Physiologically, the water we have just drunk is unable to quench our thirst this quickly. We are still dehydrated, our blood is thick and viscous, our heart is still racing, and our kidneys are still working hard to conserve water. But our brain knows that our body will stop feeling thirsty in the future and speeds up the process a little.[30]

> **PSYCHOLOGISTS VS MARKETERS: SAME WORD, DIFFERENT MEANING**
>
> When marketers and psychologists discuss the concept of perception, there is often an element of confusion or disagreement. This is because although they are using the same words, they are referring to two different concepts. When psychologists talk about perception, they focus on the psychological process by which our brain processes sensory information and assigns meaning to it (e.g. how does our brain turn the electrical signals from our eyes into a visual representation of the world around us).
>
> However, when marketers talk about perception, they are usually using the word as a synonym for 'judgement'. When they ask, *'how do consumers perceive our brand?'* they could rephrase the question as *'how do consumers judge our brand?'*. Marketers are interested in perception as a higher-level cognitive process which occurs downstream of sensory perception. Learning how the brain ascribes meaning to senses is important work and has led to important technical developments, such as developing medical implants or improving how computer screens work. However, the marketing application of this work is relatively limited, at least within most businesses. Consequently, the rest of the chapter focuses on perception from the marketing perspective.

Forming perceptions: Little clues that matter

Deciding which product to buy is tricky and as a result, shoppers often use mental shortcuts or rules of thumb to aid in the decision-making process, which is known as a *'heuristic'*. These rules may not always be right, but they normally are. The classic example being if a product is more expensive or if it comes in 'fancier' packaging, it must be higher quality. People don't always use heuristics to reach a decision, but they're more likely to depend on them when they are short on time, information or the cognitive capacity to reach a 'perfect' decision,[31] which describes the situation in which most shoppers find themselves.

Later on in the persuasion chapter, we'll take a more systematic look at the heuristics shoppers use to reach a decision, but shoppers also use seemingly trivial external cues to judge the quality of a product. By understanding these factors, marketers can dramatically change how consumers perceive their product without having to change the recipe. For example, Charles Spence's laboratory showed that consumers perceived yogurt as being 15% tastier and more expensive when they ate it from a silver spoon rather than a plastic (or lightweight metal) one.[32] Likewise, serving food on a heavy bowl or plate results in shoppers perceiving the dish as more luxurious than if the same food is served on a standard plate.[33] Even simply changing the quality of the paper that a menu is printed on makes a difference. The heavier the paper, the more high-quality guests perceive the whole dining experience to be.[34]

Unfortunately, there are some less ethical tactics to influence guests' perceptions that restaurants use as well. If food is served by an attractive server, male guests perceive their meal as tasting better, but only if they're enjoying the food. However, the reverse effect is also true as mediocre food is perceived as blander when served by unattractive servers.[35]

These tactics are not only restricted to how we perceive food or restaurants. Inputs from our five basic senses change how we perceive a product will perform.

Touch

Touch is one of the most undervalued senses when it comes to judging how a product will perform. Shoppers are more likely to depend on heuristics when they struggle to objectively judge the quality of a product, like wine, or where the results might not be immediately available, such as the quality of engine oil or shampoo. In this case, how a product and its packaging feels changes our perception. The challenge for brands is that the heuristics that shoppers use to judge a product by are not always accurate. If we take shampoo, the four attributes people use to judge its quality are: its cleansing ability, fragrance, viscosity and the amount it foams. But in reality, shampoos that do not foam can clean hair just as well as those that do. Likewise, thinner conditioners objectively work better, although consumers assume the opposite.[36]

It is essential that brands understand the heuristics shoppers use to judge their product and design a product around them. Statistically, better quality wine comes in heavier bottles,[37] which can make it tempting for cheaper wines to imitate them and also use heavier bottles. In store, most shoppers are only going to pick up the one bottle they'll buy and instead rely on the price of the wine to judge quality.[38] But when they get home, they'll have likely forgotten how much they paid for it. However, they will still hold the bottle and feel the weight of it when they serve it, which leaves a lasting impression.

Across a range of categories, shoppers associate heavier products with higher quality. When Bang & Olufsen conducted market research to understand how consumers viewed their new remote control, they unfortunately discovered that nearly all respondents hated it, but interestingly couldn't explain why. Rather than completely redesigning the remote control, the team simply added a lump of cheap metal inside the remote to make it heavier. This had no impact on the functionality, but consumers now perceived the remote more favourably and thought it was of a higher quality.[39]

While shoppers associate the weight-quality heuristic with premium products, the effect still occurs for cheaper everyday items. When a brand packaged the same liquid soap in either heavy (450g) or light (350g) packaging, the weight made a big difference. Shoppers thought the soap in the heavier bottle to have a better fragrance and to be more effective than the soap in the lighter bottle.[40]

Taste

Although we only have five basic tastes – sweet, sour, salty, bitter and umami – most of the time when people are talking about taste they are talking about flavour.[41] This may sound like just a semantic difference, but it has some significant implications for marketing. Taste is the chemicals that our tongue and mouth perceive when we eat or drink something, whereas flavour is what we experience when all of our senses and expectations are merged. Intuitively, people associate angular shapes with bitterness and round shapes with sweetness.[42] Consequently, when Australian beer drinkers tried a new craft beer, they thought it tasted 13% fruitier and perceived it had a more intense flavour when drinking from a glass with round rather than straight sides.[43] This doesn't only hold true for alcoholic drinks; the same pattern occurs when drinking hot chocolate or coffee. On average, participants found the drinks to taste 27% more bitter when served in an angular glass and 18% sweeter when the glass has a round shape.[44]

This is likely to be a case of confirmation bias. The product performs how customers think it's going to perform, and it is marketers' and product designers' role to influence this process. This confirmation effect is so strong that professionals get fooled. When researchers dyed white wine so that it looked like red wine and gave it to oenology (wine science) students, the expert panel described the wine as if it were a red wine. They were completely fooled.[45]

REAL-WORLD EXAMPLE: PSYCH IN ACTION

The UK's best-selling chocolate bar is Cadbury Dairy Milk (manufactured by Mondelez International); hence it should be no surprise that when, in 2013, Cadbury changed the shape and the recipe, there was a public outcry. They switched from the traditional square bar to a more bubble-shaped bar. Understandably, shoppers were not happy with the bar shrinking in size by 8% and the price staying the same, but they also complained that the new bar tasted 'too sweet'.[46]

But Mondelez were very clear in the fact that while they had changed the shape, the recipe remains identical. So why were consumers convinced the new bar was sweeter? The answer: the new shape. Previous research has shown that round shapes are associated with sweeter flavours, and this is true with chocolates. The same chocolate put into a round mould has a sweeter flavour than when it is put into a rectangular mould.[47] The new shape of Dairy Milk bar might be more 'on brand', but they may have accidentally altered the iconic Dairy Milk flavour without realizing.

As discussed so far, changing the shape and colour of the product changes how people think it tastes. But it is possible to not change the product and achieve the same results simply by reframing how consumers view your product. Offer your friends smoked salmon-flavoured ice cream and most people understandably will dislike it. However, serve exactly the same ice cream but call it a frozen savoury mousse and most people like it.[48] By using a different label, it activates a different set of mental criteria that shoppers use to evaluate the product, which changes our perception of its taste.

Marketers often get a bad reputation for trying to encourage people to buy products that are bad for their health. The reason is that most people assume that healthy food is less tasty than unhealthy food.[49] As soon as a chocolate bar manufacturer highlights that their chocolate contains less sugar, shoppers assume it doesn't taste as good. But it's more than that. The product physically doesn't taste as good. When female participants were given a chocolate milkshake and put into an functional magnetic resonance imaging scanner, researchers were able to see how participants' brains reacted to the milkshake. When the women thought they were drinking a regular milkshake rather than a low-fat version, they experienced greater activation in their Rolandic operculum, the part of the brain connected with the sense of taste and the ventral medial prefrontal cortex, the part of the brain associated with emotional regulation and processing.[50] Even though all participants drank the same milkshake, just thinking food is healthy really does make it taste less good.

Consequently, if a business develops a healthier version of their product, they could avoid labelling it as 'low-calorie' or the 'healthy choice' and instead use a taste-related phrase such as 'light and fresh'.[51] Consumers still understand that it is a healthy option, but as the health claim is more subtle, it doesn't trigger the negative associations with healthy food. These negative associations can be further dismissed by including hedonic claims on the packaging or menus. 'Succulent Italian Seafood Fillet' sells 28% more than 'seafood salad'. Again, it primes people to focus on the taste (and forget about the fact it is a low-calorie option).

However, it is not just a psychological reaction. In most cases, food made with more sugar, salt and fat does taste better. But marketers can use shoppers' expectations to help convince them that food made with less salt or butter tastes just as good as before. As we've shown, when we eat food, we taste what we expect. This means if your first bite is delicious, as you carry on eating, your brain stops allocating as much attention to your taste buds and focuses on other stimuli instead. Brands used this to their advantage when creating food. For example, when making a baguette, one manufacturer reduced the amount of salt in the middle but made sure the ends were properly seasoned. Based on experience, shoppers have learnt that a baguette tastes the same all the way through; its taste at the start will be the same as it tastes in the middle. So when customers bit into the end and tasted a properly seasoned baguette, they understandably assumed it would taste the same in the middle. But this wasn't the case. This meant the manufacturer was able to dramatically reduce the amount of salt in the baguette without changing the perceived taste.[52]

Vision

While colour psychology is a popular point of discussion, for the most part this book will not explore it. In marketing, it is always essential to appreciate the context, be it culture or category, and nowhere is this more important than colour psychology. Online guides suggest that red is stimulating or green is connected to nature, but these findings depend on the context. A green bottle of shampoo is likely to trigger associations of mint whereas a computer packaged in a green box is likely to be perceived as more sustainable.

Psychologists have yet to find a clear neurological link between environmental colours and any specific judgements or emotional states[53] and most research into the colour psychology is either an oversimplification or includes numerous methodological flaws.[54]

One area of research which is more robust than most is the pharmaceutical sector. Drug companies legally have to test all aspect of the products and are constantly looking for ways to optimize their products and the expectations effects, which include the products' colours. For pain medication such as paracetamol, patients have learnt to associate white tablets with pain relief, as that is what we are used to seeing. The result, white tablets are more effective at treating headaches, even when the identical medication is placed in a different colour capsule. However, if the goal of the medication is to change patients' arousal levels, either to calm or energize them, then red or blue tablets work best. People associate red with being both a stimulant and powerful, and blue with calmness and serenity.[55] As a result, medication that are these colours performs better, all thanks to expectations. (See Chapter 10 for a further discussion about expectations effect and the placebo effect.)

The associations we have with red and blue can materialize in some strange ways. For instance, in sports, teams wear different colours to help the crowd distinguish between them, often red and blue, and this colour can influence the results. In the Olympics, athletes in combat sports like boxing, taekwondo, Greco-Roman wrestling and freestyle wrestling are randomly assigned red or blue uniforms. Yet, those wearing red were more likely to win, with 16 out of 21 rounds having more red than blue winners.[56] The effect size is small, which can make it appear like a strange quirk, however, the same trend occurs outside of combat sports, with football teams[57] and rugby teams[58] playing in red performing better than those in blue, which is unfortunate news if your favourite team plays in blue.

Expectations and advertising

Running an advertising campaign is expensive, and one of the worst outcomes is not that viewers don't remember the advert (although this is certainly not ideal), but that they experience brand confusion. They can remember the advert, but they think it is advertising a different brand. Inadvertently you are paying to advertise a rivals' brands. The advert can feature your product and brand logo, but still viewers attribute it to your rival. Once again, this can be explained by expectations. If one of your rivals regularly runs an advertising campaign and you rarely do, it is understandable that viewers might expect to see an advert for your rival and therefor encode your advert as being for your rival. Surprisingly, the best factors that predict whether viewers experience brand confusion have nothing to do with brand saliency – it all comes down to money, the total advertising budget and campaign length (both for your advertising campaign and your rivals).[59]

This is not just a theoretical problem. For over a decade, Domino's Pizza sponsored *The Simpsons* in the UK, but when their contract came to an end, Channel 4 sold the rights to Pizza Hut, a rival brand. But this new partnership didn't last very long as it inadvertently led to an increase in its sales for Domino's.[60] For 10 years, viewers learnt to associate *The Simpsons* with Domino's, so when they saw a pizza advert after *The Simpsons*, they automatically assumed it was a Domino's advert, as this was what they expected to see. Once again, our brain fills in the gaps rather than paying attention to all the details.

Managing change: A question of perception

Over time, the cost of producing products rises. This means that companies are faced with a choice, either to increase the price or shrink the size of their products. If you are used to selling 12 eggs for £2.00 and thanks to inflation you need to increase the price, should you change the price to 12 eggs for £2.40 or opt to sell 10 eggs for £2.00? An economic analysis would suggest that it shouldn't make any difference as they both provide customers with the same value, but the psychology would suggest otherwise. While there is no getting away from the fact that consumers are likely to be unhappy in both scenarios, research suggests that generally reducing the size of the product and maintaining the price is a much better option.[61] Typically, research has shown that consumers are nearly four times as sensitive to a price increase as they are to a reduction in size.[62] However, as with most things there are a couple of caveats.

Firstly, the more knowledge a consumer has about marketing pricing tactics, the less likely they are to appreciate a reduction in sizing.[63] They identify that the reduction in unit size is just a price increase by another name, but worse than just being a price increase, it is a deliberate attempt to deceive the consumer, and as such consumers view this as unethical.[64] The other situation when it can sometimes make more sense to raise the price is when a product is sold in a standard unit size. Eggs are normally sold by the dozen, butter by the stick (in the US). If brands deviate from the norm, it will become more salient that they have made a change. However, if a pack of bacon is reduced from 500g to 450g, it is unlikely that most consumers will notice. The key question is, does the packaging (or product) change in an obvious manner?

REAL-WORLD EXAMPLE: PSYCH IN ACTION

Although reducing the size of a product to keep the pricing consistent is common practice within the confectionary category,[65] the example most people in the EU are likely to think about is Toblerone. In 2016, they reduced the size from 170g to 150g. This is only a 12% change, and most consumers would be unlikely to notice this change, but in this instance, there was a huge public outcry. The reason was that rather than making the chocolate bar shorter, they changed its iconic shape, increasing the gaps between the pyramids. There was an obvious change in the shape so everyone instantly recognized that they were getting less chocolate for the same price. If the bar was simply one cube shorter, it is unlikely that it would have triggered the same reaction.

This raises an important question, if a company wants to change the size of their product, how big can the change be before the customer notices? This is what psychologists refer to as the 'just noticeable difference' (JND). In most cases, marketers want to be just underneath this threshold, for example, what is the maximum amount they could increase the price by without customers noticing? However, there are times when they will want to be just over it. If marketers are going to run a special offer, they will want to make sure that the price discount is big enough for shoppers to notice, but not too large that they are giving away margin for no reason.

To predict how big a change can be before shoppers notice it, psychologists use the Weber–Fechner Law, which has two parts. Firstly, it argues that a larger stimuli requires a larger absolute change before it is noticed. Secondly, as things get more intense, people need a bigger change before they'll notice the difference.[66] From a marketing perspective, a £2 discount on a £10 steak appears like a great deal, however most people are unlikely to even notice a £2 discount on the latest iPhone, even if the economic benefits are identical. From a theoretical perspective, the Weber–Fechner Law predicts that the JND will be the same for products with an identical price. However, as with many things in life, theory does not always work in practice and marketers need to be aware of the importance of context. When researchers increased the pricing of clothing by 20%, they found that customers were far more likely to notice the price change in a traditional bricks-and-mortar store than in an online shop.[67] Likewise, consumer sensitivity to price increases differs depending on the product category, although the Weber–Fechner Law goes a long way to explain a large amount of the variation found.[68]

JND is rarely considered by marketers, if it is, it's usually only applied to price or pack size changes. But the principle can be applied to a range of other contexts. Brands are one of the most important assets any organization owns and updating a brand is fraught with danger. If your customer does not like, or even worse does not recognize, the new brand you are in trouble. Consequently, when it comes to changing a brand logo, most organizations opt to make small incremental changes that stay below the JND threshold rather than any dramatic changes. Likewise, if a company is planning on changing the ingredients they use to make a popular product, consumers are less likely to notice (and complain) if they slowly change the recipe over time rather than if they make a dramatic change overnight.[69]

Closing thoughts

Capturing consumers' attention and shaping how they perceive a product or brand is one of a marketer's key tasks, and it is a theme that this book will keep returning to. It is simply not possible to adequately cover all of the options available in one book, let alone a single chapter. However, each of the applied chapters will explore the various tactics brands can use to influence shoppers' perceptions, from advertising and copywriting to packaging and store design.

KEY POINTS

- Human attention can be categorized into types:
    - Top-down or endogenous attention: This is deliberate and controlled, and involves focusing on a specific task like looking for a specific product on a supermarket shelf.
    - Bottom-up or exogenous attention: This is quick and automatic and occurs when something automatically captures our attention, like a flashing light on a police car.
- In most cases marketers are more interested in bottom-up attention, understanding the factors that automatically capture shoppers attention. Key factors that they should focus on are:
    - Visual salience: Items with bright or contrasting packaging are more likely to capture attention and subsequently be purchased.
    - Novelty: Novel or unusual items automatically capture people's attention, driven by an evolutionary need to decide if a new stimulus poses a potential threat.
- Creativity may help capture attention, but marketers still need to ensure the viewer is motivated to engage with the message.
- When people are presented with a stimulus, their attention is initially directed to a number of key elements. These are likely to be: the most visually dominant element (especially large pictures), pictures of faces, and elements using contrasting colours. However, if we view a document or webpage, people tend to scan using an 'F pattern', initially starting in the top left and making short scans across before skimming down the left side.
- In most situations, people don't have an objective view of reality. Instead, they rely on a range of external cues to predict how a stimulus will perform – what is known as top-down processing. This is quicker and uses less energy than bottom-up processing, where the brain purely relies on immediate input from the senses. However, it can be less accurate.

PUTTING THEORY INTO PRACTICE

1   Visit a physical retailer of your choice and pay attention to which products capture your attention first. What was it about these products that made you look at them first?

2   Visit the same retailers' online stores and browse the same category. Did the same product capture your attention? If not, what caused you to focus on a different product?

3   Think of the last time you went to a restaurant or watched a celebrity chef prepare a meal on television. How do they use external cues to change the perception of their dish.

4   Imagine you are the marketing manager for a fast-moving consumer goods brand of your choice. How could you redesign the packaging to change shoppers' perception of the product?

5   If you were the brand manager for your favourite brand and you had been told that they needed to increase the price: (a) Based on the Weber–Fechner law, how much do you predict you could increase the price before shoppers noticed? (b) How would you design a research project to test your prediction?

6   Find three articles on LinkedIn discussing the psychology of colour and identify the empirical data that underpins it. Do you think this research is credible? What conclusions should marketers draw from this?

References

1   Ehrenberg-Bass Institute study, quoted in Sharp, B. (2010). *How brands grow: What marketers don't know.* OUP Australia & New Zealand
2   De Garis, H., Shuo, C., Goertzel, B., & Ruiting, L. (2010). A world survey of artificial brain projects, Part I: Large-scale brain simulations. *Neurocomputing*, 74(1–3), 3–29.
3   James, W. (1890). *The principles of psychology.* Vol. 1. New York: Henry Holt. 403–404.
4   Ramsøy, T. Z. (2015). *Introduction to neuromarketing and consumer neuroscience.* Neurons Inc.
5   Arons, B. (1992). A review of the cocktail party effect. *Journal of the American Voice I/O Society*, 12(7), 35–50.
6   Simons, D. J., & Chabris, C. F. (1999). Gorillas in our midst: Sustained inattentional blindness for dynamic events. *Perception*, 28(9), 1059–1074.
7   Drew, T., Võ, M. L. H., & Wolfe, J. M. (2013). The invisible gorilla strikes again: Sustained inattentional blindness in expert observers. *Psychological Science*, 24(9), 1848–1853.
8   Pammer, K., Sabadas, S., & Lentern, S. (2018). Allocating attention to detect motorcycles: The role of inattentional blindness. *Human Factors*, 60(1), 5–19.
9   Milosavljevic, M., Navalpakkam, V., Koch, C., & Rangel, A. (2012). Relative visual saliency differences induce sizable bias in consumer choice. *Journal of Consumer Psychology*, 22(1), 67–74. https://doi.org/10.1016/j.jcps.2011.10.002 (archived at https://perma.cc/LG78-7NT4)

10   Gidlöf, K., Anikin, A., Lingonblad, M., & Wallin, A. (2017). Looking is buying. How visual attention and choice are affected by consumer preferences and properties of the supermarket shelf. *Appetite*, 116, 29–38. https://doi.org/10.1016/j.appet.2017.04.020 (archived at https://perma.cc/ZSU5-T88Y)

11   Berns, G. S., Cohen, J. D., & Mintun, M. A. (1997). Brain regions responsive to novelty in the absence of awareness. *Science*, 276(5316), 1272–1275. https://doi.org/10.1126/science.276.5316.1272 (archived at https://perma.cc/YPE2-J6ZP)

12   Fantz, R. L. (1964). Visual experience in infants: Decreased attention to familiar patterns relative to novel ones. *Science*, 146(3644), 668–670. https://doi.org/10.1126/science.146.3644.668 (archived at https://perma.cc/H7HZ-N8PF)

13   Olsen, G. D. (1995). Creating the contrast: The influence of silence and background music on recall and attribute importance. *Journal of Advertising*, 24(4), 29–44. https://doi.org/10.1080/00913367.1995.10673487 (archived at https://perma.cc/LV5W-UUZ8)

14   Wilson, R. T., Baack, D. W., & Till, B. D. (2015). Creativity, attention and the memory for brands: An outdoor advertising field study. *International Journal of Advertising*, 34(2), 232–261. https://doi.org/10.1080/02650487.2014.996117 (archived at https://perma.cc/LV5W-UUZ8)

15   Lans, R. van der, Pieters, R., & Wedel, M. (2008). Research note—competitive brand salience. *Marketing Science*, 27(5), 922–931. https://doi.org/10.1287/mksc.1070.0327 (archived at https://perma.cc/4GSJ-XJL6)

16   Janiszewski, C., Kuo, A., & Tavassoli, N. T. (2013). The influence of selective attention and inattention to products on subsequent choice. *Journal of Consumer Research*, 39(6), 1258–1274. https://doi.org/10.1086/668234 (archived at https://perma.cc/ZY2E-NA5S)

17   Duff, B. R. L. & Faber, R. J. (2011). Missing the mark. *Journal of Advertising*, 40(2), 51–62. https://doi.org/10.2753/joa0091-3367400204 (archived at https://perma.cc/FEP2-JJHH)

18   Johnson, M. & Ghuman, P. (2020). *Blindsight: The (mostly) hidden ways marketing reshapes our brains*. BenBella Books Inc.

19   Ramsøy, T. Z. (2015). *Introduction to neuromarketing and consumer neuroscience*. Neurons Inc.

20   Rogers, S. (1992). How a publicity blitz created the myth of subliminal advertising. *Public Relations Quarterly*, 37, 12–17.

21   Broyles, S. (2006). Subliminal advertising and the perpetual popularity of playing to people's paranoia. *Journal of Consumer Affairs*, 40(2), 392–406. https://doi.org/10.1111/j.1745-6606.2006.00063.x (archived at https://perma.cc/3EP8-GXGG)

22   Locke, E. L. (1991). The Vance decision: The future of subliminal communication. *Law & Psychology Review*, 15, 375–394.

23   Karremans, J. C., Stoebe, W., & Claus, J. (2006). Beyond Vicary's fantasies: The impact of subliminal priming and brand choice. *Journal of Experimental Social Psychology*, 42(6), 792–798. https://doi.org/10.1016/j.jesp.2005.12.002 (archived at https://perma.cc/JXC4-KA8X)

24   Moore, T. E. (1988). The case against subliminal manipulation. *Psychology & Marketing*, 5(4), 297–316. https://doi.org/10.1002/mar.4220050403 (archived at https://perma.cc/PSZ8-HDAT)

25 Karremans, J. C., Stoebe, W., & Claus, J. (2006). Beyond Vicary's fantasies: The impact of subliminal priming and brand choice. *Journal of Experimental Social Psychology*, 42(6), 792–798. https://doi.org/10.1016/j.jesp.2005.12.002 (archived at https://perma.cc/F8A9-A8DZ)

26 News, B. (2015, July 20). Does subliminal advertising actually work? BBC News.

27 Broyles, S. (2006). Subliminal advertising and the perpetual popularity of playing to people's paranoia. *Journal of Consumer Affairs*, 40(2), 392–406. https://doi.org/10.1111/j.1745-6606.2006.00063.x (archived at https://perma.cc/Q4KC-RAD8)

28 Johnson, M. & Ghuman, P. (2020). *Blindsight: The (mostly) hidden ways marketing reshapes our brains*. BenBella Books.

29 Moran, J. & Desimone, R. (1985). Selective attention gates visual processing in the extrastriate cortex. *Science*, 229(4715), 782–784. https://doi.org/10.1126/science.4023713 (archived at https://perma.cc/4ZHE-9ZCZ)

30 Barrett, L. F. (2020). *Seven and a half lessons about the brain*. Picador.

31 Hertwig, R. & Herzog, S. M. (2009). Fast and frugal heuristics: Tools of social rationality. *Social Cognition*, 27(5), 661–698.

32 Spence, C., Harrar, V., & Piqueras-Fiszman, B. (2012). Assessing the impact of the tableware and other contextual variables on multisensory flavour perception. *Flavour*, 1(1), 1–12. https://doi.org/10.1186/2044-7248-1-7 (archived at https://perma.cc/44QC-4VU4)

33 Piqueras-Fiszman, B., Harrar, V., Alcaide, J., & Spence, C. (2011). Does the weight of the dish influence our perception of food? *Food Quality and Preference*, 22(8), 753–756. https://doi.org/10.1016/j.foodqual.2011.05.009 (archived at https://perma.cc/YA57-SJH7)

34 Magnini, V. P. & Kim, S. (2016). The influences of restaurant menu font style, background color, and physical weight on consumers' perceptions. *International Journal of Hospitality Management*, 53, 42–48. https://doi.org/10.1016/j.ijhm.2015.11.001 (archived at https://perma.cc/HM5B-X9QJ)

35 Lin, L., Hoegg, J., & Aquino, K. (2018). When beauty backfires: The effects of server attractiveness on consumer taste perceptions. *Journal of Retailing*, 94(3), 296–311. https://doi.org/10.1016/j.jretai.2018.04.003 (archived at https://perma.cc/SA2K-MU6E)

36 Klein, K. (2004). Evaluating shampoo foam. *Cosmetics & Toiletries magazine*. 119(10).

37 Piqueras-Fiszman, B. & Spence, C. (2012). The weight of the bottle as a possible extrinsic cue with which to estimate the price (and quality) of the wine? Observed correlations. *Food Quality and Preference*, 25(1), 41–45. https://doi.org/10.1016/j.foodqual.2012.01.001 (archived at https://perma.cc/V4Z8-B8ZX)

38 Spence, C. (2024). Cognitive influence on the evaluation of wine: The impact and assessment of price. *Food Research International*, 187, 114411.

39 Lindstrom, M. (2012). *Brand sense: Sensory secrets behind the stuff we buy*. Kogan Page.

40 Gatti, E., Bordegoni, M., & Spence, C. (2014). Investigating the influence of colour, weight, and fragrance intensity on the perception of liquid bath soap: An experimental study. *Food Quality and Preference*, 31, 56–64. https://doi.org/10.1016/j.foodqual.2013.08.004 (archived at https://perma.cc/XK5T-9HBE)

41 Spence, C. (2018). *Gastrophysics: The new science of eating*. Penguin.
42 Salgado-Montejo, A., Alvarado, J. A., Velasco, C., Salgado, C. J., Hasse, K., & Spence, C. (2015). The sweetest thing: The influence of angularity, symmetry, and the number of elements on shape-valence and shape-taste matches. *Frontiers in Psychology*, 6, 1382.
43 Mirabito, A., Oliphant, M., Van Doorn, G., Watson, S., & Spence, C. (2017). Glass shape affects the perceived taste of beer. *Food Quality and Preference*, 62, 257–261. https://doi.org/10.1016/j.foodqual.2017.05.009 (archived at https://perma.cc/5KDV-KFPB)
44 Van Rompay, T. J., Finger, F., Saakes, D., & Fenko, A. (2017). 'See me, feel me': Effects of 3D-printed surface patterns on beverage evaluation. *Food Quality and Preference*, 62, 332–339. https://doi.org/10.1016/j.foodqual.2016.12.002 (archived at https://perma.cc/2VWV-HRRR)
45 Morrot, G., Brochet, F., & Dubourdieu, D. (2001). The color of odors. *Brain and language*, 79(2), 309–320.
46 Spence, C. (2013). Unraveling the mystery of the rounder, sweeter chocolate bar. *Flavour*, 2, 1–3.
47 Ogata, K., Gakumi, R., Hashimoto, A., Ushiku, Y., & Yoshida, S. (2023). The influence of Bouba-and Kiki-like shape on perceived taste of chocolate pieces. *Frontiers in Psychology*, 14, 1170674.
48 Yeomans, M. R., Chambers, L., Blumenthal, H., & Blake, A. (2008). The role of expectancy in sensory and hedonic evaluation: The case of smoked salmon ice-cream. *Food Quality and Preference*, 19(6), 565–573. https://doi.org/10.1016/j.foodqual.2008.02.009 (archived at https://perma.cc/H8RF-L2YH)
49 Paakki, M., Kantola, M., Junkkari, T., Arjanne, L., Luomala, H., & Hopia, A. (2022). 'Unhealthy = tasty': How does it affect consumers'(un)healthy food expectations? *Foods*, 11(19), 3139. https://doi.org/10.3390/foods11193139 (archived at https://perma.cc/7V2Z-7ELE)
50 Ng, J., Stice, E., Yokum, S., & Bohon, C. (2011). An fMRI study of obesity, food reward, and perceived caloric density. Does a low-fat label make food less appealing? *Appetite*, 57(1), 65–72. https://doi.org/10.1016/j.appet.2011.03.017 (archived at https://perma.cc/JXW8-UEWT)
51 Wansink, B. & Love, K. (2014). Slim by design: Menu strategies for promoting high-margin, healthy foods. *International Journal of Hospitality Management*, 42, 137–143. https://doi.org/10.1016/j.ijhm.2014.06.006 (archived at https://perma.cc/HQT7-2UEN)
52 Spence, C. (2018). *Gastrophysics: The new science of eating*. Penguin.
53 Wise, B. K. & Wise, J. A. (1988). *The human factors of color in environmental design: A critical review*.
54 O'Connor, Z. (2011). Colour psychology and colour therapy: Caveat emptor. *Color Research & Application*, 36(3), 229–234.
55 Meissner, K. & Linde, K. (2018). Are blue pills better than green? How treatment features modulate placebo effects. International Review of Neurobiology, 139, 357–378.
56 Weiß, J., Mentzel, S. V., Busch, L., & Krenn, B. (2024). The influence of colour in the context of sport: A meta-analysis. *International Journal of Sport and Exercise Psychology*, 22(1), 177–235.

57 Attrill, M. J., Gresty, K. A., Hill, R. A., & Barton, R. A. (2008). Red shirt colour is associated with long-term team success in English football. *Journal of Sports Sciences*, 26(6), 577–582.

58 Piatti, M., Savage, D. A., & Torgler, B. (2012). The red mist? Red shirts, success and team sports. *Sport in Society*, 15(9), 1209–1227.

59 Poiesz, T. B. C. & Verhallen, T. M. M. (1989). Brand confusion in advertising. *International Journal of Advertising*, 8(3), 231–244. https://doi.org/10.1080/02650487.1989.11107108 (archived at https://perma.cc/X6F6-6SAP)

60 MarketingWeek. (2007, November 8). Domino's to sponsor The Simpsons on Channel 4. https://www.marketingweek.com/dominos-to-sponsor-the-simpsons-on-channel-4/ (archived at https://perma.cc/W39D-XF7T)

61 Gourville, J. T. & Koehler, J. J. (2004). Downsizing price increases: A greater sensitivity to price than quantity in consumer markets. *SSRN Electronic Journal*. https://doi.org/10.2139/ssrn.559482 (archived at https://perma.cc/S8S3-N69A)

62 Çakır, M. & Balagtas, J. V. (2014). Consumer response to package downsizing: Evidence from the Chicago ice cream market. *Journal of Retailing*, 90(1), 1–12. https://doi.org/10.1016/j.jretai.2013.06.002 (archived at https://perma.cc/7K2L-V3HQ)

63 Kachersky, L. (2011). Reduce content or raise price? The impact of persuasion knowledge and unit price increase tactics on retailer and product brand attitudes. *Journal of Retailing*, 87(4), 479–488. https://doi.org/10.1016/j.jretai.2011.08.001 (archived at https://perma.cc/S9SX-3JGC)

64 Gupta, O. K., Tandon, S., Debnath, S., & Rominger, A. S. (2007). Package downsizing: Is it ethical? *AI & Society*, 21(3), 239–250. https://doi.org/10.1007/s00146-006-0056-3 (archived at https://perma.cc/DS2E-8CC7)

65 Adams, A., di Benedetto, C. A., & Chandran, R. (1991). Can you reduce your package size without damaging sales? *Long Range Planning*, 24(4), 86–96. https://doi.org/10.1016/0024-6301(91)90009-d (archived at https://perma.cc/84MW-WWDU)

66 Algom, D. (2021). The Weber–Fechner law: A misnomer that persists but that should go away. *Psychological Review*, 128(4), 757.

67 Helmi, M., Xiao, S., & Nicholson, M. (2020). *The effect of price promotion on just noticeable difference in multichannel retailing*. Proceedings of the European Marketing Academy 49th.

68 Sirvanci, M. B. (1993). An empirical study of price thresholds and price sensitivity. *Journal of Applied Business Research*, 9(2), 43–49. https://doi.org/10.19030/jabr.v9i2.6075 (archived at https://perma.cc/WJB2-ZNNA)

69 Cubero-Castillo, E., Araya-Morice, A., Hernandez-Campos, D., & Araya-Quesada, Y. (2019). Salt reduction without consumer awareness using a sensory threshold approach: A case study in meat products. *Journal of Food*, 17(1), 763–769. https://doi.org/10.1080/19476337.2019.1648556 (archived at https://perma.cc/77W9-CR84)

3 | The psychology of motivation

LEARNING OBJECTIVES

- Understand how the concept of motivation has developed over time.
- Apply principles of motivational psychology to develop effective marketing campaigns.
- Analyse how businesses apply principles of gamification to create engaging products.

What is motivation?

A key aspect of a marketer's role is understanding human motivation, the driving force that shapes all behaviour. Why do some people experience a need to participate in extreme sports while others prefer collecting first-edition stamps? We not only want to understand motivation, but ultimately, we want to find ways to be able to influence motivation.

At the most basic level, motivation is the term we give to the state of tension that arises when there is a discrepancy between our desired state and our actual state. Motivation is the drive we experience to find a way to resolve this tension. However, the needs that arise can be further subdivided into innate needs (biogenic) and acquired needs.[1] We are born with innate needs and they represent all of our biological needs to survive: food, water, shelter, sex, safety etc.; whereas our acquired needs are shaped by our environment, including marketing. We might be hungry, an innate biological need, but thanks to marketing, peer pressure and how we view ourselves, we may want to satisfy this need by eating either a vegan Subway or a steak tartare, depending on the circles we move in and the marketing messages we are exposed to.

We tend to think of hunger as a physiological response, but it is important to recognize that it also includes a psychological component, where expectations will heavily influence how people feel. For example, when a team of researchers led by Steven Brown offered participants an omelette, they found that participants ate significantly less the next day when they thought they had eaten a four-egg omelette, compared with participants who thought they had eaten a two-egg omelette. In reality, all participants had only eaten a three-egg omelette.[2] Hence, when Shreddies, a breakfast cereal brand, used the slogan '*keep hunger locked up till lunchtime*', it is not just an example of marketing puffery, but is likely to shift people's expectations and change how hungry they feel.

From a psychological perspective, hunger is an interesting concept. Most people are familiar with the advice, '*don't go shopping when you're hungry or you'll end up buying more*', and it turns out to be good advice. If people go shopping when they are hungry, they are likely to buy more food,[3] and what is more, the items they purchase tend to be unhealthy.[4] In terms of evolution, this makes sense as the body is craving calories – it is what we need to survive. However, what is interesting about this phenomenon is the fact that it occurs even when we are shopping for non-food items. Researchers have shown that when people go shopping and they are hungry, they tend to buy more items, even though they are not capable of satisfying their calorific needs.[5] This finding raises some interesting implications. For people who have chosen to follow a calorie-restrictive diet, this research would suggest that they are more likely to make unplanned purchases.

Likewise, it would also suggest that online advertising is likely to be more effective before mealtimes, when people are hungry. However, robust quantitative data to support this is hard to establish. Although people might be more susceptible to impulse purchases, people's internet usage changes throughout the day.

Maslow's Hierarchy of Needs

When it comes to motivation, there is one theory that almost every marketer is familiar with – Maslow's Hierarchy of Needs. Originally proposed in 1943, Abraham Maslow (1908–1970) attempted to create a model that explained all aspects of human motivation.[6] He believed that humans have an innate desire to be the best we can, what he initially referred to as self-actualization. However, before someone can reach this stage, they need to progress through four other stages:

1 Physiological needs – Our most basic physiological needs: shelter, sex, food, water, rest.
2 Safety needs – Health, security, financial security.
3 Love and belonging needs: Intimate relationships and friends.
4 Esteem needs: Prestige and the feeling of accomplishment.
5 Self-actualization: achieving one's full potential, including creativity.[7]

The first two stages represent factors that are essential for survival, whereas the higher-order factors represent our physiological needs. However, other scholars break down the levels into growth and deficiency needs. The first four levels are deficiency needs, as an individual will be motivated by these factors when they are unmet (usually caused by deprivation, for example, not having enough food to eat, or financial security etc.). But once a deficiency need has been met, it no longer motivates us, and we are motivated by the next factor in the hierarchy. However, growth needs are a little different; once these needs become salient, the need to satisfy them does not diminish. Some would say they just keep getting stronger.

It is worth noting that while this is the model that most people are familiar with, towards the end of his life, Maslow changed it by adding an extra layer that goes above self-actualization: self-transcendence.[8] This sixth factor argues that we should focus on factors that are 'beyond the self', for example, altruism and liberation from egocentricity. This factor is rarely discussed today, although with current attitudes in the 21st century, perhaps it's worth reconsidering.

When it comes to progressing through the levels of the hierarchy, there are conflicting views over how this happens. This occurs because Maslow changed his mind about how people are motivated. In his earlier work,[9] he argued that an individual needed to complete the lower levels before progressing to the next, but in his later works he clarified that this was not the case. An individual could still be motivated by the higher-order factors, even though they have unsatisfied lower-order needs.[10] It is also the case that people not only move in one direction up the hierarchy as, unfortunately, life doesn't always go according to plan. We could break up with our partner, lose our job or even tragically lose a relative, and all of these situations could cause us to move down the hierarchy, and cause someone to concentrate on lower-order needs again.

Yet despite being widely taught, amongst psychologists, Maslow's work is widely discredited.[11] It is viewed as unscientific, both in terms of the raw data and the way he analysed his data. In order to conceptualize self-actualization, Maslow only studied 18 people, all of whom were white and highly educated, whom he defined as self-actualizers. His approach to data analysis was also highly subjective, employing a biographical approach. This is a qualitative research technique whereby it is very easy for the researchers' biases to influence the outcomes. Consequently, when researchers have attempted to empirically test Maslow's model, they have found limited, if any, scientific evidence to support it.

One other issue is rarely discussed. Despite being shown as a pyramid in virtually every textbook, Maslow never actually presented his hierarchy as a pyramid, not in his original paper nor any of his subsequent books.[12] The first example of the use of Maslow's work shown as a pyramid is by the management consultant, Charles McDermid, in an article in *Business Horizons*, in 1960. You may wonder, does this matter? But it has some significant implications as it changes how we interpret

Maslow's work. By displaying it as a pyramid, it gives the impression that you need to complete each level to progress to the next (and which, once completed, you do not go back), which is not how Maslow viewed it.

Self-Determination Theory

Today, psychologists do not use Maslow's theory, but instead the dominant model used to explain human motivation is Self-Determination Theory (SDT). This approach is based on two key findings. Firstly, SDT assumes (similar to Maslow) that humans are motivated by growth and continual improvement.[13] However, for an individual to feel motivated, three universal criteria need to be met.

- *Autonomy*: An individual needs to perceive that they are in control of their own behaviour and psychologically free to choose how to act.
- *Competence*: This is about gaining a sense of mastery over the activities they participate in.
- *Relatedness*: This is a little different to the other two dimensions as it focuses on an individual's interpersonal dimensions or how they react with other people. SDT argues that people have an intrinsic need to feel connected to other people and feel part of a community or group.[14]

While this might seem a very similar approach to Maslow in proposing a set of universal criteria that motivate everyone, there are some key differences. Maslow typically assumes that an individual is motivated by one layer at a time, whereas with SDT, an individual could be motivated by three, two or just one of these factors. The other key difference is the fact that SDT recognizes that different individuals will prioritize different factors for different decisions, rather than prescribing one set approach. Often, this approach is used to explain employee motivation, but it can also be used to predict how shoppers act. For example, using SDT, it's possible to predict whether consumers will participate in a brand co-creation campaign[15] or if a shopper will use a self-service machine at a restaurant or supermarket.[16] Shoppers who have high autonomy needs were more likely to use a self-service machine than those who do not.

Intrinsic vs extrinsic motivation

The second key finding underpinning SDT is the concept that intrinsic motivation is a more powerful motivating factor than extrinsic motivation,[17] and this has profound implications for marketers. If a consumer engages in behaviour for its own sake and enjoyment, this would be defined as intrinsically motivating. Someone might climb a mountain because they enjoy the experience and find it fulfilling, and this would be considered intrinsic motivation. However, if they climbed the same mountain because they wanted to post a photo on Instagram or receive praise from friends, then they are extrinsically motivated. In this case, their behaviour is motivated by some form of external reinforcement. Unfortunately, this distinction is something that marketers often overlook when developing behaviour change strategies.

Providing someone with extrinsic rewards undermines their intrinsic motivation. If a company gives volunteers a small financial reward for volunteering, it reduces the amount of time they volunteer for by approximately four hours per month.[18] Even parents' praise can make a difference to children. Young children draw because they enjoy it, but when their parents praise them, they start drawing, hoping to receive more praise from their parents. Once the praise stops, the children stop drawing.[19] However, if a company tries to avoid these problems by using both intrinsic and extrinsic appeals as part of the same campaign, the results are often counterproductive. Such mixed messages tend to perform worse than campaigns focusing solely on an intrinsic appeal. For instance, when Laura Edinger-Schons and colleagues tested which messages would encourage people to buy organic bed linen and fair trade coffee, they found that if a company used both an intrinsic message such as, *'Buy this green product and help protect your local environment'* alongside an extrinsic message like, *'Buy this green product and save money today'*, it made shoppers less likely to buy the produce than when either message was used on its own, but especially the intrinsic appeal.[20]

> **GIVE IT A GO**
>
> Want to see how SDT applies to you? Complete the Intrinsic Motivation Inventory, which is one of the standard tools to measure intrinsic motivation and self-regulation and has been used in numerous laboratory experiments.
>
>

Gamification

Marketers really need to be aware of this, as many campaigns focus on only providing extrinsic motivation. A great example of this is the proliferation of motivational apps for smartphones. Not only do these apps help remind people when to engage in the target activity, but they often provide rewards for the behaviour, for example, a virtual certificate for '*30 days vegetarian*', '*praise for completing your longest run on*

Strava' or '*well done for achieving the most XP in a day on Duolingo*'. The more sophisticated apps also incorporate elements of 'gamification' into their design. This involves including elements of game design into these apps, for example, having different levels, requiring users to collect tokens for completing activities or challenges where you can compete against your friends.[21] As a pure reminder, these apps work well, such as one might intend to take the contraceptive pill at 7 pm every day, but it is very easy to forget, and so a reminder via your smartphone is helpful. These reminders have been shown to work across a range of contexts, from taking medication[22] to applying sunscreen.[23]

These apps do not even need to provide an alert to trigger the target behaviour; simply creating a record of when we engaged in the target behaviour is good enough to motivate shoppers, helping make the target behaviour more salient. For example, every-body knows that we are meant to brush our teeth twice a day, but new electric toothbrushes, such as the Philips Sonicare 7000, come with an app that shows how many times you brush your teeth each day, and more importantly, for how long. If you miss a day, there is nothing you can do. You'll never be able to go back and catch up. Your app will highlight that on average you only brushed your teeth on average 1.5 times a day last month. This becomes even more effective when this record becomes public.[24]

REAL-WORLD EXAMPLE: PSYCH IN ACTION

Strava is an online running app where runners can make a public declaration about how much they intend to run each week or month. Once someone has made a public commitment, they're more motivated to maintain the behaviour as they feel like they need to maintain a consistent and positive self-image.[25] Each time you go for a run, your time, distance and heart rate is shared amongst followers, which again motivates users to run more.[26] Friends can 'give kudos', virtual rewards which again helps to motivate to run more.[27] Over time, runners tend to change their behaviour, mimicking the behaviour of the people who provide them with the most kudos.

However, Duolingo has found a way to make this even more effective. Instead of asking users to make public declarations, they take the SDT principle of relatedness one step further. Rather than just rewarding individuals for their individual activities, users can complete quests where both parties have to complete tasks. Previous research has shown that these team-based rewards and challenges are more effective than just rewarding an individual.[28]

If a company decides they are going to use gamification principles to enhance short-term motivation, there are a number of principles they can incorporate into the design to improve its effectiveness, such as leader boards, which are common in apps like Strava, Duolingo or even Fortnite. These are highly motivating when someone finishes near the top of the board, but by definition half of all users will need to finish in the bottom half, which is understandably demotivating.[29] To move up a leader board, users need to earn points. Rationally, it would make sense for an app or an incentive programme to reward us every time they engage in the target behaviour. However, well-designed apps do not do this. Instead, they are more likely to use an 'intermittent schedule of reinforcement'; one where the user never knows if they are going to be rewarded for completing the desired behaviour, or even better what the reward is. If they are rewarded every time they complete the target behaviour, we learn to associate the reward with the behaviour very quickly. But as soon as we stop getting rewarded, so does the desired behaviour. However, if we are only sometimes rewarded, then although we are slower to learn, the behaviour continues even after we stop getting rewarded.[30]

Even if a company decides to use an intermittent reward schedule, that's not the only choice they have to make; they could allocate rewards randomly, or they could 'fix' the reward schedule. Research with gamblers has shown that those who receive a big win on their first bet are likely to cash out very quickly and stop playing early compared with gamblers who do not win at the start.[31] This makes sense that the same principles could be found with app designs and reinforcement. If users think that they are going to get a reward every time, it takes away the excitement and chance, and this makes sense as humans are motivated by chance and a gamble. When shoppers were given the choice of a guaranteed 50% discount off their shopping bill or a gamble of anything from nothing to 100% off their bill (and anything in between) based on the spin of a modified roulette wheel, most people opted for the gamble[32] rather than the guaranteed saving. Shoppers were motivated by the uncertain reward because they were focusing on the reward process and not the total outcome.[33]

But that is not to say early rewards are not useful when designing an app. To motivate people to use the app in the first place, researchers have found apps that provide a reward before users engage in the primary task are more valued and motivate us further.[34] This may sound like it contradicts SDT, but there is a subtle difference. The research, which focuses on providing users with early rewards, focuses on motivating users to ensure they complete the set-up process and use the app. It does not focus on motivating users to engage in the target behaviour.

But gamification comes at a cost. People use apps such as Duolingo to learn French, but because of the gamification principles employed, users' motivation becomes more about staying in the top league, achieving their daily XP goals or collecting badges, rather than learning the language. When people use these apps, they are far more likely to engage in the target behaviour (e.g. learning a language, exercising more etc.), however if they stop using the app, then the behaviour stops. Worryingly, it drops off to a level that is worse than if they did not use the app at all.[35] This may seem confusing, but it makes sense from an SDT perspective. Before they were using any apps, they were intrinsically motivated to complete the activity, but after they start using the app, they become extrinsically motivated (especially if it is gamified).

All of this starts to undermine our intrinsic motivation and we become motivated by the extrinsic rewards. So, when the extrinsic rewards stop, so does our motivation, and ultimately the behaviour.

Novelty

While there are only three innate psychological needs as part of Self-Determination Theory (autonomy, competence and relatedness) other researchers have speculated that there may be an extra one: novelty.[36] Whether it is, or not, is still up for debate, but either way, novelty and curiosity are useful tools in the marketer's arsenal. When consumers' curiosity is sparked, whether by an email subject line, an advert or just a clickbait headline, and the consumer fails to read on further, people find themselves in a state of suspense. This state of anticipation alters their motivation, making them more likely to seek indulgent rewards. Not only that, but they may also be willing to pay more for these rewards.[37] Hence, if you are developing an advert for a luxury holiday, you could incorporate something in the background that is likely to arouse a sense of intrigue, or even incorporate some sort of riddle at the start into the story-line. Similarly, sales assistants could easily apply this technique in their interactions, using curiosity to captivate and persuade potential buyers.

The power of novelty is so strong that shoppers are often willing to accept unpleasant consequences in order to satisfy their curiosity. In laboratory-based experiments, Christopher Hsee and Bowen Ruan discovered that when participants were left in a state of suspense, they were willing to accept an electric shock[38] in return for having their curiosity satisfied. Laboratory experiment findings may be a world away from the supermarket, but we see the same pattern playing out in-store. Shoppers are prepared to accept a worse deal just to satisfy their short-term curiosity, like the roulette wheel, even if they'll feel worse about it in the long term.

So why is novelty such a powerful motivating force? When shoppers experience a sense of novelty, it's been shown to trigger a release of dopamine, a neurotransmitter which is associated with motivational salience (and not pleasure).[39] Consequently, this leads to shoppers being in a more positive mood, having a more positive outlook, and more importantly, a stronger motivation to purchase,[40] all of which are useful for marketers.

Implementation intentions

Marketers use several tactics to motivate people to change their behaviour. One of the simplest is the way they phrase or 'frame' their request. All too often marketers think that if they make a good argument and tell people the facts, then they will change their behaviour. But life rarely works like this. From a behaviour-change perspective, this is called the '*intention-behaviour gap*'; the idea that our intentions do not always turn into actions.[41] Someone may intend to get fitter, but Monday evening comes around, it's raining, and they struggle to find the motivation to go for a run. Instead of asking 'if they are going to go for a run', marketers should ask them to create an '*if-then plan*'; if X occurs, then they should do Y; what is known as an implementation intention. So, rather than simply deciding '*I'm going to study more*', an implementation intention would be reframed as '*If it is 7 pm, then I'll start revising*'.[42] It may seem like a trivial difference, but this small change makes a big difference, even when it comes to tackling some serious issues.

One of the biggest challenges doctors face is not diagnosing patients but getting patients to follow their instructions and take their medication as prescribed. But Ian Brown, Paschal Sheeran and Markus Reuber found that if they change how they spoke to their patients, they could easily change their compliance rate. When people who have epilepsy were asked to take their medication every day, the compliance rate was only 50%, but when they were asked to create their own implementation intention (e.g. 'If it is 1 pm and I'm sitting down to lunch, then I will take my tablet'), compliance shot up to 80%.[43] The same approach can be used in marketing. For example, Frank Kardes' team were trying to promote a new range of household cleaning products; they offered potential customers a demonstration of the new product in action, along with a free sample, so they could try it at home. However, the marketers tested two different ways of framing the offer. Half of the customers were simply asked whether or not they would try the product, but the other half were asked to specify exactly when, where and for what purposes they would use the product. Two weeks later, when the customers were contacted again, they found that the people who were asked to be specific in how they would use the product ended up using the product twice as often, used three times more of the product, liked the product more and ultimately were more likely to buy the product.[44]

From a psychological perspective, what is interesting is the fact that these implementation intentions do not change our motivations to achieve our goals.[45] Instead, they work by making it easier for individuals to remember the plan. The easier it is for people to remember the plan, and the stronger the association between the different components of the plan, the more likely they are to go through with their plan.

When to motivate

When people approach big life milestones, such as turning 40, 50 or 60, they often feel that it signifies the end of an era, the end of our thirties, forties or fifties. This causes people to reflect on their lives and question what they have accomplished. Consequently, as we approach the end of a decade (when we are 29, 39, 49 etc.), people are more likely to decide on sweeping changes to their lives. They are statistically more likely to enter their first marathon, have an affair or just search for meaning in life.[46] Marketers could capitalize on this and try to encourage consumers to buy a new villa in the Alps or a new motorbike when they know a consumer is 49, but it is not the most helpful tactic for marketing as it only occurs once a decade. But this *'fresh start effect'* can occur at other points in our lives. Data from Google suggests that lots of people make New Year's resolutions with the aim to better themselves as there is a dramatic increase in the volume of people searching for diets or gym membership in January[47] but a similar (albeit smaller) pattern occurs at other points of the year. People are more likely to start aspirational behaviours at the start of a new week, month, after a birthday or a key holiday.

Therefore, if marketers want to encourage customers to engage in a new goal or habit, it makes sense for them to frame it around a key milestone. This approach is not just restricted to birthdays and Christmas – there are lots of key dates in the year that can be framed as a milestone. The important thing is that the date is perceived to be a milestone. For example, most people in the US will view 20th March as just another day (unless it is your birthday or anniversary, it is unlikely to act as a fresh start). However, when Dai Hengchen framed it as 'the first day of spring', this was enough to trigger the fresh start effect[48] and motivate people to change their behaviour. The key is all about finding a key event to base your campaign around and reminding people that it serves as a fresh start.

One situation where marketers and public policy experts have struggled to motivate people to change their behaviour is saving for retirement. From a psychological perspective, people value a smaller immediate reward more than a larger future reward,[49] and when it comes to pensions, you are asking people to forgo an immediate reward for a benefit they won't receive for maybe 40 years. One approach marketers have tried to get around this problem is by asking people not to save now but to precommit to saving a percentage of their salary in the future. While it sounds like a sensible plan, the data shows it often leads to lower retirement savings overall.[50] By framing it as a choice to start saving now or in nine months' time, it gives people the impression that this is not an urgent priority. Retirement could be decades away, so people delay saving. But if you ask people to increase the amount they save each month from their next birthday (the fresh start effect), it significantly increases the number of employees who agree to start saving more.

The Cobra Effect: When marketing interventions backfire

One of the key objectives of marketers is to motivate consumers to buy their products. Unfortunately, there are numerous examples where behaviour change campaigns backfire and make the situation worse, often referred to as the Cobra Effect. The name comes from a supposed behaviour change campaign that took place in India when it was ruled by the British. At the time, Delhi was suffering from an infestation of cobras. The British government tried to motivate citizens to capture the cobras by offering them a financial reward for each cobra skin they sold to the government. However, Delhiites realized it was far safer to breed cobras, kill them and sell the skin to the government rather than catch wild cobras. Eventually, the government worked out what was going on and abandoned the scheme. Overnight, cobra farming became unprofitable, and millions of cobras were released into the wild, dramatically increasing the wild population of cobras.[51]

It is unclear whether this event occurred or if it is just an apocryphal story, but other more recent examples do exist. In 2008, the Oakland police introduced a gun buy-back scheme. Anybody could walk into a police station and sell the police their guns for $250, no catch, and no questions asked. The aim was to reduce criminals' easy access to guns but despite the scheme having a huge uptake, it was a policy disaster. Individuals were handing in their old guns and using the money to buy a better gun. Some criminals were using it as a 'safe' way to dispose of weapons that had been used in crimes, whereas other more opportunistic individuals were buying guns from people in care homes and selling them on to the police. And to make matters worse, it left the police department with a $170,000 debt.[52]

While the Cobra Effect primarily concentrates on the negative impact of financial rewards, it is important not to forget how financial incentives change consumers' motivation. As discussed earlier, providing a financial reward can undermine intrinsic motivation. But businesses and governments regularly also use fines as a tool to discourage consumers from engaging in certain behaviours or activities: driving too fast or not returning hire equipment on time. But in some situations, a small fine encourages people to engage in this behaviour.

A nursery in Israel introduced a new policy to encourage parents to pick their children up on time. The nursery shut at 4pm and most parents picked up their children on time, but occasionally a few parents were late. The nursery introduced a fine for any parents who were late. Standard economic theory would suggest that this would be a motivator, but it ended up having the opposite result; there was a dramatic increase in the number of parents picking up their children late.[53] Before the fine was introduced, parents felt guilty or ashamed if they were late. Once they knew they were going to be fined, they perceived the fine as an extra fee for supervising their children after hours. Consequently, it removed any guilt or pressure associated with picking up their children late. After all, a fine is just permission to do something, for a fee.

This goes to highlight just how complex human motivation is. There are often multiple factors motivating the same behaviour and these will not be the same in all consumers. Someone may be vegetarian because they are concerned about animal welfare, another because they want to improve their health and someone else may just choose to be vegetarian because they want to fit in with their friends. Sometimes we may not even admit these factors to ourselves.

Motivation and sustainable behaviour change

Launching sustainable products

Climate change poses a major challenge for the planet and while governments around the world are tackling the issue with various degrees of urgency, businesses are responding to pressure from consumers to launch new sustainable versions of their products. Unfortunately, a surprisingly high number of these products either fail or achieve lower sales than their conventional counterparts.[54] The reason is often relatively simple, they forget the reason why people bought the product in the first place.

A great example of this is when a company launched a 100% natural, biodegradable mountain bike chain oil. Mountain biking is a great way to explore the mountains, but despite not having an engine, it still has a negative impact on the environment. Oil flicks off the chain and soaks into the soil; consequently a biodegradable oil seemed the perfect solution. It performed just as well as traditional oil in tests, but without any of the negative environmental impacts. However, from a sales perspective, it was a total failure. The marketing campaign focused virtually exclusively on the environmental credentials of the product and ignored people's motivation for buying it in the first place: the ability to improve a bike's performance and give a faster and more exhilarating ride. Sustainability may well be a great point of differentiation, but you still need to show customers that your product will perform.

What motivates behaviour

Understanding motivation is not only important when it comes to trying to convince people to buy sustainable products; it's just as important when we are trying to change any behaviour and again, this is something that most people don't consider. Most government campaigns trying to persuade people to stop using UV sunbeds take a fact-based approach, highlighting health risks associated with sunbed use. Education-based campaigns may do a great job at increasing people's knowledge about a topic, but they don't change behaviour.[55] People use sunbeds because they want a suntan, thinking it looks attractive; therefore, if you want to persuade someone, it's more effective to use a vanity-based message, rather than a health-based message.[56] Tell people that *'using a sunbed will cause your skin to age prematurely'* or more emotively, *'How would you like it if you looked 50 when you're only 25? If so, a sunbed might be right for you.'*

The same principle applies when marketers try to develop adverts that motivate people to act against climate change. Currently, most people in Europe don't feel personally threatened by climate change. They accept that climate change is a global problem, but they are unsure what impact it will have on them; as a concept, climate change is perceived as vague, abstract and difficult for most people to understand.[57] Marketers have tried scaring people into action, but the results are mixed at best.[58]

So, how do we make climate change feel more real? Adverts need to stop making climate change feel like an abstract concept. Rather than focusing on how climate change impacts a distant corner of the world, focus on the local impact.[59] Likewise, our use of language can magnify this effect. It should be easy for people to mentally visualize the impact.[60] We may think that we are using concrete language by saying things such as 'each year 150 billion metric tons of ice is lost from the Antarctic ice sheet'. The problem is that nobody can visualize what 150 billion tons of ice looks like.

Instead, it is better for adverts to be personally relevant to the target audience. If a marketer knows that somebody is interested in skiing, they should talk about how climate change is putting their ski holidays at risk, rather than general messages about the dangers of climate change.[61] For example, an advert could target skiers to take action on climate change with messages such as '*One in eight ski resorts worldwide are projected to have no snow by 2100*'[62] or '*By 2050, 70% of Verbier and Zermatt's snow will be gone. Act now to save our alps*'.[63] Or if somebody is a keen golfer, focus on how climate change is going to threaten the local golf course, such as '*34 of the UK's best links golf courses are already threatened by climate change and sea level rising*'.[64]

While messages that focus on the melting of European glaciers are using an explicit shock tactic, when focusing on the impact of climate change close to home, it is more effective to use a hopeful message. Naturally, people resist confronting negative information and may actively choose to ignore these messages. However, if instead you focus on the global impact of climate change, then it is more effective to use a fear appeal. People pay more attention to sustainable behaviour change ads which use a fear appeal, end up having a more positive attitude towards environmental issues and are ultimately more likely to change their behaviour.[65]

Although climate change is a serious issue, it doesn't mean that any campaigns focusing on building awareness or motivating people to change their behaviour need to be dull. In fact, it is often more effective for marketing campaigns to use humour to help get their message across. While it may seem counterproductive, undermining the seriousness of the message, it is important to remember that marketers are still producing an advert, and it needs to both attract attention and be engaging. People tend to remember humorous messages more than facts alone and consequently people are more likely to remember the message, even for sustainability messages.[66] This is a lesson that public health campaigns have recently learnt. Traditionally, most health-related messages were rather sombre and fact-driven. Campaigns with the aim of raising awareness about testicular cancer focused on raw statistics like *'Testicular cancer is the most common form of cancer in young men'*.[67] But in recent years, campaigns have shifted to a more humorous tone with slogans such as *'play with your balls once a month'* or *'make your balls a bigger part of your life. Check yourself regularly'*. These cheeky innuendos resonate with the target audience, boosting engagement and ultimately awareness.[68]

Closing thoughts

While marketers often talk about motivation, it is essential for them to understand the primary factors that are driving consumer behaviour. Unfortunately, this is often harder than they'd like, as simply asking shoppers what motivates them rarely reveals genuine answers. (For a detailed overview of the challenges of research methods, see Chapter 16). It's all too easy to think about what would motivate you as a marketer, and not consider things from the shopper's perspective. In these situations, models such as Self-Determination Theory help provide marketers with an insight into the psychological mechanism which drive customer behaviour.

> **KEY POINTS**
>
> - Although Maslow's Hierarchy of Needs is one of the most commonly used models to discuss human motivation, most psychologists do not consider it a valid model due to its lack of empirical evidence.
> - Currently, the dominant model used by psychologists to measure human motivation is Self-Determination Theory. The three core components are autonomy, competence and relatedness.
> - Intrinsic motivation (engaging in behaviour for its own enjoyment) is more powerful than extrinsic motivation (behaviour driven by external rewards like praise or money).
> - Offering extrinsic rewards can undermine intrinsic motivation, leading to reduced long-term engagement in the target behaviour.
> - Rather than just asking someone to complete a task, it is more effective for marketers to frame a goal as an 'if-then plan'. Rather than saying, 'I will study more', follow through is significantly higher if the plan is 'If it's 7 pm, then I will study more'.

- When people are approaching major life milestones (like turning 30, 40 or 50), it motivates people to reappraise their life, making it more likely they will start a new habit. People are more likely to start aspirational behaviours at the start of a new week, month, after a birthday or a key holiday.

- When it comes to motivating shoppers to buy a product, marketers need to remember the primary reason why a customer buys the product in the first place. For most shoppers, environmental factors may be a secondary consideration to buying a product. It may help convince a shopper to buy 'Product A' over 'Product B', however, the shopper will still need to believe that the product will perform its primary purpose.

PUTTING THEORY INTO PRACTICE

1 Imagine you are developing a new phone app to help people train their dogs. How could you incorporate principles of both gamification and Self-Determination Theory (SDT) to encourage users to continue using the app?

2 If a government health initiative offered to financially reward unfit people for completing the 'couch to 5K' (a fitness plan where people aim to run 20–30 minutes, three times a week and then after nine weeks they aim to complete a 5km run), from an SDT perspective, what are the potential risks when the scheme ends?

3 Consider the apps that you use most on your phone. What principles of motivational psychology do they use to encourage you to keep using the apps?

4 If you had been commissioned by a fast-moving consumer goods (FMCG) brand to develop a new marketing campaign, how could you use implementation intentions to encourage customers to use their product more regularly? This is about both the psychological principle behind the campaign, but also the practical considerations, such as how you would structure your marketing campaign.

5 Develop three different advert concepts for a brand of your choice. However, each advert needs to be for the same brand and be structured around the three core components of SDT: autonomy, competence and relatedness.

6 If an FMCG brand commissioned you to design a shopper marketing campaign to be launched across a national supermarket chain to promote one of their brands, how could you use the 'principle of novelty' to encourage shoppers to interact with the display?

> **SUGGESTIONS FOR FURTHER READING**
>
> Reeve, J. (2024). Understanding motivation and emotion: 8th Edition. John Wiley & Sons.

References

1. Deckers, L. (2018). *Motivation: Biological, psychological, and environmental.* Routledge.
2. Brown, S. D., Duncan, J., Crabtree, D., Powell, D., Hudson, M., & Allan, J. L. (2020). We are what we (think we) eat: The effect of expected satiety on subsequent calorie consumption. *Appetite*, 152, 104717. https://doi.org/10.1016/j.appet.2020.104717 (archived at https://perma.cc/7SV4-AEJW)
3. Mela, D. J., Aaron, J. L., & Gatenby, S. J. (1996). Relationships of consumer characteristics and food deprivation to food purchasing behavior. *Physiology & Behavior*, 60(5), 1331–1335.
4. al, A., & Wansink, B. (2013). Appetite for destruction: Hunger leads to less healthy food choices. *JAMA Internal Medicine*
5. Xu, A. J., Schwarz, N., & Jr, R. S. W. (2015). *Hunger promotes acquisition of nonfood objects.* Proceedings of the National Academy of Sciences, 112(9), 2688–2692. https://doi.org/10.1073/pnas.1417712112 (archived at https://perma.cc/QR9X-TBFR)
6. Maslow, A. H. (1943). A theory of human motivation. *Psychological Review*, 50(4), 370–396. https://doi.org/10.1037/h0054346 (archived at https://perma.cc/JL8V-UGJG)
7. Maslow, A. H. (1943). A theory of human motivation. *Psychological Review*, 50(4), 370–396. https://doi.org/10.1037/h0054346 (archived at https://perma.cc/GAU8-PGZX)
8. Maslow, A. H. (1971). *The farther reaches of human nature.* Viking Press.
9. Maslow, A. H. (1943). A theory of human motivation. *Psychological Review*, 50(4), 370–396. https://doi.org/10.1037/h0054346 (archived at https://perma.cc/GTD6-S56X)
10. Maslow, A. H. (1987). *Motivation and personality: Third Edition.* Addison-Wesley Educational Publishers Inc.
11. Wahba, M. A. & Bridwell, L. G. (1976). Maslow reconsidered: A review of research on the need hierarchy theory. *Organizational Behavior and Human Performance*, 15(2), 212–240. https://doi.org/10.1016/0030-5073(76)90038-6 (archived at https://perma.cc/9EMX-LRXN)
12. Bridgman, T., Cummings, S., & Ballard, J. (2019). Who built Maslow's pyramid? A history of the creation of management studies' most famous symbol and its implications for management education. *Academy of Management Learning & Education*, 18(1), 81–98. https://doi.org/10.5465/amle.2017.0351 (archived at https://perma.cc/SEK6-89D5)

13 Deci, E. L. & Ryan, R. M. (1985). *Intrinsic motivation and self-determination in human behavior*. Springer. https://doi.org/https://doi.org/10.1007/978-1-4899-2271-7 (archived at https://perma.cc/X8GU-WQ77)

14 Deci, E. L. & Ryan, R. M. (2004). *Handbook of self-determination research*. Univ of Rochester Press.

15 Hsieh, S. H. & Chang, A. (2016). The psychological mechanism of brand co-creation engagement. *Journal of Interactive Marketing*, 33, 13–26. https://doi.org/10.1016/j.intmar.2015.10.001 (archived at https://perma.cc/C2MP-RQK5)

16 Leung, L. S. K. & Matanda, M. J. (2013). The impact of basic human needs on the use of retailing self-service technologies: A study of self-determination theory. *Journal of Retailing and Consumer Services*, 20(6), 549–559. https://doi.org/10.1016/j.jretconser.2013.06.003 (archived at https://perma.cc/22VQ-956Q)

17 Deci, E. L. & Ryan, R. M. (1985). *Intrinsic motivation and self-determination in human behavior*. Springer. https://doi.org/https://doi.org/10.1007/978-1-4899-2271-7 (archived at https://perma.cc/V9ZA-KH8A)

18 Freeman, R. B. (1997). Working for nothing: The supply of volunteer labor. *Journal of Labor Economics*, 15(1, Part 2), S140–S166. https://doi.org/10.1086/209859 (archived at https://perma.cc/9ZH2-VA4W)

19 Lepper, M. R., Greene, D., & Nisbett, R. E. (1973). Undermining children's intrinsic interest with extrinsic reward: A test of the 'overjustification' hypothesis. *Journal of Personality and Social Psychology*, 28(1), 129–137. https://doi.org/10.1037/h0035519 (archived at https://perma.cc/F3J2-GNW3)

20 Edinger-Schons, L. M., Sipilä, J., Sen, S., Mende, G., & Wieseke, J. (2018). Are two reasons better than one? The role of appeal type in consumer responses to sustainable products. *Journal of Consumer Psychology*, 28(4), 644–664.

21 Alsawaier, R. S. (2018). The effect of gamification on motivation and engagement. *The International Journal of Information and Learning Technology*, 35(1), 56–79. https://doi.org/10.1108/ijilt-02-2017-0009 (archived at https://perma.cc/XC5D-8EQ7)

22 Santo, K., Singleton, A., Rogers, K., Thiagalingam, A., Chalmers, J., Chow, C. K., & Redfern, J. (2019). Medication reminder applications to improve adherence in coronary heart disease: A randomised clinical trial. *Heart*, 105(4), 323. https://doi.org/10.1136/heartjnl-2018-313479 (archived at https://perma.cc/44F3-FQP8)

23 Armstrong, A. W., Watson, A. J., Makredes, M., Frangos, J. E., Kimball, A. B., & Kvedar, J. C. (2009). Text-message reminders to improve sunscreen use: A randomized, controlled trial using electronic monitoring. *Archives of Dermatology*, 145(11), 1230–1236. https://doi.org/10.1001/archdermatol.2009.269 (archived at https://perma.cc/E3WA-5XCQ)

24 Gollwitzer, P. M., Sheeran, P., Michalski, V., & Seifert, A. E. (2009). When intentions go public: Does social reality widen the intention-behavior gap?. *Psychological science*, 20(5), 612–618.

25 Cialdini, R.B. (2008). *Influence: Science and practice*, 5th ed. Boston: Pearson.

26 Russell, H. C., Potts, C., & Nelson, E. (2023). 'If It's not on Strava it didn't happen': Perceived Psychosocial implications of Strava use in collegiate club runners. *Recreational Sports Journal*, 47(1), 15–25. https://doi.org/10.1177/15588661221148170 (archived at https://perma.cc/YY32-6XT2)

27 Franken, R., Bekhuis, H., & Tolsma, J. (2023). Kudos make you run! How runners influence each other on the online social network Strava. *Social Networks*, 72, 151–164.

28 Pearson, E., Prapavessis, H., Higgins, C., Petrella, R., White, L., & Mitchell, M. (2020). Adding team-based financial incentives to the Carrot Rewards physical activity app increases daily step count on a population scale: A 24-week matched case control study. *International Journal of Behavioral Nutrition and Physical Activity*, 17(1), 1–10.

29 Östlund, F. (2020). Leaderboards in fitness applications and their effect on motivation. In *Student Conference in Interaction Technology and Design* (Vol. 64).

30 Ferster, C. B. & Skinner, B. F. (1957). *Schedules of reinforcement*. Appleton-Century-Crofts.

31 Weatherly, J. N., Sauter, J. M., & King, B. M. (2004). The 'big win' and resistance to extinction when gambling. *The Journal of Psychology*, 138(6), 495–504. https://doi.org/10.3200/jrlp.138.6.495-504 (archived at https://perma.cc/5YKP-LSC7)

32 Johnson, M. & Ghuman, P. (2020). *Blindsight: The (mostly) hidden ways marketing reshapes our brains*. BenBella Books Inc.

33 Shen, L., Fishbach, A., & Hsee, C. K. (2015). The motivating-uncertainty effect: Uncertainty increases resource investment in the process of reward pursuit. *Journal of Consumer Research*, 41(5), 1301–1315. https://doi.org/10.1086/679418 (archived at https://perma.cc/JH8G-4Q6Z)

34 Garaialde, D., Cox, A. L., & Cowan, B. R. (2021). Designing gamified rewards to encourage repeated app selection: Effect of reward placement. *International Journal of Human-Computer Studies*, 153, 102661. https://doi.org/10.1016/j.ijhcs.2021.102661 (archived at https://perma.cc/QBU8-BPF2)

35 Austin, C. G. & Kwapisz, A. (2017). The road to unintended consequences is paved with motivational apps. *Journal of Consumer Affairs*, 51(2), 463–477. https://doi.org/10.1111/joca.12135 (archived at https://perma.cc/9NEH-6XPQ)

36 González-Cutre, D., Sicilia, Á., Sierra, A. C., Ferriz, R., & Hagger, M. S. (2016). Understanding the need for novelty from the perspective of self-determination theory. *Personality and individual differences*, 102, 159–169.

37 Wiggin, K. L., Reimann, M., & Jain, S. P. (2018). Curiosity tempts indulgence. *Journal of Consumer Research*, 45(6), 1194–1212. https://doi.org/10.1093/jcr/ucy055 (archived at https://perma.cc/S3ZL-4CZH)

38 Hsee, C. K. & Ruan, B. (2016). The Pandora effect: The power and peril of curiosity. *Psychological Science*, 27(5), 659–666.

39 Berridge, K. C. & Robinson, T. E. (1998). What is the role of dopamine in reward: Hedonic impact, reward learning, or incentive salience?. *Brain Research Reviews*, 28(3), 309–369.

40 Costa, V. D., Tran, V. L., Turchi, J., & Averbeck, B. B. (2014). Dopamine modulates novelty seeking behavior during decision making. *Behavioral Neuroscience*, 128(5), 556.

41 Faries, M. D. (2016). Why we don't 'just do it'. *American Journal of Lifestyle Medicine*, 10(5), 322–329. https://doi.org/10.1177/1559827616638017 (archived at https://perma.cc/5372-SBB2)

42 Gollwitzer, P. M. (1999). Implementation intentions: Strong effects of simple plans. *American Psychologist*, 54(7), 493–503. https://doi.org/10.1037/0003-066x.54.7.493 (archived at https://perma.cc/B7C6-N2U5)

43 Brown, I., Sheeran, P., & Reuber, M. (2009). Enhancing antiepileptic drug adherence: A randomized controlled trial. *Epilepsy & Behavior*, 16(4), 634–639. https://doi.org/10.1016/j.yebeh.2009.09.014 (archived at https://perma.cc/S8LX-32RE)

44 Kardes, F. R., Cronley, M. L., & Posavac, S. S. (2005). Using implementation intentions to increase new product consumption: A field experiment. In F. R. Kardes, P. Herr, & J. Nantel, *Applying Social Cognition to Consumer-Focused Strategy* (pp. 219–233). Lawrence Erlbaum Associates.

45 Webb, T. L. & Sheeran, P. (2008). Mechanisms of implementation intention effects: The role of goal intentions, self-efficacy, and accessibility of plan components. *British Journal of Social Psychology*, 47(3), 373–395. https://doi.org/10.1348/014466607x267010 (archived at https://perma.cc/A3B6-63B4)

46 Alter, A. L. & Hershfield, H. E. (2014). *People search for meaning when they approach a new decade in chronological age*. Proceedings of the National Academy of Sciences, 111(48), 17066–17070. https://doi.org/10.1073/pnas.1415086111

47 Dai, H., Milkman, K. L., & Riis, J. (2014). The Fresh Start Effect: Temporal landmarks motivate aspirational behavior. *Management Science*, 60(10), 2563–2582. https://doi.org/10.1287/mnsc.2014.1901 (archived at https://perma.cc/5CUU-KUAW)

48 Dai, H., Milkman, K. L., & Riis, J. (2015). Put your imperfections behind you: Temporal landmarks spur goal initiation when they signal new beginnings. *Psychological Science*, 26(12), 1927–1936. https://doi.org/10.1177/0956797615605818 (archived at https://perma.cc/B68P-JCDQ)

49 Laibson, D. (1997). Golden eggs and hyperbolic discounting. *The Quarterly Journal of Economics*, 112(2), 443–478.

50 Beshears, J., Dai, H., Milkman, K. L., & Benartzi, S. (2016). *Framing the future: The risks of pre-commitment nudges and potential of fresh start messaging.* Working Paper.

51 Jr, P. W. (2021). The Cobra Effect: Kisor, Roberts, and the law of unintended consequences. *SSRN Electronic Journal*, 1(54). https://doi.org/10.2139/ssrn.3529598 (archived at https://perma.cc/PE4E-K6JG)

52 Burt, C. (2008, February 12). Cops owe $170,000 from gun buyback. East Bay Times. https://www.eastbaytimes.com/2008/02/12/cops-owe-170000-from-gun-buyback-2/ (archived at https://perma.cc/JF6H-HVTB)

53 Gneezy, U. & Rustichini, A. (2000). A fine is a price. *The Journal of Legal Studies*, 29(1), 1–17. https://doi.org/10.1086/468061 (archived at https://perma.cc/26QN-A2CB)

54 Van Doorn, J., Risselada, H., & Verhoef, P. C. (2021). Does sustainability sell? The impact of sustainability claims on the success of national brands' new product introductions. *Journal of Business Research*, 137, 182–193.

55 Lamanna, L. (2004). College students' knowledge and attitudes about cancer and perceived risks of developing skin cancer. *Dermatology Nursing*, 16. 161–4.

56 Persson, S., Benn, Y., Dhingra, K., Clark-Carter, D., Owen, A. L., & Grogan, S. (2018). Appearance-based interventions to reduce UV exposure: A systematic review. *British Journal of Health Psychology*, 23(2), 334–351. https://doi.org/10.1111/bjhp.12291 (archived at https://perma.cc/5D6B-ZCVH)

57 Corner, A. (2012). *Evaluating arguments about climate change. In Perspectives on Scientific Argumentation* (pp. 201–220). Springer, Dordrecht. http://doi.org/10.1007/978-94-007-2470-9_10 (archived at https://perma.cc/36KP-9ERH)

58 O'neill, S. & Nicholson-Cole, S. (2009). 'Fear won't do it' promoting positive engagement with climate change through visual and iconic representations. *Science communication*, 30(3), 355–379. https://doi.org/10.1177/1075547008329201 (archived at https://perma.cc/44CK-LRPG)

59 Scannell, L. & Gifford, R. (2013). Personally relevant climate change: The role of place attachment and local versus global message framing in engagement. *Environment and Behavior*, 45(1), 60–85.

60 Karlsson, H., Asutay, E., & Västfjäll, D. (2023). A causal link between mental imagery and affect-laden perception of climate change related risks. *Scientific Reports*, 13(1), 10081.

61 Chen, F., Dai, S., Zhu, Y., & Xu, H. (2020). Will concerns for ski tourism promote pro-environmental behaviour? An implication of protection motivation theory. *International Journal of Tourism Research*, 22(3), 303–313.

62 Woodford, J. (2024, March 13) One in eight ski resorts worldwide could have no snow by 2100. New Scientist. https://www.newscientist.com/article/2422017-one-in-eight-ski-resorts-worldwide-could-have-no-snow-by-2100/#:~:text=Skiing%20in%20many%20parts%20of,annual%20snow%20cover%20by%202100. (archived at https://perma.cc/LM9J-AA7U)

63 Matiu, M., Crespi, A., Bertoldi, G., Carmagnola, C. M., Marty, C., Morin, S., ... & Weilguni, V. (2021). Observed snow depth trends in the European Alps: 1971 to 2019. *The Cryosphere*, 15(3), 1343–1382.

64 McLaughlin, C. (2024, April 3). The golf courses disappearing into the sea. https://www.bbc.co.uk/news/articles/cqljjg1zq31o (archived at https://perma.cc/SEK5-F98R)

65 Lee, Y. K., Chang, C. T., & Chen, P. C. (2017). What sells better in green communications: Fear or hope?: It depends on whether the issue is global or local. *Journal of Advertising Research*, 57(4), 379–396.

66 Bonnici, T., Briguglio, M., & Spiteri, G. W. (2023). Humor helps: An experimental analysis of pro-environmental social media communication. *Sustainability*, 15(6), 5157.

67 NHS England (2020). Cancer registration statistics, England 2020. https://digital.nhs.uk/data-and-information/publications/statistical/cancer-registration-statistics/england-2020/the-3-most-common-cancers-by-gender-and-age (archived at https://perma.cc/MT86-NB7W)

68 Miller, E., Bergmeier, H. J., Blewitt, C., O'Connor, A., & Skouteris, H. (2021). A systematic review of humour-based strategies for addressing public health priorities. *Australian and New Zealand Journal of Public Health*, 45(6), 568–577.

4 | The psychology of personality

LEARNING OBJECTIVES

- Demonstrate an understanding of the historical development of personality theories and concepts.
- Evaluate how personality types can predict consumer behaviour.
- Analyse how brands can use personality traits to segment a market and produce targeted marketing campaigns.

Personality: A new approach to segmentation

Marketers spend a lot of their time trying to predict how consumers are going to behave. But in most situations, focusing on individual consumers is too expensive to be of any practical use and so we group them into segments, groups of consumers who share common traits. In an ideal world, marketers want each group to be as different as possible from each other, while ensuring that every consumer in a group is as similar as possible – no easy task. Normally expressed as *'increasing the variance between groups while decreasing the variance within groups'*, the typical approach to segmentation is to create clusters based around demographic, geographic or even behavioural variables. But just because individuals are roughly the same age (e.g. Millennials) does not mean there is a high degree of group cohesion. Relatively speaking, Millennials, Generation X and Generation Z are all diverse groups. In fact, recent research by BBH Labs has shown that there is a greater level of group cohesion amongst individuals who read the *Financial Times*, people who floss their teeth or those who work in marketing[1] than by generations.

However, psychologists have another trick up their sleeves: personality. Compared with generations, there is a much higher degree of group cohesion amongst people who share personality traits,[2] making it a far more useful tool to segment a market. At its most basic level, personality refers to 'an individual's characteristic patterns of thought, emotion, and behaviour, together with the psychological mechanisms – hidden or not – behind those patterns'.[3] This may sound fancy, but in simple terms, this is just the predictable way that a person reacts to life. Encounter a novel situation and most people react in a relatively consistent pattern of behaviour.

Although marketers spend a lot of time considering brand personality, human personality traits are rarely considered. Nonetheless, psychologists have been fascinated by personality for over a century.

Freudian marketing

One of the earliest psychologists to investigate personality was Sigmund Freud (1856–1939). In 1923, he proposed a new model of the mind (not the brain), arguing that it could be divided into three different constructs: the Id, Ego and Superego. From Freud's perspective, what is commonly referred to as a personality is the interplay between these three constructs.

At the simplest level, the Id is the most basic aspect of our personality. It is present from birth, and it is our mind's desire to achieve our most basic needs and wants; commonly referred to as the pleasure principle; our desire to have sex, drink or do almost anything that is pleasurable. However, often these behaviours are considered by society to be unacceptable, and it is the Ego's role to find a way that the desires of the Id can be satisfied without breaking societal norms. But it is not a moral compass. Our Ego has no concept of right or wrong. It's simply aware that if we engage in behaviour that breaks society's norms, then there is the chance of causing harm to oneself. Instead, our moral compass is our Superego, which starts developing about the age of five. From this age, we start to internalize a moral code based on how we are treated by our parents, peers and society as a whole.[4]

Freud's theories have been widely discredited and are now perceived to be pseudoscience rather than science,[5] but that's not to say that his approach to personality did not widely influence marketing in the 20th century. Freud was one of the first researchers to recognize that behaviour is driven not by conscious forces, but subconscious forces; the interplay between the Id, Ego and Superego. And although Freud never worked in advertising or PR, his nephew Edward Bernays (1891–1905) and another Viennese psychologist, Ernest Dichter (1907–1991) did. Between the two of them, they were responsible for some of the biggest marketing campaigns and cultural shifts of the 20th century.

Edward Bernay worked on campaigns for 'Lucky Strike' cigarettes, which for the first time made it socially acceptable to smoke. He reframed smoking not just as a habit for nicotine, but as a bold statement of feminism, freedom and independence. Bernays also played a key role in reshaping the American diet. Prior to his work, most people had relatively light breakfasts, such as fruit or porridge. He developed a marketing campaign that suggested that a protein-rich breakfast of bacon and eggs was healthier than a light breakfast, and the line 'breakfast is the most important meal of the day' was born, along with bacon being a staple of the American breakfast.

Using a Freudian analysis, both Dichter and Bernays recognized that purchasing products is as much about symbolism as it is about utilitarianism, and the marketing campaigns they developed reflected this. Dichter's work for Ivory Soap emphasized that it could wash the past and prepare you for a new start: '*Be smart, and get a fresh start with Ivory soap*'; or his work for his Esso petrol which led to the adoption of the slogan '*Put a tiger in your tank*', which symbolized the sheer power of Esso petrol and the sexual power that comes from driving.[6]

Based on Freud's work, both realized that traditional research methods were futile. If people are motivated by subconscious factors, explicitly asking them what they want or why they buy products is pointless as they are unable to answer. Instead, they changed the traditional approach of research, relying on in-depth interviews and focus groups to discover what they perceived to be the real motivation for buying and using a product. This resulted in a very different form of marketing. Rather than focusing on rational persuasion, which dominated the industry at the time, they focused on selling by developing campaigns that focused on the Id, targeting our most basic desires. For example, they argued people do not drive a sports car to get from A to B, but because it symbolizes youth and freedom.[7]

But it is not possible to discuss Dichter's work without acknowledging that a lot of the conclusions he reached are considered highly sexist today. Perhaps it is no surprise considering Dichter's work was heavily influenced by Freud. He found sex to be a motive for the majority of consumer behaviour. But it was how he believed women thought that is really outdated. He argued women wear make-up as a form of psychological therapy used to 'get rid of an awareness of personal inferiority, real or imagined'.[8] When working for General Mills promoting Betty Crocker 'pre-mixed cake mix', he concluded that housework and baking are not viewed as chores by women, but an important symbol of their status and creativity.[9]

This led to what is now one of his most famous recommendations. When Betty Crocker's first instant cake mixes launched, sales were considerably below what was predicted. Dichter argued it was because they made baking too easy; it undermined the female role in the house and undervalued it. Consequently, he recommended General Mills to change the formula. Rather than using powdered eggs, cooks were now required to add an egg to the mixture. He believed that by increasing the effort required to make the product, females wouldn't feel like their role was being undervalued. The result: sales dramatically increased. Although Dichter's recommendation may have led to an increase in sales, it probably was not for the reason he claimed. Several commentators claimed that adding an egg simply made the cakes taste better and stopped them sticking to the bottom of the pan.[10] Even if it did not change the actual taste, it seems likely that people would perceive that the cakes would taste better if made with a fresh ingredient. Despite this, his advice to advertisers consistently recommended reinforcing traditional sexual stereotypes and making explicit use of sexual appeals to sell most categories of products.[11]

Measuring personality: Myers-Briggs

Although there are a number of techniques used to measure personality, the one most people are familiar with is the Myers-Briggs Type Indicator (MBTI). And there is a good reason why we are familiar with this test. Each year, over 3.5 million people take the test in the US,[12] including employees from 89 of the Fortune 100 companies.[13] However, this number is probably a vast underestimation as it fails to include the tens of thousands of people who complete unofficial versions online every year.

This tool was originally developed by the mother and daughter team of Katherine Briggs (1875–1968) and her daughter Isabel Myers (1897–1979). They were inspired by the work of Carl Jung and wanted to develop a measure of personality based on Jung's typology. Jung argued that people could be split into two main groups: those who are 'Perceivers' and those who are 'Judgers'. But it is possible to sub-divide these categories further. Perceivers could be split into those who prefer 'Sensing' or those who are more 'Intuitive', while Judgers can be split between 'Thinkers' and 'Feelers' and all four types of people can be split into 'Introverts' and 'Extroverts'.[14]

These classifications are at the heart of the MBTI. But if you've completed the MBTI, you will notice that Jung's groupings do not perfectly align with the test. The current version of the test comprises of 93 questions, and it assigns participants to four matched pairs (rather than Jung's three). The four pairs are: Extroversion (E) vs Introversion (I), Sensing (S) vs Intuition (N), Thinking (T) vs Feeling (F) and Judging (J) vs Perceiving (P). This allows researchers to assign them to one of sixteen categories. For example, ENTJ (Extrovert, Intuitive, Thinker, Judger).

Advocates who support the use of the MBTI believe that the test results can help businesses predict how employees will behave or the products that customers will buy. Unfortunately, there is almost no academic evidence to support its use. It fails to predict how people will behave[15] and it appears to be completely unreliable. If you take the test on one day and then wait five weeks and take the test again, over 50% of people will get a completely different result.[16] However, this should not come as a surprise to psychologists. For a start, the test attempts to categorize individuals into discrete categories – you are either an extrovert or an introvert. In practice, most people are neither purely extrovert nor purely introvert, but somewhere in the middle; the distribution follows a normal distribution rather than a bimodal distribution. This is something that the MBTI does not allow for.

> **KEY TERMS**
>
> **Normal distribution**
>
> A normal distribution, sometimes known as a 'Gaussian distribution', shows how data is distributed, or spread out. When data follows a normal distribution, most values cluster near the average, with fewer appearing as you move further from the centre, and this is one of the most common patterns seen in data.
>
> **Bimodal distribution**
>
> A bimodal distribution is a less common pattern where the data has two distinct peaks, indicating that two values occur more frequently than others. When a bimodal distribution occurs, it often suggests you have two distinct groups of participants.

The other reason why the test is unreliable is the fact that it was based upon Jung's observation. While Jung was a pioneer within the field of psychology, he was working at a time when psychology was not a science. He created his initial classifications based on the observations of clinical patients, and these classifications were never subject to academic scrutiny or any attempts at replication, and even then, Myers and Briggs chose to ignore Jung's original research to suit their own needs.

Personality and the Big 5

This is not to say that all attempts to measure personality are flawed. Today, academics have developed what appears to be a robust tool kit to measure personality, the Big 5 (sometimes referred to as OCEAN). This is a trait model of personality which seeks to identify a number of stable characteristics that determine how an individual will respond to any given situation. This tool kit measures an individual on five dimensions: openness to new experiences, conscientiousness, extroversion, agreeableness and neuroticism.[17] Individuals receive a score on each of the different dimensions, but unlike the MBTI, they are not simply classified as high or low on each trait. Instead, it is a continuum with very few individuals lying on the extremes, and most people scoring somewhere in the middle. Intuitively, this makes sense. As noted previously, most people are not a pure extrovert or pure introvert, but somewhere in the middle, although we will probably be closer to one of the two extremes.

The five traits can be typically characterized as follows (Table 4.1):

Table 4.1 The typical behaviours shown by people who score high or low on each personality trait

	Low	High
Openness to experience	• Conservative • Narrow-minded • Conventional • Conforming	• Creative • Imaginative • Cultured • Intellectual
Conscientiousness	• Impulsive • Disorganized • Careless • Unreliable	• Hardworking • Dutiful • Self-disciplined • Organized
Extroversion	• Quiet • Reserved • Sombre • Passive	• Gregarious • Outgoing • Adventurous • Affectionate
Agreeableness	• Suspicious • Irritable • Uncooperative • Critical	• Altruistic • Trusting • Helpful • Good-natured
Neuroticism	• Calm • Secure • Self-satisfied • Even tempered	• Anxious • Insecure • Worried • Self-conscious

GIVE IT A GO

Want to find out what your personality type is? Complete a version of the Big 5 personality test online and see how you compare to your friends.

Unlike the MBTI, the Big 5 has been shown to be highly reliable over time. Although there are slight variations, Johanna Rantane and colleagues have shown that over a nine-year timeframe, your personality stays more or less the same.[18] The caveat to

this is that there appears to be more variation once we turn 65, especially in terms of 'openness to experience' and 'conscientiousness'.[19] Of course, major life events will result in minor changes to our personality, although interestingly, changes in our work life have a bigger impact than those in our love life (and gain-based events tend be more impactful than loss-based events).[20]

Using personality in marketing

Despite being a reliable research tool, for a long time personality appeared to have limited practical use in marketing. If a marketer wanted to identify a customer's personality, they needed to get a customer to complete a 100-item questionnaire,[21] which significantly limited their use. But today, marketers can identify someone's personality based on their social media usage,[22,23] the apps they use on their smartphone[24] or even the music they listen to on Spotify.[25] This makes sense. The pages people like on Facebook will say something about their personality.[26] It is easy to imagine that someone who 'likes' beer pong is more likely to be an extrovert.

From a research perspective, these measures are a more accurate reflection of an individual's personality than any self-report measure, or even asking our friends to review our personality.[27] Psychometric questionnaires are self-report measures, asking an individual to describe themselves, something we may not always do honestly. But when researchers analyse how someone behaves on social media, they are analysing actual behaviour. But why should marketers care?

By analysing the Big 5, psychologists can predict an individual's behaviour with remarkable accuracy. Some of this makes intuitive sense. People who score highly on neuroticism and low on openness tend to make more conservative investment decisions,[28] people who have low scores on extroversion are the least likely to use WhatsApp (or any other instant messaging service)[29] and individuals who score highly on conscientiousness, extroversion and openness are more likely to earn more.[30]

But other findings seem slightly harder to understand. For example, Christopher Soto showed that researchers can predict how likely people are to suffer from heart disease, have a healthy attachment with their romantic partner or even someone's likelihood of developing depression.[31] It might seem puzzling that personality traits can influence the risk of heart disease but consider this: a highly conscientious person is more likely to exercise regularly, drink less alcohol and follow a healthier diet, all things associated with having a healthy heart. However, it is important to point out that this approach does not allow marketers to predict how likely an individual is to suffer from heart disease. Instead, it focuses on predicting group-level effects.

Traditionally, marketers have segmented a market using demographic or psychographic variables (e.g. age, gender, interests etc.). But recently, marketers have started exploring personality as a segmentation approach, and it appears to be a highly successful one. A team led by Sandra Matz has shown that people who watch personalized adverts view them more favourably than more generic adverts with a mass market appeal.[32] But what is exciting is the fact that it's not just that people liked the adverts more; her team went on to analyse how over 3.5 million viewers behaved after viewing personalized adverts on social media. When the adverts matched the viewers' personality type, they were significantly more effective. Personalized adverts resulted in up to 40% more clicks and, more importantly, 50% more purchases.[33]

The same approach can also be used when it comes to more long-term goals. Unfortunately, most people don't save enough for the future, and this is something that marketers have tried to tackle by running ads. Once again, adverts that target our personality were far more effective at encouraging us to start saving (and achieving our saving goals) than more generic ads.[34] But what does it mean for an advert to align with an individual's personality? At the most basic level, we know that extroverts are more likely to prefer humorous[35] and loud[36] adverts. But we can take it one step further and change the style of humour an advert uses based on the viewer's personality. People who score highly on openness are more likely to appreciate nonsense jokes, whereas people who score highly on conscientiousness tend to prefer more traditional jokes (incongruity-resolution), where the joke sets up an expectation, and then surprises you by going against that expectation.[37]

Developing personalized adverts

Personality in advertising is more than just changing what jokes you use. It can mean totally redesigning the psychological appeal that an advert uses. If we continue to focus on extroverts, we know that they are more likely to be influenced by messages that are positively framed rather than negatively framed[38] and that hyperbolic discounting is more effective on extroverts than introverts.[39] This may sound rather complex but, in practice, it can be as simple as certain messages are more likely to resonate with different personality traits. We'll look at some of these in Table 4.2.

If you were designing an advert for a mobile phone and you were targeting shoppers who scored highly on neuroticism, you could frame your ad around the idea that *'help is always just a phone call away'*. Whereas if you are planning on targeting extroverts, you would be better off leading with a positive headline such as *'never miss out on a party'*.[40]

Putting personality-based messaging into action

While this might be interesting, it may seem hard to implement. How can you find a cost-effective way to personalize the adverts that somebody sees? Historically, this wouldn't be possible. But in the last 18 months, advances in artificial intelligence have made this very easy. For example, at the start of 2024, 100,000 people working for

Table 4.2 An example of the types of advertising appeals that work best for different personality types, based on research by Hirsch et al[41]

Personality	Appeal
Openness	Creativity and intellectual stimulation
Conscientiousness	Efficiency and goal pursuit
Extroversion	Excitement and Social Rewards
Agreeableness	Connection with family and community
Neuroticism	Safety and security

Publicis, a global advertising giant, received a video message from the chief executive thanking them for their hard work. But rather than this being a generic thank you, the videos were personalized, thanking the employees by name, in their first language, and in some cases even referencing their hobbies, all thanks to AI.[42] As long as you know what personality type someone is, simply changing how the message is framed is now a very simple and very cost-effective approach. No longer will this approach be restricted to the businesses with the largest budgets but it is likely to be an everyday occurrence.

While personality is normally measured using questionnaires or analysing behaviour, there is a growing body of evidence that humans are remarkably accurate at assessing someone's personality just by looking at them.[43] Researchers have shown that people can tell if someone would score high or low on three of the Big 5 traits, extroversion, conscientiousness and openness. Surprisingly, people can make these judgements accurately based on just a photo of an individual's face, even when we cannot get any cues from the clothing that someone wears, although Little and Perrett have shown that people could only successfully identify two traits, extroversion and conscientiousness.[44] People don't even need to see a photo of a face for a long time to form their first impression. Just seeing a photo of a face for as little as one-tenth of a second is enough for us to form an impression.[45]

Even if we can only successfully recognize two personality traits, this raises some interesting possibilities for marketers. Rather than just selecting a model or an actor to appear in an advert based on their looks, they might have to start considering the model's personality. How would viewers react if you were trying to sell a mortgage and the actor playing a banker is an extrovert? Do you really want an extrovert looking after your money? Or how about a salesperson who is low in conscientiousness – is this who you'd trust?

Personality and retail behaviour

Personality not only helps predict the success of an advertising campaign; it can help researchers predict how likely an individual is to go shopping or to try a new product.

Research by Ronald Goldsmith has shown that consumers who score highly on 'extroversion' and 'openness to experience' typically shop more than other consumers,[46] and consumers who score highly on 'openness to experience' are more likely to be the first to adopt new products. For example, when internet shopping was first launched, the consumers who were first to adopt it tended to score highly on 'openness to experience'.[47] Likewise, we see the same pattern when it comes to predicting which consumers are more likely to switch to eating genetically modified meat – those with high openness to experience scores.[48]

Personality can also help researchers predict how satisfied consumers are going to be with their purchases. When a team of consumer psychologists led by Sandra Matz analysed over 76,000 purchases made by consumers, they discovered the best predictor of how satisfied a customer was did not relate to how much money they spent, but what they bought. Consumers who purchased items that were linked to their personality (again, as measured by the Big 5), reported a greater satisfaction than those who purchased unrelated items.[49] We may say that money can't buy happiness, but it could just be a case that we are spending it on the wrong things, and this makes sense. People typically purchase items that align with their personality traits – presumably because they are happier with these items.[50]

Why isn't personality used more in marketing?

If personality is now so easy to measure and is such a powerful tool for predicting consumer behaviour, why is it not more widely used? Firstly, there is still a lot of confusion surrounding personality. Most people's first thought when it comes to measuring personality is the MBTI, which as we previously stated, is just as accurate at predicting a personality as a horoscope. Likewise, there are many dubious personality tests and articles on social media that claim to predict your personality. For example, what does your favourite colour say about your personality? Yet your favourite colour says nothing about your personality,[51] and each of these articles serves to undermine the credibility of personality. Secondly, personality is not something that is typically taught in marketing courses, apart from brand personality (see Chapter 7); it just remains something that marketers typically do not even consider.

While personality is clearly an effective marketing tool, it does raise some very serious ethical and practical questions. With most large supermarkets using a loyalty card programme to track purchases and large online shops offering a diverse range of products, they can clearly identify individual personality types. Currently, there is no legal reason which prevents a company from using personality variables to identify individuals with low self-control and target them, either with online adverts, emails or even direct mail.[52] But even if the legal situation does not change quickly, companies need to be aware of potential negative impacts. The Cambridge Analytica scandal really brought home the risks of personality targeting to the wider population, and triggered a lot of negative news stories.

REAL-WORLD EXAMPLE: PSYCH IN ACTION

One of the most high-profile and controversial uses of personality-based advertising was conducted by the British consultancy firm Cambridge Analytica. During the 2010s it was estimated that they collected personality data from over 87 million Facebook users without their explicit consent.[53] Initially, users installed a Facebook app, called *'this is your digital life'*. This required users to answer a mini personality questionnaire to allow Cambridge Analytica to develop a psychological profile of the user.

Worryingly, in the terms and conditions, users inadvertently gave Cambridge Analytica permission to collect data from their entire timeline (including private messages) and detailed information about a user's Facebook friends. This data was then used to produce personalized adverts that were used to support the election of Donald Trump and Ted Cruz in 2016.[54] For example, if a voter was predicted to be a Trump supporter, users would be shown photos of him winning the election and detailed instructions on how to vote. However, if a user's personality-based data suggested they might be a swing voter, instead the user would be shown images of Trump's more notable and well-respected supporters or negative information about his opponent.[55]

The way the data was captured (without users' consent and capturing data about a Facebook user's 'friends' without them ever being told) was ruled to be illegal, and Facebook was fined $5 billion by the Federal Trade Commission for privacy violations and, in the UK, the UK Information Commissioner's office issued a £500,000 fine for the data breach.[56] This not only created legal problems, but there was widespread public backlash. This is reflected by the fact that in the 12 months after the scandal broke, the number of posts, likes and shares on Facebook dropped by 20%.[57]

News about the Cambridge Analytica scandal broke in 2018, and while this is not long ago, technologically, a lot has changed in this time. One of the biggest changes has been the widespread adoption of generative AI. Potentially, this has led to a change in how people view their data being used and what they will accept. Sandra Matz and her team have already adapted their work and shown how ChatGPT can be used to create adverts based on a user's personality (based on a self-report questionnaire). The results showed that when nearly 1,800 participants were shown adverts created by ChatGPT, those that ChatGPT made using personality-based data were more effective than those that had a mass market appeal, whether promoting consumer products or encouraging action on climate change.[58]

But how would people feel when they found out these adverts were made using ChatGPT and targeted to their personality? Would we get the same negativity associated with Cambridge Analytica? This time, there was no impact; the personalized adverts continued to outperform the generic adverts. Perhaps the younger generation are more accustomed to having data captured and being used for marketing purposes. How consumers' attitudes continue to evolve is something that marketers need to be very aware of and continue to monitor.

Personality and conspicuous consumption

While personality influences how we react to adverts and what we buy, it does not explain why this occurs. However, evolutionary psychologists think the answer could lie in our distant past. They argue that we have evolved to engage in certain behaviours because it provides us with an evolutionary advantage, normally helping us find either food or a mate, and personality traits are no different. When it comes to looking for a mate, evolutionary psychologists, like Geoffrey Miller[59] and Gad Saad,[60] argue that people do not try and mate with just anybody. Instead, people have evolved to find people more attractive who give us the best chance of producing healthy and strong offspring.

Historically, people would depend on physical traits to assess the selection of a mate, known as a 'fitness indicator'. Women would be attracted to men with:

- facial symmetry: as this is interpreted as a sign of good genetic make up
- a strong jawline and pronounced cheekbones: a proxy for higher testosterone levels, indicating a stronger individual
- broad shoulders: again suggesting physical strength
- height: taller men are perceived as more dominant and protective

Whereas for men, they were traditionally attracted to:

- facial symmetry and clear skin: a sign of genetic health and hormonal balance
- youthful appearance: as fertility peaks in early adulthood, people subconsciously prioritize youth
- low waist-to-hip ratio: a waist-to-hip ratio of around 0.7 is typically perceived as the most attractive, as it again signals fertility

However, Geoffrey Miller argues that in today's world, these factors are no longer likely to predict success. Instead, people's IQ, wealth and personality traits are a better predictor of life success.[61] Consequently, to make it easier for a potential mate to assess our personality, people engage in conspicuous consumption; purchasing items with the primary purpose for other people to see, helping other people work out what our personality type is. At first glance, this sounds fanciful, but the evidence backs it up. When Vladas Griskevicius and his team introduced mating goals in men, it increased their willingness to purchase conspicuous luxury items, although it had no impact on spending on necessities. A similar pattern occurred with female participants. However, rather than changing their spending on luxury items, females whose mating goals were activated were more likely to engage in conspicuous public helping, but it had no impact on private helping.[62]

And we've all heard the stories that men who drive flashy cars have small penises, an evolutionary coping mechanism, and it turns out that this might be true. When Dan Richardson of UCL made men feel inadequate about their penis size by giving them false information about the average penis size in an online quiz (by suggesting it is roughly 7 inches, rather than the 5–6 inches it actually is), he found that men rated fast cars as more appealing when they were made to less feel well endowed.[63]

However, not everybody is equally motivated to engage in conspicuous consumption. For example, younger shoppers and especially those who are more competitive are far more likely to engage in conspicuous consumption than older shoppers.[64] Likewise, shoppers from lower socio-economic groups are also more likely to engage in conspicuous consumption,[65] which is a worry as these are often the shoppers who are least able to afford to.

Closing thoughts

Although psychologists have studied personality for over a hundred years, it has largely been ignored by marketers. This is not because marketers were ignorant of the role of personality, but because it was simply not practical to segment the market using this approach. When it was practical to use, for example, in recruitment, as it's easy to ask potential employees to complete a personality questionnaire, businesses readily embraced personality.[66] But we are now living in the world of big data. Businesses are continually capturing vast sums of data. Every keystroke you type on a website, social media post you view or interact with, the programmes you choose to stream, and of course, the product you buy using a loyalty card, is all recorded. With this data, businesses can accurately predict their shoppers' personality types and it has become a valuable segmentation tool. When this is combined with the latest developments in generative AI, it has become both feasible and viable for businesses to develop personalized adverts to target individuals. As technology continues to advance, this area is only going to grow in importance.

KEY POINTS

- Although the Myers-Briggs is one of the best-known models of personality, currently there is no academic research to support its use.
- Currently, the most accurate model of human personality is the Big 5 or OCEAN model. This measures personality on five independent dimensions: openness to new experiences, conscientiousness, extroversion, agreeableness and neuroticism.
- Behavioural measures of personality are more accurate than self-report measures.
- At a population level, personality traits are a strong predictor of behaviour. From the jobs people have, their likelihood to exercise, and even the products they will purchase.
- Advertising campaigns that are targeted to an individual's personality type are more effective than generic campaigns.
- One of the leading theories for why personality influences the products people buy is that consumers use these purchases to express their personality, to attract and retain a partner. Some argue that it is more about fitting with a social group, while evolutionary psychologists suggest that this too links back to mate attraction. Being a well-integrated member of a group signals stability and makes an individual appear more attractive as a mate.

PUTTING THEORY INTO PRACTICE

1 Write five different slogans for an advert for a new electric car. Each slogan should be targeted to a different personality type.

2 If you were the manager responsible for running a supermarket loyalty card scheme, what sort of purchases would you look at to predict a shopper's personality type? Justify your decisions.

3 Are shoppers more likely to prefer brands that reflect their actual personality traits or those of the person they aspire to be? Does it make a difference if the person is male or female?

4 Analyse the adverts that are shown to you on your personal social media pages. Which ones are tailored based on the things you 'like' and can you identify any that appear customized to reflect aspects of your personality?

5 As generative AI becomes more sophisticated, what are the implications for targeted advertising? Will only the largest companies be able to afford it or will the new advances be available to firms of all sizes?

6 Do you think personality-based marketing campaigns will be more effective for promoting physical products or services? Justify your answer.

7 What are the ethical and moral implications of brands using data about their customers' personality to create personalized adverts and recommendations?

8 From a public relations perspective, what are the risks for a company if the general public discovers they use adverts targeted to an individual's personality? Does the sector the business operates in make a difference?

SUGGESTIONS FOR FURTHER READING

Mikhailov, N. & Yankov, G. (2024). *Personality: A user's guide*. Robinson.

References

1 BBH Labs (2020). Puncturing the paradox: Group cohesion and the generational myth. https://www.bbh-labs.com/puncturing-the-paradox-group-cohesion-and-the-generational-myth/ (archived at https://perma.cc/QWV3-LRN9)

2 BBH Labs (2020). Puncturing the paradox: Group cohesion and the generational myth. https://www.bbh-labs.com/puncturing-the-paradox-group-cohesion-and-the-generational-myth/ (archived at https://perma.cc/QWV3-LRN9)

3 Funder, D. C. (2004). *The personality puzzle* (3rd edition). W. W. Norton.

4 Rennison, Ni. (2015). *Freud and psychoanalysis: Everything you need to know about Id, Ego, Super-Ego and more*. Pocket Essentials.

5 Webster, R. (2005). *Why Freud was wrong: Sin, science, and psychoanalysis* (3rd Edition). The Orwell Press.

6 Schwarzkopf, S. & Gries, R. (2010). *Ernest Dichter and motivation research, new perspectives on the making of post-war consumer culture* (S. Schwarzkopf & R. Gries, Eds.). Palgrave Macmillian. https://doi.org/10.1057/9780230293946 (archived at https://perma.cc/UE7E-Y7VT)

7 Schwarzkopf, S. & Gries, R. (2010). *Ernest Dichter and motivation research, new perspectives on the making of post-war consumer culture* (S. Schwarzkopf & R. Gries, Eds.). Palgrave Macmillian. https://doi.org/10.1057/9780230293946 (archived at https://perma.cc/6N6X-5LLN)

8 Horowitz, D. (1986). *The birth of a salesman: Ernest Dichter and the objects of desire* (Vol. 83). Daniel Horowitz.

9 Horowitz, D. (2010). From Vienna to the United States and back: Ernest Dichter and American consumer culture. In S. Schwarzkopf & R. Gries (Eds.), *Ernest Dichter and Motivation Research: New Perspectives on the Making of Post-War Consumer Culture* (pp. 41–57). Palgrave Macmillian. https://doi.org/10.1057/9780230293946_2 (archived at https://perma.cc/H6J8-MJ7C)

10 Shapiro, L. (2005). *Something from the oven: Reinventing dinner in 1950s America*. Penguin Group. https://doi.org/10.2752/155280104786577923 (archived at https://perma.cc/ZAQ9-B2DH)
11 Parkin, K. (2010). The 'sex of food': Ernest Dichter, libido and American food advertising. In S. Schwarzkopf & R. Gries (Eds.), *Ernest Dichter and Motivation Research: New Perspectives on the Making of Post-War Consumer Culture* (pp. 140–154). Palgrave Macmillian.
12 Case, P. & Phillipson, G. (2004). Astrology, alchemy and retro-organization theory: An astro-genealogical critique of the Myers-Briggs Type Indicator®. *Organization*, 11(4), 473–495. https://doi.org/10.1177/1350508404044059 (archived at https://perma.cc/7NNF-25N9)
13 Stein, R. & Swan, A. B. (2019). Evaluating the validity of Myers-Briggs Type Indicator theory: A teaching tool and window into intuitive psychology. *Social and Personality Psychology Compass*, 13(2), e12434. https://doi.org/10.1111/spc3.12434 (archived at https://perma.cc/J4CT-6HF6)
14 Jung, C. (1923). *Psychological types*. Harcourt, Brace & Company.
15 Pittenger, D. J. (1993). The utility of the Myers-Briggs Type Indicator. *Review of Educational Research*, 63(4), 467–488. https://doi.org/10.3102/00346543063004467 (archived at https://perma.cc/34S3-EAZZ)
16 Pittenger, D. J. (2005). Cautionary comments regarding the Myers-Briggs Type Indicator. *Consulting Psychology Journal: Practice and Research*, 57(3), 210–221. https://doi.org/10.1037/1065-9293.57.3.210 (archived at https://perma.cc/F5YM-25YL)
17 Costa Jr., P. T. & McCrae, R. R. (1992). The revised NEO Personality Inventory (NEO-PI-R). In G. J. Boyle, G. Matthews, & D. H. Saklofske (Eds.), *The sage handbook of personality: Theory and Assesment* (pp. 179–198). Sage.
18 Rantane, J., Metsäpelto, R.-L., Feldt, T., Pulkkinen, L., & Kokko, K. (2007). Long-term stability in the Big Five personality traits in adulthood. *Scandinavian Journal of Psychology*, 48(6), 511–518. https://doi.org/10.1111/j.1467-9450.2007.00609.x (archived at https://perma.cc/5XFQ-MH3A)
19 Allemand, M., Zimprich, D., & Martin, M. (2008). Long-term correlated change in personality traits in old age. *Psychology and Aging*, 23(3), 545–557. https://doi.org/10.1037/a0013239
20 Bühler, J. L., Orth, U., Bleidorn, W., Weber, E., Kretzschmar, A., Scheling, L., & Hopwood, C. J. (2024). Life events and personality change: A systematic review and meta-analysis. *European Journal of Personality*, 38(3), 544–568.
21 Goldberg, L. R. (1992). The development of markers for the Big-Five factor structure. *Psychological Assessment*, 4(1), 26–42. https://doi.org/10.1037/1040-3590.4.1.26 (archived at https://perma.cc/4HL4-2CQB)
22 Azucar, D., Marengo, D., & Settanni, M. (2018). Predicting the Big 5 personality traits from digital footprints on social media: A meta-analysis. *Personality and Individual Differences*, 124, 150–159. https://doi.org/10.1016/j.paid.2017.12.018 (archived at https://perma.cc/WK6V-KFFU)
23 Matz, S. C. & Netzer, O. (2017). Using Big Data as a window into consumers' psychology. *Current Opinion in Behavioral Sciences*, 18, 7–12. https://doi.org/10.1016/j.cobeha.2017.05.009 (archived at https://perma.cc/E3W7-VEMJ)

24 Stachl, C., Au, Q., Schoedel, R., Gosling, S. D., Harari, G. M., Buschek, D., Völkel, S. T., Schuwerk, T., Oldemeier, M., Ullmann, T., Hussmann, H., Bischl, B., & Bühner, M. (2020). *Predicting personality from patterns of behavior collected with smartphones*. Proceedings of the National Academy of Sciences, 117(30), 17680–17687. https://doi.org/10.1073/pnas.1920484117 (archived at https://perma.cc/D6C9-TKF5)

25 Anderson, I., Gil, S., Gibson, C., Wolf, S., Shapiro, W., Semerci, O., & Greenberg, D. M. (2021). 'Just the way you are': Linking music listening on Spotify and personality. *Social Psychological and Personality Science*, 12(4), 561–572. https://doi.org/10.1177/1948550620923228 (archived at https://perma.cc/864L-UE3C)

26 Kosinski, M., Stillwell, D., & Graepel, T. (2013). *Private traits and attributes are predictable from digital records of human behavior*. Proceedings of the National Academy of Sciences, 110(15), 5802–5805. https://doi.org/10.1073/pnas.1218772110 (archived at https://perma.cc/5XYP-RGY5)

27 Bühler, J. L., Orth, U., Bleidorn, W., Weber, E., Kretzschmar, A., Scheling, L., & Hopwood, C. J. (2024). Life events and personality change: A systematic review and meta-analysis. *European Journal of Personality*, 38(3), 544–568.

28 Jiang, Z., Peng, C., & Yan, H. (2024). Personality differences and investment decision-making. *Journal of Financial Economics*, 153, 103776.

29 Sindermann, C., Lachmann, B., Elhai, J. D., & Montag, C. (2021). Personality associations with WhatsApp usage and usage of alternative messaging applications to protect one's own data. *Journal of Individual Differences*, 42(4), 167–174. https://doi.org/10.1027/1614-0001/a000343 (archived at https://perma.cc/JSP7-GNWD)

30 Alderotti, G., Rapallini, C., & Traverso, S. (2023). The Big Five personality traits and earnings: A meta-analysis. *Journal of Economic Psychology*, 94, 102570.

31 Soto, C. J. (2018). How replicable are links between personality traits and consequential life outcomes? The life outcomes of Personality Replication Project. *Psychological Science*, 30(5), 711–727. https://doi.org/10.1177/0956797619831612 (archived at https://perma.cc/7FYY-K43M)

32 Hirsh, J. B., Kang, S. K., & Bodenhausen, G. V. (2011). Personalized persuasion. *Psychological Science*, 23(6), 578–581. https://doi.org/10.1177/0956797611436349 (archived at https://perma.cc/39WG-8KZ7)

33 Matz, S. C., Kosinski, M., Nave, G., & Stillwell, D. J. (2017). *Psychological targeting as an effective approach to digital mass persuasion*. Proceedings of the National Academy of Sciences, 114(48), 12714–12719. https://doi.org/10.1073/pnas.1710966114 (archived at https://perma.cc/4MYH-C7G6)

34 Matz, S. C., Gladstone, J. J., & Farrokhnia, R. A. (2023). *Leveraging psychological fit to encourage saving behavior*. American Psychologist, 78(7), 901–917. https://doi.org/10.1037/amp0001128 (archived at https://perma.cc/72MC-MQDP)

35 Stysko-Kunkowska, M. A. & Borecka, D. (2010). Extraversion and evaluation of humorous advertisements. *Psychological Reports*, 106(1), 44–48. https://doi.org/10.2466/pr0.106.1.44-48 (archived at https://perma.cc/97N8-KD2N)

36 Cetola, H. & Prinkey, K. (1986). Introversion-extraversion and loud commercials. *Psychology & Marketing*, 3(2), 123–132. https://doi.org/10.1002/mar.4220030208 (archived at https://perma.cc/USP2-LAD5)

37 Sulejmanov, F., Dostál, D., Grundman, V., & Ruch, W. (2024). Associations between personality and humor structure appreciation. *Current Psychology*, 43(5), 4698–4709.

38 Chang, C. (2006). Context-induced and ad-induced affect: Individual differences as moderators. *Psychology & Marketing*, 23(9), 757–782. https://doi.org/10.1002/mar.20128 (archived at https://perma.cc/Z5N9-F3A3)

39 Dohmen, T., Falk, A., Huffman, D., Sunde, U., Schupp, J., & Wagner, G. G. (2011). Individual risk attitudes: Measurement, determinants, and behavioral consequences. *Journal of the European Economic Association*, 9(3), 522–550. https://doi.org/10.1111/j.1542-4774.2011.01015.x (archived at https://perma.cc/3ZFF-A5P9)

40 Hirsh, J. B., Kang, S. K., & Bodenhausen, G. V. (2012). Personalized persuasion: Tailoring persuasive appeals to recipients' personality traits. *Psychological Science*, 23(6), 578–581.

41 Hirsh, J. B., Kang, S. K., & Bodenhausen, G. V. (2012). Personalized persuasion: Tailoring persuasive appeals to recipients' personality traits. *Psychological Science*, 23(6), 578–581.

42 Thomas, D. (2024). How AI is transforming the business of advertising. *Financial Times*.

43 Passini, F. T. & Norman, W. T. (1966). A universal conception of personality structure? *Journal of Personality and Social Psychology*, 4(1), 44–49. https://doi.org/10.1037/h0023519 (archived at https://perma.cc/B482-66HQ)

44 Little, A. C. & Perrett, D. I. (2007). Using composite images to assess accuracy in personality attribution to faces. *British Journal of Psychology*, 98(1), 111–126. https://doi.org/10.1348/000712606x109648 (archived at https://perma.cc/HQ2G-6GNX)

45 Willis, J. & Todorov, A. (2006). First impressions: Making up your mind after a 100-ms exposure to a face. *Psychological Science*, 17(7), 592–598.

46 Goldsmith, R. (2016). The Big Five, happiness, and shopping. *Journal of Retailing and Consumer Services*, 31, 52–61. https://doi.org/10.1016/j.jretconser.2016.03.007 (archived at https://perma.cc/2V3D-54NF)

47 Wang, S., Wang, S., & Wang, M. (2006). Shopping online or not? Cognition and personality matters. *Journal of Theoretical and Applied Electronic Commerce Research*, 1(3), 68–80. https://doi.org/10.3390/jtaer1030023 (archived at https://perma.cc/E2G7-FRZK)

48 Lin, W., Ortega, D. L., Caputo, V., & Lusk, J. L. (2019). Personality traits and consumer acceptance of controversial food technology: A cross-country investigation of genetically modified animal products. *Food Quality and Preference*, 76, 10–19. https://doi.org/10.1016/j.foodqual.2019.03.007 (archived at https://perma.cc/9DP7-F3CB)

49 Matz, S. C., Gladstone, J. J., & Stillwell, D. (2016). Money buys happiness when spending fits our personality. *Psychological Science*, 27(5), 715–725. https://doi.org/10.1177/0956797616635200 (archived at https://perma.cc/H3KP-ZUJT)

50 Gladstone, J. J., Matz, S. C., & Lemaire, A. (2019). Can psychological traits be inferred from spending? Evidence from transaction data. *Psychological Science*, 30(7), 1087–1096. https://doi.org/10.1177/0956797619849435 (archived at https://perma.cc/CVT2-2HVL)

51 Jonauskaite, D., Thalmayer, A. G., Müller, L., & Mohr, C. (2021). What does your favourite colour say about your personality? Not much. *Personality Science*, 2(1), e6297.

52 Gladstone, J. J., Matz, S. C., & Lemaire, A. (2019). Can psychological traits be inferred from spending? Evidence from transaction data. *Psychological Science*, 30(7), 1087–1096. https://doi.org/10.1177/0956797619849435 (archived at https://perma.cc/CVT2-2HVL)

53 Meredith, S. (2018, April 10). Facebook-Cambridge Analytica: A timeline of the data hijacking scandal. CNBC. https://www.cnbc.com/2018/04/10/facebook-cambridge-analytica-a-timeline-of-the-data-hijacking-scandal.html (archived at https://perma.cc/9BGN-M6HV)
54 Confessore, N. (April 4, 2018). Cambridge Analytica and Facebook: The scandal and the fallout so far. *The New York Times*. https://www.nytimes.com/2018/04/04/us/politics/cambridge-analytica-scandal-fallout.html (archived at https://perma.cc/67AG-SC6S)
55 Lewis, P. & Hilder, P. (2018, March 23). Leaked: Cambridge Analytica's blueprint for Trump victory. *The Guardian*. https://www.theguardian.com/uk-news/2018/mar/23/leaked-cambridge-analyticas-blueprint-for-trump-victory (archived at https://perma.cc/67AG-SC6S)
56 Wong, J. C. (2019, July 12) Facebook to be fined $5bn for Cambridge Analytica privacy violations - reports. *The Guardian*. https://www.theguardian.com/technology/2019/mar/17/the-cambridge-analytica-scandal-changed-the-world-but-it-didnt-change-facebook (archived at https://perma.cc/MQB5-4U5Q)
57 Hern, A. (2019, June 20). Facebook usage falling after privacy scandals, data suggests. *The Guardian*. https://www.theguardian.com/technology/2019/jun/20/facebook-usage-collapsed-since-scandal-data-shows (archived at https://perma.cc/8C5Q-QNXD)
58 Matz, S. C., Teeny, J. D., Vaid, S. S., Peters, H., Harari, G. M., & Cerf, M. (2024). The potential of generative AI for personalized persuasion at scale. *Scientific Reports*, 14(1), 4692.
59 Miller, G. (2010). *Spent: Sex, evolution, and consumer behavior*. Penguin Group.
60 Saad, G. (2007). *The evolutionary bases of consumption*. Mahwah, NJ: Lawrence Erlbaum.
61 Gensowski, M. (2018). Personality, IQ, and lifetime earnings. *Labour Economics*, 51, 170–183. https://doi.org/10.1016/j.labeco.2017.12.004 (archived at https://perma.cc/K9FL-24V4)
62 Griskevicius, V., Tybur, J. M., Sundie, J. M., Cialdini, R. B., Miller, G. F., & Kenrick, D. T. (2007). Blatant benevolence and conspicuous consumption: When romantic motives elicit strategic costly signals. *Journal of Personality and Social Psychology*, 93(1), 85–102. https://doi.org/10.1037/0022-3514.93.1.85 (archived at https://perma.cc/D8ZH-NFRK)
63 Richardson, D. C., Devlin, J., Hogan, J. S., & Thompson, C. (2023). Small penises and fast cars: Evidence for a psychological link. https://doi.org/10.31234/osf.io/uy7ph (archived at https://perma.cc/ZD77-NZCU)
64 Barrera, G. A. & Ponce, H. R. (2021). Personality traits influencing young adults' conspicuous consumption. *International Journal of Consumer Studies*, 45(3), 335–349. https://doi.org/10.1111/ijcs.12623 (archived at https://perma.cc/VX2N-VAKM)
65 Wang, Y., Liu, B., Lin, S., Liu, L., Wu, Y., & Cui, L. (2022). The effects of subjective socioeconomic status on conspicuous consumption. *Journal of Applied Social Psychology*, 52(7), 522–531. https://doi.org/10.1111/jasp.12876 (archived at https://perma.cc/YB3A-WFAA)
66 Neal, A., Yeo, G., Koy, A., & Xiao, T. (2012). Predicting the form and direction of work role performance from the Big 5 model of personality traits. *Journal of Organizational Behavior*, 33(2), 175–192.

5 | The role of learning and memory in marketing

LEARNING OBJECTIVES

- Critically evaluate the key theories of learning and memory and how they apply to marketing.
- Leverage theoretical insights from human memory research to design brand communications that enhance long-term memorability and strengthen brand associations.

Introduction

Marketers spend a lot of time trying to get potential customers to change their behaviour. They might encourage them to purchase a new product, use a product more regularly or even try to persuade them *not* to use a product (as, for example, in anti-smoking campaigns). If they are going to succeed, marketers need consumers to learn and remember advertising messages, because in virtually all of these situations, a customer's decision to act is made days, weeks or potentially even months after they last saw an advert. So, for an advert or marketing message to be successful, marketers need to understand the best tactics for presenting their messages positively and encouraging consumers to retain them, which means correctly encoding and storing them in their memories.[1]

With an increasing number of people shopping online, understanding how consumers remember and learn marketing messages has become even more important. When people do their weekly shop in a supermarket or are browsing in a specialist store, they walk past rows of products that act as retrieval cues, reminding them of what they need to buy. The online shopping environment is sparser. Although an online shopping page may contain adverts and promotions for various products, almost certainly tailored to the customer's demographics and known habits, promotional space is limited, and the customer may have to use a search bar. That means they need to freely recall what they wanted to buy before they start shopping.

Yet marketers need to be savvy when it comes to memory. It's not good enough for consumers to simply remember an advert for a product. Ideally, they'll remember the brand as well. Very often, consumers can clearly describe an advert, but fail to remember the brand, or worse, attribute it to a rival brand.[2]

Learning

Behaviourism

Behaviourism is one of the oldest approaches used to explain all aspects of animal behaviour, including that of humans. Unlike most psychological theories, behaviourism completely ignores people's cognitive processes, our thoughts and feelings, and instead argues that the environment can explain all aspects of behaviour. If an animal (or person) is rewarded when they carry out an activity, then they are likely to continue carrying out that activity, but if they are punished, then they are likely to stop or change their behaviour.[3]

This approach dominated psychology's academic literature until the 1950s and 1960s, partly thanks to the publication in 1913 of the American psychologist John B. Watson's (1878–1958) *Behaviourist Manifesto*.[4] In the manifesto, Watson sets out four principles that underlie what we would now call the science of behaviour change. He argued that: (a) researchers should only be interested in observable behaviour – if it cannot be measured, it should not be considered; (b) psychologists should develop laws that can be used to explain all behaviour, in any situation; (c) humans are animals and should be treated as such; (d) all behaviour, no matter how complex or trivial, can be explained by a simple stimulus-response association.

Despite no longer being in vogue amongst psychologists, Watson's principles are not obsolete. The manifesto can still provide valuable insight, although it doesn't explain all aspects of consumer behaviour and researchers will need to combine it with other cognitive approaches to learning to get a fuller picture. Although behaviourism was popular for a long period of time, it is usually separated into two distinct approaches: classical conditioning, and operant or instrumental conditioning.

Classical conditioning

Classical conditioning is the earlier of the two approaches, and it is strongly associated with the work of Russian psychologist Ivan Pavlov (1849–1936). Very early into his research into animals' digestive processes, Pavlov noticed an interesting phenomenon.

There were certain behaviours that his dogs did not need to learn. For example, whenever they were given food, they salivated.[5] Yet it was not just food that caused his dogs to salivate. The dogs learnt to salivate as soon as one of his assistants entered the room, even if they were not carrying any food. In other words, they had learnt to associate the assistant with food. If the dogs could learn to make this connection, he wondered whether the dogs could make other links. This led him to develop one of the most well-known experiments in psychology, testing to see if he could teach the dogs to connect the playing of a metronome with the presentation of their food.

When Pavlov or his assistants fed his dogs food (the unconditioned stimulus), it caused the dogs to start drooling (an unconditioned response). He then started a metronome ticking (neutral stimulus) as the food was presented to the dogs. By constantly repeating this process, the dogs learnt to associate the ticking of the metronome (conditioned stimulus) with food that caused them to start salivating (conditioning response) whenever they heard the metronome, even if no food was present. This process of learning is now known as *first-order conditioning*.[6] The reason Pavlov used a metronome rather than a bell in most of his experiments is that it allowed him to have better control over the experiment. He could ensure that the tick was the same volume, length of time and intensity, something that could not be controlled for with a bell (although he did use bells in subsequent experiments, these were electronic bells, similar to modern doorbells).[7]

Classical conditioning has come a long way since Pavlov's initial work, and researchers have refined the experimental process, with the result that we have a much better understanding of the conditions needed for learning to happen. Initially, Pavlov believed that when an animal was exposed to a cue, for example, it heard the metronome, the animal predicted that a reward would occur, and it waited to see what arrived. But new research suggests that Pavlov got it the wrong way round. When an animal receives a reward (or punishment), it looks back through its memory to work out what might have prompted this event.[8] Another change is that researchers have learnt that the pairing of the unconditioned stimulus needs to come almost immediately before the conditioned stimulus. If it doesn't, the learning effect will not be as strong[9] or may not even occur at all.

So, how does this relate to marketing? Plenty of advertising campaigns rely on classical conditioning, often without their creators realising it. For example, adverts for sports cars frequently rely on sex appeal. They feature an attractive woman (an unconditioned stimulus) as a passenger in the sports car (conditioned stimulus) and advertisers hope that, by repeatedly seeing the advert, viewers will learn to pair the two together. For this to work, the consumer needs to repeatedly see the conditioned stimulus and unconditioned stimulus together.[10] It isn't enough to see the advert only once or twice. This explains why several companies, including Coca-Cola (for Diet Coke) and Cadbury (for Cadbury's Flake), ran campaigns that consistently paired their brands with sex. However, as Cadbury retired the 'Flake Girl' in 2004, the sex pairing will have begun to weaken, eventually disappearing altogether, a process known as 'extinction'.

From a theoretical perspective, this is an example of first-order conditioning; the conditioned stimulus is paired directly with an unconditioned stimulus that is naturally rewarding. From a marketing perspective, it has relatively limited use, as the unconditioned stimulus needs to be intrinsically rewarding, which limits the number of workable stimuli. Higher-order conditioning helps to tackle this limitation, extending first-order conditioning by pairing a second neutral stimulus with the conditioned stimulus. So if Pavlov turned on the light just before ringing the bell, his dogs would start salivating when the light was turned on.

Despite Pavlov developing classical conditioning at the turn of the 20th century, it was not until 1982 that higher-order conditioning was first shown to work as a viable marketing tactic.[11] Participants were asked to watch an advert for a new pen in which the background music was either pleasant or unpleasant. At the end of the experiment, the participants were thanked and, as a reward, were shown a range of pens and told they could keep one. Participants who had heard the pleasant music as they watched the advert were more likely to choose a pen that matched the colour shown in the advert. However, participants who heard the unpleasant music were more likely to pick a pen that was different from the one shown.

Yet this finding should be taken with an element of scepticism. When James Kellaris and Anthony Cox tried to replicate this finding, they have only achieved limited success.[12] This could potentially be explained by the fact that higher-order conditioning is significantly weaker than first-order conditioning[13] and if reinforcement is not continually provided, these behaviours are more likely to become extinct in comparison with first-order conditioning.

Classical conditioning has also been suggested as a mechanism for why celebrity endorsement works (for a greater discussion about celebrity endorsement, see Chapter 9). As celebrities are likely to trigger positive feelings, they may act as an unconditioned stimulus. After repeatedly seeing a celebrity use a product or feature in an advert for the brand (conditioned stimuli), viewers may eventually develop a positive response towards the brand (a conditioned response). This explanation has been supported by experimental evidence: for example, participants who repeatedly saw images of Jennifer Aniston and hair gel together developed a more positive image of the hair gel.[14]

Stimulus generation So far, we've considered classical conditioning when an individual is constantly presented with the same stimulus. However, stimulus generalization is the idea that a stimulus that looks similar to the conditioned stimulus can produce the same conditioned response.[15] This was first shown in an unethical study where a nine-month-old baby called 'little Albert' was placed in a room with a neutral stimulus, a white fluffy toy rat. As Albert started to play with the rat, the researchers hit a large metal gong behind his head, which understandably caused Albert to cry, leaving him with a fear of rats. Yet not only did he fear rats, but he also developed a fear of other fluffy objects, including a white cloth bag, cotton balls and even Father Christmas's mask. Whenever he saw any of these, he started crying.[16]

At first, the links between stimulus generation and marketing may seem hard to find, but stimulus generalization has far more applications than just making babies cry. It can, for example, explain why the promoters of copycat brands take pains to make their products look almost identical to the premium brands they are copying. Stimulus generation can also explain why brand extension, the practice of using an existing, successful brand to promote a new product, such as Coke Zero or Dyson hand dryers, works. The positive associations from the parent brand are implicitly transferred to the new product.[17] When Brian Till and Randi Priluck created a fictitious brand of mouthwash (Garra Mouthwash) and showed participants the brand alongside a number of positive images (snow-covered mountains, picturesque beach scenes), participants rated the mouthwash more positively. However, it was not just mouthwash that participants liked more. They subsequently viewed other Garra products, such as soap, more positively too, clear experimental evidence of stimulus generalization at work.

Likewise, when brands use a copycat packaging strategy either by using a semantically similar brand name (Penguin vs Puffin) or by imitating the look of the category leader's packaging (for example, a chocolate bar with purple packaging and cows grazing on an alpine meadow mimics Milka) are also exploiting the principle of stimulus generalization. The positive brand associations that the market leader has spent a lot of time and money building subconsciously get transferred over to the rival brand. Although most shoppers object to copycat branding,[18] feeling that a company is gaining an unfair advantage, it works in influencing sales.[19,20] Unless there is a change in legislation, we are not likely to see a decrease in copycat branding any time soon.

So, where does all this leave classical conditioning and marketing? While there are numerous laboratory-based studies showing that pairing brand logos with pleasant images produces favourable brand attitudes;[21-24] there is a lack of conclusive evidence showing it works outside of a university laboratory. To date, the largest review of the literature concluded that '[there is] no convincing evidence for classical conditioning's effects on consumer behaviour'.[25] It is worth adding the caveat that this might be explained by two factors. Firstly, classical conditioning has fallen out of favour,[26] especially within consumer psychology literature, where there has been relatively little recent research exploring it. Secondly, it is exceptionally hard to design a study testing classical conditioning outside of a laboratory while controlling all other factors. Outside of a laboratory context, there are almost always other factors that could provide an alternative explanation for an experiment's results.

Operant conditioning

In all the examples we've looked at so far, we've assumed the shopper is passive, an individual being acted on by larger forces. But that's not what humans are really like – we have our own individual thoughts, opinions, emotions, interests and desires. Who we are affects exactly how all these stimuli act on us. Moreover, we can choose whether, and to what extent, we take part in the buying process. If we complete an action and like what happens next, there's a good chance we'll do it again. On the other hand, if we dislike what happens next, then we're unlikely to repeat it, unless we absolutely have to. In a marketing context, if a customer buys a product and likes it, they are receiving *positive reinforcement* and are more likely to buy the product again. The stronger the reinforcement in any given situation, the more likely we are to learn from our behaviour in that situation.

Operant conditioning works as our brains have evolved as pattern-spotting machines. Jenny Saffran, Richard Aslin and Elissa Newport have shown that children as young as eight months old automatically spot patterns between their actions and how their parents react.[27] However, operant conditioning is rather different from classical conditioning. It relies on four different approaches to modify a customer's behaviour (Table 5.1):

- *Positive reinforcement*: This relies on providing the customer with an additional positive stimulus when they behave in a particular way that makes it more likely that they will behave in the same way again. This could be a customer being given loyalty card points or a voucher whenever they do something – making repeat purchases, referring a friend or reviewing a product – that the brand would like them to do again.

- *Negative reinforcement*: With negative reinforcement, the desired behaviour is encouraged by removing a negative outcome. This is not the same as punishment (see next bullet) and many advertising campaigns rely on this approach. For example, if a customer uses suntan lotion before going to the beach, it stops them getting sunburnt. Consequently, most customers are likely to repeat the behaviour. Or maybe a customer is worried about looking older: if they use an anti-wrinkle moisturizer and they think it stops the wrinkles, their future behaviour is potentially modified by this negative reinforcement.

- *Punishment*: Within operant conditioning, the aim of punishment is to reduce subsequent behaviours. Punishment can be split into two different categories: positive punishment and negative punishment. With negative punishment, the marketer removes something desirable when a customer does something undesirable. For example, a manufacturer may cancel a warranty if the customers get their product serviced by a non-authorized dealer. On the other hand, positive punishment involves giving a negative stimulus after the undesirable behaviour has occurred. For example, if a customer fails to pay their monthly phone bill on time, they receive a fine.

Table 5.1 The four different techniques that can be used to influence behaviour from an operant conditioning perspective

	Increase Behaviour	Decrease Behaviour
Positive (add stimulus)	Positive Reinforcement	Positive Punishment
Negative (remove stimulus)	Negative Reinforcement	Negative Punishment

- *Extinction*: Just as in classical conditioning, extinction occurs when the customer is no longer rewarded or punished and the conditioned response is simply ignored, which ultimately leads to the conditioned behaviour stopping. For example, a customer may shop at a specific online store because it provides free shipping. But once they are required to pay for shipping, the likelihood of them using this service decreases.

If there are four key approaches to behaviour change, which is the best one for marketers to use? To date, research appears to suggest that positive reinforcement is the most effective at influencing behaviour[28] and the more we like the reward, the more effective it is at changing our behaviour.[29] However, there are subtle differences depending on the age of people you are trying to target. Children and teenagers are just as likely to learn from reinforcement, but punishment (such as losing points in an app) is far less effective with younger children.[30]

As individuals, it's relatively easy for us to think of a stimulus that can act as a positive reinforcement on us. The challenge for marketers is to find a reward that will appeal to all of a brand's target customers, or at least to a substantial majority of them. Providing customers with a discount is likely to be valued by the majority. But from a business perspective, the cost very quickly becomes prohibitive or the rewards will need to be so small they will nearly be meaningless or worse, insulting. To overcome this, numerous stores provide customers with abstract reward points instead, which ultimately translate into money-off vouchers in the form of loyalty cards. So, do they work?

Initially, the data appears rather unconvincing. In one experiment conducted by Joseph Bellizzi and Terry Bristol,[31] customers who regularly shopped in the target store before the loyalty card scheme was introduced were the most likely to redeem their points, although it had no impact on how much they purchased. Perhaps this shouldn't be a surprise. These customers may have experienced a ceiling effect; after all, they are already heavy buyers and there is a limit to the amount of baked beans one customer could buy. The scheme was more successful when it came to light users. These customers now purchased more items and made more regular shopping trips.[32] This would suggest that operant conditioning works, although it is worth adding a caveat. This research is nearly 20 years old and subsequent research has shown that loyalty cards only work as long as the number of competing schemes is limited and that customers are not accustomed to these schemes.[33] If all stores introduce a loyalty card, it will have no impact on customers.

But it is not just how much customers like the reward that companies need to think about. They also need to think about when the customers receive the reinforcement. The longer the delay between customers engaging in the target behaviour and receiving reinforcement, the less likely they will be to engage in the behaviour again.[34] It is also important that the customer receives the reward every time they engage in the desired behaviour. If this happens, then a behaviourist would say a contingency exists. If a customer buys a product and every time they buy the product, they receive loyalty points, a contingency exists (as receiving loyalty points is contingent on buying products from the shop). On the other hand, if we purchase a product and only sometimes receive loyalty points (or we receive points when we did not engage in the target behaviour), then there is a weak level of contingency and learning is less likely to occur.[35] However, there are pros and cons of different reinforcement schedules, and we'll explore these in the next section.

Reinforcement schedule As discussed, for operant conditioning to work, it is important for marketers to think carefully about how and when they reinforce behaviours. While you could reinforce a shopper every time they engage in a behaviour, what is known as continuous reinforcement, it is more common to use a partial reinforcement schedule. In practice, there are four main options when it comes to the partial reinforcement schedule, with each having a different impact on behaviour.

- *Fixed ratio schedule*: With a fixed ratio schedule, customers receive reinforcement (usually a reward) after a predetermined number of responses. For example, the food chain Subway offered a loyalty scheme in which, after purchasing six, six-inch Subways, you would get the seventh free. Fixed ratio schedules produce a high response rate, with our behaviour quickening as we get closer to the reward – although immediately after receiving the reward, there is usually a lull.[36] This is often called a *burst-pause pattern*.

But certain tactics can be used to help decrease these lulls. If consumers are required to collect ten stamps before receiving their reward, marketers can give customers the first two stamps for free. This causes customers to become more loyal and committed to the brand than those who did not receive the free stamps. What is interesting is that this change in behaviour is not caused by the change in the number of tokens customers need to collect but by *the perception of getting something for free*. When a car wash company offered customers loyalty cards, half of which required customers to buy eight car washes in order to receive a free car wash, and the other half required customers to collect ten stamps (but the first two stamps were already completed), they found customers were far more likely to complete the ten-point card, even though all the customers needed to complete the same number of purchases.[37]

- *Variable ratio schedule*: A variable ratio schedule is similar to a fixed ratio in that the reinforcement is provided after a set number of responses. What differs is that the number of responses required changes each time. This overcomes some of the drawbacks associated with the fixed ratio schedule, removing the lull after customers receive their reinforcement. Customers continue to engage in the scheme as there could be another reward immediately after the first. The other advantage of this system is the fact that the decay rate is slower. With the fixed interval schedule, as soon as a marketing campaign ends, customers' loyalty ends. It takes customers' loyalty longer to wane with a variable ratio schedule.[38] As with everything, this comes at a cost. This reinforcement system has a relatively slow learning curve – meaning that if a company starts using a variable ratio, it is unlikely to produce a sudden lift in sales. Instead, loyalty is built up over time and can persist even after the reward is removed.

- *Fixed interval schedule:* Whenever a store runs an annual or seasonal sale (e.g. January sales or Black Friday), they're using a fixed interval schedule. The target behaviour (in this case, buying products) is only reinforced after a predetermined length of time. It doesn't matter how many times a customer engages in the target behaviour — they're not reinforced until the end of the time period. Unsurprisingly, customers quickly recognize the pattern and put off making a purchase until they know they will receive a reward. As a result, fixed interval schedules typically result in an off-and-on pattern of behaviour[39] and this can clearly be seen by analysing sales around Black Friday. Typically, most retailers who run Black Friday sales experience a decline in sales during the run-up and then a surge in sales when the discounts are available. Due to this rather significant limitation, this approach is rarely used in education,[40] (e.g. providing students with reinforcement such as praise, after a consistent predetermined period), where most of the research into reinforcement schedules is conducted, yet it is still widely used in marketing, although that is slowly changing.

- *Variable interval schedule*: As with a fixed interval schedule, customers receive reinforcement after a set period of time. The difference with this approach is that customers never know when a reward is going to occur. This helps create a low-to-moderate rate of behaviour but avoids the on-and-off behaviour that fixed interval schedules produce.[41]

> **REAL-WORLD EXAMPLE: PSYCH IN ACTION**
>
> Although most of the research into reinforcement schedules focuses on just one of the four, it is possible to design systems that use a combination. A great example of this is Pokémon GO, a highly addictive augmented reality game that was popular in 2016. Users have to try to catch fictional characters hidden in the world around them. This uses a fixed ratio schedule: if players catch enough Pokémon, they are promoted to the next level. But after players level up, there is a risk that they might lose interest in the game (as it will take them a long time to reach the subsequent level). Consequently, game designers integrate a variable ratio and interval schedule as users never know how far they need to walk before they will find a new character, or if it will be a rare and therefore highly desirable character.
>
> Likewise, Duolingo uses a similar approach, mixing all four different reinforcement schedules. XP points are awarded after completing every lesson (a fixed ratio schedule). Occasionally, users will find a surprise chest after a lesson, but they never know when this will occur (a variable reinforcement schedule). Each day, their daily streak increases, if they complete a lesson every 24 hours (fixed interval schedule), and users can randomly receive a push notification reminding users to complete a lesson (a variable interval schedule)

Cognitive learning

Cognitive learning differs fundamentally from behaviourism as a way of understanding and predicting how humans learn. Where behaviourists adopt a 'black box model' of learning, assuming that psychologists cannot tell what is going on in a customer's head and that we therefore shouldn't waste time trying to work it out, cognitive psychologists seek to understand the mental processes that occur as we learn.

Social learning

In many ways, social learning theory can be considered a halfway point between the behavioural and cognitive approaches. A behaviourist would argue that learning can only occur when an individual receives direct feedback. Advocates of social learning, on the other hand, propose that humans are capable of learning vicariously, by watching other people and seeing what happens next. If we see someone engaging in a novel behaviour and they are then rewarded, then we are likely to mimic this behaviour. If they are punished, then understandably we'll avoid carrying out similar actions ourselves.[42]

This is not just speculation. In one experiment carried out in 1961 by Albert Bandura, Dorothea Ross and Sheila Ross, young children were shown a video of an adult attacking a large life-sized human doll; kicking it, punching it and even throwing things at the doll with the video ending in one of three different ways. Either the adult was rewarded for their behaviour, punished or nothing happened. After watching the video, the children were then placed in a room with an identical doll to play with. Those children who saw the adults rewarded for attacking the doll were far more likely to play violently with the doll than those who saw the adults being told off for this behaviour,[43] suggesting that social learning occurred. (Although it's questionable whether a modern-day ethics committee would approve this experiment.)

REAL-WORLD EXAMPLE: PSYCH IN ACTION

This idea of imitation or social learning is regularly exploited by marketers. Take the Food Dudes scheme, a marketing intervention aimed at increasing the amount of fruit and vegetables that young children eat. While in school, children watch a series of cartoons where they see the Food Dudes, a gang of four fun, cool and slightly older children, battle General Junk and the Junk Punks. The Food Dudes get their energy by eating fruit and vegetables, without which they can't beat the baddies. From a psychological perspective, the Food Dudes act as 'role models' which the children want to replicate and, as previous research has shown, children are more likely to replicate someone else's behaviour if they like that person,[44] and (with children) if the role models are the same age or slightly older.[45]

This is using social learning: the Food Dudes are positively reinforced, as they win the battle against the Junk Punks. But rather than relying solely on social learning, this initiative also uses operant conditioning, as children going through the programme receive positive rewards at lunch time (e.g. stickers) if they eat all of their fruit and vegetables.[46] Does it work? The poorest eaters of fruit and vegetables went from eating just 2% fruit at lunch to 56% after the intervention, and a similar pattern was seen with vegetable consumption, changing from 3% at baseline to 50% after the programme.[47]

Memory

To return to a marketing context, once a consumer has learnt some new information, it is essential for the marketer that they do not forget it. To maximize the chances of this occurring, marketers need to understand how memory works. Historically, psychologists would talk about a multi-store model of memory, originally proposed by Richard Atkinson and Richard Shiffrin in 1968. In this model, memory is split into three sections: sensory, short-term and long-term memory (Figure 5.1).[48] These are not three different regions of the brain, but categories that reflect how long a consumer needs to remember information for.

Sensory memory

Sensory memory is the shortest form of memory, allowing us to store information from our different senses (sight, sound, smell, touch and taste) for just as long as we need to process it and extract the key information.[49] Although we will see thousands of stimuli every hour, not all of them enter our sensory memory. We'll automatically ignore the vast majority, discarding the information they offer. If we perceive them, then they will enter our sensory memory. Visual information is only likely to be stored for about half a second, whereas auditory and haptic information lasts for approximately two seconds.[50,51] If we deem this information useful, it will then be transferred to our short-term memory.

Short-term memory

Short-term memory (STM) or working memory is where we store information that is currently being processed. As a result, most information is only stored in short-term memory for approximately 20–30 seconds.[52] Although STM stores information that we are currently processing, it has a limited maximum capacity. For a long time, it was thought that the maximum capacity varies between individuals, but most people can only hold seven items, plus or minus two,[53] what is now known as Miller's Law. However, this is not a hard and fast law but more of a general rule of thumb. The situation, context and items being recalled will change the number. For example, when people are asked to remember a list of letters or numbers without a mistake,

Figure 5.1   A visual representation of Richard Atkinson and Richard Shiffrin's multi-store model of memory

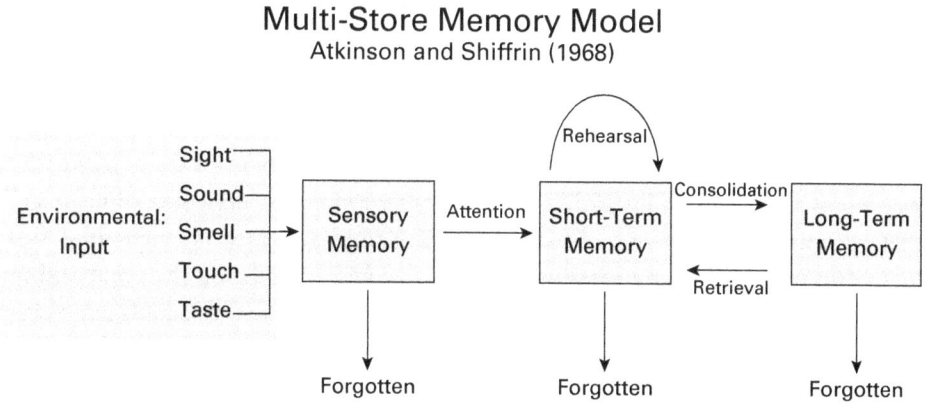

on average people could recall 7.3 letters and 9.3 numbers.[54] While our short-term memory has a limited number of 'slots', there is no limit to how much information each slot can hold. If information is presented as related groups of information, we group this information into 'chunks' that are easier to recall. So, most Swiss people would find it far easier to recall 1291, 1648, 1848 (three key dates from Swiss history), rather than 129116481848 read out as individual digits.

Presenting information in easy-to-remember formats, or at least formats that they are used to seeing, is essential. For example, William Chase and Herbert Simon found that chess masters could look at a board for five seconds and then put all the pieces in the right place. When non-chess players attempted this, they got stuck after a couple of pieces. This is not just the fact that chess players have a better memory, as they could only recreate a board if the pieces were in positions that they could plausibly end up in a game. Place the pieces randomly and they performed no better than an average person.[55]

> **GIVE IT A GO**
>
> Want to know how good your working memory is? Take a working memory test and see if you are above or below average.
>
>

Long-term memory

Long-term memory (LTM) differs from short-term and sensory memory in that it has an unlimited capacity, and once information is encoded into long-term memory it can be stored there for the rest of our lives. With such large amounts of information being stored in our LTM, it is essential for marketers to understand how each new memory is encoded.

Unfortunately, long-term memory doesn't work how most people intuitively assume. Memory is not like a video. When we recall something from the past, we don't just replay the memory. Instead, memories are stored across networks of nerve cells that are constantly changing. What's more, each time we remember something from long-term memory, we are recalling the last time we remembered the event and not the actual event. This can result in people thinking they remember details of an event that never actually happened. It's not that they are lying, they genuinely think it's true, but their memory is playing tricks on them.

The neuroscientist Jonah Lehrer is convinced he remembers one Friday night at high school, sitting on the back row of bleachers with his friends watching his school's American football team, the North Hollywood Huskies lose (yet again) while they were drinking Coca-Cola in the classic glass bottles instead of revising.[56] However, he knows this cannot have happened. So, how did this memory become so firmly implanted? Well, there are a variety of factors at play.

- *Reconstruction:* Each time we recall something, our brain reconstructs the memory, but there are always going to be gaps. In an attempt to fill in these gaps, our brains insert plausible details based on things that might have happened. For example, if you try to remember what shoes you wore during your first lecture at university, most people can't remember. But if you think back to that lecture, you'll be wearing shoes. You know you won't have been barefoot in that lecture, so your brain automatically fills in the gaps.
- *Misinformation event:* If we hear incorrect details about an event, especially details that feel highly specific, we can incorporate these details into our memory. This becomes more likely if we hear the details multiple times and from multiple sources. Then, next time we reconstruct the memory, this new detail becomes a key feature.
- *Source confusion:* Sometimes people can remember a story or an event but completely forget where they heard it. The result is that they assume the story happened to them when it didn't.
- *Association:* Memories can be influenced by related experiences. For example, if you have many similar events stored in your memory, details from different events can get mixed up.[57]

Again, this may seem like just a quirk of memory, but visual adverts are a great tool to implement false memories, which ultimately increase sales. For example, if a well-known brand creates a nostalgic ad showcasing how popular their product was in the past, it can lead viewers to believe they tried a product, leading to attitudes that are as strong, accessible and confident as if they did.[58] In the UK, lots of people claim that, as a child, Christmas didn't start until they saw the Coca-Cola *'holidays are coming'* advert.[59] However, if you are over the age of 40, this is probably a false memory, as the ad wasn't aired until 1995. Yet, this false memory helps cement the brand's position in the public consciousness.

Creating lasting memories

We often talk about individual memories, but each memory is not stored in isolation. Instead, links are formed between other existing memories, commonly referred to as Human Associative Memory (HAM) or a Network of Associations.[60,61] These networks are vital for creating successful marketing campaigns because they develop into a 'bundle of feelings, images and ideas that become connected over time'.[62] By constantly being exposed to two stimuli together, we learn to form links between the concepts, which leads to the development of stronger and longer-lasting memories.

At the neurological level, these connections can cause a change to our brain structure. Neurons in our brain communicate with each other via a process called synaptic transmission. The axon terminal in each neuron releases neurotransmitters which bind to neighbouring neurons in a process known as neural firing. When two neurons are repeatedly activated at the same time they become associated,[63] or as Donald Hebb, a Canadian neuropsychologist famously said: 'neurons that fire together, wire together'. Once these neurological pathways strengthen, messages are able to travel faster and memories become stronger. But each new memory is not only going to have links with one other concept but a range of memories and concepts. This creates a spider's web of information.

Marketers can use this web to develop stronger brands. Repeatedly pairing a brand with the same colour scheme, music or narrative can help create a strong web of associations. This can be taken a step further, too: a brand can 'borrow' from existing memories to help ensure their brand sticks in the consumer's mind. If new memories link up with information we already know, they are better encoded and less susceptible to decay.[64] The more concepts or nodes that a new memory can build upon, the stronger that memory will be. The challenge for marketers is to ensure that their brands build on nodes that produce a consistent brand image.

While associative networks explain why some memories are remembered better than others, they do not explain everything. If you think back to your childhood, the memories that you are most likely to recall are those that are most emotionally vivid.[65] This could be winning a race at sports day, being told off by a parent or embarrassing yourself in front of friends. What psychologists call the *valence* of the emotion, put simply, whether it was positive or negative, does not matter. What matters is its strength.[66] From an evolutionary perspective, our brains have evolved to prioritize emotional experiences. It doesn't matter if it's good or bad, if it can trigger a strong emotional response, our brain assumes it is important and should be remembered.[67] However, although we are more likely to remember these memories more vividly, our memory for these events is no more accurate[68] than more mundane events. Psychologists suspect this occurs because we know it's important to remember these events, so if we do forget details, our brain fills in the details as false memories.

Over time, emotional memories are still susceptible to decay like any other memory, but they are recalled better than non-emotional events.[69] This is not only the case when trying to recall memories from childhood or the distant past. We are also far more likely to remember emotional words and pictures than descriptive words and pictures.[70] From a marketing perspective, we can use this to our advantage as the principle occurs for ads as well. People are more likely to remember emotional adverts compared with neutral adverts.[71]

Not only are emotional stimuli remembered better than non-emotional stimuli, but in virtually all situations we remember images better than words.[72] Psychologists call this *the picture-superiority effect*. The only situation in which words are recalled just as well as images is when they are recalled immediately after the event. As soon as there is a delay, images win. This is usually explained by images triggering stronger mental pictures than words. It is important to point out that although emotional stimuli are more likely to be remembered, incorporating an emotional appeal into an advert may not be enough. Firstly, while viewers may remember the emotional stimuli, there is no guarantee that they will remember the brand (or even link the emotional stimuli to the brand). Secondly, even if viewers remember the advert, emotions do not automatically lead to behaviour (except in a few cases): that is the realm of motivation,[73] which, from a psychological perspective, is a very different concept (see Chapter 8).

Repetition

Another tactic that businesses can use to help customers develop strong memories is repetition.[74] Unsurprisingly, the more times we see a marketing message, the better we are at recalling it. Curiously, this effect is strongest when consumers have limited interest in the advert.[75] This quirk of memory can be used to predict which songs are most likely to reach number 1. Songs with more repetitive lyrics are dramatically more likely to reach number 1 in the charts,[76] as they are easier to remember.

While repetition works to build associations between concepts,[77] it does not work as well when it comes to learning factual information. When the BBC, the national broadcaster in the UK, changed the frequency of many of its radio stations, they conducted a saturation advertising campaign. For two months before the switch, the BBC regularly interrupted radio programmes with detailed information about the new wavelengths, with researchers estimating that regular listeners would have heard these announcements over 1,000 times.

The results: while 84% of listeners were aware that a change was occurring, virtually all listeners had no idea what frequency their favourite radio station was changing to. Only 25% of listeners attempted to describe the new frequency and their answers were no more accurate than if they simply guessed.[78] The results go to show that despite a thousand repetitions, factual information is not well remembered. Potentially, the fact that the adverts were describing an event that was going to occur in two months' time meant that viewers temporarily ignored the message. But by the end of two months, when it became crucial for listeners to remember the information, the adverts had become so tedious and repetitive that they were automatically ignored. This demonstrates that there is a balance to be struck between repetition and overkill.

So, how often should I repeat my advert? While repetition may help people remember an advert, it's not cheap. Media planners need to balance the pressure of ensuring that viewers are exposed to enough repetitions of their adverts with the need to minimize costs, which means avoiding, if they can, paying for repetitions that are not required. Psychology can help to resolve this conflict.

Intuitively, it is obvious that viewers will not consciously remember an advert if they are only exposed to it once. It is now known that most adverts have what is known as a 'wear-in' period, whereby after each additional exposure the advert becomes more effective.[79–81] But the number of repetitions needed for this is unclear. Historically, researchers argued that a viewer would need to see an advert three times before it could have any impact.[82] After seeing the advert for the first time, the viewer would ask themselves *'what is this?'*, the second time, *'what does it say?'* and the third time *'I've already seen it'*, and after this point they would start to ignore it.[83]

Today, we know this is not the case and being exposed to an advert once is enough to directly affect sales of the advertised product.[84–86] When researchers analysed the television adverts watched in 2,000 households and the brands those households purchased, they found that just seeing an advert once produces a short-term sales boost. On average, sales of advertised products were 24% higher than non-advertised products over the seven days following exposure to an advert. However, it's worth pointing out that this figure is just an average: when measured by performance, the top 20% of adverts saw a doubling of advertising spend. For 60% of all advertised brands, there was a 12% increase in share spend. This just goes to show how effective advertising is, even if most consumers do not believe that it personally affects their behaviour.[87]

Studies of memory have shown that there could also be a secondary benefit to repetition. The more you see or hear something, the more you like it, what is known as the *mere-exposure effect*.[88] This is directly relevant to advertisers, as previous research has shown that how much we like an advert is the most important factor in predicting its success, more important even than recall.[89] The original research conducted by US social psychologist Robert Zajonc involved showing participants stimuli that they had not seen before (foreign words, faces of strangers and Chinese characters) and in each case, the more they saw the stimuli, the more participants liked it. Subsequently, this research has now been directly tested in an advertising context and has been shown to work for online banner adverts[90] and television advertising.[91]

However, the mere-exposure effect appears to be slightly more complex when it comes to advertising. The effect appears to be most likely to kick in when viewers are already familiar with a brand[92] and when they only watch its adverts in a fairly superficial way. If viewers stop and think about an advert, it eventually leads to a wear-out effect, in which after a point each subsequent exposure causes us to like an advert less.[93] Unfortunately, it's hard to predict how many times we can view an advert before a wearout effect occurs, but some types of adverts seem to be more susceptible than others – those that use humour, for example.

The onset of the wear-out effect can be delayed by releasing different versions of the same advert.[94] If this is done right, the variation in the adverts will keep viewers engaged, while the similarity or continuity between them will ensure that the mere exposure effect can still work.[95] When an individual sees an advertising campaign that does not feature any variations, they quickly learn the basic message (e.g. the brand name) before any wearout occurs but tend not to experience a change of attitude towards the brand during that period. For a significant attitudinal change to occur, they have to see more repetitions: the problem is that they are more likely to get frustrated or bored by the advert before this occurs. Seeing variations of the advert delays the onset of wear-out, providing more time for a stronger attitudinal change to occur.

Does it matter when people see my adverts? So far, when discussing the 'wear-in' effects, we have not focused on *when* it's best to expose customers to repeated showings of an advert. It would make no sense for viewers to see six of the same adverts back-to-back. So, how should we space out these exposures?

One possible answer comes from a somewhat surprising domain: educational psychology. Educational psychologists have spent the last 50 or so years researching how best to teach children new concepts. One question they have explored that is directly relevant to advertisers is whether we learn new information better if it is studied a few times over a long period of time (*spaced presentation*) or if we are repeatedly exposed to the information over a short period of time (*massed presentation*). Today, the consensus is that spaced presentation is far more effective when it comes to developing strong recall.[96] The robustness of spaced presentation has been established with a wide range of stimuli, including words, sentences, photos[97,98] and, recently, adverts.[99]

Yet despite the spaced presentation effect being replicated in numerous experiments, psychologists are still not certain why it occurs.[100] One of the more popular explanations is that when we see an advert (or any stimulus) we do not just encode the advert itself, but the external context as well, forming what are known as cue-target associations.[101,102] The greater the gap between exposures, the greater the chance that we will view the advert in different situations. Even if we view the advert at home on every occasion, the situation is likely to change each time: our mental state could differ; the other adverts and programme surrounding it will differ; a multitude of other variables could have changed. Therefore, when an individual attempts to retrieve the advertisement, it is more likely that one of these retrieval cues will be present (e.g. the individual will be in a similar mood). For more information on retrieval cues, see the later section of this chapter.

If advertisers opt to use spaced presentation, they still have to make decisions about how they implement it. The simplest option is to evenly schedule the advert across the life of the campaign, but media planners may choose to use *expanding* or *condensing* spacing. Expanded spacing occurs when the viewer sees the advert regularly to begin with, then exposure becomes less frequent over time (e.g. by viewing an advert at slot 1, 2, 5 and 10 across 10 presentation slots). Condensed spacing uses the opposite approach.

So, which is more effective? Surprisingly, there is limited publicly available research investigating spacing, especially when it comes to advertising. Initially, researchers tested the phenomenon by giving participants a deck of cards which had a forename on one side and the surname on the reverse, with each card with a given combination of names appearing in the deck numerous times. Participants were given a short period of time to go through the cards and were then shown one side of a random card and asked if they knew the name on the other. Again, the results showed that cards that were distributed using massed presentation were less effective than spaced presentation. But when the results of the spaced presentation were analysed, cards distributed using expanding spacing (see previous section) outperformed those that used condensing spacing.[103] This effect has now been replicated[104] and shown to occur with advertising as well.[105]

> **GIVE IT A GO**
>
> Want to know if you have better memory for ads that use expanding, condensing or regular spacing? Test yourself online.
>
>

Forgetting

Although long-term memory is capable of holding information indefinitely, as soon as we have successfully encoded this information, we may gradually start to forget it. In most cases, the rate at which we forget information follows a standard 'forgetting curve'. Immediately after we are exposed to new information, we forget at a greater rate, but as time passes, this rate gradually slows down.[106]

This was first shown by Hermann Ebbinghaus (1850–1909), who over the course of a year learnt 169 lists of nonsensical syllables. In order to measure the rate at which he forgot these syllables, he re-learnt each list after intervals ranging from 21 minutes to a month. The longer it took him to relearn each list, the more information he had forgotten. Despite this research being over a hundred years old, the results and his forgetting curve still appear to be true today. His work has been successfully replicated, producing an almost identical forgetting curve (Figure 5.2).[107] Within the first hour of learning new information, we have forgotten 56% of it, and 24 hours later we have forgotten 67%.

Figure 5.2 An example of the Ebbinghaus forgetting curve showing how quickly people forget information over time if they don't actively try to retain this information

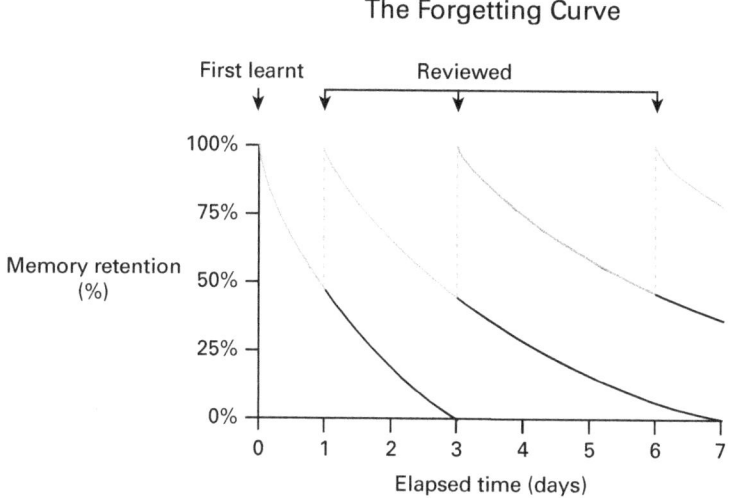

Although this research is interesting, many in marketing may question its relevance. The words Ebbinghaus learnt were all nonsense and did not link to any existing memories. This is very different from successful marketing campaigns that (marketers hope) build on existing knowledge structures and emotional memories to promote learning. Yet Ebbinghaus's forgetting curve appears to work exactly the same for emotional and personal memories. In a 2005 study, Meeter, Murre and Janssen tested over 14,000 participants' recall and recognition of news stories over the previous year.[108] After a year, participants were only able to correctly answer 31% of questions put to them about the material. But if they were asked to simply recognize news stories, they were correct about 52% of the time.

This implies two things. Firstly, it is easier to recognize information than to try and recall it unaided. This, reinforced by the fact that when 85 students were asked to draw the Apple logo, something they probably see almost every day, only one could draw it correctly. However, when shown eight different versions of the logo, half could now correctly identify the correct version; lower than most people would expect, but still demonstrating that recognition is easier than free recall.[109]

Secondly, even if we think we have forgotten information, the fact that we can recognize information means it is still in there somewhere. This gives marketers an opportunity to exploit this by using *retrieval cues*.

Retrieval cues and context-dependent memory

Retrieval cues are any stimuli that help you retrieve a memory from long-term memory. When we remember information, it is not just the target stimuli that we encode.

Instead, we encode information about the context in which we experienced the stimuli: the situation, the background music playing, the people around us, maybe even the clothes we're wearing. If the same cue is present both when information is encoded and when we try to remember it, they can help act as a trigger to access that memory.[110]

This quirk of memory was first noticed not by psychologists but by marine biologists, who noticed that although divers could easily remember the number and type of fish while underwater, they almost instantly forget what they have seen when they return to the surface,[111] which was a problem when divers were conducting underwater surveys. This led psychologists to wonder what it was about surfacing that caused the divers to forget.

Psychologists speculated that what lay behind this phenomenon was the fact that divers learnt the information in one environment but then had to recall it in another. This led them to develop one of the more unusual experiments in the history of psychological research. Divers were required to learn a list of words either on the beach or while diving. Half the divers were tested in the environment in which they learnt the words, while the other 50% were tested in the other environment. The results clearly showed that divers who learnt the words underwater were significantly better at recalling the information when tested underwater, while divers who learnt the information on the beach were far better at recalling the information on the beach. When they were asked to recall the information in the opposite environment from which they learnt it, their recall was significantly worse. This finding has now been replicated in numerous situations[112] and has even been shown to work with both mood[113] and alcohol consumption.[114]

Although scuba diving may seem rather far removed from advertising, there are several important take-home messages from this study. First, the environment in which consumers view an advert (at home) is often rather different from the one in which they are making an actual purchase decision, the big exception being if they are shopping online. A location change makes it harder for them to remember the advert. Second, very often when shoppers cannot remember an advert when shopping, it's not necessarily the case that they have forgotten the advert, but rather that they are experiencing a 'retrieval failure'. The information is still encoded in long-term memory, but they are unable to access it at that moment. All that's missing is a retrieval cue.

Retrieval cues are relatively easy to incorporate into shopper marketing campaigns. At the most basic level, when a consumer sees a brand name in a shop, it acts as a retrieval cue, helping customers remember the advert.[115] But the effect can be more subtle, too. This could include displaying pictures or characters from an advert on product packaging, or on Point of Sale displays; or the store could periodically play the same music that featured in an advert.[116] For example, Coca-Cola regularly features current chart songs in its adverts, which shoppers are highly likely to hear as they browse a supermarket, subtly reminding them about their ads.

Closing thoughts

While virtually all marketers aim for customers to learn their marketing messages, few take a systematic or evidence-based approach to achieving this objective. However, insight from psychological research can offer clear evidence-based approaches to achieving this objective. By using these findings, especially those related to the timing, frequency and rewards of marketing messages, marketers can speed up the process through which people will learn their marketing messages, ensure the memories last longer and slow down the rate at which they'll be forgotten.

> **KEY POINTS**
>
> - Behaviourism is divided into two schools of thought: classical conditioning and operant conditioning.
>   - Classical conditioning is a learning process where an originally neutral stimulus becomes associated with an unconditioned stimulus, triggering a conditioned response.
>   - In operant conditioning, the shopper plays an active role in the learning process as their behaviour is modified by reinforcement or punishment.
>   - Stimulus generalization is the idea that a stimulus that looks like the conditioned stimuli can trigger the same conditioned response, e.g. if a shopper looks at a copycat brand, it might trigger thoughts similar to those if they saw the genuine brand.
>   - Operant conditioning relies on four processes to reinforce behaviour: positive reinforcement; negative reinforcement; punishment; extinction.
>   - However, they are not usually reinforced every time a participant engages in the target behaviour. Instead, they use one of four partial reinforcement schedules: fixed ratio schedule, variable ratio schedule, fixed interval schedule and variable interval schedule.
> - The cognitive model of learning seeks to explain how people learn and how they mentally engage with the stimuli.
> - The multi-store model of memory comprises three elements: sensory memory, short-term memory and long-term memory.
>   - Sensory memory is the shortest form of memory, allowing us to store information from our different senses for a couple of seconds as our brain processes it.

- Short-term memory (STM), or working memory, is where we store information that is currently being processed. As a result, most information is only stored in short-term memory for approximately 20–30 seconds and typically comprises seven items, plus or minus two.
- Long-term memory (LTM) has an unlimited capacity, and once information is encoded into LTM, it can be stored there for the rest of our lives.
• Individual memories are not stored in isolation. Instead, links are formed between other existing memories – what is commonly referred to as Human Associative Memory (HAM) or a Network of Associations. The more links a brand has in memory, the stronger the brand will be.
• Repeatedly pairing a brand with the same colour scheme, music or narrative can help create a strong web of associations.
• Certain stimuli are more likely to be remembered: emotionally salient stimuli, images.
• When it comes to scheduling adverts, viewers are more likely to remember ads that use expanded spacing, e.g. the ads are shown a lot to start with, and then the gaps between exposure increase, rather than ads which are evenly spaced or use a condensing spacing.
• The more times we're repeatedly exposed to a stimulus, the more likely we are to recall it successfully.
• Retrieval cues are any stimuli that help you retrieve a memory from long-term memory.

PUTTING THEORY INTO PRACTICE

1 Select a loyalty scheme for a retailer that offers shoppers a reward for shopping with them. Identify what kind of reinforcement schedule the company is using and what the advantages and disadvantages of this approach are. Is there a better approach they could use?

2 Think of your favourite brand and draw a Network of Association for this brand. How could they use this information to help develop a new advert?

3 Numerous marketing campaigns make extensive use of social media influencers. How can principles of learning and memory help predict the success of these campaigns?

4 What can brands learn from the Ebbinghaus forgetting curve when it comes to scheduling advertisements?

5 According to the multi-store model of memory, why might market researchers struggle to discover what brands shoppers consider in a supermarket if they rely on interviews or questionnaires?

6 How can theories of learning and memory help media planners schedule advertisements?

SUGGESTIONS FOR FURTHER READING

Baddeley, A., Eysenck, M. & Anderson, M. (2015). Memory. 2nd ed. London: Psychology Press.

References

1. Jansson-Boyd, C. (2010). *Consumer psychology*. Open University Press.
2. Blythe, J. (2013). *Consumer behaviour* (2nd Edition). Sage.
3. O'Shaughnessy, J. (2012). *Consumer behaviour: Perspectives, findings and explanations*. Palgrave.
4. Watson, J. (1913). Psychology as the behaviorist views it. *Psychological Review*, 20(2), 158–177.
5. Pavlov, I. P. (1902). *The work of the digestive glands*. Griffin.
6. O'Shaughnessy, J. (2012). *Consumer behaviour: Perspectives, findings and explanations*. Palgrave.
7. Pavlov, I.P. (1934). A contribution to physiology of the hypnotic state of dogs. *Char. Personal*. 2, 189–200.
8. Jeong, H., Taylor, A., Floeder, J. R., Lohmann, M., Mihalas, S., Wu, B., Zhou, M., Burke, D. A., Namboodiri, V. M. K. (2022). Mesolimbic dopamine release conveys causal associations. *Science*, 378(6626), eabq6740 https://doi.org/10.1126/science.abq6740 (archived at https://perma.cc/D4QG-QVNX)
9. Miltenberger, R. (2015). *Behavior modification: Principles and procedures* (6th Edition). Wadsworth Publishing.
10. Miltenberger, R. (2015). *Behavior modification: Principles and procedures* (6th Edition). Wadsworth Publishing.
11. Gorn, G. J. (1982). The effects of music in advertising on choice behavior: A classical conditioning approach. *Journal of Marketing*, 46(1), 94–101. https://doi.org/10.2307/1251163 (archived at https://perma.cc/5ZC9-LQNZ)
12. Kellaris, J. J. & Cox, A. D. (1989). The effects of background music in advertising: A reassessment. *The Journal of Consumer Research*, 16(1), 113–118.

13 Szmigin, I. & Piacentini, M. (2015). *Consumer behaviour*. Oxford.
14 Till, B. D., Stanley, S. M., & Priluck, R. (2008). Classical conditioning and celebrity endorsers: An examination of belongingness and resistance to extinction. *Psychology and Marketing*, 25(2), 179–196. https://doi.org/10.1002/mar.20205 (archived at https://perma.cc/ZF7E-SRXV)
15 Till, B. D. & Priluck, R. L. (2000). Stimulus generalization in classical conditioning: An initial investigation and extension. *Psychology and Marketing*, 17(1), 55–72. https://doi.org/10.1002/(sici)1520-6793(200001)17:1<55::aid-mar4>3.0.co;2-c (archived at https://perma.cc/ZM38-GWG9)
16 Watson, J. B. & Rayner, R. (1920). Conditioned emotional reactions. *Journal of Experimental Psychology*, 3(1), 1–14.
17 Till, B. D. & Priluck, R. L. (2000). Stimulus generalization in classical conditioning: An initial investigation and extension. *Psychology and Marketing*, 17(1), 55–72. https://doi.org/10.1002/(sici)1520-6793(200001)17:1<55::aid-mar4>3.0.co;2-c (archived at https://perma.cc/ZM38-GWG9)
18 Van Horen, F. & Pieters, R. (2012). Consumer evaluation of copycat brands: The effect of imitation type. *International Journal of Research in Marketing*, 29(3), 246–255.
19 Van Horen, F. & Pieters, R. (2012). Consumer evaluation of copycat brands: The effect of imitation type. *International Journal of Research in Marketing*, 29(3), 246–255.
20 Warlop, L., Alba, J. W. (2004). Sincere flattery: Trade-dress imitation and consumer choice. *Journal of Consumer Psychology*, 14(1–2), 21–7.
21 Kim, J., Allen, C. T., & Kardes, F. R. (1996). An investigation of the mediational mechanisms underlying attitudinal conditioning. *Journal of Marketing Research*, 33(3), 318–13. https://doi.org/10.2307/3152128 (archived at https://perma.cc/6GHP-KU4S)
22 Priluck, R. & Till, B. D. (2004). The role of contingency awareness, involvement and need for cognition in attitude formation. *Journal of the Academy of Marketing Science*, 32(3), 329–344. https://doi.org/10.1177/0092070303257646 (archived at https://perma.cc/MX5C-JHCD)
23 Stuart, E. W., Shimp, T., & Engle, R. W. (1987). Classical conditioning of consumer attitudes: Four experiments in an advertising contex. *Journal of Consumer Research*, 14(3), 334–349. https://www.jstor.org/stable/pdf/2489495.pdf (archived at https://perma.cc/4A8S-MGC9)
24 Grossman, R. P. & Till, B. D. (1998). The persistence of classically conditioned brand attitudes. *Journal of Advertising*, 27(1), 23–31. https://doi.org/10.1080/00913367.1998.10673540 (archived at https://perma.cc/4L7Y-KTH4)
25 Pornpitakpan, C. (2012). A critical review of classical conditioning effects on consumer behavior. *Australasian Marketing Journal (AMJ)*, 20(4), 282–296. https://doi.org/10.1016/j.ausmj.2012.07.002 (archived at https://perma.cc/U6Q8-55LC)
26 O'Shaughnessy, J. (2012). *Consumer behaviour: Perspectives, findings and explanations*. Palgrave.
27 Saffran, J. R., Aslin, R. N., & Newport, E. L. (1996). Statistical learning by 8-month-old infants. *Science*, 274(5294), 1926–1928.
28 Podsakoff, P. M., Todor, W. M., & Skov, R. (1982). Effects of leader contingent and noncontingent reward and punishment behaviors on subordinate performance and satisfaction. *The Academy of Management Journal*, 25(4), 810–821.

29 Premack, D. (1959). Toward empirical behavior laws: Positive reinforcement. *Psychological Review*, 66(4), 219–233.
30 Pauli, R., Brazil, I. A., Kohls, G., Klein-Flügge, M. C., Rogers, J. C., Dikeos, D., ... & Lockwood, P. L. (2023). Action initiation and punishment learning differ from childhood to adolescence while reward learning remains stable. *Nature Communications*, 14(1), 5689.
31 Bellizzi, J. A. & Bristol, T. (2004). An assessment of supermarket loyalty cards in one major US market. *Journal of Consumer Marketing*, 21(2), 144–154.
32 Liu, Y. (2007). The long-term impact of loyalty programs on consumer purchase behavior and loyalty. *Journal of Marketing*, 71(4), 19–35. https://doi.org/10.1509/jmkg.71.4.19 (archived at https://perma.cc/SF8N-T9YS)
33 Noordhoff, C., Pauwels, P., & Schröder, G. O. (2004). The effect of customer card programs. *International Journal of Service Industry Management*, 15(4), 351–364. https://doi.org/10.1108/09564230410552040 (archived at https://perma.cc/39F4-F6G3)
34 Miltenberger, R. (2015). *Behavior modification: Principles and procedures* (6th Edition). Wadsworth Publishing.
35 Borrero, J. C., Vollmer, T. R., Wright, C. S., Lerman, D. C., & Kelley, M. E. (2002). Further evaluation of the role of protective equipment in the functional analysis of self-inurious behavior. *Journal of Applied Behavior Analysis*, 35(1), 69–72. https://doi.org/10.1901/jaba.2002.35-69 (archived at https://perma.cc/2V7P-8FD7)
36 Ferster, C. B. & Skinner, B. F. (1957). *Schedules of reinforcement*. Appleton-Century-Crofts.
37 Nunes, J. C. & Dreze, X. (2006). Your loyalty program is betraying you. *Harvard Business Review*, 84(4), 124–131.
38 Szmigin, I. & Piacentini, M. (2015). *Consumer behaviour*. Oxford.
39 Ferster, C. B. & Skinner, B. F. (1957). *Schedules of reinforcement*. Appleton-Century-Crofts.
40 Miltenberger, R. (2015). *Behavior modification: Principles and procedures* (6th Edition). Wadsworth Publishing.
41 Ferster, C. B. & Skinner, B. F. (1957). *Schedules of reinforcement*. Appleton-Century-Crofts.
42 Bandura, A. (1977). *Social learning theory*. Prentice Hall.
43 Bandura, A., Ross, D., & Ross, S. A. (1961). Transmission of aggression through imitation of aggressive models. *Journal of Abnormal and Social Psychology*, 63(3), 575–582. https://doi.org/10.1037/h0045925 (archived at https://perma.cc/KYJ2-3AA2)
44 Bandura, A. (1977). *Social learning theory*. Prentice Hall.
45 Brody, G. H. & Stoneman, Z. (1981). Selective imitation of same-age, older, and younger peer models. *Child Development*, 52(2), 717–720. https://www.jstor.org/stable/pdf/1129197.pdf (archived at https://perma.cc/6P97-VQ3R)
46 Tapper, K., Horne, P. J., & Lowe, F. C. (2003). The Food Dudes to the rescue. *The Psychologist*, 16(1).
47 Lowe, C. F., Horne, P. J., Tapper, K., Bowdery, M., & Egerton, C. (2004). Effects of a peer modelling and rewards-based intervention to increase fruit and vegetable consumption in children. *European Journal of Clinical Nutrition*, 58(3), 510–522. https://doi.org/10.1038/sj.ejcn.1601838 (archived at https://perma.cc/2XBC-B9KA)

48　Atkinson, R. C. & Shiffrin, R. M. (1968). *Human memory: A proposed system and its control processes* (K. W. Spence & J. T. Spence, Eds.). Academic Press.

49　Jansson-Boyd, C. (2010). *Consumer psychology*. Open University Press.

50　Jansson-Boyd, C. (2010). *Consumer psychology*. Open University Press.

51　Darwin, C. J. & Turvey, M. T. (1972). An auditory analogue of the sperling partial report procedure: Evidence for brief auditory storage. *Cognitive Psychology*, 3(2), 255–267. https://doi.org/10.1016/0010-0285(72)90007-2 (archived at https://perma.cc/9DF6-VR6Y)

52　Atkinson, R. C. & Shiffrin, R. M. (1971). The control of short-term memory. *Scientific American*, 225(2). https://doi.org/10.1038/scientificamerican0871-82 (archived at https://perma.cc/VNP4-JGHS)

53　Miller, G. A. (1956). The magical number seven, plus or minus two: Some limits on our capacity for processing information. *Psychological Review*, 63(2), 81–97. https://doi.org/10.1037/h0043158 (archived at https://perma.cc/64TM-M2GM)

54　Jacobs, J. (1887). Experiments on prehension. *Mind*, 12, 75–79.

55　Chase, W. G. & Simon, H. A. (1973). Perception in chess. Cognitive Psychology, 4, 55–81.

56　Lehrer, J. (2011, May 25). Ads implant false memories. Wired. https://www.wired.com/2011/05/ads-implant-false-memories/ (archived at https://perma.cc/RLD2-DHJX)

57　Brainerd, CJ. & Reyna, VF. (2005). *The science of false memory*. New York: Oxford University Press

58　Rajagopal, P. & Montgomery, N. V. (2011). I imagine, I experience, I like: The false experience effect. *Journal of Consumer Research*, 38(3), 578–594.

59　Matco, C. (2023, December 13). Coca Cola Christmas ad, keeping the tradition for over 100 years. Tech Behemoths. Available from: https://techbehemoths.com/blog/coca-cola-christmas-ad-keeping-tradition-over-years (archived at https://perma.cc/64EU-FQMH)

60　Anderson, J. R. (1983). A spreading activation theory of memory. *Journal of Verbal Learning and Verbal Behavior*, 22(3), 261–295. http://act-r.psy.cmu.edu/wordpress/wp-content/uploads/2012/12/66SATh.JRA.JVL.1983.pdf (archived at https://perma.cc/KBJ4-LUP9)

61　Keller, K. L. (1993). Conceptualizing, measuring, and managing customer-based brand equity. *Journal of Marketing*, 57(1), 1–22. https://www.jstor.org/stable/pdf/1252054.pdf (archived at https://perma.cc/TQ7J-CT37)

62　Westen, D. (2008). *The political brain: The role of emotion in deciding the fate of the nation*. PublicAffairs.

63　Hebb, D. O. (1949). *Organization of behavior: A neuropsychological theory*. Wiley.

64　Alba, J. W. & Hasher, L. (1983). Is memory schematic? *Psychological Bulletin*, 93(2), 203–231.

65　Buchanan, T. W. (2007). Retrieval of emotional memories. *Psychological Bulletin*, 761–779. https://www.ncbi.nlm.nih.gov/pmc/articles/PMC2265099/pdf/nihms41109.pdf (archived at https://perma.cc/WGJ2-G7LM)

66　Hamann, S. B., Ely, T. D., Grafton, S. T., & Kilts, C. D. (1999). Amygdala activity related to enhanced memory for pleasant and aversive stimuli. *Nature Neuroscience*, 2(3), 289–293. https://doi.org/10.1038/6404 (archived at https://perma.cc/A524-Y63Z)

67 Fox, E., Russo, R., Bowles, R., & Dutton, K. (2001). Do threatening stimuli draw or hold visual attention in subclinical anxiety?. *Journal of Experimental Psychology: General*, 130(4), 681.
68 Brown, R. & Kulik, J. (1977). Flashbulb memories. *Cognition*, 5(1), 73–99. https://doi.org/10.1016/0010-0277(77)90018-X (archived at https://perma.cc/TBF4-XDKY)
69 Levine, L. J. & Pizarro, D. A. (2004). Emotion and memory research: A grumpy overview. *Social Cognition*, 22(5), 530–554.
70 Khairudin, R., Givi, M. V., Shahrazad, W. S. W., Nasir, R., & Halim, F. W. (2011). Effects of emotional contents on explicit memory process. *Pertanika Journal of Social Science and Humanities*, 19, 17–26.
71 Friestad, M. & Thorson, E. (1986). Emotion-eliciting adversiting effects on long term memory and judgment. *Advances in Consumer Research*, 13, 111–116.
72 Childers, T. L. & Houston, M. J. (1984). Conditions for a picture-superiority effect on consumer memory. *Journal of Consumer Research*, 11(2), 643–654.
73 Baumeister, R. F., Vohs, K. D., DeWall, C. N., & Zhang, L. (2016). How emotion shapes behavior: Feedback, anticipation, and reflection, rather than direct causation. *Personality and Social Psychology Review*, 11(2), 167–203. https://doi.org/10.1177/1088868307301033 (archived at https://perma.cc/JF6J-39LB)
74 Schmidt, S. & Eisend, M. (2015). Advertising Repetition: A meta-analysis on effective frequency in advertising. *Journal of Advertising*, 44(4), 415–428. https://doi.org/10.1080/00913367.2015.1018460 (archived at https://perma.cc/6Q6B-3TS5)
75 Schmidt, S. & Eisend, M. (2015). Advertising repetition: A meta-analysis on effective frequency in advertising. *Journal of Advertising*, 44(4), 415–428. https://doi.org/10.1080/00913367.2015.1018460 (archived at https://perma.cc/6Q6B-3TS5)
76 Nunes, J. C., Ordanini, A., & Valsesia, F. (2015). The power of repetition: Repetitive lyrics in a song increase processing fluency and drive market success. *Journal of Consumer Psychology*, 25(2), 187–199.
77 Westen, D. (2008). *The political brain: The role of emotion in deciding the fate of the nation*. PublicAffairs.
78 Bekerian, D. A. & Baddeley, A. D. (1980). Saturation advertising and the repetition effect. *Journal of Verbal Learning and Verbal Behavior*, 19(1), 17–25. https://doi.org/10.1016/s0022-5371(80)90476-4 (archived at https://perma.cc/LR62-2ZW7)
79 Blair, M. H. (1998). Advertising wearin and wearout: Ten years later--More empirical evidence and successful practice. *Journal of Advertising Research*, 38(5), 7–18.
80 Blair, M. H. (2000). An empirical investigation of advertising wearin and wearout. *Journal of Advertising Research*, 40(06), 95–100.
81 Pechmann, C. & Stewart, D. W. (1988). *Advertising repetition: A critical review of wearin and wearout* (J. H. Leigh & C. R. Martin, Eds.; pp. 285–289).
82 Krugman, H. E. (1972). Why three exposures may be enough. *Journal of Advertising Research*, 12(6), 11–14.
83 Plessis, E. D. (2005). *The advertised mind*. Kogan Page Ltd.
84 Gibson, L. (1996). What can one TV exposure do? *Journal of Advertising Research*, 36(2), 9–18.
85 Jones, J. P. (1995). *When ads work*. Lexington.

86 Tellis, G. J. (1997). Effective frequency: One exposure or three factors? *Journal of Advertising Research*, 75–80. http://papers.ssrn.com/sol3/papers.cfm?abstract_id=906019 (archived at https://perma.cc/YN7B-XQLU)

87 Davison, W. P. (1983). The third-person effect in communication. *The Public Opinion Quarterly*, 47(1), 1–15. https://doi.org/10.1086/268763 (archived at https://perma.cc/3P9V-QKY8)

88 Zajonc, R. (1968). Attitudinal effects of mere exposure. *Journal of Personality and Social Psychology*, 9(2 pt 2), 1–27. https://doi.org/10.1037/h0025848 (archived at https://perma.cc/E5CJ-MK6J)

89 Haley, R. I. & Russel, A. L. (1991). The ARF copy research validity project. *Journal of Advertising Research*, 31(2), 11–32.

90 Fang, X., Singh, S., & Ahluwalia, R. (2007). An examination of different explanations for the mere exposure effect. *Journal of Consumer Research*, 34(1), 97–103.

91 Baker, W. E. (1999). When can affective conditioning and mere exposure directly influence brand choice? *Journal of Advertising*, 28(4), 31–46. https://doi.org/10.1080/00913367.1999.10673594 (archived at https://perma.cc/3SCN-7ZCY)

92 Campbell, M. C., & Keller, K. L. (2003). Brand familiarity and advertising repetition effects. *Journal of Consumer Research*, 30(2), 292–304. https://doi.org/10.1086/376800 (archived at https://perma.cc/V7DH-54XX)

93 Nordhielm, C. (2002). The influence of level of processing on advertising repetition effects. *Journal of Consumer Research*, 29(3), 371–382.

94 Gorn, G. J. & Goldberg, M. E. (1980). Children's responses to repetitive television commercials. *The Journal of Consumer Research*, 6(4), 421–424. https://doi.org/10.1086/208785 (archived at https://perma.cc/3XGC-L3NH)

95 McCullough, J. & Ostrom, T. (1974). Repetition of highly similar messages and attitude change. *Journal of Applied Psychology*, 59(3), 395–397. https://doi.org/10.1037/h0036658 (archived at https://perma.cc/5PM2-QZNN)

96 Dempster, F. (1989). Spacing effects and their implications for theory and practice. *Educational Psychology Review*, 1(4), 309–330. https://doi.org/10.1007/bf01320097 (archived at https://perma.cc/V4FC-2VS7)

97 Dempster, F. (1996). *Distributing and managing the conditions of encoding and practice* (E. L. Bjork & R. A. Bjork, Eds.; Vol. 10, pp. 317–344).

98 Crowder, R. G. (1976). *Principles of learning and memory*. Erlbaum.

99 Harvey, G. J. (2012). *Advertising repetition, spacing and variation: A laboratory study*. Bangor University.

100 Janiszewski, C., Noel, H., & Sawyer, A. (2003). A meta-analysis of the spacing effect in verbal learning: Implications for research on advertising repetition and consumer memory. *Journal of Consumer Research*, 30(1), 138–149. https://doi.org/10.1086/374692 (archived at https://perma.cc/8CBD-9C5J)

101 Glenberg, A. M. (1979). Component-levels theory of the effects of spacing of repetitions on recall and recognition. *Memory & Cognition*, 7(2), 95–112. https://doi.org/10.3758/bf03197590 (archived at https://perma.cc/SHQ6-FZ9J)

102 Melton, A. (1970). The situation with respect to the spacing of repetitions and memory. *Journal of Verbal Learning and Verbal Behavior*, 9(5), 596–606. https://doi.org/10.1016/s0022-5371(70)80107-4 (archived at https://perma.cc/GJH8-D2QY)

103 Landauer, T. & Bjork, R. A. (1978). *Optimum rehearsal patterns and name learning* (M. Gruneberg, P.E. Morns, & R. Wkyes, Eds.; pp. 625–632).

104 Cull, W., Shaughnessy, J., & Zechmeister, E. (1996). Expanding understanding of the expanding-pattern-of-retrieval mnemonic: Toward confidence in applicability. *Journal of Experimental Psychology: Applied*, 2(4), 365–378. https://doi.org/10.1037/1076-898x.2.4.365 (archived at https://perma.cc/G5AG-WR6U)

105 Harvey, G. J. (2012). *Advertising repetition, spacing and variation: A laboratory study*. Bangor University.

106 Ebbinghaus, H. (1913). *Memory: A contribution to experimental psychology* (H. A. Ruger & C. E. Bussenius, Trans.). Teachers College, Columbia University.

107 Murre, J. M. J. & Dros, J. (2015). Replication and analysis of Ebbinghaus' forgetting curve. *PLoS ONE*, 10(7), e0120644-23. https://doi.org/10.1371/journal.pone.0120644 (archived at https://perma.cc/4KNH-ECJW)

108 Meeter, M., Murre, J. M. J., & Janssen, S. M. J. (2005). Remembering the news: Modeling retention data from a study with 14,000 participants. *Memory & Cognition*, 33(5), 793–810. https://doi.org/10.3758/bf03193075 (archived at https://perma.cc/FP4X-73DV)

109 Blake, A. B., Nazarian, M., & Castel, A. D. (2015). The Apple of the mind's eye: Everyday attention, metamemory, and reconstructive memory for the Apple logo. *The Quarterly Journal of Experimental Psychology*, 68(5), 858–865. https://doi.org/10.1080/17470218.2014.1002798 (archived at https://perma.cc/HZ3D-BV6J)

110 Garretson, J. A. & Burton, S. (2005). The role of spokescharacters as advertisement and package cues in integrated marketing communications. *Journal of Marketing*, 69(4), 118–132. https://doi.org/10.1509/jmkg.2005.69.4.118 (archived at https://perma.cc/92FC-7GJ8)

111 Godden, D. R. & Baddeley, A. D. (1975). Context-dependent memory in two natural environments: On land and underwater. *British Journal of Psychology*, 66(3), 325–331.

112 Ucros, C. G. (1989). Mood state-dependent memory: A meta-analysis. *Cognition and Emotion*, 3(2), 139–169.

113 Eich, E. (1995). Searching for mood dependent memory. *Psychological Science*, 6(2), 67–75.

114 Goodwin, D. W., Powell, B., Bremer, D., Hoine, H., & Stern, J. (1969). Alcohol and recall: State-dependent effects in man. *Science*, 163(3873), 1358–1360.

115 Keller, K. L., Heckler, S. E., & Houston, M. J. (1998). The effects of brand name suggestiveness on advertising recall. *Journal of Marketing*, 62(1), 48. https://doi.org/10.2307/1251802 (archived at https://perma.cc/6474-9EFW)

116 Garretson, J. A. & Burton, S. (2005). The role of spokescharacters as advertisement and package cues in integrated marketing communications. *Journal of Marketing*, 69(4), 118–132. https://doi.org/10.1509/jmkg.2005.69.4.118 (archived at https://perma.cc/92FC-7GJ8)

PART TWO
Consumer psychology in action

6 | The psychology of copywriting: Words that sell

LEARNING OBJECTIVES

- Create engaging, persuasive and memorable copy by understanding the development of the English language.
- Use principles from prospect theory to create more persuasive copy that can be used across a variety of different touchpoints.
- Understand how marketers need to change their writing style based on the message objectives.

Finding the right words

For marketers, finding the right words to persuade can be tricky. It often feels like there are dozens of words that all mean the same thing. Do we want to describe our product as brilliant, amazing or fabulous? While a linguist could describe the difference between each of these words, most people would probably use them interchangeably. Yet there are subtle differences, and finding the right word can make or break a marketing campaign. Take, for example, a charity running a fundraising campaign. Most of the time they ask for a donation it's clear and everybody understands what they are asking for. But Phyllis Wang, Yuwei Wang and Yuwei Jiang showed that instead of asking for a donation, if charities ask for a 'gift' people typically give 29% more.[1] This is because using the word gift implies that we are closer to the charity, whereas the word donation implies that we are distant from them. Previous research has shown that if we feel socially distant from someone, we are understandably less likely to help them. Recognizing these differences is the art of good copywriting, helping us to establish a close and personal connection with our shoppers.

Thinking of the English language in particular, why is it that we have so many words seemingly all meaning the same thing? To answer this question, we need a (brief) history lesson. The English we speak today has evolved from a melting pot of other languages. Each time what we now refer to as Great Britain was invaded, the conquerors left traces of their languages behind (Table 6.1). Originally, the people of Britain used to speak several different Celtic languages, but when the Roman emperor Claudius invaded in AD 43, he introduced Latin. The Romans ruled over most of England and Wales until the early 5th century, and during this time, they united England and Wales into the Kingdom of Britannia, unifying the tribes under one system of government. Not only this, but under their rule, they protected the country from invading tribes. But after they left, the country was unprotected and by AD 600 Britannia had been invaded by three tribes from northern Germany and Denmark: the Angles, the Saxons and the Jutes – what we now refer to as the Anglo-Saxons, who spoke North Sea Germanic. The next major change to the English language occurred when the Vikings invaded. The first raid took place at Lindisfarne in AD 793 off the Northumberland coast and they introduced Old Norse to the country. Their rule was relatively short, as in 1066 William the Conquer invaded England and Wales, bringing with him Norman French, and today approximately 45% of the English words we use have a French origin.

Each time there was an invasion, the new language didn't replace the old language, but we simply added the new language to the mix. So, if we go back to our example of brilliant, amazing and fabulous, brilliant has a French origin, amazing is from Old English and fabulous traces its origin back to Latin. You may be wondering why this

Table 6.1 A selection of English words of Anglo-Saxon origin paired alongside the equivalent English words of French origin

Anglo-Saxon	French	Anglo-Saxon	French
Ask	Inquire	Heaven	Celestial
Build	Construct	High	Elevated
Burn	Incinerate	Need	Require
Buy	Purchase	Next	Adjacent
Died	Deceased	Share	Proportion
Eat	Consume	Small	Diminutive
Fair	Equitable	Smell	Odour
Forgive	Pardon	Talk	Converse
Good	Favourable	Thinking	Pensive
Grow	Cultivated	Understand	Comprehend

matters, but a word's origin directly impacts its power to persuade. This occurs because although the new languages were assimilated into English, not everybody would use them. For example, when William the Conquer invaded, the Norman French that he spoke was only used by the ruling classes, whereas the commoners continued to use Anglo-Saxon. This distinction remains a thousand years later. When we want to sound formal or eloquent, we subconsciously use words with a French origin, whereas more everyday words have an Anglo-Saxon origin.

Although it is a generalization, words with an Anglo-Saxon origin are normally shorter, harder in sound and more concrete, which leads them to be more persuasive than words with a French origin.[2] Hence, when Churchill said 'Short words are best, and old words when short are best of all',[3] what he was really advising is to avoid using words with a French origin. You would never tell your child to 'go and sanitise your chamber' (both sanitise and chamber are words of French origin), we'd say 'go and clean your room'.

And the latest academic research has shown that Churchill was right. When a large language model analysed people reading over 35,000 documents, they found that people were 25% more likely to finish reading an article if it contained simple and familiar words, or to put it another way, words that they found easier to read.[4] Unfortunately, when it comes to writing anything, whether it's an email, report or even a webpage, people tend to use words with a French origin, even if they are words we wouldn't normally use if we were talking with someone.

In a similar vein, it is also a good idea to avoid using technical jargon or acronyms in our writing as, unless the reader is familiar with them, it just adds to their confusion. Unfortunately, people who feel like they are in a position of lower status (e.g. working at a lower-rank university, when speaking with our bosses, etc.) are more likely to use jargon or acronyms in their writing.[5] This is true whether we are writing or speaking, and it occurs because in most cases people feel like they are being judged and they want to fit in. As a result, they are more concerned with how they are being evaluated rather than the clarity of their writing.

Abstract vs concrete language

While words with an Anglo-Saxon origin are generally easier for the brain to process, they also have a second advantage. People find words with an Anglo-Saxon origin more concrete, meaning that it is easier to create a mental picture in our minds.[6] Think of the words 'burn' vs 'incinerate'. One conjures up a vivid image, whereas the other feels more like a term from a government report. Not only does this change the tone of our writing, but it makes it easier for the reader to process quickly. When reading, the easier it is to conjure up an image for a word in our mind, the faster our brain can process it.[7] All of this explains why Mark Sadoski, Ernest

Goetz and Maximo Rodriguez have shown that the best predictor of a reader's ability to understand, pay interest to and ultimately recall information that they've read is a text's concreteness.[8] Copywriting is all about taking the reader on an emotional journey, and when we use more concrete language, this is easier to achieve.

But it doesn't only help make your text more memorable, it can also result in your customers being more satisfied. This doesn't only occur when people are reading copy; the same principle works when speaking to customers. When we're talking with someone, we want them to feel like they are being listened to, and that we're paying attention to what they are saying. There are different ways of doing this but one of the simplest is to make sure you use concrete rather than vague language. So, if they ask for something, it is better to repeat back exactly what they asked for rather than using vague language. For example, if a customer in a restaurant has just told you that they have a wheat allergy, it's much better to say, '*I'll talk to the chef about your wheat allergy*' rather than just saying '*I'll tell them about your issue*'. Or if someone asks for you to get a t-shirt, make sure you refer to it as a t-shirt and not just a top.[9]

Ensuring we are precise in our use of language forces us to listen and pay more attention to what our customers are saying, and this changes how shoppers reflect on their interaction. Because they feel like they are being listened to, they have a more positive perception of the person they are talking to and ultimately are more likely to make a purchase.[10] A very small change but one which makes a big difference with minimal costs.

Effects of not being precise

However, sometimes we are inadvertently vague in our use of language. We might be making a claim that we don't feel overly confident about, so we include a number of weasel words or qualifiers. These are words such as may, might, help, could or possibly, to name only a few. These are words that 'appear substantial but upon closer look, they disintegrate into hollow meaninglessness'.[11] A good example of claims that use these words would be 'Effectively fights 7 signs of ageing. Reviving skin to look up to 10 years younger in 4 weeks' or 'Brighten, whiten, freshen, and save up to 30% per load'. At first glance, these both sound like solid claims, but on closer inspection, they both say 'up to'.

From a shopper's perspective, these words undermine the credibility of the claim.[12] If a marketer can avoid using them, they should, but sometimes they have to, because either they are not 100% convinced in what they are saying or their lawyers aren't convinced. If this is the case, it is important to understand the situation in which people are going to be viewing these claims. If shoppers are only paying casual attention to an advert, what psychologists often refer to as a '*low involvement*' scenario, then the use of weasel words is less critical. If it's a TV advert, shoppers are only going to be paying casual attention to the message and they will often not even hear these words. But if a marketer is running an advert on the underground, where people are quite likely to look at the adverts on the commute home, then they could be in trouble. These commuters might be highly involved and think carefully about the claim and your choice of wording.

When using concrete language goes wrong

But, as ever, there is one situation where using concrete language can backfire, and this is when you are pitching a new business. Based on everything we know about concrete language you would imagine that you want to make it as easy as possible for investors to visualize your company as a success but it turns out that more abstract language in a pitch can work in your favour. Before Uber became a household name and they were trying to attract investment, they described the company in one of two ways: either '*a smartphone app that makes it easier to get a taxi, connecting passengers and drivers and reducing wait times.*' or '*a transportation solution that is convenient, reliable and readily accessible to everyone*'. The first proposition follows the rules of good copywriting. It uses short, common, and concrete words, and is easy to understand; whereas, after reading the second proposition, you are still not certain what a transportation solution company is. It was the second, more abstract version that resonated with investors.[13]

This is not a cherry-picked example. A team of researchers analysed all the decisions made by a group of angel investors. They reviewed all the pitches made to the investors, not just the successful ones, and the same pattern emerged. Founders who used more abstract language in their pitches were more successful in securing an investment.[14] Without realising it, their use of abstract language changed how investors viewed both the investment opportunity and them. By using abstract language, they weren't viewed as just another founder looking for funding for their company. Instead, they are more likely to be viewed as a forward-looking visionary, not only focusing on this business opportunity, but also going to develop future business ventures. As for this investment, it suddenly seemed like a better opportunity. The market was perceived as bigger with more room to expand[15] and, as the market was perceived as bigger with more growth potential, it attracted more investments.

The use of concrete language is one way that we can make our writing more engaging and persuasive, but another approach is to make the reader feel more involved. Although there are numerous ways you can do this, an underused way is to avoid using a verb and change it to a noun.[16] While this may sound rather technical (and if your knowledge of English grammar is limited, rather intimidating), it's a very simple change to make. Rather than saying, '*you go running*', change it to '*you are a runner*'. It may seem a small difference, but it changes how people think about themselves. To say that you go running suggests that while you do run, it may not be a permanent state or a key part of your self-identity. After all, how many people's New Year's resolution has been to go running three times a week, but when a cold, wet and miserable February evening comes around, they decide it's better to sit on the sofa watching TV. But if you are 'a runner', it suggests that this is a more permanent state, it's part of your identity.

REAL-WORLD EXAMPLE: PSYCH IN ACTION

Rather than asking '*Do you read the Economist?*' it would be far stronger to change it to '*Are you an Economist reader?*' Apple famously used this approach in their 'Get a Mac' campaign, more commonly known as '*Hello, I'm a Mac. And I'm a PC.*' which ran from 2006 to 2009. Rather than just suggesting that someone uses a Mac, they positioned the product as if it was a central part of a person's identity. They may not have added 'er' to the end of a verb, as in runner, climber or reader, but the principle is exactly the same.

Another approach that can be used to hook the reader in and get them to engage with our writing is to ensure that both our headline and body content includes the second person pronoun – words such as you, your, you'll and yourself. Second-person pronouns may not grab our attention as effectively as if the article was tailored and used our name, but when someone reads the word 'you' they assume that the message is directly referring to them and not a generic individual. As a result, they process the message in more detail, ultimately leading them to feel more attached to the brand. So, if you were trying to sell a cloud computing service, the headline 'Keeping your data safe' works better than 'Keeping data safe'. The data backs this up: people are far more likely to like, share and comment on posts that use second-person pronouns.[17]

Prospect theory: Gains, losses and risk

While copywriters have to find the right words to persuade, they also have to decide how to frame a message. This is because they can present exactly the same factual information in different ways. For example, when it comes to selling beef mince, they could either describe it as being 95% fat-free or 5% fat. Mathematically, both say exactly the same thing, but it is unsurprising that shoppers see the percentage-free option as being healthier, and are more likely to buy it, with this effect becoming stronger the higher the fat level (e.g. 90% fat-free vs 10% fat).[18] Sometimes marketers may not even consider that there is an alternative way to frame a message, or it is not obvious which frame will be the most powerful.

When most marketers attempt to persuade shoppers to change their behaviour, their automatic tendency is to focus on the positives. We tell customers what they will gain if they start using our products. For example, *'Sign up to our health plan and save 20% on your next purchase'*. From a technical perspective, this is what psychologists would call a gain frame (shoppers are being given a 20% saving). However, although we're naturally inclined to use a gain frame, research by Eyal Gamliel and Ram Herstein has shown that it is normally more effective if a message is phrased so that it emphasizes what the customer loses out on by not making a purchase, or what is known as a loss frame. *'If you don't sign up to our health plan, your next purchase will cost 20% more'*.[19] From an economic perspective, there is no difference between the two offers, but in practice, one is far more persuasive than the other.

If both offers are exactly the same, what causes this difference? The answer is *Prospect Theory*. Originally proposed by Daniel Kahneman and Amos Tversky in 1979,[20] Prospect Theory demonstrated that people don't make decisions in a rational, logical manner, but rather the majority of our decisions are driven by emotions and how they make us feel. Emotionally, the brain feels a loss very differently to the equivalent gain. Roughly speaking, the emotional impact of a loss is between 1.5 and 2.5 times greater than that of an equivalent gain. Or to put it in real terms, if you lost £10, you'd need to find £25 to balance out this loss.[21]

REAL-WORLD EXAMPLE: PSYCH IN ACTION

Airlines regularly overbook, as usually not all their passengers turn up. However, if they do all turn up, they offer to pay passengers not to travel (along with free tickets for the next available flight and accommodation at a nice hotel). But being a business, airlines do not want to pay more than they need to, so how do they decide what to pay? Well, they run a reverse auction. They'll offer to pay people $100 not to fly; if nobody or not enough people take the offer, they'll increase it to $200 until the flight isn't overbooked and this is where we can see loss aversion in action.

In 2022, Delta overbooked a flight from Grand Rapids to Minneapolis by eight people. So how much did they have to pay to convince eight out of 208 people to give up their seats? $500, $1,000, maybe $1,500. In the end, the auction reached $10,000 before eight people were willing to give up their seats.[22] Out of the 208 passengers, some will have had essential meetings, others will have had weddings or christenings that couldn't be missed. But it seems that most people felt like they already 'owned' their ticket and their seat, and it caused them to overvalue how much it was worth, something they may come to regret when they think what $10,000 dollars could buy them. This shows the power of ownership; customers do not like to give up what they perceive they already own and this is something that marketers can use to their advantage. When writing copy, be sure to use language that suggests that your audience already owns the product.

What marketers can learn from TV gameshows

Gameshows are all about giving contestants a chance to win money, and normally, when people talk about winning, they're using a gain frame. But producers have an intuitive understanding of Prospect Theory, even if they've never heard of it. The jeopardy and excitement come not from watching someone potentially win a life-changing amount of money, but from seeing someone potentially lose all this money.

In *Who Wants to Be a Millionaire?*, if the contestant gets the final question wrong, they will lose £450,000. Yes, they still walk away with £50,000, but it feels like a loss. In *Deal or No Deal*, you could be offered the chance to walk away with £30,100, or risk it and select one of two boxes. One box contains 10p, the other £100,000, again potentially losing £30,099.90. And in *The Million Pound Drop*, the contestant starts with a million pounds in cash and need to answer eight multiple-choice questions. Each question has four possible answers. To answer a question they need to put the money over a trapdoor. If they get the question correct, the door remains closed; get it wrong and the door opens, and the contestant watches the money vanish before their eyes. Not only does this use loss aversion, but they really ramp up the psychology by playing up the visual saliency of losing money.

Designing a gameshow around a loss frame rather than a gain frame has two big advantages. For the audiences, it helps to build the excitement and drama in the programme, creating more drama. But it also changes how the contestant reacts. It makes every decision seem bigger, causing them to slow down and reflect on their choices, which again ramps up the tension.

Successful marketers use the same principle of loss aversion, highlighting what customers will be missing out on if they don't act, for example, offering customers a free one-month trial, knowing that a lot of customers will continue paying for access rather than giving up something they already have access to. Salespeople's marketing patter can focus on what customers will be giving up if they don't buy the product today. Even loyalty programmes can use this approach, showing that without a loyalty card, customers will have to pay more (rather than focusing on the cost saving).

Message framing and healthcare

At first glance, this would suggest that the situation doesn't matter, marketers should always aim to use a loss frame, not just when it comes to talking about price but with the risks of not doing something. For example, if you were trying to encourage someone to take calcium supplements, you have the option of framing it in one of two ways, as outlined in Table 6.2.

Table 6.2 Two different messages that can be used to encourage people to take a calcium supplement. One option uses a gain frame, whereas the other uses a loss frame[23]

Gain Frame	Loss Frame
Building strong bones during childhood, adolescence and early adulthood is your best defence against developing osteoporosis later in life. Are you taking steps to prevent osteoporosis developing? If you get enough calcium now you can: 1. Increase your chances of developing strong and healthy bones 2. Reduce your risk of osteoporosis What are the *benefits* of getting enough calcium? • Getting enough calcium promotes strong bone growth • Adequate calcium intake decreases your chances of getting osteoporosis later in life • Eating calcium-rich foods can prevent painful fractures and spinal deformities like humpback and stooped posture	Not building strong bones during childhood, adolescence and early adulthood is your worst defence against preventing osteoporosis later in life. Are you failing to take steps to prevent osteoporosis developing? If you do not get enough calcium now you can: 1. Increase your chances of developing weak and brittle bones 2. Increase your risk of osteoporosis What are the *risks* of not getting enough calcium? • Not getting enough calcium causes poor bone growth • Inadequate calcium intake increases your chances of getting osteoporosis later in life • Not eating calcium-rich foods can lead to painful fractures and spinal deformities like humpback and stooped posture

As with most things in psychology, it is not that simple. When you are trying to motivate someone to look after their health, the frame you should use depends on what type of behaviour you want to motivate. When you are trying to persuade someone to engage in preventative behaviour, for example wear sunscreen in a heat wave, take vitamin tablets or brush their teeth twice a day, then a gain-framed message is more effective. However, if you're trying to persuade people to detect a condition (for example, encouraging females to go for a smear test, persuading young men to check for signs of testicular cancer, or even encouraging someone to take a pregnancy test), then in these conditions a loss frame is more effective.[24]

This occurs because of the way we perceive risk. We take vitamin tablets or wear sunscreen as we're trying to prevent ourselves from falling ill or getting sunburnt. It's risk avoidance behaviour. In contrast, the goal of detection behaviours is identifying if we have any pre-existing health issues. Consequently, we perceive this behaviour as psychologically risky – it might reveal that we have cancer or that we are pregnant, and we know that loss-framed messages are more effective with risky or uncertain outcomes.[25]

Message framing: In practice

As a rough rule of thumb, in most situations when you are trying to persuade someone to do something, it is more effective to express the risks in a negative frame but provide your solution using a gain or positive frame. Or to put it another way, you should start off by highlighting the fact that they might lose something, but then use positive language to demonstrate how you can solve this problem. This works because people are risk-averse for gains (we don't want to avoid losing our winnings) but are risk-seeking with losses,[26] that is we'll take risks to avoid a loss. For example, if you were selling car insurance you could lead with a headline that emphasizes the risk of not making a purchase '*Can you afford £350 to replace a broken windscreen?*', but you then follow it up with your solution in a positive term '*95% of customers protected with XXX insurance don't have to pay anything to replace a chipped windscreen!*' or '*Imagine losing every photo from your wedding day. With XXX Cloud Storage, you'll never have this problem*'.

The power of a story

Once we've worked out how we want to frame an issue, we still need to make sure people remember and engage with it. Using concrete and Anglo-Saxon language is one way to achieve this, but another approach is to tell stories. When we're trying to persuade someone, we are presenting them with a lot of information in a short space of time and one way that we make sense of complex information is to turn it into a story in our mind.[27] The better the story, the more persuasive it is. Not only are stories persuasive, but they also help people remember information. Gordon Bower and Michal Clark, of Stanford University, have shown that when people were presented with a random list of facts, people could only recall 13%, but when these facts were presented as part of a story, people could now remember 93%,[28] a 615% increase.

But rather than letting the shopper create a story for themselves, it is better if the marketer remains in control and creates the story for them. After all, a well-told story not only captures our imagination and is unforgettable, but is a highly powerful persuasion tool. This is the case even when we are trying to persuade shoppers to buy a product that we'd assume is normally driven by specifications and performance, such as smart TVs, mobile phones or computers. When a team of psychologists led by Mario Cassar redesigned the marketing material for Smart TVs, they found that shoppers were more likely to believe the material when it was told as a story, rather than just emphasising the technical specs. More importantly, not only were they more likely to believe the material, but they were also more likely to purchase the TV.[29]

The right story can also help break down barriers. This can be especially useful when it comes to selling products that shoppers may find embarrassing to buy, such as condoms, sanitary products or lice treatments. In these situations, it is often more effective to use a humorous appeal rather than an informative-based message.[30] Shoppers find a humorous message more exciting, which increases the likelihood of them making a purchase.

REAL-WORLD EXAMPLE: PSYCH IN ACTION

Worryingly, using stories to persuade has been shown to work in numerous different contexts, including court cases. When jurors deliberate, they attempt to construct a story. The easier it is for the evidence to fit into a narrative, the more plausible it is, and the more likely they are to be persuaded. Consequently, successful lawyers attempt to make it as easy as possible for the jury to construct a plausible narrative. Rather than asking witnesses to reveal everything they know about the incidents, questions should be asked so that the evidence is presented as the story unfolds, which in most cases is in chronological order.[31] When the prosecution presents a narrative, and the witnesses are called in the order that they appear in the story, 78% of jurors agreed with the prosecution. However, when the witnesses appeared in a different order, only 31% of jurors agreed with the prosecution as the evidence was perceived as being less credible[32] even though the evidence and the witness statements were identical.

While lawyers must work within strict parameters when it comes to crafting a story, making sure they don't bend or reinvent the truth, marketers have more flexibility. They can decide who should be the central character and carefully craft their story arch. Marketers are often tempted to try to introduce multiple characters into the story; the thought process is that the more people that feature in the story, the more likely there will be a character that will resonate with the reader or viewer. For example, they'll make sure there is a male and female character, people of different races and ages.

Unfortunately, this approach ends up being less successful. The more characters introduced, the less the viewer gets to know each individual character. This is especially challenging when you are trying to tell a complete story in just a single paragraph or two. But stories that focus on a single character end up triggering a greater range of emotions from the reader and we feel more empathy for the protagonist, which directly impacts our purchasing behaviour.[33] It is for this reason that fundraising campaigns are more effective if the focus is on a single identified victim rather than concentrating on the thousands of people in need.[34] It is much easier to feel empathy for a single starving 7-year-old girl who is so unwell she can't go to school, rather than the 4 million children in the UK who are not getting enough to eat.

Another advantage of using a story is the fact that a lot of the time, anecdotal evidence, aka a story, is more persuasive than statistics, but this depends on the situation. When the person you are trying to persuade is emotionally engaged, anecdotal evidence is typically more persuasive than statistical evidence. However, where they are not emotionally engaged, statistical evidence is more persuasive than anecdotal evidence.[35] Hence, when it comes to convincing policymakers of the importance of seatbelts for children, statistical evidence is the most successful, but when it comes to persuading parents, anecdotal evidence works best.[36]

Sometimes marketers like to play it safe and use both an anecdote and statistics, but when they do this, shoppers tend to ignore the statistics and just focus on the story. For example, when doctors told patients that 90% of patients treated with Tamoxol (a fictitious drug used to treat internal worms) made a full recovery, but then talked about one of their previous patients, participants focused on the past patient. For example, if the story said *'Pat's decision to undergo Tamoxol resulted in a poor outcome. The worm was not completely destroyed. The disease resumed its course. At 1-month post treatment, Pat was blind and had lost the ability to walk'*, only 39% of participants opted to go for treatment. However, when the story was positive saying *'Pat's decision to undergo Tamoxol resulted in a positive outcome. The entire worm was completely destroyed. Doctors were confident the disease would not resume its course. At 1-month post treatment, Pat's recovery was certain.'*, 88% of participants opted for the treatment.[37] The statistical information hasn't changed, but people don't remember this.

This suggests that stories are always the best way to persuade and in most cases they are, especially when the person you are trying to convince is not highly engaged in the process, for example while passively watching a television advert. Likewise, if the facts you have to work with are relatively weak, presenting them in an engaging story is a fantastic approach. People focus on the story and consequently, do not end up critically thinking about the argument you're making, they just accept it as part of the story. However, if you have just one or two key facts, then in this case it often makes more sense to present them in isolation and not part of a narrative.[38] This is because these facts stand up to scrutiny and you are happy for people to think carefully about them. However, this only works when you have one or two facts in isolation.

Making sense of numbers

While using a story may be more persuasive, there will be times where we want to use statistics. Unfortunately, our intuition of how to use numbers is often wrong. Archaeological evidence, such as the Ishango bone found in the Democratic Republic of Congo (a bone with notches on it used for counting), suggests that humans have been using numbers for an estimated 40,000 years.[39] However, the use of numbers by early humans was relatively simplistic, counting to perhaps 30.[40] Today, people can do multiplication in their heads, understand fractions and quickly compare percentages, but it takes more cognitive effort. This effect is so strong that when Morteza Malali and colleagues asked participants to perform maths tasks, and recorded their brain activity using an electroencephalogram (EEG) (see Chapter 16 for an overview of EEG) and heart rate using an ECG, they could tell with over 98% accuracy if someone was doing sums or just resting as they could easily detect the increase in cognitive load.[41]

A great example of this occurs when marketers use statistics. Gut instinct tells us to use a precise number as we think it will make us sound more credible and intellectual. For example, if we're talking about last quarter's sales, we might report them as being 'worth £2,890,000', yet it would be far more effective if we rounded this number to 'nearly 3 million'.[42] This makes the number more user-friendly, and, importantly, more memorable. When Huy Nguyen asked people to read a newspaper article that contained several different statistics, people were much better at recalling the facts when they were rounded rather than being precise. When the article included precise stats, only two out of five readers were able to accurately remember the statistic, but when the journalists rounded the numbers, three out of five readers could accurately remember the numbers.

Unfortunately, often the numbers we want to talk about are percentages. While humans may struggle with numbers, the situation is even worse when it comes to both percentages and fractions.[43] When people use whole numbers, they are something that can be visualized and at least vaguely understood. Yet it does not matter how many marketing meetings we've been forced to sit through where percentages and fractions are thrown around, people struggle to visualize them. Consequently, rather than saying 40% or 60%, it is more effective to reframe this as 'two out of five' or 'three out of five'. It is far easier for us to imagine what two out of five people look like, bringing the percentage to life. However, if we have the word count, we can elevate this even more by turning it into a mini story. For example, rather than simply saying '28% *of UK men do not always wash their hands after using the bathroom*', it's both more salient and emotional to say, '*at least 1 in every 4 men you shake hands with at work will not have washed their hands after using the bathroom*'.

Unfortunately, people are even worse at dealing with percentages when we're dealing with numbers that are over 100%. Consider a company launching a new model of a battery-powered vacuum cleaner that has a 125% longer run-time than the competition. Most people's gut intuition is the fact that the vacuum's battery will last 25% longer than the competition, not 100% longer + 25% more.[44] Their estimation is off by exactly 100%! Instead of talking in percentages, it would be far more effective to say, '*The battery on our vacuum lasts over twice as long as the competition*'. By avoiding numbers altogether, we're making our writing more readable.

Comparisons

Another approach that people instinctively use to make numbers easier to appreciate is to use comparisons. Again, these help us to visualize what the numbers mean. The challenge is to make sure we select the right visual metaphor. For example, a business might claim that *'if we stacked all the biscuits we sold last year, it would create a tower taller than Mount Everest'*. While this may sound impressive, it's not the most powerful statement. The problem is the fact that most people don't know how tall Mount Everest is. Even if you do know that Everest is 8,849m, this is just an abstract fact and is not something you can easily visualise. Most photos of Everest are taken from Base Camp, which is already at 5,364m, so even a photo doesn't help. You could have just as easily said Mont Blanc, which despite being nearly half as tall, would give the statement the same impact.

Instead, it makes more sense to use an analogy using things that we are familiar with. This often means rather than finding the biggest thing we can possibly compare our number to, it's best to find a smaller and more relatable comparison. For example, Chip Heath and Karla Starr argue that rather than saying *'97.5% of the world's water is salt water. Of the 2.5% that's freshwater, over 99% is trapped in glaciers and snowfields. In total, only 0.025% of the water on the globe is drinkable by humans and animals'*, this comparison could be reframed using everyday items, and not even mention any numbers: *'Imagine a gallon jug filled with water, with three ice cubes next to it. All of the water in the jug is salt water. The ice cubes are the only freshwater, and humans can only drink the drops that are melting off each.'*

Sometimes, when it comes to creating these comparisons, we need to get a little creative. Rather than making a comparison to something physical, it can sometimes be useful to convert numbers to time. By converting large numbers to time, it can make the differences much simpler to understand. For example, most people know that a billion is bigger than a million, but don't realize just how different these two numbers are. Convert them to time, and the difference is obvious. A million seconds is 12 days, a billion seconds is 31 years and a trillion seconds is 31,688 years!

Probabilities

This approach also works well when it comes to describing the odds of something occurring. We all know the odds of winning the lottery are small, but it is hard to appreciate just how small they are. The odds of winning the US Powerball are 1 in 292,201,338, but this doesn't mean much to most people. Convert this into time and it is a lot easier to appreciate it: 'Imagine having to guess which second of a day someone is thinking of – any date, hour, minute, and second from the time they're born to the time they turn 9. If you can guess the number, you win the lottery, sounds easy'.[45]

In the UK, there has been a lot of discussion about the building of a new high-speed railway (HS2), with very strong feelings on both sides. However, part of the issue is the fact that the numbers involved are just so big. The estimated cost of building the track from London to Birmingham (a distance of 134 miles) was predicted to be £44.6 billion in 2019. But just like when we were talking about the height of Everest, people really struggle to comprehend just how big a billion is. But if we reframe this and instead of talking about the total cost we break it down into a smaller unit, the cost per inch, the numbers become more understandable – HS2 would cost £5,253 per inch!

When talking about probabilities, we want our estimates to be perceived as credible, but there are some occasions when this is more important than others. If we are talking to investors or even just our manager and they want to know how long until a new product is ready to launch, there are a number of ways we can answer this question. We could either say that the product will be ready to launch in three weeks or we could say 21 days, both are saying exactly the same thing, but we perceive the two answers differently. When we're using smaller units (e.g. days rather than weeks), people perceive that our estimates are more credible.[46] It doesn't just work when talking about days versus weeks, the same pattern occurs when talking about minutes and hours. If we're describing how long the battery will last on a mobile phone, an estimate of 540 minutes is seen as more accurate than 9 hours. This occurs because people subconsciously perceive larger units (like hours) as being vague and less precise.

How to apologize

It doesn't matter what business you operate in, at some point things are going to go wrong. The wrong product can get sent out, orders lost or just a simple breakdown in communication. Either way, it means that you're going to have to apologize; it's just how you go about it. Understandably, most people feel slightly uncomfortable about apologizing. Saying sorry means admitting you made a mistake, but when a lot of people apologize, they try and avoid admitting they made a mistake by using the passive voice. Rather than saying, *'I'm sorry, I made a mistake'* (which uses the active voice), they prefer to say, *'I'm sorry, a mistake was made'*.

When apologizing, people intuitively prefer to use the passive voice because it diffuses responsibility. It feels like you don't have to admit that you made a mistake, and from a grammatical perspective this is true. In the active voice, the subject (I) performed the action, but when we use the passive voice, the structure of the sentence is flipped. Now the subject is being acted upon by the verb, it seems like somebody else made the mistake and not them. But despite feeling natural, shoppers are aware of this and intuitively distrust the passive voice. As a result, they view apologies in the passive voice as a non-apology.[47]

So, how should we say sorry? From a psychological perspective, a successful apology needs to comprise six elements: (1) an expression of remorse over the conflict; (2) an acceptance of responsibility for the harmful behaviour; (3) an admission of injustice or wrongdoing; (4) an acknowledgement of harm and/or victim suffering; (5) a promise to do better in the future; and (6) an offer to repair the damage done.[48] But is it a case of just simply ticking those boxes and it's job done? Probably not. As Guy Doza points out, if you accidentally reversed over your neighbour's cat and said, '*I am so sorry. It is my fault. I was wrong. I can see that you're upset. It won't happen again. I'll get you a new cat*', you're not going to get very far. It may contain every aspect that an apology needs, but it is missing the art of rhetoric. Psychology can give you the building blocks, but we still need rhetorical flair to make it work.

Saying sorry is not a miraculous cure for all. If our apology includes a 'promise to do better in the future', which it should, shoppers will hold us to a higher standard, expecting more from us in the future. By saying sorry, it can help to restore shoppers' trust, but if we let them down again, they feel angrier than if we had made no apology at all.[49] And if we keep having to make repeated apologies after numerous bad experiences, research shows that these repeated apologies end up making the situation worse than if we made fewer apologies.

REAL-WORLD EXAMPLE: PSYCH IN ACTION

If a business makes a mistake and it is a genuine one off and they handle it well, it can actually work in their favour. For example, Uber is a taxi company where people book a taxi by using an app. With 5 million rides booked each day, it is understandable that a small number will arrive late but this has a significant impact on their business. If a customer's Uber arrived more than 5 minutes late, customers typically spent 5–10% less on the platform in the future (assuming there was no apology given), meaning a significant loss of revenue for the business. With so much money at stake, Basil Halperin led a team of researchers and tested how customers reacted to different forms of apologies. Across six different markets, 1.5 million riders whose Uber was more than 5 minutes late received one of four different messages. These were either a control (no message), a basic apology, a $5 voucher but no apology, or an apology with a $5 voucher.

Over the next 84 days, the researchers tracked them to see if the apology made any difference. Those who had just received an apology were less likely to use Uber, resulting in a loss of revenue of 6.4%. However, those who received the voucher and an apology were more likely to use Uber in the next couple of months.[50] We call this the service recovery paradox. But, it wasn't just the fact that they received $5 that led to the increase in usage. Users who received a random $5 voucher were less likely to use Uber in the future than those who received an apology and a $5 coupon after a late ride. While we don't know for certain why this occurs, psychologists speculate that shoppers perceive it as a sign of reassurance. We know that if the company makes a mistake in the future, we'll trust them that they'll go out of their way to put it right for us, because that's what they did this time.

While the Uber study is the largest investigation into the service recovery paradox, it is not the only one. Across 21 different experiments, researchers consistently show that shoppers who experience a breakdown in service end up more satisfied than those who didn't, assuming they receive a true apology and a gesture of goodwill.[51] What is less convincing is whether it impacts repurchase intention and corporate reputation; this is an area where more research needs to be conducted with larger samples.

Dealing with shoppers who haven't paid

While sometimes we have to apologise for mistakes that we have made, other times we have to deal with customers who make mistakes – frequently they've not paid on time. In this situation, there are a couple of ways we can deal with this. We can either send a gentle reminder, because after all, we all make mistakes, or we can send a more serious letter. Intuitively, we may feel that the second option is likely to be the more successful, after all, who wants to have to deal with the threat of legal proceedings?

While the logical thing to do after receiving a threatening letter would be to tackle the issue straight away, often this is not what happens. People are worried, scared and end up burying their heads in the sand, hoping that the issue will go away. But if the tone of the letter is changed so that instead of being threatening, it is warmer, more accessible and clearly explains what the customer needs to do, the outcome is a lot better.

REAL-WORLD EXAMPLE: PSYCH IN ACTION

Unsurprisingly, a lot of students leave writing their dissertations until the last minute. This means in the weeks before the deadline, they will have taken out numerous books from the library to complete their thesis. Once they've submitted their thesis, normally their final piece of university work, they have far better things to do than worry about returning library books, and unfortunately, a significant number of students take the books with them when they leave. Considering the cost of academic textbooks, this means universities across the country are losing tens of thousands of pounds' worth of books. Universities respond in a typical bureaucratic fashion, sending out threatening letters written in a very formal tone, sometimes even claiming that the student wouldn't be allowed to graduate unless they return all books. For example, students would receive a letter stating '*Attached are details of your current library loans and/or fines. If you are a final year student, please return all loans, and clear all debts no later than Xth June 20XX. Should you fail to do so, you will be considered to be an official library debtor, which may jeopardize your final degree award'.*

Bangor University changed the tone of the letter so that instead of being threatening, it is warmer, more accessible and clearly explains what the student needs to do using simple language. For example, the new letter said *'Every year we have to chase departing students for unreturned items and outstanding fines. As you can imagine, it's hard to improve our service to students when we have to spend our funds replacing books that people have forgotten to return. If you still have any of our books, or there are fines you haven't paid, you need to get in touch with us now. What you need to do: You can bring books back to any Library site in Bangor— the Main Library, Deiniol Road or the Normal Site. You can return books anonymously by using our Self-Serve machines— you don't have to see us Library staff again if you don't want to!'* The results, students were 28% more likely to comply with the new letter and did so faster.[52] It's important to note that it wasn't just the tone of the letter that changed, they also made it clearer what action the students needed to take.

It's not just the tone that needs to be important; you need to make sure your instructions are clear. Evidence to support this comes from a range of sources, including one slightly surprising one: the redesign of a court summons. At first glance, you might think that the design of a court summons is going to be irrelevant. No matter how a summons is designed, you are going to read it carefully, ensuring you attend court on the right day and at the right time. However, in practice, this is not the case. Of the 250,000 summons issued in New York, 100,000 people failed to turn up. Or to put it another way, 40% of people failed to turn up to court and were issued with an arrest warrant. Consequently, a team of behavioural scientists were brought in to see if they could understand what the issue was and to redesign the form.

A brief look at the summons and the issues were obvious. For a start, it was not clear what the form was; simply having the title '*Complaint/Information*'. Even if they did read the form, it was confusing what they should do next, and if they had any questions, there was no obvious contact information. The redesign solved all these issues. The form had a clear and explicit title: Criminal Court Appearance Ticket. It provided step-by-step instructions on what the people needed to do, and in which order and if they still had questions, there was clear contact information. These changes may sound small, but the implications were significant. After switching to the new design, the failure to appear dropped from 47% to 40.8%, a relative reduction of 13%.[53] This may not sound like a huge change, but in practice, this meant that 30,000 fewer arrest warrants were issued, saving the city $140,000.

Closing thoughts

While writing is often seen as more of an art than a science, this doesn't mean marketers can't take a scientific approach to improving their communication. Through A/B testing and carefully designed experiments, researchers can identify which appeals and messages resonate most with consumers and yield the best conversion rates. And by applying principles from psychology, there is a better chance that marketers' experiments will be successful. But the best results occur where marketers collaborate with a skilled writer. These people know how to transform scientific insights into compelling content that aligns with the brand and delivers results.

KEY POINTS

- When trying to persuade native English speakers, it is more effective to use words with an Anglo-Saxon origin.
- Writing that uses more concrete language is more persuasive and memorable than vague or abstract writing. The one exception to this rule is when trying to persuade someone to invest in a business venture.
- Avoid using weasel words like may, might, help, could or possibly in your writing as it undermines your credibility.
- Writing that makes the reader feel more involved is more engaging. When writing headlines, changing the verb to a noun can help make the reader more engaged. 'Do you read *The Economist*?' vs 'You are a reader of *The Economist*?'
- Losses loom larger than gains – when writing headlines or offers, it is normally more effective to use a negative frame than a gain frame.
- People find stories more memorable and persuasive than statistics and isolated facts.
- If you do need to use a statistic:
  - Find a way to conceptualize it. Don't talk about an abstract number but relate it to something people understand. Don't say a product has a 100% bigger battery – say the product battery now lasts twice as long.
  - Rather than talking about 40%, say two out of five people.
- If a business needs to make an apology, it is best to use the active voice, rather than the passive voice.
- In most cases, warmer, more accessible language is more engaging than threatening writing or writing in legal language.

PUTTING THEORY INTO PRACTICE

1. Find eight different adverts online and identify if they are using a gain or loss frame. Try and rewrite the headline using the opposite frame.

2. Find eight different statistics that companies have used in their adverts or website copy. See if you can find two different ways to reframe each statistic to make it easier for shoppers to relate to.

3. Download the technical specification for a technical product like a computer, smart speaker or a mobile phone. Find a way to turn this technical specification into a story that a salesperson could use while speaking with a customer.

4. Climate change is one of the biggest threats facing our planet. Find a number of statistics from journal articles published in the last five years discussing climate change and then use these statistics to form a story to encourage people to adopt more sustainable behaviour – remember to reframe the statistics to make it more relatable.

5. Write an apologetic email to a disgruntled customer. Make sure your email includes the six elements of the apology. How could you benefit from the service recovery paradox?

SUGGESTIONS FOR FURTHER READING

Berger J. (2023). Magic words: What to say to get your way. New York: Harper Business

Heath C. & Starr K. (2022). Making numbers count. London: UK. Penguin

References

1. Wang, P. X., Wang, Y., & Jiang, Y. (2022). Gift or donation? Increase the effectiveness of charitable solicitation through framing charitable giving as a gift. *Journal of Marketing*, 87(1). https://doi.org/10.1177/00222429221081506 (archived at https://perma.cc/J2F2-2LXP)
2. Schiess, W. (2019). *Legal writing nerd*. CreateSpace Publishing, Germany.
3. The Economist (2004) Out with the long. https://www.economist.com/leaders/2004/10/07/out-with-the-long (archived at https://perma.cc/W4DX-W5PQ)
4. Berger, J., Moe, W. W., & Schweidel, D. A. (2023). What holds attention? Linguistic drivers of engagement. *Journal of Marketing*, 87(5), 793–809.

5   Brown, Z. C., Anicich, E. M., & Galinsky, A. D. (2020). Compensatory conspicuous communication: Low status increases jargon use. *Organizational Behavior and Human Decision Processes*, 161, 274–290.
6   Farnsworth, W. (2020). *Farnsworth's classical English style*. David R. Godine, Publisher, Incorporated.
7   Gerwien, J., Filip, M., & Smolik, F. (2023). Noun imageability and the processing of sensory-based information. *Quarterly Journal of Experimental Psychology*. 17470218231216304
8   Sadoski, M., Goetz, E. T., & Rodriguez, M. (2000). Engaging texts: Effects of concreteness on comprehensibility, interest, and recall in four text types. *Journal of Educational Psychology*, 92(1), 85.
9   Packard, G. & Berger, J. (2021). How concrete language shapes customer satisfaction. *Journal of Consumer Research*, 47(5), 787–806.
10 Packard, G. & Berger, J. (2021). How concrete language shapes customer satisfaction. *Journal of Consumer Research*, 47(5), 787–806.
11 Vidaković, M. M. & Janjić, Z. D. T. (2017). Weasel claims in advertisements in English and Serbian. *Proceedings of the Faculty of Philosophy in Pristina*, 47(1). https://doi.org/10.5937/ZRFFP47-12305 (archived at https://perma.cc/X4RA-V6ZE)
12 Hassan, L. M. Parry, S., & Shiu, E. (2022). Exploring responses to differing message content of pictorial alcohol warning labels. *International Journal of Consumer Studies*, 46(6), 2200–2219.
13 Berger, J. (2023). *Magic words*. Harper Business. New York, US.
14 Huang, L., Joshi, P., Wakslak, C., & Wu, A. (2021). Sizing up entrepreneurial potential: Gender differences in communication and investor perceptions of long-term growth and scalability. *Academy of Management Journal*, 64(3), 716–740.
15 Berger, J. (2023). *Magic words*. Harper Business. New York, US.
16 Gelman, S. A. & Heyman, G. D. (1999). Carrot-eaters and creature-believers: The effects of lexicalization on children's inferences about social categories. *Psychological Science*, 10(6), 489–493.
17 Cruz, R. E., Leonhardt, J. M., & Pezzuti, T. (2017). Second person pronouns enhance consumer involvement and brand attitude. *Journal of Interactive Marketing*, 39(1), 104–116.
18 Sanford, A. J., Fay, N., Stewart, A., & Moxey, L. (2002). Perspective in statements of quantity, with implications for consumer psychology. *Psychological Science*, 13(2), 130–134.
19 Gamliel, E. & Herstein, R. (2007). The effect of framing on willingness to buy private brands. *Journal of Consumer Marketing*, 24(6), 334–339. https://doi.org/10.1108/07363760710822918
20 Kahneman, D. & Tversky, A. (1979). Prospect Theory: An analysis of decision under risk. *Econometrica*, 47(2), 263–291.
21 De Martino, B., Camerer, C. F., & Adolphs, R. (2010). Amygdala damage eliminates monetary loss aversion. *Proceedings of the National Academy of Sciences*, 107(8), 3788–3792.

22 Carley, C. (2022, June 28). Delta reportedly shelled out $80,000 in compensation for that Grand Rapids to Minneapolis flight! Eye of the Flyer. https://eyeoftheflyer.com/2022/06/28/delta-bump-80000-grand-rapids-michigan/ (archived at https://perma.cc/Y7H6-EA72)

23 Gerend, M. A. & Shepherd, M. A. (2013). Message framing, it does a body good: Effects of message framing and motivational orientation on young women's calcium consumption. *Journal of Health Psychology*, 18(10), 1296–1306.

24 Rothman, A. J. & Salovey, P. (1997). Shaping perceptions to motivate healthy behavior: The role of message framing. *Psychological Bulletin*, 121, 3–19.

25 Rothman, A. J., Martino, S. C., Bedell, B. T., Detweiler, J. B., & Salovey, P. (1999). The systematic influence of gain-and loss-framed messages on interest in and use of different types of health behavior. *Personality and Social Psychology Bulletin*, 25(11), 1355–1369.

26 Kahneman, D. & Tversky, A. (1979). Prospect Theory: An analysis of decision under risk. *Econometrica*, 47, 263–91.

27 Mello, R. (2001). The Power of storytelling: How oral narrative influences children's relationships in classrooms. *International Journal of Education and the Arts*, 2(1).

28 Bower, G. H. & Clark, M. C. (1969). Narrative stories as mediators for serial learning. *Psychonomic Science*, 14, 181–182. https://doi.org/10.3758/BF03332778 (archived at https://perma.cc/Q4MR-KHKW)

29 Cassar, M. L., Caruana, A., & Konietzny, J. (2021). Facts or story? The impact of website content on narrative believability and purchase intention. *Journal of Marketing Communications*, 1–20. https://doi.org/10.1080/13527266.2021.1929408 (archived at https://perma.cc/FD7V-D8LT)

30 Barney, C. & Jones, C. L. E. (2023). Laughing in the face of embarrassment: Humorous marketing messages, excitement, and embarrassing products in retail. *Psychology & Marketing*, 40(5), 979–994.

31 Lempert, R. (1991). Telling tales in court: Trial procedure and the story model. *Cardozo L. Rev.*, 13, 559.

32 Pennington, N. & Hastie, R. (1992). Explaining the evidence: Tests of the Story Model for juror decision making. *Journal of Personality and Social Psychology*, 62(2), 189. https://psycnet.apa.org/doi/10.1037/0022-3514.62.2.189 (archived at https://perma.cc/8Y73-ELKJ)

33 Johnson, M., Detter, L., & Ghuman, P. (2018) *Individually driven narratives facilitate emotion and consumer demand*. EuroMedia 2018.

34 Small, D. A., Loewenstein, G., & Slovic, P. (2013). Sympathy and callousness: The impact of deliberative thought on donations to identifiable and statistical victims. In *The Feeling of Risk* (pp. 51–68). Routledge.

35 Freling, T. H., Yang, Z., Saini, R., Itani, O. S., & Abualsamh, R. R. (2020). When poignant stories outweigh cold hard facts: A meta-analysis of the anecdotal bias. *Organizational Behavior and Human Decision Processes*, 160, 51–67. https://doi.org/10.1016/j.obhdp.2020.01.006 (archived at https://perma.cc/3FE3-KNC8)

36 Wagenaar, W. A. & Keren, G. B. (1986). The seat belt paradox: Effect of adopted roles on information seeking. *Organizational Behavior and Human Decision Processes*, 38(1), 1–6. https://doi.org/10.1016/0749-5978(86)90022-1 (archived at https://perma.cc/N6QG-WC4C)

37 Freymuth, A. K. & Ronan, G. F. (2004). Modelling patient decision-making: The role of base-rate and anecdotal information. *Journal of Clinical Psychology in Medical Settings*, 11, 211–216.

38 Krause, R. J. & Rucker, D. D. (2020). Strategic storytelling: When narratives help versus hurt the persuasive power of facts. *Personality and Social Psychology Bulletin*, 46(2), 216–227. https://doi.org/10.1177%2F0146167219853845 (archived at https://perma.cc/6H63-RR23)

39 Everett, C. (2017). Numbers and the making of us: Counting and the course of human cultures. *Harvard University Press*. pp. 35–36.

40 Everett, C. (2017). Numbers and the making of us: Counting and the course of human cultures. *Harvard University Press*. pp. 35–36.

41 Jafari Malali, M., Sarbaz, Y., Zolfaghari, S., & Khodayarlou, A. (2024). The influence of mental calculations on brain regions and heart rates. *Scientific Reports*, 14(1), 18846.

42 Nguyen, H. A., Hofman, J. M., & Goldstein, D. G. (2022, April). *Round numbers can sharpen cognition*. In Proceedings of the 2022 CHI Conference on Human Factors in Computing Systems (pp. 1–15).

43 Heath, C. & Starr, K. (2022). *Making numbers count*. London: UK. Penguin.

44 Fisher, M. & Mormann, M. (2022). The off by 100% bias: The effects of percentage changes greater than 100% on magnitude judgments and consumer choice. *Journal of Consumer Research*, 49(4), 561–573.

45 Heath, C. and Starr, K. (2022). *Making numbers count*. London: UK. Penguin.

46 Zhang, Y. C. & Schwarz, N. (2012). How and why 1 year differs from 365 days: A conversational logic analysis of inferences from the granularity of quantitative expressions. *Journal of Consumer Research*, 39(2), 248–259.

47 Eisinger, R. M. (2011). The political non-apology. *Society*, 48(2), 136–141.

48 Doza, G. (2022). *How to apologise for killing a cat*. Canbury Press, London, UK.

49 Halperin, B., Ho, B., List, J. A., & Muir, I. (2022). Toward an understanding of the economics of apologies: Evidence from a large-scale natural field experiment. *The Economic Journal*, 132(641), 273–298.

50 Halperin, B., Ho, B., List, J. A., & Muir, I. (2022). Toward an understanding of the economics of apologies: Evidence from a large-scale natural field experiment. *The Economic Journal*, 132(641), 273–298.

51 De Matos, C. A., Henrique, J. L., & Alberto Vargas Rossi, C. (2007). Service recovery paradox: A meta-analysis. *Journal of Service Research*, 10(1), 60–77.

52 Heather, E., Hilton, B., Nelson, P., & Heaton, T. (2014). Behaviour change and copy: Tackling Bangor University Library and Archives Service debts. *Journal of Direct, Data and Digital Marketing Practice*, 16, 105–114.

53 Fishbane, A., Ouss, A., & Shah, A. K. (2020). Behavioral nudges reduce failure to appear for court. *Science*, 370(6517), eabb6591.

7 | The psychology of branding

LEARNING OBJECTIVES

- Understand how businesses can develop a strong brand identity.
- Critique the design of brand logos and brand names from a psychological perspective.
- Measure the strength of a brand using a range of experimental techniques.

What is a brand?

The idea of a brand is at the heart of much of modern-day marketing, and understandably so. By the time a child in the US reaches their tenth birthday, on average they will have learnt to recognize between 300–400 different brands,[1] and the impressions formed in childhood will last into adulthood, influencing how they interact with these brands for the rest of their life. This highlights an important characteristic: a brand is not just a logo, but a powerful tool that changes our expectations about how a product or person will behave. However, in the past, the terms 'brand' and 'logo' were used interchangeably.

The American Marketing Association (AMA) still defines a brand as 'A name, term, design, symbol, or any other feature that identifies one seller's goods or service as distinct from those of other sellers',[2] whereas psychologists, and most professional marketers, focus on a definition that emphasizes mental associations. For example that a brand is a 'complex abstract mental representation' of a product(s), covering 'the functional, sensory/perceptual, and emotional qualities' associated with both the product(s) and the company selling/making it.[3] While the difference between the two may appear to be semantics, it has important implications for brand management. The marketing definition implies that a brand is something that the business creates and controls. But a psychologist would argue that a brand is a collection of associations and expectations, and as such, can't be controlled, although marketers can influence them. These are the associations that determine how shoppers will behave.

Product expectations

Expectations are powerful. In 1995, a 29-year-old builder was working on a building site and rather than climb six feet down a ladder, he took a shortcut and jumped down. Unfortunately, he landed on a 15cm tall nail that had been dropped and was pointing up, which went straight through his work boot and into his foot. Understandably, he collapsed to the floor, screaming a few choice expletives. When he got to the hospital, a doctor gently touched the nail to work out exactly where it was located, and he let out a huge scream. It quickly became apparent that he was going to need painkillers – and a lot of them. First, they injected him with the midazolam, the standard approach, but it did nothing. In the end, they had to use fentanyl, a drug 100 times stronger than morphine, before they could take his boot off and look at his foot. By this point, you've probably already guessed what the doctors saw. The nail completely missed the foot, going between the big and second toe. The pain was all in his head.[4]

While it might seem easy to dismiss this story as just the case of one individual who was having a panic attack, this isn't the case. Doctors have been aware of the power of expectations to shape treatments for over a 100 years – the placebo. Placebos are medical interventions that from a scientific perspective should have no impact on patient wellbeing (e.g. a sugar pill), yet they make us feel better simply because we believe they will. Numerous studies have shown that these placebos can reduce how much pain a patient experiences, reducing feelings of sickness or even increasing their energy levels.[5] If you really want to boost the power of your placebo, receive it as an injection rather than a tablet[6] as most people assume that an injection is for more serious conditions than tablets. But the real surprise is the fact that a placebo works, even if you know you're being given a placebo[7] – a doctor can tell you that they are giving you a placebo injection with no active ingredients, and yet you still feel better.

The world of medicine may seem different to marketing and branding, but branding is all about influencing people's expectations. Pharmacists may tell a patient that a generic paracetamol is just as effective as a branded paracetamol, as the active ingredients are identical, but this isn't strictly true. In a double-blind trial where participants don't know which is the branded pill and which is the generic, the pharmacist will be right – there will be no difference between the two. But we don't live in a double-blind world. The branded product comes with a certain element of kudos. It comes in a fancier packet and the tablet might be sugar-coated so they taste nicer, the result being that patients who had a headache and were given generic medication labelled with a leading brand name reported it as more effective than the patients who were given the same tablets but labelled with a generic name.[8] The brand name changed the product's performance.

These effects can occur in any domain. People often act drunk because they think they should be. When researchers gave students a drink and told them it was alcoholic (when it was actually alcohol free), they acted drunk, becoming more aroused by erotic stimuli.[9] This effect becomes even more pronounced when you tell someone they are drinking a branded product. When drinking a vodka Red Bull cocktail, students acted as if they were 51% more drunk than when they were given just a vodka cocktail.[10] Not only this, but the men in the study took more risks in an online game and were more sexually confident. Red Bull's brand stands for *'energy, risk-taking and adventure'*. As a result, when you drink a 'vodka Red Bull' these associations change how we behave.

Building a brand: It's all about associations

If a brand is never fully owned by a company but is simply a collection of associations, the best a company can do is influence these associations. By repeatedly pairing the brand with the same positive experiences, images, sounds, ideas or events, shoppers become 'conditioned' or learn to associate these concepts with the brand. A great example is Red Bull. For nearly 30 years, they have partnered with extreme sports ranging from rock climbing and snowboarding to Red Bull Air Racing. By repeatedly seeing Red Bull paired with these events, it has led consumers to perceive Red Bull as exciting, edgy and extroverted.

From a neurological perspective, these associations lead to a change in our brain structures. Every time our brains react to a stimuli, an electrical impulse triggers either the formation of a new synaptic connection or it strengthens an existing connection. This is what Hebb described as *'what fires together, wires together'*[11] and the more often the synapses fire together, the stronger the association becomes (See Chapter 5).

Repeatedly viewing two ideas together results in consumers linking the ideas, but this takes time, with some experts arguing it can take up to 10 years for a brand to develop a clear position in a shopper's mind.[12] So, while building associations is straightforward, few brands execute it successfully, as corporate marketing often adopts a short-term philosophy. Brand managers typically only stay in a role 2–3 years, and a newly appointed brand manager wants to stamp their own vision on a brand. These changes may not seem drastic, but they slow down an already slow process.

This also explains why approximately 50% of all rebrands fail.[13] Brand redesigns can involve throwing away all the associations that a business has spent multiple decades building. Despite the millions that a business may spend on advertising, you can't just 'buy' mental associations; it will take time. Yet sometimes a rebrand may be necessary as a business wants to leave all of the negative associations behind. Some of the best examples of rebrands come from the food sector (Table 7.1). For

Table 7.1 Examples of renamed food products

Old Name	New Name
Chinese Goosebery	Kiwi Fruit
Patagonian Toothfish	Chilean Sea Bass
White Spider Crab	Cornish King Crab
Megrim Sole	Cornish Sole
Whore's Eggs	Sea Urchin
Rapeseed Oil	Canola Oil
Soybean Curd	Tofu
Locus	Sky Prawns
Dog Fish	Rock Salmon

example, in the 1970s, sales of Patagonian toothfish were relatively low. This was a concern because, at the time, Patagonian toothfish were one of the more sustainable fish from the Southern Ocean. It didn't matter how it was cooked or who prepared it, people were put off by the name and the negative connotations it conjured up. As a result, Lee Lantz, a US fish wholesaler, decided to increase sales to the North American consumer market by rebranding it as Chilean Sea Bass. The result was that sales increased by over 1,000% and it is now sold as Chilean Sea Bass globally.[14]

This is not an isolated example. A number of foods that most people have heard of used to have a very different name. In a restaurant context, changing a dish's name to make it sound more appealing increases sales by 43%.[15]

Does a brand need to be unique?

When it comes to creating a brand, most marketing experts suggest you need to develop a proposition that is totally unique in the market. When customers think about your brand, it should trigger a set of thoughts and feelings that are completely different to your rivals. Yet if you think about this carefully, you'll realize that this is naive. The average European supermarket contains 30,000 SKUs (stock keeping units) – can they all be unique to one another? Consider Coca-Cola, one of the most valuable brands in the world – is there anything truly unique about their brand proposition? Everyone will articulate the proposition differently, but at its heart, it is about *'creating refreshing and uplifting drink that brings people together in the emotional moments that matter'*. There is nothing particularly distinctive about this, but what makes it so powerful is the consistency. Their position has remained virtually unchanged for over 100 years. They launched their first Christmas advert in 1931, featuring Father Christmas and variations of the same ad are still running today.

Even if a brand pulls off the impossible and comes up with a truly unique proposition, there is no evidence that it increases the likelihood that the brand will succeed. When a group of psychologists explored the associations shoppers had with 94 brands across eight different sectors, they found there was no correlation between whether the brand had built up unique associations and whether shoppers bought the brand.[16] Instead, the key to creating a successful brand is developing strong associations rather than unique associations.

This occurs because, in most cases, shoppers don't see brands as being distinct from one another. A marketer planning on launching a new brand of toothpaste will have spent weeks, if not months creating a clear brand identity. They will understand the smallest differences between Craft, Oral-B and Elmex. But as 99% of shoppers are not overly invested in the category, they don't notice these differences. Unless there are significant functional differences (especially price and location), shoppers just don't see brands as different from each other.[17] This is not to say that brand differentiation does not exist: it does, but it explains far less variation in what gets bought when compared to other factors. The best predictor is the product's availability, both physically (e.g. distribution) and mentally (is the brand name top of mind?)[18]

This should not be taken as evidence that branding is not important. Branding is essential, not just for business success, but survival. But it should change how marketers think about building a brand. When it comes to building a new brand, marketers should prioritize building brand recognition and not brand differentiation. After all, one of the best predictors of what gets bought in a supermarket is brand recognition – people buy brands they recognize.[19]

Building brands

Creating emotional brands

Apart from a stable brand image, what else is it that makes a brand successful? Some hints can be found by analysing the so-called Pepsi Paradox. The Pepsi Paradox is the phenomenon whereby in a blind taste test most people prefer the taste of Pepsi, yet when they are given a choice between Coca-Cola and Pepsi, they claim to prefer the taste of Coca-Cola. So, what is it about the Coca-Cola brand that people prefer?

It is widely talked about that emotions are key to decision-making, and this is backed up by neuroscience. Researchers recreated the Pepsi Paradox experiment with three different groups of people; healthy volunteers, patients who had experienced damage to the ventromedial prefrontal cortex (vmPFC), the part of the brain associated with regulating and inhibiting our responses to emotions, and patients who had brain damage, but not in the vmPFC. As expected, in the first part of the task, all three groups preferred the taste of Pepsi in a blind taste trial. But when the researchers revealed which brand they were drinking, the majority of participants with a healthy brain and those with a non-vmPFC brain lesion now claimed to prefer Coca-Cola. However, participants who had damage to their vmPFC experienced no change in attitude. They still preferred Pepsi.[20]

So, what does this show? Firstly, successful branding is clearly connected to emotions. This makes sense at a number of levels. While emotions do not trigger behaviour[21] (that is, motivation), they do help us in remembering information. When we try to recall a memory from childhood, it is likely that what we come up with will be something emotionally salient; a first kiss, winning a race at sports day or maybe the death of our first pet. But just because a memory is emotional does not make it permanent. Emotional memories are susceptible to decay like any other memory, but they are recalled better than non-emotional events.[22] This is useful for brand management because if a brand is consistently paired with emotional imagery or movies, people are more likely to remember them.[23]

The ultimate objective of any marketing campaign is to increase sales and the same is true of emotion-based branding. It's pointless developing a memorable campaign that fails to increase sales. When researchers analysed 996 different advertising campaigns from 1980 to 2010, they found that emotion-based campaigns (those that focus on System 1) typically fail to generate a short-term lift in sales but do lead to a long-term (3+ year) sales increase.[24] In contrast, campaigns that focus on a rational appeal, concentrating, for example, on the benefits or value of a product or product range, delivered a short-term increase in sales but failed to turn these short-term gains into stable long-term growth.

Findings like this have led some marketers to completely focus on emotion-based campaigns. However, it's important not to get too carried away with brand-first strategies. While there's nothing wrong with creating emotional adverts with compelling storylines, it's important that marketers are aware of two things. First, the brand should be incorporated into the advert's storyline and not simply be dropped in as a logo at the end. If it is, viewers may well remember the advert, but they are unlikely to associate it with the brand. Second, when creating an advert, marketers need to be very aware of the mental associations that it will create. Are they suggesting attributes that they want associated with their brand? Do they contradict the brand image? It takes a long time for consumers to develop a clear image of a brand, so constantly introducing new concepts to a brand runs the risk of just confusing customers and diluting the message.

But this idea of creating an emotional connection is not only limited to adverts. For some brand managers, their ultimate goal is to convince shoppers to form an emotional relationship with their brand. The only catch is that most people don't want a relationship with a brand. Take bleach. For most people, bleach isn't something we think about very often, and we certainly don't want a relationship with a bleach brand. Hence, across the market there are relatively few brands that have a strong emotional relationship with their customers.[25] The only brands most people follow on social media are connected to their self-identity (or ones that offer discounts). Someone interested in the outdoors might follow brands connected to climbing, snowboarding or paragliding, whereas a new parent might be interested in brands connected to babies. But they don't want to follow a bleach brand.

What makes a great logo?

Word marks vs logos: Does it make a difference?

While a brand is far more than just a logo, there is no avoiding the fact that a logo is a key part of a brand's identity. The logo is the visual representation of the brand, and as shoppers have a stronger memory for brand logos than they do for brand names,[26] they play an important role. This makes complete sense. After all, people have a fantastic ability to recognize pictures. Flash an image in front of someone, and several days later they are able to recognize if they've seen it before with 90% accuracy.[27] Try to do the same thing with words and people struggle.[28] This has led some commentators to argue that wordmarks don't make for great logos (hint, probably best not to mention this to Google), but this overlooks a number of key facts.

Firstly, it assumes that we process a wordmark as if it were any other word. But when we see a wordmark, such as the Google logo, we don't read it as a word; instead we recognize it as a picture. This is an important distinction because our brains process words and pictures differently,[29] with images being processed quicker than words[30] (but not 60,000 times quicker, which is often cited), and in most cases, people pay more attention to images.[31]

How to optimize a logo or wordmark?

This doesn't mean that wordmarks don't make effective logos, it just comes down to the situation. If you are trying to introduce a new brand to the market, shoppers typically prefer a wordmark to an image-based logo.[32] This is because when people are unfamiliar with a brand, they hunt for clues about what it stands for. What is it? What do they do? What should they expect from the brand? While a picture-based logo will give some of these clues, it's easier to interpret this from words, assuming the brand name says something about the company, such as Flash or Lyft. However, once they become familiar with the brand and they've learnt to associate the name with the logo, this effect vanishes, and shoppers now prefer image-based logos. The implications of this are two-fold. Firstly, when talking about brands, most people automatically think about the Googles and Apples of this world, but these are the exceptions. Most brands are relatively small, with a limited budget, and they struggle to build brand awareness. Consequently, for these brands, a distinctive wordmark may be more effective.

However, the second implication does not only apply to wordmarks, but also visual logos. Wordmarks outperformed picture-based logos because shoppers found them more descriptive. And we can use this principle when it comes to designing new picture-based logos. Take the Costa Coffee logo. Although it includes the word 'coffee' which certainly helps make the link to the product more salient, it also includes a picture of a coffee bean to make this link obvious. This is important because the clearer the logo links to the product, the more positively shoppers perceive the logo to be – which results in higher sales.[33] Businesses can choose how they make this link, either with a descriptive brand name, or visually, but when launching a new brand into the market and shoppers have no knowledge about the brand at all, the link should be obvious.

There are a couple of caveats to this. Clearly, if you are selling a product towards which shoppers have a less favourable attitude, for example, palm oil, or a cesspit-emptying company, it is not a good idea to make the link any more salient than it needs to be. If you do, the stronger the visual link to the product category, the worse the sales are. The second caveat is that once a logo becomes well-known, people recognize it almost instantly. If they've learnt to associate it with the appropriate category, there is no need for the logo to be as descriptive. Hence why there are lots of well-established brands like Ikea, Nivea or Pepsi who don't follow this rule and it doesn't hurt them at all.

If a brand opts for a wordmark, the fact that people perceive them as an image rather than a word means that some of the standard rules we associate with processing words don't apply. For example, when writing headlines, it's best to avoid using block capitals as people are typically 20% slower to read block capitals than sentence case. But as shoppers perceive wordmarks as images, this isn't the case. Shoppers make different inferences depending on whether the logo is written in either uppercase or lowercase. If a logo is written in block capitals, shoppers typically perceive the brand to be more premium than wordmarks written in lower case.[34] Consequently, if you're targeting shoppers who are cost-conscious or at least trying to save money, then they are more likely to buy brands whose logo is in lowercase. But this does come at a cost. Logos written in block capitals are perceived as being more credible and having more authority[35] – you'll just have to make a judgement call about which is more important to your brand.

What makes a good brand name?

It is not just the image that is key to a successful logo; the name is also vital. Take a look in both the professional and academic marketing literature and you'll find a plethora of guidelines suggesting how to come up with the perfect name. While we will steer clear of precise recommendations, the psychological literature makes several recommendations that all link back to the same concept – how easy it is for shoppers to process.

Unlike naming a child, when it comes to creating a brand, marketers can come up with anything. They can use a person's name, select a word from any language or even just make up a new word. While it might be tempting to create your own word, as it makes it easier to trademark, this approach comes with a few risks. Shoppers are better able to recall a brand name when it is a real word than a made-up word. However, when it comes to recognition, people are more accurate at recognizing brand names that are made-up words.[36] Made-up words are unique, which means they don't fit into any existing memory structures, making them harder to remember without prompts or hints. But the fact that they are so unique makes them easier to recognize. Consequently, newly created words might perform better for products bought from bricks-and-mortar stores where shoppers browse, but if the majority of sales occur online, where shoppers can search for specific products, established words may be the best course of action.

If a marketer decides to create a new word to represent their brand, it's still a good idea not to get too crazy. Whatever name they come up with, it should still follow the linguistic rules of their customers' language. Tetley, Haribo and Lucozade are not 'words', but they are easy to pronounce as they follow the standard pronunciation in English. This is important as the easier it is to pronounce, the more likely people are to like it.[37]

But some brands have opted for a halfway house. Rather than making a word up, they use an existing word but deliberately spell it wrong. For example, Lyft, Fiverr or Krispy Kreme. Unfortunately, despite its popularity, shoppers are less likely to buy brands with these spelling errors. When sports fans were sitting in a stadium, waiting for the big game to start, researchers offered fans the chance to try a new brand of fizzy drink. When the drink was called 'Clear' fans were 13.6% more likely to try it than when they offered them 'Klear'. Exactly the same trend happened when they tested the concept with iPhone apps. There was nearly a 20% decrease in the number of people who downloaded an app called 'Daily Gainz' than when it was called 'Daily Gains'.[38] This occurs because shoppers felt that these unconventional names are a direct attempt to manipulate shoppers and as such it triggers reactance.

On the other hand, if a brand opts to use an existing word that's spelt correctly, it helps if the word relates to something tangible in the real world, something customers can visualize. For example, it is very easy to imagine a concept like an Apple, Shell or Red Bull, but names such as IBM or KFC which have no stand-alone meaning are far harder to visualize. The easier it is for shoppers to imagine, the better their recall and recognition of the logo[39] – once again processing fluency in action.

The final trick marketers need to be aware of when deciding on a brand name is how long it should be. Most of the time, marketers are trying to remove the friction from a purchase decision. This would suggest that it's better to have a shorter brand name as it's easier for people to process, but this doesn't appear to be true for all. Typically, brands with a one-syllable name are more suited for basic brands, whereas longer brand names are better suited for luxury.[40] In both English and French, polysyllabic words are rarer, so people consider them to be more complex, distant and abstract, and when they are used in a brand name, they feel more luxurious.

Brand ownership: The face of the brand

It is a marketer's dream for shoppers to form an emotional relationship with a brand, but achieving this isn't easy, especially when a brand can be seen as a faceless corporation. To make it easier for shoppers to relate to a brand, over one in five brands now feature a human name as part of the branding[41] – think Mr Kipling, Trader Joe's or Ben & Jerry's Ice Cream. This helps make a brand appear more personable, trustworthy and approachable. This works because most shoppers assume the brand is named after the founder, making it feel real. But usually this isn't the case. Neither Aunt Bessie, Mr Kipling, nor Uncle Ben (now Ben's Original) ever existed; they are just inventions of a marketing department.

So, if a marketer is going to invent a persona to front their brand, are there gender considerations? For products that are handmade (or at least perceived as being handmade), women prefer to buy from other women, as they subconsciously like to support women in industry. In contrast, men aren't bothered whether the product is made by a man or a woman[42] – hence, brands with feminine names tend to perform better. This doesn't only apply to bespoke products, exactly the same trend occurs with fast-moving consumer goods (FMCG); overall, shoppers prefer brands with female names and are more likely to buy them.[43]

Just take a look at the Interbrand list of Best Global Brands (a list of the most valuable brands based on financial performance, brand strength and value) and you won't be surprised to find that only 36% of brands have a masculine name (55% of brands had a feminine name and 9% were neutral). When it comes to FMCGs, feminine brand names outperform masculine names, not because women want to support women, but because stereotypically women are perceived as being warmer. When we perceive someone as warmer, we also associate them as being more trustworthy, friendly and sincere – all traits that are fantastic for a brand.

But opting for a gendered name will always come with an inherent risk, as companies may be nervous about playing up to potentially sexist stereotypes. Launching a new brand of household cleaner and naming it Mrs Jones will likely offend many people, leading them to query: why did they call it Mrs Jones and not Mr Jones? Just look at the criticism both Amazon and Apple received for giving a female voice to their voice assistants (Siri and Alexa). The BBC ran an article headlined 'Alexa, are you making me sexist?', whereas Le Monde read 'Les assistants vocaux renforcent les stéréotypes sexists' (Voice assistants reinforce gender stereotypes). In an attempt to avoid offending anybody, some brands opt for a gender-neutral name such as Jamie, Jordan or even create a new name. Yet we automatically classify a name as either male or female.

People intuitively associate a name as being feminine if it (a) has more syllables, (b) ends in a vowel sound, especially schwa, rather than a consonant, (c) stresses the second (or multiple) syllable(s).[44] Hence, people are more likely to assume that 'Nestlé' sounds feminine but 'Next' is masculine. This means that if a brand is creating a name from scratch, they have options in influencing audience perceptions.

The final decision a marketer needs to make when using a person's name for a brand is whether they should include the possessive or not. Although it sounds grammatically complicated, the possessive is simply whether you include an apostrophe after the noun. For example, Tracy's skis, Charlotte's motorbike or Françoise's lunch. While an English teacher would suggest that brands should always include the apostrophe (as the apple pies belong to Mr Kipling), often they opt not to. Sometimes this is purely a design decision. When the logo is shrunk to fit on a business card, details like an apostrophe can get lost. But shoppers make inferences from factors even as trivial as this. People are more likely to buy a brand, spend more on it and give the product a more glowing review online if it includes the possessive[45] – although this is only true for unknown brands. This occurs because in all our English classes, we've been taught that an apostrophe after a person's name implies ownership. If someone is confident enough to own a brand (even if they're fictional), it improves the credibility.

So, what does all this mean for marketers?

If you're reading this and thinking that your current brand logo doesn't follow these rules, don't panic. We're not saying that if a brand does not follow these rules, it cannot be successful. A number of the examples we've cited break the rules and are very successful: IBM, FedEx or AT&T, to name only a few. But when developing a brand from the start, it's always best to stack the odds in your favour wherever possible. And this is even more important for new small businesses. These businesses often have smaller marketing teams and budgets and will appreciate any help they can get to compete against more established brands. But if you've already got a successful brand, and it breaks the rule, there is no point in changing. You've spent a lot of time and money developing a brand. And who needs the stress of a brand redesign?

Sonic branding

As we said earlier, a brand is more than just a visual logo. If you asked people to describe the Netflix logo, most people would describe a red N. But when a customer logs into their Netflix account, they'll hear the 'ta-dum' sound, which for most people is just as recognizable as the logo. And this is not a new trend. Anyone who used a Windows computer in the late 1990s will be intimately familiar with both the Intel and Windows 95 start-up noises. This is not just a case of marketing departments trying to find creative ways to spend their budget. Brands that have a sonic brand tend to have more success.[46] While correlation does not equal causation, there is good evidence that sonic branding helps.

Different regions of our brain process different sensory inputs, so if a customer sees and hears a brand at the same time, it means that more brain regions are engaged simultaneously which leads to the creation of stronger memories. Not only do sonic brands help foster stronger memories, but they are capable of triggering positive emotions, and lead to a greater level of emotional engagement.[47]

Just as designing the right visual logo is tricky, coming up with a sonic logo is not easy either. It shouldn't be a surprise that the best-performing sonic logos are more positive, upbeat and generally sound happy.[48] In western cultures, this means composing these logos in a major key. When music is written in a major key, it intuitively sounds more positive, whereas people perceive music written in a minor key to sound negative or sad.[49] However, sonic brands are not like normal songs or symphonies. Whereas symphonies last 35 minutes and a pop song lasts on average 3:30, a sonic brand will be over in a matter of seconds. Both the Netflix tune and the Intel 'bong' are over in under three seconds. Composers need to convey a lot of information and associations very quickly and as a result everything is, or at least should be, carefully considered.

With only two bars to work with, composing a tune that is distinctive, catchy and memorable is not easy. But distinctiveness is an interesting concept within marketing. Brands want to be different to the norm, but not too different. The bestselling pop songs sound different to everything else in the charts, but also recognizable,[50] and there is no difference for sonic brands. Sonic brands with fewer notes sound familiar, whereas logos with lots of different notes are more complicated for the brain to process, and sound less familiar. As with most things in life, the best course of action is somewhere in the middle. Typically, customers are more willing to pay for brands when a sonic logo features six unique notes than when a brand uses either three or nine notes.[51]

In a similar vein, the instruments chosen make a big difference to how the brand is perceived, as different instruments trigger different associations. Sonic logos which heavily feature guitar or have a synth bass line are perceived as being more rugged, whereas sonic logos that are based around a piano or flute are thought of as being more sophisticated.[52] If a brand wants to be perceived as more masculine, brass instruments work best, whereas woodwind (flute, clarinet) taking centre stage is perceived as more feminine.[53] All of this contributes to a brand's personality.

Brand personality

Although great care is taken in crafting a name and a logo, most marketers believe it is essential that it represents something, and this is where brand personality comes in.

Within psychology, personality refers to the combination of the characteristics, patterns of thought, feelings and behaviour that make up an individual's character (see Chapter 4). Brand personality is the same concept: people anthropomorphise the brand, using the same language to describe it as they would a person. Brands are abstract concepts, intangible and hard to describe, but by thinking of them as a person, or at least entities capable of possessing human characteristics, people can easily describe a brand as cool, exciting or macho. Marketers often talk about brand 'traits', 'characteristics' or 'values', the sort of abstract nouns we would more usually apply to people.

In order to help marketers talk about brand personality consistently, researchers have developed a standardized language and metrics to measure them. Currently the dominant approach is Aaker's Brand Personality Scale.[54] Having been cited over 16,743 times, it is one of the most cited marketing articles of all times. Aaker describes a brand on five independent dimensions: sincerity, excitement, competence, sophistication and ruggedness. It is important to emphasize that this is a multi-dimensional model, and an individual brand is ranked on each of the five scales, so a brand could score highly on one scale and low on the other four. Scoring high or low on any one scale is not necessarily a good or bad thing, but merely a way to describe the different characteristics of a brand, helping marketers understand what makes it different from its competitors.

From a psychological perspective, Aaker's model is interesting because there is an overlap between this framework and the dominant model to measure human personality: the Big 5 personality traits (see Chapter 4).[55] Sincerity is similar to the Big 5's 'agreeableness', excitement relates to 'extroversion' and competence equates to 'conscientiousness'. However, the final two dimensions (sophistication and ruggedness) are unique to brand personality. But just because something can be measured doesn't mean it should be. How useful is brand personality as a tool? Although there is some evidence that people choose brands similar to their own personality,[56] this appears to be relatively weak. People who are extroverts buy different brands to people who are neurotic. But extroverts don't necessarily buy brands that are positioned as exciting. Instead, they're motivated by different claims (see Chapter 4 on personality).

> ### GIVE IT A GO
>
> Review two different brands using Aaker's Brand Personality questionnaire and compare the results. Are the results what you expected?
>
>

Worse, there is some evidence to suggest Aaker's model is just an artificial construct, dreamed up by researchers. When researchers showed participants three different garden rocks as stimuli and asked each participant to complete Aaker's brand personality questionnaire for the rocks, they found that each rock had its own unique and statistically stable personality on 41 of the 42 different components, leading researchers to develop detailed personalities for each rock[57] despite the fact that rocks clearly have neither a personality nor a brand.

This isn't to suggest that brand personality isn't a useful concept, if used wisely. As we've suggested earlier, one of the key factors that predicts brand success is presenting a consistent brand message over time. Aaker's brand personality can help marketers to ensure that each new advert or social media post are all perceived as the same, and that brand image is not consistently changing and presenting a different message with every new campaign.

As well as providing marketers with a standardized language to describe how shoppers perceive a brand, it also helps to untangle the relationship between brand personality, brand trust and brand commitment. Typically, brands that have a distinctive personality are more trusted and shoppers are more committed to them.[58,59] From a theoretical perspective, it does not matter which of the five aspects of brand personality you choose to emphasize, all have a positive impact on improving brand relationship, brand strength and purchase intention.[60] However, it is still worth remembering that although having a distinctive brand personality can help, it is still not as important as ensuring shoppers recognize your brand.

The double jeopardy of marketing

This links back to one of the few empirical laws of marketing – the double jeopardy law. This proposes that brands with less market share are in that situation because they have fewer buyers (jeopardy number 1), and secondly, these buyers are less loyal (jeopardy number 2).[61] At face value, this may seem blindingly obvious, but when you explore the causes, it has far-reaching implications when it comes to brand building. Firstly, it means that brand growth is primarily driven by market penetration and not by improving customer loyalty.[62] You may have heard the statistic, that if a credit card company could retain 5% more customers, they could double their profits.[63] Yet despite featuring in the *Harvard Business Review*, there is no data to support it; it was just a hypothetical thought experiment, and a flawed one at that.

The full scenario proposes that if a credit card company lost 10% of its customers each year, then the average customer lifespan would be 10 years. If the company could improve the turnover rate to 5% then the average customer lifespan would increase to 20 years. A drop from 10% to 5% is a change of 5 percentage points, not 5%. In practice, this is a 50% decrease, a mammoth undertaking. Secondly, the thought experiment didn't consider company profitability but customer profitability.

If a brand wants to grow, they should always focus on attracting new customers, not getting existing customers to buy more. This principle has been shown to occur in all countries, sectors and for products as diverse as detergents to aviation fuels.

The second point is that it is impossible to increase customer loyalty without increasing market share. To improve loyalty, brands need to win more customers (and not the other way around). Even in situations when a business has its customers locked in, such as when they use a subscription business model, improving brand salience improves loyalty. A 1% increase in brand salience is associated with a lower defection rate of 0.25%.[64]

So why does this link to branding? The double jeopardy law occurs for two reasons: mental availability and physical availability. Larger brands have better physical availability as they are sold in more locations, but it is not just the number of outlets that gives them an advantage. The bigger the brand, the more facings they have in a store, which increases the likelihood that shoppers will buy them, or at the very least consider buying. This explains the second advantage larger brands have: mental availability. People think about these brands more.

For brand managers, the key takeaway is that the larger the brand, the easier it is for shoppers to think about it, improving mental availability. For any brand, but especially smaller or challenger ones, they need to prioritize brand building and getting their name out more. If they're investing money and time in brand building, it is important that they present a consistent brand image, and it won't hurt to be distinctive – but they should remember that brand building is the primary focus. Keeping your existing customers loyal is not a bad move, but it won't help growth. Eventually, the double jeopardy law will catch up with them, and the business will decline.

Brand myths

No ski holiday to Switzerland would be complete without at least one cheese fondue, that traditional meal eaten by 'vachers' (cowherds) on the alpine pastures all over Switzerland for centuries. The only catch is this story isn't strictly true. While the Greek historian Homer may have eaten a variation of a fondu over 3,000 years ago, for the last 2,000 years it has been a very regional dish that wasn't popular. That is, until the Swiss Cheese Union got involved in the 1930–50s and thought it was a perfect way to encourage people to eat more cheese.[65] The same approach was successfully used in the UK with the introduction of the *'ploughman's lunch'*. Dairymen never ate cheese and pickle, washed down with a pint of ale. This was a marketing campaign developed by the Milk Marketing Board in the 1960s to, once again, sell more cheese. Both campaigns were highly successful because they created beautiful stories that shoppers can believe in and play up the idea of heritage and nostalgia from a bygone era.

In a similar vein, historic brands such as Cartier (1847), Twining's (1706) and Stella Artois (1366) all trade off their heritage as it helps to promote trust, brand attachment and commitment, which all ultimately increases purchase intention.[66] But if a brand doesn't have history on their side, they can take a leaf out of the milk marketing group's playbook. If you are launching a new drink, you could use an old-fashioned bottle, design the label using a heritage font, and show a nostalgic rural landscape as part of your logo. It doesn't take much for your brand to be seen as traditional. After all, the ciabatta was invented by Italian bakers to compete with the French baguette in 1982, Baileys was launched in 1974 and the New York Roll, the sushi classic sold in supermarkets (and petrol stations) around the world, was created in 1979. Which means that all three of these products are younger than Leonardo DiCaprio, Heidi Klum and Dwayne (the Rock) Johnson.

Clearly, nostalgia won't be the right approach for all brands, but for hedonistic products, it makes more sense to play up to nostalgia or at least the emotive nature of the brand. Products that are positioned as 'scientifically developed' are seen by shoppers as being both reliable and credible, but also cold and lacking emotions,[67] not what you want when it comes to selling a hedonic product. Which is exactly the reason why if you see an advert for Werther's Original, they always feature an image of the 'developmental kitchen'. It doesn't look anything like a factory, but almost resembles an alpine kitchen.

Brand rituals

Although advertising is probably the most common way to create an emotional connection with a brand, some take it one step further and attempt to turn the process of consuming their products into an emotional moment linked with the brand. One way of achieving this is by creating a brand ritual, an act they hope customers will perform before consuming their product. Before eating a Kit-Kat, lots of people first rub the foil wrapper, causing the brand logo to stand out, before breaking the fingers apart while still in the wrapper. Likewise, if you're familiar with Oreos, you might remember their advertising suggests that they are best eaten by twisting the biscuit apart, licking the filling and putting it back together before finally dunking it in milk and eating it.

And most people know that it takes 119.5 seconds to pour the perfect pint of Guinness, but again this is part of the brand ritual created by a marketer. Back in 1996, bar staff were trying to persuade customers not to order a Guinness because it took too long to pour. But Guinness tried to turn this into an advantage and created a ritual out of it. The glass needs to be held at a perfect 45-degree angle, the Guinness should be poured in hitting the side and filled up until the glass is three-quarters full and then left to rest for 90 seconds. Once it's settled, the glass should be topped up.

Although at first these rituals can just look like gimmicks, they can become a key part of the product experience and even lead to greater enjoyment of the product by consumers.[68] When researchers gave participants an unknown brand of chocolate and asked them to '...*without unwrapping the chocolate bar, break it in half. Unwrap half of the bar and eat it. Then unwrap the other half and eat it.*' They found that participants rated the chocolate as being more flavoursome, valuable and deserving of being savoured than by people who ate the chocolate normally. Consumers do not experience increased enjoyment when they simply make random gestures before eating the chocolate; it has to be the specified ritual. Psychologists believe this occurs because performing a ritual causes shoppers to be more involved in the moment, making consumption itself more of an experience and all the positive results this triggers.

Branding and social norms

Building a brand image takes time, so marketers are always looking for shortcuts. From a scientific point of view, brands are more appealing once we see other people using them,[69] a form of social proof. If everyone is making the same decision, we defer to their wisdom, believing that everybody '*can't be making the wrong decision*'.[70] We may not be making the best decision, but it is unlikely to be a terrible choice. Hence, social norms are powerful tools to influence consumer behaviour.[71]

Restaurants will use phrases like 'family favourite', online shops tell customers how many units they've sold, and KickStarter campaigns will highlight how many backers they have already received, all to reinforce how popular the product is. It's a small intervention but powerful. When energy companies tried to persuade households to use less electricity, they tested four different adverts. The first two adverts focused on the different benefits associated with using less electricity – the fact that they could save money or the environmental benefits. The third advert focused on households' moral responsibility to use less electricity, whereas the fourth used a social norm appeal, highlighting that most other people are already trying to reduce their electricity consumption. The advert based around social norms was the only one that changed consumers' behaviour in both the short and long term.[72]

Although social norms are powerful, people are more likely to use social norms when they're unsure how to act.[73] For example, if someone is on a first date and wants to make a good impression but isn't a wine expert, they are likely to order one of the bestselling wines, thinking there must be a reason it is popular. But there are different ways that businesses can use social norms in their campaigns. They can emphasize how most people behave, what is known as a descriptive norm, such as 'most people regularly recycle their plastic bottles' or a company could emphasize what most people think, for example, 'Most people believe recycling is important', what is known as an injunctive norm. If a brand is attempting to motivate potential customers to change their behaviour, such as to buy a product, it is far more effective to use a descriptive norm, whereas if a company is aiming to change attitudes, it is more effective to use an injunctive norm.[74]

At first, this would suggest that all organizations should focus on descriptive norms rather than injunctive norms, but this decision is more complicated for political parties, lobby groups or even charities. Which objective is more important for a political party such as the Green Party/Les VERT-E-S suisses? Do they want to focus on convincing people to vote for them, or instead, is it more important to change people's attitudes towards sustainability and environmental issues?

REAL-WORLD EXAMPLE: PSYCH IN ACTION

When Alapcin, a German shampoo for men, entered the UK market, they used two different tag lines. *'German engineering for your hair'* and *'Germany's best-selling shampoo for men'*. Both of these lines used a different psychological mechanism to help build up brand associations and encourage people to try the product.

For most of the 20th and early 21st century, it wasn't considered masculine to focus on one's appearance. As a result, rather than using a vanity-based message, such as emphasizing that shampoo will make your hair stronger, reduce split ends or make your hair glossier, which you typically find with shampoos targeted at women, they built on the positive mental associations people already had developed towards Germany. Germany is well known for its engineering prowess, with brands such as BMW, Mercedes-Benz and Bosch. Consequently, they opted to use language more familiar with electrical products, e.g. *'recharge your hair during washing'*. Not only was this perceived as more masculine, but it helped to differentiate the product from other shampoos already on the market.

The second message 'Germany's best-selling shampoo for men' made use of a descriptive norm. People are often creatures of habit and are unlikely to switch brands unless something changes. For a FMCG, this is often that their usual product is sold out or a rival product is on special offer. However, by telling people that Alapcin is the best-selling shampoo for men, it helps reassure people that the product works – people in Germany wouldn't consistently buy the product if it didn't do its job. But when a new brand is supported by a national marketing campaign pushing a novel message (*German engineering for your hair*), and the fact that people know that the product is already used, this can be enough to get people to switch brands.

Measuring brand strength

Introduction

As brands are such a powerful tool, companies understandably want to measure their strength, and see how they compare to their rivals. A quick search online will reveal hundreds of different lists charting the most valuable brands. Yet most of these lists are either based on the firm's financial performance, or even less helpfully, marketing professionals' expert opinions. However, psychologists might be able to help. Over the years, they have developed a range of different experiments that can be used to measure participants' attitudes to a variety of things, and these can easily be modified to include branding.

Implicit association test

When researchers first started investigating racism, they quickly realized they could not simply ask someone if they were racist, as the results would be meaningless. Not only is it wrong and unlawful, but society as a whole explicitly disapproves of racism, so if people are asked about what they think about ethnic minorities and they hold racist views, they hide this. Researchers refer to this as the '*social desirability bias*' and needed to develop a new test that did not rely on self-reporting. This led to the creation of the Implicit-Association Test (IAT).

Technically, the IAT is a measure of associative knowledge between two different concepts. From the point of view of a participant, the IAT is just a simple sorting task. They are asked to sort a series of words and images into different categories and the time it takes to categorize words provides researchers with an insight into their attitudes.

In the original racism experiment, participants were asked to sort a selection of faces into two categories: light-skinned faces or dark-skinned faces. Next, participants were presented with a selection of positive or negative words and asked to categorize them into good or bad. The third and fourth stage involves the faces and words being presented together; the only difference between the two stages is that the categories are counterbalanced: first, dark-skinned is paired with good and in the next stage dark-skinned is paired with bad.[75] This seemingly odd method allowed researchers to measure the strength of the association between the two concepts via priming. The first image the participant sees primes their reaction to the second stimulus. If a participant associates two concepts together, they will be slightly faster at responding. For example, someone with a racial bias will be faster to respond when pairing a dark-skinned face with negative words than they would when a dark-skinned face is paired with a positive word.

Originally developed to measure implicit racial attitudes, this task has been modified to measure brand attitudes.[76] Rather than presenting participants with faces, in the modified test they have to categorize brand logos or photos of products. Excitingly, the results of this study appeared to be a better predictor of participants' actual behaviour than measuring attitudes via a questionnaire. However, it is important to add a few caveats. First, an IAT is not an absolute measurement of brand attitude. All it can do is give a relative judgement between two different concepts. So, if researchers compared Coca-Cola with Pepsi and the results suggested that users preferred Pepsi to Coca-Cola, this does not imply that participants do not like Coca-Cola – just that they prefer Pepsi.

Second, IATs are not reliable at an individual level. When designing psychometric tests, one of the standard techniques to assess their reliability is to ask the same participant to complete the test twice, under the same conditions, and calculate how closely the two results correlate. For a test to be considered reliable, statisticians generally expect a test to correlate at above 0.7, although 0.8 is preferable. However, the IAT is relatively weak, with correlation scores in the range of 0.32–0.65).[77] Considering these low scores, most academics (including the developers of the IAT) now agree that the IAT cannot be used to predict how an individual will behave,[78] only to understand group behaviour.

As well as the IAT's reliability being questioned, there's some debate over its scientific underpinnings. When data from 14,900 participants was analysed, it revealed that IAT results only explained 5.5% of participants' actual behaviour.[79] Despite this, IATs remain popular with market researchers. More work needs to be done to validate the science behind them. To date, the vast majority of the academic research exploring IATs' reliability and validity has focused on racial attitudes. Further work is needed to measure the reliability and validity of the test when measuring brand attitudes.

> **GIVE IT A GO**
>
> Want to get a better understanding of how an IAT works? Take an IAT and see what your implicit brand attitude is. How does your score compare to your friends?
>
>

Attentional blink

Another experimental approach that can be used to measure brand strength is the attentional blink. The attentional blink exploits a strange quirk of the visual system. After something grabs your attention, there is a very short period of time, approximately

200–500msec, where your attention is unavailable for noticing other things.[80] This is normally shown in laboratory studies where stimuli such as letters, numbers or pictures are flashed on the screen in quick succession and participants are asked to spot one individual letter. Virtually all participants can spot the target letter, however they are unable to accurately recall what letters come next. Yet certain stimuli are capable of jumping out of this attentional blink. When the experiment is repeated but with the participant's name shown after the target stimulus, the results changed. Participants have no problem spotting their name, although the effect *only* worked for their name. If it was a different name or a random word, then this was blanked.[81] Certain stimuli jump out from the attentional blink because they are personally more relevant to us.

As the attentional blink is all about personal relevance, a number of psychologists have adopted this approach to develop a Cognitive Brand Strength Index (CBSI). However, rather than using the participant's name after the target stimuli, this time it's replaced with a brand logo. The experiment is repeated numerous times, and the brand is placed in different positions after the target stimuli. The closer the brand can go to the target stimuli and still be recognized, the more personal relevance the brand is to participants and the higher the brand's CBSI score. This test appears to have relatively strong predictive value as the higher the CBSI score, the more likely people are to purchase the product.

Iowa Gambling Task

The final psychological experiment that has been modified to measure brand loyalty is the Iowa Gambling Task (IGT). The IGT is a simple decision-making task, structured as a game in which participants can win or lose notional amounts of cash in a card game. Each participant is presented with four decks of cards. They are told that each deck contains cards that will either reward or penalize them and that the aim of the game is to win as much money as possible. In reality, the decks have been carefully stacked so that two decks are good, and two are bad. After drawing ten cards from the bad deck, participants will typically have earned $1,000 in rewards but lost $1,250 in penalties. On the good decks, the rewards are much smaller, but more consistent: after drawing ten cards, participants would typically earn $500 but incur penalties of only $250.[82] Typically, most participants will learn to only draw from the good decks after selecting about 30 cards.[83] So, what happens when you place brand logos on the decks?

When a well-liked brand logo is placed on a bad deck, participants are initially more likely to select it and are much slower to realize that it is a bad deck. Participants will only start to switch decks after 100 draws.[84] In contrast, when disliked brands are placed on a good deck, participants avoid these decks to begin with and are even slower to switch decks. After 100 draws, they generally haven't switched at all. As this switching behaviour appears to be standardized, researchers can place different brands on the decks and, depending on when participants learn the task, researchers can calculate their level of brand love or brand hate.

GIVE IT A GO

Want to get a better understanding of how the IGT works? Take an IGT and see what your implicit brand attitude is. How does your score compare to your friends'?

Closing thoughts

Developing a strong brand is at the heart of most modern-day marketing, whether promoting a product, a place or even a personality on social media. Yet, despite being a core component of a company's marketing strategy, a brand can never truly be 'owned' by a company. While a brand's logo and visual identity can be trademarked to stop rivals from using them, the brand itself is ultimately owned by the public. It resides in the thoughts and feelings that come to mind when people hear the brand name. The only way for a brand to build these mental associations is by consistently pairing itself with specific stimuli, giving shoppers the opportunity to learn to link the two concepts together. For instance, if a brand wants to be perceived as sophisticated or stylish, it makes sense for it to sponsor or partner with actors and events renowned for their style and elegance. Over time, brand managers will want to understand how successful this process is, and this is where marketers will want to measure both brand strength and brand attitudes. While self-report measures can give an indication of this, to understand the deeper associations people have towards brands, experimental testing can be useful.

KEY POINTS

- A brand is far more than just a logo; it encompasses all of the thoughts, feelings and emotions a consumer experiences when they think of an organization, place or person.
- Brands shape shoppers' expectations about how a product or organization will perform and often these become self-fulfilling prophecies.
- When consumers consistently see a brand paired with the same associations, it starts to build a stable and strong brand image.

- It is more important for a brand to build consistent brand associations than unique associations.
- New or relatively unknown brands benefit from having a more descriptive brand logo or name; either a picture or a name which helps explain what the brand does.
- Brand names don't have to be existing words, but they should read like a word in the shopper's native language.
- Brands that are associated with a person (e.g. Mr Kipling or Ben & Jerry's Ice Cream) typically perform better than those that aren't.
- Convincing shoppers to create an 'implementation intention', an 'if–then statement' is more effective at changing behaviour than just giving them a reason to change their behaviour.
- Although Aaker's brand personality scale is the most commonly used, there are questions over what it measures. However, it is a useful tool to ensure that new brand assets adopt a consistent approach.
- Experimental methods are more robust at measuring brand attitudes than self-report measures as they are not influenced by social desirability bias. However, they work best at measuring group attitudes rather than individual attitudes.
- Although the Implicit Association Test (IAT) is the best-known measure of implicit attitudes, there are questions about its reliability.
- A branded Iowa Gambling Task and a branded attentional blink may have more potential than the IAT to measure implicit brand attitudes.

PUTTING THEORY INTO PRACTICE

1. Imagine you are the marketing manager for a new start-up offering campervan hire across Europe. Come up with three different brand names and logo concepts for this start-up that should work from a psychological perspective.

2. For a sector of your choice, select six brand logos, three from market leaders and three from relatively new entrants or small brands. Critique these logos from a psychological perspective, highlighting what they do well and what could be improved.

3. Developing a strong brand is all about building consistent mental associations. If you were the brand manager of a brand of your choice, how would you go about establishing these associations?

4. How could a restaurant that specializes in haute cuisine use the principle of brand rituals to enhance the dining experience?

5. If you were working at a market research firm and a client asked you to determine how strong their brand is in comparison to their rival, what procedure would you propose and why?

> **SUGGESTIONS FOR FURTHER READING**
>
> Johnson, M. & Misiaszek, T. (2022). *Branding that means business*. Economist Books.

References

1. Johnson, M. & Ghuman, P. (2020). *Blindsight: The (mostly) hidden ways marketing reshapes our brains*. BenBella Books.
2. American Marketing Association (2017). Dictionary: Definitions of marketing. https://www.ama.org/resources/Pages/Dictionary.aspx?dLetter=B (archived at https://perma.cc/26YW-VLS5)
3. Intriligator, J. (2017, September). *Applied consumer psychology*. Bangor University.
4. Fisher, J. P., Hassan, D. T. & O'Connor, N. (1995). Minerva. *BMJ*, 310, 70. https://doi.org/10.1136/bmj.310.6971.70 (archived at https://perma.cc/9G8B-BFAQ)
5. Hrobjartsson, A. & Gøtzsche, P. C. (2010). Placebo interventions for all clinical conditions. *Cochrane Database of Systematic Reviews*, 1, 1–451.
6. Lasagna, L. (1955). Placebos. *Scientific America*, 193, 68–71. https://doi.org/10.1038/scientificamerican0855-68 (archived at https://perma.cc/3E82-4N9M)
7. Charlesworth, J. E., Petkovic, G., Kelley, J. M., Hunter, M., Onakpoya, I., Roberts, N., ... & Howick, J. (2017). Effects of placebos without deception compared with no treatment: a systematic review and meta-analysis. *Journal of Evidence-Based Medicine*, 10(2), 97–107.
8. Branthwaite, A. & Cooper, P. (1981). Analgesic effects of branding in treatment of headaches. *British Medical Journal*, 282(6276), 1576–1578.
9. Hull, J. G. & Bond, C. F. (1986). Social and behavioral consequences of alcohol consumption and expectancy: A meta-analysis. *Psychological Bulletin*, 99(3), 347–360. https://doi.org/10.1037/0033-2909.99.3.347 (archived at https://perma.cc/D8F4-SWVG)
10. Cornil, Y., Chandon, P., & Krishna, A. (2017). Does Red Bull give wings to vodka? Placebo effects of marketing labels on perceived intoxication and risky attitudes and behaviors. *Journal of Consumer Psychology*, 27(4), 456–465.
11. Hebb, D. O. (1949). Organization of behavior: A neuropsychological theory. Wiley.
12. Ritson, M. (2017). Mark Ritson: Burberry has a big challenge to replace Christopher Bailey. *Marketing Week*. https://www.marketingweek.com/2017/11/01/burberry-christopher-bailey/ (archived at https://perma.cc/N54R-CHQX)
13. Miller, D., Merrilees, B., & Yakimova, R. (2014). Corporate rebranding: An integrative review of major enablers and barriers to the rebranding process. *International Journal of Management Reviews*, 16(3), 265–289.
14. The Economist (2022, July 7) To hook American diners, an invasive species of carp gets a new name. https://www.economist.com/united-states/2022/07/07/to-hook-american-diners-an-invasive-species-of-carp-gets-a-new-name (archived at https://perma.cc/36FK-X4G2)

15 Gavrieli, A., Attwood, S., Wise, J., Putnam-Farr, E., Stillman P., Giambastiani, S., Uprichard J., Hanson, C., & Bakker, M. (2022). Appealing dish names to nudge diners to more sustainable food choices: a quasi-experimental study. *BMC Public Health* 22, 2229. https://doi.org/10.1186/s12889-022-14683-8 (archived at https://perma.cc/929D-EPHR)

16 Romaniuk, J. & Gaillard, E. (2007). The relationship between unique brand associations, brand usage and brand performance: Analysis across eight categories. *Journal of Marketing Management*, 23(3-4), 267–284. https://doi.org/10.1362/026725707X196378 (archived at https://perma.cc/2ED4-Y8HT)

17 Romaniuk, J., Sharp, B., & Ehrenberg, A. (2007). Evidence concerning the importance of perceived brand differentiation. *Australasian Marketing Journal*, 15(2), 42–54. https://doi.org/10.1016/S1441-3582(07)70042-3 (archived at https://perma.cc/F62K-8CCN)

18 Macdonald, E. K. & Sharp, B. M. (2000). Brand awareness effects on consumer decision making for a common, repeat purchase product: A replication. *Journal of Business Research*, 48(1), 5–15.

19 Sharp, B. & Romaniuk, J. (2016). *How brands grow*. Melbourne: Oxford University Press.

20 Koenigs, M. & Tranel, D. (2008). Prefrontal cortex damage abolishes brand-cued changes in cola preference. *Social Cognitive and Affective Neuroscience*, 3(1), 1–6. https://doi.org/10.1093/scan/nsm032 (archived at https://perma.cc/3HPR-2M9J)

21 Baumeister, R. F., DeWall, N. C., Vohs, K. D., & Alquist, J. (2008). Does emotion cause behavior (apart from making people do stupid, destructive things)? (C. R. Agnew, D E Carlston, W G Graziano, & R. J. Kelly, Eds.; pp. 1–30). http://assets.csom.umn.edu/assets/128887.pdf (archived at https://perma.cc/Y9GC-AXM2)

22 Levine, L. J. & Pizarro, D. A. (2004). Emotion and memory research: A grumpy overview. *Social Cognition*, 22(5), 530–554. https://doi.org/10.1521/soco.22.5.530.50767 (archived at https://perma.cc/VR5Y-ET3P)

23 Khairudin, R., Givi, M. V., Shahrazad, W. S. W., Nasir, R., & Halim, F. W. (2011). Effects of emotional contents on explicit memory process. *Pertanika Journal of Social Science and Humanities*, 19, 17–26.

24 Binet, L., & Field, P. (2013). *The long and the short of it: Balancing short and long-term marketing strategies*. Institute of Practitioners in Advertising.

25 Alvarez, C. & Fournier, S. (2016). Consumers' relationships with brands. *Current Opinion in Psychology*, 10, 129–135.

26 Ghosh, T., Sreejesh, S., & Dwivedi, Y. K. (2022). Brand logos versus brand names: A comparison of the memory effects of textual and pictorial brand elements placed in computer games. *Journal of Business Research*, 147, 222–235. https://doi.org/10.1016/j.jbusres.2022.04.017 (archived at https://perma.cc/9EUK-8BYL)

27 Standing, L., Conezio, J., & Haber, R. N. (1970). Perception and memory for pictures: Single-trial learning of 2500 visual stimuli. *Psychonomic Science*, 19(2), 73–74. https://doi.org/10.3758/BF03337426 (archived at https://perma.cc/AGC9-Z5S3)

28 Shepard, R. N. (1967). Recognition memory for words, sentences, and pictures. *Journal of Verbal Learning and Verbal Behavior*, 6(1), 156–163. https://doi.org/10.1016/S0022-5371(67)80067-7 (archived at https://perma.cc/DGA5-HPE2)

29 Grady, C. L., McIntosh, A. R., Rajah, M. N., & Craik, F. I. (1998). *Neural correlates of the episodic encoding of pictures and words*. Proceedings of the National Academy of Sciences, 95(5), 2703–2708. https://doi.org/10.1073/pnas.95.5.2703 (archived at https://perma.cc/XK5M-MCUC)

30 Hockley, W. E. & Bancroft, T. (2011). Extensions of the picture superiority effect in associative recognition. *Canadian Journal of Experimental Psychology*, 65(4), 236–244. https://doi.org/10.1037/a0023796 (archived at https://perma.cc/9DR7-MAPL)

31 Pieters, R. & Wedel, M. (2004). Attention capture and transfer in advertising: Brand, pictorial, and text-size effects. *Journal of Marketing*, 68(2), 36–50. https://doi.org/10.1509/jmkg.68.2.36.27794 (archived at https://perma.cc/7SZ8-C424)

32 Morgan, C., Fajardo, T. M. & Townsend, C. (2021). Show it or say it: How brand familiarity influences the effectiveness of image-based versus text-based logos. *Journal of the Academy of Marketing Science*, 49, 566–583. https://doi.org/10.1007/s11747-020-00760-0 (archived at https://perma.cc/N6M3-N9ZF)

33 Luffarelli, J., Mukesh, M., & Mahmood, A. (2019). Let the logo do the talking: The influence of logo descriptiveness on brand equity. *Journal of Marketing Research*, 56(5), 862–878. https://doi.org/10.1177/0022243719845000 (archived at https://perma.cc/7SZ8-C424)

34 Yu, Y., Zhou, X., Wang, L., & Wang, Q. (2022). Uppercase premium effect: The role of brand letter case in brand premiumness. *Journal of Retailing*, 98(2), 335–355. https://doi.org/10.1016/j.jretai.2021.03.002 (archived at https://perma.cc/9FMJ-NDH6)

35 Xu, X., Chen, R. & Liu, M. W. (2017) The effects of uppercase and lowercase wordmarks on brand perceptions. *Marketing Letters*, 28, 449–460. https://doi.org/10.1007/s11002-016-9415-0 (archived at https://perma.cc/52RV-CVZG)

36 Lerman, D. & Garbarino, E. (2002). Recall and recognition of brand names: A comparison of word and nonword name types. *Psychology & Marketing*, 19(7-8), 621–639.

37 Bao, Y., Shao, A. T., & Rivers, D. (2008). Creating new brand names: Effects of relevance, connotation, and pronunciation. *Journal of Advertising Research*, 48(1), 148–162.

38 Costello, J. P., Walker, J., & Reczek, R. W. (2023). 'Choozing' the best spelling: Consumer response to unconventionally spelled brand names. *Journal of Marketing*, 87(6), 889–905.

39 de Lencastre, P., Machado, J. C., & Costa, P. (2023). The effect of brand names and logos' figurativeness on memory: An experimental approach. *Journal of Business Research*, 164, 113944. https://doi.org/10.1016/j.jbusres.2023.113944 (archived at https://perma.cc/8K8Z-Q2YK)

40 Pathak, A., Velasco, C., Petit, O., & Calvert, G. A. (2019). Going to great lengths in the pursuit of luxury: How longer brand names can enhance the luxury perception of a brand. *Psychology & Marketing*, 36(10), 951–963. https://doi.org/10.1002/mar.21247 (archived at https://perma.cc/944C-QBTA)

41 Khamitov, M. & Puzakova, M. (2022). Possessive brand names in brand preferences and choice: The role of inferred control. *Journal of the Academy of Marketing Science*, 1–20.

42 Schnurr, B. & Halkias, G. (2022). Made by her vs. him: Gender influences in product preferences and the role of individual action efficacy in restoring social equalities. *Journal of Consumer Psychology*. https://doi.org/10.1002/jcpy.1327 (archived at https://perma.cc/LDK4-3GFB)

43 Pogacar, R., Angle, J., Lowrey, T. M., Shrum, L. J., & Kardes, F. R. (2021). Is Nestlé a lady? The feminine brand name advantage. *Journal of Marketing*, 85(6), 101–117.

44 Pogacar, R., Angle, J., Lowrey, T. M., Shrum, L. J., & Kardes, F. R. (2021). Is Nestlé a lady? The feminine brand name advantage. *Journal of Marketing*, 85(6), 101–117.

45 Khamitov, M. & Puzakova, M. (2022). Possessive brand names in brand preferences and choice: The role of inferred control. *Journal of The Academy of Marketing Science*, 1–20.

46 Lindstrom, M. (2011). *Brand sense: Sensory secrets behind the stuff we buy*. Simon and Schuster.

47 Kemp, E., Cho, Y. N., Bui, M., & Kintzer, A. (2023). Music to the ears: The role of sonic branding in advertising. *International Journal of Advertising*, 1–21.

48 Scott, S. P., Sheinin, D., & Labrecque, L. I. (2022). Small sounds, big impact: Sonic logos and their effect on consumer attitudes, emotions, brands and advertising placement. *Journal of Product & Brand Management*, 31(7), 1091–1103.

49 Smit, E. A., Milne, A. J., Sarvasy, H. S., & Dean, R. T. (2022). Emotional responses in Papua New Guinea show negligible evidence for a universal effect of major versus minor music. *PLOS One*, 17(6), e0269597. https://doi.org/10.1371/journal.pone.0269597

50 Berger, J. (2023). *Magic words*. Harper Business, London, UK.

51 Krishnan, V., Kellaris, J. J., & Aurand, T. W. (2012). Sonic logos: Can sound influence willingness to pay?. *Journal of Product & Brand Management*, 21(4), 275–284.

52 Puligadda, S. & VanBergen, N. (2023). The influence of sound logo instruments on brand personality perceptions: An investigation of brand ruggedness and sophistication. *Journal of Business Research*, 156, 113531. https://doi.org/10.1016/j.jbusres.2022.113531 (archived at https://perma.cc/WNB7-LQ3L)

53 Techawachirakul, M., Pathak, A., Motoki, K., & Calvert, G. A. (2023). Sonic branding of meat-and plant-based foods: The role of timbre. *Journal of Business Research*, 165, 114032.

54 Aaker, J. (1997). Dimensions of brand personality. *Journal of Marketing Research*, 34(3), 347–356. https://doi.org/10.2307/3151897 (archived at https://perma.cc/YP64-XNUB)

55 Digman, J. M. (1990). Personality structure: Emergence of the five-factor model. *Annual Review of Psychology*, 41(1), 417–440. https://doi.org/10.1146/annurev.ps.41.020190.002221 (archived at https://perma.cc/V2NB-KZ7N)

56 Maehle, N. & Shneor, R. (2010). On congruence between brand and human personalities. *Journal of Product & Brand Management*, 19(1), 44–53. https://doi.org/10.1108/10610421011018383 (archived at https://perma.cc/AH2M-47MB)

57 Avis, M., Forbes, S., & Ferguson, S. (2014). The brand personality of rocks. *Marketing Theory*, 14(4), 451–475. https://doi.org/10.1177/1470593113512323 (archived at https://perma.cc/JW7N-6EZP)

58 Fournier, S. (1998). Consumers and their brands: Developing relationship theory in consumer research. *Journal of Consumer Research*, 24(4), 343–353.
59 Fournier, S. & Yao, J. L. (1997). Reviving brand loyalty: A reconceptualization within the framework of consumer- brand relationships. *International Journal of Research in Marketing*, 14(5), 451–472. https://doi.org/10.1016/S0167-8116(97)00021-9 (archived at https://perma.cc/TB5B-HWFC)
60 Eisend, M. & Stokburger-Sauer, N. E. (2013). Brand personality: A meta-analytic review of antecedents and consequences. *Marketing Letters*, 24, 205–216.
61 Ehrenberg, A. S. C. (1996). Towards an integrated theory of consumer behaviour, *Journal of the Market Research Society*, 11(4), 305–37.
62 Sharp, B. & Romaniuk, J. (2016). *How brands grow*. Melbourne: Oxford University Press.
63 Reichheld, F. F. (1990). Zero defections: Quality comes to services. *Harvard Business Review*.
64 Romaniuk, J. & Sharp, B. (2003). Brand salience and customer defection in subscription markets. *Journal of Marketing Management*, 19(1-2), 25–44.
65 Raboud-Schüle, I. (2010). *History of cheese fondue. A matter of taste: Part 2*.
66 Rose, G. M., Merchant, A., Orth, U. R., & Horstmann, F. (2016). Emphasizing brand heritage: Does it work? And how?. *Journal of Business Research*, 69(2), 936–943.
67 Philipp-Muller, A., Costello, J. P., & Reczek, R. W. (2022). Get your science out of here: When does invoking science in the marketing of consumer products backfire? *Journal of Consumer Research*. https://doi.org/10.1093/jcr/ucac020 (archived at https://perma.cc/D2M2-E2PB)
68 Vohs, K. D., Wang, Y., Gino, F., & Norton, M. I. (2013). Rituals enhance consumption. *Psychological Science*, 24(9), 1714–1721. https://doi.org/10.1177/0956797613478949 (archived at https://perma.cc/8V4C-63EP)
69 Lebreton, M., Kawa, S., d'Arc, B. F., Daunizeau, J., & Pessiglione, M. (2012). Your goal is mine: Unraveling mimetic desires in the human brain. *Journal of Neuroscience*, 32(21), 7146–7157.
70 Cialdini, R. B., Wosinska, W., Barrett, D. W., Butner, J., & Gornik-Durose, M. (1999). Compliance with a request in two cultures: The differential influence of social proof and commitment/consistency on collectivists and individualists. *Personality and Social Psychology Bulletin*, 25(10), 1242–1253.
71 Rhodes, N., Shulman, H. C., & McClaran, N. (2020). Changing norms: A meta-analytic integration of research on social norms appeals. *Human Communication Research*, 46(2-3), 161–191.
72 Nolan, J. M., Schultz, P. W., Cialdini, R. B., Goldstein, N. J., & Griskevicius, V. (2008). Normative social influence is underdetected. *Personality and Social Psychology Bulletin*, 34(7), 913–923.
73 Higgs, S. (2015). Social norms and their influence on eating behaviours. *Appetite*, 86, 38–44.
74 Melnyk, V., van Herpen, E., & Trijp, H. (2010). The influence of social norms in consumer decision making: A meta-analysis. *ACR North American Advances*, 37, 463–464.

75 Greenwald, A. G., McGhee, D. E., & Schwartz, J. L. K. (1998). Measuring individual differences in implicit cognition: The implicit association test. *Journal of Personality and Social Psychology*, 74(6), 1464.

76 Maison, D., Greenwald, A. G., & Bruin, R. H. (2004). Predictive validity of the implicit association test in studies of brands, consumer attitudes, and behavior. *Journal of Consumer Psychology*, 14(4), 405–415. https://doi.org/10.1207/s15327663jcp1404_9 (archived at https://perma.cc/3F68-UELM)

77 Singal, J. (2017). Psychology's favourite tool for measuring racism isn't up to the job. https://www.thecut.com/2017/01/psychologys-racism-measuring-tool-isnt-up-to-the-job.html (archived at https://perma.cc/PY7Q-H94E)

78 Greenwald, A. G., Banaji, M. R., & Nosek, B. A. (2015). Statistically small effects of the Implicit Association Test can have societally large effects. *Journal of Personality and Social Psychology*, 108(4), 553–561. https://doi.org/10.1037/pspa0000016 (archived at https://perma.cc/GL2T-J555)

79 Greenwald, A. G., Poehlman, T. A., Uhlmann, E. L., & Banaji, M. R. (2009). Understanding and using the Implicit Association Test: III. Meta-analysis of predictive validity. *Journal of Personality and Social Psychology*, 97(1), 17–41. https://doi.org/10.1037/a0015575 (archived at https://perma.cc/S4EM-KKE7)

80 Raymond, J. E., Shapiro, K. L., Arnell, K. M., & Arnell, K. M. (1992). Temporary suppression of visual processing in an RSVP task-all attentional blink. *Journal of Experimental Psychology: Human Perception and Performance*, 18(3), 849–860.

81 Shapiro, K. L., Caldwell, J., & Sorensen, R. E. (1997). Personal names and the attentional blink: A visual 'cocktail party' effect. *Journal of Experimental Psychology: Human Perception and Performance*, 23(2), 504–514.

82 Bechara, A., Damasio, A. R., Damasio, H., & Anderson, S. (1994). Insensitivity to future consequences following damage to human prefrontal cortex. *Cognition*, 50(1–3), 7–15. https://doi.org/10.1016/0010-0277(94)90018-3 (archived at https://perma.cc/8YDF-TRMB)

83 Davies, J. L. & Turnbull, O. H. (2011). Affective bias in complex decision making: Modulating sensitivity to aversive feedback. *Motivation and Emotion*, 35(2), 235–248. https://doi.org/10.1007/s11031-011-9217-x (archived at https://perma.cc/8PT7-BUFS)

84 Peatfield, N., Parkinson, J., & Intriligator, J. (2012). Emotion-based learning is biased by brand logos. *Applied Cognitive Psychology*, 26(5), 694–701. https://doi.org/10.1002/acp.2847 (archived at https://perma.cc/XLL7-GPBW)

8 | The psychology of advertising

LEARNING OBJECTIVES

- Understand how the context in which an advertisement is viewed changes its effectiveness.
- Analyse the different tactics that encourage viewers to engage with advertisements and examine how these tactics differ across different media platforms.
- Critically evaluate the role of brand identity in advertising.

Introduction

When advertisers speak to psychologists, they are often focused on making sure their advert will be easy for viewers to learn and that they won't be able to forget. However, for an ad to be successful, it needs to do more than just be memorable – it ultimately needs to persuade people to change their behaviour. This is exactly the sort of question that psychologists have been investigating for the last 70 years. However, it is important to recognize that the marketing landscape has changed dramatically since 2000. For the latter half of the 20th century, the primary media advertisers were considered to be newspapers, billboards, magazines, radio, television and cinema. But since the introduction of the internet and social media, advertising is no longer a one-way broadcast medium. Consumers can now share content and interact directly with a brand. Consequently, this chapter will explore traditional approaches to advertising while the next chapter focuses on the unique challenges of applying these principles to social media. Just because something has been shown to work with traditional advertising doesn't mean it will work on social media.

Does advertising change behaviour?

It can feel like advertising is ubiquitous in modern society. While it's not possible to know how many advertisements we see each day, numerous blogs suggest 5,000 ads a day, whereas others suggest it is nearer 3,600. However, if we stop to think about these numbers and analyse them, we'll realize they almost certainly can't be true. If we take the lower estimate and assume that someone looks at each ad for just five seconds, that would mean that person spends five hours a day looking at ads. Whatever the actual number is, it is clear to see that advertising has had a large impact on society. The reason we give diamond engagement rings is an ad campaign first launched by De Beers in the 1940s.[1] The concept of 'casual Friday' or 'dress down Friday' was a campaign to sell Hawaiian shirts promoted by the Hawaiian Fashion Guild.[2] And the idea *'breakfast is the most important meal of the day'* is not based on medical research but was an advertising slogan from 1867 used to sell Grape Nuts breakfast cereal and later adopted in the 1920s by Edward Bernays to promote bacon and eggs for breakfast.[3]

Yet some people still argue that advertising doesn't work, or more often, they claim that advertising works, but not on them, what is known as the *'third person effect'*.[4] While it's true that the effectiveness of advertising is decreasing over time,[5] possibly because there is more advertising than there used to be, it still works. It is important to note that it remains more effective in the long run, at the early stage of a product's lifecycle and for more durable products than for non-durable goods.

When designing a marketing campaign of any sort, but especially with adverts, there is always a tension between focusing on short-term versus long-term gains. Ads aimed at short-term growth typically adopt a more informational focus, for instance, letting shoppers know about a new product or highlighting that Supermarket X offers 5,000 items at lower prices than Supermarket Y. These straightforward messages drive a short-term bump in sales, but this does not necessarily convert to long-term success.

When Les Binet and Peter Field analysed the Institute of Practitioners in Advertising advertising effectiveness database, a database which contains over 30 years' worth of campaign data for more than 700 brands, they were able to identify which types of adverts had the greatest impact on consumer behaviour.[6] Their conclusion was that the adverts that had the greatest long-term impact on sales were those focused on brand building. Instead of offering viewers a rational reason to buy the product, these adverts typically highlight the brand's personality, story or values, helping make the brand more salient. They typically rely on an emotional appeal and a more creative execution.

This is not to say that there isn't a place for brand activation (marketing tactics designed to trigger an immediate engagement and interaction with the brand) or that brands should ignore it. In fact, Binet and Field recommend that a brand should split its time and money 60:40. While 60% of their ads should focus on long-term brand building, the other 40% should focus on more short-term sales activation. This often means using a mixture of more emotional or fame-based campaigns with more targeted activation campaigns. However, brands should avoid trying to achieve both objectives within a single advertisement. Each campaign should have a clear focus – either brand building or tactical. Adverts that attempt to do both tend to underperform on both metrics.

Am I watching the programme or the adverts?

It doesn't matter if a brand is running a short-term or long-term campaign, best practice suggests that marketers should view things from the consumer's perspective,[7] and things are no different when it comes to advertising. Unfortunately, this is something that is often forgotten. It doesn't matter how beautifully crafted an advert is, marketers need to remember people slumped on the sofa watching TV or doom-scrolling social media probably don't want to see any adverts. The reality is that most people are only going to pay passive attention towards ads or see them in their peripheral vision.

In an ideal situation, consumers would pay close attention to adverts. However, even if they only see an advert briefly, it is enough to change what they buy.[8] In a study by Stewart Shapiro, Deborah MacInnis and Susan E. Heckler, a small advert was placed on the side of a newspaper, promoting either carrots or a tin opener. The advert was placed halfway down the left-hand column and participants were asked to just read the middle column (Figure 8.1). When researchers analysed what shoppers claimed they'd buy after reading the article, they found that people were far more likely to buy carrots when they saw the ad for carrots in their peripheral vision or a tin opener when that appeared in their peripheral vision.

This idea extends beyond print media and into other forms of advertising, such as television. People stream TV because they want to watch the programmes, not the adverts. It may sound obvious, but a brand's advert is going to be squished in between programmes and the type and content of those programmes will influence viewers' ability to recall the ads they see.

Rather than investigating the effects of individual programmes, Tavassoli, Shultz and Fitzsimons looked at two key variables: involvement and enjoyment. They found that, in most situations, there is an inverted relationship between programme involvement and both advert recall and attitude.[9] As viewers' involvement with a programme increases from low to moderate levels, the adverts surrounding it become more effective. However, as viewers become more involved, it hits a point where the adverts start to become less effective. Related to this, the more people like the programme they are watching, the less effective they are at recalling the adverts surrounding it.[10]

Figure 8.1 An example of the three different newspapers given to participants in Shapiro, MacInnis, & Heckler (1997) experiment. In each case participants were only asked to read Column B each time

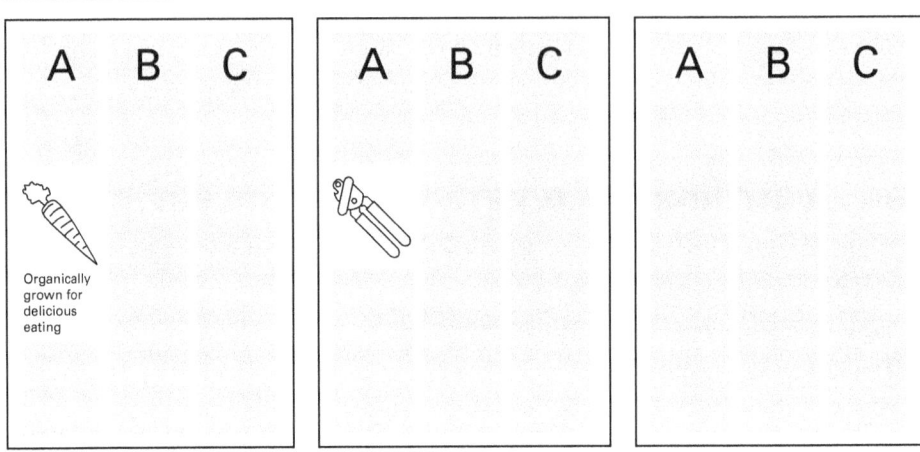

This can be explained by the change in viewers' *arousal* levels. When viewers are highly aroused (compared with moderately aroused), they tend to process the adverts more superficially.[11] The more involved in the programme, the higher the arousal levels are likely to be. It's quite easy to imagine this sort of situation for yourself: if you're casually watching something on TV that you're enjoying but not massively engaged with, you might still have quite a bit of attention and interest to spare for the adverts in the breaks. If, however, you're gripped by a really exciting, emotional, funny, disturbing or absorbing narrative, it's likely that you'll give scant attention to the adverts or even get annoyed or impatient with them for breaking the flow of your engagement.

This presents advertisers with a bit of a dilemma. The most popular programmes, the ones that offer exposure to the greatest possible audience, are also likely to be those that viewers are most aroused by. In other words, they offer a larger audience but less engagement. Shrewd advertisers and buyers address this problem with good advert design. For high involvement programmes (e.g. thrillers or major sporting events), it makes more sense for adverts to be relatively simple, and perhaps be brand-oriented rather than product-oriented, allowing highly involved viewers to process the ad and learn the message without demanding too much of their heavily diverted attention.[12] Yet it is not just the viewer's involvement that can change. Watching a television programme can change the viewer's mood as well as their arousal levels,[13] and again, this affects how an advert performs. Viewers in a positive mood tend to have a more positive attitude towards the advertised product and are ultimately more likely to purchase the advertised product than viewers in a negative mood.[14]

If someone is watching a sad programme, this can have several negative impacts for advertisers. Mathur and Chattopadhyay have shown that for low-involvement products, negative emotions triggered by the programme can be transferred to the product, so viewers end up with a more negative view of the product.[15] For high-involvement products, the situation isn't great either. Viewers in a negative mood are less likely to process the advert as deeply. On its own, this is not necessarily a negative. Lots of adverts are very successful using the peripheral route to persuasion. But when viewers are in a negative mood, the advert is less likely to trigger related thoughts and feelings in our associated network (see Chapter 5 on memory), reducing the effectiveness of the advert.[16] Consequently, if you know your advert is going to be shown during a sad programme, it makes more sense for the advert to rely more on peripheral persuasion techniques rather than logic.[17]

KEY TERMS

The central and peripheral routes to persuasion are the two different ways that marketers can persuade people according to the Elaboration Likelihood Model developed by Richard Petty and John Cacioppo.[18] The central route attempts to persuade using facts and logic, whereas the peripheral route attempts to persuade by focusing on peripheral cues. Table 8.1 shows how a marketer could try selling a razor using both the central and peripheral routes.

Table 8.1 Two different approaches to promoting a razor. One using the central route to persuasion, whereas one uses the peripheral route to persuasion

Central route	Peripheral route
Why not try our latest razor featuring our patented state-of-the-art, five-bladed system, a flexible pivot head and anti-friction coating, adapting to your unique facial contours, ensuring a smoother and more efficient shave every time.	Upgrade your grooming game with the razor that everyone's talking about! With a sleek new design and premium feel, it's no wonder this razor is the most used razor by players in the champions league.
Clinical studies show that our new design reduces skin irritation by 30% compared to other brands, providing you with the closest shave possible, with fewer strokes.	And with limited edition colour, it's more than just a shave – it's a statement. Don't miss out on the chance to own the razor that combines luxury with performance.
Choose the razor that's backed by science and trusted by professionals.	Get yours today!

The case for matching ads to programmes

The extent to which the content of adverts matches or reflects programme content can also have an effect. Intuitively, people assume that it's best for an advert to be directly relevant to the programmes around it. Typically, viewers are better able to recall an advert when the advertised product is related to the programme that follows the break.[19]

Interestingly, if the product was related to the programme *before* the break, individuals' recall is significantly worse.[20] Rather than the television programme priming viewers' memory, elements of the advert and the programme merge together in a process known as '*meltdown*'. This makes it harder for the viewer to successfully differentiate between the programme and the advert, leading to significantly poorer recall of the advert.

Advertising and branding

All too often, creative directors produce beautiful adverts with amazing, engaging, emotional storylines but can forget that the point of an advert is to sell something. To identify whether an advert falls into this trap, Bob Levenson, a hugely influential copywriter of the 1960s, created a simple test. 'If you look at an ad and fall in love with the brilliance of it, try taking the product out of it. If you still love the ad, it's no good'.[21] Yet this mantra is more than just an industry myth. Commercial research by Millward Brown,[22] analysing how easily UK shoppers could identify and recall the brand featured in an advert, and the sales it subsequently generated, showed a very strong correlation of .88, where a perfect correlation would be 1. In other words, the easier shoppers could identify and recall the brand in the advert, the more it drove actual sales.

So how can an organization increase the branded memorability of their adverts? It's not as simple as repeating the product or brand name throughout the advert. When Millward Brown analysed 1,404 different adverts, they found there was little relationship between the number of times a brand was mentioned and brand memorability.[23] Similarly, it doesn't matter when the brand is first mentioned in the advert, as, again, there is only a very weak correlation between viewers' ability to recall what the advert is for and when the brand is first mentioned (.105).

This can be explained by the fact that most viewers are unlikely to remember an advert in its entirety but instead recall one or two key points. As shown in the memory chapter, there are three points we are most likely to remember. The first item in a sequence (the *primacy effect*), the last element in a sequence (the *recency effect*)[24] and the most emotionally salient point (the *peak-end rule*).[25] When it comes to branded memorability, the peak-end effect appears to be the most important.

This creates both an opportunity and a challenge for marketing. In advertising, the single element that the viewer is likely to recall is called the '*creative magnifier*' and marketers need to ensure that this moment is branded. However, if a marketer gets this wrong and places the branding immediately after the creative magnifier, it can be one of the least effective moments to do so. The creative magnifier is typically the most emotionally salient point in the advert. People are typically focusing on this moment and fail to process what comes next, meaning the branding that follows is unlikely to be remembered.[26] This effect only lasts a second or two, but with television adverts costing thousands, every second counts and brands try and compress as much as possible into every second.

Co-branding: Are two brands really better than one?

Advertising is a great tool, but unfortunately, it can be rather expensive, especially if a company plans to run a national or even international campaign across multiple platforms. As a result, some brands opt to run a co-branding campaign, partnering with a second brand to split the costs. For example, a manufacturer of gin might choose to partner with another company that makes tonic, and between them, they can promote gin and tonics. As a tactic, this has a lot going for it on paper. First, it helps to reduce the costs, but secondly, the two brands can 'borrow' associations that the other brand has already built up. For example, if shoppers already viewed the gin brand as luxurious, the tonic brand might want to partner with that gin brand as they hope that they will be seen in a similar way – conditioning in action (as discussed in Chapter 5).

Unfortunately, this approach comes with a number of risks. Just like with any marketing, the more messages you try to get across, the less likely it is that the viewer will remember any of them. For example, data from Millward Brown's Link project argues that by including two messages in an ad, the chances that someone will remember either message drops by 35%.[27]

Similarly, when adverts use co-branding, Cathy Nguyen has shown that viewers are far less likely to remember either brand that featured in the advert,[28] which is ultimately the goal of advertising. Despite this, some marketers may think that the trade-off is worth it. If this is the case, then they need to design the ad carefully. In a TV ad, if the two brands are introduced together, then viewers have a lower brand evaluation for the less-known brand. However, if the two brands are introduced separately, after seeing the ad, evaluations of the lesser-known brand improve.[29]

Print and billboard advertising

Television advertising may be the most glamorous and expensive form of advertising, but unless a brand has a very generous budget, this is unlikely to be an option.

Instead, their marketing efforts are more likely to focus on digital, print or billboard ads. So, how best to brand them? All too often, when designing print ads, marketers place their logo in the bottom right corner. Unfortunately, this is a bad idea, as this place is known as the *corner of death*. From an eye-tracking perspective, Dan Hill has shown people spend on average 1.7 seconds looking at a print advert, but the lower right-hand corner is the second to last place people look on the page (the last place for an A4 print ad is the right-hand side, what's known as the *alley of death*).[30]

So, how should you brand a print or billboard ad? Lex Meurs and Mandy Aristoff showed 187 Dutch outdoor adverts to participants using a tachistoscope, a device used to display pictures for a specific length of time, and accurately measured how long it took participants to recognize the brand and product in the advert. They concluded that, where possible, brands should try to avoid having lengthy headlines, large body copy and avoid including the brand name in the headline. Long headlines and a large amount of body copy can put people off and delay product and brand recognition. Likewise, including a brand name in the headline reduces the ad's appeal.[31] Instead, having a clear photo of the product and clear and consistent branding really helps product recognition and to viewers liking the ad.

This is why it is crucial for brands to follow a clear set of visual guidelines, consistently using the same colour palette, typeface and overall look and feel. Over time, shoppers learn to associate these elements with the brand, allowing them to recognize an advert more quickly than if each advert used a different font, colour scheme or photography style.

Advertisement imagery

Including a picture of the product in an ad works because, in virtually all cases, the first element that captures the viewer's attention is the image.[32] But a good image needs to do more than be aesthetically appealing. Subtle cues that initially appear irrelevant have a significant impact on an advert's success. A good example of this is how the photo is lit. In virtually all situations, photos are lit from above as we are used to sunlight coming from above. However, consumers' natural tendency is to assume that the light source is not directly above, but slightly to the left and as a result they prefer photos that are lit from the left.[33]

Artists intuitively understand this preference. Visiting the Louvre in Paris, 72% of all portraits in the gallery are lit from the left, as it makes the portraits more appealing. Jennifer Hutchison, Nicole Thomas and Lorin Elias have taken this approach and extended it to advertising. They have shown that if advertisers light their adverts from the left, these adverts are more effective than those lit from the right.[34] Viewers perceive the product more positively and, more importantly, are more likely to purchase the product. Interestingly enough, this phenomenon appears to be strongest when targeting younger consumers. As people age, this left bias starts to wane, and people start to prefer photos that are lit directly above. While most photographers subconsciously know this, and light images from the left, it is not uncommon for designers to flip the photo, so the image works better with the rest of the design, undoing the photographer's natural instinct.

The left/right bias has an importance beyond lighting. When photographing a product to use in an advert, photographers need to think carefully. Is the product set up for a right- or left-handed person? You might wonder how, say, a yoghurt could be biased towards a left- or right-handed person, but small cues will make a difference. Do you place the spoon on the left or right side of the carton? How about a trigger on a bottle of bleach: is it oriented so that you would naturally grab it with your left or right hand? So why is this important? Well, the affordances of a product can change how easily a customer can imagine using that product, and this directly affects their purchase intentions.[35] When Ryan Elder and Aradhna Krishna showed participants an advert for a smooth vanilla yoghurt, with either the spoon on the right or left side of the bowl, purchase intention was nearly 20% higher when the spoon was placed on the side of the bowl that matched a consumer's dominant hand. As 90% of people are right-handed, it makes sense if adverts and product packaging target right-handers.

The 'perfect' smile

Not all adverts focus solely on the product. Many also include photos of people, and from what we know of the psychology involved, this makes sense. Humans have evolved as social creatures and, as such, people are naturally drawn to images of people's faces.[36] In adverts, the model is usually smiling;[37] this often leads to viewers evaluating the message more favourably.[38] Unfortunately, not all smiles are created equal. Smiles can either be classed as genuine or polite.[39] Genuine smiles (sometimes known as Duchenne's smile) are what spontaneously occur when you are happy, as the cheek muscles (the zygomatic major) cause the corners of our lips to rise up in the classic smile. But it is more than that; the smile reaches our eyes as the orbicularis oculi muscles contract temporarily (commonly known as crows' feet).

Polite smiles are fundamentally different. Rather than being an instinctive reaction, we pull a polite smile when we feel that the situation requires us to smile. This could be when we hear a bad joke or if a friend asks us if we like their new outfit (and we do not). But it is not just the context that defines the difference between smiles. With a polite smile, the corner of our lips will still rise, but that's it; the smile does not reach our eyes. While the two may sound similar, if we are presented with two faces, one showing a polite smile, the other a genuine smile, most people can easily identify which is which.[40] Even children as young as six or seven can identify these differences.[41]

When it comes to marketing and producing adverts, it is important for firms to ensure that models feature genuine rather than polite smiles. Research conducted in food outlets has shown that servers who have a genuine smile receive bigger tips than those who only smile politely,[42] and product packaging that features genuine smiles outperforms polite smiles.

This effect also applies in a supermarket context. When Philip Adcock redesigned the packaging for a leading mouthwash brand sold in UK supermarkets, he replaced the model's polite smile with a genuine one. He then tested the impact of his new design by selling the original packaging in some supermarkets and the redesigned version in others. The results: sales of the new product featuring the genuine smile were 12% higher.[43] One small design change led to a large impact on sales.

While the smile is important, other researchers argue that marketers need to be aware of a model's facial expressions as a whole. Numerous psychologists argue that we have six core emotions (anger, disgust, fear, happiness, sadness and surprise, and a seventh, contempt, is sometimes added) and that each emotion has its own unique physiological fingerprint.[44] This idea was originally proposed by Carl-Herman Hjortsjö, but it was the work of Paul Ekman in 1978 that really extended this concept. Because it was unclear if facial expressions were a learnt reaction or an innate response, Ekman went to Papua New Guinea to research one of the few surviving Palaeolithic cultures that had yet to have contact with the western world. He showed the tribespeople photos of people pulling one of the six different facial expressions and asked them to create a story, guessing what had happened just before the photo was taken. The stories the tribespeople told perfectly matched the facial expressions, suggesting that our understanding of facial expressions is universal and instinctive.[45]

While sounding convincing, it is important to note that Ekman's research is controversial, and most psychologists now discount his findings. Research led by Erika Siegel analysing how 8,400 different participants reacted to a range of emotional states, shows that there does not appear to be a *consistent* physiological response to each emotional state, and that variation appears to be the norm.[46] As such, using facial expressions as a research technique seems unreliable at best,[47] and hence companies such as Microsoft have phased out AI-powered facial analysis tools that claimed to identify participants' emotional states from videos and pictures after it proved to be unreliable.[48]

But even if facial expressions are an unreliable research tool, marketers need to be aware of them because people think they can recognize people's emotions based on their facial expressions.[49] This would suggest that when it comes to developing adverts, photographers and videographers need to be very aware of the expression their models are showing. They may be smiling, but is their expression showing happiness, disgust or, even worse, contempt? It is not hard to imagine a situation where a model could be caught showing the wrong emotion. Imagine a model who does not have any children being asked to cuddle a baby and pretend that they are the parent. If the model is uneasy with children, and moments before the photo is taken, the baby was crying, what expression is the model going to be showing, however hard he or she tries to force a smile? Likewise, if a model is asked to wear some clothes they think are unfashionable, what expression is going to be on their face?

The eyes

Looking into someone's eyes can help reveal a lot about them and their interaction with you, which is why when we're talking with someone, we tend to focus primarily on the other person's eyes.[50,51] So how does this relate to adverts? Assuming a print or billboard ad is using a positive emotional appeal, it is more effective for the model to not look directly at the viewer. If they do, it can feel intimidating and lower overall engagement with the ad. However, if a government is running an informational advert or using a negative emotional appeal, such as part of a drink-drive campaign, it can be more effective for the model to look directly at the viewer.[52] In these situations, you want the viewer to feel like they are being held accountable, and looking directly at the audience is one way to achieve this. The downside is that viewers will spend less time looking at the ad when the model is looking straight at the viewer,[53] meaning your message needs to be quick and easy to process.

If the model is not going to be looking directly at the viewer, then we can use their eye-gaze to help ensure they read the headline or pay attention to the call to action. If we see people looking in a certain direction, most people tend to follow the gaze, as we want to know what they are looking at. Hutton and Nolte have shown that if the model in an advert is looking at your headline, call to action or even QR code, the viewer is also more likely to look at it.[54] In practice, this meant that viewers are better able to both recognize and recall the brand more successfully when the model is looking at the brand.[55] There are only two catches. Firstly, this effect doesn't work when the model is a famous celebrity. Celebrities capture and hold our attention. Consequently, we spend most of our time looking at the celebrity and are less likely to notice the branded message or call to action.[56] Secondly, if the goal of an advert is to make the viewer feel personally accountable, such as in a demarketing campaign asking viewers when they last flushed a wet wipe down the toilet, or a charity appeal questioning when they last made a donation, it is more effective for the model to look directly at the viewer rather than the call to action. Looking directly at the audience increases their sense of personal responsibility, making viewers more likely to comply with the advert's message.[57]

To think or not to think?

Normally, an advertiser's goal is to make sure that the viewer's brain doesn't have to work too hard to process an advert. This is because people generally find exerting mental effort unpleasant.[58] The harder our brain needs to work to process a stimulus (what psychologists call '*processing fluency*', the less people like it.[59]

This means making sure that the advert is visually simple, that any text is large and easy to read, and the visuals use clear contrast colours. For television adverts, the advert should include a number of familiar elements, such as faces or settings, and the key messages or points should be repeated a number of times to make it easier for people to learn (including repeating the advert). Although ads may like to surprise the viewer, they should still feel natural, not out of place. However, there are times when marketers will deliberately make an advert harder to process.

Rather than making sure the message is perfectly clear, they'll ask the reader to create part of the message. For example, when Cancer Research UK ran an ad campaign highlighting that obesity is the biggest 'preventable' cause of cancer, rather than just explicitly stating this, the advert said: '*OB_S_ _ Y is a cause of cancer*' or '*Guess what is the biggest preventable cause of cancer after smoking?*' It seems odd, but asking people to come up with part of the stimulus means that they are far better at remembering the message.[60] The reader is required to think more deeply about the message, making it more memorable. Hence when people were asked to read a list of five different brand names, as shown in Table 8.2, participants were 14% better at recalling the list when the brand name had one letter missing out of the name than when they were spelled correctly.[61]

Another similar tactic to encourage deeper processing of an advert is to use a rhetorical question in the headline[62] or to use a metaphor. At first glance, a metaphor might make no sense, until you stop to think about it. Since people dislike not understanding a reference, they pause to think about it, making these ads more effective at changing behaviour.[63] Not only are they more effective at changing behaviour, people are also more likely to remember these adverts and the target brand.[64]

The only catch is that if a brand is using a metaphor, be it a visual or lexical one, they want to make sure that the audience understands it. When a viewer 'solves' a metaphor, they feel a sense of accomplishment, meaning they view the advert more positively.[65] But if they can't, the reverse is true, with viewers perceiving both the advert and the brand negatively.[66] Hence, it makes more sense to use a metaphor when you know that your viewer is likely to have the time or motivation to engage in your message, such as on a tram or train.

Table 8.2 The stimuli used in Shotton, Treharne, & Burnett's 2020 study

List 1	List 2
HSBC	H_BC
Ford	F_rd
McDonald's	McD_nald's
Amazon	Amaz_n
Facebook	F_cebook

Humour and advertising

An alternative approach to increase engagement could be to use humour. Despite what marketers may convince themselves of, consumers don't sit around talking about adverts. But if they are going to talk about an advert with friends, there is a good chance it will be a funny ad. It's not just that these adverts are talked about more, but they *can* be more successful, assuming humour is used appropriately. On average, people pay more attention to humorous adverts, like these adverts more and, most importantly of all, like the brand more. The only downside is the fact that it can negatively impact the brand's credibility[67] – but this is only likely to be an issue for a 'serious' brand, for example, an investment bank.

If a brand does opt to use humour, research shows that generally consumers prefer ads that make use of clever jokes – a joke where the viewer needs to make a mental connection to 'solve' the joke. Just like with a metaphor, when brands use clever jokes, viewers have a more positive brand attitude and are more likely to engage with the brand.[68] A great example of this is an advert from *The Economist* that uses the line '*I never read The Economist: Management trainee. Aged 42*'. It's funny (assuming you're a reader of *The Economist*), and helps to position *The Economist* as the sort of newspaper read by successful business people. But it's hard to argue that it's not a little arrogant, which is a dangerous combination for a brand. Haakon Brown has shown that when brands are perceived to be arrogant, their current users of the product like the brand more but people who don't buy the brand end up having a worse view of the brand,[69] and are less likely to buy the brand. This is a problem, as the only long-term sustainable way to grow a brand is to win new customers. Convincing current users to buy more will not drive growth in the long term.[70]

Brand managers might be nervous about using humour, as it may not fit with their brand image (which is a legitimate concern) or they may think it's not appropriate for their product category, such as personal hygiene products. But if done well, this is not the case. Humorous ads often perform better than informative campaigns, the style of adverts the above category normally runs. They can help counteract the negative reaction people have when buying these products which increases the likelihood they'll actually buy them.[71]

The risk is that humour is subjective. What one person finds funny, someone else might not or, worse, will find it distasteful.[72] Brands need to make sure that they sufficiently understand their audience to ensure their jokes land. Secondly, brands need to ensure that the humour is linked to the brand. When viewers remember the joke, they also need to be able to remember the brand or message – hopefully both.

Advertisement copy

Although the image may be the first thing that captures a viewer's attention, virtually all adverts will also include words — or 'copy'. In the context of print and online adverts, small changes to the way copy is written or presented have a big impact on its effectiveness. While Chapter 6 explores how marketers need to choose the right words, they also need to display them correctly – getting the right font, typesetting and spacing. Often, if a naive advertiser wants their message to jump out, they place the message in block capitals. Unfortunately, this is usually a bad idea as people find text written in block capitals less legible,[73] and Miles Tinker has shown it takes people significantly longer to read text written in block capitals compared to copy written in sentence case, somewhere between 10–20% longer depending on the individual.[74]

This occurs because words written in lowercase have more distinctive shape patterns. As we learn to read, we are regularly exposed to the same words over and over again, and we learn to recognize their shapes, rather than reading each individual letter.[75] This would suggest that when designing a billboard that is going to be placed somewhere where people are only going to see the ad for a short time (e.g. next to a road), it makes sense to avoid block capitals. But there are some situations where block capitals may make sense. Most of the research investigating legibility explores how capitals affect the reading of text close up. When reading text from a distance of over 17 feet, the uppercase headlines are perceived as more legible,[76] although this might be explained by the fact that block capitals are slightly larger than lower-case letters of the same font size. Given the choice, it probably makes more sense to increase the size of your message rather than using block capitals.

Sexual appeal in advertising

There has always been a lot of controversy over the use of sexual appeal in advertising. This is perhaps unsurprising, considering that globally 28% of all adverts featured some degree of female nudity (e.g. wearing a bikini or revealing clothing) and 13% feature male nudity (e.g. topless man).[77] Is it appropriate in the 21st century? What impact does it have, and more importantly, is it effective? While the first question needs to be answered by society as a whole, consumer psychologists can help answer the other questions.

Advertisers have historically been keen to use it because of the belief that sex sells. From an evolutionary perspective, this makes sense. Humans have evolved to be attracted to and pay attention to sexual cues.[78] If an advert features an attractive scantily-clad individual, it grabs our attention. But the simple fact that sex grabs attention does not automatically make it an effective advertising tool, as we'll see.

When researchers analysed 78 different studies, they discovered that viewers are more likely to remember adverts that use sex appeal than those that do not.[79] But does the fact that people are more likely to remember sexualized adverts imply that sexualization is a good idea? The problem is, it's not just the advert that we need to remember; viewers need to remember the brand, too. When, in another study, brand recall was tested in the context of sexualized advertising, it was shown that there is no significant impact on viewers' ability to recognize or recall the ad. While it's easy to point to isolated examples, such as Axe/Lynx, Dolce & Gabbana, or Old Spice, who successfully use sensual imagery in their ads, these appear to be isolated examples and not the norm.

The ultimate test of an advert is whether it makes us more likely to buy the product. When researchers tested this, there was no significant difference between adverts that used sexual appeal and those that did not.[80] But what is more worrying is that ads that make use of it have been shown to have a negative effect on the way that consumers ultimately perceive the brand, assuming the product is not connected to sex (e.g. a beauty product).

> **NATURE OR NURTURE?**
>
> Researchers and sociologists have argued about whether society teaches us that we should pay attention to sexual imagery or if it is an evolved tendency. To try to answer this question, a team of researchers investigated how a group of participants responded to sexual imagery in advertising. But the participants were unusual: instead of being humans, they were rhesus macaques (a very social monkey). In a variation on a classical conditioning paradigm, the researchers showed the monkeys a variety of different brand logos. Each logo was paired with an image of either (a) a male macaque with a high social status; (b) a male macaque with a low social status; or (c) the genitals of a female macaque. Later, the monkeys were shown just the logos and they had to select their favourite. The monkeys preferred the brands that were paired with dominant males or female genitals.[81]

The situation appears to be even more problematic on social media. Marketers can get preoccupied by easy-to-measure metrics such as likes and reshares. Posts that make use of sex appeal are interacted with more than those that don't, but this engagement doesn't convert into sales;[82] partly because these posts are viewed as less credible[83] and partly because they are distracting. But even if a brand decides not to use an explicit sexual appeal, there is still the temptation to use a highly attractive model. Whether this is morally right is up for society to decide, however, the business case is more complex than we may first think.

Outside of advertising, people on Kiva (a platform similar to JustGiving) are more likely to donate more money to more attractive, less overweight people, and those who have a lighter skin colour.[84] A one-standard-deviation increase in attractiveness meant that person reached their funding target 11% quicker. Likewise, a one-standard-deviation increase in obesity meant that they were 12% slower to reach their funding target. Even just having a photo of someone of the opposite sex on a website where people make donations is enough to increase the average donation size, for both men and women, although the effect is strongest for males.[85]

As for advertising, if you're promoting a product which is connected to making someone look more attractive or enhancing their appearance, such as a beauty product, it makes sense to use highly attractive models. Likewise, if a brand is trying to encourage men to purchase more high-status products, it is more effective for the advert to feature physically dominant male models.[86] However, if your product is connected to solving a practical problem, it makes no difference whether you use a highly attractive model or an average-looking model[87] and, in many ways, it is easier for people to relate to a normal-looking model than a perfect-looking model.

Reactance theory

Whether we like to admit it or not, advertising is a direct attempt to influence people. It could be trying to persuade people to vote for a political candidate, recycle more rubbish or buy a particular breakfast cereal. But directly manipulating people carries risks. We've all probably experienced this. For example, if you tell a child that they are not allowed to play outside, they suddenly want to do just that. At a psychological level, what the child is experiencing is *reactance*.[88]

Reactance occurs when we feel like our freedom to act is being threatened and the only way we can restore this freedom is to rebel against the instructions. Consequently, when we are aware that someone is deliberately trying to persuade us to do something, it can actually have a boomerang effect, causing us to be less likely to comply with their wishes.[89] Take unskippable ads on YouTube; we may get frustrated that we're being forced to watch the advert and so we may start to feel that we like the brand less.

In a series of five controlled laboratory experiments, researchers showed that when participants were shown brand names vs slogans, brands primed people to spend more, whereas slogans had a reverse priming effect. They actually lead people to spend less.[90] The authors speculate that the advertising slogans triggered a reaction as consumers perceived the slogan as a deliberate attempt to persuade them to buy certain products. In contrast, they did not view branding as a persuasion tactic; they simply thought of it as a label.

Yet advertisers can avoid the risk of reactance if they are careful. Rather than explicitly telling people to do something and risk taking away the viewer's autonomy, they can give reasons why you should do something but let people make up their own mind. Hence, instead of saying '*don't drink and drive*', they might say: '*Can you afford to lose your job if you get caught drink driving?*' Or if they wanted to use a less logical appeal (the peripheral route to persuasion in the Elaboration Likelihood Model), they could use a message such as: '*Your friends don't drink and drive…*' or even just use a celebrity saying, '*If I've had a drink, I'll call an uber*'.

Online, the risk of reactance is just the same, but different things are capable of triggering reactance. From an advertising perspective, one exciting opportunity is the ability to personalize adverts. Depending on a user's previous online behaviour, marketers can change which adverts a user sees, or even the content of these adverts – personalizing the imagery or even the slogan used. Ads that are targeted to a person's interest, location and age outperform those that don't.[91] However, some people find hyper-personalized adverts too much, which can trigger reactance[92] – unless they've given consent. Brands need to get this balance right. Yet reactance is complex; it is possible for an advert to trigger reactance (a negative emotion) and still persuade.[93] People can feel an emotional frustration at being forced to do something, but still comply. In this case, the brand needs to weigh up the pros and cons in each situation. Is the change in behaviour or the emotional damage more important in the long run?

REAL-WORLD EXAMPLE: PSYCH IN ACTION

In 2022, the Mayor of London's office, in collaboration with Ogilvy Consulting, launched the 'Say maate to a mate' campaign, an initiative aimed to encourage young men not to engage in sexist banter or to make sexist jokes. Most people may have thought that the odd sexist joke isn't a problem, but it establishes a social norm that it is acceptable to view women as sexual objects – which can ultimately lead to violence against women. In the past, adverts which tried to tackle this issue have targeted the people making the comments directly and tried to persuade them to change their behaviour, but this ad tried something different.

A key cornerstone of behaviour change is the idea that it is a lot easier to convince someone to start a new behaviour than it is to stop an existing behaviour. So rather than the ad trying to persuade young men to stop making sexist jokes, they wanted their friends to call out any jokes that went too far by saying '*maate*'. From a psychological perspective, this was a shrewd move. They weren't trying to stop a behaviour, but to start a new behaviour, which helps avoid reactance. While you're still being told not to do something, it is a lot better to be told by your friends, rather than the government. People want to fit in with their friends, so if they realize their friends disapprove of something, they are less likely to repeat that action. Secondly, by having a large number of billboards around London, it created a social norm, that it was acceptable to call out such behaviour, when in the past people might have felt uncomfortable to do so. Finally, according to WPP's 2024 report, it created an acceptable language for everybody to use and get behind.[94]

The risk of advertising avoidance

While most marketers recognize the fact that viewers are only going to pay passive attention to their adverts, there are times when viewers will actively try to avoid them.

When we are actively engaged in a task, like watching a video, and something gets in the way, we subconsciously learn to ignore the distracting stimulus. Indirectly, we are training ourselves to ignore it, and this leads us to develop a negative perception of the distraction.[95] While this effect was originally demonstrated in a laboratory experiment with participants looking for random visual patterns, the same effect has now been shown to occur with ads online. Duff and Faber's 2011 article discussed how, when adverts were placed on a website and the user was actively trying to ignore them, they ended up developing a negative attitude towards the brand, even when they were not consciously aware of the brand in the advert[96] – what's known as the '*Distractor Devaluation Effect*'. The size of this effect all comes down to how easy the consumer finds the information to ignore.

Conventional wisdom dictates that online ads should be as similar as possible to the main content on the webpage. Unfortunately, this could actually make the distractor devaluation effect worse. Because viewers find it harder to distinguish between what's advertising and what's content, they subconsciously work harder to ignore the adverts – magnifying the effect. In an ideal world, you want the content of your ad to be relevant to the viewers of the website, but for it to be obvious to the viewer that it is not part of the site.

What happens if a brand stops advertising?

At some point, when budgets get tight, brands may be tempted to stop advertising or at least reduce the amount they advertise. So, is this a good business decision or will it just make the situation worse? From a research perspective, it's a hard question to answer as there is no way to do a randomized control study. However, by tracking how the market share of 365 US brands, across different sectors, changed after they stopped advertising for at least 12 months, researchers can begin to get some answers. On average, a brand's market share declined by 10% after one year of no advertising, 20% after two years and 28% after three years relative to the last advertised year.[97] However, there was a large degree of variation between brands and even sectors. Typically, consumer goods that are bought relatively infrequently suffered a bigger drop in sales when compared to goods that are bought more frequently. Either way, stopping advertising may save a small amount of money in the short term, but it will cost you a lot more money in the mid to long term.

Closing thoughts

Advertising is a key part of an organization's communication strategy and by applying insights from psychology, businesses can significantly improve the effectiveness of their campaigns. This doesn't mean brands need to start from scratch. Often, simply making small adjustments to existing brand assets can have a big impact. Simple changes like repositioning a brand logo, altering lighting angles or switching the font all have an impact. And when all these subtle tweaks are combined, the overall effect can be substantial.

> **KEY POINTS**
>
> - On average, the most successful brands spend 60% of their advertising budget on long-term brand building and the other 40% on more short-term sales activation campaigns.
> - Viewers don't need to look directly at an advert for it to change our behaviour; seeing things in our peripheral vision can change our behaviour.
> - Adverts are more effective when viewers are moderately engaged with the programme they surround, but as engagement or enjoyment increases further, viewers become less attentive to the ads because their heightened arousal levels cause them to process ads more superficially.
> - When watching an advert, the moment people are most likely to remember is the most emotionally salient point, hence this moment needs to be branded.
> - With print adverts, images capture attention more than text.
> - For adverts that are only glanced at, they need to be very easy to process. However, if people have the time or motivation to engage with an advert, they can encourage elaboration, which leads to a more memorable ad.
> - Adverts that use jokes are typically more memorable and persuasive, whereas adverts that use sex are often more likely to grab people's attention, but less likely to change behaviour.
> - Rather than explicitly telling people to do something, it is more effective to suggest a course of action and let the viewer make up their own mind.

PUTTING THEORY INTO PRACTICE

1 When it comes to creating an advertisement, what tactics can encourage people to engage with the advert, but are unlikely to positively change consumer behaviour? Can you find five examples of adverts that make these mistakes?

2 Imagine you have been briefed to produce a print advert to encourage 18–25 year olds to not binge drink. What principles and tactics would you use in your advert? Would these principles still be appropriate if you were going to try to encourage the same viewers to buy fast-moving consumer goods?

3 Watch the advertisements that appear during a television show or YouTube video of your choice. How might the content of the programme influence your perception of the ads shown during the break? If you were a brand manager for one of the ads, would you want to change its scheduling?

4 Find an example of an advert where the marketer has deliberately decreased the ad's processing fluency. Do you think that this has made the advert more or less successful, bearing in mind the context in which the ad will be viewed?

5 When creating an advertisement, marketers must balance short-term sales targets with long-term brand-building objectives. How might an advert aimed at short-term sales differ from one focused on long-term brand building? Consider what you've learnt in the chapter on learning and memory as well.

6 Watch a sample of television adverts on YouTube and identify the most emotionally salient point or the creative magnifier. Was this moment appropriately branded? If not, how could you change the design of the advert to make the brand more memorable.

7 Imagine you are the creative director at an advertising agency, and you've been asked to produce a billboard advert promoting an electric razor. Provide creative direction for your designer for the choice of model in the advert and how you'd like the advert to look.

SUGGESTIONS FOR FURTHER READING

Ferrier, A. & Fleming, J. (2014). *The advertising effect*. Oxford University Press, US.

Du Plessis, E. (2008). *The advertised mind: Groundbreaking insights into how our brains respond to advertising*. Kogan Page, London, UK.

References

1. Twitchell, J. (2001). *Twenty ads that shook the world: The century's most groundbreaking advertising and how it changed us all*. Crown.
2. Garber, M. (2016, 25 May). Casual Friday and the 'end of the office dress code'. *The Atlantic*. https://www.theatlantic.com/entertainment/archive/2016/05/casual-friday-and-the-end-of-the-office-dress-code/484334/ (archived at https://perma.cc/NEJ4-JLSE)
3. Nassara, M. (2024). They lied to you: How a marketing campaign became science. Medium. https://medium.com/@miminassara/how-a-marketing-campaign-became-science-44c160bd7af3 (archived at https://perma.cc/TH8S-T26W)
4. Eisend, M. (2017). The third-person effect in advertising: A meta-analysis. *Journal of Advertising*, 46(3), 377–394.
5. Sethuraman, R., Tellis, G. J., & Briesch, R. A. (2011). How well does advertising work? Generalizations from meta-analysis of brand advertising elasticities. *Journal of Marketing Research*, 48(3), 457–471.
6. Binet, L. & Field, P. (2013). *The long and the short of it: Balancing short and long-term marketing strategies*. Institute of Practitioners in Advertising.
7. Lemon, K. N. & Verhoef, P. C. (2016). Understanding customer experience throughout the customer journey. *Journal of Marketing*, 80(6), 69–96.
8. Shapiro, S., MacInnis, D. J., & Heckler, S. E. (1997). The effects of incidental ad exposure on the formation of consideration sets. *Journal of Consumer Research*, 24(1), 94–104. https://doi.org/10.1086/209496 (archived at https://perma.cc/DVX9-V8U9)
9. Tavassoli, N. T., Shultz, C., & Fitzsimons, G. J. (1995). Program involvement: Are moderate levels best for ad memory and attitude toward the ad? *Journal of Advertising Research*, 35(5), 61–72. https://faculty.fuqua.duke.edu/~gavan/bio/GJF_articles/program_involvement_jar_95.pdf (archived at https://perma.cc/5KRV-5A7F)
10. Furnham, A., Gunter, B., & Walsh, D. (1998). Effects of programme context on memory of humorous television commercials. *Applied Cognitive Psychology*, 12(6), 555–567.
11. Shapiro, S., MacInnis, D. J., & Park, C. W. (2002). Understanding program-induced mood effects: Decoupling arousal from valence. *Journal of Advertising*, 31(4), 15–26. https://doi.org/10.1080/00913367.2002.10673682 (archived at https://perma.cc/EZ4H-T7MC)
12. Tavassoli, N. T., II, C. J. S., & Fitzsimons, G. J. (1995). Program involvement: Are moderate levels best for ad memory and attitude toward the ad? *Journal of Advertising Research*, 35(5), 61–72.
13. Newell, S., Henderson, K., & Wu, B. (2001). The effects of pleasure and arousal on recall of advertisements during the Super Bowl. *Psychology and Marketing*, 18(11), 1135–1153. https://doi.org/10.1002/mar.1047 (archived at https://perma.cc/MX36-NESX)
14. Owolabi, A. B. (2009). Effect of consumers mood on advertising effectiveness. *Europes Journal of Psychology*, 4, 118–127.
15. Mathur, M. & Chattopadhyay, A. (1991). The impact of moods generated by television programs on responses to advertising. *Psychology and Marketing*, 8(1), 59–77. https://doi.org/10.1002/mar.4220080106 (archived at https://perma.cc/T8R4-E7VF)

16 Mathur, M. & Chattopadhyay, A. (1991). The impact of moods generated by television programs on responses to advertising. *Psychology and Marketing*, 8(1), 59–77. https://doi.org/10.1002/mar.4220080106 (archived at https://perma.cc/HVN4-MTNV)

17 Aylesworth, A. B. & MacKenzie, S. B. (1998). Context is key: The effect of program-induced mood on thoughts about the ad. *Journal of Advertising*, 27(2), 17–31. https://doi.org/10.1080/00913367.1998.10673550 (archived at https://perma.cc/789V-TYQR)

18 Petty, R. E. & Cacioppo, J. T. (1986). *The elaboration likelihood model of persuasion* (pp. 1–24). Springer New York.

19 Furnham, A., Bergland, J., & Gunter, B. (2002). Memory for television advertisements as a function of advertisement-programme congruity. *Applied Cognitive Psychology*, 16(5), 525–545. https://doi.org/10.1002/acp.812 (archived at https://perma.cc/8PV7-6K4J)

20 Furnham, A., Gunter, B., & Richardson, F. (2002). Effects of product-program congruity and viewer involvement on memory for televised advertisements. *Journal of Applied Social Psychology*, 32(1), 124–141.

21 Levenson, B. (1988). *Bill Bernbach's book: A history of the advertising that changed the history of advertising*. Villard Books.

22 Brown, M. (2005). *Brands and advertising*. Sage.

23 Brown, M. (2005). *Brands and advertising*. Sage.

24 Glanzer, M. & Cunitz, A. R. (1966). Two storage mechanisms in free recall. *Journal of Verbal Learning and Verbal Behavior*, 5(4), 531–360.

25 Fredrickson, B. L. & Kahneman, D. (1993). Duration neglect in retrospective evaluations of affective episodes. *Journal of Personality and Social Psychology*, 65(1), 45–55.

26 Shapiro, K. L., Raymond, J. E., & Arnell, K. M. (1997). The attentional blink. *Trends in Cognitive Sciences*, 1(8), 291–296.

27 Kurtzman, W. (2019, October 8). Too many messages! Coleman Insights. https://colemaninsights.com/coleman-insights-blog/too-many-messages (archived at https://perma.cc/N4AN-TAD4)

28 Nguyen, C., Romaniuk, J., Faulkner, M., & Cohen, J. (2018). Are two brands better than one? Investigating the effects of co-branding in advertising on audience memory. *Marketing Letters*, 29(1), 37–48.

29 Cunha Jr, M., Forehand, M. R., & Angle, J. W. (2015). Riding coattails: When co-branding helps versus hurts less-known brands. *Journal of Consumer Research*, 41(5), 1284–1300. https://doi.org/10.1086/679119 (archived at https://perma.cc/YK2W-5FZM)

30 Hill, D. (2010). *About face: The secrets of emotionally effective advertising*. Kogan Page.

31 Van Meurs, L. & Aristoff, M. (2009). Split-second recognition: What makes outdoor advertising work?. *Journal of Advertising Research*, 49(1), 82–92.

32 Pieters, R. & M, W. (2004). Attention capture and transfer in advertising: Brand, pictorial, and text-size effects. *Journal of Marketing*, 68(2), 36–50. https://doi.org/10.1509/jmkg.68.2.36.27794 (archived at https://perma.cc/2743-42SE)

33 Sun, J. & Perona, P. (1998). Where is the sun? *Nature Neuroscience*, 1(3), 183–184. https://doi.org/10.1038/630 (archived at https://perma.cc/4KBX-4EKT)

34 Hutchison, J., Thomas, N. A., & Elias, L. (2011). Leftward lighting in advertisements increases advertisement ratings and purchase intention. *Laterality: Asymmetries of Body, Brain and Cognition*, 16(4), 423–432. https://doi.org/10.1080/13576501003702663 (archived at https://perma.cc/Y2RX-5AEJ)

35 Elder, R. S. & Krishna, A. (2012). The 'visual depiction effect' in advertising: Facilitating embodied mental simulation through product orientation. *Journal of Consumer Research*, 38(6), 988–1003. https://doi.org/10.1086/661531 (archived at https://perma.cc/X5JT-YHVJ)

36 Theeuwes, J. & Stigchel, S. V. der. (2006). Faces capture attention: Evidence from inhibition of return. *Visual Cognition*, 13(6), 657–665. https://doi.org/10.1080/13506280500410949 (archived at https://perma.cc/GG9H-HLLJ)

37 Petroshius, S. M. & Crocker, K. E. (1989). An empirical analysis of spokesperson characteristics on advertisement and product evaluations. *Journal of the Academy of Marketing Science*, 17(3), 217–225. https://doi.org/10.1007/bf02729813 (archived at https://perma.cc/B59N-CFNA)

38 Berg, H., Söderlund, M., & Lindström, A. (2015). Spreading joy: Examining the effects of smiling models on consumer joy and attitudes. *Journal of Consumer Marketing*, 32(6), 459–469.

39 Shore, D. M. & Heerey, E. A. (2011). The value of genuine and polite smiles. *Emotion*, 11(1), 169–174. https://doi.org/10.1037/a0022601 (archived at https://perma.cc/GL3J-VNKW)

40 Frank, M. G., Ekman, P., & Friesen, W. V. (1993). Behavioral markers and recognizability of the smile of enjoyment. *Journal of Personality and Social Psychology*, 64(1), 83–93.

41 Gosselin, P., Perron, M., & Maassarani, R. (2009). Children's ability to distinguish between enjoyment and non-enjoyment smiles. *Infant and Child Development*, 15. https://doi.org/10.1002/icd.648 (archived at https://perma.cc/4QML-H7RL)

42 Bujisic, M., Wu, L. L., Mattila, A., & Bilgihan, A. (2014). Not all smiles are created equal. *International Journal of Contemporary Hospitality Management*, 26(2), 293–306. https://doi.org/10.1108/ijchm-10-2012-0181 (archived at https://perma.cc/PLN8-L4BQ)

43 Harvey, G. J. (2018). The power of a smile. consumerpsych.co.uk

44 Ekman, P. & Friesen, W. V. (1978). *Manual for the facial action coding system*.

45 Ekman, P., Friesen, W. V., O'sullivan, M., Chan, A., Diacoyanni-Tarlatzis, I., Heider, K., ... & Tzavaras, A. (1987). Universals and cultural differences in the judgments of facial expressions of emotion. *Journal of Personality and Social Psychology*, 53(4), 712

46 Siegel, E. H., Sands, M. K., Noortgate, W. V. den, Condon, P., Chang, Y., Dy, J., Quigley, K. S., & Barrett, L. F. (2018). Emotion fingerprints or emotion populations? A meta-analytic investigation of autonomic features of emotion categories. *Psychological Bulletin*, 144(4), 343–393. https://doi.org/10.1037/bul0000128 (archived at https://perma.cc/URW4-4KJ8)

47 Barrett, L. F., Adolphs, R., Marsella, S., Martinez, A. M., & Pollak, S. D. (2019). Emotional expressions reconsidered: Challenges to inferring emotion from human facial movements. *Psychological Science in the Public Interest*, 20(1), 1–68.

48 Vincent, J. (2022). Microsoft to retire controversial facial recognition tool that claims to identify emotion. *The Verge*. https://www.theverge.com/2022/6/21/23177016/microsoft-retires-emotion-recognition-azure-ai-tool-api (archived at https://perma.cc/2ZMB-XSC9)

49 Guarnera, M., Hichy, Z., Cascio, M., Carrubba, S., & Buccheri, S. L. (2017). Facial expressions and the ability to recognize emotions from the eyes or mouth: A comparison between children and adults. *The Journal of Genetic Psychology*, 178(6), 309–318. https://doi.org/10.1080/00221325.2017.1361377 (archived at https://perma.cc/5ZKE-JGHJ)

50 Droulers, O. & Adil, S. (2015). Perceived gaze direction modulates ad memorization. *Journal of Neuroscience, Psychology, and Economics*, 8(1), 15–26. https://doi.org/10.1037/npe0000029 (archived at https://perma.cc/D9VG-MX22)

51 Sæther, L., Belle, W. V., Laeng, B., Brennen, T., & Øvervoll, M. (2009). Anchoring gaze when categorizing faces' sex: Evidence from eye-tracking data. *Vision Research*, 49(23), 2870–2880. https://doi.org/10.1016/j.visres.2009.09.001 (archived at https://perma.cc/5ZKE-JGHJ)

52 To, R. N. & Patrick, V. M. (2021). How the eyes connect to the heart: The influence of eye gaze direction on advertising effectiveness. *Journal of Consumer Research*, 48(1), 123–146. https://doi.org/10.1093/jcr/ucaa063 (archived at https://perma.cc/5WK7-TXAC)

53 Sajjacholapunt, P. & Ball, L. J. (2014). The influence of banner advertisements on attention and memory: Human faces with averted gaze can enhance advertising effectiveness. *Frontiers in Psychology*, 5, 997. https://doi.org/10.3389/fpsyg.2014.00166 (archived at https://perma.cc/K9DW-46WY)

54 Hutton, S. B. & Nolte, S. (2011). The effect of gaze cues on attention to print advertisements. *Applied Cognitive Psychology*, 25(6), 887–892. https://doi.org/10.1002/acp.1763 (archived at https://perma.cc/M8XP-JGJG)

55 Droulers, O. & Adil, S. (2015). Perceived gaze direction modulates ad memorization. *Journal of Neuroscience, Psychology, and Economics*, 8(1), 15–26. https://doi.org/10.1037/npe0000029 (archived at https://perma.cc/6Q3W-XJ3Q)

56 D'Ambrogio, S., Werksman, N., Platt, M. L., & Johnson, E. N. (2023). How celebrity status and gaze direction in ads drive visual attention to shape consumer decisions. *Psychology & Marketing*, 40(4), 723–734. https://doi.org/10.1002/mar.21772 (archived at https://perma.cc/H9SM-HBFL)

57 Adil, S., Lacoste-Badie, S., & Droulers, O. (2018). Face presence and gaze direction in print advertisements: How they influence consumer responses—An eye-tracking study. *Journal of Advertising Research*, 58(4), 443–455. https://doi.org/10.2501/JAR-2018-004 (archived at https://perma.cc/2B6K-CT4N)

58 David, L., Vassena, E., & Bijleveld, E. (2024). The unpleasantness of thinking: A meta-analytic review of the association between mental effort and negative affect. *Psychological Bulletin*, 150(9). https://doi.org/10.1037/bul0000443 (archived at https://perma.cc/2S57-SU8M)

59 Reber, R., Winkielman, P., & Schwarz, N. (1998). Effects of perceptual fluency on affective judgments. *Psychological Science*, 9(1), 45–48.

60 Jacoby, L. L. (1978). On interpreting the effects of repetition: Solving a problem versus remembering a solution. *Journal of Verbal Learning and Verbal Behavior*, 17(6), 649–667.

61 Shotton, R., Treharne, M., & Burnett, L. (2018). Unpublished study on the generation effect, as cited in Shotton, R. (2018). *The Choice Factory: 25 behavioural biases that influence what we buy*. Harriman House.

62 Ahluwalia, R., & Burnkrant, R. E. (2004). Answering questions about questions: A persuasion knowledge perspective for understanding the effects of rhetorical questions. *Journal of Consumer Research*, 31(1), 26–42.

63 Lee, S. Y., Jung, S., Jung, H. Y., Choi, S. T., & Oh, S. (2019). Imagination matters: Do consumers' imagery processing and self-regulatory goals affect the persuasiveness of metaphor in advertising?. *International Journal of Advertising*, 38(8), 1173–1201.

64 Beard, E., Henninger, N. M., & Venkatraman, V. (2022). Making ads stick: Role of metaphors in improving advertising memory. *Journal of Advertising*, 1–18. https://doi.org/10.1080/00913367.2022.2089302 (archived at https://perma.cc/RSD6-MCXH)

65 Barthes, R. (1986). *Rhetoric of the image*. Hill and Wang.

66 Dehay, E. K. & Landwehr, J. R. (2019). A MAP for effective advertising: The metaphoric advertising processing model. *AMS Review*, 9(3), 289–303.

67 Eisend, M. (2009). A meta-analysis of humor in advertising. *Journal of the Academy of Marketing Science*, 37, 191–203.

68 Howe, H. S., Zhou, L., Dias, R. S., & Fitzsimons, G. J. (2022). Aha over haha: Brands benefit more from being clever than from being funny. *Journal of Consumer Psychology*, 33(1) 107–114. https://doi.org/10.1002/jcpy.1307 (archived at https://perma.cc/5E45-J4GG)

69 Brown, H. T. (2012). So What if I don't have an iPhone? The unintended consequences of using arrogance in advertising. *Journal of Applied Business Research (JABR)*, 28(4), 555–562.

70 Sharp, B. & Romaniuk, J. (2016). *How brands grow*. Melbourne: Oxford University Press.

71 Barney, C. & Jones, C. L. E. (2023). Laughing in the face of embarrassment: Humorous marketing messages, excitement, and embarrassing products in retail. *Psychology & Marketing*, 40(5), 979–994. https://doi.org/10.1002/mar.21775 (archived at https://perma.cc/97A5-TS4P)

72 Dore, M. (2020). Intertextuality and failed taboo humour in advertising. The European *Journal of Humour Research*, 8(3), 99–114.

73 Breland, K. & Breland, M. K. (1944). Legibility of newspaper headlines printed in capitals and in lower case. *Journal of Applied Psychology*, 28(2), 117–120.

74 Tinker M. A. (1954). The effect of slanted text upon the readability of print, *Journal of Educational Psychology*, 45, 287–291. In Tinker, M. (1965) *Bases for Effective Reading*. Lund Press. p. 136.

75 Weisenmiller, E. M. (1999). *A study of the readability of on-screen text*.

76 Paterson, D. G. & Tinker, M. A. (1946). Readability of newspaper headlines printed in capitals and in lower case. *Journal of Applied Psychology*, 30(2), 161–168. https://doi.org/10.1037/h0060093 (archived at https://perma.cc/P6MM-ZUBD)

77 Nelson, M. R. & Paek, H.-J. (2008). Nudity of female and male models in primetime TV advertising across seven countries. *International Journal of Advertising*, 27(5), 715–744. https://doi.org/10.2501/s0265048708080281 (archived at https://perma.cc/LWR3-RNMG)

78 Maner, J. K., Gailliot, M. T., Rouby, D. A., & Miller, S. L. (2007). Can't take my eyes off you: Attentional adhesion to mates and rivals. *Journal of Personality and Social Psychology*, 93(3), 389–401. https://doi.org/10.1037/0022-3514.93.3.389 (archived at https://perma.cc/52MP-JXSR)

79 Wirtz, J. G., Sparks, J. V., & Zimbres, T. M. (2018). The effect of exposure to sexual appeals in advertisements on memory, attitude, and purchase intention: A meta-analytic review. *International Journal of Advertising*, 37(2), 168–198. https://doi.org/10.1080/02650487.2017.1334996 (archived at https://perma.cc/JP7P-TGYG)

80 Wirtz, J. G., Sparks, J. V., & Zimbres, T. M. (2018). The effect of exposure to sexual appeals in advertisements on memory, attitude, and purchase intention: A meta-analytic review. *International Journal of Advertising*, 37(2), 168–198. https://doi.org/10.1080/02650487.2017.1334996 (archived at https://perma.cc/JP7P-TGYG)

81 Acikalin, M. Y., Watson, K. K., Fitzsimons, G. J., & Platt, M. L. (2018). Rhesus macaques form preferences for brand logos through sex and social status based advertising. *PLoS ONE*, 13(2), e0193055-13. https://doi.org/10.1371/journal.pone.0193055 (archived at https://perma.cc/EH4Z-6XK7)

82 Stewart, K., Dalakas, V., & Eells, D. (2022). Does sex sell? Examining the effect of sex appeals in social media ads on engagement with the ad and actual purchase. *Journal of Marketing Communications*, 1–14. https://doi.org/10.1080/13527266.2022.2072367 (archived at https://perma.cc/R7FH-29RL)

83 Su, Y., Kunkel, T., & Ye, N. (2021). When abs do not sell: The impact of male influencers conspicuously displaying a muscular body on female followers. *Psychology & Marketing*, 38(2), 286–297. https://doi.org/10.1002/mar.21322 (archived at https://perma.cc/C785-ZHNG)

84 Jenq, C., Pan, J., & Theseira, W. (2015). Beauty, weight, and skin color in charitable giving. *Journal of Economic Behavior & Organization*, 119, 234–253. https://doi.org/10.1016/j.jebo.2015.06.004 (archived at https://perma.cc/85UY-9CUP)

85 Sisco, M. R. & Weber, E. U. (2019). Examining charitable giving in real-world online donations. *Nature Communications*, 10(1), 3968. http://dx.doi.org/10.1038/s41467-019-11852-z (archived at https://perma.cc/353H-KDH4)

86 Otterbring, T., Ringler, C., Sirianni, N. J., & Gustafsson, A. (2018). The Abercrombie & Fitch effect: The impact of physical dominance on male customers' status-signaling consumption. *Journal of Marketing Research*, 55(1). https://doi.org/10.1509/jmr.15.0247 (archived at https://perma.cc/K8ND-LZ2Q)

87 Bower, A. B. & Landreth, S. (2001). Is beauty best? Highly versus normally attractive models in advertising. *Journal of Advertising*, 30(1), 1–12.

88 Brehm, J. W. (1966). *A theory of psychological reactance* (W. Burke, D. Lake, & J. Paine, Eds.). Academic Press.

89 Worchel, S. & Brehm, J. W. (1970). Effect of threats to attitudinal freedom as a function of agreement with the communicator. *Journal of Personality and Social Psychology*, 14(1), 18–22.

90 Laran, J., Dalton, A. N., & Andrade, E. B. (2011). The curious case of behavioral backlash: Why brands produce priming effects and slogans produce reverse priming effects. *Journal of Consumer Research*, 37(6), 999–1014. https://doi.org/10.1086/656577 (archived at https://perma.cc/T83V-FG3A)

91 De Keyzer, F., Dens, N., & De Pelsmacker, P. (2022). Let's get personal: Which elements elicit perceived personalization in social media advertising?. *Electronic Commerce Research and Applications*, 55, 101183.
92 Chen, Q., Feng, Y., Liu, L., & Tian, X. (2019). Understanding consumers' reactance of online personalized advertising: A new scheme of rational choice from a perspective of negative effects. *International Journal of Information Management*, 44, 53–64.
93 Amarnath, D. D. & Jaidev, U. P. (2021). Toward an integrated model of consumer reactance: A literature analysis. *Management Review Quarterly*, 71, 41–90.
94 WPP (2024) Ogilvy: Mayor of London's say maate to a mate. https://www.wpp.com/en/featured/work/2024/02/ogilvy-say-maaate-to-a-mate (archived at https://perma.cc/823T-Z4ET)
95 Raymond, J. E., Fenske, M. J., & Tavassoli, N. T. (2003). Selective attention determines emotional responses to novel visual stimuli. *Psychological Science*, 14(6), 537–542. https://doi.org/10.1046/j.0956-7976.2003.psci_1462.x (archived at https://perma.cc/26U6-T4KD)
96 Duff, B. R. L. & Faber, R. J. (2011). Missing the mark. *Journal of Advertising*, 40(2), 51–62. https://doi.org/10.2753/joa0091-3367400204 (archived at https://perma.cc/YCM5-NU7U)
97 Phua, P., Hartnett, N., Beal, V., Trinh, G., & Kennedy, R. (2023). When brands go dark: A replication and extension: examining market share of brands that stop advertising for a year or longer. *Journal of Advertising Research*, 63(2), 172–184.

9 | The psychology of social media: Likes, shares and sales

LEARNING OBJECTIVES

- Understand the factors that lead posts to be effective on social media.
- Evaluate the factors that are likely to lead to a successful partnership between a brand and influencers.
- Learn how to create a social media posting plan and schedule that will help build up the company's brand equity and directly increase sales.

Social media: Democratizing marketing?

It is impossible to ignore the role that social media plays in a firm's marketing strategy today. Thirty years ago, if you wanted to reach a mass audience, your choices were relatively limited. You were forced to rely on advertising and your options were television, radio, magazine or billboards. But thanks to social media, sole traders with a minimal marketing budget can now reach a global audience, with a novel idea and a little luck. As a result, online advertising, and especially social media advertising, is bigger business than ever. In 2022, $567 billion was spent on online advertising.[1] That's the same as every person on earth spending $71 a year on online advertising, and this figure is only set to grow.

But what makes life both tricky and exciting is the fast pace of change. What works today may not work tomorrow. The basic psychological principles that underpin human behaviour never change, but social media platforms regularly change their algorithms, which can mean that what works one month may not necessarily work the next. In a similar vein, over time, the popularity of different platforms changes. As of 2025, the most popular platforms in the EU, Switzerland and the UK, based on the number of active users, were Facebook, YouTube, Instagram, TikTok, Twitter (now X), and LinkedIn. However, since the platforms are constantly looking to make their sites appealing, they continually tweak their algorithm. What worked before may no longer work now. Consequently, brands need to understand both psychology and the algorithm to succeed.

This presents a challenge not only for marketers but also for academics trying to understand the psychology behind social media. Also, because platforms are proprietary to their developers, researchers are often unable to run controlled A/B experiments, isolating specific features for testing. As a result, the volume of academic research in this area remains relatively sparse compared to the more traditional forms of advertising, despite its growing importance to brands.

The development of influencer marketing

While most people know of influencer marketing and crowdfunding, they assume it is a recent development. But like most aspects of marketing, they have a far more complicated history than we assume. Influencer marketing can trace its origin back to 1765 and Josiah Wedgwood, a potter, and arguably the founder of modern marketing. He recognized the power of celebrity, and at the time, there was no bigger celebrity than Queen Charlotte, wife of King George III. He was already supplying the Queen with porcelain and as the British people looked up and aspired to be like royalty, he launched a range of pottery called '*Queensware*' and took out adverts in national newspapers highlighting the fact that it was used by the Queen.

As for crowdfunding, the first campaign was run by the famed publisher Joseph Pulitzer in 1885, to pay for the Statue of Liberty. Although the Statue of Liberty was a diplomatic gift from the French and paid for by their government, the US were required to pay for the large granite plinth the statue sits on. In 1885, this cost $250,000 to build or nearly $4.2m in today's prices, and unfortunately, the US was $83,333 short. Rather than asking for corporate sponsors, Joseph Pulitzer ran a campaign in his newspaper, *The New York World*, asking members of the public to give what they could. This raised $100,000, from over 160,000 donors, which was enough to cover the costs and the leftover money was given as a gift to the sculptor.[2] There is no record of the term crowdfunding being used in the 19th or early 20th century, but this was no different to the sort of campaigns we now see on GoFundMe, Indiegogo or FundRazr, etc.

Does social media work?

It may seem like every business is active on social media, but this doesn't mean it's going to be an effective strategy for all. So, what does the data say? Well, the good news is that a brand's social media page is often more important than marketers realize. Many marketers, and especially digital marketers, focus on easy-to-measure metrics such as likes, comments or shares of owned social media posts. And while these metrics aren't a proxy for sales or even brand loyalty, research by Blend Ibrahim does suggest a strong relationship between social media activity and brand equity.[3] Rather than conducting a single study, Ibrahim conducted a meta-analysis, identifying all the studies that tried to answer the question between 2010 and 2019 and merged their results into one large analysis. This provides a much more robust analysis than any single study. Taken together, this showed a medium-to large effect size, suggesting social media activity does lead to greater brand equity.

But the primary objective of marketing is to increase sales. While this can be difficult to quantify, one of the most robust analyses to date, a meta-analysis by Georgia Liadeli and colleagues which combined the results from 86 studies across 31 industries and 17 countries, showed that for business-to-consumer brands, posting on a company's owned social media pages regularly is nearly three times as effective at increasing sales than traditional advertising.[4] However, to get the best out of social media, brands need to ensure there is a diverse range of content. Emotionally engaging content is the most effective at driving social media engagement (such as gaining likes and reshares), which is essential for ensuring your content reaches a wider audience based on the way the algorithms work. But more informational-based content has a stronger impact on increasing sales.

Building a following

Before a brand or influencer can begin to take advantage of social media, they first need to build a following. Regardless of the platform, this requires the user to post regularly and for people to interact with your post. How you get people to interact with your posts will differ depending on what type of following you want to build and the content you post. For celebrities or brands who post lifestyle content, the stories and posts that get the most engagement share content about people with whom they have close ties, such as family, friends and even romantic partners.[5] We may have never met the celebrity posting these stories, but these personal stories help us to feel closer to them, making them appear warmer, more relatable and ultimately more authentic. This effect can be magnified further by the language used in a post.

While most viewers tend to ignore the captions on visual platforms like Instagram or TikTok, if an influencer uses language such as I, we, me etc., once again viewers feel more connected, and these posts do better.

It may seem a trivial effect, but using first-person language changes how people encode the information. Firstly, it makes it easy for the viewer to see the post from the influencer's perspective, which makes the content more emotionally salient. It also weakly leverages the 'self-referencing effect',[6] the idea that people remember information better when they relate to it themselves. When a post uses 'I' or 'we', it makes it feel more like a story and the viewer can put themselves in the narrator's position, which leads to the content being more memorable. Secondly, according to Social Presence Theory, which refers to the extent that someone is perceived as a real person in mediated communications,[7] the more authentic and human a person seems, the more influence they have. Using first-person language helps create this presence, making it feel as if there is a real person behind the screen. This reduces the psychological distance and makes the content feel like a genuine conversation rather than a one-way broadcast.[8]

But it is important that not all posts feel the same. When João Oliveira led a team of researchers who analysed over 60,000 posts from the 100 leading brands on Twitter, they found a pattern as to which posts had the most interaction. Tweets that were the most emotionally engaging were the most liked,[9] although surprisingly, they were less likely to be reshared. But this shouldn't be taken as evidence that all posts should be emotionally engaging. If all posts are engaging, the viewer quickly becomes habituated to this and they feel normal, rather than emotionally engaging. When readers look at your timeline, there needs to be an emotional journey, with some posts being more engaging than others.

Sometimes brands and influencers take a shortcut when it comes to growing their followers. Rather than growing organically by having their content found and reshared, brands can launch promotional campaigns encouraging people to follow them. Although there are lots of different ways this can work, most use a variation of the following theme. Brands will put up a post offering people the chance to win a fantastic prize, for example, a free weekend ski break for two. To enter, all you need to do is (a) like this post, (b) comment below, tagging a friend who you would like to share this holiday with, (c) follow this account, (d) the person you tagged must also like and follow the account. They will then choose a winner at random from the comments. Hopefully, this will increase their number of followers, but by encouraging people to interact with the posts, it also means that the algorithm will share your posts with more people. With more people seeing your posts, your followers should increase.

Sometimes, brands take this one step further, especially if they have an online shop and they can identify loyal customers. Rather than just running a competition on social media, they ask, or perhaps more accurately, they bribe their customers to recommend a friend to follow them on social media. If they do, and their friend follows the brand, they can get a reward – perhaps 10% off their next order. If a brand does plan on running this sort of campaign, what reward works best? For weaker brands, it is best for them to offer non-monetary rewards such as free products rather than a discount on their next order.[10] Both approaches are effective at getting customers to recommend their friends, but friends are more likely to accept a recommendation when they receive a free gift. Understandably, people are suspicious if they realize that their friends are paid to recommend them and question their motivation. Can we really trust their recommendations?

Instead, a better approach is to offer a reward to both parties and to be honest about it. If an existing customer recommends a friend and doesn't tell them that they are getting something in return, it can feel like they are telling a half-truth or lying by omission. But just like any relationship, if customers are honest and explain that the deal is good for both parties, research has shown that the receiver will be less suspicious and more likely to accept the offer.[11] However, certain rules need to be followed. Firstly, being open only works when the reward for the existing customer is equal to or less than the friend's reward. If the reward for the existing customer is bigger, the potential new customer feels that the process isn't fair and as a result, they don't want to cooperate, a variation of the 'Prisoner's Dilemma'. The second caveat is that the business offering the reward must make it clear the reward is paid for by the company and doesn't come out of the new client's spending.

WHAT IS THE PRISONER'S DILEMMA?

The Prisoner's Dilemma is a thought experiment developed by Merrill Flood and Melvin Dresher in 1950. They described a scenario where two members of a criminal gang have been arrested and are in solitary confident in prison. However, the police don't have enough evidence to charge them on the primary charge, so they plan on sentencing them on a lesser charge, which will result in a year in prison. But they simultaneously offer both prisoners an offer: if they testify against their partner, they will go free, but their partner will face three years in prison on the main charge. But if both prisoners testify against each other, they will each face two years in jail. Both prisoners know the same deal is being made to the other prisoner but they don't know what decision they'll reach.[12]

The idea of the dilemma illustrates that when people act purely in their own self-interest, it often leads to worse outcomes for everyone involved. This is because when everyone engages in selfish behaviour, it prevents the group from reaching an optimal outcome, punishing all involved.

Implementing influencer marketing strategies

Just like with television adverts, brands need to decide whether to use a famous celebrity or an everyday person to front their campaigns on social media. However, on social media, the distinction between an everyday person and a celebrity has become blurred with the introduction of influencers. Thirty years ago, the only way you could become a celebrity was to feature on television, radio or publish a book, with the media acting as a gatekeeper. But social media has democratized the process. Anybody can create a YouTube or Instagram channel, providing advice on topics ranging from make-up tutorials, van conversions or even just how to wire a plug. Considering influencers can have followers ranging from thousands to multiple millions, it is easy to appreciate the importance they play in modern marketing campaigns.

So, which should you use, a traditional celebrity or an influencer? While celebrities are better at capturing attention than non-celebrities, this often doesn't convert to sales, or at least the sales are not as high as you would expect considering how many people view the posts.[13] People are fascinated by celebrities, which is why they attract attention, but it is also the reason why it doesn't convert to sales. People focus on the celebrity at the expense of any marketing messages. They are more interested in noticing (and judging) what haircut or what clothing the latest celebrity is wearing, rather than reading the headline or looking at the product you are trying to sell. However, there is still a balancing act to strike here. The conversion rate may be less good, but in the crowded world of social media, where people are consistently being bombarded by photos and messages, just getting people to stop and look at your message is a challenge, and it may be worth the trade-off.

But this trade-off will depend on what you are selling. Celebrities need to be perceived as authentic and relevant to the product they are endorsing. If you are attempting to sell an off-grid battery pack for 'van life', it's probably best not to opt for Taylor Swift to front your campaign. Ignoring the fact that hiring Taylor Swift would be outside the budget for virtually every company, it is hard to imagine her roughing it in a self-converted camper van. In this situation, Linan Ren and colleagues have shown that a more authentic 'real' person is going to be far more persuasive,[14] and this is where influencers fit in. They live for their hobbies and are perceived as experts. If they recommend a product, it carries far more weight than a celebrity who we know is being paid to endorse it. But the internet is full of influencers and the challenge for marketers is to find the right influencer to promote their product and work out how to structure the campaign. Luckily, research can provide some clear guidance.[15]

A research team led by Fine Leung of Hong Kong University analysed nearly 6,000 sponsored posts from 2,412 influencers posting on behalf of 850 different brands. To ensure the results were generalizable, they ensured the brands spanned across 29 categories including beauty products, e-commerce platforms, food and beverages, electronics, apparel, and personal care. The researchers considered how much each influencer was paid and the number of reposts, comments and likes each post achieved. Their main seven findings were as follows.

1 *Follower count.* It may seem a very obvious point, but you want to select someone with a relatively large following. Given the choice between collaborating with six influencers who each have a relatively modest follower count or a single influencer whose follower count is equal to the six influencers combined, it's often better to select the influencer with the higher follower count overall. Thanks to social proof, influencers with a large number of followers are perceived as more credible. When it comes to following someone for their expertise (rather than their looks or lifestyle), followers may be interested in the topic, but are not experts. Consequently, it can be hard for them to determine if they're credible or not. But if lots of people are following them, it suggests that they're both credible and producing high-quality content.

The exact number of followers you want an influencer to have will depend on your budget, and your campaign objective and message. For short-term relationships or when brands are looking for immediate bump in sales, brands should be looking for macro-influencers. Influencers with the broadest reach possible within their niche, and the posts should be more information-focused. However, if the aim is to establish a long-term relationship with the goal of helping build up the brand image, relatively smaller influencers who post emotional and more personal stories which feature the brands[16] are a better bet.

However, it is worth noting that there are opposing views when it comes to what provides best value. Maximilian Beichert from Bocconi University analysed nearly two million purchases driven by posts from influencers across Europe. His research suggested that nano influencers, those with fewer than 10,000 followers, provided better value for money. Because of their relatively small audience, they typically charge $50 per post, about the cost of the free product they are promoting. Yet on average, these posts generate around $1,000 in sales. In contrast, influencers with over 100,000 followers can charge over $1,000 per post but their content typically leads to about $6,000 increase in sales.[17]

2 *Posting frequency.* Fine Leung's research also concluded that companies are looking for an influencer who posts about five times per week. This hits the sweet spot where they are posting enough to build a large following, and drive a high

level of engagement, but not so much that it clutters a viewer's timeline. When one person or company posts incessantly, it very quickly becomes annoying, and readers skip their posts. Conversely, people who don't post frequently enough are not perceived to be as trustworthy or up to date. Just like with Goldilocks, this is not too much, or not too little.

3 *Brand/influencer fit.* When brands are looking for an influencer to work with, they want to find someone who posts content that is related to their brand or company. However, it is important that the influencer's content is not too closely related to the company. If both the brand and influencer are posting content that is virtually interchangeable, then they are competing against each other for attention. The influencer's followers are going to be loyal to them; hence there is a risk that they are unlikely to leave their social media accounts. In an ideal world, the brand needs to produce content that explores a similar topic but needs to be novel enough that readers are intrigued and motivated to click on any links.

4 *Influencer originality.* We are living in a world where there is more content being produced than ever. In June 2022, more than 500 hours of videos were uploaded every minute onto YouTube – that's 30,000 hours of content per hour.[18] Influencers are consistently competing with each other to produce novel content for their followers. And while some continue to create new content, others simply replicate video ideas and posts from their rivals. From a partnership and sponsorship perspective, creators who produce a higher percentage of original content appear both more knowledgeable and authentic, which means their posts generate a higher rate of engagement. It just requires marketers to be able to differentiate between novel and replicated content.

5 *Post positivity.* Posts that are more positive than normal attract the most engagement. But the key is for the posts to be only slightly more positive than average. People are naturally sceptical and aware that social media is not real life. When we view posts that are all unduly positive, we perceive them as disingenuous and not reflective of real life. Consequently, it's best for brands not to be associated with influencers who continually post overtly positive messages. That's not to say that you want to collaborate with a brand that consistently posts negative messages either. It is about finding collaborations with people who produce positive content, but that doesn't feel removed from real life.

6 *Brand links:* It may sound obvious, but brands need to make sure that any influencers they work with link to their official social media accounts or web pages. Some influencers can be reluctant to do this, feeling that it can undermine their credibility and impartiality. Yet from the consumer's perspective, it adds important context, resulting in more effective campaigns.

> **7** *Launching new products*: Brands have lots of reasons why they may want to collaborate with an influencer, but a popular motivation is to promote the launch of a new product. Unfortunately, when influencers post about a new product, these posts have a significantly lower engagement rate than their equivalent posts which don't discuss new products. Consumers of social media are savvy; they recognize that posts by influencers which endorse products are probably paid for. It's exactly the same reason why product placement often outperforms TV adverts. Given the choice, the best combination is if a company can afford to run a product placement and TV ads, but if this isn't an option, the next most effective option is product placement on its own, then followed by just a TV ad campaign.[19] Television does a great job at building brand awareness and getting your name out there, but shoppers are sceptical of the messages. When it comes to social media, partnerships that go beyond product launches tend to be the most successful.

In a similar vein, brands are looking for influencers who don't endorse too many products.[20] If an influencer is seen to be endorsing multiple brands, viewers think that they are less authentic, and just endorsing multiple products to earn money. As a result, consumers are less likely to copy their behaviour or believe their recommendations.

Celebrities and social media

If a brand does opt for a celebrity to front their campaign on social media, there is a similar set of guidelines for brands developed by Johannes Knoll and Jörg Matthes to help marketers select the right face for their campaign. Although some of the principles seem strange or counterintuitive, it's worth remembering that they were calculated after analysing the results of 46 different experiments testing how over 10,000 users of social media reacted to different posts.[21] The most important factors are listed first:

1 *Male celebrities*: From a purely statistical perspective, male celebrities typically resulted in more positive attitudes and led to higher sales. It is assumed this occurs because even today, people still subconsciously believe that male celebrities have more expertise and prestige. However, it is important to note that there will be category differences, and brands have a moral responsibility to ensure that their ads are representative of the population at large. Sometimes, just because something is more effective doesn't mean it is the right thing to do.

2 *Implicit endorsements are better than explicit endorsements*: Normally, when brands pay celebrities to endorse a product, they expect them to explicitly endorse the product, saying something like '*I love my new XXX hairdryer*'. Yet social media posts from celebrities that don't explicitly endorse the product, but instead just feature it prominently in their videos or posts, are more effective at convincing people to buy the target product.

3 *Celebrity brand fit*: Just like with influencers, campaigns that have a good fit between the celebrity and the brand are more successful.

4 *Quality seals and awards are more effective than celebrity endorsements*: Celebrity endorsements are useful at encouraging sales, but it is important to remember that they are not as effective as a brand receiving awards or external quality seals.

5 *Actors generally perform better than other celebrities*: When endorsing products on social media, actors typically perform better compared to models, musicians and TV hosts of similar prominence).

Crafting a winning post

Regardless of whether it is a brand posting about their product or an influencer aiming to build up their profile, they want to know how to create engaging posts. When celebrities or influencers post about other people rather than themselves, these posts are far more likely to be reshared. However, stories that focus on themselves are still shared more often than when they just list facts about themselves.[22] As with many aspects of marketing, engaging stories are what hooks people in, and brands should look to partner with people who tell stories. For more information about storytelling, see Chapter 6.

Unfortunately, while influencers and celebrities may be great at promoting themselves, without guidance, they often struggle when it comes to promoting sponsored products. For example, if a company that manufactures sports massage guns (a tool to give yourself a deep tissue massage after exercise) partnered with a celebrity, typically you end up with a video where they simply say '*I love to use my XXX massage gun after a run*'. Yet these are exactly the sort of posts that are least likely to be shared or interacted with. Instead, in this case, a more effective approach would be to post a short reel featuring an athlete just after finishing a run. They could be speaking directly to the camera, reflecting on what went well and what they'd like to improve next time, all while casually using the massage gun. Importantly, the massage gun is never explicitly mentioned or acknowledged.

It's not just the story that's important, but the images. Although it differs by platform, social media is primarily a visual medium, dominated by videos and photos. But from a sales perspective, the sort of images that perform best go against the standard marketing rules. From an evolutionary perspective, humans are instinctively drawn to faces. They capture our attention, hence ads that feature faces typically perform best[23] – but not on social media. Yes, selfies taken featuring a product receive 28% more likes compared to someone just holding a product. However, when it comes to increasing sales, viewers were 7% more likely to buy the product when the post just showed someone holding the product and the face is out of shot.[24] But why is this?

A person's face automatically captures our attention, but it causes us to focus on the person in the photo. Instead of imagining what it would be like if we were using the product (*the endowment effect*), we look at the person in the image instead. Hence, numerous brands will show someone touching their product online, but you can't see the person's face. This helps to make it easier for us to imagine we're touching the product and increases the feeling of psychological ownership of the product,[25] even though we've not bought it yet. This is a similar tactic to the one discussed in Chapter 6, where marketers are encouraged to use language that implies the target audience already owns the product.

This effect works even when it comes to promoting physical locations, which will hopefully have a special, positive meaning, such as a wedding venue or holiday location. When people saw ads for two different locations, one featuring people in the photo, and one that didn't, in both cases, viewers were 29% more likely to book the option where the photos don't show anybody.[26] Perhaps, this explains why so many travel influencers take photos with their back to the camera while facing a stunning view. However, if a brand is selling a physical product, showing someone touching the product (but you can't see their face), it helps create a connection to the hand on-screen.

Getting your timing right

Having a content strategy is one thing, but coming up with ideas of what to post multiple times a week is a challenge, which is why companies take advantage of national awareness days or special days, be it Mother's Day, Valentine's Day, or even something less conventional, such as International Talk Like a Pirate Day. It may feel contrived, but from a pure sales perspective, these days are critical. For example, when an online pet shop launched an email marketing campaign promoting 25% off, it was almost twice as effective when it was linked to a made up promotional day[27] than when they offer 25% on a normal day.

Yet companies need to think about the timing of their posts around these days, especially if they are offering a discount. Research by Huixin Deng, Liyin Jin and Qian Xu showed that if a national chain of flower shops posted on Mother's Day that they were offering a 15% discount on all bouquets of flowers, then shoppers are likely to react negatively.[28]

At best, they find these posts unhelpful and at worst exploitative. By the time you see a post promoting flowers on Mother's Day, it's probably a little late for you to do anything about it. But if the same chain of shops launched the same post with the same 15% discount, shoppers in advance of Mother's Day (and deleted the post on Mother's Day) then viewers would react more favourably. This time they think that the company is helping them out, rather than just taking advantage of the situation. Of course, if you're not running a specific promotion or explicitly trying to sell something, but just raising awareness then your timing doesn't matter. For example, if on International Dog Day a company posted a photo of all their staff with their dogs, that's fine. But if you asked people to upload a photo of their dog to get a discount on the day, it's a different story.

It's not just a case of working out which day to post, businesses also need to decide what time to post. While the best time to post will be slightly different for every business, it will also change depending on the nature of the post. If the post is promoting more virtuous content, such as promoting companies' charitable initiatives, educational content or promoting responsible content, then these messages typically resonate best in the morning.[29] However, if the post promotes vice content, for example, if the post makes explicit use of sex appeal, risky humour or encourages people to eat or drink too much unhealthy food, then these posts perform better during the evening. Intuitively, this makes sense; we often start the day with the best of intentions but after three unplanned meetings and a lot of coffee, these can go out of the window. By this point in the day, vice content is more likely to appeal to how we feel.

Being open: What happens when you label a post as an ad

Regardless of whether you opt for a traditional celebrity or influencer, brands need to recognize that by using influencers the line between paid and earned content gets confused. Brands typically provide influencers with their product, but they don't have creative control like they would with a traditional advert. For example, a ski resort might provide a prominent influencer with a free lift pass and accommodation, hoping they'll share what a fantastic time they'll have with their thousands of followers, but they don't know what they'll say. Even so, regulators and social media platforms are changing the rules. In 2017, Instagram first added the 'paid partnership tags' and, in 2019, the EU introduced the 'Unfair commercial practice directive' which entered into force in 2022, which means that brands must disclose if any collaborations with influencers are a paid partnership, which includes providing free products. This just means that influencers need to tick the *'paid partnership with...'* button if it's a sponsored post and use the hashtag '#ad'.

Some influencers try to get creative and use the word, *'sponsored'* rather than *'advertising'* but ultimately this doesn't make any difference.[30] However, it makes sense for brands to want to avoid disclosing these paid relationships as these disclosures decrease the post's effectiveness.[31] However, this doesn't mean that brands should dismiss influencers as a channel. Even after an influencer discloses that a post is sponsored, users still spend more time engaging with sponsored posts than non-sponsored posts.[32]

Closing thoughts

Social media has become an increasingly vital part of any business's marketing strategy, and based on the current evidence, this is unlikely to change any time soon. Yet it is potentially one of the easiest areas for marketers to optimize. Social media platforms are built with experimentation in mind. Marketers can test what happens when they post different types of content and receive near instant feedback in the form of likes and click-through rates. This means that while marketers should use academic research as a starting point, they should continue to test what works for their specific audience, developing their own best practice guidelines tailored to their industry.

> **KEY POINTS**
>
> - For B2C brands, owned social media is nearly three times as effective as traditional advertising.
> - Emotionally engaging content is more effective at driving social media engagement, while informational-based content is more effective at increasing sales. However, it's crucial for brands to maintain a balanced mix of both. Only posting informational-based posts will result in followers losing interest and potentially stop following the brand
> - Assuming a celebrity and social media influencer have a similar follower count, brand partnership with influencers are typically more successful. People typically focus on the celebrity and ignore the branded message they're paid to post. In contrast, influencers are more relatable for most people.
> - When partnering with brands or celebrities, it is important to select people who:
>   o have a large follower count
>   o post regularly, but not too often
>   o post content that is related to the brand, but not too similar that the branded messages get lost or ignored
>   o produce content that is original and different to other influencers.
> - When selling location-based services, photos or videos that don't feature people perform better at converting likes to sales than those that do include people.

PUTTING THEORY INTO PRACTICE

1 Select a brand of your choice that sells a physical product, either using a direct-to-consumer model or selling via a retailer. Select five different influencers that could be used to endorse the brand, and justify your choices based on academic research.

2 Select an Instagram influencer(s) of your choice and find five posts where they have endorsed a product. Work out whether these posts are optimized to either drive engagement or increase sales. From the brand's perspective, what would they like the influencer to do differently in each of these posts?

3 For a brand of your choice, design a competition that they could run which would help increase their follower count on social media.

4 Imagine you are the social media manager for a brand of your choice. Create a posting plan for the next month – this needs to identify what day and time each post is going out, and the basic nature of each post. Make sure you include a mixture of factual and emotional posts, and highlight if you are going to collaborate with any influencers.

5 If you were the marketing manager of a fast-moving consumer goods brand and you had the opportunity to sponsor either one traditional celebrity or an influencer with a large following, which would you select and why? What would need to change for you to change your mind?

SUGGESTIONS FOR FURTHER READING

Federer, J. (2020). *The hidden psychology of social networks: How brands create authentic engagement by understanding what motivates us.* McGraw Hill: US.

References

1 Statista (2025). Advertising revenues of digital pure player media owners worldwide in 2024 and 2025. https://www.statista.com/statistics/237974/online-advertising-spending-worldwide/ (archived at https://perma.cc/LR77-87UT)
2 BBC (2013). The Statue of Liberty and America's crowdfunding pioneer. BBC News, UK.
3 Ibrahim, B. (2022). Social media marketing activities and brand loyalty: A meta-analysis examination. *Journal of Promotion Management*, 28(1), 60–90.

4   Liadeli, G., Sotgiu, F., & Verlegh, P. W. (2023). A meta-analysis of the effects of brands' owned social media on social media engagement and sales. *Journal of Marketing*, 87(3), 406–427.
5   Chung, J., Ding, Y., & Kalra, A. (2023). I really know you: How influencers can increase audience engagement by referencing their close social ties. *Journal of Consumer Research*, 50(4). https://doi.org/10.1093/jcr/ucad019 (archived at https://perma.cc/38B6-22RW)
6   Rogers, T. B., Kuiper, N. A. & Kirker, W. S. (1977). Self-reference and the encoding of personal information, *Journal of Personality and Social Psychology*, 35(9), 677–678.
7   Gunawardena, C. N. (1995). Social presence theory and implications for interaction collaborative learning in computer conferences. *International Journal of Educational Telecommunications*, 1(2/3), 147–166.
8   Osei-Frimpong, K. & McLean, G. (2018). Examining online social brand engagement: A social presence theory perspective. *Technological Forecasting and Social Change*, 128, 10–21.
9   Oliveira, J. S., Ifie, K., Sykora, M., Tsougkou, E., Castro, V., & Elayan, S. (2022). The effect of emotional positivity of brand-generated social media messages on consumer attention and information sharing. *Journal of Business Research*, 140, 49–61. https://doi.org/10.1016/j.jbusres.2021.11.063 (archived at https://perma.cc/BV3K-453T)
10 Jin, L. & Huang, Y. (2014). When giving money does not work: The differential effects of monetary versus in-kind rewards in referral reward programs. *International Journal of Research in Marketing*, 31(1), 107–116. https://doi.org/10.1016/j.ijresmar.2013.08.005 (archived at https://perma.cc/BAW9-TPLC)
11 Xu, M., Yu, Z., & Tu, Y. (2023). I will get a reward, too: When disclosing the referrer reward increases referring. *Journal of Marketing Research*, 60(2), 355–370. https://doi.org/10.1177/00222437221117113 (archived at https://perma.cc/SD9G-UULD)
12 Poundstone, W. (1993). *Prisoner's Dilemma: John Von Neumann, Game Theory, and the Puzzle of the Bomb*. Anchor Books.
13 Yang, L. & Yang, Q. (2023). Evaluating the influence of celebrity endorsement in advertising: Insights from eye-tracking analysis. *Finance & Economics*, 1(4). https://doi.org/10.61173/gg4pvj23 (archived at https://perma.cc/5H9W-CGGP)
14 Ren, L., Lee, S. K., & Chun, S. (2023). The effects of influencer type, regulatory focus, and perceived authenticity on consumers' purchase intention. *International Journal of Consumer Studies*. https://doi.org/10.1111/ijcs.12898 (archived at https://perma.cc/8NE9-8EWF)
15 Leung, F. F., Gu, F. F., Li, Y., Zhang, J. Z., & Palmatier, R. W. (2022). Influencer marketing effectiveness. *Journal of Marketing*, 86(6), 93–115. https://doi.org/10.1177/00222429221102889 (archived at https://perma.cc/UQC4-4YP2)
16 Gross, J. & Von Wangenheim, F. (2022). Influencer marketing on Instagram: Empirical research on social media engagement with sponsored posts. *Journal of Interactive Advertising*, 22(3), 289–310.
17 Beichert, M., Bayerl, A., Goldenberg, J., & Lanz, A. (2024). Revenue generation through influencer marketing. *Journal of Marketing*, 88(4), 40–63.

18 Ceci, L. (2025, June 20). Hours of video uploaded to YouTube every minute 2007–2022. Statista. https://www.statista.com/statistics/259477/hours-of-video-uploaded-to-youtube-every-minute/#:~:text=Hours%20of%20video%20uploaded%20to%20YouTube%20every%20minute%202007%2D2022&text=As%20of%20June%202022%2C%20more,newly%20uploaded%20content%20per%20hour. (archived at https://perma.cc/Z52K-WXAP)

19 Gamage, D., Jayasuriya, N., Rathnayake, N., Herath, K. M., Jayawardena, D. P. S., & Senarath, D. Y. (2023). Product placement versus traditional TV commercials: New insights on their impacts on brand recall and purchase intention. *Journal of Asia Business Studies*, 17(6). https://doi.org/10.1108/JABS-04-2022-0126 (archived at https://perma.cc/Z6JK-ED3U)

20 Borchers, N. S., Hagelstein, J., & Beckert, J. (2022). Are many too much? Examining the effects of multiple influencer endorsements from a persuasion knowledge model perspective. *International Journal of Advertising*, 1–23. https://doi.org/10.1080/02650487.2022.2054163 (archived at https://perma.cc/KD3L-PWHZ)

21 Knoll, J. & Matthes, J. (2017). The effectiveness of celebrity endorsements: A meta-analysis. *Journal of the Academy of Marketing Science*, 45, 55–75. https://doi.org/10.1007/s11747-016-0503-8 (archived at https://perma.cc/G4R7-NY36)

22 Aleti, T., Pallant, J. I., Tuan, A., & Van Laer, T. (2019). Tweeting with the stars: Automated text analysis of the effect of celebrity social media communications on consumer word of mouth. *Journal of Interactive Marketing*, 48(1), 17–32. https://doi.org/10.1016/j.intmar.2019.03.003 (archived at https://perma.cc/4F48-9LNF)

23 Guido, G., Pichierri, M., Pino, G., & Nataraajan, R. (2019). Effects of face images and face pareidolia on consumers' responses to print advertising: An empirical investigation. *Journal of Advertising Research*, 59(2), 219–231.

24 Hartmann, J., Heitmann, M., Schamp, C., & Netzer, O. (2021). The power of brand selfies. *Journal of Marketing Research*, 58(6), 1159–1177.

25 Webb Luangrath, A., Peck, J., Hedgcock, W., & Xu, Y. (2020). *Virtual touch facilitates psychological ownership of products in virtual reality*. ACR North American Advances.

26 Lu, Z. Y., Jung, S., & Peck, J. (2023). It looks like 'theirs': When and why human presence in the photo lowers viewers' liking and preference for an experience venue. *Journal of Consumer Research*, 51(2). https://doi.org/10.1093/jcr/ucad059 (archived at https://perma.cc/Z62Q-22BR)

27 Zane, D. M., Reczek, R. W., & Haws, K. L. (2022). Promoting Pi Day: Consumer response to special day-themed sales promotions. *Journal of Consumer Psychology*, 32(4), 652–663. https://doi.org/10.1002/jcpy.1271 (archived at https://perma.cc/T29F-ZYB8)

28 Deng, H., Jin, L., & Xu, Q. (2022). 'Right' on the day: How the timing of date-specific promotions influences consumer responses. *Psychology & Marketing*, 39(2), 429–440. https://doi.org/10.1002/mar.21607 (archived at https://perma.cc/PZ2D-8XJH)

29 Zor, O., Kim, K. H., & Monga, A. (2022). Tweets we like aren't alike: Time of day affects engagement with vice and virtue tweets. *Journal of Consumer Research*, 49(3), 473–495. https://doi.org/10.1093/jcr/ucab072 (archived at https://perma.cc/VL8Q-8U6K)

30 Lee, S. & Kim, E. (2020). Influencer marketing on Instagram: How sponsorship disclosure, influencer credibility, and brand credibility impact the effectiveness of Instagram promotional post. *Journal of Global Fashion Marketing*, 11(3), 232–249.
31 Chung, Y. J., Lee, S. S., & Kim, E. (2023). The effects of influencer types and sponsorship disclosure in instagram sponsored posts. *Journal of Current Issues & Research in Advertising*, 44(2), 193–211.
32 Gross, J. & Von Wangenheim, F. (2022). Influencer marketing on Instagram: Empirical research on social media engagement with sponsored posts. *Journal of Interactive Advertising*, 22(3), 289–310.

10 | The psychology of pricing

LEARNING OBJECTIVES

- Critically analyse the psychological mechanisms that influence how consumers perceive prices.
- Create a pricing strategy that encourages consumers to purchase a more expensive product option.

Introduction

Look in any marketing textbook and you're bound to find a chapter exploring pricing. Pricing is a key component of the marketing mix, the so-called Four Ps of *product*, *price*, *place* and *promotion*. Yet these textbooks generally focus on the strategic implications of pricing. For example, should an organization use 'penetration pricing' or 'price skimming' when they launch a new product? In this chapter, we're going to look beyond individual strategies and instead consider the overall psychological impact of price.

Paying is painful

Nobody likes paying for things, and at some point, most of us will have referred to the process as painful.[1] To talk in terms of pain isn't an exaggeration. If you analyse someone's brain when they are paying for something they think expensive, you'll find increased activation in a region of the brain called the *insula*.[2] This region is typically activated when we experience a number of different emotions and sensations, of which physical pain is one. While everybody will experience physical pain when it comes to paying, the feeling is stronger for some people, and these people are more reluctant to spend their money. However, when a recession hits, it is these shoppers who cut their spending back far more dramatically than the 'average' shopper.[3]

Yet shoppers only experience pain if they perceive the product as expensive. While it's possible for marketers to objectively measure the price of a product, the way shoppers perceive price is far more fluid. This is because in most situations, shoppers do not mentally process (or *encode*, to use the technical term) the actual price of a product, but simply whether it is cheap, average or expensive.[4] So, rather than remembering that a cup of Earl Grey from our local café costs £3.99, we just remember that it's expensive. This presents several opportunities for businesses. There are a variety of psychological tactics that marketers can use which change how shoppers perceive a product's price, either increasing or decreasing the amount of pain a customer experiences.

Framing: It's a question of how you look at it

Poor decisions by marketers, and by customers themselves, can actually make the process of paying more painful. For example, choosing to pay for a product with cash feels more painful than if we pay by credit or debit card.[5] This is because when we pay with cash, the act of paying becomes more salient: you have to physically hand over money, making you more aware of the cash leaving your possession. (To a psychologist, *saliency* is the extent to which a particular fact, situation or event is present in an individual's conscious consideration.) On the other hand, if you pay using a credit card or gift certificate, the transaction is emotionally less vivid, and so we are likely to spend more.[6] When paying by cash, we're less likely to make impulse purchases. When Thomas and colleagues analysed the shopping habits of 1,000 households for six months, they found that shoppers who used credit or debit cards to pay for their purchases were more likely to purchase food items classified as impulse purchases (and their shopping baskets were also more unhealthy).[7]

This is one of the reasons why casinos use gambling chips. If you are playing roulette, you're more likely to stop and think if you had to physically put your cash on 'red 7'. You can see the money that you're potentially (or probably) about to lose. If, on the other hand, you just put a few casino chips on 'red 7', you're already one step removed from the money. You'll feel less physical pain if you lose (at least until you get home) and this is why people gamble far more when using chips than cash.[8]

But in a post-Covid world, how we pay for goods has changed. For purchases under £100, contactless payments have become the norm in the UK. But people no longer just use a contactless credit or debit card; instead people are just as likely to pay by mobile phone or smartwatch. And just as the previous research suggests, people who pay using their mobile are at a much higher risk of overspending.[9] But if you use contactless payment, and you want to try to reduce your spending, there is something you can do about this. Changing a setting on your phone or watch so that it vibrates each time you pay has been shown to slightly reduce this effect.[10] This small vibration is enough to make paying that little more salient, which makes you more cautious with your spending.

Paying by mobile phone doesn't just mean we are likely to overpay, it changes what we buy; it increases the likelihood you'll purchase more hedonistic products.[11] This is because mobile phones are no longer a solely functional tool: we associate them with a hedonic mindset as we use them for social activities (e.g. social media, browsing the internet etc.) In contrast, if we pay with a smartwatch, although we spend more money on hedonistic items than if we had used cash, it would not feel as costly if we're paying via our smartphone. This is because, despite the hi-tech nature of smartphones, they're still more associated with functional benefits, rather than social.

It's not only the payment method that can make the pain of paying more salient. Another decision marketers make that will influence the amount of pain customers experience is *when* we make them pay. If customers pay for a product before they consume it, they get the experience of pain out of the way and can then focus on the benefits they receive from using the product. If you ask customers to pay after they consume it, you're making the payment more salient.[12] This can mean that a shopper's lasting experience of the product might be negative because of what psychologists refer to as the Peak-End Effect, the idea that consumers do not remember or judge an experience based on the whole experience but focus on a few key moments: the most emotionally salient moment and the feeling we experience at the end[13] (see Chapter 8). In this case, this is the pain associated with paying.

Surprisingly, subtle features, such as the way the prices are written, can change our perception. When a team of psychologists, led by Sybil Yang from Cornell University, changed how the price was written in an upmarket restaurant in New York, they found that customers spent significantly less if the menu featured the words 'dollar' or the '$ symbol before the price' (e.g. $12). Although they didn't explicitly explore the psychological mechanism, it's likely that including the dollar symbol reinforces the fact that customers are about to make a payment, increasing the saliency. Simply removing the dollar symbol from a menu can increase customers' total spend.[14]

In another example, the price £4.99 can be perceived very differently, depending on how it is written (Figure 10.1). Showing the price as black text on a white background can cause customers to perceive it as more expensive; unsurprisingly, prices with discount symbols next to them, or with an old price crossed out, seem cheaper.[15]

Simply removing the comma from a price changes the way we see it. Research has shown that people feel $1,599 to be more expensive than $1599.[16] That's because we encode numeric information in three different ways simultaneously: as an Arabic numeral (say, 32), as a sound ('thirty' and 'two') and as a magnitude, e.g. small or

Figure 10.1 An example of two price tags, the left-hand label makes the prices feel more expensive, whereas the label on the right makes the product feel cheaper

large.[17] Including the comma in $1,599 changes the way we encode the auditory information. We are more likely to encode it as 'one thousand, five hundred and ninety-nine' (10-syllables) rather than 'fifteen hundred and ninety-nine' (8-syllables). Prices that contain a greater number of syllables take more cognitive energy to process and, consequently, we perceive them to be larger.[18] This effect holds true even if we read a price that is written as a number and do not say the price out loud. All three systems of encoding are still engaged.[19]

This Triple-Code Model of memory offers other opportunities to influence the way we encode prices. The third system involves encoding a price as a magnitude, but this is a relative concept. Determining if £99 is expensive or not depends on what we're comparing it with. But there is an overlap between our visual and numerical concepts of size.[20] For example, when participants are presented with two numbers and asked to decide which number is greater, their response time is quicker when the larger number is displayed in a larger font[21] – an effect similar to the Stroop task.

GIVE IT A GO

The Stroop task is a classic experiment within psychology. Participants are asked to name the colour of the ink a word is printed in, which becomes more difficult when the word itself spells out a different colour. For example, the word blue is printed in red ink. Think it's easy? Give it a go and see how well you do!

Comparative pricing

While the Triple-Code Model of memory may sound like an academic curiosity, marketers can use this effect to help make a new sale price feel lower than the original price. If the sale price is displayed in a smaller font than the original price, it creates a visual difference between the physical size of the number and the size of the amount it represents, causing participants to view the new price as more attractive and leading to higher sales.[22] But it's not just the size of the font that's important. Simply increasing the horizontal distance between the two prices causes consumers to perceive a greater difference between them.[23] If marketers do not have room on a label to move the prices further apart, it could be hypothesized that a similar effect could be achieved by displaying the two different prices in different colours, although this has yet to be shown in studies.

Changing the location of the old and new price can change how we feel about a price (Figure 10.2). To make a price feel more expensive, it helps if we place the price at the top of an advert or label. Then, when it comes to the new (hopefully) lower price, you want to put it at the bottom of the label. This is because all European languages write from left to right. When we write, number one goes on the left of the page and ten goes on the right. Likewise, one goes at the bottom of the page and ten goes at the top. Consequently, we associate higher numbers as being on the top and lower numbers on the bottom.[24] Just like with the Stroop task, when things are placed where we expect them, we read them faster, and it influences our perception.

In the above examples, we've concentrated on comparisons of different prices on the same item (e.g. between the normal price and sale price). But when it comes to shopping, consumers generally compare the price of one item with other products. In most situations, these are implicit comparisons. The consumer decides for themselves to compare prices, but a popular marketing tactic is to invite customers to compare prices, especially if you are the cheapest! For example, a local supermarket may ask you to compare the prices of the leading brand of razors and the store's own brand. This is referred to as an explicit comparison, and it can have some unintended consequences. When consumers are explicitly asked to compare prices, rather than going for the cheaper product, consumers are more likely to go for the established brand as it is perceived as being less risky (or they may even avoid making a purchase at all).[25] For example, when participants were asked to bid on items on eBay with an opening bid of $1.99, half of shoppers were allocated to a shop where they could see the same product listed in another auction for 99 cents and the other half for $6.99. The results were clear. Shoppers paid far more for products when it was shown next to products costing $6.99. However, if the experimenters told the participants to compare prices, they found that participants became far more cautious, bidding less. And the surrounding products became irrelevant. It turns out it's far better to let shoppers make their own comparisons.

From a marketer's perspective, what is important is ensuring that your customers compare your product to the 'right' other products. Initially, this sounds obvious, but it's an important distinction. When Nestlé launched the home espresso machine back in 1986, the obvious comparison was to pre-ground coffee. At today's prices, a cup of coffee made using an espresso machine costs about 90p to £1.35, depending on the flavour you buy. In contrast, a cup of coffee made using Nestle's Gold Blend costs about 5p a cup. But Nestlé framed the Nespresso so you aren't comparing it to an instant coffee. Instead, you are comparing the price to a cup of coffee from Starbucks or Tim Hortons. Suddenly, it doesn't seem so expensive!

The consideration set doesn't even have to be a similar product. If you are a fan of extreme sports, there is a good chance that you'll have a gear room full of expensive toys: kayaks, snowboards, paragliders, surfboards etc. In comparison to these items, personal insurance seems like nothing, yet companies struggle to convince people to buy it. They'd rather spend their money on another exciting bit of kit. In this instance, a company might use a 'loss appeal': 'What might happen if you injured yourself? If you break both your legs, can you afford 10 weeks off work?'

Asymmetrical dominance (the decoy effect)

If we know consumers are going to make implicit comparisons, then as marketers we should be sure we understand how we can use this to our advantage. Consumers compare for a simple reason: it is often hard to determine a product's absolute value, so we need to use a reference point. We can make one product look like it provides better value by introducing a *decoy product*.

One of the most powerful examples of this is provided by Dan Ariely,[26] who described a marketing campaign produced by *The Economist*. Readers had the option of subscribing to the newspaper's web-only content for $59 a year, the print edition for $125 a year, or a combined offer of print and web access for $125, the same price as the print edition. At first, it seems like the print-only option is a mistake. Surely nobody would choose it, knowing they can get the digital and print edition for the same price? And, indeed, when Dan Airely tested the campaign, this is exactly what he found – nobody took up the print-only subscription. When students were asked to choose one of the three subscription packages, 84% selected the combination deal and only 16% chose the online-only subscription. So if nobody was actually choosing the middle option, what was the point of it? That's when things became interesting. When he tested the campaign but removed the print-only option, he found a significant shift in consumers' preferences. This time, only 32% of participants selected the print and digital option, and 68% of participants went for the digital subscription.

Figure 10.2 An example of a company using the decoy effect to make their more expensive product feel like a better purchase

This suggests that the middle or decoy option plays a pivotal role in the decision-making process, in that it changes the way we perceive the other options. We find it quite hard to decide which provides the best value for money between Option A and Option B, when A and B are somewhat similar. But by including a decoy option which is similar to Option B (but clearly inferior), it causes us to perceive Option B as more valuable, a perception we then generalize when we compare it to Option A.

Yet this is not an isolated example. The same effect has been shown when Simonson and Tversky gave students the choice of $9 in cash or a nice pen worth $9. 64% of students opted for the cash and the remainder went for the pen. But when a decoy option of an ugly cheap pen was introduced, it made the expensive pen appear more desirable. In those circumstances, only 52% of students opted for the cash, 46% selected the nice pen and, bizarrely, 2% of students chose the cheap pen.[27]

The compromise effect

Retailers can also create a different type of decoy to influence consumers' choices. When a group of participants were asked to decide which digital camera they wanted to buy, given a choice of either a low-price Minolta SLR camera or a mid-price Minolta SLR camera, participants' purchases were split 63:37 between the two options, with most students opting for the cheaper model. But when a third choice was introduced into the mix, a high-end Minolta SLR camera, students' preferences shifted substantially. This time, only 31% of students opted for the low-price camera, 46% went for the mid-price camera and 23% chose the high-end camera.[28] Including the high-end model changed the way the students' decision was framed. Previously, the participants were faced with choosing either a basic or expensive option. The presence of the luxury model allowed them to frame their choice of the first high-end camera as the best of both worlds, a compromise between cost and extra features.

This isn't restricted to the laboratory. Numerous companies exploit it, although some probably unwittingly. For example, Williams-Sonoma was one of the first companies to introduce bread makers to the domestic market. The first breadmaker they launched cost $275, but sales were sluggish. However, rather than dropping the product, they conducted some market research and decided to launch a new model. This new model was slightly larger, included more advanced features and as a result, cost double the price. Again, the new product didn't sell very well, but sales of the old model doubled.[29] The new, more expensive model acted as a reference point that helped consumers decide if they were getting good value or not.

Charm pricing: It's all in the nines

It would be almost impossible to discuss the psychology of pricing without considering *charm pricing* (sometimes just called psychological pricing). Charm pricing is the idea that retailers price a product at one or five pence below a round number. So rather than a product being priced at £10, it's priced at £9.99 or £9.95. This is one of the most-used pricing tactics, with approximately 60% of all advertised prices ending in a nine.[30]

So why do companies use charm pricing? When viewed from a cognitive perspective, it's clear that there is virtually no difference between £10 and £9.99. Consequently, conventional psychological theory (e.g. the Weber–Fechner law – see Chapter 2) would suggest that it shouldn't change customers' price perception. But both sales data and market research show that this is not the case. For example, Anderson and Simester[31] conducted an experiment investigating the impact of charm pricing in a mail-order catalogue aimed at women. The catalogue mostly sold moderately priced clothing, and in most cases, the products were priced using whole numbers ending in a nine (e.g. $29, $39 etc.). For the study, the researchers produced a number of different versions of the catalogue, pricing the same items at different prices (e.g. $34, $39 or $44). The results clearly support the use of charm pricing. When a dress was priced at $34, 16 units were sold, at $39, 21 units were sold and at $44, 17 units were sold. Increasing the price of the dress from $34 to $39 led to a 23% increase in sales. However, the absence of statistical difference in sales of identical items priced at $34 and $44 in different versions of the catalogue highlights the fact that consumers are unable to determine an item's objective value and need to make a decision based on relative comparison.

It's easy to think this is a cherry-picked example to prove a point. But when Troll and colleagues reviewed every experiment they could find investigating charm pricing, 69 in total, testing over 40,000 shoppers, they found that charm pricing had a small but positive impact on sales, without harming shoppers' perception of the quality of the product.[32] However, it is important to note that while on average the results increased, there was a relatively high degree of variation in the results, with it not always working.

While it is hard to predict when charm pricing will work, there are some hints. When shopping, we're often forced to make a comparison between two prices for the same item, typically a 'normal' price and a discounted sale price. When there is a large difference between prices, it's easy to work out which price is cheaper, therefore we don't tend to rely on the left-most digit in the number. However, when the prices are similar, we rely on our snap estimates of the numbers, using what psychologists call an heuristic model of decision-making, and consequently place a greater emphasis on the left-hand digit. In those circumstances, charm pricing is more effective.[33]

While self-report research techniques may have their flaws (see Chapter 16), in this case, they can help to provide some insight as to why charm pricing is so powerful. If a business increases the price of a product from 99p by 1p, so that it now costs £1.00, shoppers respond as if the price has been increased by more than 20p. Unfortunately, most businesses fail to appreciate this and as a result, they can end up leaving about 1–4% margin on the table.[34] Yet the real-world sales data suggests that this might be an underestimation.

REAL-WORLD EXAMPLE: PSYCH IN ACTION

In 2019, Lyft, a US-based ride-sharing app, trialled switching to a charm pricing strategy and measured what impact it had on customer demand. Over seven months, Lyft made over 600 million offers to potential customers across the US, of which 65% were accepted. The data showed that changing the price from $15 to $14.99 had roughly the same impact on demand as a price change from $15.99 to $15. Consequently, if the results of this experiment were rolled out across the whole company permanently, it would increase profits by $160m per year.[35]

Although the exact psychological mechanism for charm pricing is not fully understood, it is speculated that as we read from left to right (in western cultures), we start to process the price even before we finish reading it. So, when reading £4.99, our brain has already encoded the four even before we have read the nine, hence it is perceived as cheaper, even though there's only a penny's difference between the two prices.[36] But new eye-tracking research has started to question whether we really do read prices from left to right. Laurent and Vanhuele, a team of French scientists, showed that when we first look at a price, we focus between the first third and the middle of the price. We usually look to the left but subsequent eye movements are as often to the left as to the right;[37] either way, it looks like researchers will keep exploring this topic for a little while more.

Unfortunately, the use of charm pricing can come at a cost: pricing a product at £99.99 may make it appear cheaper, but it can also create a negative implication about the product's quality.[38] If a company is selling a luxury product, they are less likely to use charm pricing, because they don't want you to be focusing on price or value when you make your purchase decision; instead, it's all about emotions and feeling. But when a product is being discounted, marketers understand that customers are thinking in terms of value. In that situation, they are more likely to use charm prices.

Expectation effects

So far in this chapter, we've been exploring how brands can make their prices feel lower, but high prices are not always a negative. In fact, in some cases, they can increase sales. Shoppers may use the price as a heuristic to judge a product's quality: the more expensive the product is, the higher quality we perceive it to be (this is sometimes called the *Price-Quality Heuristic* or even the 'marketing placebo').[39]

This has led to a number of surprising results, such as the case of a jewellery store whose staff were struggling to sell some turquoise jewellery. They had tried a range of promotional tactics, but nothing was working. Eventually, the manager decided that she needed to accept a loss and sell them at a significant discount. She left a note for her employees to discount them by a half. However, her employees misunderstood and instead doubled the price. Within a week, all of the products had been sold, increasing the price made them appear to be of higher quality and thus more desirable.[40]

Changing our expectations of a product can actually change how well a product functions. For example, when a team of scientists gave participants a fake pain relief tablet and then proceeded to give them a series of small electric shocks, people who thought the pill cost $1.50 experienced less pain than those who were told the pill cost $0.10. What's interesting is that as the scientists increased the voltage, the pills 'protective' effect became even stronger for the more expensive pill.[41]

Yet this effect is not limited to medication. A similar effect has been shown when people are asked to try wine. Participants were shown a bottle of wine with the price clearly marked and asked to try it. They were then asked to report how pleasant they found the wine. As expected, the more expensive the wine, the better they claimed it tasted.[42] But relying on self-report data is problematic; participants may not have actually thought the wine tasted better, but due to societal expectations, they felt obliged to say the more expensive wine tasted better. But, further research has shown this is not the case. In a subsequent study, participants were asked to taste wine while lying in an fMRI scanner (a research tool used to measure blood flow in the brain – see Chapter 16). Before tasting the wine, half of the participants were told they were drinking $90 wine and the other half were told they were drinking $10 wine, although in reality they were all drinking the same wine. The results showed that participants who thought they were drinking $90 rather than $10 wine experienced more activation in the Medial Orbotofrontal Cortex, a part of the brain associated with pleasantness. This finding suggests participants were not just conforming to social expectations but really did believe that the supposedly more expensive wine tasted nicer.[43]

While this is compelling evidence, generally, if you are going to be drinking a $90 bottle of wine, it will accompany a lavish meal you are sharing with a partner or good friends. Consequently, it would be fair to say that the study has poor ecological validity, *the extent to which the findings of a study can be generalized to a real-life context*. Unfortunately, from a legal and ethical perspective, it would be hard to test this in a retail context, as it would involve deceiving customers.

REAL-WORLD EXAMPLE: PSYCH IN ACTION

Balthazar is an upmarket brasserie in New York that serves traditional French food. When customers order wine, rather than serving it in the bottle, they pour it into decanters and bring that to your table. This can make it challenging for the sommelier to ensure that the right wine is sent to the right table. Normally, it is not a problem, but on one occasion, there was a mix-up. A group of four Wall Street businessmen ordered a Bordeaux First Growth Mouton Rothschild 1989, the most expensive wine on the menu, costing $2,000. Across on the other side of the restaurant, a young couple were on a date. They ordered an $18 pinot, the cheapest wine on the menu, and, you guessed it, the two decanters got muddled up. Neither of the customers noticed the difference. In fact, the businessmen praised their wine's purity.[44] They simply tasted what they expected to taste. The price of the wine set their expectation (although perhaps the alternative takeaway is that most people cannot tell the difference between cheap and extremely expensive wine).

While research shows that the price-quality heuristic is a consistent finding, there are some questions about the longevity of the effect. When we're standing in a shop looking at the shelves, virtually everybody believes that more expensive products are better quality. However, if we buy an expensive product and take it home, over time we can start to feel disillusioned with the product if the product's quality doesn't live up to the expensive price.[45]

Services and price

Services have four unique characteristics that make promoting them different to physical goods: intangibility, inseparability, variability and perishability. These characteristics can influence how they are priced: services being intangible means that customers can't touch or see the product when deciding whether or not to purchase, making the decision feel more risky. And because it is harder to evaluate service, it means that buyers and sellers are more likely to disagree over the price than they are for a physical good.[46]

From a marketing perspective, this may seem like a negative, but there are advantages as well. Customers are more willing to accept a price increase for an experience than a physical product. This comes down to the unique characteristics of a service: by definition a service varies, and as a result, customers expect a unique experience. Go to a restaurant on two different days and order exactly the same dishes and your experience will be different. It is for this reason that shoppers are prepared to accept a price increase for a service but find it unreasonable to pay more for a product when they are receiving exactly the same product.[47]

How to justify a price increase

But what should you do if you're selling a physical product and you need to increase your prices? It turns out that often, honesty is the best course of action. One reason why shoppers object to price rises is that they don't understand the costs. If you're in a restaurant, you may look at the ingredients on your plate and think that you could cook this meal for only a few pounds at home. But you forget to factor in the cost of the kitchen staff, waiting staff, rent, heat and utilities etc.

This is not only true for a restaurant but physical products as well. Take a rucksack that costs £36.35; the business might have to pay costs of £12.92 for materials, £5.13 for handwear, £10.16 in labour, £1.81 in tax and £5.83 in transport. When these costs are explained to shoppers, they are nearly 30% more likely to buy.[48] Consequently, if you're going to increase your prices, it helps to explain why you're going to do so.

However, one area where shoppers frequently complain about price transparency is when booking airline tickets. Book with any budget airline and you'll quickly find that the advertised price is not what you pay. If you want to take a suitcase with you, book a seat or even just take hand luggage, you'll have to pay extra. From a technical perspective, this is known as partition-based pricing (where the price of an item is broken down into subcomponents, but which can't be bought individually). The research consistently shows that the added complexity and cognitive effort required for shoppers to process the price leads consumers to think that the price is unfair.[49]

Surprisingly, this finding holds true for both B2B and B2C customers. While we would expect corporate customers to prefer to negotiate heavily to secure the lowest price possible, it still seems that people would prefer to pay a flat fee rather than a pay-per-use, even if it works out more expensive for them (although the effect is weaker for B2B customers).[50] Understandably, if past usage is highly variable or if shoppers have a close relationship with the seller, they're more likely to opt for a flat fee if they're given the choice.[51]

If partition pricing irritates shoppers so much, why do so many companies use it? There are two main advantages. Firstly, it provides businesses with a lower headline price which can be used for advertising and price comparison websites, but more interestingly, it changes how people remember the price.

When shoppers view a partitioned base price, nearly one in four completely ignore the surcharges when thinking about how much they paid in total, and even if shoppers remembered they had to pay a surcharge, over half underestimated just how much they were forced to pay.[52] Consequently, when a business uses partition-based pricing, shoppers are far more likely to make a purchase, even if they moan about it. It is worth mentioning that companies do need to be careful when using partition-based pricing: unlike in the United States, in the EU and Switzerland, companies can't advertise the price without including taxes.

But there is a way you can use a variation of partition-based pricing which is both legal and encourages people to buy more premium products instead. Rather than just stating that the regular product costs £199 and the premium version costs £259, it's more effective to say a regular item costs £199 and the premium version just costs £60 more.[53] By using this differential price approach, shoppers don't just focus on the total, instead they focus on the price difference, which makes the product feel cheaper.

Precise pricing

When determining how to price a product, retailers have the choice of either using a round price (e.g. £100) or a more precise price (e.g. £112). If they opt to use a round number, consumers may perceive these prices as too perfect. Shoppers can be sceptical that the product really costs £500 or £1,000 (potentially believing that it has been rounded up and is now overpriced).[54] For example, when participants were told the retail price of a product (e.g. a plasma television, basketball etc.) and asked to estimate the wholesale price (the price the store paid for the product), participants who were shown a round retail price (e.g. $5,000) thought of a significantly lower wholesale price compared to participants who were shown a precise price (e.g. $4,988).

This finding can frequently be seen in real-world sales data. When researchers analysed five years' worth of house sales data from Alachua County, Florida, they found that houses initially priced with an odd price (e.g. $494,500) sold at a price closer to the initial asking price than houses that were priced with round numbers (e.g. $500,000).[55] This effect of precise prices being perceived as better value is magnified when consumers are faced with situations where they are unfamiliar with the price or the product category,[56] for example, when buying a car or a new computer (two categories where most of us make purchases infrequently).

Processing fluency

When it comes to being precise, retailers can decide whether to include decimal places or not. Exactly how many pennies or centimes are used at the end of a price may seem like a minor decision, especially for higher value goods, but it influences sales. This is because prices that don't include pence or cents are processed more fluently than those that do.[57] Processing fluency is the ease with which the brain processes information.[58] In general, the easier we process information, the more positively we reflect on the associated experience. Consequently, when it comes to emotional process where we rely on 'Type 1' emotional decision-making, round prices often 'just feel right', but if we are attempting to use a non-heuristic decision (e.g. rational decision-making), we prefer non-round numbers.

If our brain can process prices or the nature of a product easily (in a fluent way, to use the language of psychologists), we view them, perhaps mistakenly, in a more positive light.[59] Consequently, if display prices or labels are in a font that is difficult to read, it increases the likelihood that consumers will defer making a purchase decision.

In one study, customers were asked to choose between two cordless phones, with the price information written for each phone in different typefaces; one easy to read and the other more difficult. When the typeface was easy to read, only 17% of customers put off making a purchase, but when the typeface was hard to read, this increased to 41%.[60] The researchers concluded that customers mistakenly believed the difficulty they experienced reading the text was caused by the challenge they had in deciding which product to buy. To make matters worse, when information is written in a hard-to-read font, people are less likely to believe it.[61]

However, there is one plus side. If a shopper did decide to make a purchase, they were more satisfied with their purchases in the long term. Shoppers recognized that they spent more time deliberating (because the information was harder to process), but as a result, assumed that as they put more thought into the purchase, they must be happy with the decision (see Figure 10.4 for an example).[62]

While processing fluency as theory has replicated across different cultures, there are cultural differences in how people read a font. For example, if a font is written in an angular font, such as DIN (rather than a more rounded font like Century Gothic), Japanese shoppers feel the pain of payment more acutely, and as a result, are more

Figure 10.3 An example of two labels. One is written in a clear and easy-to-read font, whereas the other is written in a more complex font. As shoppers' brains need to work harder to process this information, they perceive the product as more expensive

hesitant when it comes to making a purchase.[63] However, when the experiment was replicated with North American shoppers, they found that the roundedness of the font made no difference at all.

There are other ways marketers can use processing fluency to make promotional offers feel right. From a very young age, we learn a series of set number combinations: numbers that add up to ten, our times tables and so on. If retailers create special offers that use these patterns, consumers can process them more fluently and, in consequence, perceive them in a more positive light than they otherwise might.[64] For example, in one study, customers perceived four small pizzas and up to six toppings for $24 as more appealing than four small pizzas with unlimited toppings for $24. This is because 4 times 6 is 24 and consequently, it just feels right to us, even if we don't consciously know why.

Pricing: It's all a matter of timing

When we go shopping, we tend to see paying as an unpleasant necessity. But the point at which we first encounter a product's price changes how we view that product. If we're shopping online and order the search results by price, it means we are likely to encounter the price first, even before we view the product. This primes us to make our purchasing decisions based on economic value. If we purchase everyday, utility-type products – things like washing up liquid and toilet paper – this is a good thing from a marketer's point of view; research shows that consumers who focus on the price before looking at the product are more likely to make a purchase than those who view the product first.[65] However, the reverse is true when it comes to luxury products. Consumers who view the price first are less likely to make a purchase. This is because luxury goods retailers want customers to focus on how the product makes them *feel*. In other words, they want the purchase decision to be driven by emotions (System 1) rather than by logic (System 2). When selling a luxury watch, marketers will focus on the status and symbolism of the product. If consumers are primed to focus on the price and functional attributes of the product, they are less likely to buy.

Marketers are well aware of this, as you can see if you flick through the advertising in a large-circulation newspaper. Adverts from supermarkets and other dealers in essential or near-essential items – things like groceries, mid-range and budget furniture and some types of electronic goods – will often feature prices, price reductions and price-oriented offers. Adverts for luxury goods like high-end watches and jewellery will rarely feature prices. You can see the same effect at work even within product categories. Adverts for budget or family cars will often feature a price, typically expressed as a seemingly low monthly figure for hire-purchase. Adverts for high-end cars rarely do.

Another approach that can cause consumers to focus on price in a restaurant context is to list all prices in columns and to use leader dots[66] – full stops linking the food description to the price, like this:

Pot of Earl Grey……………………………………………..£2.50

By listing the prices in columns, and using leader dots, the restaurant has inadvertently turned their menu into a giant price list. It is encouraging diners to make their food choice based on the products' value – which just makes the price more salient – not what they will enjoy the most about the product.

Anchoring

We've established that it makes a difference *when* we encounter a product's price, but there are still more factors we need to bear in mind. Sometimes the first price we encounter when shopping can *anchor* or influence our sense of value. *Anchoring* is our tendency to rely too heavily on the first piece of information offered when making decisions. Think about a restaurant menu. If the first item you see is a steak tartare, with fries and a béarnaise sauce costing £30, you may not order this dish, but it sets your expectations about how much you're going to spend. Consequently, you're likely to spend significantly more than if the first dish was a jacket potato with cheese and beans costing £5.50, even if every item on the menu was identical. Consequently, when restaurant menu items are placed in descending order, i.e. the most expensive items are listed first, shoppers tend to spend on average 10% more than if the cheaper items are listed first.[67]

But when it comes to reading a menu, most people don't read the top item first and instead start halfway down the middle pages. But to ensure that customers are anchored to a nice high price, designers will place an eye-catching graphical element above the more expensive sections, increasing the likelihood that customers will focus on the expensive items, thereby creating a high price anchor.[68]

Many marketers overlook this simple approach, even if they are aware of the technique, often thinking it won't work for low-value items or where there isn't much variation in the price of products. When a local pub changed the order in which the beers were listed on the menu from ascending to descending, the average price paid for a beer increased by 4%.[69] Nothing else changed. The menu still contained the same 13 beers, but listing them as $10, $9, $8, $8, $7, $7, $7, $7, $6, $5, $4, $4 and $4 rather than the reverse caused people to order a more expensive drink.

REAL-WORLD EXAMPLE: PSYCH IN ACTION

But it's not just a product's price that can act as an anchor in a consumer's mind. Several apparently irrelevant factors can also anchor our perceptions of value. For example, in a lecture, Dan Airely[70] asked his students to write down the last two digits of their social security number as values next to photos of several items, including bottles of rare wine, Belgian chocolates, cordless keyboards etc. So, if their social security number ended with 76, they wrote $76 next to each item. They were then asked to write down how much they would pay for each item. However, unlike many psychology experiments, this was not a hypothetical decision; the students were taking part in an auction. The student who wrote down the highest amount would effectively win the auction for that item… and have to pay for it.

Before entering their bids, the students were explicitly reminded that the social security number price they had written next to the products was a random number and didn't mean anything. Yet, students with a higher social security number were *still* willing to pay significantly more for all of the products (Table 10.1). Students with social security numbers ending in the range from 80 to 99 ended up bidding between 216% and 346% more for the products compared to students with the lowest range of social security numbers (from -00 to -19).

Table 10.1 Results of the experiment

Rank of SSN	Cordless Trackball	Cordless Keyboard	Average Wine	Rare Wine	Design Book	Belgium Chocolate
Lowest Fifth	$8.64	$16.09	$8.64	$11.73	$12.82	$9.55
2nd Lowest Fifth	$11.82	$26.82	$14.45	$22.45	$16.18	$10.64
Middle Fifth	$13.45	$29.27	$12.55	$18.09	$15.82	$12.45
2nd Highest Fifth	$21.18	$34.55	$15.45	$24.55	$19.27	$13.27
Highest Fifth	$26.18	$55.64	$27.91	$37.55	$30.00	$20.54

This phenomenon has direct implications for marketing. The first thing we encounter when shopping for a product can act as an anchor, even if it's not a price. Consequently, retailers should think about what messages customers see before they enter a store. A sign saying *'Over 60,000 products in stock'* could be a powerful message.

Closing thoughts

When it comes to discussing prices, marketers understandably spend most of their time focusing on the big decisions. For example, if the product is sold for €30, will customers be prepared to buy it at that price? However, this overlooks the fact that prices can be relatively flexible (to a degree) in a consumer's mind. Most of the time, they are not encoded perfectly and this gives marketers a lot of control over how they are perceived. But all too often, these decisions are not given due consideration by marketers. The way a price label, a menu or even an advert (which shows the product's price) is designed can often be left to graphic designers. While they may be brilliant at creating an attractive and sophisticated-looking marketing asset, they are often not experienced in understanding how consumers perceive a price. Consequently, some of the decisions that they make can inadvertently make a product feel more expensive than necessary. This is where a knowledge of psychology and considering all parts of the consumer journey will make a big difference.

KEY POINTS

- When consumers pay for a product that they perceive to be expensive, it triggers physical pain.
- Shoppers don't usually remember or encode the product exactly. Instead, they recall if it was cheap, about right or expensive.
- The more salient the payment is, the more pain it causes. Hence, paying by cash is more painful than paying by credit card, mobile phone or tokens.
- People feel prices are lower when they don't include a comma: £1,199 vs £1199.
- If we ask shoppers to compare our price to our rivals, they can become sceptical. It's often far more effective to let shoppers make a comparison themselves.
- By including a 'decoy' product, a slightly worse version of a brand's high-end product, it can encourage shoppers to buy the high-end product.
- Charm pricing, pricing a product just below a round number (e.g. £99 vs £100), encourages people to make a purchase.
- If a company needs to increase its prices, it helps to be open and explain why the prices are increasing.
- The easier it is for consumers to cognitively process prices, the lower the prices are perceived to be.
- When consumers are anchored to a high price – for example, an unrelated high number (e.g. tell shoppers how many thousand units have been sold) – it encourages shoppers to spend more.

PUTTING THEORY INTO PRACTICE

1 Visit a website of your choice and review their approach to pricing. How could you optimize their pricing tactics by using principles from psychology?

2 What differences in pricing tactics might there be between a luxury watch retailer and a budget supermarket?

3 Apart from using explicit references to price, how might a brand use the principle of anchoring to influence how consumers feel about their prices?

4 Design a menu for a restaurant of your choice. Try to influence your patrons to purchase a more expensive dish (and feel good about their choice). Think about the location of each item on the menu, its price and how you display it.

5   Imagine you were working for a water company. They are planning to introduce a new pricing structure to encourage households to be more sustainable and use less water. Previously, customers would pay XXX per litre of water they used. Now they will pay XXp for the first 5,000 litres they use in a month, XXXp for the next 5,001–9,999 litres they use and XXXp per litre they use of 10,000 litres. Write a letter to consumers explaining this change (including a table explaining the changes) so that the pricing structure doesn't feel unfair.

6   If you were the manager of a company providing guided adventure holidays in the Swiss alps and you needed to increase your prices, how might you go about explaining this decision to your consumers?

7   Paying for products is psychologically painful. What creative techniques could a cruise line use to make paying feel less painful and encourage guests to make more purchases once they're on board?

8   Find a price list for a car company, including all the optional extras (and their associated costs). Redesign this price list so that it encourages customers to include several optional extras when making a purchase.

SUGGESTIONS FOR FURTHER READING

Ariely, D. (2010). *Predictably irrational: The hidden forces that shape our decisions.* New York: Harper Perennial.

Poundstone, W. (2011). *Priceless: The hidden psychology of value.* Richmond: Oneworld.

References

1   Prelec, D. & Loewenstein, G. (1998). The red and the black: Mental accounting of savings and debt. *Marketing Science*, 17(1), 4–28. https://doi.org/10.1287/mksc.17.1.4 (archived at https://perma.cc/V2LV-YVZY)
2   Knutson, B., Rick, S., Wimmer, G. E., Prelec, D., & Loewenstein, G. (2007). Neural predictors of purchases. *Neuron*, 53(1), 147–156. https://doi.org/10.1016/j.neuron.2006.11.010 (archived at https://perma.cc/NXJ4-PN78)
3   Gladstone, J. J. & Masters-Waage, T. C. (2024). When paying is (even more) painful: Personality-based heterogeneity in consumption responses to economic hardship. *Social Psychological and Personality Science*, 15(3), 264–274.
4   Adaval, R. & Monroe, K. B. (2002). Automatic construction and use of contextual information for product and price evaluations. *Journal of Consumer Research*, 28(4), 572–588. https://doi.org/10.1086/338212 (archived at https://perma.cc/B2Q7-KJ5U)

5   Prelec, D. & Loewenstein, G. (1998). The red and the black: Mental accounting of savings and debt. *Marketing Science*, 17(1), 4–28. https://doi.org/10.1287/mksc.17.1.4 (archived at https://perma.cc/9J4U-3JP3)

6   Raghubir, P. & Srivastava, J. (2008). Monopoly money: The effect of payment coupling and form on spending behavior. *Journal of Experimental Psychology: Applied*, 14(3), 213–225. https://doi.org/10.1037/1076-898x.14.3.213 (archived at https://perma.cc/7F7M-5XUU)

7   Thomas, M., Desai, K. K., & Seenivasan, S. (2011). How credit card payments increase unhealthy food purchases: Visceral regulation of vices. *Journal of Consumer Research*, 38(1), 126–139. https://doi.org/10.1086/657331 (archived at https://perma.cc/9J4U-3JP3)

8   Lapuz, J. & Griffiths, M. D. (2010). The role of chips in poker gambling: An empirical pilot study. *Gambling Research: Journal of the National Association for Gambling Studies* (Australia), 22(1), 34–39.

9   Ahn, S. Y. & Nam, Y. (2022). Does mobile payment use lead to overspending? The moderating role of financial knowledge. *Computers in Human Behavior*, 134, 107319.

10 Manshad, M. S. & Brannon, D. (2021). Haptic-payment: Exploring vibration feedback as a means of reducing overspending in mobile payment. *Journal of Business Research*, 122, 88–96.

11 Yu, Y., Peng, X., & Wang, L. (2023). The impact of mobile payment on hedonic preference. *Journal of Interactive Marketing*, 58(2-3), 151–166.

12 Prelec, D. & Loewenstein, G. (1998). The red and the black: Mental accounting of savings and debt. *Marketing Science*, 17(1), 4–28. https://doi.org/10.1287/mksc.17.1.4 (archived at https://perma.cc/9J4U-3JP3)

13 Fredrickson, B. L. & Kahneman, D. (1993). Duration neglect in retrospective evaluations of affective episodes. *Journal of Personality and Social Psychology*, 65(1), 45–55.

14 Yang, S. S., Kimes, S. E., & Sessarego, M. M. (2009). Menu price presentation influences on consumer purchase behavior in restaurants. *International Journal of Hospitality Management*, 28(1), 157–160. https://doi.org/10.1016/j.ijhm.2008.06.012 (archived at https://perma.cc/C8GJ-VYXS)

15 Barden, P. (2013). *Decoded*. John Wiley & Sons.

16 Coulter, K. S., Choi, P., & Monroe, K. B. (2012). Comma N' cents in pricing: The effects of auditory representation encoding on price magnitude perceptions. *Journal of Consumer Psychology*, 22(3), 395–407. https://doi.org/10.1016/j.jcps.2011.11.005

17 Dehaene, S. (1989). The psychophysics of numerical comparison: A reexamination of apparently incompatible data. *Perception & Psychophysics*, 45(6), 557–566.

18 Coulter, K. S., Choi, P., & Monroe, K. B. (2012). Comma N' cents in pricing: The effects of auditory representation encoding on price magnitude perceptions. *Journal of Consumer Psychology*, 22(3), 395–407. https://doi.org/10.1016/j.jcps.2011.11.005 (archived at https://perma.cc/XQ6H-5R79)

19 Dehaene, S. (1992). Varieties of numerical abilities. *Cognition*, 44(1–2), 1–42. https://doi.org/10.1016/0010-0277(92)90049-N.

20 Coulter, K. S. & Coulter, R. A. (2005). Size does matter: The effects of magnitude representation congruency on price perceptions and purchase likelihood. *Journal of Consumer Psychology*.

21 Dehaene, S. (1989). The psychophysics of numerical comparison: A reexamination of apparently incompatible data. *Perception & Psychophysics*, 45(6), 557–566.
22 Coulter, K. S. & Coulter, R. A. (2005). Size does matter: The effects of magnitude representation congruency on price perceptions and purchase likelihood. *Journal of Consumer Psychology*.
23 Coulter, K. S. & Norberg, P. A. (2009). The effects of physical distance between regular and sale prices on numerical difference perceptions. *Journal of Consumer Psychology*, 19(2), 144–157. https://doi.org/10.1016/j.jcps.2009.02.008 (archived at https://perma.cc/V8DP-B8GT)
24 Barone, M. J., Coulter, K. S., & Li, X. (2020). The upside of down: Presenting a price in a low or high location influences how consumers evaluate it. *Journal of Retailing*, 96(3), 397–410.
25 Dholakia, U. M. & Simonson, I. (2005). The effect of explicit reference points on consumer choice and online bidding behavior. *Marketing Science*, 24(2), 206–217. https://doi.org/10.1287/mksc.1040.0099 (archived at https://perma.cc/AEW4-WZFV)
26 Ariely, D. (2008). *Predictably Irrational*. Harper.
27 Simonson, I. & Tversky, A. (1992). Choice in context: Tradeoff contrast and extremeness aversion. *Journal of Marketing Research*, 29(3), 281–295. https://doi.org/10.2307/3172740 (archived at https://perma.cc/R35P-YRG3)
28 Simonson, I. & Tversky, A. (1992). Choice in context: Tradeoff contrast and extremeness aversion. *Journal of Marketing Research*, 29(3), 281–295. https://doi.org/10.2307/3172740 (archived at https://perma.cc/R35P-YRG3)
29 Buell, B. (2000). The limits of one-to-one marketing. *Stanford Business*, 68(4).
30 Holdershaw, J., Gendall, P., & Garland, R. (1997). The widespread use of odd pricing in the retail sector. *Marketing Bulletin*, 8.
31 Anderson, E. T. & Simester, D. I. (2003). Effects of $9 price endings on retail sales: Evidence from field experiments. *Quantitative Marketing and Economics*, 1(1), 93–110. https://doi.org/10.1023/a:1023581927405 (archived at https://perma.cc/MT2B-5SHS)
32 Troll, E. S., Frankenbach, J., Friese, M., & Loschelder, D. D. (2024). A meta-analysis on the effects of just-below versus round prices. *Journal of Consumer Psychology*, 34(2), 299–325.
33 Thomas, M. & Morwitz, V. G. (2005). Penny wise and pound foolish: The left-digit effect in price cognition. *Journal of Consumer Research*, 32(1), 54–64. https://doi.org/10.1086/429600 (archived at https://perma.cc/F4PZ-E5X3)
34 Strulov-Shlain, A. (2021). *Firms as model-free decision makers – Evidence from a reform*. Working Paper.
35 List, J. A., Muir, I., Pope, D., & Sun, G. (2023). Left-digit bias at Lyft. *Review of Economic Studies*, 90(6), 3186–3237.
36 Dehaene, S. (1997). *The number sense: How the mind creates mathematics*. Oxford University Press.
37 Laurent, G. & Vanhuele, M. (2023). How do consumers read and encode a price?. *Journal of Consumer Research*, 50(3), 510–532.
38 Schindler, R. M. & Kibarian, T. M. (2001). Image communicated by the use of 99 endings in advertised prices. *Journal of Advertising*, 30(4), 95–99. https://doi.org/10.1080/00913367.2001.10673654 (archived at https://perma.cc/QD24-X5MM)

39 Rao, A. R. (2005). The quality of price as a quality cue. *Journal of Marketing Research*, 42(4), 401–405. https://doi.org/10.1509/jmkr.2005.42.4.401 (archived at https://perma.cc/5DTZ-32YS)
40 Cialdini, R. B. (1993). *Influence: Science and practice*. HarperCollins.
41 Waber, R. L. (2008). *The role of branding and pricing on health outcomes via the placebo response*. Doctoral dissertation, Massachusetts Institute of Technology.
42 Schmidt, L., Skvortsova, V., Kullen, C., Weber, B., & Plassmann, H. (2017). How context alters value: The brain's valuation and affective regulation system link price cues to experienced taste pleasantness. *Nature Scientific Reports*, 7(1), 1–13. https://doi.org/10.1038/s41598-017-08080-0 (archived at https://perma.cc/E6VR-T47B)
43 Plassmann, H., O'Doherty, J., Shiv, B., & Rangel, A. (2008). Marketing actions can modulate neural representations of experienced pleasantness. *Proceedings of the National Academy of Sciences*, 105(3), 1050–1054. https://doi.org/10.1073/pnas.0706929105 (archived at https://perma.cc/6JL4-ER64)
44 Mercer, C. (2020, October 24). NY restaurant couple mistakenly served $2000 Mouton 1989 after ordering $18 Pinot. *Decanter*. https://www.decanter.com/wine-news/new-york-restaurant-mistake-mouton-rothschild-1989-446051-446051/ (archived at https://perma.cc/NN58-UR8U)
45 Kurz, J., Efendić, E., & Goukens, C. (2023). Pricey therefore good? Price affects expectations, but not quality perceptions and liking. *Psychology & Marketing*, 40(6), 1115–1129.
46 Nguyen, P. & Wang, X. (2024). The influence of non-physicality of goods on disparities in seller–buyer valuations: A meta-analysis. *Journal of Consumer Psychology*, 34(3), 445–465.
47 Bastos, W. (2019). Now or never: Perceptions of uniqueness induce acceptance of price increases for experiences more than for objects. *Journal of Consumer Psychology*, 29(4), 584–600.
48 Mohan, B., Buell, R. W., & John, L. K. (2020). Lifting the veil: The benefits of cost transparency. *Marketing Science*, 39(6), 1105–1121.
49 Homburg, C., Totzek, D., & Krämer, M. (2014). How price complexity takes its toll: The neglected role of a simplicity bias and fairness in price evaluations. *Journal of Business Research*, 67(6), 1114–1122.
50 Kienzler, M., Kowalkowski, C., & Kindström, D. (2021). Purchasing professionals and the flat-rate bias: Effects of price premiums, past usage, and relational ties on price plan choice. *Journal of Business Research*, 132, 403–415.
51 Kienzler, M., Kowalkowski, C., & Kindström, D. (2021). Purchasing professionals and the flat-rate bias: Effects of price premiums, past usage, and relational ties on price plan choice. *Journal of Business Research*, 132, 403–415.
52 Morwitz, V. G., Greenleaf, E. A., & Johnson, E. J. (1998). Divide and prosper: Consumers' reactions to partitioned prices. *Journal of marketing research*, 35(4), 453–463.
53 Köcher, S., Husemann-Kopetzky, M., Schirmbeck, M., Hess, M., Gmeindl, F., & Hess, S. (2024). A conceptual replication of the differential price framing effect in the field. *Marketing Letters*, 35(1), 159–170.

54 Janiszewski, C. & Uy, D. (2008). Precision of the anchor influences the amount of adjustment. *Psychological Science*, 19(2), 121–127. https://doi.org/10.1111/j.1467-9280.2008.02057.x (archived at https://perma.cc/UKV9-7TEF)

55 Plassmann, H., O'Doherty, J., Shiv, B., & Rangel, A. (2008). Marketing actions can modulate neural representations of experienced pleasantness. *Proceedings of the National Academy of Sciences*, 105(3), 1050–1054. https://doi.org/10.1073/pnas.0706929105 (archived at https://perma.cc/6JL4-ER64)

56 Thomas, M., Simon, D. H., & Kadiyali, V. (2010). The price precision effect: Evidence from laboratory and market data. *Marketing Science*, 29(1), 175–190. https://doi.org/10.1287/mksc.1090.0512 (archived at https://perma.cc/N5XG-E832)

57 Wadhwa, M. & Zhang, K. (2015). This number just feels right: The impact of roundedness of price numbers on product evaluations. *Journal of Consumer Research*, 41(5), 1172–1185. https://doi.org/10.1086/678484 (archived at https://perma.cc/KLG9-GPAP)

58 Alter, A. L. & Oppenheimer, D. M. (2009). Suppressing secrecy through metacognitive ease: Cognitive fluency encourages self-disclosure. *Psychological Science*, 20(11), 1414–1420. https://doi.org/10.1111/j.1467-9280.2009.02461.x (archived at https://perma.cc/23RZ-5RZS)

59 Lee, A. Y. & Labroo, A. A. (2004). The effect of conceptual and perceptual fluency on brand evaluation. *Journal of Marketing Research*, 41(2), 151–165. https://doi.org/10.1509/jmkr.41.2.151.28665 (archived at https://perma.cc/L2YF-EMVA)

60 Novemsky, N., Dhar, R., Schwarz, N., & Simonson, I. (2007). Preference fluency in choice. *Journal of Marketing Research*, 44(3), 347–356. https://doi.org/10.1509/jmkr.44.3.347 (archived at https://perma.cc/AS22-DY6C)

61 Reber, R. & Schwarz, N. (1999). Effects of perceptual fluency on judgments of truth. *Consciousness and Cognition*, 8(3), 338–342. https://doi.org/10.1006/ccog.1999.0386 (archived at https://perma.cc/CXN4-WMW8)

62 Jain, G., Shrivastava, S., Nayakankuppam, D., & Gaeth, G. J. (2020). (The lack of) fluency and perceptions of decision making. *Journal of Marketing Communications*, 27(6). https://doi.org/10.1080/13527266.2020.1815072 (archived at https://perma.cc/G5JV-6PPQ)

63 Park, J., Velasco, C., & Spence, C. (2022). 'Looking sharp': Price typeface influences awareness of spending in mobile payment. *Psychology & Marketing*, 39(6), 1170–1189. https://doi.org/10.1002/mar.21651 (archived at https://perma.cc/49LH-GCZ6)

64 King, D. & Janiszewski, C. (2011). The sources and consequences of the fluent processing of numbers. *Journal of Marketing Research*, 48(2), 327–341. https://doi.org/10.1509/jmkr.48.2.327 (archived at https://perma.cc/4JZ3-97PZ)

65 Karmarkar, U. R., Shiv, B., & Knutson, B. (2015). Cost conscious? The neural and behavioral impact of price primacy on decision making. *Journal of Marketing Research*, 52(4), 467–481. https://doi.org/10.1509/jmr.13.0488 (archived at https://perma.cc/JA7N-B625)

66 Poundstone, W. (2011). *Priceless: The hidden psychology of value*. Oneworld Publications.

67 Huff, S. C. (2021). Money on the table: Increasing revenue through menu order. *Journal of Digital & Social Media Marketing*, 9(3), 275–283.

68 Poundstone, W. (2011). *Priceless: The hidden psychology of value*. Oneworld Publications.

69 Suk, K., Lee, J., & Lichtenstein, D. R. (2012). The influence of price presentation order on consumer choice. *Journal of Marketing Research*, 49(5), 708–717. https://doi.org/10.1509/jmr.11.0309 (archived at https://perma.cc/6F9Q-S4UJ)

70 Ariely, D., Loewenstein, G., & Prelec, D. (2003). 'Coherent arbitrariness': Stable demand curves without stable preferences. *The Quarterly Journal of Economics*, 118(1), 73–105.

11 | The psychology of price promotion and competitions

LEARNING OBJECTIVES

- Design and create effective price promotion campaigns for brands.
- Explain how situational and category factors influence the effectiveness of special offers.
- Analyse the psychological factors that will influence the success or failure of promotional competitors.

Introduction: How do shoppers react to special offers?

While marketers may want to avoid offering price discounts or running promotional competitions, it is often unavoidable as retailers can insist on discounts to secure listings, especially new brands needing to find ways to encourage shoppers to try their products. Yet despite their prevalence, marketers don't fully understand them. Virtually all approaches drive sales, but not all are equally effective. So why, when you walk around a supermarket, do you see a mixture of buy one get one free (BOGOF), 50% off or 50% extra free? From a behavioural perspective, surely one is more effective than the other? When running special offers, researchers estimate that brands are giving away a third more margin than they need to generate the same levels of sale. Luckily, psychologists have investigated this topic for the last 40 years and have run over 500 different experiments, providing marketers with some clear answers.

Price discounts

Of all the price promotion techniques, by far the simplest are discounts – just temporarily reducing the price of your products. Not only are they simple, but they're popular with customers. Given the choice, shoppers prefer a 50% discount to the equivalent Buy One Get One Free deal. However, in some ways, this is a false equivalence. Although stores do offer 50% discounts and BOGOF deals, they are relatively rare. Instead, it is more common for retailers to offer a more modest discount or a modest increase in pack sizes for no increase in price.

From an economic perspective, as long as the offers are matched, it shouldn't make any difference – but prospect theory would predict the opposite. People are more sensitive to losses than gains, which suggests that price discounts will outperform xx% free. However, new research has shown that this is not always the case. If the retailer offers what shoppers consider to be a very small price discount, shoppers prefer the equivalent percentage free.[1] Although we don't know why this occurs, it is possible that it comes down to Just Noticeable Difference (JND) – see Chapter 2. The price reduction is so small that we don't even consider it a discount. Once the discount increases to a more meaningful amount, shoppers are more likely to prefer price discounts over the equivalent pack increase – as prospect theory would predict.

Yet care needs to be taken when running price promotions. Brands offer their product on promotion hoping to encourage people who use their rival products to switch to them. And if you take a superficial look at the sales data, it seems to support this conclusion. Price discounts result in a short-term spike in sales, but when the campaign ends, there is a slump before sales level off again.[2] This suggests that any increase in sales occurs because consumers are stockpiling, rather than winning shoppers from rival brands. In fact, it is estimated that only 33% of the sales bump comes from brand switching;[3] the rest is stockpiling.

Improving effectiveness

As shown in the pricing chapter, most shoppers aren't aware exactly how much a product costs. Hence, when it comes to running a price promotion, brands need to remind shoppers what the old price was to reinforce the idea that the new product is offering better value. However, while this usually works,[4] if the price discount is very small (or at least feels small), it is best to avoid mentioning the old price.

Another simple change that can make price discounts more effective is to simplify them. Most people didn't like maths at school and that doesn't change the older we get. Yet when we're looking at the old and new price of a product and trying to calculate the potential saving, it can feel like we are back in school and doing a maths test. From a shopper's perspective, this has a bigger impact than we may realize. The harder our brain needs to work to process a price change (the poorer the processing fluency), the less likely we are to make a purchase. So, marketers should aim to simplify the maths.

This doesn't necessarily mean changing the price of the item, but can simply mean changing how we write the price. At school, we learn to do subtractions by writing the large number on the left and the small number on the right (e.g. 10 – 5 = 5). Consequently, when it comes to writing a before-and-after price, the maths is easier if the smaller number is to the right of the large number or below it on the tag (e.g. 'Was £10 now £5') (Figure 11.1). But if the price discount is either very small or very high, the effect is reversed.[5] Another way you can make the price easier to process is by ensuring the ending of the discounted price is the same as the original price. If the original price was £12.99, where possible, the discount price should be £10.99 and not £10.50. When the ending of the sales price and original price are the same, most shoppers perceive the discounted price to be cheaper and as a result, sales increase.[6]

This occurs even when the discount is not quite as good. For example, when shampoo was put on a special offer and the price was reduced from £4.89 to £3.89, shoppers thought the discount was 12% more than if it had been discounted from £4.92. Likewise, shoppers were nearly 20% more likely to buy an electric fan and think that the price was nearly 25% cheaper when the price endings were consistent.

Although an exciting finding, there are some limitations, as it only works with more complicated prices. If the price is only two digits, i.e. £21, then the maths is relatively straightforward, and the effect disappears. However, once there are decimal places or there are three digits involved, the complexity of the maths increases, and the effect occurs.

While it is best practice to simplify prices, some retailers use shoppers' poor understanding of percentages to their advantage and make the offers feel more appealing. Instead of offering a 30% discount, some retailers offer a 10% discount and then a further 20% discount on the original price (Figure 11.2). From the shoppers' perspective, they perceive two gains as better than a single gain[7] – even if the final price is the same. It feels intuitively logical to present the larger discount first (e.g., initially a 20% discount, followed by a 10% discount), but the opposite is more effective. By starting with the smaller discount and building, it creates the perception that the total discount is larger.[8] In practice, the margin you give away is identical, but by breaking the discount into two parts, it will feel different to the shopper – which translates to sales.

Discount codes

Regardless of how the discount is framed, it is usually automatically applied to your purchase. But the exception to this rule is when shopping online, where it is common for shoppers to have a discount code that they type in as they check out and the price

Figure 11.1 An example of two price discounts

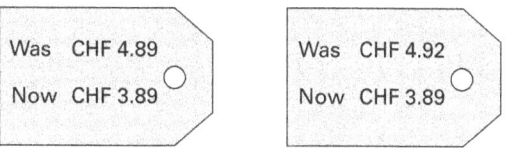

Figure 11.2 An example of percentage discounts

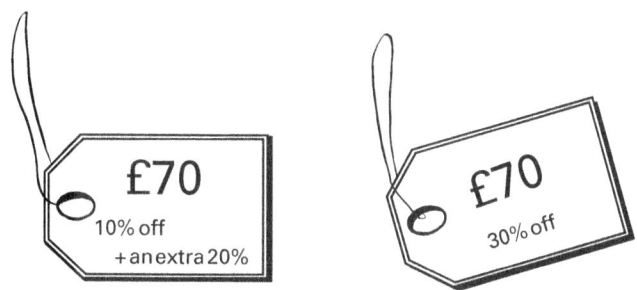

is reduced. Businesses are normally advised to make the shopping experience as frictionless as possible, reducing the number of webpages you need to visit to make a purchase, so why manually enter the discount before checking out?

The answer is saliency. If a retailer gives a shopper a discount, they want them to notice and appreciate it. If the discount is instantly applied, there is a good chance that shoppers won't notice it. But if they have to stop and manually type in a discount code, you are making them engage in the process. Normally, paying is a negative, triggering psychological pain, but now at the checkout, you get a boost when you see just how much you save – dialling down the pain. Surprisingly, this effect is even stronger when it comes to high-value purchases[9] – the cost of these purchases is even higher, so the perceived savings are even greater, increasing the effect.

Product bundles

When it comes to encouraging shoppers to buy more, often retailers don't just use a simple discount, but instead they offer a discount only if you buy two or three of the same product. For example, rather than paying £2.50 for a cider, you could buy '3 ciders for £5'. Once again, this presents a number of opportunities and challenges. Is it best to run a headline campaign that says: '*3 ciders for £5*' or '*£5 for 3 ciders*'?

By listing the price first, shoppers focus on the money that they're spending to make a purchase. If the quantity is first, shoppers focus on what they are going to receive, and consequently, sales are higher.[10] While it is always a good idea to frame the offer like this, the effect is stronger when the number of items included in the offer is higher than the price paid, for example, '*24 cans of cider for £10*'. This is because the number of items on offer has an anchoring effect, resulting in shoppers focusing on the quantity (in this case, 24) and they falsely infer that the price is a more attractive deal. But product bundles are not only used to promote fast-moving consumer goods (FMGCs); they are also just as likely to be used with high-end products. If you're buying a three-piece sofa set (a corner chair, three-person sofa and a two-person sofa), the retailer might offer a discount for buying all three.

Considerations for product bundles

However, careful consideration needs to be given when creating product bundles as there are drawbacks.

Firstly, shoppers are less likely to return a product that is bought as part of a bundle, as it changes how they perceive the offer. From a financial perspective, '*Buy a snowboard and bindings for €500*' is identical to '*buy a snowboard for €500 and get a free pair of bindings*'.[11] By receiving a '*free gift*' with our purchase, we not only receive a functional benefit, but a hedonic one as well. We feel better about our purchase, and this causes us to evaluate it in a more positive light.

The second risk with a product bundle occurs if you include a cheaper product as part of the package. Surprisingly, this can cause shoppers to think the bundle is worth less – what is known as the Presenter's Paradox. This seems illogical, but when shoppers were asked how much they would be prepared to pay for an iPod Touch, and an iPod cover, the average amount was $242. But when asked how much they'd pay for an iPod Touch, an iPod cover, AND a free download (objectively a better package), they were only willing to pay $177. For some reason, they thought the more expensive package was worth $65 less. So, what was going on? Once more, it's an anchoring effect, but this time shoppers are anchored to a lower price. The cheapest item acts as an anchor and stays in the shoppers' mind when they are trying to work out how much the items are worth, dragging down the estimation of the entire package value.[12]

This effect doesn't always occur, but it is most likely to happen when the main product in the bundle is expensive, even if shoppers aren't certain of the product's value. For example, if we're buying a computer, most people don't know how much an individual one is worth. You could easily be paying anywhere from £300 to over £10,000, depending on the specification and unless you are into computers, you may struggle to work out where an individual model sits in this range. Consequently, we look for cues to make a judgement and an anchoring effect is more likely to occur. Retailers need to encourage shoppers to focus on the most expensive product in a high-end product bundle, encouraging them to anchor on this product or try to make sure all the products are relatively similar in value.

Marketers often think that the more products are in the bundle, the more attractive it will be, but in reality, the opposite is true. In practice, it is better to offer a smaller bundle with a high percentage discount, rather than a larger bundle that has the same percentage discount.[13]

To keep things fresh, supermarkets are constantly developing innovative ways of offering product bundles, often based around occasions. Leading up to a major sporting event, supermarkets will offer deals such as 'buy a pizza and get two bottles of cider for free', encouraging shoppers to make an experience of watching the event. From a marketing perspective, it's a great proposition, but when running this promotion, is it best to offer the pizza as the free gift or the cider? The answer turns out to be relatively simple. Shoppers are statistically more likely to purchase a bundle when the target product (the product they were initially looking at purchasing) is promoted as the free gift.[14] So, when running the promotion in the cider aisle, it would make sense to promote the cider as the free gift, but if the same promotion were run in the pizza aisle, the opposite would be best.

If a retailer can't afford to offer the product completely free, they could opt to offer the second item at a discount instead. In this situation, the effect still occurs, but the importance of location is less important. Likewise, if you are trying to recreate this promotion online, the effect is even smaller. Shoppers are intuitively more suspicious of promotions online, as they are so used to being targeted by the algorithm that they've become intuitively suspicious. Consequently, people question these promotions far more than seeing the same promotion in a bricks-and-mortar store.

Buy one get one free

Probably the most famous variation of a product bundle is the BOGOF deal. Even ignoring the amusing name, there is a lot going on from a psychological perspective. From a rational and mathematical perspective, it should not make any difference if an offer is framed as a BOGOF or a deal offering a 50% discount if you buy two items, but shoppers don't think like this. Instead, people consider a BOGOF in terms of additional gains, whereas discount deals are perceived in the form of reduced losses.[15] As a rule of thumb, shoppers prefer percentage-off deals compared to BOGOF deals[16] (which makes sense when considered through the lens of prospect theory).

Prospect theory shows that *'losses loom larger than gains'*.[17] What this means is that from a psychological perspective, people are more affected by things they lose rather than what they gain (see Chapter 6). This explains why shoppers prefer price reductions in comparison to pack enlargements.[18] With a larger pack, shoppers focus on additional gains – how much more product do you get for your money, whereas money off is again perceived as a reduction in losses (the money you must pay for a product).

However, like most aspects of psychology, there are exceptions to this rule. The most obvious example is where a promotional deal requires shoppers to purchase a specific number of items to qualify for a discount, for example, buy one, get 50% off subsequent purchases. As soon as there are prerequisites, the promotion feels overly complicated, and they tend to get ignored. This preference is so strong that shoppers frequently opt for the BOGOF deal over the percentage deal – even if it is objectively a worse deal – in an attempt to simplify the maths![19] People recognize and understand what a BOGOF deal is. As soon as shoppers are required to purchase a specific number of an item to qualify for a discount, these offers feel too complex, and instead, shoppers follow their gut instinct and select the simple deal.[20]

Some brand managers criticize BOGOF deals and feel that they don't work. After analysing their sales data, they notice that a significant percentage of shoppers only buy one item and leave the second item, even though it's free. But this does not usually occur across all offers and can be explained by the category. For example, BOGOF deals perform better for non-vice products such as vegetables, rather than vice products (such as chocolates or cakes).[21] This is because shoppers impose limits on themselves. By definition, we prefer vice products, but we also know that they are unhealthy. If we buy a bar of chocolate, we don't have the self-control and quickly eat it. Consequently, in an attempt to limit how much we eat, shoppers sometimes decide to leave the second item in an attempt to limit how many cakes or chocolate they eat.

So, when it comes to promoting vice products, it's better to avoid offering a BOGOF deal and instead use a percentage-off deal. We can use the money off as a justification to treat ourselves to a 'tarte tatin', but it doesn't encourage us to overconsume quite as much![22]

BOGOF DEALS VS PERCENTAGE OFF – A MATHS TEST!

At times, shopping can resemble a maths exercise. Unfortunately, this would be a test that most people would fail. In one study, participants were asked to determine which promotion provides the best value for money between:

- '50% Off Multiple Purchases'
- 'Buy One, Get One Free'
- 'Buy Two, Get 50% Off'

Only 18% of participants realized that the deals were identical. Instead, the vast majority of participants preferred the 50% off deal, 21% preferred the BOGOF deal and only 4% liked the 'Buy Two, Get 50% Off'. This highlights that, wherever possible, prices should be presented in the simplest way to ensure that people don't get confused.

From a psychological perspective, this highlights the importance of message framing, and there are some simple guidelines to help advise businesses. When the price of a product is under £100, it makes sense to describe any money off in terms of percentages, but when it costs more than £100, it is best to describe the absolute discount as it will sound larger. Going from £20 to £15 is a £5 saving, but when framed as 25% off, it appears much larger. Care needs to be taken when discussing percentages, as most people have a poor understanding of percentages and easily get confused.

Shoppers frequently perceive '150% of 100' and '150% more than 100' as the same offer. Yet mathematically, they are very different. 150% of 100 is 150, whereas 150% more than 100 is 250 – that's a difference of 100% but shoppers do not realize. This has some interesting implications when it comes to how you describe any product changes to shoppers. If you are launching a new battery-powered Bluetooth speaker and the battery life is increased from 4 hours to 9 hours, it would be more effective to say that the battery life is doubled rather than that you have increased it by 125%. Technically, doubling the battery life is smaller than 125% but, intuitively, people don't realize this. We have enough other tasks to concentrate on when we're shopping; we don't need to make life even more complicated.

Free gifts

When shoppers are thinking about making a big purchase but are unsure whether to go ahead with it, sales staff may offer a free gift as encouragement. If you are undecided about buying a car, the salesperson might offer you free alloy wheels or a cycle rack: while we think of them as an upgrade, they are a free gift. Despite typically associating free gifts with cheaper purchases, they are just as common at the top end of the market. For example, 50% of sales of Esteè Lauder products (a high-end perfume brand) included a free gift.[23]

From a business perspective, offering a free gift makes a lot of sense. On average, shoppers value these gifts 2.4 times more than they cost the seller,[24] probably because of the endowment effect (see Chapter 6), and if the customer is on the fence about buying a product, it is often enough to persuade them, making their purchase seem like a better deal. However, by throwing in a free gift, it changes how we see both the main product and the gift. Usually, when a product is offered as a free gift, shoppers now think it's less valuable than if it is sold as a standalone product. Surprisingly, it is not only the 'freebie' that is considered less valuable but there is a carryover, where any similar products are also viewed as less valuable. However, if the free product is paired with a premium brand, some of the premium associations we have with that brand rub off on the free product, increasing its perceived value.[25]

But what happens when the promotion ends? Does the fact that the product was offered as a freebie have a lasting impression? If a product is offered as a free gift with a more expensive purchase and the promotion ends, shoppers are still willing to pay more for the free item than if the same product were offered with a heavy discount.[26] This is because when a product is discounted, it anchors our expectations as to what the product is worth. However, if the product is offered for free, the number zero doesn't act as an anchor. Consequently, we don't view it as a 'true' price. Cognitively, we may know that a price reduction is not the real price, but it is still able to anchor our expectations.

Free trial periods

In today's economy, with more companies selling services and especially subscriptions, businesses have learnt to modify the 'free gift' and offer a free trial to new subscribers. Rather than having to decide what the free gift is, the decision is to work out how long to offer a free trial for. Intuitively, people assume that the longer the free trial, the more likely customers are to convert and subscribe, but when researchers tested a free 7-day, 14-day and 30-day free trial, they discovered that the 7-day free trial was the most effective.[27] The argument is that the longer the trial, the more chance people have to use it and build up a habit. But shorter trials encourage more intensive product usage, increasing the likelihood that we'll buy the product.

REAL-WORLD EXAMPLE: PSYCH IN ACTION

Take a free trial of Netflix. If we're only given it for seven days, we're likely to watch it intensively, making the most of the trial. When it ends, we think of how much we've watched and think we can't really live without it. If we're offered a 30-day free trial, we'll still watch it, but we don't have the same time pressure. As a result, we don't watch it as intensively, especially towards the end of the trial – the point when we need to decide if we're going to subscribe or not.

Loyalty schemes and discounts

While price discounts are popular, they can usually only be run for a short period of time – otherwise the discount becomes the regular price. To combat this, many retailers have introduced loyalty programmes; unfortunately, though, most have a limited impact on sales. Statistically, people who have a store loyalty card do spend more money,[28] but this is not necessarily a causal relationship. It's just a case that heavy shoppers are more likely to sign up to a loyalty card in the first place.

This is not to argue that loyalty programmes have no impact. Firstly, they are highly effective at gathering large amounts of personalized data about shoppers. This data can be used both to create personalized adverts and offers, and to generate revenue as the retailer might sell the data to third parties. In 2023, it is estimated that stores like Tesco and Sainsbury's made an estimated £300m selling this data.[29]

Loyalty cards can increase customers' lifetime value, albeit with one major caveat. If multiple retailers offer loyalty cards in a similar geographic region, then the effect of the loyalty card is dramatically reduced.[30] Considering the average US household belongs to 21.9 loyalty programmes and actively engages in 9.5 programmes,[31] this is a real issue. Retailers need to question what the purpose of their loyalty card scheme is: market research or sales promotion?

Loyalty system tiers

Not all loyalty programmes operate in the same way. At a simple level, they can be divided into two groups: relatively simple schemes and complex tiered reward programmes. The effectiveness of each differs considerably. The relatively simple programmes, such as Subway's '*order 6 x 6-inch Subways and get the 7th free*', were historically viewed by experts as ineffective.[32] However, new research questions this. An experiment measuring the behaviour of 5,500 customers at a chain of male barbers showed that the introduction of a simple loyalty programme (customers received $5 discount on every $100 they spent across visits) resulted in a significant increase in store loyalty.[33] Over a five-year period, this increase in loyalty equated to an increase in customer lifetime value of 29.5%. Interestingly, the increase in loyalty did not occur uniformly for all customers. The effect was more pronounced for both heavy and light clients and weakest for moderately loyal customers.

The second set of loyalty programmes uses a tiered system (for example, '*Book 15 nights in XXX hotel chain in 12 months and become a Platinum member*'). This style of loyalty scheme is popular within the hospitality and travel sector as it operates on a very different psychological perspective to the simple approaches. The simple approaches work on two key psychological principles: behaviouralism (the idea that people will repeat behaviour they are rewarded for – e.g. loyalty points/stamps – and avoid behaviour they are punished or not rewarded for),[34] and the Zeigarnik principle (the idea that people don't like unfinished tasks).[35] Instead, tiered loyalty programmes exploit the idea of '*conspicuous consumption*', the need for status and a sense of belonging to a higher group. Typically, tiered programmes have been shown to be more effective, but they work best when there are at least three tiers. It allows for a clearer relationship for 'elite' members and users find the system intuitively easier to understand.[36]

All loyalty schemes work slightly differently, but most give shoppers vouchers to redeem depending on how much they spend. Each store will implement this in a slightly different way. Some provide shoppers with a money-off voucher that they can spend on any product in store, whereas some larger companies adopt a slightly more sophisticated approach looking for patterns in shoppers' spending. If an individual shopper spends £45 on a typical supermarket shop, they may get a money-off voucher, but only if they spend £53. Or perhaps the retailer notices that they typically buy toilet rolls every five weeks. In this case, four weeks after they last bought some toilet roll, they'll be sent a coupon that can only be redeemed against toilet roll.

Depending on whether the voucher can be redeemed against all products or a specific category should change how the offer is presented. When this discount can be redeemed against all products, it's in the retailer's best interest to present the discount as a percentage off rather than £X off, whereas if the discount only applies to specific products, it makes sense to frame the discount as £X off. Percentage-off coupons encourage shoppers to spend more, as the more they spend, the more they save, but £X off makes it simpler for us to understand how much we are saving when making an individual purchase.[37]

Communicating value

Novel promotional mechanisms

With a range of promotional mechanisms to choose from, what typically works best? If you ask shoppers what they prefer, the answer is almost unanimous – cheaper products. No fancy BOGOF or 15% extra free, they just want to pay less. Promotional mechanisms perform great in market research, but often don't result in the jump in sales expected.

It's not the fact that shoppers don't appreciate price discounts, but retailers can communicate it more effectively. Whenever retailers offer a price discount, there is normally a poster saying something similar to: '*40% off the regular price*'. However, in one study, when retailers tried framing it as '*Pay 60% of the regular price*', shoppers thought they were saving more, and importantly, were more likely to make a purchase.[38] However, there are some caveats to this effect, namely that it is primarily driven by novelty. If this approach became the industry norm, or if promotions across an entire online store were framed like this, the effect would disappear. As the effect is driven by novelty, there are further opportunities for retailers, such as using an unusual colour or font to communicate the discount – but again this needs to be used sparingly. The second caveat is that the effect only works for low-involvement shoppers. For shoppers who are already emotionally invested in their purchase, the fact that the message is framed using a novel mechanism will not result in them being any more engaged in their purchase decision; but for habitual shoppers, this can shift which offer they find the most tempting.

Another option brands and retailers have is to change the way that they describe their promotions. In most situations, companies describe price promotions as '*now XX% cheaper*' a gain-framed message. But retailers have tried reframing this as '*x% higher*' and in this situation, sales nearly doubled.[39] If the normal price was £100, then your two messages are either '*now 25% off*' or '*was 33% more expensive last week*'. Mathematically, it's the same deal, but 33% off seems like a better price (25/75 = 0.33 vs 25/100 = 0.25).

This effect is more pronounced under certain conditions. Firstly, with consumers who are less numerate, and secondly, when the absolute discount is relatively low. In practice, this means the effect is likely to be more relevant for retailers whose primary customers are older or from a lower socio-economic background. Of course, this does raise ethical considerations as these consumers are likely to be more vulnerable.

Promotional limits: Is there too much of a good thing?

Probably the most widely used tactic to increase the appeal of a special offer is scarcity claims (such as 'limited time offers', 'for two weeks only' or 'only three products per customer'). These restrictions were originally intended to stop the offer from selling out too quickly, but they unexpectedly made the offer more appealing. When a supermarket ran a series of adverts over 80 weeks, they found that on average the ads increased sales by 202%, however, the 44 ads that featured a quantity restriction increased sales by 544%.[40]

When viewing the ads, shoppers used the restriction as a source of information. If you are limited in how many units you can buy, it suggests the product is highly desirable – a form of social proof. But restrictions also serve as an anchor. Normally, when shopping, the default number of units we plan on purchasing is one, but when we see an anchor telling us that the offer is limited to '*three units per customer*', we interpret that the expected number of units to purchase is three.

The way a shopper reacts to a restriction is always going to depend on the specific type of restriction used. In each case, shoppers will make a different inference about the promoted product. If there is a quantity limit, this implies that a restriction is needed to reduce stockpiling (aka the product is highly desirable). In contrast, when shoppers are required to spend a certain amount to qualify for the deal, we assume the product quality will not be as high. In essence, shoppers create a hierarchy of quality based on the restrictions imposed. If shoppers think purchase limits offer the highest quality, then time limits and finally purchase preconditions offer the lowest quality – with this effect being strongest for unfamiliar brands.[41]

This isn't the only reason why shoppers will doubt the quality of a product. If a discount seems too big and there is no justification provided for it, shoppers will be highly sceptical. If the price is accurate, then the only thing that could be wrong is the product. If shoppers can be encouraged to physically touch and interact with the product, it can dispel these doubts.[42] Most of us aren't experts and touching a product won't provide us with much relevant information, but if a retailer is confident enough to let us handle and interact with the product, they clearly believe in their product.

Legal considerations

If you've ever worked for a large corporation, it can sometimes feel that you can't make any decision without consulting the lawyers, and running promotions is no different. Lawyers often like to leave themselves some '*wiggle room*' and rather than making definitive claims, they will say something like '*up to 50% off, while stocks last*'. But as soon as customers see the words '*up to*', they assume they'll get a discount, but it will be nowhere near the advertised percentage. Unsurprisingly, this leads people to trust the brands less.[43]

If a retailer is vague about the end date of a promotion, it can trigger two conflicting thoughts. We recognize that it is probably a cynical attempt to drive sales in the short term, but we still think '*what happens if this offer ends sooner and I miss out?*' The answer to this question depends on the offer. If the offer itself is believable, e.g. '*15% off while stocks last*', shoppers are likely to react positively and not think that '*while stocks last*' is a cynical marketing ploy. However, if the discount feels implausible, such as '*up to 70% off*', shoppers become cynical of the whole promotion, disbelieving all of it – especially for high ticket items.[44]

Paradox of choice and promotions

As shown in Chapter 12, marketers are often nervous about the paradox of choice; the idea that if you asked shoppers what they would like, they claim they would like a bigger range of products to choose from, but this results in lower sales. While this is a more complex and controversial finding, often not occurring, the belief that it might happen still influences how promotions are run.

Marketers frequently opt to only offer one product on promotion at a time. Their theory is that if two products are being promoted, shoppers will be unable to decide which is the better deal and won't buy anything. Unfortunately, this appears to be a mistake for a number of reasons. Sales data shows that shoppers are more likely to make a purchase when there are two products on promotion rather than one.[45]

When researchers offered shoppers the choice of either '*A Sony DVD player for $299*' or the choice of either '*a Sony DVD player for $299 or a Philips DVD player for $289*', demand was 2.5 times greater when two products were on special offer. We don't fully understand the mechanism at play here, but psychologists think it occurs because shoppers feel that they have more autonomy and are in control of the situation, where multiple deals are on promotion. If a shop only has one product on special offer, consumers perceive that the store is trying to manipulate them into buying that product. This is reactance theory in action – the idea that when our psychological freedom to act is threatened, we seek to regain control,[46] even if it means acting economically irrationally (passing up on a good deal)

The long-term implications of promotions

While price discounts are a great way to drive sales in the short term, they come at a cost. Deep price discounts may increase sales today, but they hurt sales when prices return to normal. Typically, once a brand starts to regularly discount a product, even a non-premium product, research shows it takes around three to five years for shoppers to feel happy paying the full price for that product again.[47] Brands can offer one-off discounts without any issues, but once shoppers regularly see the same product on promotion, they get anchored to paying a low price. But if the retailer provides an explanation as to why a product is being discounted, it reduces the impact of the anchor. The reason doesn't have to be overly complex; simply explaining that you're selling off last season's stock is enough.

When retailers force brands to run a price promotion, there are steps brands can take to minimize the anchoring effect. Rather than simply displaying the price as '*was £12.99 now £9.99*', if they display the price in terms of the percentage discount, it stops the anchoring effect from occurring.[48] Unfortunately, it does make the discount feel slightly smaller, but this is often worth it. Shoppers are now focusing on the percentage price change, and not the new price, hence the anchoring effect does not occur.

But what happens in the long term if you don't offer a price discount but instead run a non-monetary promotion (such as 20% extra free or offer a free gift with a purchase). Here, the research consistently demonstrates that non-price promotions have a more positive impact on brand attitude in the long run than price promotions.[49] This occurs not only because they avoid the anchoring effect, but also due to framing. When a free gift is offered or some other form of non-monetary promotion, it does not influence our internal reference price to the same extent.

Cracking the code: Why context matters

New products and hedonism

Launching a new product is always going to be tricky. In most cases, shoppers are going to have their preferred products, so in order to tempt shoppers to try a new product, brands often run a special offer. But what offer is most effective? It depends on how your potential customers view your new product. If the new product is perceived as innovative, shoppers understandably feel that the purchase is riskier. Will the product work as described? Is it going to do what they hoped for? Consequently, they are not likely to want to stockpile it, and so it's not best to use a BOGOF deal or 50% off your second purchase. Instead, it's better to offer a simple financial discount. However, if the product is perceived to be less innovative, then consumption discounts can work.[50]

In a similar vein, shoppers react differently to promotions for hedonistic and non-hedonistic products. When shopping, we need to justify our purchases to ourselves. For utilitarian products, that is easier to do because they are something that we need, e.g. cleaning products, toiletries or other essentials. Nobody wants to purchase these items, but if we want to live in a clean house and look presentable, then they're things we need.

But it is a very different situation when it comes to hedonistic products and indulgent treats. Even the most optimistic shopper is going to struggle to explain why they *need* to buy chocolates, wine and a pain au chocolat (or three). However, if a luxury product is on offer, it makes it easier for us to justify buying it. Consequently, if we see pain au chocolat on a BOGOF deal, we might find the deal not the most tempting. We can justify buying one pain au chocolat, but two might be pushing it. And this is why in most situations, non-quantity promotions (e.g. price discounts, rebates, coupons and loyalty rewards) are more successful when it comes to promoting hedonistic products in comparison to utilitarian products.[51] It's also the reason why financial conditional promotions (e.g. *'get a £10 discount if you spend over £60'*) are more successful for hedonistic products[52] – we're looking for an excuse to buy hedonistic products and justifying it to ourselves.

As an aside, this is also the same reason why a marketing campaign that promises to donate 5% of its profits would work much better for a company that sells hedonic and indulgent products than one that sells utilitarian products.[53] We're looking to find a reason to buy these products, and the charitable appeal makes the perfect excuse.

This isn't the only practical reason why shoppers may avoid buying a product on a BOGOF deal. How many times have you bought something, like a new toilet seat from Amazon, only to get targeted emails a month later suggesting you buy more. Unless you're a business, there is a limit to how many toilet seats you're going to need. Similarly, if you are trying to encourage consumers to buy a product that isn't consumable (such as glassware or bathmats), then 50% off promotions are likely to be more effective than BOGOF deals.[54] It may be a fantastic deal, but if shoppers can't easily store the product at home, then they aren't going to buy multiples of it.

Own brands, national brands and unbranded products

A lot of the research into branding focuses on large international brands with global recognition and turnover in the multiple millions. Yet unless you work for a global organization, this is not likely to be the situation that you face. It's an unfortunate truth, but shoppers perceive deals on national brands more favourably than when exactly the same offer is run on both private label and generic brands.[55] Shoppers have a more favourable attitude towards national brands and view them as being more prestigious than own branded or unbranded products and hence get more excited when these products are on promotion. This is why lots of retailers put banners in the store windows advertising discounts on national brands, using this as a loss leader to encourage customers into the store.

Ending deals

As the saying goes, all good things must come to an end, and the challenge for brand managers is how they manage this transition without irritating shoppers who have missed out on the deal. This is not a hypothetical problem; both the academic and commercial literature have shown that when a promotion ends and a customer can't buy the product at the price they thought, they feel angry towards the brand and seek to punish it by switching to a rival brand instead.[56] This scenario is made all the more common by the way most brands run their promotions, using what is referred to as a 'hi-lo' pricing strategy. The prices start off high (the regular price) and then are discounted for a short period, before reverting to the regular everyday price. However, some companies have started trialling a new approach. Rather than the price reverting straight back to the normal price, they use a graduated price, what psychologists call a '*steadily decreasing discount*', or SDD.

A good example of this in practice is by Boden. Rather than ending the promotion suddenly, they initially offer a 15% discount for three days, followed by 13% off for a day, 11% off for a day and 10% off for a day, before returning merchandise to its original price. This may seem like an overly complicated approach for retailers, but shoppers are used to it – albeit in a very different context. This is how season tickets are priced for most ski resorts and even some football clubs.

In a supermarket context, this graduated return to normal prices has been shown to be more effective than either using everyday low prices or the hi-lo pricing approach.[57]

This occurs for several reasons. Firstly, when shops use a steadily decreasing discount, it increases the likelihood that customers will visit the store. Secondly, it also increases the likelihood that shoppers will buy the product, as seeing the price gradually rising acts as a clear signal that the price is going to rise even further in the future, prompting shoppers to buy now. Contrast this with the traditional hi-lo pricing strategy. If a special offer has just ended, you're likely to begrudge having to pay full price for the same product, and as a result, don't buy it – unless you really have to. But with an SDD, if a shopper misses the initial price discount, there is a second and a third opportunity to purchase at a discounted price. Yes, the discount will not be as good and we'll be slightly irritated that we didn't get the best deal, but we are less resentful, resulting in a more positive relationship with the brand.

Regardless of how a brand chooses to end the deal, there will be one date when it finally ends, and the business will want to motivate as many people as possible to buy before then. One reason why many shoppers delay making a purchase is that they feel they have lots of time and they can come back another day. So, brands want to make the deadline feel as close as possible. Two simple approaches can achieve this. The first involves changing how the deadline is communicated. Rather than stating the deadline as a calendar date (e.g. 22 August), it is more effective to state that the sale ends in 12 days' time.[58] Once again, this reframe changes our perspective, making the deadline more salient. It causes us to focus on the fact that it is fast approaching, motivating us to act.

Secondly, retailers can slightly change the size of the discount they offer. Normally, our aim is to make the discount feel as big as possible, so given the choice between a 7.7% discount or an 8% discount, retailers would opt for the 8%. After all, using round numbers makes it easier for people to remember. But when it comes to special offers, this is not always the best course of action as it can reduce shoppers' intention to buy. When retailers offer a more precise discount, shoppers have the perception that the offer is going to run for a shorter period of time, and as such are more likely to buy the promoted product today.[59]

GIVE IT A GO

We've created an online shop selling a range of pizzas. However, there are a number of special offers available: (a) 50% off multiple purchases; (b) buy one, get one free; and (c) buy two, get 50% off. Which promotion results in the highest sales?

Competitions

The perfect prize

An alternative to a special offer is a competition. But for a competition to be effective, you have to offer an alluring prize. Headline-grabbing prizes such as cash, a luxury car or even a house do a great job at attracting attention, but they need to be supplemented with smaller prizes. When it comes to analysing consumer behaviour and attitude, most shoppers prefer a price structure which offers both major and minor prizes.[60] The smaller prizes increase people's perception that they might win, which motivates them to enter.

However, there is an exception to this rule. If the campaign is primarily targeting current or existing users, and the campaign is more about presenting new information to them, then it is more effective to offer a limited number of major prizes.[61] In this situation, the structure of the competition should be more about fostering enjoyment and promoting the hedonistic nature of the competition.

You may think that the best large prize is a lot of cash. This way, the winner can spend it on exactly what they want. If you offered a luxury holiday, it's hard to know what will appeal to the most people. One person's dream holiday might be sitting on the beach in 35°C heat doing nothing, whereas somebody else would be much happier getting up at 7 am to go snowboarding in -20°C. However, this is also the limitation of cash. A CHF 100,000 prize might sound fantastic, but shoppers need to use their imagination to work out how they will spend it.

This is not a drawback for shoppers who are highly involved or who are paying attention to the ads. They are prepared to invest the cognitive energy required to process the message and their imagination can run wild, creating scenarios of how they will spend the money. But the majority of consumers will process the message passively and will have a low level of involvement.[62] Cash prizes do not automatically imply a specific use, so contestants must use their imagination more actively.[63] As a result, positive emotions are more difficult to anticipate, and result in people tending to have lower-level emotional engagement in the competition.

This problem can be overcome by careful design of the promotional material. You can still state the prize is a CHF 100,000, but it's best to emphasize all the different things you do with the money. Pay off your mortgage, buy a luxury campervan, take a year off work and travel around the world. The poster or packaging just needs to do something to make contestants visualize what the money means for them.

As for the number of headline prizes on offer, there is no point in offering multiple headline-grabbing prizes if they are all drawn at the same time (for example, five luxury skiing holidays to be won). Most consumers have limited experience of entering competitions, and as such, struggle to estimate the odds of winning. They don't see that the odds of winning are any better if you offer one luxury prize or 20 luxury prizes. In simple terms, increasing the number of headline prizes dramatically increases the cost to the company but doesn't increase the likelihood that people will participate[64] – unless there is a dramatic increase in the number of prizes on offer.

Instead, people place a greater weighting on the value of the prize rather than the number of prizes. If a trade-off needs to be made between the number of identical prizes to offer, and the value of these prizes, managers should offer fewer prizes with a higher value. From a practical point of view, once competition organizers have selected a headline-grabbing prize, they get better value for money by promoting the competition rather than increasing the number of prizes available to win.

Factors influencing participation rates

Removing friction

As with most aspects of marketing, it is usually a good idea to remove friction from your competition; the easier it is to enter, statistically, the more entrants you are likely to get. This explains why competitions such as raffles, simple quizzes or interactive quizzes are popular with competitors.[65] The exception to this rule is if you have a highly educated target audience. In this scenario, it can make sense to use a quiz and deliberately increase the level of difficulty or challenge to enter. Research indicates that well-educated people enjoy intellectual challenges ('academic traps') associated with these competitions[66] – they're not just entering to win the prize but for the challenge and to prove something to themselves. This explains why more intellectual newspapers feature sudoku-style puzzles as competition mechanisms.

The other exception to this rule is when you want your competition to appeal to existing consumers who are already brand loyal. Asking a technical or complex brand question appeals to these loyal consumers, and while this will result in fewer people entering, it means that the business creates a database of more engaged consumers.

Delayed gratification and hyperbolic discounting

Another bias that influences participation in a competition is delayed gratification and hyperbolic discounting. Psychological research has demonstrated that most people prefer a small reward immediately rather than waiting for a large reward in the future.[67] In laboratory conditions, psychologists often test this by offering participants the choice to receive £10 now or £15 in a month; most participants opt for the £10 now. When this is applied to competitions, the evidence suggests that if the prize draw is a long time in the future, then participants are less likely to enter. This is especially true when it comes to smaller prizes. Participants just don't feel like it's worth entering. Consequently, it is normally considered best practice for there to be multiple opportunities to win, with a staggered draw element. This increases people's perceptions of winning, encourages repeat entry and avoids any problems of delayed gratification.[68] However, this is more important when the campaign's focus is:

- driving sales
- building product awareness
- building consumer engagement
- developing partnerships with suppliers

Closing thoughts

When it comes to running a successful price promotion, retailers need to think carefully about the psychology behind it. While offering a large discount may drive a short-term boost in sales, it can also mean sacrificing more margin than necessary. In many cases, a well-positioned, smaller discount can be just as effective, or even more effective, if properly designed. By understanding how shoppers perceive numbers and promotions, retailers can design promotions that maximize impact without unnecessarily eroding profits.

> **KEY POINTS**
>
> - Shoppers prefer percentage off deals compared to BOGOF deals. Given the choice, shoppers' order of preference is 50%, then BOGOF and finally 'Buy Two, Get 50% Off'.
> - Non-quantity-based promotions (e.g. price discounts, rebates, coupons and loyalty rewards) are more effective at promoting indulgent products, as shoppers are looking for excuses to justify buying them.
> - Launch price promotions towards the end of the month – most people are paid at the end of the month, so budgets are tighter and price promotions become more attractive.
> - When running price promotions, you need to display the old and new price – shoppers don't remember the old price, so can't tell how good a deal it is.
> - Wherever possible, prices should be presented in the simplest way possible to ensure that people don't get confused.
> - When reducing a product's price, the discounted price should have the same ending as the original price. If the original price was £12.99, the discounted price should be £10.99 not £10.50. This causes shoppers to perceive the discount as bigger, increasing the likelihood of a purchase being made.

- If the product costs under £100, describe the money off as a percentage, but if it is over £100, describe the absolute discount.
- Where possible, remove the confusion by using more concrete language. If you increase the pack size from four cans to nine, it's more effective to say 'over twice the size' than 125% extra.
- Where possible, don't end a price promotion suddenly. Gradually reduce the value of the promotion. For example, offer a 15% discount for two weeks, followed by 10% off for four days, and 5% off for three days, before returning the merchandise to its original price.
- Promotions are more effective when two products are promoted simultaneously – shoppers feel less manipulated.
- How you describe a discount changes its effectiveness. Saying '*3 ciders for £5*' is more effective than '*£5 for 3 ciders*'.
- If a product is not consumable (such as glassware or bathmats etc.), then framing a promotion as 50% off is more effective than a BOGOF promotion.
- Bundles are more effective when the target product is promoted as the free gift. If a retailer were promoting a package of a 'pizza and a pint', they would be better off describing the pizza as free in the pizza aisle and the beer as free in the beer aisle.
- Headline-grabbing prizes, such as a large cash prize, a luxury car etc., are great at attracting attention but do little to encourage people to enter.
- People are more likely to enter a competition where the prize structure includes a mixture of major and minor prizes.
- There is no point in offering multiple headline-grabbing prizes if they are all drawn at the same time. Shoppers do not perceive that offering one or five prizes increases their odds of winning the competition.

PUTTING THEORY INTO PRACTICE

1 Imagine you are the brand manager of an FMCG brand of your choice. If your biggest client demands a price promotion, what price promotion would work best for your brand and why?

2 If a new hotel chain wanted to introduce a loyalty card scheme, how would you design the initiative?

3 Review an online supermarket of your choice and its special offers. How might you reconceptualize these offers to improve their effectiveness?

4 From a brand management perspective, what are the risks of running a price promotion? Are there any steps that a brand manager could take to minimize these risks?

5 What are the risks of using product bundles to sell products?

6 Imagine you are the marketing manager of a large ski resort. You want to run a large competition to collect emails that can be used in future marketing campaigns. What would be the best mix of prizes to encourage a large number of entrants?

References

1 Palazon, M. & Delgado-Ballester, E. (2009). Effectiveness of price discounts and premium promotions. *Psychology & Marketing*, 26(12), 1108–1129. https://doi.org/10.1002/mar.20315 (archived at https://perma.cc/4WUG-GRSU)

2 Dawes, J. (2004). Assessing the impact of a very successful price promotion on brand, category and competitor sales. *Journal of Product & Brand Management*, 13(5), 303–314. https://doi.org/10.1108/10610420410554395 (archived at https://perma.cc/TB48-AEUS)

3 Van Heerde, H. J., Gupta, S., & Wittink, D. R. (2003). Is 75% of the sales promotion bump due to brand switching? No, only 33% is. *Journal of Market Research*, 40(4), 481–491. https://doi.org/10.1509/jmkr.40.4.481.19386 (archived at https://perma.cc/C6BM-4AYM)

4 Krishna, A., Briesch, R., Lehmann, D. R., & Yuan, H. (2002). A meta-analysis of the impact of price presentation on perceived savings. *Journal of Retailing*, 78(2), 101–118. https://doi.org/10.1016/S0022-4359(02)00072-6 (archived at https://perma.cc/TK6Q-SQ4M)

5 Biswas, A., Bhowmick, S., Guha, A., & Grewal, D. (2013). Consumer evaluations of sale prices: Role of the subtraction principle. *Journal of Marketing*, 77(4), 49–66. https://doi.org/10.1509/jm.12.0052 (archived at https://perma.cc/SR9M-VSUU)

6 Hung, H. H., Cheng, Y. H., Chuang, S. C., Yu, A. P. I., & Lin, Y. T. (2021). Consistent price endings increase consumers perceptions of cheapness. *Journal of Retailing and Consumer Services*, 61, 102590. https://doi.org/10.1016/j.jretconser.2021.102590 (archived at https://perma.cc/D2JL-WQMY)

7 Kahneman, D. & Tversky, A. (1979). Prospect Theory: An analysis of decision under risk. *Econometrica*, 47(2), 263–291. https://doi.org/10.2307/1914185 (archived at https://perma.cc/32ZE-ME3P)

8 Gong, H., Huang, J., & Goh, K. H. (2019). The illusion of double-discount: Using reference points in promotion framing. *Journal of Consumer Psychology*, 29(3), 483–491. https://doi.org/10.1002/jcpy.1102 (archived at https://perma.cc/UG85-A2QA)

9 Jia, H., Huang, Y., Zhang, Q., Shi, Z., & Zhang, K. (2023). Final price neglect in multi-product promotions: How non-integrated price reductions promote higher-priced products. *Journal of Consumer Research*, 50(6). http://dx.doi.org/10.1093/jcr/ucad045 (archived at https://perma.cc/5BM9-696L)

10   Bagchi, R. & Davis, D. F. (2012). $29 for 70 items or 70 items for $29? How presentation order affects package perceptions. *Journal of Consumer Research*, 39(1), 62–73. https://doi.org/10.1086/661893 (archived at https://perma.cc/Y556-98VD)

11   Lee, S. & Yi, Y. (2019). 'Retail is detail! Give consumers a gift rather than a bundle': Promotion framing and consumer product returns. *Psychology & Marketing*, 36(1), 15–27. https://doi.org/10.1002/mar.21154 (archived at https://perma.cc/JA8G-HQ8F)

12   Weaver, K., Garcia, S. M., & Schwarz, N. (2012). The presenter's paradox. *Journal of Consumer Research*, 39(3), 445–460. https://doi.org/10.1086/664497 (archived at https://perma.cc/J6SV-2E3H)

13   Krishna, A., Briesch, R., Lehmann, D. R., & Yuan, H. (2002). A meta-analysis of the impact of price presentation on perceived savings. *Journal of Retailing*, 78(2), 101–118. https://doi.org/10.1016/S0022-4359(02)00072-6 (archived at https://perma.cc/9VAT-T9JE)

14   Liu, M. W., Wei, C., Yang, L., & Keh, H. T. (2022). Feeling lucky: How framing the target product as a free gift enhances purchase intention. *International Journal of Research in Marketing*, 39(2), 349–363. https://doi.org/10.1016/j.ijresmar.2021.07.001 (archived at https://perma.cc/WJH2-JDRY)

15   Diamond W. D. & Sanyal, A. (1990). The effect of framing on the choice of supermarket coupons. In *NA - Advances in Consumer Research Volume 17* (eds. Goldberg, M. E., Gorn, G., & Pollay, R. W.) Provo, UT: Association for Consumer Research (488–493).

16   Diamond W. D. & Sanyal, A. (1990). The effect of framing on the choice of supermarket coupons. In *NA - Advances in Consumer Research Volume 17* (eds. Goldberg, M. E., Gorn, G., & Pollay, R. W.) Provo, UT: Association for Consumer Research (488–493).

17   Kahneman, D. & Tversky, A. (2013). Prospect theory: An analysis of decision under risk. In *Handbook of the Fundamentals of Financial Decision Making: Part I* (99–127). https://doi.org/10.1142/9789814417358_0006 (archived at https://perma.cc/D2U6-64A5)

18   Hardesty, D. M. & Bearden, W. O. (2003). Consumer evaluations of different promotion types and price presentations: The moderating role of promotional benefit level. *Journal of Retailing*, 79(1), 17–25. https://doi.org/10.1016/S0022-4359(03)00004-6 (archived at https://perma.cc/7G8U-654A)

19   Gordon-Hecker, T., Pittarello, A., Shalvi, S., & Roskes, M. (2020). Buy-one-get-one-free deals attract more attention than percentage deals. *Journal of Business Research*, 111, 128–134. https://doi.org/10.1016/j.jbusres.2019.02.070 (archived at https://perma.cc/AF3M-GH6W)

20   Hardesty, D. M. & Bearden, W. O. (2003). Consumer evaluations of different promotion types and price presentations: The moderating role of promotional benefit level. *Journal of Retailing*, 79(1), 17–25. https://doi.org/10.1016/S0022-4359(03)00004-6 (archived at https://perma.cc/3Z3K-5AGC)

21   Wertenbroch, K. (1998). Consumption self-control by rationing purchase quantities of virtue and vice. *Marketing Science*, 17(4), 317–337. https://doi.org/10.1287/mksc.17.4.317 (archived at https://perma.cc/B6YC-KZVR)

22   Mishra, A. & Mishra, H. (2011). The influence of price discount versus bonus pack on the preference for virtue and vice foods. *Journal of Marketing Research*, 48(1), 196–206. https://doi.org/10.1509/jmkr.48.1.196 (archived at https://perma.cc/29WW-XKPC)

23   Raghubir, P. (2004). Free gift with purchase: Promoting or discounting the brand?. *Journal of Consumer Psychology*, 14(1–2), 181–186. https://doi.org/10.1207/s15327663jcp1401&2_20 (archived at https://perma.cc/9Q7M-HE8U)

24   Hudik, M., Karlíček, M. & Říha, D. (2023), 'Do consumers appreciate promotional gifts?', *Journal of Consumer Marketing*, 40(3), 305–314. https://doi.org/10.1108/JCM-09-2020-4109 (archived at https://perma.cc/LNB3-TD9X)

25   Raghubir, P. (2004). Free gift with purchase: Promoting or discounting the brand?. *Journal of Consumer Psychology*, 14(1–2), 181–186. https://doi.org/10.1207/s15327663jcp1401&2_20 (archived at https://perma.cc/3XKT-CSW7)

26   Palmeira, M. M. & Srivastava, J. (2013). Free offer ≠ cheap product: A selective accessibility account on the valuation of free offers. *Journal of Consumer Research*, 40(4), 644–656. https://doi.org/10.1086/671565 (archived at https://perma.cc/B4SS-8VTL)

27   Yoganarasimhan, H., Barzegary, E., & Pani, A. (2023). Design and evaluation of optimal free trials. *Management Science*. 69(6), 3220–3240. https://doi.org/10.1287/mnsc.2022.4507 (archived at https://perma.cc/FW9E-WLWA)

28   Meyer-Waarden, L. (2007). The effects of loyalty programs on customer lifetime duration and share of wallet. *Journal of Retailing*, 83(2), 223–236. https://doi.org/10.1016/j.jretai.2007.01.002 (archived at https://perma.cc/87T4-GEKC)

29   The Times (2023, December 10) How Tesco and Sainsbury's made £300m out of your loyalty cards. https://www.thetimes.com/business-money/markets/article/tesco-sainsburys-loyalty-card-oyster-nectar-9mcqtlrqd (archived at https://perma.cc/2U7J-R8HB)

30   Meyer-Waarden, L. (2007). The effects of loyalty programs on customer lifetime duration and share of wallet. *Journal of Retailing*, 83(2), 223–236. https://doi.org/10.1016/j.jretai.2007.01.002 (archived at https://perma.cc/GHS6-SFCB)

31   Berry, J. (2013). The 2013 COLLOQUY Loyalty Census. COLLOQUY Industry Report. https://www.yumpu.com/en/document/view/51626903/the-2013-colloquy-loyalty-census (archived at https://perma.cc/6HXX-W8BK)

32   Sharp, B. & Sharp, A. (1997). Loyalty programs and their impact on repeat-purchase loyalty patterns. *International Journal of Research in Marketing*, 14(5), 473–486. https://doi.org/10.1016/S0167-8116(97)00022-0 (archived at https://perma.cc/Z8NU-P93L)

33   Gopalakrishnan, A., Jiang, Z., Nevskaya, Y., & Thomadsen, R. (2021). Can non-tiered customer loyalty programs be profitable?. *Marketing Science*, 40(3), 508–526. https://doi.org/10.1287/mksc.2020.1268 (archived at https://perma.cc/AAU8-CXG3)

34   Ferster, C. B. & Skinner, B. F. (1957). *Schedules of reinforcement*. Appleton-Century-Crofts.

35   MacLeod, C. M. (2020). Zeigarnik and von Restorff: The memory effects and the stories behind them. *Memory & cognition*, 48(6), 1073–1088

36   McCall, M. & Voorhees, C. (2010). The drivers of loyalty program success: An organizing framework and research agenda. *Cornell Hospitality Quarterly*, 51(1), 35–52. https://doi.org/10.1177/1938965509355395 (archived at https://perma.cc/D8W9-GGXJ)

37 Montazeri, S., Tamaddoni, A., Stakhovych, S., & Ewing, M. (2021). Empirical decomposition of customer responses to discount coupons in online FMCG retailing. *Journal of Retailing and Consumer Services*, 58, 102340. https://doi.org/10.1016/j.jretconser.2020.102340 (archived at https://perma.cc/7HDG-7FYJ)

38 Kim, H.M., Kramer, T. (2006). 'Pay 80%' versus 'get 20% off': The effect of novel discount presentation on consumers' deal perceptions. *Market Letters*, 17, 311–321. https://doi.org/10.1007/s11002-006-9309-7 (archived at https://perma.cc/56ZT-YAGL)

39 Guha, A., Biswas, A., Grewal, D., Verma, S., Banerjee, S., & Nordfält, J. (2018). Reframing the discount as a comparison against the sale price: Does it make the discount more attractive? *Journal of Marketing Research*, 55(3), 339–351. https://doi.org/10.1509/jmr.16.0599 (archived at https://perma.cc/ET7T-2H6D)

40 Inman, J. J., Peter, A. C., & Raghubir, P. (1997). Framing the deal: The role of restrictions in accentuating deal value. *Journal of Consumer Research*, 24(1), 68–79. https://doi.org/10.1086/209494 (archived at https://perma.cc/76RA-YXEZ)

41 Inman, J. J., Peter, A. C., & Raghubir, P. (1997). Framing the deal: The role of restrictions in accentuating deal value. *Journal of Consumer Research*, 24(1), 68–79. https://doi.org/10.1086/209494 (archived at https://perma.cc/76RA-YXEZ)

42 Yazdanparast, A. & Kukar-Kinney, M. (2023). The effect of product touch information and sale proneness on consumers' responses to price discounts. *Psychology & Marketing*, 40(1), 146–168. https://doi.org/10.1002/mar.21755 (archived at https://perma.cc/DT3M-8V7T)

43 Tan, S. J. & Chua, S. H. (2004). 'While stocks last!' Impact of framing on consumers' perception of sales promotions. *Journal of Consumer Marketing*, 21(5), 343–355. https://doi.org/10.1108/07363760410549168 (archived at https://perma.cc/5TCX-HJDJ)

44 Tan, S. J. & Chua, S. H. (2004). 'While stocks last!' Impact of framing on consumers' perception of sales promotions. *Journal of Consumer Marketing*, 21(5), 343–355. https://doi.org/10.1108/07363760410549168 (archived at https://perma.cc/5TCX-HJDJ)

45 Mochon, D. (2013). Single-option aversion. *Journal of Consumer Research*, 40(3), 555–566. https://doi.org/10.1086/671343 (archived at https://perma.cc/4LTR-C4YB)

46 Brehm, J. W. (1966). *A theory of psychological reactance*. Academic Press.

47 Piercy, N. F., Cravens, D. W., & Lane, N. (2010). Marketing out of the recession: Recovery is coming, but things will never be the same again. *The Marketing Review*, 10(1), 3–23. https://doi.org/10.1362/146934710X488915 (archived at https://perma.cc/C4V9-2ZJH)

48 DelVecchio, D., Krishnan, H. S., & Smith, D. C. (2007). Cents or percent? The effects of promotion framing on price expectations and choice. *Journal of Marketing*, 71(3), 158–170. https://doi.org/10.1509/jmkg.71.3.158 (archived at https://perma.cc/SKJ4-WRQS)

49 Yi, Y. & Yoo, J. (2011). The long-term effects of sales promotions on brand attitude across monetary and non-monetary promotions. *Psychology & Marketing*, 28(9), 879–896. https://doi.org/10.1002/mar.20416 (archived at https://perma.cc/343Y-V93R)

50 Lowe, B. & Barnes, B. R. (2012). Consumer perceptions of monetary and non-monetary introductory promotions for new products. *Journal of Marketing Management*, 28(5-6), 629–651. https://doi.org/10.1080/0267257X.2011.560889 (archived at https://perma.cc/M2SM-WV7Mq)

51 Kivetz, R. & Zheng, Y. (2017). The effects of promotions on hedonic versus utilitarian purchases. *Journal of Consumer Psychology*, 27(1), 59–68. https://doi.org/10.1016/j.jcps.2016.05.005 (archived at https://perma.cc/NPT9-GMU6)

52 Nigam, A., Dewani, P., Behl, A., & Pereira, V. (2022). Consumer's response to conditional promotions in retailing: An empirical inquiry. *Journal of Business Research*, 144, 751–763. https://doi.org/10.1016/j.jbusres.2022.02.051 (archived at https://perma.cc/TGH8-CSKD)

53 Strahilevitz, M. & Myers, J. G. (1998). Donations to charity as purchase incentives: How well they work may depend on what you are trying to sell. *Journal of Consumer Research*, 24(4), 434–446.

54 Li, S., Sun, Y., & Wang, Y. (2007). 50% off or buy one get one free? Frame preference as a function of consumable nature in dairy products. *The Journal of Social Psychology*, 147(4), 413–421. https://doi.org/10.3200/SOCP.147.4.413-422 (archived at https://perma.cc/6GP9-YFPQ)

55 Krishna, A., Briesch, R., Lehmann, D. R., & Yuan, H. (2002). A meta-analysis of the impact of price presentation on perceived savings. *Journal of Retailing*, 78(2), 101–118. https://doi.org/10.1016/S0022-4359(02)00072-6 (archived at https://perma.cc/J8ZN-KHMQ)

56 Biraglia, A., Usrey, B., & Ulqinaku, A. (2021). The downside of scarcity: Scarcity appeals can trigger consumer anger and brand switching intentions. *Psychology & Marketing*, 38(8), 1314–1322. https://doi.org/10.1002/mar.21489 (archived at https://perma.cc/9MMX-LJAB)

57 Tsiros, M. & Hardesty, D. M. (2010). Ending a price promotion: Retracting it in one step or phasing it out gradually. *Journal of Marketing*, 74(1), 49–64. https://doi.org/10.1509/jmkg.74.1.49 (archived at https://perma.cc/3GD7-SFD9)

58 Jeong, Y., Hwang, S., & Suk, K. (2023). Ten days (vs. May 10) make you rush: The effect of time descriptions on task scheduling. *Journal of Applied Social Psychology*, 53(2), 121–133. https://doi.org/10.1111/jasp.12933 (archived at https://perma.cc/53BF-F7ZB)

59 Jha, S., Biswas, A., Guha, A., & Gauri, D. (2024). Can rounding up price discounts reduce sales?. *Journal of Consumer Psychology*, 34(2), 343–350. https://doi.org/10.1002/jcpy.1384 (archived at https://perma.cc/CBD2-TFQV)

60 Chen, C., Huang, J., Su, S., & He, F. (2012). A comparison of probabilistic prize promotion schemes. *Social Behaviour and Personality*, 40(7), 1183–1194. https://doi.org/10.2224/sbp.2012.40.7.1183 (archived at https://perma.cc/SK3Q-AFMW)

61 Ogden, S., Minahan, S., & Bednall, D. (2017). Promotional competitions: A taxonomy of campaign framing choices integrating economic, informational, and affective objectives. *Journal of Promotion Management*, 23(4), 449–480. https://doi.org/10.1080/10496491.2017.1297971 (archived at https://perma.cc/6YD4-T2C4)

62 Cacioppo, J. T. & Petty, R. E. (1984). *The elaboration likelihood model of persuasion.* ACR North American Advances.

63 Santini, F. D. O., Vieira, V. A., Sampaio, C. H., & Perin, M. G. (2016). Meta-analysis of the long-and short-term effects of sales promotions on consumer behavior. *Journal of Promotion Management*, 22(3), 425–442. https://doi.org/10.1080/10496491.2016.1154921 (archived at https://perma.cc/K5PR-QFYD)

64 Laporte, S. & Laurent, G. (2015). More prizes are not always more attractive: Factors increasing prospective sweepstakes participants' sensitivity to the number of prizes. *Journal of the Academy of Marketing Science*, 43(3), 395–410. https://psycnet.apa.org/doi/10.1007/s11747-014-0389-2 (archived at https://perma.cc/JKF4-F9KG)

65 Kalra, A. & Shi, M. (2010). Consumer value-maximizing sweepstakes and contests. *Journal of Marketing Research*, 47(2), 287-300. https://doi.org/10.1509/jmkr.47.2.287. (archived at https://perma.cc/XPN5-UFCP)

66 Kalra, A. & Shi, M. (2010). Consumer value-maximizing sweepstakes and contests. *Journal of Marketing Research*, 47(2), 287–300. https://doi.org/10.1509/jmkr.47.2.287. (archived at https://perma.cc/XPN5-UFCP)

67 O'Donoghue, T. & Rabin, M. (2000). The economics of immediate gratification. *Journal of Behavioral Decision Making*, 13(2), 233–250. https://doi.org/10.1002/(SICI)1099-0771(200004/06)13:2%3C233::AID-BDM325%3E3.0.CO;2-U (archived at https://perma.cc/K85G-664L)

68 Ogden, S., Minahan, S., & Bednall, D. (2017). Promotional competitions: A taxonomy of campaign framing choices integrating economic, informational, and affective objectives. *Journal of Promotion Management*, 23(4), 449–480. https://doi.org/10.1080/10496491.2017.1297971 (archived at https://perma.cc/J77W-N5P7)

12 | Psychology in the aisles: Psychological influences in the shopping environment

LEARNING OBJECTIVES

- Understand how the design of a retail environment influences consumer behaviour.
- Analyse the psychological mechanisms by which environmental cues influence consumer behaviour.

Designing the perfect bricks-and-mortar store

Designing a new store is a complex process bringing together architects, visual merchandisers and brand strategists, but it is essential not to ignore the role that consumer psychology plays. Without it, architects and merchandisers will create a beautiful looking store, but one that does not encourage shoppers to spend more. For example, in the UK, shoppers' natural tendency is to walk around a supermarket in an anticlockwise direction.[1] Although there is no clear psychological evidence why, it has been suggested that this occurs because the majority of consumers are right-handed.[2] Yet architects frequently design stores that encourage consumers to walk in a clockwise direction, for example by placing the door on the left-hand side. Shoppers enter from the left, but their natural tendency is to immediately turn 'right'. This causes them to walk straight into customers who are queuing, causing irritation for everyone.[3]

Shoppers' implicit desire to walk in an anticlockwise direction can be overridden by careful design. When Collin Payne and his team stuck ten six-foot-long by three-foot-wide green arrows on the supermarket floor in New Mexico, 90% of shoppers followed the arrows, even though they did not know where they were being directed.[4] But if painting large arrows on a shop floor might feel too overt, the same effect can be generated using more subtle cues. Retailers can design a 'raceway' or an ideal path for customers by using differently coloured carpets or tiles to guide them through the store. When Christopher Kalff and Gerhard Strube from the University of Freiburg tried this, 74% of shoppers followed this new path, without even being aware that the store was guiding them.[5] Alternatively, if you want to guide shoppers to a specific shelving unit or temporary display, you could place stickers on the floor representing footprints, and again, shoppers subconsciously follow them.[6]

But how do researchers know if these interventions work? Understanding how shoppers walk around a store used to be a challenge, but technological advances have changed this. By placing RFID (radio frequency identification) chips in shopping trolleys, and using data generated from digital CCTV cameras, researchers can accurately track the path individual shoppers take around supermarkets.[7-11] Prior to this, it was commonly believed that most consumers engaged in 'considered shopping';[12] walking up and down every aisle, but we now know this is not the case.[13] Data collected by Jeffrey Larson, Eric Bradlow and Peter Fader by placing RFID tags in shopping trolleys at supermarkets in the Western US showed that shoppers spend most of their time walking around the perimeter of the store or the 'power aisle' (the aisle that divides the store in half). They typically only make short trips down individual aisles, selecting what they need before returning back to the perimeter.

From a marketer's perspective, they want shoppers to explore as much of the store as possible, as the more of the store they see, the more chance they have of making unplanned purchases. To this extent, there are a range of techniques available. Placing the more popular items near the end of the aisles encourages shoppers to enter the aisle. Once they enter, there is a good chance they will continue to explore the rest of the aisle.[14] However, for this to work, product placement is key. Items shouldn't be positioned in the middle, as they may not be visible from the aisle entrance. Shoppers typically pause at the end of an aisle to decide whether it's worth exploring. Placing products about a third of the way down allows them to be seen and draws them in. Once they've walked a third of the way down, they often decide to continue walking. Conversely, if the item is placed only a quarter of the way in, customers may select what they need and immediately return to the main shopping path, reducing exposure to other products.

A second approach you could use is to change the height of the shelves and the width of the aisles. Typically, supermarket shelves are approximately two meters tall, comfortably taller than the average shopper, meaning that they can't see over them. When shoppers are surrounded by tall shelving, it creates an environment where shoppers feel like the environment is controlling them,[15] what Albert Mehrabian and James Russel would characterize as a 'dominating' environment. This decreases the likelihood that they will walk down these aisles and even if they do, shoppers are less likely to make a purchase. This feeling of claustrophobia is made worse if the store's ceiling is low or the aisles are narrow and long, with no gaps. This explains why most supermarkets have high ceilings even though it dramatically increases the heating costs.

REAL-WORLD EXAMPLE: PSYCH IN ACTION

An easy way you could overcome the problem of a 'dominating' retail environment is to decrease the height of the shelves and make the aisles slightly wider. But this comes at a cost. It dramatically decreases the number of products a store can sell, and as such a compromise is needed. Rather than using traditional vertical shelves, innovative stores could use shelves that slightly slope away from shoppers. These give the illusion that the aisles are wider but without dramatically reducing the total number of aisles in a store.[16] This approach has been used in a range of stores, including Iceland, a UK supermarket. Other approaches involve shortening the aisles and including more breaks, so shoppers are free to walk into a different aisle.

Surprisingly, how shoppers perceive the width of an aisle is not fixed. An aisle that seems nice and wide to begin with quickly feels crowded when there are other shoppers with trolleys in the aisle, and that's before retailers make the aisle narrower by adding promotional displays. As soon as shoppers feel like a shop is crowded, there is a risk that they will leave and potentially may not return.[17] When Gilbert Harrell, Michael Hutt and James Anderson analysed how 600 shoppers walked around a supermarket, they found that when it became more crowded, not only did customers fail to purchase everything they initially intended to, they also reported being less satisfied with the purchases they had made,[18] leading to an all-round negative experience.

Decompression zone: Getting you into the mood to buy

When entering a store, be it a supermarket or computer store, the first area shoppers enter is considered the decompression zone.[19] This is the area at the very front of the store, and it is designed to slow customers down and put them in a shopping mindset. Before someone enters a store, they are generally not focused on shopping. If they've driven, they are likely to be concentrating on getting from the car and into the store as quickly as possible (and often out of a wet and windy car park). Researchers, such as Paco Underhill, have shown that most customers are likely to be walking significantly faster than their normal browsing pace and they don't slow down when they immediately enter the store. People can easily walk 30m before transitioning from 'purposely walking' to 'browsing mode' and as such this means they often miss products, special offers or adverts placed at the entrance of the store.

To help shoppers make this transition quicker, marketers could include 'speed bumps' or design features that force shoppers to slow down. This could be double doors, swinging barriers, a 90-degree turn as customers walk in, or products on special offer placed prominently. These speed bumps are not necessarily designed to sell but encourage consumers to start browsing sooner.

Some premium stores also have a greeter at the entrance, who welcomes customers as they enter. Some managers feel this is a waste of an employee's time, but Swedish researchers Otterbring, Ringler, Sirianni and Gustafsson have shown that when a retailer employs a greeter, shoppers spend more, feel more satisfied with the store, and have a more positive perception of employees in the store.[20] Not only this, but greeters have the unexpected benefit of decreasing shoplifting as they act as a visible presence.[21]

Most of the principles described so far can apply to both store design and shopping centre or shopping mall design. However, there is one key difference, and this specifically applies to the entrance. A good shop shouldn't intentionally confuse shoppers as they enter. If shoppers are confused, it puts them in a bad mood, and this reflects badly on the brand. But in the 1970s and 1980s, this was a key objective when it came to designing shopping centres. What became known as the '*Gruen Effect*' or '*Gruen Transfer*', named after Australian Architect Victor Gruen.

If someone walks into a store and is met with an intentionally confusing layout or lots of 'glitz', they are likely to lose track of their original intentions, making them more susceptible to impulse purchases.[22] The reason this proved more popular with shopping centres rather than individual stores is that if there was any frustration, this was directed at the shopping centre, which is far less damaging.

Is there too much of a good thing?

If you ask shoppers if they want a large or smaller range of products to choose from, they will inevitably say they want the biggest choice possible. The greater the range, the greater the odds they will find something that meets their needs. However, in 2000, a paper was published by Iyengar and Lepper that questioned this.

Although shoppers think they want more choices, having too many options reduces the likelihood of them making a purchase. When faced with an overwhelming number of products, they struggle to decide which one they want and are more likely to defer the decision altogether, ultimately leaving without buying anything.[23] Even if they do decide to buy something, they tend to be less satisfied with their purchase as they wonder if they would have been happier if they had opted for something different.

This was famously demonstrated in what has become a classic experiment. When a garden centre was selling jam, they alternated the number of jam flavours they put out on display. Some days the display only had six flavours, other days the display had 24 varieties. And this change led to a significant difference in sales. When there were only six varieties of jam on display, 30% of customers bought one, but when there were 24 on offer, only 3% of customers bought some jam. This choice overload effect has been given as one of the reasons for Aldi and Lidl's phenomenal success in recent years, as they have far fewer stock keeping units (SKUs) than a traditional store.

But like many psychological findings, in recent years, this result has been questioned, with numerous studies attempting to replicate it and a lot of the time failing.[24] So, under what circumstances is it a good idea to reduce shoppers' choices and when does more choice help? When Chernev, Böckenholt and Goodman analysed the results of 99 different experiments together, they found the choice overload was only an issue when:[25]

- shoppers want to make a quick and easy choice.
- making the right choice is important to you, or you are selling complex products (for example, investment decisions or insurance products).
- the options are difficult to compare.
- customers are unclear about their preferences.

This explains why most supermarkets don't suffer from choice overload despite the huge choice of products. However, if a retailer or brand feels like choice overload is a potential problem, they have a couple of options that don't necessarily involve reducing the product range. For example, if a store sells 20 different types of walking boots, they can divide them into five sections: high-altitude boots, winter boots, summer boots, lightweight boots and approach shoes. Now, rather than having to decide between 20 boots, shoppers just need to decide between five models.

The second option involves changing how products are displayed on the shelf. By taking the exact same number of products and displaying them horizontally rather than vertically, consumers perceive there to be a greater variety,[26] without actually increasing the number of SKUs. This occurs because humans have binocular vision (our eyes are arranged horizontally), so we find it easier to scan the shelves left and right, rather than vertically. Consequently, when products are arranged horizontally, shoppers find it easier to process the information, and we think there is more variety (an example of perceptual fluency), and this ultimately leads customers to select a greater variety of products.

But it is important to keep in mind what type of shopper is likely to be in the category. Suppose the category is dominated by 'grab and go shoppers', people who are looking for their usual brand of hair gel. In that case, it makes more sense to display products vertically, as it makes it quicker and easier to spot the brand we're looking for. However, if shoppers are here to browse, such as 'considered shoppers', and are likely to purchase different versions of the same products (e.g. macaroons or pastries), it makes more sense to arrange the products horizontally, to encourage consumers to engage in variety-seeking behaviour, which will ultimately result in more products being bought.

Store layout and shopping time

Ask most shoppers where the staple items, such as bread and milk, are located in a supermarket and they will say they are at the back, forcing them to walk around the rest of the store. To a certain extent, this is true. Hui, Bradlow and Fader have shown that the longer a customer spends in a store, the more items they are likely to purchase,[27] and as a typical customer only explores about a third of the area in a supermarket,[28] increasing the distance they walk can have a dramatic impact on sales. If you can increase the distance a customer walks by just 10%, this increases unplanned spending by 17%.[29]

This makes it sound like retailers should try to keep customers in the store for as long as possible, but there is a downside. The longer a consumer spends in the store, the slower they are to make their purchases.[30] As the shopping visit increases in length, the less efficient the shopping becomes.[31] This can partly be explained because although consumers tend to purchase products in a logical order, the route they take around the store is highly inefficient, and the longer the visit, the more inefficient the route becomes, as highlighted in Table 12.1. When shoppers are buying items they buy frequently (e.g. milk, bread etc.), then they are likely to select a more efficient route, as they know where these items are. But, if you force shoppers to walk around the majority of the store just to select the few items they want, understandably they get irritated and it puts customers off returning to the store.[32]

Table 12.1 Average spend per minute in a US supermarket, based on time spent in-store (adapted from data from Sorensen, 2009)

Shopping Trip Length (mins)	Spend Speed ($/minute)
5	6.6
10	2.34
20	1.9
30	1.6
40	1.2
50	1
60	0.9

In an attempt to save money, some supermarkets, like Tesco (UK) or COOP & Migros (Switzerland), have opted for 'scan as you shop'. Shoppers use a small handheld scanner or their phone and they scan the barcodes of items they want to buy as they shop. This way, instead of scanning everything at checkout, they just pay for what they've already scanned. This makes checkout quicker, but Grewal, Noble, Ahlbom and Nordfält discovered an unintended benefit of this system. It slows shoppers down as they shop. They have more time to notice other products and information on the shelf, and as a result, end up spending more and making more impulse purchases.[33] What's exciting from the retailer's perspective is that shoppers don't feel like they are being intentionally slowed down; instead they feel more in control of their budget, meaning they have a more positive shopping experience.

The contagion effect

When traveling around a supermarket, different products are clearly separated into distinct areas, for example a frozen goods aisle, international food, cleaning products etc. While this makes it easier for customers to find products, it also has a second advantage. Researchers Morales and Fitzsimons discovered that when products are placed next to each other, shoppers perceive that attributes from one product transfer from one to the other.[34] For example, when researchers placed packaged products such as lard and rice cakes next to each other (so that the products touch), shoppers rated the rice cakes as having a higher fat content compared to when the products were placed simply 'near' each other. This is not a one-off effect; the same effect has been shown when food products come into contact with non-food products. Customers rated a sealed packet of cookies as less appealing when the packaging touched a sealed pack of sanitary towels.

In many ways, this is counterintuitive as both the cookies and rice cakes were in sealed packages and there was no way any physical properties could transfer. The other remarkable aspect of this study is the longevity of this effect. Customers' attitude towards the product not only changes when the products are in contact with one another, but this attitude change appears to be fixed. The effect is also magnified by the ease with which consumers can imagine the products touching each other. If a product is packaged in a transparent container, allowing customers to actually see the product (common with food products), it's far easier for customers to imagine the products touching, intensifying this effect – even though consumers are completely unaware.

Shelf help: Displaying products

Eye-tracking research by Chen, Burke, Hui and Leykin has shown that when shoppers walk down an aisle, they naturally pay more attention to products on their right-hand side and those that are placed about 40cm below eye-level.[35] This is the result of simple biology. When people walk, they are looking ahead, but most people's posture isn't great. Rather than holding their head up straight, it tilts slightly forward, and as a result they are more likely to notice products just below eye-level. As for the right-sided bias, psychologists suggest this occurs because 90% of people are right-handed, and we're more likely to look towards our dominant hand.

This insight isn't just an academic curiosity, it is something retailers actively capitalize on. It is often said in retail, 'unseen is unsold', and as such some retailers charge brands to place their products in more prominent positions. If you want to promote your product on the end of an aisle, in most large stores you need to pay a listing fee; some stores even have listing fees for placing products at eye level, or the right-hand side. Brands are willing to pay this because in a supermarket one of the best predictors of whether your product is going to be bought is just how long someone spends looking at it.[36]

But unfortunately, not all attention is equal. If a brand has the choice of doubling the number of product facings they have in a store or the opportunity to place their product on the middle shelf, they should always go with doubling the number of facings.[37] Shoppers naturally look near the middle shelf when walking around a store, but when they stop to browse, they use the middle shelf as a reference point. Once shoppers have stopped moving, having more facings, eye-catching packaging or signage becomes more important than being just below eye-level.

Retailers who don't charge a listing fee have more freedom in how they merchandise their shelves, allowing them to create layouts that encourage shoppers to buy more. For example, light colour products typically sell better when they're on the top shelves, and dark coloured products sell better at the bottom.[38] This layout feels naturally 'right' to shoppers and improves their processing fluency. People have learnt that light comes from above, like sunlight or artificial lights, and these cast shadows lower down. Placing darker-coloured products on lower shelves mimics this familiar pattern, aligning with what our brains instinctively expect.

Positioning products: Solo or group?

However, when it comes to selling luxury and more expensive products, it is not just colour that marketers need to be aware of – physical space matters too. According to research by O'Guinn, Tanner and Maeng,[39] luxury products need space to 'breathe' as shoppers expect these products to have empty space around them to reflect their status.

If you were looking in a jeweller and saw a Patek Philippe watch on its own, you'd intuitively assume it was more expensive or prestigious than five or six Girard Perregaux watches displayed together. Without space, we automatically assume the products aren't as luxurious. This is true whether we are looking at products in person or on a website. As well as setting expectations, displaying products on their own makes price disparities less evident and makes it less likely that shoppers will make a purchase decision based on price rather than status.

It is not only luxury products that it helps to position on their own. When selling hedonistic products, it helps if they are displayed on their own or next to other more guilt-providing products which can act as a decoy.[40] Alaoui, Valette-Florence and Cova argue that shoppers need to justify their purchases to themselves and if there is a considerably cheaper or healthier product next to what they are thinking of buying, it makes the task considerably harder. Consequently, some retailers will deliberately include a significantly more expensive or unhealthy product next to the target product. They don't expect to sell many of these items, but it gives the shoppers an excuse: 'I may not have needed X, but at least I didn't buy Y, which was far more expensive'. Whereas, if there are lots of cheaper products nearby, it makes this self-rationalization process far harder.

Staying organized

But regardless of how retailers display products, they can make life easier for shoppers by keeping the shelves organized. Typically, shoppers pay less attention to individual products in a visually complex or messy shopping environment, as this triggers a negative emotional reaction.[41] Hence, most major supermarkets pay staff to tidy displays and make sure products are on the right shelf and the labels are facing forward.

At some point, even the best-run shop is going to sell out of some items. If shoppers see a few products 'sold out' in a large store, it increases the likelihood that they will purchase more of other items. Tian, Chen and Xu argue that the sold-out items act as a form of 'social proof', signalling that other people are buying lots of items, which makes the store and its remaining products feel more desirable.[42] However, if too many products are sold out, the effect is reversed, and people are less likely to buy anything and just find the whole shopping experience frustrating.

If a store has sold out of a product, some companies will put a simple sign up, letting shoppers know so they don't search in vain. But the wording of this message is key. If it simply says 'Unavailable', or '*Out of stock*', it gives the impression that the store can't manage their supply chain, which will irritate shoppers even more. However, retailers can avoid this problem by changing the messaging. Instead, if it says '*Sold Out*', it makes it look like the product is highly desirable, and not just the fact you can't manage your stock. Shoppers will still be irritated, but less so, and if you can let them know when it will be back in stock, this minimizes irritation even further.

REAL-WORLD EXAMPLE: PSYCH IN ACTION

The Body Shop, a global beauty brand, uses sold-out signs as the perfect opportunity for both brand building and to increase sales. Rather than saying a product is sold out, they include a sign that says, '*Sorry I'm so popular I've run out, have a look for me online at thebodyshop.com*'. This reframes the situation and turns it into a positive. Rather than looking like poor stock management, they're using it as an example of 'social proof'; highlighting that their products are so popular they keep selling out.

Waitrose, an upmarket UK supermarket chain, uses a similar reframing when it comes to promoting unsold items from their boulangerie. Each morning, their croissants and pastries are made fresh, and anything unsold at the end of the day is thrown away. If it gets late in the afternoon and there are still some unsold, most other supermarkets will offer a big discount and promote them as 'reduced for quick sale'. But Waitrose does something a little different. They drop the price slightly and promote them as 'too good to waste'. If they offered a 50% discount, like most of their rivals, it sets shoppers' expectations that the croissants are sub-quality. Whereas Waitrose has reframed the offer as 'too good' rather than 'going off' and are able to keep the price higher.

Buying something new

When a product is out of stock, it is normally a bad thing. But it can present opportunities for retailers. Shoppers who regularly buy the same item from the same store will know exactly where it is on shelf, and will pick it up on autopilot. The behaviour has become so automatic that they don't consider anything else. To demonstrate just how blind habitual consumers are, Schmidtke, Watson, Roberts and Vlaev switched the location of a best-selling product and a new product. Sales of the original product fell dramatically and the new product sales increased,[43] suggesting shoppers were operating on autopilot.

This clearly shows that without some external intervention, shoppers are unlikely to change what they buy. This could be that their usual product is out of stock, the entire section is redesigned or a new Point of Sale (POS) display has been introduced. This is especially true for shoppers who've bought the same product for a long period of time and whose habits become engrained. The longer you've bought a product, the less likely you are to try something new,[44] which potentially explains why younger shoppers are more likely to be new buyers in a product category. Hence new and growing brands tend to have a higher proportion of younger shoppers.[45] But it is important to remember that correlation does not equal causality. Simply targeting younger shoppers does not guarantee that a brand will grow.

Are all shoppers the same?

It is important not to overgeneralize and say that all shoppers always act on autopilot. Philip Adcock realized that people typically shop in one of five different ways,[46] whether they are in a supermarket, a department store or an outdoor superstore. Understanding who predominantly shops in your category should change your marketing.

- *Grab & Go Shoppers:* These shoppers aren't shopping but simply replacing products they have run out of. The purchases they make are driven by habits, and there needs to be a serious disruption to shift behaviour. Unless you invest in point-of-sale displays or their normal product has sold out, it is highly unlikely that these shoppers will change their behaviour.
- *Impulse Shoppers:* These shoppers only decide what they want to buy at the fixture. They spend very little time at the fixture and also decide what to purchase very quickly. They're looking for something tempting, and easy to buy, where they don't have the opportunity to think twice about it. Packaging needs to capture attention and almost instantly 'wow' them. They are not going to read all the different claims made on the packaging, but their purchase decision is driven by the product photo and maybe one key claim that stands out.
- *Inexperienced Shoppers:* These are often new shoppers to a category who don't know exactly what they are looking for. They are motivated and are looking for information to help with their purchase. However, they typically have a low

threshold for information and are prone to walk away if they're interrupted or can't find the information they are after. Information needs to be easy to find and understand, and as such infographics and iconography work really well in explaining why they should buy a particular product.

- *Experiential Shoppers:* These shoppers don't rely solely on visual cues; for them, shopping is an enjoyable experience, even if they're just browsing. They're not in a rush and are happy to take their time, exploring the category, learning about products and enjoying the overall experience.

- *Considered Shoppers:* These shoppers take their time at the fixture and consider their options. They are highly influenced by the power of brands, special offers and new product development. Yet, in order to reach a decision, they need time, space and information. These are the shoppers who are going to attempt to reach a purchase decision using rational, considered decision-making. This doesn't necessarily mean you need to give them leaflets. Depending on the product and how expensive it is, the information they need may simply be on the back of the packaging, but they have to be able to pick it up and read it.

These shopper types are not like personality traits. People are not always a 'Grab & Go shopper' and will adopt different profiles depending on the shop and even the section of the store. For example, in a supermarket, someone might be a 'Grab & Go shopper' when it comes to buying their regular brand of tomato ketchup, but if they go to the herbal tea section and are looking for something a little different, they might become a 'considered shopper'.

Typically, different categories will have a different mix of shoppers. Some will be predominantly more 'grab & go' shoppers, while others will be more 'experiential' shoppers. Brands need to understand what type of shoppers dominate their product category and make sure their packaging, secondary packaging and POSs are optimized for who is currently in the category, or potential new shoppers.

Impulse purchases

The design of any retail space should make shopping enjoyable but also encourage shoppers to make unplanned or impulse purchases. And this is where physical stores have a significant advantage over online stores. Commercial sales data has shown that people are twice as likely to make impulse purchases in a physical store than when shopping online.[47] How likely they are to make an impulse purchase will depend on the design of the store and decisions shoppers have made before they walk in.

We've all heard the advice, 'don't go shopping when you're hungry, as you'll buy more food', and this is true. But Xu, Schwarz and Wyer, a team of researchers from the University of Minnesota, demonstrated that you are not only likely to buy more food items but buy more of everything, even non-food items.[48] Simply being hungry activates the concept of acquisition in the brain in general; people are not only looking to satisfy their desire for calories but acquiring items in general. Although it's not been reliably demonstrated in an academic context, some companies have started running ads or messages that remind shoppers that they're hungry as they shop.

REAL-WORLD EXAMPLE: PSYCH IN ACTION

It's not just being hungry that is a bad idea; it turns out that shopping after a coffee is just as problematic. When retailers offered shoppers a complimentary cup of coffee before entering a supermarket or department store, they found that people spent over 50% more and bought 30% more than those who were offered a free glass of water or decaf,[49] suggesting the effect is caused by caffeine and not reciprocity. But it is not just that shoppers bought more, it changed what shoppers bought. People bought more nonessential products like scented candles or fragrances and in the supermarket, shoppers bought more hedonistic and richer (aka delicious) foods.

This potential explains why a number of leading supermarkets, including Waitrose, offer customers with a loyalty card a free coffee when they visit the store. Not only do they benefit from the principle of 'reciprocation', but it encourages customers to spend more.

Individuals experiencing a reduced sense of personal control are more likely to purchase indulgent or vice products, such as unhealthy foods and beverages. Under conditions of stress or perceived lack of agency, people are more likely to engage in self-licensing, making small indulgences, as a means of reasserting control. This coping mechanism can have a measurable impact on purchasing behaviour.[50] While it is ethically dubious to play on shoppers' insecurities, some brands have run messages highlighting how hard or busy life is and have just coincidentally promoted vice products.

But regardless of what is going on in a shopper's life, impulse purchases are driven by making the process easier. Shoppers need to be able to clearly see the product and pick it up. This explains why in a supermarket, shoppers are less likely to make an impulse purchase in the freezer section. Commercial research conducted by Philip Adcock showed that when freezer doors are present, the number of people reading product information drops from 31% to 9%, grab-and-go shopping behaviour decreases by 13% and most worryingly, the number of shoppers who make a purchase dropped by 29%.[51] This is because, to buy anything, shoppers are required to open the freezer door before picking up the product. Not only does this make it slightly harder to see the product through fogged glass, but it creates a natural pause. This small break is enough for shoppers to reconsider if they really need another frozen pizza.

Placing doors on fridge and freezers in a supermarket would considerably reduce a stores electricity bill. It's been estimated that this change would cut a typical supermarket's electricity bill by an average of 33%, and if the five largest supermarket chains in the UK did this, it would reduce the UK's electricity usage by 1%.[52] However, currently stores believe that the impact on sales means it is not worth it.

The importance of touch

One of the key reasons why some shoppers like going to a physical store rather than shopping online is that they get to see, and more importantly touch the products before they buy them. It may seem like a small difference, but this shouldn't be overlooked. As Catherine Jansson-Boyd has demonstrated, when shoppers can touch a product, they evaluate it more favourably and the likelihood that they'll purchase it increases.[53] This occurs for a variety of reasons, one of which is the endowment effect, that is, the idea that shoppers value something more if they own it. Yet this suggests that they don't have to physically own a product; simply touching it in-store is enough to trigger the endowment effect.[54]

REAL-WORLD EXAMPLE: PSYCH IN ACTION

Unfortunately, lots of brands make it difficult for shoppers to touch their products. Shoppers want to pick up products like loose leaf teas to be able to smell them. Yet to protect their products, brands wrap them in cellophane so you can't smell them, meaning shoppers don't bother picking them up. This isn't only an issue for food products. Numerous household products from can openers to garden hose attachments now come in blister packs.

When consumer psychologist Philip Adcock redesigned the packaging of a hosepipe spray nozzle for a leading garden tool manufacturer, he replaced the traditional blister pack with a more interactive design that featured a cutout. This allowed shoppers to pick up the product, squeeze the trigger a few times. The result? Sales jumped by 23%. Without the opportunity to touch and interact with the product, those additional sales would likely have been lost.

The shopping trolley: The 'greatest salesman' around

In a supermarket, surprisingly trivial things can influence how much people buy, like whether they use a basket or a trolly. Carrying a shopping basket around a store puts a strain on the arm and Dutch researchers Bram van Den Bergh, Julien Schmitt and Luk Warlop have shown that this makes us more likely to purchase 'vice' products,[55] such as cakes and fizzy drinks.

However, this is not to suggest that retailers should avoid using shopping trollies. If shoppers decide not to use a shopping trolley, they are limited on how much they can carry (either what they can physically carry in their arms or a basket). Once they reach this limit, they stop being motivated to search for more products, stop paying attention to marketing stimuli and usually head to the checkout.[56] Using a shopping trolley makes it easier to carry more items, but it also provides a hint to customers telling them how many items they are expected to purchase. Larsen and Sigurdsson, a pair of Nordic researchers, were able to influence consumers to purchase more fruit and vegetables, just by changing the trolley. Rather than using a standard trolly, they modified it by dividing it into different compartments, with each item labelled with what is meant to be placed in it (e.g. fruit and vegetables, other groceries etc.). The larger the compartment, the more money people spent on that category of items.[57]

In recent years, the size of the trolley has got bigger. As Martin Lindstrom has demonstrated, as the trolley doubles in size, shoppers typically buy 40% more.[58] This occurs because people use the size of the trolley as a cue as to how much they should buy. They presume the size of the trolley represents the amount that they should buy on a typical shop.

The trolley of the future

Today, researchers are changing the design of trolleys. For example, some stores are experimenting with dividing the shopping trolley into different sections (e.g. meat, fruit & veg etc.). The theory is, the larger the section, the more of these items shoppers are likely to buy. And this appears to work. In one experiment where the shopping trolley was divided into 'Meats & Treats' and 'Fruit & Veggies', they found the size of the section directly influenced how much people spent. In the control condition (with no divide), shoppers spent on average $10.36 on fruit and vegetables. When the trolley included a fruit & vegetables section that took up 35% of the trolley, shoppers spent $11.85 on fruit and vegetables. But when the researchers increased this to take up 50% of the trolley, shoppers now spent $13.40 on fruit and vegetables, nearly a 30% increase.[59] Although the researchers were using this tactic to encourage shoppers to purchase more healthy food items, the same approach could be used to sell more high-margin items, it just depends on the store's motivation.

Other retailers are experimenting with more hi-tech solutions, incorporating a small tablet into the handle of the trolley. Products in store contain a small RFID chip and as soon as shoppers place an item in the trolley, they get instant feedback, for example, a running total of how much they've spent. It may seem counterintuitive, but when real-time feedback was provided to budget-conscious shoppers in Atlanta, Georgia, it resulted in them spending 34% more.[60] Regardless of whether they had feedback or not, budget-conscious shoppers stayed under budget. The difference was that without feedback they spent 79.2% of their budget, but with feedback they spent 94.6% of their intended budget, resulting in a less stressful shopping experience. However, for shoppers who weren't cost-conscious, providing real-time feedback caused them to spend 24.9% less. Providing real-time feedback simply made the role of price more salient. But if a store has done a good job at segmenting the market and understands who their target market is, they should be able to understand if this is an intervention they want to implement or not.

This intervention is likely to be prohibitively expensive for most physical stores to implement, but it would be relatively simple for the idea to be incorporated into an e-retail environment. What would be cheaper for stores to implement is to change the design of the trolleys' handles. Currently, most trolleys have a long horizontal handle. As you push it, this works the triceps muscles in your arm. This may not sound very important, but previous research has shown that triceps activation is associated with rejecting things. For example, when we push something away that we do not like, our triceps are activated. However, if we are pulling something towards our body, our biceps are activated. Estes and Streicher, a pair of academics, redesigned the trolley so it activated our biceps as it was pushed.

Shoppers using the traditional trolleys spent on average €22, but when using the new trolleys, they spent on average €29 – a 25% difference in spending.[61] And unlike a lot of experiments, this was not looking at hypothetical purchases made in a laboratory context. The researchers created these new trolleys and introduced them into a major supermarket. Participants were unaware that they were taking part in an experiment, as they were just doing their normal shopping.

At first glance, this finding appears to be too good to be true. Perhaps the change in behaviour was caused by novelty? After all, people have used the same design of trolleys for years. Perhaps this quirky new design increased involvement? But in a follow-up experiment, the researchers tested the effect of horizontal, vertical and parallel handles. Both the vertical and parallel handles were novel, but only the parallel handles increased sales – suggesting that their initial hypothesis (the activation of the flexor muscles) was correct.

Olfactory cues: The smell of success

New age meets science

Olfactory marketing is the use of aromas for marketing purposes. Although this may sound rather 'new age', numerous studies have shown that ambient aromas produce physiological changes in people, such as reducing anxiety levels, mood states and stress levels.[62] This is not just a case that participants believe the aromas reduced their stress and anxiety levels, but by measuring their Galvanic Skin Response and how their brain responds using EEG, researchers are able to measure physiological changes, confirming that aromas make a clear difference.

Aromas are of particular interest to marketers for two reasons. From an evolutionary perspective, aromas helped us to determine if a stimulus was potentially dangerous or beneficial.[63] (Consequently, aromas can trigger an immediate reaction and influence shoppers without them having to pay conscious attention towards the aroma).[64] Secondly, as soon as we walk into a shop, we cannot help but be influenced by the aroma.

REAL-WORLD EXAMPLE: PSYCH IN ACTION

One of the first academic experiments to demonstrate that smells could be used for marketing was conducted in a Las Vegas Casino by Alan Hirsch in 1995.[65] While a casino may sound like a strange setting to research shopping behaviour, it was selected for good reason. If the research was conducted in a shop, although they could measure if sales increased, they could not explain why this occurred. It might be that the aroma induced a positive mood amongst sales staff, triggering them to become more helpful and thereby increasing sales, or it could be that the aroma directly influenced consumers. By conducting the experiment in a casino with just slot machines, it removed the sales staff, allowing researchers to directly understand what was influencing gamblers' behaviour.

Two identical rooms full of one-arm-bandits were selected. These are gambling machines where users pull a lever on the side and it causes the reals to spin; if the three 'windows' show the same icon, the gambler wins a cash prize. In one room, the researchers introduced a faint, suitably ambient aroma, while the other room was used as a control condition. Although money gambled in the control condition increased by 3%, takings increased by 45% in the experimental condition (the room with the aroma). Even more remarkably, when they replicated the experiment but increased the intensity of the aroma, takings increased by 53%.[66] This finding appears to suggest that by simply increasing the intensity of an aroma, sales will increase. But like most things, the situation is a little more complicated. This is because aromas that we find pleasant in low doses can quickly become unpleasant as the concentration increases.[67]

Getting this intensity correct is vital for brands. Not only does the intensity impact our liking of the aromas, but it can change how we perceive both products and brands. For example, when brand logos were presented in a room with an aroma, participants preferred the brands presented with a more intense aroma, but only up to a point. As the intensity increased, participants' ratings of the brands started to decrease.[68]

Aromas and decision-making

While retailers can use aromas to change customers' attitudes towards brands, they can also be used to persuade customers to purchase specific products. When John McDonnell diffused the smell of coconut oil while customers browsed in a travel agent, it increased the likelihood that customers would book a beach holiday compared to those who visited when no aroma was present.[69] Although the research did not explore the psychological mechanism, this probably occurred as most people associate the smell of coconut with sunny locations, which led them to think of suntan lotion and beach holidays.

While this provides evidence that using product-specific aromas can work, it is not without risk. Unlike a travel agency, most shops stock multiple products, making it very challenging to use a smell to promote a specific product. One of the most common examples given of olfactory marketing is the idea that supermarkets pump the smell of fresh bread to increase sales.[70] While the smell of fresh bread primes the sales of baked goods, it can actually have a negative impact on overall sales. This is because baked goods are relatively bulky and large, so they quickly fill up shoppers' trolleys and baskets. Consequently, when customers realize that their basket is fuller than they expected, they decide they should probably not buy so much. But as baked goods tend to have a relatively low profit margin, the end result is a lower profit for the store. Consequently, rather than using product-specific aromas, it makes more sense to release a generic pleasant aroma in the store. When Brenda Soars tested this approach in a supermarket, she found that customers had a more positive evaluation of the store, and it resulted in a 14% increase in sales.[71]

Aromas and segmentation

While some stores choose to use just one aroma across the store, other shops use aromas to help segment different areas. This not only helps to differentiate between areas, but also has a remarkable impact on sales. For example, when researchers introduced a spicy honey-like aroma into the menswear department and a subtle vanilla aroma into the female department, sales nearly doubled in comparison with a control condition.[72] Unlike the casino study, this increase in sales was not attributed to the aroma being pleasant, but to the gendered nature of the aromas. To test this hypothesis, the researchers reversed the aromas, pairing the masculine spiced honey aroma with the female clothing and diffusing the vanilla aroma around the menswear department. This time, the aromas had a negative effect, with sales lower than before any aromas were used.

Aromas and memory

REAL-WORLD EXAMPLE: PSYCH IN ACTION

While aromas can be used to help differentiate between different areas of the store, they can also be used to help make the shopping experience more memorable. Victoria's Secret, one of the largest retailers of luxury lingerie, developed a unique blend of potpourri, which is distributed throughout its stores and placed in customers' shopping bags after they make a purchase.[73] When the consumer arrives home and opens the packaging, they experience the aroma once again, reminding the customer that they bought their new lingerie at Victoria's Secret. This works by exploiting a psychological phenomenon known as the Proust Effect.

The Proust Effect proposes that when someone is exposed to a distinctive aroma, it is capable of taking them back to when they first experienced it.[74] Although there was plenty of anecdotal evidence supporting the theory, it wasn't until 2012 that Toffolo and Smeets provided the first academic evidence to substantiate it. Participants were asked to watch an upsetting video focusing on incidents including car accidents and the Rwandan genocides. However, while watching these videos, the smell of cassis was infused around the room, while neutral music was played in the background and coloured lights lit up the back wall.

A week later, the participants returned to the laboratory and were asked to recall their memories of the film. Those who were exposed to the scent of cassis during the recall session provided significantly more detailed information and rated their memories as more unpleasant and emotionally arousing than those who were simply re-exposed to the music. Interestingly, lighting was found to be just as effective as aroma in serving as a retrieval cue.[75]

A possible explanation as to why aromas act as such effective retrieval cues lies in the human ability to recall aromas in comparison with other stimuli. When asked to remember verbal and visual information, we experience a steady decline over time, although the greatest delay occurs immediately after exposure.[76] In comparison, our ability to immediately recall an aroma is relatively poor. When Engen and Ross exposed participants to one aroma followed immediately by a second, and then asked them to determine whether the two were the same, participants were accurate only about 70% of the time.[77] In comparison, our ability to recall visual stimuli in these situations is almost perfect, at about 99%.[78] But the big difference comes with long-term retrieval. When researchers exposed participants to an aroma three months later and asked if participants recognized it, accuracy only declined by 3%. By contrast, when the same study was repeated with visual cues, accuracy declined to 58%.

In the mood for shopping

Another key reason why aromas are popular with marketeers is their ability to trigger emotional reactions in their customers.[79] Although it is obvious that customers will spend more time in a store that they enjoy,[80] previous research by Morris and Schnurr has shown that shoppers who are in a positive mood spend approximately 12% more than shoppers who are not. It is likely that this effect occurs because customers who are in a positive mood tend to evaluate all stimuli they view (in this case products) in a positive light.[81,82] Not only do happy customers spend more, but they evaluate the store in a more positive light[83] and are far more likely to make a spontaneous purchase.[84]

Yet we often hear about shoppers who engage in 'retail therapy' when they are in a bad mood. Although shoppers in a bad mood don't spend as much as shoppers in a positive mood overall, they will frequently buy a couple of products to make themselves feel better. Rick, Pereira and Burson suggested this occurs because when people feel sad, buying things helps them feel that they have more control over their life, which reduces sadness, at least in the short term.[85] But what happens when shoppers are already angry before shopping? Surprisingly, shoppers are more focused and make more goal-oriented choices. Not only this, but they're less likely to delay making a choice, are less likely to compromise and end up being more satisfied with their choices than those who were fearful, sad or feeling neutral. In short, being angry can make your shopping experience more focused and fruitful.[86]

Although it may appear that influencing a shopper's mood is beyond the control of retailers, there are a number of surprisingly trivial manipulations experimental psychologists have created that can be used to induce or put shoppers into a positive mood. For example, giving shoppers an unexpected gift (something as small as a few sweets),[87] a free coffee or listening to happy music will induce a positive mood in shoppers.[88] But what makes a song sound happy? In western cultures, music written in a major key sounds positive whereas songs in a minor key sound sad and induce a negative mood. However, this is not a universal effect, and only occurs in western countries.[89]

The power of music

Introduction

When walking around most shops you are likely to hear music playing in the background. Although this might be chosen at random, stores that carefully consider their playlist can use it to influence shoppers' behaviour. As Duncan Herrington has shown, at the most basic level, customers generally prefer shopping in stores that play music,[90] and background music has also been shown to make shoppers more loyal and create a pleasurable shopping experience.[91] Importantly, this translates to sales as shoppers spend more time and money in these stores.[92] But like most aspects of psychology, it's a little more complex than it first appears.

It is not just a case of playing music and expecting sales to improve; retailers need to get the right music at the right volume. Just as fast-tempo music has been shown to cause drivers to drive faster and commit more driving offenses,[93] the same can be found in a supermarket. Experiments by Ronald Milliman have shown that when a supermarket increased the tempo of the background music from 72 beats per minute to 94, shoppers walked around the store significantly faster.[94] On the other hand, if a store plays music which is slightly quieter and slower, shoppers tend to linger in store for longer.[95] From a retailers perspective, this is advantageous as playing slow tempo music increased sales turnover by 40%.[96] This occurs because consumers walking around the store slower spend more time browsing, giving them more opportunity to make impulse purchases. This was regardless of whether shoppers were aware of the music playing.

But it may not just be a case of playing slow-tempo music. New research led by Klemens Knoferle suggests that it all depends on the mode of the music as well as the tempo. When slow-tempo music was played in a major key (which generally sounds brighter and happier), it had no impact on customers' spending. However, when slow-tempo music was played in a minor key (which usually sounds sadder and moodier) it positively impacted sales.[97] It is also important to get the volume of the music right. Playing music that customers find to be too loud has been shown to cause customers to spend less time in store.[98] Again, we cannot make sweeping statements about the correct volume levels as this will partly depend on the age of the customer. Yalch and Spangenberg have shown that younger shoppers reported spending more time in store when there was background music playing, however older shoppers spent more time in store when there was foreground music instead.[99] However, this study relied on self-report measures, so we do not know if actual shopping time changed.

Rather than relying on self-report measures, Yalch and Spangenberg have subsequently tried to replicate this study by measuring actual shopping time. When music was played that shoppers were familiar with, they thought that they spent less time shopping than they actually did. However, if background music was played that they didn't listen to, they felt like they spent more time shopping.[100]

REAL-WORLD EXAMPLE: PSYCH IN ACTION

Cafés are typically busiest around lunchtime and early evening, with quieter periods throughout the rest of the day. The quiet periods pose a significant challenge for managers. Not only are people not spending, but if a café appears empty, it can deter potential customers, as a lack of atmosphere can make the space feel uninviting.

In a novel experiment, Tesco, a UK supermarket with in-store cafés, found a clever way to manage café traffic using background music. During quieter periods, they played slower-tempo music. This encouraged customers to linger longer, creating a livelier atmosphere that attracted more people to dine in. This also had the added benefit of encouraging customers to purchase a slice of cake or a second coffee (items with a high profit margin). Conversely, during peak hours, the goal shifted to increasing table turnover. To encourage faster dining, Tesco played upbeat, fast-tempo music. The result: customers ate more quickly and spent less time in the café, allowing more people to be seated and boosting overall sales efficiency.

Whether we enjoy shopping or not, certain aspects get on most people's nerves, such as queuing. By changing the tempo of the background music, it can change our perception of time.[101] If we are queuing and the music is generally quite slow, customers perceived that they were waiting for less time than they actually were. This effect holds true for up to 15 minutes, although once customers are forced to wait for over 18 minutes, background music does not make any difference.

An arousing experience

But what's going on? Why can listening to music change what people buy? Listening to calming (slow tempo) music or smelling aromas such as lavender changes customers' arousal levels.[102] If customers are in a shop that is playing fast-tempo music or has diffused the smell of citrus, this causes physiological changes, such as our palms starting to get slightly clammy, our heart rate and blood pressure to rise.[103] While we may notice these changes, we struggle to understand what causes them.[104] One of the most extreme examples of this occurred as part of the Capilano Bridge experiment conducted by Donald Dutton and Arthur Aron.

They asked male participants to walk across the Capilano Bridge in British Columbia. This is a 140-metre-long rope bridge, about 1.5 metres wide, that towers

70 metres above a fast-flowing river below. As you walk across it, you can feel the bridge sway and creak, and if you are brave enough to look down, you can watch the white water of the river below.

Researchers asked male participants to walk across the bridge, but halfway across, they walked past a female experimenter. She asked if they would be willing to complete a short questionnaire. Finally, she showed them a photo of a lady covering her face and asked the participants to create a back-story to explain the image. In case any of the participants had any questions about the experiment, she gave them her phone number so they could call her; later, nearly 50% of the participants contacted her, often to ask her out on a date. However, when they repeated the study but instead of asking participants to walk across the Capilano bridge, they walked along a 'safe' sturdy wooden bridge only a few feet from the ground, they found very different results. This time only 12.5% of participants called the researcher and the stories they invented describing the women were far less sexual in nature. In fact, participants on the Capilano Bridge were almost twice as likely to have a sexually suggestive narrative.[105]

Why is this relevant to retail design? Well, the participants on the Capiliano Bridge were more likely to call the female participants because they mistakenly believed they were attracted to her. They were standing on the bridge with their heart rate pounding and their palms slightly clammy; these are two signs of being in love (or at least in lust). They mistakenly thought their increased arousal was caused by the attractive female and not the extreme drop. The same process can occur in a supermarket. Our arousal levels can be raised by external cues, but as customers we do not notice this. Instead, we think it is more likely to be caused by other cues, for example, the products, increasing the odds that we buy them.

Priming

An alternative psychological explanation as to why background music changes shoppers' behaviour is priming.[106] Conceptual priming is an implicit memory effect whereby exposure to one stimulus causes us to think about related concepts, which triggers a change in our behaviour.[107] For example, experiments by Charles Areni and David Kim have shown that playing classical music rather than Top 40 chart music causes customers to spend more money in a wine store in a large US city.[108] The researchers observed shoppers' behaviour between 6.00 pm and 11.00 pm every Friday and Saturday. During this time, they played either classical music or Top 40 hits, switching which type of music was used on Fridays and Saturdays to keep things fair. The choice of which music to play on which day was random, and they skipped collecting data on any dates when outside events, like holidays or special occasions, might have affected the results. It is hypothesized that consumer behaviour changed because most people associate classical music with upper-class wealthy individuals; consequently, individuals end up buying more expensive upper-class products.

Similarly, over a two-week period, Adrian North, David Hargreaves and Jennifer McKendrick played stereotypical French or German music in the wine aisle of a UK supermarket. When the store played stereotypical French music, they experienced an increase in the sale of French wine; the French music triggered thoughts of France. This finding may not be too much of a surprise as France has a reputation for producing world-class wine. What is remarkable is that the same effect occurred when stereotypical German music was played instead; this time sales of German wine increased.[109]

Does this suggest supermarkets can prime customers to buy anything? Probably not! In the wine study, shoppers were probably already going to buy wine; they just didn't know what type of wine before entering the aisle. Hence, playing either German or French music just nudged shoppers towards the wine they selected. However, if a customer walked into a store and knew exactly the variety of wine they wanted to buy, then background music would have no impact on their behaviour.

Priming in a supermarket is not just restricted to music; aromas and visual cues can also be used to prime customers. For example, shoppers who were exposed to the smell of pain au chocolat, were far more likely to purchase high-calorie desserts than customers who were exposed to no aromas.[110] Likewise, when shoppers are encouraged to bring their own reusable bags to the supermarket, it causes them to buy both more environmentally friendly products and indulgent products.[111] Bringing a reusable bag primes shoppers to focus on sustainability issues, but it makes us feel virtuous. Giving us a license to make other indulgent decisions after.

But caution is necessary when talking about priming. As a technique, priming gained considerable popularity, if not notoriety, amongst psychologists in the 1990s and early 2000s when several laboratory studies were able to show that seemingly irrelevant tasks could prime participants to change their behaviour in remarkable ways. For example, Ap Dijksterhuis and Ap Knippenberg asked participants to spend five minutes describing either professors (who are stereotypically perceived as intelligent) or football hooligans (who are not); those participants who described professors performed 13% better on a simulated IQ test than those primed to think of hooligans.[112] But in the last decade, researchers have started questioning the credibility of priming. When Michael O'Donnell led a global team of researchers from 40 different laboratories and they tried to replicate this study testing 4,493 participants,[113] they failed to find the same result, with no difference between groups.

Worryingly, this is not one study failing, as numerous classic priming studies have failed to be replicated.[114-116] Thanks to research by John Bargh, Mark Chen and Lara Burrows, it was widely believed that asking participants to complete a scrambled sentence task with words including grey, bingo, wrinkles and knitting would prime participants to think of older people. Participants were told they were just completing a task relating to their language ability and at the end of the research, they were thanked and allowed to leave. However, this is when things got interesting.

The researchers measured the speed that the participants walked down the corridor after the experiment. Those who were primed to think of older people walked significantly slower than those who were in the control condition.[117] But once again, Stéphane Doyen and her team failed to replicate the results.[118]

So where does this leave the priming literature? Should it be consigned to the past along with Freudian psychology? Maybe not. To date, the priming studies that have failed to be replicated fall within 'social priming'. For social priming to work, it relies on the prime triggering the same thoughts and feelings amongst all participants. The closer the behaviour is associated with the prime, it would appear the more likely the effect can be replicated. So, diffusing the smell of chocolate around a supermarket is likely to prime consumers to want chocolate; it is not a large conceptual leap. However, asking participants to imagine professors and hoping that this will then trigger them to think about someone intelligent (rather than an old individual with a bad fashion sense) is more of a stretch.

Let there be light

Whenever customers enter a shop, it needs to be adequately lit to comply with health and safety legislation. Yet, lighting should be viewed as more than just functional and is another tool in a marketer's arsenal. When Areni and Kim investigated the impact of lighting in a wine store, they found that customers handled more wine when the light was brighter. Interestingly, this did not result in any more time spent in the store, or more sales.[119] But lighting can be used to direct customers' attention within a store. By increasing the intensity of lighting of certain displays, stores caused customers to spend more time at these displays and to touch more products,[120] and touching normally results in higher sales.

Lighting is not all about brightness; it is also about the colour of the light. Retailers can keep the brightness of the lighting the same, but by changing the colour, it can produce very different results amongst consumers. When the lighting is warm, consumers found the products less arousing, more approachable and more pleasurable than when the products were lit by cooler whiter lighting.[121]

While virtually all the research that explores lighting focuses on artificial lighting, it is worth remembering that for thousands of years we relied on either the sun or fire for lighting and it appears that we still have a preference for natural daylight over electrical lighting. School children perform better in schools with more windows,[122] and there is a growing body of evidence supporting the impact of Seasonal Affective Disorder, a form of depression caused by a shortage of daylight.[123] This effect appears to hold true in retail as shoppers spend more money when there's more daylight.[124] This is not a case that more people go to the shops on days when the weather is good, but the average spend per person is higher on sunny days. When a team of researchers led by Heschong analysed sales data over an 18-month period for a large chain retailer, sales per square foot were higher in stores with more natural daylight (when controlling for all other variables).[125]

This has some interesting implications for retailers, as although most shops have large windows at the front, they are frequently blocked with large adverts promoting special offers, blocking the daylight from entering the store. Likewise, although it will be difficult to install more windows in a shop, something as simple as using photos and imagery of sunlight in-store should increase shoppers' willingness to pay.

Of course, the impact of the weather does have a small impact on shoppers' spending. Natalie Rose and Les Dolega have shown that variations in the weather explain 3.5% of the differences in daily sales.[126] Most of this makes intuitive sense; on hotter days sales increase, and when the weather is bad (e.g. it's raining, windy or too humid) sales decrease. But some shops are hit more than others. The effect is far greater for stores on the high street than those based in an out-of-town shopping centre. For shops located on the high street, changes to the weather explain up to 5.5% of sales variance, whereas it's less than 1% for shops in out-of-town shopping centres. When it comes to shopping on the high street, people are more exposed to the impact of the weather than if they've driven.

Interestingly, Rose and Dolega's research discovered regional differences across the UK. They found that weather had a stronger effect on shopping habits in London, while the influence was less pronounced in the southwest and northern regions of the UK. Although they didn't determine the difference, they suspected it was because of the prevailing weather conditions. In the southwest and northern parts of the UK, there are stronger coastal winds, higher rates of rain and lower average temperatures). Poor weather is just a fact of everyday life, so people get used to it. Conversely, people living in London, on average 10°C warmer than nearby rural areas and which receives only half the annual rainfall compared to the rest of the UK, are less accustomed to adverse weather, making its impact more significant.

Unfortunately, while changes in the weather may influence how much shoppers buy, there is not a lot that stores can do about it. But by looking at the long-range forecast, stores can understand what products shoppers are more likely to buy and stock up. For example, if the temperature passes 26°C in the UK, sales of rosé are higher than the sales of red and white wine combined![127] More generally, if there is heavy rain, sales of footwear, clothing, cosmetics and even beverages are dramatically down (especially beer in the summer), and sales of books and DIY equipment increase.[128]

Closing thoughts

When it comes to designing a new store, it's easy to understand why marketers focus on designing an aesthetically pleasing one. However, a well-designed store needs to be more than just good looking. It needs to be practical and encourage shoppers to make a purchase, and this is where psychology plays a part. Shoppers will pick up on subtle cues from the environment that will change what they buy. This should not be left to chance but should be underpinned by the latest scientific research.

> **KEY POINTS**
>
> - When people first enter a store, their natural tendency is to walk around in an anticlockwise direction.
> - Shoppers tend to subconsciously follow visual cues on the floor, such as arrows or coloured tiles to guide them around a store.
> - In a large store, shoppers do not walk up and down every aisle, but tend to walk around the perimeter or power aisle, and then just visit the relevant aisles to buy the products they're interested in before returning to the perimeter or power aisle.
> - If a store feels claustrophobic, such as when it has narrow aisles, a low ceiling or is crowded, shoppers tend to spend less time shopping and purchase fewer items.
> - The choice overload effect, the idea that people won't make a purchase when there is too much choice, only occurs under very specific situations.
> - Shoppers are most likely to purchase items on their right-hand side and just below eye-level.
> - There are five different types of shoppers: Grab & Go, Impulse, Inexperienced, Experiential and Considered. Shopper types are fluid and context-dependent, with people adopting different behaviours based on the store or product category. Brands must understand the dominant shopper types in their specific category and adjust their packaging and in-store marketing accordingly.
> - People are more likely to make a purchase when they're able to touch and interact with the product.
> - When people are in a positive mood, they are more likely to make more purchases. Simple things like giving shoppers an unexpected gift or playing positive music can induce a positive mood as people shop.
> - Shoppers tend to walk more quickly through a store when fast-tempo music is playing, and more slowly when slower music is playing.
> - Ambient aromas in a store can influence what shoppers purchase by triggering specific pre-established associations.
> - Retailers can use different aromas to segment store areas, which can boost sales. For example, using gender-congruent aromas can nearly double sales.

- Lighting in the retail environment should be more than just functional; it will influence the likelihood that customers will handle a product and which products they focus on.
- Humans prefer natural light to artificial light and shops with more natural daylight tend to have higher sales.

PUTTING THEORY INTO PRACTICE

1 Using the classification developed by Philip Adcock to explain the five different shopping styles, how might a pharmacy change the way it merchandizes cold and flu medication to appeal to different shopper types?

2 Imagine you worked for a high-end jewellery store, and you were asked to create a playlist of songs that could be played for the next three hours. What songs would you select and why?

3 Think about your local supermarket. How can Mehrabian and Russell's concept of dominance be used to explain how long people are likely to spend shopping there? Are there any simple changes they could make to encourage customers to spend more?

4 If you were the marketing manager for a boutique fashion store, why might you want customers to be in a positive mood? What simple techniques could you use to induce a positive mood in your customers?

5 Visit either your nearest department store in person or its e-commerce platform. Based on Chernev, Böckenholt and Goodman's research, are they likely to suffer from choice overload? If they are, how might they overcome this problem?

6 Visit an e-commerce website that sells products you're interested in (e.g. pet food, climbing shoes or perfume). Choose a specific category and list all the products within it. How would you physically display or merchandise these products in a bricks-and-mortar store? Explain how psychological principles have informed your merchandizing decisions.

7 Visit your local supermarket and draw a floor plan. What psychological principles will guide how shoppers will walk around the store. What changes would you suggest to optimize the layout?

8 Impulse shopping often accounts for a significant proportion of a retailer's sales. What tactics can a business use to encourage customers to make impulse purchases?

9 Large retailers often use a 'decompression zone' at the entrance of their stores to ease customers into the shopping journey, but how could a smaller independent retailer use the same concept to encourage their customers to spend more?

> **SUGGESTIONS FOR FURTHER READING**
>
> Underhill, P. (1999). *Why we buy: The science of shopping.* New York: Simon & Schuster.

References

1. Groeppel-Klein, A. & Bartmann, B. (2007). Anti-clockwise or clockwise? The impact of store layout on the process of orientation in a discount store. *ACR European Advances*, 8, 415–416.
2. Underhill, P. (2000). *Why we buy.* Simon and Schuster.
3. Sorensen, H. (2009). *Inside the mind of the shopper.* Pearson Prentice Hall.
4. Payne, C. R., Niculescu, M., Just, D. R., & Kelly, M. P. (2014). Shopper marketing nutrition interventions. *Physiology & Behavior*, 136, 111–120. https://doi.org/10.1016/j.physbeh.2014.03.029 (archived at https://perma.cc/WBP3-XRQK)
5. Kalff, C. & Strube, G. (2009). Background knowledge in human navigation: A study in a supermarket. *Cognitive Processing*, 10(2), 225–228. https://doi.org/10.1007/s10339-009-0287-6 (archived at https://perma.cc/Y8AY-XHMX)
6. Albarrak, L. Y. (2022). *Designing and evaluating technologies to guide and nudge navigational decision-making* (Doctoral dissertation, University of Bristol).
7. Kholod, M., Takai, K., & Yada, K. (2011). *Clockwise and anti-clockwise directions of customer orientation in a supermarket: Evidence from RFID Data* (Vol. 6883, pp. 304–309). Springer Berlin Heidelberg. https://doi.org/10.1007/978-3-642-23854-3_32 (archived at https://perma.cc/DJ2C-C5ES)
8. Yada, K. (2009). String analysis technique for shopping path in a supermarket. *Journal of Intelligent Information Systems*, 36(3), 385–402. https://doi.org/10.1007/s10844-009-0113-8 (archived at https://perma.cc/T6XW-SMS6)
9. Kholod, M., Takai, K., & Yada, K. (2011). *Clockwise and anti-clockwise directions of customer orientation in a supermarket: Evidence from RFID Data* (Vol. 6883, pp. 304–309). Springer Berlin Heidelberg. https://doi.org/10.1007/978-3-642-23854-3_32 (archived at https://perma.cc/EL2J-ADE4)
10. Yada, K. (2009). String analysis technique for shopping path in a supermarket. *Journal of Intelligent Information Systems*, 36(3), 385–402. https://doi.org/10.1007/s10844-009-0113-8 (archived at https://perma.cc/2BS3-7HBA)
11. Nguyen, K., Le, M., Martin, B., Cil, I., & Fookes, C. (2022). When AI meets store layout design: A review. *Artificial Intelligence Review*, 55(7), 5707–5729.
12. Adcock, P. (2011). *Supermarket shoppology.* Writersworld Limited.
13. Larson, J. S., Bradlow, E. T., & Fader, P. S. (2005). An exploratory look at supermarket shopping paths. *International Journal of Research in Marketing*, 22(4), 395–414. https://doi.org/10.1016/j.ijresmar.2005.09.005 (archived at https://perma.cc/PMY7-SMPQ)

14 Sorensen, H. (2005). *Management implications* (P. S. Fader, Ed.).
15 Mehrabian, A. & Russell, J. A. (1974). *An approach to environmental psychology*. The MIT Press. http://books.google.com/books?id=EthOAAAAMAAJ&printsec=frontcover (archived at https://perma.cc/LMR2-YNWA)
16 Sorensen, H. (2009). *Inside the mind of the shopper*. Pearson Prentice Hall.
17 Machleit, K., Eroglu, S. A., & Mantel, S. (2000). Perceived retail crowding and shopping satisfaction: What modifies this relationship? *Journal of Consumer Psychology*, 9(1), 29–42. https://doi.org/10.1207/s15327663jcp0901_3 (archived at https://perma.cc/TF2B-E6XT)
18 Harrell, G. D., Hutt, M. D., & Anderson, J. C. (1980). Path analysis of buyer behavior under conditions of crowding. *Journal of Marketing Research*, 17(1), 45–51. https://doi.org/10.2307/3151115 (archived at https://perma.cc/V7ZY-GMA8)
19 Underhill, P. (2000). *Why we buy*. Simon and Schuster.
20 Otterbring, T., Ringler, C., Sirianni, N.J., & Gustafsson, A. (2013). *Entering consumption: A greeter at the store entrance positively influences customers' spending, satisfaction, and employee perceptions*. Paper presented at Association for Consumer Research (ACR) North American Conference, Chicago, October 3–6, 2013.
21 Cardone, C. & Hayes, R. (2012). Shoplifter perceptions of store environments: An analysis of how physical cues in the retail interior shape shoplifter behavior. *Journal of Applied Security Research*, 7(1), 22–58.
22 Weiss-Sussex, G. & Bianchini, F. (Eds) (2006). *Urban mindscapes of Europe*. Brill Academic Publishers (p. 92).
23 Iyengar, S. S. & Lepper, M. R. (2000). When choice is demotivating: Can one desire too much of a good thing? *Journal of Personality and Social Psychology*, 79(6), 300–322. https://doi.org/10.1017/cbo9780511618031.017 (archived at https://perma.cc/SR8H-66DE)
24 Scheibehenne, B., Greifeneder, R., & Todd, P. M. (2010). Can there ever be too many options? A meta-analytic review of choice overload. *Journal of Consumer Research*, 37(3), 409–425.
25 Chernev, A., Böckenholt, U., & Goodman, J. (2015). Choice overload: A conceptual review and meta-analysis. *Journal of Consumer Psychology*, 25(2), 333–358.
26 Deng, X., Kahn, B. E., Unnava, H. R., & Lee, H. (2016). A 'wide' variety: Effects of horizontal versus vertical display on assortment processing, perceived variety, and choice. *Journal of Marketing Research*, 53(5), 682–698. https://doi.org/10.1509/jmr.13.0151 (archived at https://perma.cc/6C6T-7DFP)
27 Hui, S. K., Bradlow, E. T., & Fader, P. S. (2009). Testing behavioral hypotheses using an integrated model of grocery store shopping path and purchase behavior. *Journal of Consumer Research*, 36(3), 478–493. https://doi.org/10.1086/599046 (archived at https://perma.cc/8SAX-ABRH)
28 Hui, S. K., Inman, J. J., Huang, Y., & Suher, J. (2013). The effect of in-store travel distance on unplanned spending: Applications to mobile promotion strategies. *Journal of Marketing*, 77(2), 1–16. https://doi.org/10.1509/jm.11.0436 (archived at https://perma.cc/SNQ6-CUVT)
29 Sorensen, H. (2009). *Inside the mind of the shopper*. Pearson Prentice Hall.

30 Sorensen, H. (2009). *Inside the mind of the shopper*. Pearson Prentice Hall.
31 Hui, S. K., Fader, P. S., & Bradlow, E. T. (2009). The traveling salesman goes shopping: The systematic deviations of grocery paths from TSP optimality. *Marketing Science*, 28(3), 566–572. https://doi.org/10.1287/mksc.1080.0402 (archived at https://perma.cc/3K9N-FRFS)
32 Reid, R. & Brown, S. (1996). I hate shopping! An introspective perspective. *International Journal of Retail & Distribution Management*, 24(4), 4–16. https://doi.org/10.1108/09590559610119910 (archived at https://perma.cc/C29W-6Y28)
33 Grewal, D., Noble, S. M., Ahlbom, C. P., & Nordfält, J. (2020). The sales impact of using handheld scanners: Evidence from the field. *Journal of Marketing Research*, 57(3), 527–547. https://doi.org/10.1177/0022243720911624 (archived at https://perma.cc/85DF-6B9M)
34 Morales, A. C. & Fitzsimons, G. J. (2007). Product contagion: Changing consumer evaluations through physical contact with 'disgusting' products. *Journal of Marketing Research*, 44(2), 272–283. https://doi.org/10.1509/jmkr.44.2.272 (archived at https://perma.cc/9BB8-SHJ9)
35 Chen, M., Burke, R. R., Hui, S. K., & Leykin, A. (2021). Understanding lateral and vertical biases in consumer attention: An in-store ambulatory eye-tracking study. *Journal of Marketing Research*, 58(6), 1120–1141. https://doi.org/10.1177/0022243721998375 (archived at https://perma.cc/3MQC-9T29)
36 Gidlöf, K., Anikin, A., Lingonblad, M., & Wallin, A. (2017). Looking is buying. How visual attention and choice are affected by consumer preferences and properties of the supermarket shelf. *Appetite*, 116, 29–38. https://doi.org/10.1016/j.appet.2017.04.020 (archived at https://perma.cc/7CPN-Q6JV)
37 Chandon, P., Hutchinson, J. W., Bradlow, E. T., & Young, S. H. (2008). *Does in-store marketing work? Effects of the number and position of shelf facings on attention and evaluation at the point of purchase*. Unpublished working paper, Center for Global Research and Education, INSEAD–Wharton School Alliance, Fontainebleau.
38 Sunaga, T., Park, J., & Spence, C. (2016). Effects of lightness-location congruency on consumers' purchase decision-making. *Psychology & Marketing*, 33(11), 934–950.
39 O'Guinn, T. C., Tanner, R. J., & Maeng, A. (2015). Turning to space: Social density, social class and the value of things in stores. *Journal of Consumer Research*, 42(2). https://doi.org/10.1093/jcr/ucv010 (archived at https://perma.cc/NH8K-EESM)
40 Alaoui, M. D., Valette-Florence, P., & Cova, V. (2022). How psychological distance shapes hedonic consumption: The moderating role of the need to justify. *Journal of Business Research*, 146, 57–69. https://doi.org/10.1016/j.jbusres.2022.03.046 (archived at https://perma.cc/VQ3K-EQ3R)
41 Ketron, S. (2018). Perceived product sizes in visually complex environments. *Journal of Retailing*, 94(2), 154–166 https://doi.org/10.1016/j.jretai.2018.04.001 (archived at https://perma.cc/XC8S-N58W)
42 Tian, J., Chen, R., & Xu, X. (2022). A good way to boost sales? Effects of the proportion of sold-out options on purchase behavior. *International Journal of Research in Marketing*, 39(1), 156–169. https://doi.org/10.1016/j.ijresmar.2021.04.002 (archived at https://perma.cc/P4JS-9KWP)

43 Schmidtke, K. A., Watson, D. G., Roberts, P., & Vlaev, I. (2019). Menu positions influence soft drink selection at touchscreen kiosks. *Psychology & Marketing*, 36(10), 964–970. https://doi.org/10.1002/mar.21248 (archived at https://perma.cc/BWR3-9ZAZ)

44 Riefer, P. S., Prior, R., Blair, N., Pavey, G., & Love, B. C. (2017). Coherency-maximizing exploration in the supermarket. *Nature Human Behaviour*, 1(1), 1–4. https://doi.org/10.1038/s41562-016-0017 (archived at https://perma.cc/EKF4-SY4B)

45 Anderson, K. & Sharp, B. (2010). Do growing brands win younger consumers? *International Journal of Market Research*, 52(4), 433–441. https://doi.org/10.2501/S1470785309201387 (archived at https://perma.cc/B324-RBTT)

46 Adcock, P. (2011). *Shoppology – Inside the mind of the customer*. Shopping Behaviour Xplained Ltd: UK.

47 LivePerson. (2013). The connecting with customers report: A global study of the drivers of a successful online experience. LivePerson Inc. Retrieved from http://thecustomerconnection.nl/docs/member94427/The%20connecting%20with%20customers%20report.pdf (archived at https://perma.cc/PN95-R389)

48 Xu, A. J., Schwarz, N., & Wyer Jr, R. S. (2015). Hunger promotes acquisition of nonfood objects. *Proceedings of the National Academy of Sciences*, 112(9), 2688–2692. https://doi.org/10.1073/pnas.1417712112 (archived at https://perma.cc/CB7K-NU38)

49 Biswas, D., Hartmann, P., Eisend, M., Szocs, C., Jochims, B., Apaolaza, V., Hermann, E., López, C. M., & Borges, A. (2022). Caffeine's effects on consumer spending. *Journal of Marketing*, 87(2). https://doi.org/10.1177/00222429221109247 (archived at https://perma.cc/PM38-EYZY)

50 Lunardo, R., Jaud, D., & Jaspers, E. (2022). Engagement in vice food and beverage consumption: The role of perceived lack of control. *Psychology & Marketing*, 39(12), 2221–2239. https://doi.org/10.1002/mar.21708 (archived at https://perma.cc/78XY-VMXC)

51 Shopping Behaviour Xplained (2018, March 28). Study sees fridge doors as sales barrier. Cooling Post. https://www.coolingpost.com/features/study-sees-fridge-doors-sales-barrier/ (archived at https://perma.cc/UR75-XFV9)

52 Pigott, P. (2021, November 7). Climate change: Fridge doors could save 1% of UK electricity use. BBC News. https://www.bbc.co.uk/news/uk-wales-59141894 (archived at https://perma.cc/CL38-W57R)

53 Jansson-Boyd, C. V. (2011). Touch matters: Exploring the relationship between consumption and tactile interaction. *Social Semiotics*, 21(4), 531–546. https://doi.org/10.1080/10350330.2011.591996 (archived at https://perma.cc/BX3M-HS9F)

54 Shu, S. & Peck, J. (2007). To hold me is to love me: The role of touch in the endowment effect. In *NA – Advances in Consumer Research Volume 34*, Fitzsimons, G. & Morwitz, V. (Eds.) Association for Consumer Research (513–514).

55 Bergh, B. V. den, Schmitt, J., & Warlop, L. (2011). Embodied myopia. *Journal of Marketing Research*, 48(6), 1033–1044. https://doi.org/10.1509/jmr.09.0503 (archived at https://perma.cc/33AH-3Z9B)

56 Larsen, N. M. & Sigurdsson, V. (2019). What affects shopper's choices of carrying devices in grocery retailing and what difference does it make? A literature review and

conceptual model. *The International Review of Retail, Distribution and Consumer Research*, 29(4), 1–33. https://doi.org/10.1080/09593969.2019.1581074 (archived at https://perma.cc/XD2Z-9AS8)

57 Wansink, B., Soman, D., & Herbst, K. C. (2017). Larger partitions lead to larger sales: Divided grocery carts alter purchase norms and increase sales. *Journal of Business Research*, 75, 202–209. https://doi.org/10.1016/j.jbusres.2016.06.023 (archived at https://perma.cc/K69R-URB3)

58 Lindstrom, M. (2012). *Brandwashed: Tricks companies use to manipulate our minds and persuade us to buy*. Kogan Page Publishers. London, UK.

59 Wansink, B., Soman, D., & Herbst, K. C. (2017). Larger partitions lead to larger sales: Divided grocery carts alter purchase norms and increase sales. *Journal of Business Research*, 75, 202–209. https://doi.org/10.1016/j.jbusres.2016.06.023 (archived at https://perma.cc/NE3B-PYS7)

60 Van Ittersum, K. Wansink, B., Pennings, J. M., & Sheehan, D. (2013). Smart shopping carts: How real-time feedback influences spending. *Journal of Marketing*, 77(6), 21–36. https://doi.org/10.1509/jm.12.0060 (archived at https://perma.cc/45GU-97KS)

61 Estes, Z. & Streicher, M. C. (2021). Getting a handle on sales: Shopping carts affect purchasing by activating arm muscles. *Journal of Marketing*, 86(6). https://doi.org/10.1177/00222429211061367 (archived at https://perma.cc/22QB-7XCV)

62 Herz, R. S. (2009). Aromatherapy facts and fictions: A scientific analysis of olfactory effects on mood, physiology and behavior. *International Journal of Neuroscience*, 119(2), 263–290. https://doi.org/10.1080/00207450802333953 (archived at https://perma.cc/2R9B-CVHK)

63 Spence, C. (2015). Leading the consumer by the nose: On the commercialization of olfactory design for the food and beverage sector. *Flavour*, 4(1), 1–15. https://doi.org/10.1186/s13411-015-0041-1 (archived at https://perma.cc/LZ44-AJHD)

64 Ward, P., Davies, B. J., & Kooijman, D. (2007). Olfaction and the retail environment: Examining the influence of ambient scent. *Service Business*, 1(4), 295–316. https://doi.org/10.1007/s11628-006-0018-3 (archived at https://perma.cc/JMV4-WCU4)

65 Hirsch, A. R. (1995). Effects of ambient odors on slot-machine usage in a Las Vegas casino. *Psychology and Marketing*, 12(7), 585–594. https://doi.org/10.1002/mar.4220120703 (archived at https://perma.cc/P5ZQ-VUEA)

66 Hirsch, A. R. (1995). Effects of ambient odors on slot-machine usage in a Las Vegas casino. *Psychology and Marketing*, 12(7), 585–594. https://doi.org/10.1002/mar.4220120703 (archived at https://perma.cc/P5ZQ-VUEA)

67 Gulas, C. S. & Bloch, P. H. (1995). Right under our noses: Ambient scent and consumer responses. *Journal of Business and Psychology*, 10(1), 87–98. https://doi.org/10.1007/bf02249272 (archived at https://perma.cc/7KWH-7DFX)

68 Ramsøy, T. Z. (2015). *Introduction to neuromarketing & consumer neuroscience*. Neurons Inc.

69 McDonnell, J. (2002). Sensorial marketing for those who can wait no longer. In *1st International Conference on Sensorial Marketing*, Abdelmajid, A. (Ed.).

70 Ward, P., Davies, B. J., & Kooijman, D. (2007). Olfaction and the retail environment: Examining the influence of ambient scent. *Service Business*, 1(4), 295–316. https://doi.org/10.1007/s11628-006-0018-3 (archived at https://perma.cc/7KWH-7DFX)

71 Soars, B. (2009). Driving sales through shoppers' sense of sound, sight, smell and touch. *International Journal of Retail & Distribution Management*, 37(3), 286–298. https://doi.org/10.1108/09590550910941535 (archived at https://perma.cc/7DNR-GGAT)

72 Spangenberg, E. R., Crowley, A. E., & Henderson, P. W. (1996). Improving the store environment: Do olfactory cues affect evaluations and behaviors?. *Journal of Marketing*, 60(2), 67–80.

73 Goldkuhl, L. & Styvén, M. (2007). Sensing the scent of service success. *European Journal of Marketing*, 41(11/12), 1297–1305. https://doi.org/10.1108/03090560710821189 (archived at https://perma.cc/6BZU-TDSP)

74 Krishna, A. (2012). An integrative review of sensory marketing: Engaging the senses to affect perception, judgment and behavior. *Journal of Consumer Psychology*, 22(3), 332–351. https://doi.org/10.1016/j.jcps.2011.08.003 (archived at https://perma.cc/H2JS-6APF)

75 Toffolo, M. B. J., Smeets, M. A. M., & Hout, M. A. van den. (2012). Proust revisited: Odours as triggers of aversive memories. *Cognition & Emotion*, 26(1), 83–92. https://doi.org/10.1080/02699931.2011.555475 (archived at https://perma.cc/69MQ-SLK4)

76 Peterson, L. & Peterson, M. J. (1959). Short-term retention of individual verbal items. *Journal of Experimental Psychology*, 58(3), 193–198. https://doi.org/10.1037/h0049234 (archived at https://perma.cc/349U-RDLF)

77 Engen, T. & Ross, B. M. (1973). Long-term memory of odors with and without verbal descriptions. *Journal of Experimental Psychology*, 100(2), 221–227. https://doi.org/10.1037/h0035492 (archived at https://perma.cc/XLL4-6CPH)

78 Shepard, R. N. (1967). Recognition memory for words, sentences, and pictures. *Journal of Verbal Learning and Verbal Behavior*, 6(1), 156–163. https://doi.org/10.1016/s0022-5371(67)80067-7 (archived at https://perma.cc/MHZ9-Q2B9)

79 Bell, S. & Bell, C. P. (2007). Future sense: Defining brands through scent. *The Journal of the Marketing Society*, 38, 60–62.

80 Robert, D. & Rossiter, J. R. (1982). Store atmosphere: An environmental psychology approach. *Journal of Retailing*, 58(1), 34–57.

81 Isen, A. M., Shalker, T. E., Clark, M., & Karp, L. (1978). Affect, accessibility of material in memory, and behavior: A cognitive loop? *Journal of Personality and Social Psychology*, 36(1), 1–12. https://doi.org/10.1037/0022-3514.36.1.1 (archived at https://perma.cc/LZ2Y-KBUQ)

82 Morris, W. N. & Schnurr, P. P. (1989). *Mood*. Springer Verlag.

83 Babin, B. J. & Darden, W. R. (1996). Good and bad shopping vibes: Spending and patronage satisfaction. *Journal of Business Research*, 35(3), 201–206. https://doi.org/10.1016/0148-2963(95)00125-5 (archived at https://perma.cc/M4L5-NCEG)

84 Ozer, L. & Gultekin, B. (2015). Pre- and post-purchase stage in impulse buying: The role of mood and satisfaction. *Journal of Retailing and Consumer Services*, 22(C), 71–76. https://doi.org/10.1016/j.jretconser.2014.10.004 (archived at https://perma.cc/BQB3-W2DD)

85 Rick, S. I., Pereira, B., & Burson, K. A. (2014). The benefits of retail therapy: Making purchase decisions reduces residual sadness. *Journal of Consumer Psychology*, 24(3), 373–380.

86   Khan, U., DePaoli, A., & Maimaran, M. (2019). The unique role of anger among negative emotions in goal-directed decision making. *Journal of the Association for Consumer Research*, 4(1), 65–76.
87   Estrada, C. A., Isen, A. M., & Young, M. J. (1997). Positive affect facilitates integration of information and decreases anchoring in reasoning among physicians. *Organizational Behavior And Human Decision Processes*, 72(1), 117–135. https://doi.org/10.1006/obhd.1997.2734 (archived at https://perma.cc/YXS3-J36J)
88   Martin, M. (1990). On the induction of mood. *Clinical Psychology Review*, 10(6), 669–697. https://doi.org/10.1016/0272-7358(90)90075-l (archived at https://perma.cc/888T-8SDR)
89   Smit, E. A., Milne, A. J., Sarvasy, H. S., & Dean, R. T. (2022). Emotional responses in Papua New Guinea show negligible evidence for a universal effect of major versus minor music. *Plos one*, 17(6), e0269597. https://doi.org/10.1371/journal.pone.0269597 (archived at https://perma.cc/BFT9-HR9E)
90   Herrington, J. D. (1996). Effects of music in service environments: A field study. *Journal of Services Marketing*, 10(2), 26–41. https://doi.org/10.1108/08876049610114249 (archived at https://perma.cc/T6UQ-DX86)
91   Garlin, F. V. & Owen, K. (2006). Setting the tone with the tune: A meta-analytic review of the effects of background music in retail settings. *Journal of Business Research*, 59(6), 755–764. https://doi.org/10.1016/j.jbusres.2006.01.013 (archived at https://perma.cc/PJ3C-5FB5)
92   Andersson, P. K., Kristensson, P., Wästlund, E., & Gustafsson, A. (2012). Let the music play or not: The influence of background music on consumer behavior. *Journal of Retailing and Consumer Services*, 19(6), 553–560. https://doi.org/10.1016/j.jretconser.2012.06.010 (archived at https://perma.cc/YNL5-JGFW)
93   Brodsky, W. (2001). The effects of music tempo on simulated driving performance and vehicular control. *Transportation Research Part F: Traffic Psychology and Behaviour*, 4(4), 219–241. https://doi.org/10.1016/s1369-8478(01)00025-0 (archived at https://perma.cc/9ZRJ-RX7Q)
94   Milliman, R. E. (1982). Using background music to affect the behavior of supermarket shoppers. *The Journal of Marketing*, 46(3), 86–91. https://doi.org/10.2307/1251706 (archived at https://perma.cc/SZR9-9287)
95   Garlin, F. V. & Owen, K. (2006). Setting the tone with the tune: A meta-analytic review of the effects of background music in retail settings. *Journal of Business Research*, 59(6), 755–764. https://doi.org/10.1016/j.jbusres.2006.01.013 (archived at https://perma.cc/WP2K-HFZV)
96   Milliman, R. E. (1982). Using background music to affect the behavior of supermarket shoppers. *The Journal of Marketing*, 46(3), 86–91. https://doi.org/10.2307/1251706 (archived at https://perma.cc/SZR9-9287)
97   Knoferle, K. M., Spangenberg, E. R., Herrmann, A., & Landwehr, J. R. (2012). It is all in the mix: The interactive effect of music tempo and mode on in-store sales. *Marketing Letters*, 23(1), 325–337. https://doi.org/10.1007/s11002-011-9156-z (archived at https://perma.cc/5YRY-X8K2)

98   Smith, P. C. & Curnow, R. (1966). 'Arousal hypothesis' and the effects of music on purchasing behavior. *Journal of Applied Psychology*, 50(3), 255.
99   Yalch, R. F. & Spangenberg, E. R. (1988). An environmental psychological study of foreground and background music as retail atmospheric factors. 106–110.
100 Yalch, R. & Spangenberg, E. (1990). Effects of store music on shopping behavior. *Journal of Consumer Marketing*, 7(2), 55–63.
101 Oakes, S. (2003). Musical tempo and waiting perceptions. *Psychology and Marketing*, 20(8), 685–705. https://doi.org/10.1002/mar.10092 (archived at https://perma.cc/Q5KD-MKNL)
102 Turley, L. & Milliman, R. (2000). Atmospheric effects on shopping behavior: A review of the experimental evidence. *Journal of Business Research*, 49(2), 193–211. https://doi.org/10.1016/s0148-2963(99)00010-7 (archived at https://perma.cc/KU2B-M8KF)
103 Knoferle, K. M., Spangenberg, E. R., Herrmann, A., & Landwehr, J. R. (2012). It is all in the mix: The interactive effect of music tempo and mode on in-store sales. *Marketing Letters*, 23(1), 325–337. https://doi.org/10.1007/s11002-011-9156-z (archived at https://perma.cc/A6QN-KXHD)
104 Dutton, D. G. & Aron, A. P. (1974). Some evidence for heightened sexual attraction under conditions of high anxiety. *Journal of Personality and Social Psychology*, 30(4), 510–517. https://doi.org/10.1037/h0037031 (archived at https://perma.cc/5TGX-FDJC)
105 Dutton, D. G. & Aron, A. P. (1974). Some evidence for heightened sexual attraction under conditions of high anxiety. *Journal of Personality and Social Psychology*, 30(4), 510–517. https://doi.org/10.1037/h0037031 (archived at https://perma.cc/5TGX-FDJC)
106 North, A. C., Hargreaves, D. J., & Mckendrick, J. (1999). The influence of in-store music on wine selections. *Journal of Applied Psychology*, 84(2), 271–276. https://doi.org/10.1037/0021-9010.84.2.271 (archived at https://perma.cc/F2HW-DJMK)
107 Ferguson, M. J. & Bargh, J. A. (2004). How social perception can automatically influence behavior. *Trends in Cognitive Sciences*, 8(1), 33–39. https://doi.org/10.1016/j.tics.2003.11.004 (archived at https://perma.cc/6PDU-AMVS)
108 Areni, C. S. & Kim, D. (1993). *The influence of background music on shopping behavior: Classical versus Top-Forty music in a wine store*. Association for Consumer Research, NA-20. https://www.researchgate.net/profile/David-Kim-22/publication/309255897_The_influence_of_background_music_on_shopping_behavior_Classical_versus_top-forty_music_in_a_wine_store/links/62f422feb8dc8b4403d33107/The-influence-of-background-music-on-shopping-behavior-Classical-versus-top-forty-music-in-a-wine-store.pdf (archived at https://perma.cc/2NF5-D7HG)
109 North, A. C., Hargreaves, D. J., & Mckendrick, J. (1999). The influence of in-store music on wine selections. *Journal of Applied Psychology*, 84(2), 271–276. https://doi.org/10.1037/0021-9010.84.2.271 (archived at https://perma.cc/M35V-3GAW)
110 Chambaron, S., Chisin, Q., Chabanet, C., Issanchou, S., & Brand, G. (2015). Impact of olfactory and auditory priming on the attraction to foods with high energy density. *Appetite*, 95(C), 74–80. https://doi.org/10.1016/j.appet.2015.06.012 (archived at https://perma.cc/PL3A-SVUZ)

111 Karmarkar, U. R. & Bollinger, B. (2015.) BYOB: How bringing your own shopping bags leads to treating yourself, and the environment. *Journal of Marketing*, 79(4), 1–15. https://doi.org/10.1509/jm.13.0228 (archived at https://perma.cc/M6ZX-24WH)

112 Dijksterhuis, A. & Knippenberg, A. van. (1998). The relation between perception and behavior, or how to win a game of Trivial Pursuit. *Journal of Personality and Social Psychology*, 74(4), 865–877. https://doi.org/10.1037/0022-3514.74.4.865 (archived at https://perma.cc/NB7X-WDTK)

113 O'Donnell, M., Nelson, L. D., Ackermann, E., Aczel, B., Akhtar, A., Aldrovandi, S., Alshaif, N., Andringa, R., … Zrubka, M. (2018). Registered Replication Report: Dijksterhuis and van Knippenberg (1998). *Perspectives on Psychological Science*, 13(2), 268–294. https://doi.org/10.1177/1745691618755704 (archived at https://perma.cc/YA8F-JVX8)

114 Pashler, H., Coburn, N., & Harris, C. R. (2012). Priming of social distance? Failure to replicate effects on social and food judgments. *PLoS ONE*, 7(8), e42510-6. https://doi.org/10.1371/journal.pone.0042510 (archived at https://perma.cc/Q8SX-G7DW)

115 Harris, C. R., Coburn, N., Rohrer, D., & Pashler, H. (2013). Two failures to replicate high-performance-goal priming effects. *PLoS ONE*, 8(8), e72467-9. https://doi.org/10.1371/journal.pone.0072467 (archived at https://perma.cc/G8U9-7TE2)

116 Shanks, D. R., Newell, B. R., Lee, E. H., Balakrishnan, D., Ekelund, L., Cenac, Z., Kavvadia, F., & Moore, C. (2013). Priming intelligent behavior: An elusive phenomenon. *PLoS ONE*, 8(4), e56515-10. https://doi.org/10.1371/journal.pone.0056515 (archived at https://perma.cc/T2ZD-GM8B)

117 Bargh, J. A., Chen, M., & Burrows, L. (1996). Automaticity of social behavior: Direct effects of trait construct and stereotype activation on action. *Journal of Personality and Social Psychology*, 71(2), 230–244. https://doi.org/10.1037/0022-3514.71.2.230 (archived at https://perma.cc/87UK-RE3N)

118 Doyen, S., Klein, O., Pichon, C.-L., & Cleeremans, A. (2012). Behavioral priming: It's all in the mind, but whose mind? *PLoS ONE*, 7(1), e29081. https://doi.org/10.1371/journal.pone.0029081 (archived at https://perma.cc/W7H2-A4RG)

119 Areni, C. S. & Kim, D. (1994). The influence of in-store lighting on consumers' examination of merchandise in a wine store. *International Journal of Research in Marketing*, 11(2), 117–125. https://doi.org/10.1016/0167-8116(94)90023-x (archived at https://perma.cc/EYG6-G5X6)

120 Summers, T. A. & Hebert, P. R. (2001). Shedding some light on store atmospherics: Influence of illumination on consumer behavior. *Journal of Business Research*, 54(2), 145–150. https://doi.org/10.1016/s0148-2963(99)00082-x (archived at https://perma.cc/S6F6-FCZS)

121 Park, N. K. & Farr, C. A. (2007). The effects of lighting on consumers' emotions and behavioral intentions in a retail environment: A cross-cultural comparison. *Journal of Interior Design*, 33(1), 17–32. https://doi.org/10.1111/j.1939-1668.2007.tb00419.x (archived at https://perma.cc/XA7H-NRCL)

122 Heschong, L., Wright, R. L., & Okura, S. (2002). Daylighting impacts on human performance in school. *Journal of the Illuminating Engineering Society*, 31(2), 101–114. https://doi.org/10.1080/00994480.2002.10748396 (archived at https://perma.cc/GM8T-TKHY)

123 Eagles, J. M. (2003). Seasonal affective disorder. *The British Journal of Psychiatry*, 182(2), 174–176. https://doi.org/10.1192/bjp.182.2.174 (archived at https://perma.cc/WX9A-J6RN)

124 Kliger, D., Raviv, Y., Rosett, J., Bayer, T., & Page, J. (2015). Seasonal affective disorder and seasoned art auction prices: New evidence from old masters. *Journal of Behavioral and Experimental Economics*, 59, 74–84.

125 Heschong, L., Wright, R. L., & Okura, S. (2013). Daylighting impacts on retail sales performance. *Journal of Illuminating Engineering Society*, 31(2), 21–25. https://doi.org/10.1080/00994480.2002.10748389 (archived at https://perma.cc/EE6G-FDWR)

126 Rose, N. & Dolega, L. (2022). It's the weather: Quantifying the impact of weather on retail sales. *Applied Spatial Analysis and Policy*, 15(1), 189–214. http://dx.doi.org/10.1007/s12061-021-09397-0 (archived at https://perma.cc/UPX3-8DVD)

127 Majestic Insider Knowledge (n.d.). What makes official rosé weather? https://www.majestic.co.uk/blog/inside-knowledge/what-makes-official-rose-weather (archived at https://perma.cc/ZR2S-LZJ6)

128 Bertrand, J. L. & Parnaudeau, M. (2017). No more blaming the weather: a retailer's approach to measuring and managing weather variability. *International Journal of Retail & Distribution Management*, 45(7/8), 730–761.

13 | The psychology of online shopping

LEARNING OBJECTIVES

- Understand how people view and navigate an e-commerce website.
- Critically evaluate the role that customer reviews and recommendations have in influencing online purchasing decisions, and analyse the implications for e-commerce businesses.
- Analyse the psychological techniques used by designers to create e-commerce platforms that encourage shoppers to spend more.

A new approach to retail

Bricks-and-mortar stores were the dominant approach to selling in the 20th century, but we are now in a different world. Sales online now account for over one in every four retail sales made,[1] and this figure is increasing. However, as shoppers cannot touch, feel or interact with the products, they instead have to rely on just the product description and photos. This can be an advantage as it gives marketers greater control over what information shoppers have available to make their decision with. Unlike in a physical shop, customers can read reviews and marketers can control the order in which shoppers see the products or dynamically change the offers based on the time of the day, things that have not previously been possible.

How do people read a webpage?

With businesses spending significant money developing their website and e-commerce platform, it would be nice to think that visitors fully engage with them, reading all information. Unfortunately, this is extremely rare.[2] Instead, most visitors just scan the page, either looking for specific information or for something to capture their attention. However, the way people scan a webpage is not random. Eye-tracking research has shown that people browse a website using one of seven standard patterns, regardless of whether they are using a mobile or laptop:[3]

- *F-pattern:* This is the most well-known pattern, although it is commonly misunderstood. Users read or scan across the upper part of the content area or block, (but not the whole webpage), then scan down the left-hand side before scanning right again, creating an F-shaped pattern. This means that it is the first lines of text and the first words on the left of a webpage which are looked at most. However, this pattern only occurs for people who read from left to right. In countries where people read from right-to-left, a reverse F-pattern occurs.

    From a design perspective, this is less than ideal as visitors tend to only engage superficially with the content and a lot of the key information is ignored. However, if a website is redesigned to make more extensive use of subheadings and sections, it decreases viewers' reliance on this pattern and encourages people to process the content more deeply.

- *Z-pattern or Gutenberg:* Whereas the F-pattern is more common for text heavy content blocks, people are more likely to use the Z-pattern on pages where the user does not need to scroll down and that are relatively content-light, such as landing pages. As implied by the name, viewers read the webpage in the shape of a Z, starting in the top left, moving horizontally before scanning to the bottom left before looking to the bottom right.

    From a design perspective, the most important information needs to be placed along this Z axis. However, certain areas are more important than others. The top left corner is where visitors initially look, and marketers should ensure this area will motivate visitors to continue browsing the rest of the page. The next area viewed is the top right, however brands should avoid placing any calls to action (C2A) here. Any C2A will disrupt a reader's flow and will stop them exploring the rest of the page. While people will look at the bottom left, of the four areas, people spend the least time looking here. Consequently, it's not best for any key information to be placed here. The final area where people look is the bottom right-hand corner – making it the perfect place for the C2A to be placed.

- *Layer cake pattern:* Whereas the F-pattern focuses on how viewers read a content block, the layer cake pattern looks at the page as a whole. Viewers scan the heading and subheadings but skip the text below each section, unless a heading looks relevant. Objectively this is the most effective way for visitors to process a website, but it only works when a website makes effective use of subheadings. Consequently, marketers need to think carefully about their subheadings, ensuring they motivate users to read the relevant section.

- *List bypassing pattern:* Although people are more likely to engage with bullet point lists than a block of text, the start of each bullet point needs to be different. When each bullet points starts with the same words, people are less likely to engage as they assume there will be duplication.
- *Spotted pattern:* When shoppers are looking for specific information, maybe a phone number or a specific product in an online shop, visitors skip large chunks of text and instead just scan for that specific feature.
- *Lawnmower pattern:* For webpages that include grids (such as when displaying products in an online shop or comparison tables) shoppers typically start reading at the top left, read across the row then read the next row below, but from right to left. Readers use this pattern as it is the easiest way to compare between products. Therefore designs need to make sure comparison tables make it easy for visitors to use the lawnmower pattern. This can be achieved by: (a) having fixed column headers, so readers always know which column they are reading; (b) allowing readers to hide columns they're not interested in (so the two columns a shopper is comparing are next to each other; (c) make sure all columns that have a yes/no answer are grouped together (so as not to disrupt the pattern).
- *Commitment pattern:* This is unlike any of the other patterns as it involves shoppers reading the entire page rather than just scanning. This is only likely to occur if the shopper is highly motivated, such as when making a high-involvement purchase.[4]

No matter which pattern a shopper uses, designers should develop a webpage so that it can be scanned easily. However, it is also important for a website to look visually appealing, and these two objectives can be contradictory. Including a mixture of text and images helps tell a coherent story. Originally, these were designed using an 'aligned layout'; the text blocks were on the left and images on the right. But to make a webpage more aesthetically interesting, most sites now use a 'zigzag' layout, alternating the position of text and images.

So how does this change the way people view the webpage? Well, it depends on what type of imagery the website uses. If the imagery contains useful information (such as showcasing the product, demonstrating how it can be used or how to assemble it) then both layouts are equally effective.[5] However, if the imagery is purely decorative and doesn't provide the user with any meaningful information, the zigzag layout is less effective. Shoppers want to avoid wasting their time and quickly learn that the imagery is purely decorative. But when the position of this information keeps moving, it makes it harder for the user to ignore it, increasing the cognitive load required to view the website.

This has some significant implications for how websites are designed.

1 Marketers should think carefully about the first image that is shown. If this image is purely decorative, visitors are likely to assume that the rest of the images are also decorative.

2. In countries where people read from left to right, make sure the information in the top left block will motivate people to read on. It doesn't matter if this is a picture or text, it has to provide the reader with a reason to continue scanning the rest of the content.

3. Ensure that any text blocks and decorative images are aligned (and make sure that the decorative image is not higher than the corresponding text block). If a decorative image is slightly higher than the associated text, it is likely to capture more of the shopper's attention and as a result, visitors pay less attention to the text.

4. There is a place for decorative imagery. As shown in the branding chapter, constantly pairing a brand with the same type of imagery can help establish and build a brand identity. But from an eye-tracking perspective, it is best to place these images aligned on the left, ensuring that they are viewed in users' peripheral vision. The exception to this rule is if there are only 2–3 rows, in which case it is OK for the content to be staggered.

Navigating online shops

While eye-tracking studies show how visitors read a single webpage, on their own they don't explain how shoppers browse and navigate between pages. But marketers need to be able to understand the complete journey. While it is important not to overgeneralize, as this journey will differ depending on the store and category, there are some general rules.

When buying products from an online supermarket, rather than using the search bar to look for specific products, 95% of shoppers browse via *'virtual departments'*.[6] Once on the relevant category page, for low involvement or habitual purchases most shoppers will add the product direct to their basket from here, rather than clicking on the product page,[7] meaning that any extra information on the product page is completely ignored. When users do use the search bar, they are more likely to be searching for specific product categories, e.g. 'gluten-free pizza' or 'Swiss chocolate' rather than searching for a specific brand.[8]

Once a user has clicked on a virtual department or even searched for a specific term, the products are usually presented in a grid format as it is the most effective way to showcase a large range of products simultaneously. However, for retailers who sell a smaller range of products, they can be more creative in their layout. Rather than using a grid or matrix layout, they can opt to list the products horizontally or vertically. The advantage of this approach is that rather than only displaying a product photo, product name and price, retailers are able to include a little more information on the virtual department page. You may think this is not a big deal as a shopper can always click on the product page information to find out more, but when it comes to low involvement purchases or items that the person regularly buys, they don't need the extra detail from the product page.

The decision on whether to use a vertical or horizontal layout is more than just an aesthetic choice. The layout changes what products people buy. If the products are displayed horizontally, people are more likely to avoid purchasing any product on the edge, instead opting for a middle option.[9] It is not a large effect, but consistent. One retailer found that shoppers selected the middle option 23% of the time, compared to the 20% that probability would predict.[10] This may seem like a small change, but it equates to a 15% difference, and for a large retailer these add up quickly; brands need to think carefully about where they place their most profitable products.

Likewise, the layout also changes the criteria that shoppers use to make a purchase decision. When a vertical layout is used, shoppers are more likely to use concrete features to reach a decision, such as the price, whereas when a horizontal layout is used, shoppers are more likely to make a decision based on product quality and its primary features.[11] But it is not just the layout that needs to be considered; the order that products are shown is critical. As shown in the pricing chapter, people spend approximately 10% more when the default order products are shown is from high to low.[12] But this may not be a good idea for all brands. As well as producing an anchoring effect, listing prices in a descending order causes shoppers to focus on the product benefits. But for brands focusing on selling products for a low price in high volume, it makes more sense to list the products in ascending order.[13] This is likely to be the case for budget stores. Their products will be cheaper than the competition but are unlikely to be as feature-rich.

Buy-it-now

With most shoppers not clicking on the product page, the role of the 'buy-it-now' or 'add to basket' button is critical. When one website added the feature, they found that shoppers placed 43% more orders, bought 36% more items and, more importantly, the average spend went up by 28.5%.[14] This should not be a surprise; previous commercial research by the Baymard Institute has shown that 22% of shoppers who added products to their basket but didn't complete their purchase claimed that this was because the checkout process was too long or too complicated.[15] To change behaviour, it is more effective to make the target behaviour easier (aka remove friction), rather than trying to motivate someone to perform the behaviour.[16] Yet web designers often overlook the power of friction.

Filling out an online form may not seem like a big deal; shoppers must register on any website before buying anything, but it can be enough to stop a sale. In the US, parents could register online to receive regular text messages with strategies to help their children revise more effectively. When the process required parents to fill out a form to sign up, only 1% registered. However, when the process was simplified to texting the word 'enrol' to a phone number, participation increased to 11%.[17]

Adding a 'buy-it-now' button not only removes friction, but with thought, they can be used to encourage people to order more. On most websites, the button will add one product to the basket, but some online supermarkets now allow shoppers to specify how many units get added. Some retailers have become more creative and changed the layout, for example featuring three buttons: 'buy 1', 'buy 2' and 'buy 3'. Although it creates a slightly more cluttered looking webpage, it changes the way shoppers think about their purchase decision. Using the traditional approach causes shoppers to ask themselves *'do I want to buy the product?'*, whereas this new approach reframes the question as *'how many should I buy?'*.[18]

While this research originally focused on the B2C domain, there is no reason why the same approach could not work in a B2B context. Rather than having buttons offering shoppers the option to order one, two or three, the defaults could be 50, 100 or 200. It could be hypothesized that this might be even more effective, as it implies to clients that these are the default number of units that other clients order from the wholesaler. However, based on what we discussed earlier about anchoring, the first button shoppers see should be the 200 option, and not the 50, to encourage shoppers to select the larger option.

The final factor marketers should consider is the design of the button. Eye-tracking research has shown that shoppers are naturally drawn to round buttons and, as a result, the click-through rate is higher for curved rather than square buttons.[19] So, what's driving this behaviour? The authors of the research believe that it is driven by evolution. People have learnt to associate curvy elements with being more friendly, unlike angular designs, which draws shoppers' attention.

Recommendations, defaults and online shopping

It may sound obvious but online retailers need to focus on converting visitors from browsers to shoppers. The average conversion rate for the top 100 US e-commerce websites is only 4.6%,[20] meaning that if 100 people visit the site, less than five people are going to buy something (although the range varies from 0.95% to 18.4% depending on the site). Unlike a traditional store, e-commerce platforms are dynamic and they can prioritize different products based on what's going on in the world or shoppers' previous purchases. Personalized recommendations require more sophisticated data analysis, but it's a highly effective way to encourage people to buy something.[21]

REAL-WORLD EXAMPLE: PSYCH IN ACTION

When Migros, the largest Swiss supermarket, implemented personalized recommendations, sales of the recommended product increased by 0.3%.[22] When you consider how many products are sold across a country, these small differences add up. However, it is important for brands not to be overly simplistic in their data analysis. Rather than only considering sales of recommended products, brands need to think about indirect sales, non-recommended products from categories first introduced to them by the recommendations, that wouldn't otherwise be bought. In this case, Migros sales revenue increased by over 60% – a huge change.

If redesigning the homepage to provide fully personalized recommendations proves too complex, a simpler alternative is to offer suggestions based on items the customer is currently browsing, similar to Amazon's *'frequently bought together'* feature. While Amazon doesn't release official sales data, estimates suggest that 34% of their total sales are driven by customers adding something to their basket via these recommendations.[23] This is not a quirk of shopping on Amazon. When one of North America's five largest online retailers implemented a 'customers who bought this item also bought' feature, their purchase rate increased by over 30%.[24]

One reason this approach is so effective is that these recommendations appear near the end of the shopping journey. In almost all retail settings, suggestions made later in the customer journey tend to be more impactful[25] as shoppers perceive them to be tailored to their current browsing activity rather than based on their historic purchases. Websites like Amazon and COOP.ch sell virtually everything, from stationery to make-up, meaning the same visitor might be shopping for very different things on different occasions. This can make recommendations based on previous search history irrelevant. On the other hand, recommendations based on what the shopper is currently browsing (e.g. 'People who looked at this item also viewed…') are perceived as more relevant and, consequently, more helpful.

But not all the products that are given prominence on a website are based on a shopper's previous purchases. Sometimes, retailers are just trying to push products with a higher profit margin or when they have too much of a specific product in stock. But rather than just relying on visual salience to promote these products, brands will sometimes position the target product as the 'default' option. When shoppers are unsure about what to buy, they often look for cues, such as which option is preselected. Take buying travel insurance. It can be really confusing deciding what level of excess you need and the level of coverage you require for your baggage, technical equipment, and cancellation and travel disruption. Travelers are free to customize their coverage option to what suits their needs and budget, but retailers will often provide a default or suggested level of coverage, by putting the movable bar in a certain place. When two equally appealing products are displayed but one is presented as the 'default option,' that option is chosen 27% more often than the alternative.[26]

Defaults work because shoppers intuitively assume that retailers have selected the default option for a reason; it must be the best option for most people (even if this isn't factually true). However, when a shopper knows exactly what they want, they buy this, regardless of the default. Defaults only work when the customer is either uncertain of what to buy (e.g. what level of coverage they need for travel insurance), or they are not motivated to reach a decision.[27] Take the children's meals at Disney World. When Disney changed the default options from a fizzy drink and curly fries to squash and fruit or vegetables, children ended up consuming 21% fewer calories, 44% less fat and 43% less sodium.[28] Parents were still free to order their normal regular fries, but most parents didn't bother to change.

REAL-WORLD EXAMPLE: PSYCH IN ACTION

Searching for a book on Amazon, most shoppers are likely to know exactly which book they want to buy, and as such defaults are unlikely to influence their choice. However, most people haven't thought about the format of the book. Do they want a hardback, paperback, e-book or audiobook? Amazon will auto-select one version as the default, increasing the likelihood that this format is purchased.

Defaults are popular not just because they are easy to implement, but because they can work alongside other psychological tactics. Good marketers are always looking to use a range of psychological tactics when designing a website. But it is important to remember that in most cases the impact of behavioural interventions is not cumulative. Using two interventions simultaneously is more effective than using one, but not twice as effective. However, defaults work really well when combined with social norms.[29] Consequently, if a retailer positions a product as the default, they should think about how they describe or justify why it is the default option. For example, they could describe the product as *'our most popular option'*, *'family favourite'* or even just *'our best-selling'*. These changes reassure customers why this product has been positioned as the default, making it feel less like a blatant attempt at manipulation.

But care needs to be taken with defaults. If the default option is set to be something that is too expensive or not appropriate, then understandably, shoppers will feel irritated. Not only will they not purchase it, but it can decrease the likelihood that they'll return to that establishment.[30] When New York City cab drivers were paid in cash, the default tip was 10%. However, when the city introduced a digital payment system and passengers could select a pre-determined tip amount of either 20%, 25% or 30%, the average tip increased to 22%.[31] But passengers who were not prepared to pay the 20% suggested were more likely to avoid tipping altogether, rather than enter a custom amount.

The risk in using any form of psychological intervention to influence shoppers' behaviour is that if they realize what the business is doing, they'll react badly. When it comes to using defaults, the risk is greater as it's more obvious than changing whether products are listed in ascending or descending price order. However, it's easy for a company to overcome these challenges.

Michaelsen et al showed that when a retailer was open with shoppers and told them they use defaults, to simplify the shopping process, shoppers are free to ignore the defaults, they are less likely to feel manipulated, and surprisingly, it doesn't reduce the effectiveness of the defaults.[32] But for this to work, Michaelsen et al concluded that getting the timing right is crucial. Brands must disclose their use of defaults before shoppers have decided what to buy. If this information is revealed afterwards, shoppers will have a negative reaction to the brand.

Scarcity appeals

Virtually all online shops will use some form of psychological technique to persuade, but the most commonly used are scarcity and urgency.[33] This is the idea that people value something more when it is rare[34] and when it comes to retail, products that are scarce, such as being nearly sold out are liked and bought more than products that are readily available.[35] Consequently, you'll see messages such as: *'only 10 products left in stock'*, *'flash sale ends in 48 hours'* or brands launching a limited-edition version. For example, Triumph motorcycles launched a James-Bond-themed edition of the Tiger 900, and the website highlighted that the bike was *'strictly limited to just 250 motorcycles'*. Each of these messages employs scarcity but the psychological mechanism behind each of them is slightly different, meaning they should be used in different circumstances.

Highlighting that a product is nearly sold out (e.g. only 10 left in stock) uses demand-based scarcity. Flash sales emphasize time-based scarcity (e.g. *sale ends in 48 hours*) and limited-edition models use supply-driven security. Of the three approaches, time-based scarcity appeals usually lead to the biggest upsurge in sales, whereas demand-based appeals have the smallest effects.[36] However, this doesn't mean that time-based appeals are going to be right for all brands or all situations. When promoting low involvement or utilitarian products, such as a chocolate bar, it's best for a brand to use a demand-based appeal. This approach not only leverages scarcity but also taps into social proof. If there are only four units left, the product must be popular as it is selling out. In contrast, for higher involvement products, time-based appeals drive the most sales. In these cases, people have already decided if they want to buy the product but need a small nudge or excuse to buy today, hence highlighting that the product is only available in September encourages shoppers to buy it sooner. Finally, when selling experiences or luxury items, research shows that supply-based appeals, like limited editions, are most effective. These emphasize exclusivity and position the product as a status symbol, enhancing its desirability.

It is not just the product that makes a difference; it also matters if you are buying for yourself or someone else. When buying a gift, there is always pressure. Have I bought the right option and will the other person like it? Consequently, most people are motivated by a desire to reduce the risk and uncertainty of their decision. If a product is proving popular, it suggests that it must be a fairly safe bet that whoever you're buying it for will like it. Consequently, it is more effective to use a social norm-based appeal than a scarcity appeal.[37] Hence, around Christmas time, when lots of people are shopping for gifts, it might be a good time to boost the use of social norm appeals. However, when shoppers are buying for themselves, scarcity-based messages tend to be more effective. This is because most people like to think of themselves as unique, who don't simply follow the crowd (even if the data suggests otherwise). As a result, scarcity appeals resonate well, reinforcing the idea of exclusivity and individuality.

Urgency is the most commonly used tactic for e-retailers, though it's not necessarily the most powerful. If shoppers cannot decide between two products, and they are unfamiliar with both brands, they typically buy the product with the highest sales level. However, if the sales are similar, or at least shoppers perceive the sales to be similar, then shoppers opt for the product with the lowest remaining stock levels.[38] Again, this is a case of shoppers deferring to social norms and only if shoppers perceive the sales level as similar, does the fear of missing out (FOMO) take over. For this to work, retailers don't need to state the exact sales level, which is likely to be commercially sensitive. Instead, it is good enough for a retailer to list a product as 'top ten best-selling business psychology books' or flag a product as a best-selling cooking sauce.

GIVE IT A GO

Visit our experimental online shop and test whether social norms or scarcity appeals have the biggest impact on sales.

Recommendations, testimonials and reviews

As shoppers can't physically interact with a product, most websites will feature testimonials and quotes from delighted customers or experts who are willing to endorse the product. These are different from product reviews but involve pulling out a quote from a review or endorsement and giving it a prominent position on the website; a little like the testimonials you sometimes find on the back cover of a novel or a film poster. But who is the best person to provide these quotes? Should a website use a celebrated expert or instead use the 'common-man' appeal, featuring a quote from an everyday person that the shopper could relate to? Once more, the answer depends on the type of product being sold. If the company is attempting to sell a product where it is relatively hard to judge the quality of a product, it usually makes more sense to feature a quote from an expert.[39] If most shoppers are unable to objectively tell the quality of a product, their evaluation is predominantly influenced by their prior expectations and an expert testimonial or endorsement will really shape this.

A good example of this could be when it comes to selling a bottle of wine or a new snowboard. In both cases, an average wine drinker or snowboarder may struggle to appreciate the difference between a great product and a good product. Instead, they are going to rely on external cues, such as price, brand reputation and expert endorsement. However, if a brand is selling a product where it is very easy to judge the quality, or at least if a shopper likes it or not (such as a film or a book), it is best to use an endorsement from someone the customer can relate to. It doesn't matter what your expectations are, if you sit watching a film and you're not enjoying it, it is very obvious – prior expectations will have a limited impact.

In this situation, rather than just pulling out one or two quotes, it's much better to highlight that a large number of people have enjoyed the product, such as '*over a thousand five-star reviews*'. Product reviews hopefully remove the risk of shopping online, as they showcase what most shoppers think, not just a few hand-picked examples. While this sounds like a great idea, the research suggests that in practice, these reviews are often not overly useful for shoppers. On Amazon, over half of all reviewers give their purchases five stars (out of five) and the average rating is 4.2 stars.[40] This produces a J-shaped distribution, with most reviews getting a 4 or 5, a few 1-star reviews, and virtually nothing in between. Intuitively, this makes sense – if someone is really happy with a product, they are going to be motivated to leave a review to let others know about it, but why so few negative reviews? Society reinforces the idea that people shouldn't directly criticize others, and even online where reviewers are relatively anonymous, this idea still proliferates, hence people are less likely to leave negative reviews, even when they are underwhelmed by a product.[41]

Intuitively, most shoppers are aware of this bias. Rather than focusing on how many stars a product has been given, most shoppers now focus on reading written reviews.[42] When they look at all the reviews posted online, most people spend less time focusing on the positive reviews and instead choose to focus on the negative reviews, especially females.[43] Hence, it is really important for shoppers to be able to filter reviews based on star rating. However, when it comes to scanning the reviews, not all are perceived equally. In general, shoppers think a review is more helpful if it is clear, easy to read and uses emotionally engaging language.

But with businesses being able to purchase fake reviews,[44] this has understandably led shoppers to be sceptical. To overcome this, many online stores now display a 'verified purchase' badge from customers who bought the product from their store. It's a small change, but shoppers trust these reviews more.[45] Similarly, brands can take steps to humanize reviewers. Rather than simply asking for a review, retailers can encourage reviewers to upload a profile photo and share a brief biography to accompany their review. For instance, on a website selling running gear, a reviewer might describe themselves as 'an enthusiastic trail runner exploring the Alps around Valais'. These subtle details help position the reviewer as an expert, making their reviews more trusted.[46] Similarly, including a photo can further reinforce the reviewer's authenticity, though people are generally more willing to do this when leaving positive reviews.[47]

If a site doesn't include these features, shoppers will subconsciously look for other clues in the way the review is written to decide if it's genuine. Real customers do not just talk about the positives, but they will highlight some of the downsides.[48] Consequently, rather than just asking customers to review their purchases, bold companies might ask customers what they like about the product and whether there are any features that other shoppers need to be aware of. While it doesn't directly ask shoppers to focus on the negatives, it is likely to make the negatives a little more salient in the shopper's mind. Hence, shoppers are more likely to write a review that will acknowledge a product's weaknesses as well as its strengths.

Yet there is also another unexpected benefit of phrasing the question like this. It increases the likelihood that the reviewer will write in the present rather than the past. The distinction between 'the cheese fondue was delicious' and 'the cheese fondue is delicious' is subtle but it matters. Reviews written in the present tense feel more certain and persuasive, ultimately making shoppers more likely to purchase the product.[49] A review written in the past tense implies that something was true at the time it was written, but it might not be now. A review that says 'Saas-Fee is great' not only implies that the place is currently great, but it removes the subjective, suggesting the place will be fun for others as well.

Building on this, brands can increase engagement with product reviews by encouraging customers to upload photos or a short video to support their review. These 'hybrid reviews,' combining text and visuals, are perceived as not only more believable but also more helpful.[50] This is likely because humans are naturally drawn to images and often pay more attention to visuals than text.[51] Readers instinctively seek visuals that reinforce what's written, creating a more compelling and trustworthy impression. If a review claimed the product packaging was damaged in shipping, by including a photo, the potential customer can look at the damage and decide if this is a problem for them. As a result, when asking shoppers to upload photos as part of their review, the instructions should encourage them to focus on key parts that other shoppers might find important, rather than simply taking a photo of the whole product.

When to ask for a review

The challenge for brands is when to ask customers to review their purchases. Many retailers include a note with the parcel, encouraging shoppers to leave a review immediately after receiving the product. However, these early reviews are unlikely to be particularly useful. Shoppers can comment on delivery speed and their initial impressions, but such reviews often lack depth, as the customer may not yet have had a chance to use the product. But if you wait a couple of weeks, shoppers will have used their purchase. Some might assume this delay risks missing the opportunity as customers could become too busy to respond but the data tells a different story. If a brand asks customers to review a product as soon as they receive the product, it decreases the likelihood that they'll write one, especially for younger shoppers.[52] It can leave people feeling irritated and pressurized, triggering what's known as reactance (see Chapter 8). In contrast, when brands wait a week or two before reaching out, customers are more likely to leave a thoughtful review.

So how long should you wait to ask? The answer depends on your product. How much time will it take for customers to form a realistic evaluation of it? For standardized products such as bottled water, canned soups or a ream of paper, brands can ask for reviews quickly. These products are homogeneous, and generally most people know what to expect when they order them. Hence, it is not a problem to ask for a review quickly. But when it comes to evaluating a product, such as new home speakers or a bread maker, people will need time to use the product and understand how it performs in different situations. For these products, it is better to wait a couple of weeks or even longer before you ask for shoppers' thoughts.

How to take product photos that sell

Selecting the right product photography for an online shop is vital. Logically, it would make sense for shoppers to depend more on the text description as it provides more factual information, but Townsend and Kahn have shown that shoppers prefer visual information; what psychologists refer to as the visual preference heuristic.[53] But photos are even more important than we often realize. Shoppers process pictures quicker than words,[54] they trigger more emotions than words[55] and in most situations, they are more memorable.[56] Hence, it should be no surprise that getting the right photos will lead potential shoppers to trust the website more and it increases the likelihood they'll make a purchase.[57] But what is the right photo?

Lifestyle shots vs product shots

The most basic decision art directors and photographers need to make is how to showcase the product. Should it be on its own, commonly on a plain white background, or is it best to show the product in use? Arguments can be made for both approaches. Using a white background allows the product to be the centre of attention, whereas showing the product in a naturalistic environment makes it easier for a shopper to imagine using the product at home.

From a psychological perspective, the key to successful product photography is processing fluency; how easy is it for our brains to process information? The easier a stimulus is for our brain to process, the more we like it.[58] However, arguments could be made that both options could improve fluency. An image with no distractions is simple for the brain to understand because we can only focus on the product, but viewing the product in context provides the viewer with extra cues as to how it should be used, while only marginally increasing the complexity of the image.[59]

But research by Maier and Dost has shown that contextual cues dramatically improve processing fluency, causing viewers to like the photos more, and evaluate the product more favourably.[60] Similarly, showing a product physically close to the problem it solves leads shoppers to believe the product is more effective.[61] People believed a cream that treats muscle aches was over 20% more effective when they saw the product was positioned next to a picture of a sprained muscle. By positioning the product alongside the problem it solves, people infer a stronger connection between the two.

Unfortunately, this is not always possible. Several leading online retailers' brand guidelines require the product photos that suppliers submit to show their product without any background surfaces, creating the illusion that the products are floating in mid-air. But there are little tricks that can still improve these photos and keep within retailer guidelines. By showing the products with a very basic digital background that provides some depth cues, dramatically improves a photo's ability to sell.[62] It doesn't matter if you are selling durable products such as mugs, chairs or handbags, or consumables such as wine, soup or chocolate, the effect holds true.

In each of these product photos where there is a basic digital background, the designers have also included a product shadow to help embed the product to the background. When people first look at images, they are unlikely to consciously notice the shadow as their attention is focused on the product. However, whether the backdrop is digital or real, shoppers are more likely to purchase a product when it includes a shadow. This is because, across various product categories, people tend to associate heavier items with higher quality[63] (see Chapter 2). However, this effect only applies to products that shoppers expect or want to be heavy. For items where being lightweight is desirable, like a laptop, adding a shadow can be counterproductive.

The challenge with looking at any photo, but especially one with a minimalist or no background, is that shoppers find it very hard to judge a product's size. Looking at a photo of a chocolate brownie, it can be hard to tell if it's only going to feed one, or if it's large enough to feed a family of four. Some retailers overcome this by including an extra photo that includes a reference object next to the product; perhaps a ruler or an item that everybody can relate to, such as a can of fizzy drink. This allows shoppers to quickly judge the size of the product, increasing trust in the photo.[64]

E-commerce or m-commerce

When discussing online retail, it is important to recognize that how consumers use the internet is changing. Globally, over half of all websites are now accessed via a mobile phone, excluding tablets.[65] However, people are not just viewing on their phone, and then making a purchase on a desktop. In Switzerland, 52% of all retail sales were made from a mobile, whereas in the UK it's 56%.[66] This has led to a change in the type of images that sell. Initially, brands would upload a product photo; the photo shown online was identical to the product that consumers could buy in a physical store. But the size of the two items is very different. A frozen pizza box is likely to be over 30cm across, but a photo of the product viewed on a mobile will be less than 2cm across. Details that can easily be seen in store vanish when viewed on a mobile.

As a result, brands have developed a new simplified version of their packaging which they use online for both mobiles and desktops. Shoppers should be able to look at a product image in the size it appears on a mobile screen (typically 16 x 16mm) and correctly identify the 4Ws:

a Who is the brand? Normally this is the brand name that shoppers will be looking for.

b What is the product? Is it dog food, bleach or hair gel?

c Which variety is it? What characteristics distinguish one product from another, be it flavour, fragrance or model. For example, is this a thin-crust loaded cheese pizza or a tiger-crust cheese medley pizza?

d How much of it is there? What size is the product or how many units does the shop get?

Any element on the packaging that doesn't answer these questions should be removed, as it's likely to be a distraction.

The big question is, does it just make the category feel easier to shop or does it increase sales of the target brand? When Unilever tested the concept with their Magnum ice creams, a billion-dollar brand, they found that switching to mobile-optimized imagery led to an increase in sales of 24%[67] when shopping from a mobile. Of course, as they were one of the first to make this switch, they gained a big advantage, but if brands don't make this change and every other brand does, they will be at a significant disadvantage.

Mobile commerce also changes how shoppers interact with an image. All smartphones have a touch screen, allowing shoppers to pinch to zoom in or use gesture control to see the product from different angles. This seemingly small change has a significant impact: shoppers evaluate the product more favourably, are more likely to make a purchase and are even willing to pay a higher price.[68] Interestingly, this effect is more pronounced for shoppers who prefer physically touching products in shops.[69]

In a store, the simple act of touching a product is enough to increase a shopper's sense that they already own an item, even if they haven't actually purchased it.[70] Psychologists believe the same effect occurs when using a touchscreen to shop. Interacting with the product photo increases a variation of the *'endowment effect'*. This is a robust psychological phenomenon that has been discussed across numerous studies. When university students were given a branded mug and were subsequently asked how much they would sell it for, the average price was $4.50. However, when a different group of students were asked how much they'd pay to buy the identical mug, this time the students were only prepared to pay $2.25. In theory, these two values should be the same – it's the same mug, the only difference is the fact one group already owned the mug, which explains a 100% difference in values.[71] Just as in a physical store, it is a good idea to get shoppers to touch your product; in an e-commerce store, it's a good idea for shoppers to interact with product images using gesture control.

A good photo: It's all in our imagination

Photos are a powerful tool for selling products because they help shoppers imagine themselves using the product; the easier it is to imagine using the product, the more likely we are to buy it. And there are some really simple tricks for photographers to make it easier for shoppers to imagine using the product. When taking a photo of a 'grabbable' product, make sure that the product is orientated so that someone could pick it up in their right hand. When viewing an advert for 'a smooth vanilla yoghurt', purchase intention was nearly 20% higher when the spoon was orientated to match the dominant hand of the viewer[72] and since around 90% of the population is right-handed, it's logical to design adverts for right-handed shoppers.

Even if your product is non-grabbable, such as rugs, furniture or even art, photographers and stylists can benefit from the same effect. When setting up such lifestyle shots, if 'haptic cues' can be included, something that is unrelated to the product but that can be held (e.g. a wine glass), it should be positioned so that the viewer would naturally pick it up with their right hand. Even though the haptic cue is completely unrelated to the target product, it still increases shoppers' purchase intention for the target product.[73]

Once you have the right photography, marketers need to decide how many photos to show. In the past, brands would only have the choice of including one or two photos in print catalogues, but online it is not uncommon to see 10+ photos shown. Intuitively, people would assume that the more photos included, the better. However, if an online shop includes lots of photos, it can cause more doubt and uncertainty, which results in the product appearing less distinctive.[74] This is unrelated to the paradox of choice, but it changes how shoppers decide. Including lots of photos causes the shopper to focus on individual features rather than processing the product in a Gestalt manner. However, this could work in a brand's favour if they want you to consider multiple factors.

Yet marketers need to focus on more than just the photos that appear in the web shop. When designing their website, the products are probably going to feature prominently on the site. So, how best to showcase them? Should they be shown in isolation or should the entire range be shown in one photo? The answer depends on the product being sold and its cost. If the product is relatively cheap or modestly priced, it's best to show lots of the product in one photo. However, when the product is expensive, like a luxury whisky, it's far better to show the product in isolation.[75] By showcasing a group of products together, it diminishes the pain of paying for a product, making the product feel less expensive. However, for premium products, they want their brand to be perceived as exclusive and even expensive, so they can benefit from the price-quality heuristic (see Chapter 10) and the scarcity principle.

The last step: Check-out

One of the drawbacks of online shopping is that unless the product is a digital download, it needs to be shipped. Shoppers have to wait to receive their product and either the business or the customer will need to pay for postage. It may sound like a cliché, but shoppers are happier paying CHF 25 for a product that includes free shipping than paying CHF 20 and having to pay CHF 5 for postage.[76] However, by changing the way this offer is framed can make it more effective. Rather than framing the offer as free postage, the product should still cost CHF 20, and postage cost CHF 5, but when the customer comes to check out, there is a special promotion that deducts CHF 5 from the total bill.[77] This works because it makes the money off, the CHF 5 promotion, feel more salient, rather than just offering free postage, even if the absolute value is the same.

However, lots of websites won't offer these discounts automatically. Instead, retailers will email shoppers a discount code which, when entered, gives customers free shipping or maybe discounts on certain products. Some brand managers feel that these campaigns are ineffective because of the low number of people who redeem the offers. But this ignores the fact that these campaigns can drive lots of traffic to the websites. When Sahni, Zou and Chintagunta ran 70 different experiments for an online store, sending out 52,043 emails with discount codes, they found that sales increased by 37%. However, 90% of this increase was not generated by shoppers buying products that were on offer, but buying other products. Even the week after the offers ended, sales were still 19% higher than the same week the previous year.[78]

But how will a customer react when they come to check out if they don't have a discount code? Most shoppers will find this frustrating, as nobody likes the idea that others are paying less for the exact same item. This often leads them to search online for a code. If they can't find one, there's a good chance they might abandon their purchase and buy the same item from a competitor, sometimes even paying fractionally more just to 'punish' the original store. This doesn't mean retailers should stop using discount codes, but rather should rethink how they design their webpages. If the discount code box is redesigned, so that it reads *'enter discount code here'* inside the box and removing the 'apply' button, the discount box becomes less conspicuous. This way, when a shopper is scanning the webpage to check they've filled in all the boxes, it is not obvious that they haven't entered a code, increasing the likelihood that a shopper without a code will still make a purchase.[79]

Closing thoughts

With shoppers making purchases online, it is essential for retailers to design effective web stores. This requires marketers to have a detailed understanding of both principles of user experience and consumer psychology, which have been described in this chapter. However, in some ways, it is easier than designing a traditional bricks-and-mortar store. This is because with the click of a few buttons retailers can quickly change the look and feel of their website, changing the photos, the placement and colour of buttons or even how products are described. Psychological theory will predict what should work best, but marketers should always run experiments (what are commonly referred to as A/B tests by industry professionals) to test whether the concepts work for their sites.

> **KEY POINTS**
>
> - Most shoppers navigate a website using one of seven standard eye-tracking patterns: F-Pattern, Z-Pattern (Gutenberg), Layer Cake Pattern: List Bypassing Pattern: Spotted Pattern: Lawnmower Pattern: Commitment Pattern.
> - For low-involvement purchases, most shoppers add things directly to their basket using the 'buy it now' button and don't click on the product page. Hence, retailers need to ensure the most important details are on the search page.

- Purchase recommendations are more effective when made later in the shopping journey rather than at the beginning.
- Shoppers uncertain about what to buy are more likely to follow default suggestions, especially when paired with social norm appeals.
- Scarcity appeals are more persuasive when shoppers are buying for themselves, while social norm appeals work better for gifts or purchases intended for others.
- Online reviews influence shoppers most when written in the present tense, balanced with both pros and cons, and supported by photos. Encourage reviewers to share what they liked and mention any features other shoppers should know about.
- For expensive purchases, wait a couple of weeks before asking for reviews to increase participation. For inexpensive items like commodities, immediate review requests focusing on delivery and packaging are fine.
- Products showcased in lifestyle settings sell better than those displayed on plain backgrounds.
- Shoppers browsing on mobile devices feel more engaged with products when they can interact with photos (e.g. zooming or rotating).

PUTTING THEORY INTO PRACTICE

1 Visit five different websites, making sure you select a mixture of e-commerce sites and general brand websites. Identify which eye gaze pattern shoppers are likely to use to navigate each site. Based on your findings, evaluate whether the placement of any elements should be changed to improve usability or effectiveness.

2 Visit an e-commerce site of your choice and see how many psychological techniques you can identify. Of the techniques you've identified, which do you think will be the most effective?

3 Using your smartphone, take a selection of product photos that you could upload to an e-commerce website. Make sure that you think about how your photos are optimized to encourage shoppers to buy more.

4 Imagine you are the marketing manager for a new online e-retailer selling products of your choice. Storyboard the look and feel of your website using pencil sketches. This should be a simple and easy-to-understand visual overview of your website, highlighting key design elements such as location of menus, header, footer, content sections and product photos.

5   Visit the website of your local supermarket on a desktop or laptop. Imagine you were asked to redesign the website to optimize it for viewing on a mobile. What changes would you make?

6   If you were the marketing manager for a company selling travel insurance, how could you ethically use principles of social norms or defaults to influence travellers' purchase of insurance?

SUGGESTIONS FOR FURTHER READING

Kumar, A. (2024). *Psychology UX Design: Psychological laws and effects | Gamification | Biases (English Edition)*. BPB Publications.

References

1   Office for National Statistics (2024). Internet sales as a percentage of total retail sales (ratio) (%). https://www.ons.gov.uk/businessindustryandtrade/retailindustry/timeseries/j4mc/drsi (archived at https://perma.cc/3SMN-RQ8D)

2   NN/G group (2023). *How people read online report, 2nd edition*. https://www.nngroup.com/reports/how-people-read-web-eyetracking-evidence/ (archived at https://perma.cc/5N39-KBMR)

3   NN/G group (2023). *How people read online report, 2nd edition*. https://www.nngroup.com/reports/how-people-read-web-eyetracking-evidence/ (archived at https://perma.cc/3FRY-4C5Y)

4   NN/G group (2023). *How people read online report, 2nd edition*. https://www.nngroup.com/reports/how-people-read-web-eyetracking-evidence/ (archived at https://perma.cc/3FRY-4C5Y)

5   NN/G group (2023). *Zigzag image -Text layouts make scanning less efficient*. https://www.nngroup.com/articles/zigzag-page-layout/ (archived at https://perma.cc/GY8G-Q34Z)

6   Benn, Y., Webb, T. L., Chang, B. P., & Reidy, J. (2015). What information do consumers consider, and how do they look for it, when shopping for groceries online?. *Appetite*, 89, 265–273.

7   McKinsey & Company. (2015). The digital path to purchase: How consumers navigate online retail environments. Unpublished commercial report.

8   Harvey, G. J., Gordon, A., Evershed, J., Schilling, T., Van Loo, E., & Devlin, J. (2025). Virtual carts and cognitive choices: Simulating online shopping for behavioral experiments. Manuscript submitted for publication to Behavior Research Methods.

9   Kim, J., Hwang, E., Park, J., Lee, J. C., & Park, J.(2019). Position effects of menu item displays in consumer choices: Comparisons of horizontal versus vertical displays. *Cornell Hospitality Quarterly*, 60(2), 116–124.

10 Rodway, P., Schepman, A., & Lambert, J. (2012). Preferring the one in the middle: Further evidence for the centre-stage effect. *Applied Cognitive Psychology*, 26(2), 215–222. https://doi.org/10.1002/acp.1812 (archived at https://perma.cc/GK8C-9VQX)

11 Mukherjee, S. (2022). Vertical vs. horizontal presentation formats result in different consumption choices due to construal priming. *Journal of Consumer Behaviour*. https://doi.org/10.1002/cb.2062 (archived at https://perma.cc/M8FN-ZNTK)

12 Huff, S. C. (2021). Money on the table: Increasing revenue through menu order. *Journal of Digital & Social Media Marketing*, 9(3), 275–283.

13 Mukherjee, S. (2022). When does the price presentation order impact choices? Dispositional and situational moderators for the price order effect. *International Journal of Consumer Studies*, 46(6), 2153–2166. https://doi.org/10.1111/ijcs.12775 (archived at https://perma.cc/UD59-RG5P)

14 Unal, M. & Park, Y. H. (2023). Fewer clicks, more purchases. *Management Science*, 69(12), 7317–7334.

15 Baymard Institute (n.d.). 49 cart abandonment rate statistics 2025. https://baymard.com/lists/cart-abandonment-rate (archived at https://perma.cc/N2FH-HSPL)

16 Luo, Y., Li, A., Soman, D., & Zhao, J. (2023). A meta-analytic cognitive framework of nudge and sludge. *Royal Society Open Science*, 10(11), 230053.

17 Bergman, P., Lasky-Fink, J., & Rogers, T. (2020). Simplification and defaults affect adoption and impact of technology, but decision makers do not realize it. *Organizational Behavior and Human Decision Processes*, 158, 66–79.

18 Duke, K. E. & Amir, O. (2022). The importance of selling formats: When integrating purchase and quantity decisions increases sales. *Marketing Science*. https://doi.org/10.1287/mksc.2022.1364 (archived at https://perma.cc/2EL8-JDA6)

19 Biswas, D., Abell, A., & Chacko, R. (2024). Curvy digital marketing designs: Virtual elements with rounded shapes enhance online click-through rates. *Journal of Consumer Research*, 51(3), 552–570.

20 Gudigantala, N., Bicen, P., & Eom, M. (2016). An examination of antecedents of conversion rates of e-commerce retailers. *Management Research Review*, 39(1), 82–114.

21 Alves, G., Jannach, D., de Souza, R. F., Damian, D., & Manzato, M. G. (2024). Digitally nudging users to explore off-profile recommendations: Here be dragons. *User Modeling and User-Adapted Interaction*, 34(2), 441–481.

22 Dias, M. B., Locher, D., Li, M., El-Deredy, W., & Lisboa, P. J. (2008, October). *The value of personalised recommender systems to e-business: A case study*. In Proceedings of the 2008 ACM conference on Recommender systems (291–294).

23 Medium (2019, June 10). How frequently bought together increases your sales. https://medium.com/recommendation-kit/how-frequently-bought-together-increases-your-sales-75b49052cbea (archived at https://perma.cc/J2LJ-AXLM)

24 Lee, D. & Hosanagar, K. (2019). How do recommender systems affect sales diversity? A cross-category investigation via randomized field experiment. *Information Systems Research*, 30(1), 239–259.

25 Pöyry, E., Hietaniemi, N., Parvinen, P., Hamari, J., & Kaptein, M. (2017). *Personalized product recommendations: Evidence from the field*. Proceedings of the 50th Hawaii International Conference on System Sciences.

26 Jachimowicz, J., Duncan, S., Weber, E., & Johnson, E. (2019). When and why defaults influence decisions: A meta-analysis of default effects. *Behavioural Public Policy*, 3(2), 159–186. https://doi.org/10.1017/bpp.2018.43 (archived at https://perma.cc/S5SM-BS4M)

27 Dhingra, N., Gorn, Z., Kener, A., & Dana, J. (2012). The default pull: An experimental demonstration of subtle default effects on preferences. *Judgment and Decision Making*, 7(1), 69–76.

28 Peters, J., Beck, J., Lande, J., Pan, Z., Cardel, M., Ayoob, K., & Hill, J. O. (2016). Using healthy defaults in Walt Disney World restaurants to improve nutritional choices. *Journal of the Association for Consumer Research*, 1(1), 92–103. https://doi.org/10.1086/684364 (archived at https://perma.cc/C4F3-XVMT)

29 Buchanan, T. M., Buchanan, J., Diedericks, D., & Davis, L. (2023). I'll have what she's having: (Social) perceptions of default options and implications for marketing and decision making. *International Journal of Consumer Studies*, 47(2), 509–522. https://doi.org/10.1111/ijcs.12847 (archived at https://perma.cc/N52F-G3FM)

30 Colby, H., Li, M., & Chapman, G. (2020). Dodging dietary defaults: Choosing away from healthy nudges. *Organizational Behavior and Human Decision Processes*, 161, 50–60.

31 Haggag, K. & and Paci, G. (2014). Default tips. *American Economic Journal: Applied Economics*, 6(3), 1–19. https://doi.org/10.1257/app.6.3.1 (archived at https://perma.cc/V8XR-X9V2)

32 Michaelsen, P., Nyström, L., Luke, T. J., & Hedesström, M. (2021). Downstream consequences of disclosing defaults: Influences on perceptions of choice architects and subsequent behavior. *Comprehensive Results in Social Psychology*, 1–24. https://doi.org/10.1080/23743603.2021.1983720 (archived at https://perma.cc/6J2M-5NAJ)

33 Mathur, A., Acar, G., Friedman, M. J., Lucherini, E., Mayer, J., Chetty, M., & Narayanan, A. (2019). Dark patterns at scale: Findings from a crawl of 11K shopping websites. *Proceedings of the ACM on human-computer interaction*, 3(CSCW), 1–32.

34 Brock, T. C. (1968). Implications of commodity theory for value change. In A. G. Greenwald, T. C. Brock, & T. M. Ostrom (Eds.), *Psychological foundations of attitudes* (243–275). New York: Academic Press.

35 Amaldoss, W. & Jain, S. (2005). Pricing of conspicuous goods: A competitive analysis of social effects. *Journal of Marketing Research*, 42, 30–42.

36 Barton, B., Zlatevska, N., & Oppewal, H. (2022). Scarcity tactics in marketing: A meta-analysis of product scarcity effects on consumer purchase intentions. *Journal of Retailing*, 98(4), 741–758. https://doi.org/10.1016/j.jretai.2022.06.003 (archived at https://perma.cc/M6UD-237V)

37 Wu, L. & Lee, C. (2016). Limited edition for me and best seller for you: The impact of scarcity versus popularity cues on self versus other-purchase behaviour. *Journal of Retailing*, 92(4), 486–499. https://doi.org/10.1016/j.jretai.2016.08.001 (archived at https://perma.cc/SQV4-RXV8)

38 He, Y. & Oppewal, H. (2018). See how much we've sold already! Effects of displaying sales and stock level information on consumers' online product choices. *Journal of Retailing*, 94(1), 45–57.

39 Keh, H. T. & Sun, J. (2018). The differential effects of online peer review and expert review on service evaluations: the roles of confidence and information convergence. *Journal of Service Research*, 21(4), 474–489.

40 Rocklage, M. D., Rucker, D. D., & Nordgren, L. F. (2021). Mass-scale emotionality reveals human behaviour and marketplace success. *Nature Human Behavior*, 5, 1323–1329. https://doi.org/10.1038/s41562-021-01098-5 (archived at https://perma.cc/S9S7-XQWG)

41 Hydock, C., Chen, Z., & Carlson, K. (2020). Why unhappy customers are unlikely to share their opinions with brands. *Journal of Marketing*, 84(6), 95–112.

42 Agnihotri, A. & Bhattacharya, S. (2016). Online review helpfulness: Role of qualitative factors. *Psychology & Marketing*, 33(11), 1006–1017.

43 Chen, T., Samaranayake, P., Cen, X., Qi, M., & Lan, Y. C. (2022). The impact of online reviews on consumers' purchasing decisions: Evidence from an eye-tracking study. *Frontiers in Psychology*, 13. https://doi.org/10.3389%2Ffpsyg.2022.865702 (archived at https://perma.cc/Q39D-WBP9)

44 He, S., Hollenbeck, B., & Proserpio, D. (2022). The market for fake reviews. *Marketing Science*, 41(5), 896–921.

45 Kokkodis, M., Lappas, T., & Kane, G. C. (2022). Optional purchase verification in e-commerce platforms: More representative product ratings and higher quality reviews. *Production and Operations Management*, 31(7), 2943–2961.

46 Thomas, M. J., Wirtz, B. W., & Weyerer, J. C. (2019). Determinants of online review credibility and its impact on consumers' purchase intention. *Journal of Electronic Commerce Research*, 20(1), 1–20.

47 Qiu, K. & Zhang, L. (2024). How online reviews affect purchase intention: A meta-analysis across contextual and cultural factors. *Data and Information Management*, 8(2), 100058.

48 Cheung, C. M. Y., Sia, C. L., & Kuan, K. K. (2012). Is this review believable? A study of factors affecting the credibility of online consumer reviews from an ELM perspective. *Journal of the Association for Information Systems*, 13(8), 2.

49 Packard, G., Berger, J., & Boghrati, R. (2023). How verb tense shapes persuasion. *Journal of Consumer Research*, 50(3), 645–660.

50 Wu, R., Wu, H. H., & Wang, C. L. (2021). Why is a picture 'worth a thousand words'? Pictures as information in perceived helpfulness of online reviews. *International Journal of Consumer Studies*, 45(3), 364–378. https://doi.org/10.1111/ijcs.12627 (archived at https://perma.cc/N63X-7JX5)

51 Pieters, R. & Wedel, M. (2004). Attention capture and transfer in advertising: Brand, pictorial, and text-size effects. *Journal of Marketing*, 68(2), 36–50.

52 Jung, M., Ryu, S., Han, S. P., & Cho, D. (2023). Ask for reviews at the right time: Evidence from two field experiments. *Journal of Marketing*, 87(4), 528–549.

53 Townsend, C. & Kahn, B. E. (2014). The 'visual preference heuristic': The influence of visual versus verbal depiction on assortment processing, perceived variety, and choice overload. *Journal of Consumer Research*, 40(5), 993–1015. https://doi.org/10.1086/673521 (archived at https://perma.cc/E8LM-4JCP)

54 Schlochtermeier, L. H., Kuchinke, L., Pehrs, C., Urton, K., Kappelhoff, H., & Jacobs, A. M. (2013). Emotional picture and word processing: An fMRI study on effects of stimulus complexity. *PLoS One*, 8(2), e55619. https://doi.org/10.1371/journal.pone.0055619 (archived at https://perma.cc/7DMG-U7WS)

55 Lee, L., Amir, O., & Ariely, D. (2009). In search of homo economicus: Cognitive noise and the role of emotion in preference consistency. *Journal of consumer research*, 36(2), 173–187. https://doi.org/10.1086/597160 (archived at https://perma.cc/4N9B-U9QM)

56 Childers, T. L. & Houston, M. J. (1984). Conditions for a picture-superiority effect on consumer memory. *Journal of consumer research*, 11(2), 643–654. https://doi.org/10.1086/209001 (archived at https://perma.cc/Y7EU-T7NH)

57 Di, W., Sundaresan, N., Piramuthu, R., & Bhardwaj, A. (2014, February). *Is a picture really worth a thousand words? On the role of images in e-commerce*. In Proceedings of the 7th ACM international conference on Web search and data mining (pp. 633–642).

58 Brakus, J. J., Schmitt, B. H., & Zhang, S. (2014). Experiential product attributes and preferences for new products: The role of processing fluency. *Journal of Business Research*, 67(11), 2291–2298.

59 Maier, E. & Dost, F. (2018). The positive effect of contextual image backgrounds on fluency and liking. *Journal of Retailing and Consumer Services*, 40, 109–116. https://doi.org/10.1016/j.jretconser.2017.09.003 (archived at https://perma.cc/H727-3DE6)

60 Maier, E. & Dost, F. (2018). The positive effect of contextual image backgrounds on fluency and liking. *Journal of Retailing and Consumer Services*, 40, 109–116. https://doi.org/10.1016/j.jretconser.2017.09.003 (archived at https://perma.cc/UQA6-GLY3)

61 Chae, B., Li, X., & Zhu, R. (2013). Judging product effectiveness from perceived spatial proximity. *Journal of Consumer Research*, 40(2), 317–335.

62 Brylla, D. & Walsh, G. (2020). Scene sells: Why spatial backgrounds outperform isolated product depictions online. *International Journal of Electronic Commerce*, 24(4), 497–526. https://doi.org/10.1080/10864415.2020.1806470 (archived at https://perma.cc/PX8C-9XF8)

63 Piqueras-Fiszman, B. & Spence, C. (2012). The weight of the bottle as a possible extrinsic cue with which to estimate the price (and quality) of the wine? Observed correlations. *Food Quality and Preference*, 25(1), 41–45.

64 Dang, A. & Nichols, B. S. (2024). The effects of size referents in user-generated photos on online review helpfulness. *Journal of Consumer Behaviour*, 23(3), 1493–1511.

65 Ceci, L. (2025, January 28). Percentage of mobile device website traffic worldwide from 1st quarter 2015 to 4th quarter 2023. Statista. https://www.statista.com/statistics/277125/share-of-website-traffic-coming-from-mobile-devices/#:~:text=Mobile%20accounts%20for%20approximately%20half,percent%20of%20global%20website%20traffic (archived at https://perma.cc/63JJ-YX5P)

66 Statista Research Department (2025, April 8). Mobile commerce in the United Kingdom – statistics & facts. Statista. https://www.statista.com/topics/5888/mobile-commerce-in-the-uk/#topicOverview (archived at https://perma.cc/K5V7-9QQ3)

67 University of Cambridge (2018, February 7). Newly-developed image guidelines will improve mobile shopping experience worldwide. https://www.cam.ac.uk/research/news/newly-developed-image-guidelines-will-improve-mobile-shopping-experience-worldwide (archived at https://perma.cc/9AS9-C8XR)

68 Liu, Y. (2023). How and why a touchscreen interface impacts psychological ownership and its downstream consequences. *Journal of Retailing and Consumer Services*, 70, 103182. https://doi.org/10.1016/j.jretconser.2022.103182 (archived at https://perma.cc/CU6V-K26E)

69 Hattula, J. D., Herzog, W., & Dhar, R. (2023). The impact of touchscreen devices on consumers' choice confidence and purchase likelihood. *Marketing Letters*, 34(1), 35–53. https://doi.org/10.1002/mar.21817 (archived at https://perma.cc/DR3X-9W36)

70 Peck, J. & Shu, S. B. (2009). The effect of mere touch on perceived ownership. *Journal of Consumer Research*, 36(3), 434–447.

71 Kahneman, D., Knetsch, J., & Thaler, R. (1990). Experimental tests of the endowment effect and the Coase Theorem. *Journal of Political Economy*, 98(6), 1325–1348.

72 Elder, R. S. & Krishna, A. (2012). The 'visual depiction effect' in advertising: Facilitating embodied mental simulation through product orientation. *Journal of Consumer Research*, 38(6), 988–1003. https://doi.org/10.1086/661531 (archived at https://perma.cc/3DKA-JXM3)

73 Maille, V., Morrin, M., & Reynolds-McIlnay, R. (2020). On the other hand…: Enhancing promotional effectiveness with haptic cues. *Journal of Marketing Research*, 57(1), 100–117. https://doi.org/10.1177/0022243719878390 (archived at https://perma.cc/D7G4-SN5M)

74 Jia, J. S., Shiv, B., & Rao, S. (2014). The product-agnosia effect: How more visual impressions affect product distinctiveness in comparative choice. *Journal of Consumer Research*, 41(2), 342–360. https://doi.org/10.1086/676600 (archived at https://perma.cc/6AWR-LLML)

75 Guo, T., Zhong, S., Wang, X., & Li, G. (2022). Does product display quantity increase purchase intention? The mediation of diminished pain of payment. *Journal of Research in Interactive Marketing*, 16(1), 101–117. https://doi.org/10.1108/JRIM-08-2020-0163 (archived at https://perma.cc/2LB6-EHV9)

76 Fanani, Y. D. (2023). Shopee pay free shipping promotion moderation on customer satisfaction. *Journal of Social Science and Business Studies*, 1(1), 27–41.

77 Shehu, E., Papies, D., & Neslin, S. A. (2020). Free shipping promotions and product returns. *Journal of Marketing Research*, 57(4), 640–658.

78 Sahni, N. S., Zou, D., & Chintagunta, P. K. (2017). Do targeted discount offers serve as advertising? Evidence from 70 field experiments. *Management Science*, 63(8), 2688–2705. https://doi.org/10.1287/mnsc.2016.2450 (archived at https://perma.cc/Q25A-GJUM)

79 Xia, L., Monroe, K. B., & Cox, J. L. (2004). The price is unfair! A conceptual framework of price fairness perceptions. *Journal of Marketing*, 68(4), 1–15. https://doi.org/10.1509/jmkg.68.4.1.42733 (archived at https://perma.cc/RZ34-VFXR)

14 | The psychology of packaging

LEARNING OBJECTIVES

- Analyse the psychological impact of product packaging on consumer expectations, perceived value and purchase intention.
- Critically evaluate the assumptions shoppers make based on the imagery and font choice used on packaging.
- Understand how the visual hierarchy influences the way shoppers perceive product packaging.

Introduction

Ask any fast-moving consumer goods (FMCG) marketer and they will tell you just how important product packaging is, with some even referring to it as the fifth P of marketing.[1] From a practical perspective, packaging needs to protect the product and keep it safe during transport, but it plays an even more important marketing function, potentially making or breaking a sale. In a cluttered retail environment, product packaging needs to capture the shoppers' attention. If a shopper doesn't notice a product, they can't buy it. Even if they do look at a product, this does not automatically mean they are going to buy it, but it does act as a marketer's last opportunity to influence a decision before they make a purchase, meaning the messaging on the packaging is essential.

Visual salience and customer attention

Conceptually, most marketers understand this, but they still underestimate the challenge of getting noticed in-store. In a supermarket, shoppers spend on average just

34.35 seconds in the cereal aisle and in that time they will have glanced at over 29 different products. The situation is no better in other categories. Shoppers spend 38.2 seconds in the pasta aisle, looking at 33 products, and in the yogurt aisle they spend just 32 seconds looking at 29 products.[2] That means that in reality most shoppers will spend a second or less looking at the majority of products, and in that time, they will have decided whether to buy it or not.

With so many products all competing for shoppers' attention, marketers need to understand '*bottom-up attention*'; the factors that automatically capture shoppers' attention and cause them to look at these items (see Chapter 2). However, just because a shopper looks at a product, even for a considerable amount of time, it does not necessarily mean that they like it. Eye-tracking should not be used as a proxy for liking.[3] A product may automatically capture shoppers' attention, even if they don't like it. However, this should also not undervalue the importance of visual salience. In a supermarket, visual saliency is a better predictor of what gets bought than individual brand preferences.[4]

Just imagine walking down the wine aisle in a supermarket. You may have decided you want to buy a bottle of white wine, potentially even a French wine, but you most likely don't have a strong brand preference. This is exactly the sort of scenario where visual salience dictates what gets bought. Even if a shopper knows what brand they want to buy and looks to find it on a shelf (top-down attention), if they can't find it on the shelf within 8–10 seconds, they often walk away without making a purchase or buy a substitute product instead.[5] So, how can brands make sure their products get noticed? While some of the tactics discussed in the advertising chapter are relevant here, there are specific principles that marketers need to be aware of.

For example, brands like to use creative or novel packaging to try to capture shoppers' attention. If shoppers are confronted with a wall of products that all look similar, but there is one product that looks different, it's going to stand out. This is what's known as the Von Restorff or isolation effect.[6] But how different does a product need to be to stand out? The answer depends on the category. If we go back to that wine aisle where virtually every bottle looks the same, it doesn't take much for one product to stand out. Just consider wine sold by JP Chenet in a Josephine bottle – its wonky shape causes it to stand out on the shelf.

It is not just a case of using unusual shapes to attract attention, but simply including an unconventional element as part of the packaging can be enough to capture a shopper's attention, which can lead to them making an impulse purchase. Something as simple as the packaging featuring an unusual texture, message or even just an emoji can trigger a sense of curiosity, which leads to higher sales.[7] However, this effect only occurs when it comes to unplanned purchases. If shoppers are going into a computer store and they know that they want to purchase a specific model of external hard drive, quirky packaging is unlikely to influence a shopper – unless their desired model is out of stock.

The challenge for designers when it comes to creating novel packaging is to get the balance right between creating something that looks different to the rivals, but making sure shoppers recognize what the product is. If a brand gets carried away and produces a product that looks radically different to the category norms, it can hurt sales.[8] Considering how little time shoppers spend looking at a product, they need to quickly understand what a product is and how to use it. Take JP Chenet's Josephine bottle. It still looks like a bottle of wine, but it's a little 'quirky'. Likewise, the trend for 'moonshine' to be sold in what appears to be jam jars. It conjures up the associations with moonshine's history, but jam jars are not that different to a glass bottle, so from the shopper's perspective, it's not too challenging. Just like with copywriting, the most successful brands use novelty in moderation when it comes to packaging design.

Visual hierarchy

With shoppers spending so little time looking at any individual product, it means that in reality, shoppers are not going to notice all the features on the product's packaging. Instead, by changing the relative size, colour and positioning of different design elements, what's known as the visual hierarchy, marketers can predict which features shoppers are going to look at first. People have learnt that if an element is larger, it is usually more important, hence people read the largest text first.[9]

Marketers can use this to their advantage, ensuring that shoppers look at the most important aspect of a product first. For instance, if you were selling frozen pizza, you may want shoppers to notice the brand name first, then the type (stuffed crust). Then you'd direct their attention to an enticing product photo, before finally to the flavour (sweet honey BBQ). By changing the relative size and prominence of each component, marketers can predict how shoppers will engage with the pack.

Unfortunately, if marketers can't decide which element to emphasize, they sometimes try to give equal prominence to all elements. This leads to a cluttered design, with shoppers' attention being pulled towards all elements simultaneously, which increases the cognitive demand required to process the design. Rather than encouraging people to look at all of the design, people end up not engaging with packaging at all. When packaging has a clear visual hierarchy, shoppers like the design more and it leads to higher sales.[10]

The challenge for marketers is to think of all the information that needs to go on the front of a pack and determine its relative importance. However, there are often different ways of conveying the same information. In our pizza example, the flavour of the pizza could be described either using words, pictures or a combination of the two. While words are able to describe more specific information than a picture, in most cases, imagery is more effective at quickly indicating product variety.[11] As shoppers are naturally drawn to images rather than words, the packaging designer of our pizza example could showcase a picture of a honey dipper to indicate the flavour. Not only are images processed quicker than words,[12] but they also trigger more emotions than words,[13] meaning that it's easier for a shopper to imagine what the product will taste like, leading to higher sales.[14]

This is especially true if a brand is targeting children. When researchers showed 125 children (aged 4 to 11) a selection of cereal boxes and asked them to draw the packaging from memory, the results were striking. In 78% of cases, the most memorable feature was the brand logo, especially if it was bold and simple. The next key feature, with 68% of participants focusing on it, was the colour scheme. With younger children, it was more important for the colour scheme to make use of bright, bold colours to stand out and be memorable. The third most memorable detail was the shape of the packaging. Although most cereals come in standard rectangular boxes, any product that broke the mould was much more likely to be remembered. And what about the text on the packaging? Unsurprisingly, it barely registered, with only 35% of children (and mainly the older ones) recalling any details written on the packaging.[15]

Product and line extensions

When a brand is launching a product extension, package designers need to demonstrate clearly that the new product is related to the parent brand but need the product to have its own visual identity. From a visual hierarchy perspective, in this situation, the most important feature for shoppers to initially focus on is the parent brand.[16] Line extensions work because the positive mental associations that shoppers have built up with the parent brand are transferred to the new product via stimulus generalization (see Chapter 5). For this to work, brands need shoppers to focus on the established brand name first – something designers need to remember when creating a visual hierarchy.

However, to ensure the new product has its own visual identity, 9 out of 10 designers use colour to differentiate the new product from the original. Unfortunately, colour is often less useful than designers think. When designing packaging in isolation, colour is a fantastic way to differentiate between brands or product variants. For example, the packaging for 'Brylcreem' hair gel is nearly identical across its 'Original,' 'Anti-Dandruff' and 'Lite' versions; the only distinguishing factor is colour. The 'Original' comes in red, 'Lite' in blue and 'Anti-Dandruff' in green. Unfortunately, this differentiation does not always work in a supermarket. With so many different brands using different colour schemes, the designers' carefully crafted colour system can quickly get lost.[17] Instead, in this situation, imagery and pictures are more effective to help differentiate between products in a range.

Persuading shoppers to buy

With packaging being a marketer's last chance to persuade shoppers to buy their product, there is a temptation to try to provide as much information as possible. This temptation is made all the greater because shoppers are more likely to believe claims made on packaging than in other mediums, such as advertising.[18] Shoppers expect advertising as a medium to try to persuade us, and therefore they are sceptical of it, yet surprisingly, the same is not true of packaging. With packaging, the product is right next to the claim being made, making shoppers feel that it is easier for them to verify any claims printed on the packaging. The result is that shoppers think that marketers are less likely to make exaggerated claims on packaging than they are on advertising.

Packaging text

Unfortunately, even if shoppers are more likely to believe the claims printed on a product's packaging, it is still not a good idea to list too many. Firstly, eye-tracking research has shown that shoppers are more likely to pay attention to products with a simpler or cleaner design.[19] The more cluttered your packaging is, the harder it is for shoppers to notice any individual claim on it.[20] This occurs because as a design includes more elements, it increases the cognitive load required to process the packaging.[21] And the more effort a shopper has to put in, the less likely they are to remember any claim.[22] Secondly, the more claims, or reasons why a shopper should buy your product, are listed on the packaging, the more sceptical a shopper starts to become. Once a product starts to include four or more claims, shoppers start to view all the claims with scepticism.[23] Is it really possible that a new razor can: have an ergonomic handle, feature a new anti-clog design, contain a rust-resistant blade, and be recommended by dermatologists?

This means that designers need to think carefully about what will convince a shopper to buy one brand and not another, and only emphasize these points. However, even if you know what will motivate a shopper, it is important to communicate these points as succinctly as possible, while still making it easy for shoppers to visualize what you are saying. If you were selling a bespoke coffee, it is normally described using language like *'sweet'*, *'acidic'* or *'mild'*. This may help coffee connoisseurs understand what the coffee will taste like, but for most shoppers, these are abstract constructs which are hard to intuitively understand. Likewise, we have exactly the same problem if language such as *'exciting'*, *'refreshing'* or *'appealing'* is used. It sounds good, but fundamentally, these words don't mean much. Instead, it is far more effective to use source-based words; words like honey, chocolate or pear, which are far easier to visualize, and we know what they taste like.[24] When packs describe food using these words, shoppers are more likely to buy the product and more importantly, think the product will taste better.

But even if a coffee brand has decided to use more descriptive words on its packaging, how should it convey this information? Should these adjectives just be put on the packaging in isolation or should they be part of a short claim? Once more, the correct answer comes down to what is more effective at triggering visual memories. When reading an isolated adjective, it can be hard for it to conjure up a clear mental image, whereas a short sentence can trigger a mental picture. Hence, it is usually best for claims to take the form of a short sentence.[25]

When designing packaging, there are some features that legally have to be included, such as quantity. Buy a bottle of shampoo and it will give a quantity, such as 500ml. While this allows shoppers to make a comparison between different products and work out if it provides value for money, visualizing 500ml is not the easiest. Instead, research has shown that marketers should include the volume but also reframe it to give shoppers something they can relate to, like the average number of washes you get from each bottle. This approach doesn't only works for liquids. When it comes to selling chocolate, rather than simply saying 200g of chocolate, say 40 pieces as well. Shoppers find these intuitive units more persuasive and, as a result, are prepared to pay up to 49% more.[26] Of course, the legal information has to be included as well, but marketers can get creative with extra information.

Packaging imagery

While text is great at highlighting specific product features, it is not the best at triggering hedonic or sensory experiences. Instead, imagery is more effective at quickly triggering an emotional reaction, and it works in a similar way to branding. Good branding is all about building mental associations between different concepts. When shoppers see imagery on packaging, it can activate thoughts in a way that words simply can't. If a brand is trying to convince shoppers that their coffee is strong and rich, rather than simply stating this, they could opt to use a visual metaphor, using imagery that symbolizes strength and power, such as a lion or a fortress. These work because our brain processes images more intuitively than text-based claims. But it is not just a case of selecting the right imagery: it needs to be positioned correctly on the pack to maximize its effect. If a brand wants to symbolize that their food is light and fluffy by using imagery of bubbles or feathers on their packaging, these need to be placed on the top to reinforce the metaphor. Whereas if a beer brand uses a symbol of a castle to represent strength, this should be on the bottom of the bottle.[27]

While brands use a diverse range of visual metaphors on their packaging, one of the most commonly used is brand mascots. Think Tony the Tiger, Colonel Sanders or Captain Birdseye. These mascots personify the brand, helping shoppers form an emotional connection and making it more memorable. People are better at remembering something tangible, like a brand mascot, than they are an abstract concept.[28] This is really important from both a branding and packaging perspective. To persuade shoppers to buy something, marketers typically emphasize a reason to believe in it. For example, Gaviscon, medication for heartburn and indigestion, includes the claim *'It's fast, and is longer lasting than antacids'*. Rationally, it makes sense but it's hard to remember. Consequently, they supplement this tag line with a brand mascot: a fireman, squirting water to put out a fire. Visually, this is far easier for people to remember and is a perfect visual metaphor for the product.

To ensure these characters are engaging, they are often portrayed as a hero or villain. Neither approach is necessarily better than the other, but the category will make a difference. Typically, hero characters work better for vice foods and villains work best for virtuous foods. By using a hero character, it can make unhealthy foods appear less harmful, whereas a villainous character can make virtuous foods appear a little more fun and appealing.[29]

But when it comes to selling over-the-counter pharmaceutical products, such as cough medicine to adults or Gaviscon as in the above example, there is a risk to using an anthropomorphized version of their product or mascot on their packaging. Although these characters are distinctive and allow the company to build an ownable asset, unfortunately, they can trigger the wrong associations. Understandably, products targeting children use cartoon characters to appeal to their audience. But as medication for children is less powerful than the adult version, shoppers instinctively believe packaging that uses these characters will be less effective, and as a result they are prepared to spend less money on these products.[30] However, this is only going to be an issue for new brands on the market. Once a brand becomes established, shoppers will have already formed an opinion about how the product will perform.

Mixing text and imagery

Take a look at any product and you'll see that virtually all will use a mixture of text and images. Traditionally, neuroscientists argued that when it came to presenting visual information, images should go on the left and the text on the right. This is because the brain processes visual information from opposite fields. Stimuli in the left visual field are first received by the right hemisphere, while those in the right visual field go to the left hemisphere. As the right hemisphere is better suited to process pictorial information and the left is more logical and verbal, placing the image on the left-hand side of the text enhances the processing of the whole message.[31]

From a theoretical perspective, this should work, but only under very specific conditions. When viewing an online shop, a shopper's field of vision is limited to the screen. Not only this, but virtually all web shops are responsive, meaning text and images are automatically resized to fill the screen. In a physical store, however, marketers have no control over what appears in a shopper's field of vision. Just because an image is placed on the left side of a package doesn't mean it will actually appear in the shopper's left visual field. It is highly probable that a different product is in the field of vision. When researchers have tested this idea on packaging, they've found the opposite is true. Packs work best when the text elements are on the left-hand side and pictorial elements are on the right-hand side.[32] When packs are designed like this, shoppers end up spending more time looking at the packs.

Bringing products to life: The power of photography

As shown in the advertising chapter, people are naturally drawn to pictures rather than text, and the same is true for product packaging. When browsing, shoppers are most likely to look at the imagery on the packaging first, which is why, in most cases, the product is featured on the packaging. For single items like an external hard drive, the image just needs to be a clear and attractive representation of the product. However, when it comes to food items and the pack contains multiple products (e.g. a pack of pain au chocolat), marketers need to decide how many pictures of the product to show. Is it best to show a large photo of the product or a photo which features multiple products? In most cases, it is more effective to show more of your products. For example, if your packaging shows twelve pains au chocolat rather than three, shoppers intuitively assume that the pack contains more units, making the product more appealing.[33] Cognitively, they know how many units the pack contains, but it still influences their subconscious perception. Interestingly, this effect not only has an impact while shopping, but also changes how quickly shoppers consume the product at home. The more photos of the product on the packaging, the quicker they'll eat the products (and need to replace them).

But showing multiple copies not only influences our perception of quantity, but also changes how effective people think a product will be. If you're buying flea treatment and multiple images of the product are shown, shoppers are more likely to assume the treatment is more effective.[34] People have been shown to assume an energy drink would give them 10% more energy when there were 15 bottles on the front rather than just one. This occurs due to a Gestalt effect, where people mentally group products together rather than viewing them individually. As a result, we assess their combined impact, rather than evaluating each product on its own.

Managing consumer scepticism

Understandably, people are sceptical of product photographs. It is all too easy for a photo to be airbrushed or digitally altered so it doesn't actually reflect reality. Even without digitally altering a product, photographers can get creative and use optical illusions to make a product appear bigger. When looking at a picture, people judge the size of items based on their relative size to other items in the image. This is why illusions such as the Ponzo illusion or the Delboeuf illusion work. When two converging lines (which look like train tracks) disappear into the distance and two horizontal bars, which are the same length, are placed on the tracks, people automatically assume the higher bar looks longer.[35]

If a company sold a meat pie in a sealed cardboard box, it could use a similar visual trick when photographing the product for its packaging. Instead of using horizontal lines to influence perception, they could change the size of the plate on which the product is placed . Using a smaller plate gives the illusion that the pie looks larger than it is, which will make it look more appealing. Beyond making the product look bigger, people also think they will be fuller after eating the same amount of food served on a small plate.[36]

To ensure shoppers do not feel like they have been deceived, some designers will include a transparent window so that shoppers can see the product inside. This is especially useful when it comes to selling food products as shoppers perceive the food as being fresher, of higher quality and are ultimately more likely to purchase the product when the packaging includes a window.[37] If a pack designer wants to include a see-through window, they need to think carefully about where they position it. Shoppers intrinsically prefer packaging where the window is on the right-hand side. All things being equal, they find the design more attractive and, as a result, think the food will be tastier, although more research is needed to understand why this occurs.[38] Likewise, the shape of this window makes a difference, with shoppers preferring circular windows to square windows or triangles, and again, this impacts purchase intention.[39] If a brand does opt to use a triangle window, perhaps because their brand identity revolves around triangles, then the triangle should be pointing upwards. However, once more, psychologists are not clear what the underlying mechanism is for this behaviour.

Including a transparent window not only increases the likelihood that people will buy your product, but also changes how quickly people consume it, which influences how quickly they will need to buy it again. For example, when attractive snacks such as sweets are served in transparent packaging, consumers eat up to 88% more.[40] In the transparent packaging, they are sitting there tempting you to have another one. It is much easier to resist eating something which we can't see.[41]

Interestingly, this effect is strongest for smaller items, such as sweets, rather than larger items like croissants or bread rolls. This is because of what psychologists call *the monitoring effect*.[42] If you bought eight croissants from a supermarket and placed them in a brown paper bag, you could eat two and you wouldn't notice. However, if the paper bag had a big transparent window, it would be obvious that you've eaten 25% of them, which might encourage you to slow down. In contrast, if you continually graze on a packet of small sweets, you don't notice them gradually going down. The result: large food items sell best in opaque packaging with a small transparent window. This still tempts consumers, but makes it less obvious how quickly they are consuming the product.[43]

Inferences: Decoding what isn't said

While packaging will make a number of explicit claims, shoppers also make a number of inferences based on just the look of the packaging. When it comes to buying packaged food, people automatically assume that products with simple or minimalist packaging are going to be made with fewer ingredients,[44] which is important considering the recent trend against ultra-processed foods. But it does make a difference what products you are trying to sell. If you are designing the packaging for a private label or own-brand product, you often have to battle shoppers' preexisting expectations. People often wrongly assume that these products are of lower quality and that the brands have made compromises in selecting cheaper ingredients. If the packaging is relatively simple, it can reinforce this expectation. Hence, for own-brand products, more indulgent packaging typically sells better. We see exactly the same pattern for other indulgent items like desserts. Shoppers expect desserts to be complex and made from lots of indulgent ingredients, and the packaging should reflect this, typically avoiding a minimalist design.

In addition to the style and shape, the colour of the packaging plays a role in influencing expectations. Not only does the colour of packaging help attract attention (as discussed in Chapter 2) but with food it shifts people's expectations. People instinctively assume that food will have a more intense flavour if the packaging makes use of more saturated colours or if the packaging comes in an angular shape rather than a round shape.[45] At home, this influence on taste is relatively small, but in a supermarket, when a shopper is deciding between two different raspberry yoghurts, one in a round, pale red carton and the other in a square, deeper red carton, this subtle difference can be enough to sway their choice. And after all, it is the critical moment in the supermarket that brands care most about.

But just like when it comes to painting a room, with packaging, marketers have a choice of a matte or gloss finish. Packaging with a gloss finish is shiny, reflective and more vibrant, whereas a matte finish is more muted in colour and non-reflective. While it may seem to be a purely aesthetic choice, shoppers have learnt that natural and organic food items tend to come in packaging with a matte finish. If shoppers see a food item with a matte finish, they automatically assume that it is going to be more natural, it will taste better and most importantly, are more likely to buy it.[46] What's more, the effect is strongest for food items that shoppers generally think of as artificial. Likewise, shoppers perceive food that comes in glossy packaging to be less healthy and lower quality.[47] Marketers just need to be aware that because organic and healthy products are typically more expensive, shoppers associate natural-looking packs with being more expensive.[48]

The halo effect

Although most of the research in this chapter has focused on the food category, the same principles can be applied to other categories. For example, people assume that food products that come in more attractive packaging taste better, and similarly, in the make-up category, shoppers assume that make-up that comes in beautiful packaging will work better, encouraging people to buy it.[49] Both cases are examples of the 'halo effect' in action. If a product excels on one attribute, we automatically assume that it will excel on other unrelated variables. But although the halo effect occurs across categories, the effect is more pronounced under certain circumstances.

When a product is made by a well-known brand, shoppers tend to rely on the brand name as a guarantee of quality, rather than judging the quality of the packaging. Similarly, if the packaging clearly highlights a unique selling point that sets the product apart from competitors, packaging quality becomes less significant. However, if all other factors are equal, shoppers pay closer attention to small details, like the quality of the packaging, to make a decision.

Judging whether packaging is attractive or not can feel like a subjective decision, but there are some objective criteria that can help, at least in certain categories. Humans anthropomorphize inanimate objects. Whether rightly or wrongly, society typically associates tall and slim figures with being more elegant and classier. As a result, when looking at make-up or perfume, people perceive brands that come in tall, narrow bottles as being more expensive and luxurious than those that come in shorter packaging,[50] which directly influences how much someone is willing to pay for the product. It is exactly the same mechanism that explains why most shoppers intuitively assume that feminine fragrances will have a smooth bottle, and more masculine scents have a rough texture,[51] and when the texture and scent align, shoppers prefer the product.

REAL-WORLD EXAMPLE: PSYCH IN ACTION

Same product, different audience: how do you redesign packaging so that men feel comfortable buying exfoliation cream?

It is estimated that 25% of all men in Britain spend £25 a month or more on grooming products, resulting in the global market being worth an estimated $73.66 billion. Yet despite being part of the daily washing regime for millions of people, men are assumed to be uncomfortable talking with others about their grooming practices. So how do brands reposition a product that was almost solely aimed at women and make men feel comfortable using it? One key change is to radically change the packaging.

Tweaking the brand name

While there is nothing in the name L'Oréal that explicitly signals masculinity or femininity, the original name is L'Oréal: Paris, which could conjure up more feminine associations (Paris is associated with luxury and sophistication). Consequently, L'Oréal tweaked the name from L'Oréal: Paris to L'Oréal: Men's Expert (and hiding Paris in the O). To overcome any preexisting associations that people might have towards it, they made sure on the version targeting men that 'Men's Expert' is just as prominent as the name L'Oréal. They have also changed the typeface, dropping the gold which represents luxury, sophistication and elegance and instead placed 'Men's Expert' in a heavy and compressed typeface – again, a more masculine typeface.

Shape and colour

Although both products are the same size (100ml), the packaging is a different shape. They've switched from a tall narrow packaging, which triggers associations of elegance and sophistication, to one which is shorter and wider, again two traits more associated with masculinity. The existing product, like most skin cleaning products, is white as it implies fairness. However, it can also trigger connotations of purity and innocence, stereotypically less associated with masculinity. What colours can you use to imply cleanliness without triggering femininity? Grey is a good compromise. Equally important is the visual patterns it creates. We've been socialized to associate straight lines, angularity and solid geometry with masculine traits, whereas flowing curves are perceived to be more feminine. Hence, the new packaging uses big bold blocks of colour.

Trademarks

The trademark is changed from '*DERMO-EXPERTISE*' to '*Active Defence System*'. Rather than using the more conventional words such as protection or cleanse, they've chosen to create a trademark that sounds strong and tough. They've avoided using the more traditional words, such as protection or soothing, but still imply that the product is scientifically developed. However, the graphical way the trademark is displayed conjures up imagery that you would traditionally see with sport, another sign that it is permissible for men to buy.

Likewise, the name of the product is also changed from White Perfect to White Activ, reinforcing the sport connotations. Rather than emphasizing that people use the product for aesthetic reasons (the primary purpose of the product), it enables men to have an excuse for the purchase.[52]

Typeface

When designing a product, marketers need to carefully consider the typeface used. Often, this is left to the designer, who chooses a typeface based on aesthetic criteria, but shoppers will make inferences about the product based on the typeface. When it comes to selling more hedonistic products, shoppers prefer handwritten style fonts, whereas for functional or utilitarian products shoppers prefer a more standard font.[53] For example, when a chocolate bar manufacturer produced two identical versions of their bar, the only difference being the font of the brand name, the bar with the handwritten font was bought more often. The handwritten font appeared in 17.2% of shopping baskets, compared to just 3.4% for the bar with the traditional font.

Even if a brand opts for a more traditional typeface, there is a huge range of options to choose from. In Chapter 2, we explored how the physical shape of a product changes its flavour. Chocolate is perceived as being sweeter when it comes in a round shape, compared to the same chocolate that comes in a square shape. But packaging designers can use the same psychological principles. The simplest way to do this is by changing the typeface used. When it comes to selling sweets or chocolates, it is best to use a rounder typeface, such as the logo for Twirl, Wispa, Chomp, Picnic, Flake or Caramel chocolates. But if you are selling food that is more associated with bitter flavours, such as coffee, then it is best to use an angular font – as shown by the font choice for coffee brands Maxwell House, Starbucks or Nescafé Azera.[54]

The same effect can be achieved by changing the physical shape of the packaging. With cheese served in triangular packaging, something which is very angular, it is perceived to have a stronger, sharper taste.[55] While this is relatively easy to implement for cheese, as it's traditionally sold in triangle blocks, for most other products, such as pizza or coffee, it would be harder to sell. However, there is an easy workaround. Rather than changing the physical shape of the product, a brand could change the colour scheme of the product. If they wanted the product to be seen as having a stronger flavour or being associated with bitter flavours, they could use blocks of colour on the packaging to create triangles or angular shapes, whereas if they wanted to emphasize a product as being sweet, they could use more flowing round colour blocks as part of their design.[56]

Secondary packaging

When it comes to designing packaging, most designers automatically focus on the primary packaging; the packaging that protects the product, be it the milk carton, the cat food tins or the box in which a mobile phone arrives. However, it is important not to forget how the design will interact with any secondary packaging. The purpose of secondary packaging is to group individual SKUs together to both protect them and make it easier to transport and handle. Rather than sending wine to supermarkets as individual bottles, they are typically placed in a box of six, and it is these boxes that are considered secondary packaging.

While bottles of wine are generally taken out of the secondary packaging before being placed on the shelves, this is not true for all products and especially products sold in discount stores. In these stores, it is not uncommon for the secondary packaging to be placed directly onto the shelves. For example, cans of food are often placed on a shelf in a cardboard tray to make life easier for staff. Although it is obvious that the primary and secondary packaging need to work together; this means that a brand shouldn't place any critical information on the packaging somewhere that is going to be covered by the secondary packaging.

CIGARETTES

Governments around the world have recognized the power of packaging and used it as a tool to try to reduce the number of people who smoke. Canada, Australia, France and the UK have made it a requirement for cigarettes to be sold in unbranded packaging. While initially it hasn't changed the number of people smoking, it has changed the brands people are buying. After the introduction of plain packaging, more people have switched to buying budget or value brands[57] rather than big names. If people can't see you're smoking a big-name brand, what's the point in spending more money? This could be considered conspicuous consumption in action.

But this is not the only change that you see. Within both Switzerland and the EU, all cigarette packages need to include a health warning. In Switzerland, these are not small labels but are legally required to cover 48% of the front and 63% of the back of the pack. However, despite these warning labels, there is a real risk that shoppers quickly get used to (or 'habitualize') these labels and ignore them. This is more than just a theoretical risk, as five years after these were introduced, people had learnt to completely ignore them and the benefits were more or less negated.[58] Hence, to slow this wear out, Switzerland rotates through a set of 14 images. After two years, a new set of 14 images is introduced. It is well established that people are drawn to novel stimuli and attention fades over time.[59] Regularly changing the images encourages people to pay attention to the warning messages.

Closing thoughts

It is easy to assume that successful packaging is all about creating something that stands out from the competition and looks attractive. While that certainly helps, packaging plays a much bigger role. It is a marketer's last chance to convince shoppers to choose their product and to shape expectations about how the product will perform. Luckily for marketers, what 'grabs' a shopper's attention and sets their expectations is not random but can be predicted in advance, with the right understanding of psychology. As with many elements of marketing, successful packaging is an equal partnership between creative inspiration and scientific underpinning.

But when designing packaging, it is important for marketers to remember the context in which the pack will be viewed. It doesn't matter how beautiful a design looks in isolation, this is unlikely to be how a consumer views it, especially at the moment of truth. A brand's packaging needs to work on a shelf in a store or when viewed on a website. Likewise, thought needs to be given to how a product is going to be merchandized. Will the product be placed next to another product? If so, this is likely to change how the product appears. Will it stop shoppers from seeing essential information that is written on the sides? When focusing on psychological interventions, it is important not to forget the practical considerations as well.

> **KEY POINTS**
>
> - In a large store, shoppers typically spend less than a second looking at each product. In this time, shoppers will decide whether to buy the product or not.
> - When designing packaging, marketers need to know the criteria shoppers use to make a purchase decision and ensure the visual hierarchy of their packaging reflects this (e.g. Is brand name more important than price? Is flavour more important than brand name?).
> - Visual salience, ensuring your product stands out, is one of the best predictors of what will get bought in a busy store.
> - Using colour to differentiate between line or product extensions is often less effective in-store as rival products compete for attention.
> - When designing packaging, it is best not to include more than four claims (or reasons to buy). Once you make more than four, shoppers start to be sceptical of all claims and disbelieve them.
> - People struggle to visualize and remember abstract concepts in comparison to things that are more tangible. Hence, it is best to use imagery or language that makes it easier to visualize your product. Rather than saying 500g of chocolate, say 20 servings instead.

- When selling a product with a specific purpose (e.g. cough sweets, baking powder etc.), people assume that the product will be more effective if the packaging shows lots of images of the products, e.g. a pile of cough sweets.
- When buying food items, shoppers are more likely to buy products where they can physically see the product (assuming the food looks attractive). If the pack contains a 'see-through' window, it is best for this to be circular in shape and on the right-hand side of the pack.
- People assume that food items that come in packaging featuring multiple colours will be made with lots of ingredients. This can be beneficial for desserts and treats but isn't always great for savoury dishes.
- Shoppers associate tall, slim packaging as being more elegant and classier than shorter and wider packaging, and this reflects how much they are prepared to pay.
- When selling FMCGs online, brands use a different version of their packaging to make it easier for shoppers to identify the product from small photos.
- When designing a product, designers need to ensure that the primary packaging works alongside the secondary packaging. Are any key features of the packaging blocked by the secondary packaging?

PUTTING THEORY INTO PRACTICE

1 Visit a website for an online supermarket and select three products that are designed well from a psychological perspective and three where the design could be improved. (a) From a psychological perspective justify your choices; (b) What changes would you suggest are made to the weaker designs?

2 Imagine you are the marketing manager for a company selling (a) external hard drives; (b) anti-dandruff shampoo; (c) cough medicine. For each of these products, determine what the visual hierarchy is.

3 Imagine you are the marketing manager for Hellmann's mayonnaise. How could you redesign their packaging to reinforce the taste superiority claim?

4 If you were working for a product design agency and you were asked to create a new pack design for a popcorn brand, how would you go about it? Think about (a) making sure the product is visually salient on the shelf; (b) convincing shoppers to buy the product in store; (c) encouraging shoppers to eat the product.

5 Why are product photos critical when it comes to designing product packaging? What techniques can you use to optimize the photos used?

6 What are the legal, ethical and business implications of using either the Ponzo illusion or the Delboeuf illusion to make a food item look larger than it is on product packaging?

7 Marketers frequently use eye-tracking to assess the effectiveness of their packaging designs. What can the results of eye-tracking reveal to a marketer when it comes to packaging design?

8 What techniques are available to marketers to make a product easier to visualize? Find examples of brands that use these techniques on their packaging.

SUGGESTIONS FOR FURTHER READING

Klimchuk, M. R. & Krasovec, S. A. (2013). *Packaging design: Successful product branding from concept to shelf.* John Wiley & Sons.

References

1 Dimitrieska, S. & Bilic, S. (2023). Packaging as the 5th P of marketing. *Economics and Management*, 20(2), 134–143.
2 Gidlöf, K., Anikin, A., Lingonblad, M., & Wallin, A. (2017). Looking is buying. How visual attention and choice are affected by consumer preferences and properties of the supermarket shelf. *Appetite*, 116, 29–38.
3 García-Madariaga, J., López, M. F. B., Burgos, I. M., & Virto, N. R. (2019). Do isolated packaging variables influence consumers' attention and preferences?. *Physiology & Behavior*, 200, 96–103.
4 Milosavljevic, M., Navalpakkam, V., Koch, C., & Rangel, A. (2012). Relative visual saliency differences induce sizable bias in consumer choice. *Journal of consumer psychology*, 22(1), 67–74.
5 Young, S. H. (2010). *Winning at retail: Insights from 35 years of packaging & shopper research*. Illinois: In-Store Marketing Institute.
6 Parker, A., Wilding, E., & Akerman, C. (1998). The von Restorff effect in visual object recognition memory in humans and monkeys: The role of frontal/perirhinal interaction. *Journal of Cognitive Neuroscience*, 10(6), 691–703.
7 Das, M., Balaji, M. S., Paul, S., & Saha, V. (2023). Being unconventional: The impact of unconventional packaging messages on impulsive purchases. *Psychology & Marketing*. https://doi.org/10.1002/mar.21865 (archived at https://perma.cc/Z4MT-EREY)
8 Shukla, P., Singh, J., & Wang, W. (2022). The influence of creative packaging design on customer motivation to process and purchase decisions. *Journal of Business Research*, 147, 338–347. https://doi.org/10.1016/j.jbusres.2022.04.026 (archived at https://perma.cc/JC4P-SK6M)

9   Pasquale, M. R., Butcher, L., & Teah, M. (2024). (Relative) size matters: A content analysis of front-of-packaging cue proportions and hierarchies. *Journal of Product & Brand Management*, 33(6), 783–800.

10 Urano, Y., Kurosu, A., & Todorov, A. (2019). *Good visual hierarchy is good design*. Princeton University Department of Psychology, Social Perception Lab.

11 Ward, E., Romaniuk, J., Trinh, G., Dawes, J., & Beal, V. (2024). How to signal product variety on pack: An investigation of color and image cues. *International Journal of Market Research*, 66(1), 46–72.

12 Schlochtermeier, L. H., Kuchinke, L., Pehrs, C., Urton, K., Kappelhoff, H., & Jacobs, A. M. (2013). Emotional picture and word processing: An fMRI study on effects of stimulus complexity. *PLoS One*, 8(2), e55619. https://doi.org/10.1371/journal.pone.0055619 (archived at https://perma.cc/X4YQ-NRL8)

13 Lee, L., Amir, O., & Ariely, D. (2009). In search of homo economicus: Cognitive noise and the role of emotion in preference consistency. *Journal of Consumer Research*, 36(2), 173–187. https://doi.org/10.1086/597160 (archived at https://perma.cc/DK5L-MW28)

14 Jaud, D. A. & Melnyk, V. (2020). The effect of text-only versus text-and-image wine labels on liking, taste and purchase intentions. The mediating role of affective fluency. *Journal of Retailing and Consumer Services*, 53, 101964.

15 McNeal, J. U. & Ji, M. F. (2003). Children's visual memory of packaging. *Journal of Consumer Marketing*, 20(5), 400–427.

16 Ward, E., Romaniuk, J., Trinh, G., Dawes, J., & Beal, V. (2024). How to signal product variety on pack: An investigation of color and image cues. *International Journal of Market Research*, 66(1), 46–72.

17 Ward, E., Romaniuk, J., Trinh, G., Dawes, J., & Beal, V. (2024). How to signal product variety on pack: An investigation of color and image cues. *International Journal of Market Research*, 66(1), 46–72.

18 Fajardo, T. M. & Townsend, C. (2016). Where you say it matters: Why packages are a more believable source of product claims than advertisements. *Journal of Consumer Psychology*, 26(3), 426–434.

19 Clement, J., Kristensen, T., & Grønhaug, K. (2013). Understanding consumers' in-store visual perception: The influence of package design features on visual attention. *Journal of Retailing and Consumer Services*, 20(2), 234–239. https://doi.org/10.1016/j.jretconser.2013.01.003 (archived at https://perma.cc/7FNK-6MEM)

20 Bialkova, S., Grunert, K. G., & van Trijp, H. (2013). Standing out in the crowd: The effect of information clutter on consumer attention for front-of-pack nutrition labels. *Food Policy*, 41, 65–74.

21 Pleyers, G. (2024). Visual complexity in product design: How does the degree of elaborateness of the front-pack image impact consumers' responses?. *Journal of Consumer Behaviour*, 23(3), 1418–1445.

22 Grzyb, T., Dolinski, D., & Kozłowska, A. (2018). Is product placement really worse than traditional commercials? Cognitive load and recalling of advertised brands. *Frontiers in Psychology*, 9, 1519.

23 Shu, S. B. & Carlson, K. A. (2014). When three charms but four alarms: Identifying the optimal number of claims in persuasion settings. *Journal of Marketing*, 78(1), 127–139. https://doi.org/10.1509/jm.11.0504 (archived at https://perma.cc/5PXZ-GB2Y)

24 Hazebroek, B. K. & Croijmans, I. (2023). Let's talk over coffee: Exploring the effect of coffee flavour descriptions on consumer imagery and behaviour. *Food Quality and Preference*, 105, 104757.

25 Solja, E., Liljander, V., & Söderlund, M. (2018). Short brand stories on packaging: An examination of consumer responses. *Psychology & Marketing*, 35(4), 294–306. https://doi.org/10.1002/mar.21087 (archived at https://perma.cc/L4YH-BE8Z)

26 Monnier, A. & Thomas, M. (2022). Experiential and analytical price evaluations: How experiential product description affects prices. *Journal of Consumer Research*, 49(4), 574–594. https://doi.org/10.1093/jcr/ucac010 (archived at https://perma.cc/8DVE-957Z)

27 Fenko, A., De Vries, R., & Van Rompay, T. (2018). How strong is your coffee? The influence of visual metaphors and textual claims on consumers' flavor perception and product evaluation. *Frontiers in Psychology*, 9, 53.

28 Xiao, X., Zhao, D., Zhang, Q., & Guo, C. Y. (2012). Retrieval of concrete words involves more contextual information than abstract words: Multiple components for the concreteness effect. *Brain and Language*, 120(3), 251–258.

29 Masters, T. M. & Mishra, A. (2019). The influence of hero and villain labels on the perception of vice and virtue products. *Journal of Consumer Psychology*, 29(3), 428–444.

30 Chang, C. T., Lee, H. C., Lee, Y. K., & Wang, T. P. (2023). "I Doubt It Works!" the negative impacts of anthropomorphizing healthcare products. *Journal of Business Research*, 164, 114008. https://doi.org/10.1016/j.jbusres.2023.114008 (archived at https://perma.cc/G6FW-DKCT)

31 Kalat, J. W. (2012). *Biological psychology*. 11th edition. Sage.

32 Otterbring, T., Shams, P., Wästlund, E., & Gustafsson, A. (2013). Left isn't always right: Placement of pictorial and textual package elements. *British Food Journal*, 115(8), 1211–1225.

33 Madzharov, A. V. & Block, L. G. (2010). Effects of product unit image on consumption of snack foods. *Journal of Consumer Psychology*, 20(4), 398–409.

34 Vanbergen, N., Irmak, C., & Sevilla, J. (2020). Product entitativity: How the presence of product replicates increases perceived and actual product efficacy. *Journal of Consumer Research*, 47(2), 192–214.

35 Prinzmetal, W., Shimamura, A. P., & Mikolinski, M. (2001). The Ponzo illusion and the perception of orientation. Perception & Psychophysics, 63(1), 99–114.

36 Peng, M. (2017). How does plate size affect estimated satiation and intake for individuals in normal-weight and overweight groups?. Obesity Science & Practice, 3(3), 282–288.

37 Simmonds, G., Woods, A. T., & Spence, C. (2018). 'Show me the goods': Assessing the effectiveness of transparent packaging vs. product imagery on product evaluation. *Food Quality and Preference*, 63, 18–27. https://doi.org/10.1016/j.foodqual.2017.07.015 (archived at https://perma.cc/U43Q-BPQZ)

38 Simmonds, G., Woods, A. T., & Spence, C. (2018). 'Seeing what's left': The effect of position of transparent windows on product evaluation. *Foods*, 7(9), 151. https://doi.org/10.3390/foods7090151 (archived at https://perma.cc/GTJ8-Y84D)

39 Simmonds, G., Woods, A. T., & Spence, C. (2019). 'Shaping perceptions': Exploring how the shape of transparent windows in packaging designs affects product evaluation. *Food Quality and Preference*, 75, 15–22. https://doi.org/10.1016/j.foodqual.2019.02.003 (archived at https://perma.cc/TR6C-3JMQ)

40 Simmonds, G. & Spence, C. (2019). Food imagery and transparency in product packaging. *Multisensory Packagings*, 49–77. https://doi.org/10.1007/978-3-319-94977-2_3 (archived at https://perma.cc/83ME-YE8U)

41 Wansink, B., Hanks, A. S., & Kaipainen, K. (2016). Slim by design: Kitchen counter correlates of obesity. *Health Education & Behavior*, 43(5), 552–558.

42 Deng, X. & Srinivasan, R. (2013). When do transparent packages increase (or decrease) food consumption? *Journal of Marketing*, 77(4), 104–117. https://doi.org/10.1509/jm.11.0610 (archived at https://perma.cc/5JD7-77HW)

43 Deng, X. & Srinivasan, R. (2013). When do transparent packages increase (or decrease) food consumption?. *Journal of Marketing*, 77(4), 104–117. https://doi.org/10.1509/jm.11.0610 (archived at https://perma.cc/5JD7-77HW)

44 Ton, L. A. N., Smith, R. K., & Sevilla, J. (2024). Symbolically simple: How simple packaging design influences willingness to pay for consumable products. *Journal of Marketing*, 88(2), 121–140.

45 Becker, L., van Rompay, T. J., Schifferstein, H. N., & Galetzka, M. (2011). Tough package, strong taste: The influence of packaging design on taste impressions and product evaluations. *Food Quality and Preference*, 22(1), 17–23.

46 Marckhgott, E. & Kamleitner, B. (2019). Matte matters: When matte packaging increases perceptions of food naturalness. *Marketing Letters*, 30, 167–178.

47 De Kerpel, L., Kobuszewski Volles, B., & Van Kerckhove, A. (2020). Fats are glossy but does glossiness imply fatness? The influence of packaging glossiness on food perceptions. *Foods*, 9(1), 90.

48 Orth, U. R., Campana, D., & Malkewitz, K. (2010). Formation of consumer price expectation based on package design: Attractive and quality routes. *Journal of Marketing Theory and Practice*, 18(1), 23–40. https://doi.org/10.2753/MTP1069-6679180102 (archived at https://perma.cc/PQ7S-6RWD)

49 Sundar, A., Cao, E. S., & Machleit, K. A. (2020). How product aesthetics cues efficacy beliefs of product performance. *Psychology & Marketing*.

50 Chen, H., Pang, J., Koo, M., & Patrick, V. M. (2020). Shape matters: Package shape informs brand status categorization and brand choice. *Journal of Retailing*, 96(2), 266–281.

51 Krishna, A., Elder, R. S., & Caldara, C. (2010). Feminine to smell but masculine to touch? Multisensory congruence and its effect on the aesthetic experience. *Journal of Consumer Psychology*, 20(4), 410–418.

52 Cheong, H. F. & Kaur, S. (2015). Legitimising male grooming through packaging discourse: A linguistic analysis. *Social Semiotics*, 25(3), 364–385. https://doi.org/10.1080/10350330.2015.1026650 (archived at https://perma.cc/8SE8-U7V2)

53 Schroll, R., Schnurr, B., & Grewal, D. (March 2018). Humanizing products with handwritten typefaces. *Journal of Consumer Research*, 45(3), 648–672. https://doi.org/10.1093/jcr/ucy014 (archived at https://perma.cc/DY22-KTMR)

54 Velasco, C., Woods, A. T., Hyndman, S., & Spence, C. (2015). The taste of typeface. *i-Perception*, 6(4). https://doi.org/10.1177/2041669515593040 (archived at https://perma.cc/V692-TQ5E).

55 Veflen, N., Velasco, C., & Kraggerud, H. (2023). Signalling taste through packaging: The effects of shape and colour on consumers' perceptions of cheeses. *Food Quality and Preference*, 104, 104742.

56 Gil-Pérez, I., Rebollar, R., Lidón, I., Martín, J., van Trijp, H. C., & Piqueras-Fiszman, B. (2019). Hot or not? Conveying sensory information on food packaging through the spiciness-shape correspondence. *Food Quality and Preference*, 71, 197–208.

57 Scollo, M., Zacher, M., Coomber, K., Bayly, M., & Wakefield, M. (2015). Changes in use of types of tobacco products by pack sizes and price segments, prices paid and consumption following the introduction of plain packaging in Australia. *Tobacco Control*, 224(2), ii66. https://doi.org/10.1136/tobaccocontrol-2014-052071 (archived at https://perma.cc/9Q5D-22P3)

58 White, V., Bariola, E., Faulkner, A., Coomber, K., & Wakefield, M. (2015). Graphic health warnings on cigarette packs: How long before the effects on adolescents wear out?. *Nicotine & Tobacco Research*, 17(7), 776–783.

59 Belton, C. A. & Sugden, R. (2018). Attention and novelty: An experimental investigation of order effects in multiple valuation tasks. *Journal of Economic Psychology*, 67, 103–115.

15 | The science of persuasion

LEARNING OBJECTIVES

- Understand the psychological underpinnings of a successful negotiation.
- Analyse the difference between high-involvement and low-involvement decision-making processes.
- Evaluate how brands use habit-forming techniques to change behaviour.

Introduction

The goal of marketing is to change behaviour, be it voting intention, what products people buy or even how someone looks after themselves. Throughout the other chapters, we've explored how brands can achieve this without rationally trying to persuade someone explicitly. However, there will be times when a business will need to use rational arguments to persuade. Unfortunately, despite what we may like to think, a lot of the time our audience is not fully engaged in what we're saying. Consequently, it is important for brands to appreciate this and change how they frame their arguments depending on the audience's engagement level, even if using a rational argument.

The elaboration likelihood model

Initially, the early research into persuasion kept coming up with contradictory findings. Techniques that worked in one situation would fail when replicated in another. This led Richard Petty and John Cacioppo,[1] two psychologists, to review the literature and work out what was going on. They recognized that most academic research into persuasion involved testing students in a laboratory environment, which meant that these early studies had poor '*ecological validity*' (they failed to represent real-world conditions). As most of the previous chapters have shown, in reality, shoppers usually only pay passive attention to marketing stimuli (like vaguely watching an advert while streaming a film or scrolling social media). In the experiments, the subjects were being paid and expected to pay attention to the experiment.

Without realizing it, these laboratory studies had created a high-involvement scenario where the audience is cognitively engaged. From a psychological perspective, the key difference between this and a low-involvement scenario is the effort with which the audience is prepared to think about the arguments being made, what has become known as the '*Elaboration Likelihood Model*' (Figure 15.1). If someone is highly motivated to make the right decision, then 'the central route' is best. This focuses on the individual merits of an argument and the person will weigh up the pros and cons before deciding what to do. In a marketing context, motivation is normally higher when it comes to making risky purchases; either an expensive item or one related to the shoppers' self-identity (where they may feel like they may be judged if they purchase the wrong item). Take a professional mountaineer purchasing a new pair of skis; they're likely to invest in the decision, as skiing is central to their self-identity, but also because financially it is a big investment.

In contrast, when it comes to deciding what brands of toothpaste to buy, for most people this will be a relatively low-risk, and low-involvement purchase. In which case, the '*Peripheral route*' will be more appropriate. Rather than focusing on the logical reason to buy a product, with the peripheral route, shoppers rely on external cues or heuristics (mental shortcuts that aid in the decision-making process) to decide whether to buy a product or not. A shopper might infer that a product is high

Figure 15.1 A graphical representation of the Elaboration Likelihood Model as developed by Petty and Cacioppo (1986)

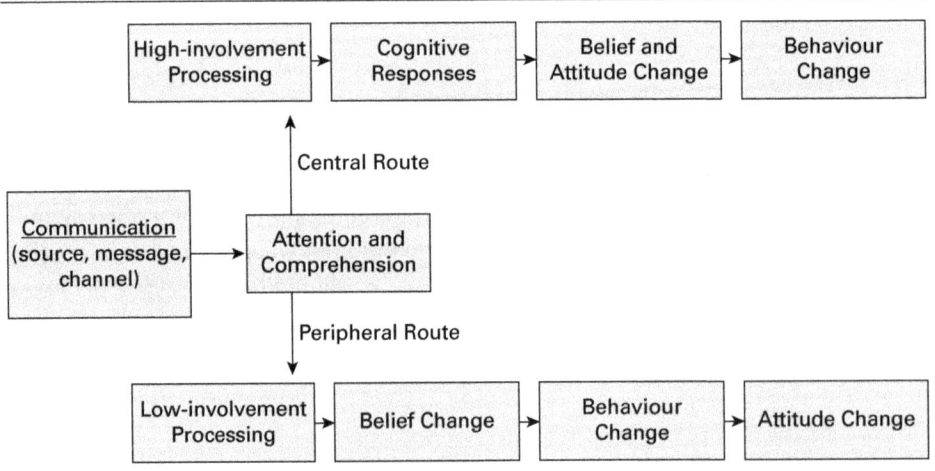

quality if it is endorsed by a credible celebrity[2] (e.g. a TV chef recommending a stock cube), it comes in fancy packaging[3] or if lots of other people have already bought it[4] (social norms). This has led some commentators to suggest that shoppers are making 'irrational' decisions, but this is not the case. They are just finding a more efficient way to make low-risk decisions.

While nobody knows for certain how many decisions a person makes each day, estimates suggest it is around 33,000 to 35,000.[5] Yet not all decisions are equally important, for example, should I put my left or right sock on first? People don't have the mental effort or enthusiasm to analyse each decision carefully, and this is why they rely on heuristics or mental shortcuts to help. The decisions may not be perfect, but they are also unlikely to be terrible. For example, if a couple are trying to decide whether they should eat in a specific restaurant, and they notice it looks full, this implies that it must be popular, as people keep coming back – so the food must be ok. If anything, using heuristics is a rational way to allow people to spend more time focusing on the decisions that matter.

With 35,000 decisions to make every day, what impact does it have on the quality of the decisions people make? In the past, psychologists believed that the brain was like a muscle. Run a half marathon and most people will feel it in their legs. Make a lot of decisions in a short time period, the more fatigued we feel. Historically, the research also showed that when people experienced decision fatigue, they also became more impulsive and made poorer decisions.[6] In effect, people gave up on using the central route to reach a decision. Place a bowl of chocolates in front of someone and tell them not to eat them and most people can resist them. However, give them a difficult task to complete at the same time and most people will succumb to temptation and eat at least one chocolate – evidence for decision fatigue.[7]

With findings like this, decision fatigue and the related concept, ego depletion, quickly became part of the accepted academic model, partly because the model makes intuitive sense. Unfortunately, during the replication crisis in the 2010s, researchers started questioning these findings. Most of these early studies were laboratory-based and some were found to be flawed. When researchers repeated these experiments with much larger sample sizes and using more robust methods, the findings didn't materialize.[8,9] Likewise, there may be alternative explanations to explain findings in a supermarket, such as more special offers and unhealthy purchases being placed at the tills near the end of a shopping trip.

Rational persuasion

Constructing a narrative: Order matters

Although most of the 35,000 decisions people make every day are trivial, there will be a few important decisions, and these are the ones where the central route is used.

This could include a pitch situation, buying an expensive item or deciding where to go on our holiday. Under these situations, people invest the time and effort to think about the arguments made, but this doesn't mean that they are not susceptible to heuristics, too.[10]

For example, experienced high court judges are just as susceptible to anchoring (as described in Chapter 10) as lay individuals, even though they are meant to avoid using heuristics. Enough and Mussweiler have shown that when the prosecution requests a lengthy custodial sentence, it influences and anchors the judge's decision, leading to a harsher sentence, despite judges being trained to avoid such biases.[11] This means that even when making rational arguments, brands need to think about how we present our argument so that it can appeal to both the central and peripheral route. For example, in a pitch, businesses often have numerous reasons why a client should work with them. The challenge lies in deciding which order to present these arguments. This is a more critical decision than many people realize, as simply adding more arguments fails to help to persuade, unless they are organized and structured coherently.[12]

From a memory perspective, researchers know that the audience is most likely to remember the first or last arguments made and tends to forget those in the middle.[13] But where do you place your strongest argument – first or last? The answer depends on how many arguments you are going to make and when you make them. If you plan on making just two arguments in quick succession, then your audience is most likely to remember the first argument – *the primacy effect*. However, if there is a long gap between your arguments, for example, you make your first point, talk about something else, perhaps a case study, and then make your second argument, your audience is most likely to remember the second argument – *the recency effect*.[14]

But it does not matter how good your product is, there will always be a reason for someone not to buy it. The question is whether it is a good idea to acknowledge these weaknesses or not. While it might be nice to hope that your audience won't notice these flaws, the likelihood is that they will, and if they don't, your competitors are almost certainly going to tell them. Consequently, if only using positive information, there is a strong likelihood that the audience will become sceptical and assume that important flaws are being deliberately concealed. However, if several small negative points are openly disclosed, people are more likely to believe the overall presentation.

This holds true when the audience is highly engaged, such as in a marketing pitch or a court case,[15] but also in advertising, assuming the audience is engaged.[16] In a court case, raising a negative point first allows the lawyer to shape the narrative and influence any counterarguments the audience might consider. With advertising, again it makes your message seem more credible, and it makes it less likely the viewer will consider any other product flaws, and ultimately increases the likelihood the viewer will buy the products. However, this does require viewers to be actively watching and listening to the message and not just passively engaged. This is because before introducing any negative information, marketers first need to convince the audience to believe in their primary argument. Only then can they introduce the negative information and finally finish with a strong argument. If the audience is only passively engaged, there is a risk they could remember the one negative message, and nothing else, depending on when they looked up from their phone.

However, when it comes to ordering arguments, the worst thing a brand can do is lead with a relatively weak argument. From a memory perspective, this is a mistake as the first argument is likely to be the main thing people remember, but it can also prevent your audience from being persuaded by what is said next. When the audience recognizes that the first argument is weak, they automatically assume that any subsequent argument will also be unconvincing. Consequently, they are less likely to believe whatever is said next or, at the very least, scrutinize it more carefully,[17] even if it is a compelling reason. Without realizing it, the speaker has made the audience immune to their arguments, hence the name coined by William McGuire '*the inoculation effect*'.

> **GIVE IT A GO**
>
> Want to know if you are susceptible to the primacy and recency effect? Test yourself online and see which adverts you remember best.
>
>

How to persuade when interest is low

While marketers hope that their audience is paying close attention to what they're saying, unfortunately, this is often not the case. While disheartening, especially if you're delivering a presentation, it can be used to your advantage. This is because when people are not listening carefully, they often confuse argument quantity with quality.[18] Listeners are persuaded more by the volume of arguments made, rather than the quality of each argument. However, even if your argument is relatively superficial, it is possible to make it appear more persuasive. Simply repeating the same argument multiple times makes it seem more believable, even when the audience knows the message is objectively false – what is known as the '*illusory truth effect*'.[19] But if you don't have the luxury of time, such as in a presentation and can't repeat an argument, simply telling people that you have already told them about this information (e.g. '*as I previously stated*') can recreate the illusory truth effect, albeit to a lesser extent.[20]

This effect is not only used in presentations and pitches but frequently in adverts. However, shrewd advertisers can both magnify the effect and make it feel less apparent by ensuring the audience hears the same message from multiple sources.[21] This doesn't just mean repeating the same message across different mediums (e.g. an omnichannel campaign) but involves ensuring the target audience hears different people repeating the same messages. When researchers analysed how 11,000 different ads performed, they discovered that adverts which were the more persuasive were those that featured multiple people repeating the key message.[22]

However, for the illusory truth effect to occur, a message needs to be framed correctly. While marketers often use rhetorical questions to boost engagement, this limits the size of the illusory truth effect.[23] Instead, to trigger this effect, the statement must be phrased in the declarative form – a clear, straightforward assertion. Simply asking a question encourages the audience to elaborate on the statement and question whether it makes sense or not.

If you are presenting on your own, it is challenging to repeat the same message in a different voice, but there are other options available to increase the believability of your statements. This includes making sure you include the word *'because'* in your answers. This works as people have learnt that when someone says because, they follow it up with a reason to support their belief. If they are listening carefully, then the quality of their justification is important, but when the audience is only passively engaged, they often just assume what comes next is a quality argument[24] – even if in reality the argument is relatively meaningless. For example, when a complete stranger approached a line of people queuing to use a photocopier and asked if they could skip the queue by saying *'Excuse me, I have five pages, may I use the copier?'*, 60% of people agreed. However, when they said, *'May I use the copier, because I need to make some copies?'*, 93% of people let the researchers skip the queue. In this case, the reason was completely meaningless. The only reason anybody would want to use the copier would be to make some copies. In fact, providing a reason, such as explaining the fact that you were in a rush, only increased compliance, to 94%.

Asking for a favour

When it comes to asking for a favour or persuading someone to change their behaviour, how you frame and ask the question is critical. But before focusing on message framing, the simplest way to increase the odds that someone will agree with your request is to ask it in-person. Typically, when making a request, asking in-person is 34 times more effective at getting a yes than asking via email.[25] By asking in-person, there is an implicit element of trust conveyed that is lost in email. If it's not possible to ask in-person, asking via the phone is still better than via email. Even if people ask a favour in-person, it can be tempting, especially if we're in a rush, to just ask the favour, but it is important to build rapport first. This is because people are naturally more influenced by people we know and like.[26] It's also why good salespeople make sure they make a note of their clients' children's names, favourite sports-teams or even where they last went on holiday.[27] This way, when they're chatting and know the child's birthday is coming up, they can ask what they have planned. This shows the illusion of genuine interest, which builds a personal connection, increasing compliance.[28]

Once a client manager has developed rapport with a client, it is still often not a good idea to lead with the main request. Just as businesses can '*prime*' or '*anchor*' shoppers' expectations, which will influence how much they are prepared to pay for a product, a similar tactic can be used to increase the chances they will agree with your request, a process known as '*target-chuting*'. Instead of starting with the main question, the speaker first asks a broad, generic question that almost everybody agrees with. Once the audience agrees to the first question, the real question is asked. As people have agreed with the first question, they are more likely to agree with the follow-up question as well.[29] For example, when a team of scientists asked students if they would sign up for a newsletter and in return, they would be given a free soft drink, only 33% agreed. But if they first asked, '*Do you consider yourself an adventurous person?*' (of which 97% agreed), and then asked for their email, 76% now agreed.

Of course, nobody likes feeling that they are being manipulated. For some people, even the offer of a free drink in exchange for signing up to a mailing list can feel like manipulation. If they do, the only way they can react is to find a way to establish their independence and ignore the request. But simply adding eight extra words, '*but you are free to accept or refuse*' gives people the illusion they are more in control of the situation and are less likely to experience reactance (the feeling that their freedom to act is threatened). The result is that they are more likely to agree with your request.[30]

REAL-WORLD EXAMPLE: PSYCH IN ACTION

It is not unheard of for unscrupulous developers to use a variation of target-chuting to show widespread support for their next project, when this might not be the case. Hypothetically, if an energy company planned to build a large wind farm near a village, most locals would likely object if asked directly '*Do you support the building of the new wind farm in your area?*'. However, if instead they asked multiple questions, where the answer to each question 'primed' the response to the next, the energy company could show greater support for this initiative. This could be achieved by asking:

1 Do you appreciate nature? (a question most people agree with)
2 Do you believe in man-made climate change?
3 Are you in favour of initiatives that promote sustainability and clean energy solutions?
4 Do you support the building of the new wind farm in your local area?

If you believe in man-made climate change, you would appear hypocritical if you didn't support initiatives that promote sustainability and clean energy. Likewise, if you support initiatives promoting clean energy, then why wouldn't you support the building of a wind farm in your local area? When the developer reveals the results to the planning committee, they only reveal the results of Question 4.

While target-chuting is a powerful tool to encourage agreement, salespeople need to be cautious about using this approach, or at least use it selectively. Initially, it may appear that the simplest way to use this technique is to try and persuade a shopper to make a small initial purchase and then convince them to upgrade, what is known as '*the foot in the door technique*'. For a sales associate, this can feel less intimidating than trying to persuade a customer to purchase a more expensive model. Unfortunately, it usually results in lower sales. Instead, it is more effective to lead with a large request that is almost certainly going to be rejected (metaphorically having the door slammed in your face) and then follow up with a smaller request[31] – hence the name '*face in the door*'.

It sounds counterintuitive, but the effect was first shown trying to persuade students to volunteer to give up their Saturday morning to take a group of '*juvenile delinquents*' to the zoo. When the researchers randomly approached students who were walking around campus and asked if they would be willing to volunteer, amazingly, 17% of students agreed. However, if instead the researchers initially asked students if they would be prepared to spend two hours every weekend for the next two years acting as a counsellor for the juvenile delinquents, everybody said no. But when the researchers immediately followed up with the small request and asked if they'd be prepared to give up their Saturday morning and take the juvenile delinquents to the zoo, this time half of the students agreed – nearly a 200% increase.[32] However, would the students feel manipulated and consequently not show up? Follow-up studies suggest this isn't a concern. When marketers just make the small request, only 50% of people showed up and completed the volunteering. But when the '*face in the door*' technique was used, 85% of people turned up and completed their volunteering.[33]

Sales assistants don't necessarily need to suggest the most expensive model to use the '*face in the door*' technique. Instead, they could recommend a customer purchase a large quantity of a product. In the Austrian alps, a cheesemonger tried to persuade shoppers to buy an overly generous quantity of cheese. When everybody said no, they suggested a more 'normal' quantity. However, by recommending the larger portion first, sales nearly tripled.[34] But if the cheesemonger draws attention to their first suggestion, highlighting how impractical it was, stating: '*Well, that's probably really too much. After all, you have to carry the cheese all the way down to the valley*', sales increased four-fold. So, what's going on? The answer comes down to the principle of reciprocity.

Reciprocity

When asking for a favour, psychologists have shown that it is more effective to give the other person something first. Humans have evolved as social creatures, with complex sets of social rules and norms. When someone gives us something for nothing, it triggers a moral obligation to find a way to return the favour,[35] even if we are not consciously aware of this. With the '*face in the door*' technique, when the vendor makes the initial large request that is turned down, and they then follow it up with a smaller, more reasonable one, the client feels as if the vendor has made a concession. In effect, they've given them something and in return, they feel obliged to return the favour, which they can do by agreeing to the request.[36]

The principle of reciprocity is why most companies have policies that prevent staff from accepting gifts from both prospective and current agencies or suppliers. Research by Richard Beltramin has shown that, on average, when a marketing agency gave a brand manager an unexpected $40 gift, the brand manager immediately increased the work they gave to the agency. This boost wasn't limited to a single order; over the next six months, the agency continued to receive more work, with sales typically increasing by 615% compared to pre-gift levels.[37]

However, in a B2B context, not all businesses benefit equally from the principle of reciprocity. If a supplier already has a strong relationship with a client, then the effect is stronger.[38] Likewise, it is better for the gift to be implicit rather than explicit, which can feel like a bribe! Hence, if a marketing agency wanted to showcase its packaging design credentials, they might leave behind samples of packaging created for previous clients. And if this happened to include work for Fortnum & Mason, a luxury department store in London, this might be a subtle way to leverage the principle of reciprocity without being obvious.

While most discussions about reciprocity in a marketing context focus on B2B transactions, it is easy to apply the same principles in a B2C environment. Visit a jewellery store and it is common for the sales associate to offer customers a complimentary cup of tea or glass of wine while the client is browsing. This does more than just leveraging reciprocation, as it encourages the customer to stay in the store for longer, which gives the sales associate more time to build a rapport. Secondly, it also induces a positive mood,[39] and shoppers typically spend 12% more when they are in a good mood versus a negative mood.[40]

It may be obvious that this tactic is financially viable for high-end retailers such as jewellers, but marketers may question whether it is profitable when promoting low-value items. This is because in a B2B context, the size of the gift correlates with the size of the order placed. But if a retailer only sells low-value items, financially, it makes no sense to offer a large free gift. However, in a B2C setting, seemingly trivial gifts influence how much shoppers spend. When a fast-food restaurant offered everybody who walked in a small free yoghurt, the average order value increased from

$7.11 to $10.41,[41] nearly a 50% uplift. Even just giving shoppers a friendly compliment as they enter a department store[42] is enough to change behaviour.

Yet many retailers do not realize they're using reciprocation. Whenever a shop offers customers a free sample, they are inadvertently using the principle of reciprocation. Logically, the argument is that shoppers can try the product and decide if they like it, reducing the risk of buying something new, but this isn't the whole story. A winery tested this idea by offering half the visitors a free sample of their wine and the other half had the chance to buy a small glass, which virtually all customers bought. This meant that all customers knew if they liked the wine or not, yet visitors who received the free sample ended up spending 37% more than those who paid for it. This is reciprocation in action.[43]

REAL-WORLD EXAMPLE: PSYCH IN ACTION

While businesses are good at using this approach, charities are the true experts. They often send letters asking for a donation, but instead of simply asking for a gift, these letters frequently include a small gift, perhaps a pen or at Christmas time, themed Christmas cards. People won't think too much about these items or even consider them a gift, but they change behaviour. In a large-scale field experiment, Armin Falk sent over 10,000 letters to people asking for donations. However, in one-third of the letters he included a free Christmas card, in the second third he included four free Christmas cards, and the other third acted as a control and included no free gift. By including one free Christmas card, the average donation increased by nearly 10%. With four free Christmas cards, donations increased by over 65%.[44]

Negotiations

In western Europe, customers typically don't negotiate when shopping, but it doesn't mean that marketers don't need to be skilled in the art. Whether it is negotiating a salary or discussing a contract's value, numbers will need to be discussed and agreed upon. For most people, this can be a daunting process, and they go into a negotiation with the goal of trying to reach a compromise where both parties meet in the middle... just slightly closer to their target price. But by using a structured framework informed by psychology, marketers can increase the likelihood they'll achieve their goals.

As shown earlier in the chapter, people are more likely to compromise or agree with people they like. Building rapport in a negotiation is more than just about getting the other person to like you; it is about demonstrating to the other party that you are listening and understand their position. Discussing the problem from their perspective can allow a negotiator to discover hidden stumbling blocks that they may not openly admit to.[45] But more than that, when people feel that the other person understands their situation, it increases their influence and power later on in a negotiation.[46]

It may sound obvious, but this means actively listening to what the other person is saying, being fully engaged or present in the conversation, thinking about what is being said and understanding the intent behind the words used.[47] If someone is talking quickly, it might imply they are nervous or anxious, whereas if they speak slowly, they could be tired or trying not to give anything away. But it is not just about focusing on the words used; it can also involve picking up on body language and also being aware of what our body language implies. Everybody wants to feel like they are being listened to – good listeners will nod in the right place or make encouraging noises to encourage the other person to carry on talking.[48]

MARKETING MYTHS

At some point you have probably been told '*93% of all communication is non-verbal, what you say is not as important as how you say it*'. Numerous online training courses cite the ratio of 55% of communication is body language, 38% is the tone of voice, and 7% is the words spoken.[49] But have you ever stopped to think about it? If we take this claim at face value, this means that if you stopped someone on the street and asked for directions to a wine bar on the other side of town, you should be able to understand 93% of their directions based on their tone of voice and gestures alone. Now, pointing and gesturing can get you so far, but even with a good dose of luck, I'm not overly confident I'll make it to the wine bar.

The statistic comes from the work of a psychologist called Albert Mehrabian, but it vastly oversimplifies his findings. Mehrabian was only interested in relatively simple communication in relation to feelings and attitudes. This is obvious when you look at the experiment in detail.[50] Participants didn't watch a whole conversation; instead they watched an experimenter saying nine words in isolation. Three words were positive (dear, honey and thanks), three neutral (oh, maybe and really) and three negative (brute, don't and terrible). Each word was said three times, either in a positive, neutral or negative way, and participants were asked to determine if they believed what the experimenter said, or how it was said. Unsurprisingly, people trusted the tone and facial expressions more. So, for emotional content, Mehrabian's work can be applied to a marketing context, but when it comes to any other sort of communication, the content is far more important.

Active listening during negotiations

Active listening is a key attribute of building *'tactical empathy'*, which is understanding the feelings, emotions and motivation that the other person is experiencing. However, even when the negotiator is paying close attention, it can still be easy to misinterpret the emotion the other person is experiencing. This is why it is important to *'label'* what the other person is feeling by saying something like *'It seems like'* or *'it sounds like'*.[51] One thing to be mindful of is beginning a statement with *'I think'*. Tactical empathy is centred on understanding the other person's emotions, but beginning a statement with *'I think'* shifts the focus from their feelings to your perspective, potentially undoing all of the good work the negotiator has just done.

Once a negotiator has labelled an emotion, it is important for them to be silent, ideally for at least four seconds, to give the other person time to process what has just been said and respond. This is the same tactic that counsellors use when speaking with clients. People don't like silence and tend to speak to fill these gaps,[52] providing more information to the person they're speaking with.

Mirroring

Another subtle way to encourage collaboration and agreement is 'mirroring'. People naturally like others who are similar to themselves.[53] From a social psychology perspective, researchers normally focus on whether two parties share similar interests or come from similar backgrounds,[54] hence the importance of finding these connections in the rapport-building stage. But if a skilled negotiator subtly mirrors the other person's body language and words they use,[55] they end up being liked more[56] and have a better success rate.[57]

For a lot of people, mirroring can feel unnatural, especially the first time they try it. Consequently, to start using it, professional negotiators recommend repeating the last three words that the other person says, or at least the three critical ones. For example, if the other person said *'We lost pretty big on an investment, and it created a strain amongst the management team'*, a simple response that uses mirroring would be to say *'Losing big on an investment is tough. A lot of us have been there.'*[58] And with practice, this will become more natural and less awkward.

Asking the right questions

The goal for many negotiators is to let the other person do most of the talking, especially at the beginning of the conversation. While the other person is likely to volunteer some information, you will probably need to ask questions. But by being skilful in the questions asked will not only reveal new information, but it can shift the balance of power and encourage the person to see things from your perspective.

However, ask the wrong question, or even ask the right question but in the wrong way, and the other person can feel like they are being interrogated. If this happens, they can quickly get defensive and experience reactance, which makes them less receptive and more likely to reject your suggestions.

It is best to avoid close-ended questions, such as questions that start with: *'can'*, *'is'*, *'are'*, *'do'* or *'does'*. While unlikely to trigger reactance, these questions can easily be answered with a simple yes or no. Ask, *'Do you think your price is a little high?'* and it doesn't reveal anything, nor does it change how the other person will think about the situation. But the bigger problem is that it can create a stilted conversation. When discussing figures and finances, this is not a huge problem, but if you are still trying to build rapport and factfinding, this can be an issue.[59] Instead, it is better to use *'calibrated questions'* – questions that are designed to extract as much information as possible but still keep the conversation flowing. One way of achieving this is by asking questions that use the journalists' 5Ws: *'What, How, Who, When and Where'*.

Of these five questions, the best two to lead with are 'what and how'. Questions such as *'How did you come up with those figures?'* or *'What are we trying to achieve here?'* will hopefully make the other person feel like they are in control of the situation, while simultaneously encouraging them to reveal more information, and potentially bringing them around to your side. However, although it can be tempting to ask *'why'*, it needs to be used with caution. In any language, when 'why' is used in negotiation, it will almost always come across as an accusation. Ask *'Why did you reject our offer?'* and the other person will understandably get defensive, which is not what you want in a negotiation. Instead, the goal is to find the common ground where a compromise can be found.

Discussing figures

At some point in any negotiation, be it the value of a contract or a pay rise, figures will need to be discussed. One of the best ways to ensure that you achieve your target figure is to use a six-step process that uses a range of psychological techniques known as the Ackerman Method. For example, if a marketer were negotiating the cost of a new website, the six steps would be as follows.

1. Initially, decide on a target price, the price you want to pay or be paid. They may want to pay their agency CHF 13,000.
2. Initially offer 65% of your target price – in this case, CHF 8,450.
3. Assuming the first offer is rejected, make three more offers. The first at 85% of your target price (CHF 11,050), next 95% (CHF 12,350), and finally your target price (CHF 13,000).
4. Each time the other person makes an offer that is not good enough, reject it, but try and avoid using the word 'no'. Show empathy and rephrase it using phrases

such as: *'How am I supposed to do that?'*, *'I'm afraid we can't do that'*, or *'That doesn't work for us'*.

5 When it comes to making the final offer, avoid using a round number like CHF 13,000 but suggest a more precise number such as CHF 13,150.

6 If the target amount is rejected, include a nonmonetary item or two, even if it's something that the other party does not necessarily want. For example, providing slightly more advantageous payment terms.[60]

From a psychological perspective, the Ackerman Method works for a number of reasons. By increasing your offer from 65% of your target amount to 85%, 95% and finally 100%, it gives the impression that you are being squeezed to your absolute maximum, which encourages the other person to not push as hard. Next, the final price is a non-round figure, and this causes people to assume that there must be a reason for you to select such an odd figure. Finally, by including a nonmonetary item or two, it really reinforces the fact that you want to reach a compromise but have hit the absolute financial limit and have nothing more to give.

As part of this process, it will be inevitable that several of the initial offers will need to be rejected. However, the aim is to use the concept of no, but without explicitly using the word no. In a negotiation, saying no is one of the most assertive things that can be done, as it shifts the balance of power to the person saying no. While this sounds like it should be a good thing, successful negotiation involves making the other person perceive that they are in control of the process. As soon as they feel like they have lost control of the situation, they are going to be less receptive to any suggestions or counteroffers made in an attempt to reinstate control over the situation. This is why skilled negotiators will use phrases such as *'How do you think that price would work for me?'* and will only use the word no to make a point.

Experts in persuasion

It doesn't matter if an individual is using either the central or peripheral route, people are more likely to agree with their requests and follow their recommendations if they are perceived as an expert[61] or a person in authority; what is known as the *authority principle*.[62] When using the peripheral route, the audience is more likely to judge the quality of the messenger rather than the message itself.[63] Hence, if a doctor recommends getting a flu jab, people are unlikely to think about the reason given and just trust the information because it came from a doctor. In contrast, with the central route, people will think carefully about the arguments made but give a greater weighting to information from experts.

Consequently, it is essential for experts to establish their credentials in the audience's mind before attempting to persuade them. Unfortunately, this is something which is frequently overlooked. Take physiotherapists – they often get frustrated when their patients fail to follow their advice when they leave hospital. For patients with a sports injury, this just slows down their recovery, but for patients recovering from a stroke, there is a very good chance that if they don't complete their exercises, they won't be able to live independently. Yet despite this incentive, most patients failed to follow their advice. The reason was that patients didn't see the physiotherapists as having equal credibility with doctors, despite the fact that physiotherapy is their specialism. However, when the physios put copies of their degree certificates on their office walls, along with any awards or prizes they had won, reinforcing their status as an expert, patient compliance increased by 34%.[64]

Unfortunately, the cues people use to determine expertise can be relatively easy to replicate. For example, doctors are perceived as being more credible and their advice is more believable when they're wearing white coats. Worryingly, this effect is even more pronounced for female doctors than male doctors.[65] However, it is not only the general public who are susceptible to this bias. Even doctors are susceptible to the same effect, finding recommendations from doctors more credible when they are wearing white coats.[66] This is why doctors and dentists in adverts are always seen wearing a white coat.

Likewise, it is worth experts experimenting with different ways to describe their titles and qualifications. Although people within an industry will understand the jargon, people outside the sector may not. Within a university, most people will understand the difference between a doctor and a professor, but outside the sector they don't. Hence, when a pharmaceutical company ran online seminars for vets, they tested how altering the speaker's description changed the sign-up rate. They tried three different variations. Firstly, they described the speaker with the letters after their name giving their academic qualification (e.g. Dr Lara Gut-Behrami DVM, PhD, DACVM (SAIM)). Secondly, they included the speaker's job title and affiliation (e.g. Dr Lara Gut-Behrami, Orthopaedic surgeon, Heartland Veterinary Referral Centre). Finally, they listed their specialism (e.g. Dr Lara Gut-Behrami, Board Certified Specialist in Small Animal Surgery). It may seem like a trivial difference, but the speaker was seen as more of an expert and more trustworthy when the qualifications were listed than when their specialism was given.

GIVE IT A GO

Collect data and see if participants are more likely to sign up to a webinar with an expert who lists their title, qualification or speciality.

But an individual does not need a PhD nor any formal qualifications to benefit from the authority principle. It is enough for someone to demonstrate how much time and effort they have invested in learning a skill. This is because people confuse effort with value, what's known as *'the labour illusion'*. For example, an estate agent recommended 10 apartments to prospective buyers and told them one of two stories, either that the list was generated by a computer program and it only took the agent an hour to compile, or that they had spent nine hours going through their records by hand and compiling the list. When clients believed the estate agent had spent more time preparing the list, they thought the agent's work was of higher quality.[67] This is why behavioural science experts like Phil Agnew promote their newsletter by saying: '*I spend 18 hours each week turning marketing psychology into readable newsletters.*' The key for marketers is to demonstrate to clients how much work they do that clients don't get to see.

Potentially, this is why price comparison websites do not reveal the search results instantly, and the results are not revealed all at once. Instead, there is a short pause, and the results are revealed one by one, giving the illusion it's working to find the best deals. In fact, when researchers tested this, and the results took 60 seconds to be revealed after pressing 'search', users were actually happier with their experience than when the results were revealed instantly.[68]

Peripheral routes to persuasion

Most of this book has focused on persuading consumers through the peripheral route. Rather than revisiting each technique in detail, it is useful to highlight two key checklists that summarise the most common methods of persuasion when using the peripheral route: the MINDSPACE[69] approach and the EAST framework.[70] Both frameworks were developed to guide policymakers in how they could use behavioural science to form public policy.

The MINDSPACE framework

Messenger: Rather than focusing on what has been said, people are influenced by who is communicating. For example, a doctor (or even an actor who plays a doctor on TV) is viewed as more credible recommending medication than an engineer. But it is not just the speaker that is important, the medium makes a difference. A news article is viewed as less credible on social media than on a 'traditional' news channel.[71]

Incentives: People have a stronger desire to avoid punishments than gain rewards,[72] which is why marketing campaigns such as 'Don't sign up to a loyalty card today and your shopping will be 20% more expensive' is more effective than the reverse, 'Sign up for a loyalty card today and save 20%' (see Chapter 6 on message framing).

Norms (social): When people are unsure how to act, people look to what other people are doing in a similar situation and copy them.[73] Hence, marketers use phrases such as 'our best-selling product' (see Chapter 7).

Defaults: When people are uncertain which option is the best one for them, they are most likely to select the default option.[74] For example, most people will opt for the standard computer and won't customize it (see Chapter 13).

Salience: People spend more time looking at items in our environment that are visually salient[75] or stand out. This could be because of the product's size, colour, brightness or shape compared to the items surrounding it (see Chapter 14 for a detailed review of how marketers can use these principles when designing new product packaging).

Priming: Individuals are subconsciously influenced by factors in their environment that they may not be aware of.[76] For example, playing stereotypical French music in a supermarket increases the sales of French wine[77] (see Chapter 12).

Affect: People's decisions are shaped by their current mood states. For example, shoppers spend on average 12% more when they are in a positive mood compared to a negative mood[78] (see Chapter 12).

Commitment: People like to behave in a consistent manner and expect reciprocal actions (see previous section on reciprocal actions increasing sales).

Ego: In most situations, people act in a way that supports their (positive) self-image. For example, men donate more to charity when asked by a female fundraiser whom they find attractive than by a woman whom they are not attracted to,[79] suggesting that this behaviour is triggered by trying to form a positive image of themselves.

The EAST framework

Easy: People are more likely to do something if it is easier to do. Marketers can make the decision-making process easier for shoppers by using defaults[80] (see Chapter 13), remove friction[81] (see Chapter 13) or just by simplifying the message (see Chapter 6).[82]

Attractive: People are more likely to do something if it's attractive. This could mean thinking about what rewards people get for engaging in the target behaviour[83] (see Chapter 5 on learning) or making a message stand out[84] (see Chapter 2 on attention).

Social: See Norms in the MINDSPACE model

Timely: The same message can be more or less effective depending on when a person hears it. People are more likely to change their behaviour around major life events[85] (see Chapter 3) or when habits are disrupted. Likewise, more immediate rewards or punishments are more effective than things we receive in the future.[86]

But both models are not free of criticism. The models were developed without using a clear theoretical framework,[87] which has led some academics to question whether they include the most important variables. Secondly, while these tactics may be ideal for tackling relatively simple behaviours, they may be less appropriate to tackle more complicated behaviours with multiple root causes.

Habits

While the MINDSPACE framework is useful when people are making decisions using the peripheral route, it is worth remembering that with people having to make tens of thousands of decisions every day, rather than making the minimal effort of using the peripheral route, often people tend to simply repeat their previous decisions when faced with the same choice, eventually creating a habit. While the term habit is used colloquially, it does have a strict psychological definition. For a behaviour to qualify as a habit, it must meet three criteria according to Verplanken and Wood: (a) *minimal awareness* – the person must engage in the behaviour without actively focusing on it; (b) *efficiency* – the behaviour can be performed alongside other activities; and (c) *lack of control* – the behaviour occurs without deliberate intention or conscious thought.[88]

It is estimated that up to 45% of the decisions we make daily are habitual,[89] which for marketers can be either a blessing or a curse. If shoppers are regularly buying your products, they are unlikely to switch, however, if they are not, it is challenging to convince shoppers to switch. In a supermarket, eye-tracking data shows that 67% of purchases are habitual, with shoppers going straight to the product they want and that they don't even glance at any alternatives.[90] In most cases, shoppers only switch if something disrupts their routine, such as their usual product is sold out, a visually distracting point-of-sale display or the store has been redesigned.

These seemingly small changes break a shopper's routine as most habits are context dependent. If people visit a different store, they make different purchases.[91]

For a behaviour to become habitual, there need to be three elements: (a) a trigger or cue, (b) routine and (c) reward.[92] If a shopper's behaviour is compared to a computer program, the trigger is what starts the program running.[93] When people are trying to get fit and start exercising, often it is not running that is the hard part, it's finding the motivation to get out of the door in the first place. However, if someone goes for a run at the same time every day after work, it can become a habit. If an individual comes home from work and changes out of their work clothes straight away, this acts as a prompt, reminding them to go for a run.

Next comes the role of routine. Habits are automatic because the brain has learnt how to perform certain tasks automatically, freeing up capacity to focus on other tasks. If each day on the way to work you get off the tram at the same spot and grab a coffee and croissant from your favourite boulangerie, you know exactly where you are going and you walk there on autopilot without thinking. However, for the habit to be learnt, there needs to be repetition.

> **MARKETING MYTHS**
>
> It is a common myth that it takes just 28 days to form a habit, which is why fitness programmes like the '*28-Day Ab Challenge*' are popular. The idea is that if you repeat the behaviour daily for a month, it becomes habitual. Unfortunately, it takes an average of 66 days to form a habit, but it can be considerably longer for more complex behaviour. For instance, a simple task like drinking a glass of water at breakfast can become habitual after just 18 days, while more complex behaviours can take up to 254 days, or may never become habitual.[94] This challenge is reflected in a study where 96 people committed to forming a new healthy habit, repeating the behaviour at least once a day for 84 days. At the end of the period, only 41% of participants had successfully formed a new habit.

Practice makes perfect

The key to forming any new habit is not just repetition but performing the same behaviour at the same time each day, or at least in the same situation.[95] Keeping the contextual cues consistent speeds up habit formation. A great example of this in action comes from the pharmaceutical sector. While a number of pills need to be taken with food, sometimes companies recommend that they are taken with a meal, because the meal acts as a prompt, increasing compliance.[96] It's easy to forget to take a tablet every four hours, but if you need to take it with food, each time you sit down for a meal, it reminds you to take your tablet. This doesn't just work for medication, but the principle can be applied to building any new habits. Rather than trying to establish a new habit from scratch, it is easier to link the new behaviour to an already established habit.[97]

When a brand launched a saline nasal spray, the idea being that people should wash the dust and pollen out of their nose each day, amazingly, they found that getting shoppers to buy the product was only half the battle. They could convince shoppers to buy the product, but consumers would forget to use it once they got it home. But when they suggested that the product should be used as part of their bedtime routine, washing their nose straight after they'd brushed their teeth, an already established habit, usage increased, resulting in higher sales.

While marketers are usually focusing on trying to build new habits, these principles can also be used to break existing habits. If someone is trying to stop eating an unhealthy lunch at work, it is a lot easier to break the habit if the environment is altered.[98] Hence, if you start a new job, or even just move to a new office, it is the best time to change what you eat. It's the same reason why so many companies sponsor universities' freshers fairs. By being in a new situation, so many existing habits will have been broken, and it is the perfect time to establish new ones – *the fresh start effect*.[99]

Likewise, as shown earlier, it takes a long time for a new habit to form, and brands need to be creative to make sure the new habitual behaviour is repeated without any breaks. When it comes to the contraceptive pill, most doctors advise women to take it at the same time every day, often with a meal, or just before bed. This way, the action of eating a meal or brushing your teeth acts as a reminder, or cue, to take it. However, depending on the contraceptive pill being used, it only needs to be taken for the first 21 days of the menstrual cycle. However, if you have to take a tablet for three weeks and then have a week off, there is a very real risk that the individual would easily forget to start taking it again. Considering the consequences of forgetting to take a tablet can be considerable, pharmaceutical companies sell pills in batches of 28 pills. However, the last seven pills are placebos – they have no medical purpose, but are simply included to ensure that women don't fall out of the habit of taking their pill.[100]

For some people, rather than trying to remember to take the pill every day, or drink a glass of water with lunch, they opt to use apps on their phone to act as a reminder. These apps provide a notification at the same time every day, or when the user arrives at a certain location (e.g. the cafeteria at work), reminding the user to do something. Objectively, they work, as people using apps do engage in the target behaviour more, but it stops a habit forming.[101] Take away the app, and the behaviour stops occurring. The notification acts as the cue, which triggers the behaviour, rather than any specific cue in our environment. From a brand perspective, this is not necessarily a problem as the target behaviour still occurs, but brands just need to remember how critical the app is and continue to invest in it.

Rewarding habits

The final stage in habit formation is reward. This is what motivates the user to engage in the behaviour and reinforces the behaviour before the task becomes automatic. Initially, when discussing rewards, most people automatically think of extrinsic or tangible rewards, such as financial rewards or praise from friends, but intrinsic rewards, such as doing something for the pleasure or feeling of accomplishment, are just as important.[102] In fact, new research from a self-determination theory perspective has shown that intrinsic rewards are more important because extrinsic rewards can slow down or even stop habits from forming. A petrol station might provide commuters with 10% off their shopping at a local supermarket if they have a car wash between 15:30 and 19:00 on a Friday each week. The goal is that shoppers will get into the habit of washing their cars on the way home from work. This is likely to work in the short term, but once the reward stops, the behaviour stops.[103] The key is for brands to remember that extrinsic rewards only help form habits where achieving the reward does not become the performance goal.[104] Just think, how many people engage in Duolingo every day to keep their streak freeze alive rather than to learn French. Consequently, considering that in most cases it is not financially feasible for brands to continually reinforce behaviour with external rewards, it is worth focusing on intrinsic rewards.

Closing thoughts

While persuasion can feel like a dark art, by adopting a more structured approach, a marketer can increase the likelihood they will achieve their goals. The key is for marketers to understand how a consumer is going to approach the decision-making process. If they are willing to invest the time and effort in making a well-thought-out decision, then a marketer should focus their efforts on using a more rational argument, but still remember that their audience is going to use some form of heuristic processing to evaluate the argument. However, if their audience is not invested in this decision, then marketers should focus on optimizing the message for heuristic processing – and this is where frameworks like MINDSPACE are useful. It is a simple question, but one where marketers really do need to be honest. Far too often, we like to think that our customers are as invested in our product as we are. But in reality, most shoppers are not overly invested in what brand of bleach they buy.

> **KEY POINTS**
>
> - When shoppers are motivated to listen to an argument, the central route to persuasion is effective. Individuals make decisions based on the pros and cons of an argument.
> - For shoppers who are not invested in analysing the pros and cons of an argument, they use the peripheral route or heuristic approach to decision-making.
> - To optimize a message for the central route, marketers should lead and end with their strongest argument and repeat it numerous times. A marketer can acknowledge a counterargument in the middle, but they need to acknowledge the arguments against it.
> - When sales associates are trying to persuade, it's better to lead with a large offer they know will be rejected than start with a small offer and upsell once the customer agrees.
> - People are more likely to agree to a request if they first receive a small free gift or favour.
> - Negotiators are more successful when they ask calibrated questions and label the other party's emotion. Likewise, the principle of anchoring (Chapter 10) should be used when discussing figures.
> - If the audience is not invested in a topic, it is more effective to use the peripheral route to persuasion. The MINDSPACE (Messenger, Incentives, Norms, Defaults, Salience, Priming, Affect, Commitments and Ego) and EAST frameworks (Easy,

Attractive, Social and Timely) provide a clear overview of the most popular techniques available to marketers.

- When the same behaviour is regularly repeated, it can become a habit. On average, a behaviour needs to be repeated for 66 days to become a habit, but it can be up to 254 days and some behaviour will never become habitual.
- For a behaviour to become a habit, there need to be three elements: (a) a trigger or cue, (b) routine and (c) reward.

PUTTING THEORY INTO PRACTICE

1 Identify five arguments you've engaged with in the last six months which you've processed using the central route to persuasion. What factors caused you to use the central route rather than the peripheral route?

2 Find three adverts on YouTube that use the central route to persuasion. How would you redesign the advert to optimise it for the peripheral route to persuasion?

3 Select a controversial political topic that sharply divides public opinion. Write a speech to convince someone to agree with your perspective. Think about where you position your strongest/weakest arguments and whether you acknowledge any counterarguments. Explain why you've structured your speech as you have.

4 Imagine you are the marketing manager of the Student Union bar. How could you use the power of habits to increase sales? How would you structure this campaign?

5 If you were tasked by the government to ensure recent graduates saved more for their retirement, how could you use either the MINDSPACE or EAST framework to achieve this objective?

6 How could a brand use the authority principle in a marketing campaign to encourage people to switch to electric vehicles?

7 If you were going to ask your boss for a pay rise, how could you use the Akermann method?

8 What are the ethical implications of using the principle of reciprocity in a B2B negotiation? Could it be argued that the principle of reciprocity is a form of manipulation?

9 Find a speech made by a politician and identify what psychological techniques they are using. Make sure you consider both the central and peripheral route.

10 How could the marketing manager of an adventure tour company use the face-in-the-door technique when trying to sell packages to potential guests?

> **SUGGESTIONS FOR FURTHER READING**
>
> Clear, J. (2018). *Atomic habits: Tiny changes, remarkable results: An easy & proven way to build good habits & break bad ones.* NY: Avery, Penguin Random House.
>
> Voss, C. & Raz, T. (2016). *Never split the difference: Negotiating as if your life depended on it.* Random House.

References

1. Petty, R. E. & Cacioppo, J. T. (1986). The elaboration likelihood model of persuasion. *Advances in Experimental Social Psychology*, 19, 123–205.
2. Petty, R. E., Cacioppo, J. T., & Schumann, D. (1983). Central and peripheral routes to advertising effectiveness: The moderating role of involvement. *Journal of Consumer Research*, 10(2), 135–146.
3. Van Ooijen, I., Fransen, M. L., Verlegh, P. W., & Smit, E. G. (2017). Packaging design as an implicit communicator: Effects on product quality inferences in the presence of explicit quality cues. *Food Quality and Preference*, 62, 71–79.
4. Burchell, K., Rettie, R., & Patel, K. (2013). Marketing social norms: Social marketing and the 'social norm approach'. *Journal of Consumer Behaviour*, 12(1), 1–9.
5. Reill, A. (2023). *A simple way to make better decisions.* Harvard Business Review.
6. Baumeister, R. F., Bratslavsky, E., Muraven, M., & Tice, D. M. (2018). Ego depletion: Is the active self a limited resource?. In *Self-Regulation and Self-Control* (pp. 16–44). Routledge.
7. Yim, M. Y. C. (2017). When shoppers don't have enough self-control resources: Applying the strength model of self-control. *Journal of Consumer Marketing*, 34(4), 328–337.
8. Hagger, M. S., Wood, C., Stiff, C., & Chatzisarantis, N. L. (2010). Ego depletion and the strength model of self-control: A meta-analysis. *Psychological Bulletin*, 136(4), 495–525. https://doi.org/10.1037/a0019486 (archived at https://perma.cc/A4ZF-SYE7)
9. Vohs, K. D., Schmeichel, B. J., Lohmann, S., Gronau, Q. F., Finley, A. J., Ainsworth, S. E., et al (2021). A multisite preregistered paradigmatic test of the ego-depletion effect. *Psychological Science*, 32(10), 1566–1581.
10. Khan, H. H., Naz, I., Qureshi, F., & Ghafoor, A. (2017). Heuristics and stock buying decision: Evidence from Malaysian and Pakistani stock markets. *Borsa Istanbul Review*, 17(2), 97–110.
11. Enough, B. & Mussweiler, T. (2001). Sentencing under uncertainty: Anchoring effects in the courtroom 1. *Journal of Applied Social Psychology*, 31(7), 1535–1551.
12. Ta, V. P., Boyd, R. L., Seraj, S., Keller, A., Griffith, C., Loggarakis, A., & Medema, L. (2022). An inclusive, real-world investigation of persuasion in language and verbal behavior. *Journal of Computational Social Science*, 5(1), 883–903.

13 Murdock Jr, B. B. (1962). The serial position effect of free recall. *Journal of Experimental Psychology*, 64(5), 482.
14 Forgas, J. P., Cooper, J., & Crano, W. D. (2011). *The psychology of attitudes and attitude change*. Psychology Press.
15 Williams, K. D., Bourgeois, M. J., & Croyle, R. T. (1993). The effects of stealing thunder in criminal and civil trials. *Law and Human Behavior*, 17(6), 597–609.
16 Eisend, M. (2006). Two-sided advertising: A meta-analysis. *International Journal of Research in Marketing*, 23(2), 187–198.
17 McGuire, W. J. (1964). Inducing resistance to persuasion: Some contemporary approaches. In *Advances in Experimental Social Psychology*, Vol. 1, ed Berkowitz L. (New York, NY: Academic Press;), 191–229.
18 Petty, R. E. & Cacioppo, J. T. (1984). The effects of involvement on responses to argument quantity and quality: Central and peripheral routes to persuasion. *Journal of Personality and Social Psychology*, 46(1), 69.
19 Hassan, A. & Barber, S. J. (2021). The effects of repetition frequency on the illusory truth effect. *Cognitive Research: Principles and Implications*, 6(1), 38.
20 Mattavelli, S., Corneille, O., & Unkelbach, C. (2023). Truth by repetition … Without repetition: Testing the effect of instructed repetition on truth judgments. *Journal of Experimental Psychology: Learning, Memory, and Cognition*, 49(8). https://doi.org/10.1037/xlm0001170 (archived at https://perma.cc/KGZ6-8L6R)
21 Harkins, S. G. & Petty, R. E. (1987). Information utility and the multiple source effect. *Journal of Personality and Social Psychology*, 52(2), 260–268. https://doi.org/10.1037/0022-3514.52.2.260 (archived at https://perma.cc/V9SA-EBUC)
22 Chang, H. H., Mukherjee, A., & Chattopadhyay, A. (2022). More voices persuade: The attentional benefits of voice numerosity. *Journal of Marketing Research*. https://doi.org/10.1177/00222437221134115 (archived at https://perma.cc/UNB2-9XJX)
23 Mattavelli, S., Bianchi, C., & Motterlini, M. (2025). 'Questioning' the Truth Effect: Processing information in interrogative form reduces (but does not cancel) repetition-induced truth. *Memory and Cognition*. https://doi.org/10.3758/s13421-025-01742-9 (archived at https://perma.cc/BRF3-5226)
24 Langer, E. J., Blank, A., & Chanowitz, B. (1978). The mindlessness of ostensibly thoughtful action: The role of 'placebic' information in interpersonal interaction. *Journal of Personality and Social Psychology*, 36(6), 635–642. http://dx.doi.org/10.1037/0022-3514.36.6.635 (archived at https://perma.cc/HZA2-3UNY)
25 Roghanizad, M. M. & Bohns, V. K. (2017). Ask in person: You're less persuasive than you think over email. *Journal of Experimental Social Psychology*, 69, 223–226. https://doi.org/10.1016/j.jesp.2016.10.002 (archived at https://perma.cc/5YNX-5V85)
26 Cialdini, R. B. (2009). *Influence: Science and practice* (Vol. 4, pp. 51–96). Boston: Pearson education.
27 Beatty, S. E., Mayer, M., Coleman, J. E., Reynolds, K. E., & Lee, J. (1996). Customer-sales associate retail relationships. *Journal of Retailing*, 72(3), 223–247.
28 Burger, J. M. (2011). Fleeting attraction and compliance with requests. In *The Science of Social Influence* (pp. 155–166). Psychology Press.
29 Cialdini, R. (2016). *Pre-suasion: A revolutionary way to influence and persuade*. Simon and Schuster.

30 Carpenter, C. J. (2013). A meta-analysis of the effectiveness of the 'but you are free' compliance-gaining technique. *Communication Studies*, 64(1), 6–17. https://doi.org/10.1080/10510974.2012.727941 (archived at https://perma.cc/H27T-W5PY)
31 Rodafinos, A., Vucevic, A., & Sideridis, G. D. (2005). The effectiveness of compliance techniques: Foot in the door versus door in the face. *The Journal of Social Psychology*, 145(2), 237–240.
32 Cialdini, R. B., Vincent, J. E., Lewis, S. K., Catalan, J., Wheeler, D., & Darby, B. L. (1975). Reciprocal concessions procedure for inducing compliance: The door-in-the-face technique. *Journal of Personality and Social Psychology*, 31(2), 206.
33 Miller, R. L., Seligman, C., Clark, N. T., & Bush, M. (1976). Perceptual contrast versus reciprocal concession as mediators of induced compliance. *Canadian Journal of Behavioural Science/Revue canadienne des sciences du comportement*, 8(4), 401.
34 Ebster, C. & Neumayr, B. (2008). Applying the door-in-the-face compliance technique to retailing. *The International Review of Retail, Distribution and Consumer Research*, 18(1), 121–128.
35 Ridley, M. (1997). *The origins of virtue*. UK: Penguin.
36 Turner, M. M., Tamborini, R., Limon, M. S., & Zuckerman-Hyman, C. (2007). The moderators and mediators of door-in-the-face requests: Is it a negotiation or a helping experience?. *Communication Monographs*, 74(3), 333–356.
37 Beltramin, R. F. (2000). Exploring the effectiveness of business gifts: Replication and extension. *Journal of Advertising*, 29(2), 75–78.
38 Bodur, H. O. & Grohmann, B. (2005). Consumer responses to gift receipt in business-to-consumer contexts. *Psychology & Marketing*, 22(5), 441–456.
39 Westermann, R., Spies, K., Stahl, G., & Hesse, F. W. (1996). Relative effectiveness and validity of mood induction procedures: A meta-analysis. *European Journal of Social Psychology*, 26(4), 557–580.
40 Morris, W. N. & Schnurr, P. P. (1989). *Mood*. Springer Verlag.
41 Friedman, H. H. & Rahman, A. (2011). Gifts-upon-entry and appreciatory comments: Reciprocity effects in retailing. *Journal of International Marketing Studies*, 3(3), 161–164.
42 Friedman, H. H. & Friedman, E. (1996). The effect of an appreciatory comment on sales: Reciprocity in a retailing context. *Central Business Review*, 15, 25–26.
43 Kolyesnikova, N. & Dodd, T. H. (2009). There is no such thing as a free wine tasting: The effect of a tasting fee on obligation to buy. *Journal of Travel & Tourism Marketing*, 26(8), 806–819.
44 Falk, A. (2004). *Charitable giving as a gift exchange-evidence from a field experiment*. IZA Discussion Papers, No. 1148.
45 Galinsky, A. D., Maddux, W. W., Gilin, D., & White, J. B. (2008). Why it pays to get inside the head of your opponent: The differential effects of perspective taking and empathy in negotiations. *Psychological Science*, 19(4), 378–384.
46 Voss, C. & Raz, T. (2016). *Never split the difference: Negotiating as if your life depended on it*. Random House.
47 Saragih, H. S. (2024). Genuine small talk, rapport, and negotiation outcomes in B2B relationship. *Journal of Business & Industrial Marketing*.

48 Holmes, O. W. (1997). Active listening. *Counselling Skills for Dietitians*, 59.
49 Lapakko, D. (2007). Communication is 93% nonverbal: An urban legend proliferates. *Communication and Theater Association of Minnesota Journal*, 34(1), 2.
50 Mehrabian, A. (1972). *Nonverbal communication*. New Brunswick: Aldine Transaction.
51 Voss, C. & Raz, T. (2016). *Never split the difference: Negotiating as if your life depended on it*. Random House
52 Sharpley, C. F., Munro, D. M., & Elly, M. J. (2005). Silence and rapport during initial interviews. *Counselling Psychology Quarterly*, 18(2), 149–159.
53 Hampton, A. J., Fisher Boyd, A. N., & Sprecher, S. (2019). You're like me and I like you: Mediators of the similarity–liking link assessed before and after a getting-acquainted social interaction. *Journal of Social and Personal Relationships*, 36(7), 2221–2244.
54 Rand, T. M. & Wexley, K. N. (1975). Demonstration of the effect, 'similar to me,' in simulated employment interviews. *Psychological Reports*, 36(2), 535–544.
55 Van Swol, L. M. (2003). The effects of nonverbal mirroring on perceived persuasiveness, agreement with an imitator, and reciprocity in a group discussion. *Communication Research*, 30(4), 461–480.
56 Kühn, S., Müller, B. C., Van Baaren, R. B., Wietzker, A., Dijksterhuis, A., & Brass, M. (2010). Why do I like you when you behave like me? Neural mechanisms mediating positive consequences of observing someone being imitated. *Social Neuroscience*, 5(4), 384–392.
57 Voss, C. & Raz, T. (2016). *Never split the difference: Negotiating as if your life depended on it*. Random House
58 MasterClass (2021, September 20). How to use mirroring as a negotiation tactic. https://www.masterclass.com/articles/mirroring-negotiation-guide (archived at https://perma.cc/6X5J-99EW)
59 Truong, M., Fast, N. J., & Kim, J. (2020). It's not what you say, it's how you say it: Conversational flow as a predictor of networking success. *Organizational Behavior and Human Decision Processes*, 158, 1–10.
60 Voss, C. & Raz, T. (2016). *Never split the difference: Negotiating as if your life depended on it*. Random House.
61 Klucharev, V., Smidts, A., & Fernández, G. (2008). Brain mechanisms of persuasion: How 'expert power' modulates memory and attitudes. *Social Cognitive and Affective Neuroscience*, 3(4), 353–366.
62 Cialdini, R. B. (2009). *Influence: Science and practice* (5th ed.). Pearson Education.
63 Petty, R. E. & Cacioppo, J. T. (1984). Source factors and the elaboration likelihood model of persuasion. *Advances in Consumer Research*, 11(1), 668–672.
64 Cialdini, R. B. (2001). Harnessing the science. *Harvard Business Review*, 79(9), 72–79.
65 Rehman, S. U., Nietert, P. J., Cope, D. W., & Kilpatrick, A. O. (2005). What to wear today? Effect of doctor's attire on the trust and confidence of patients. *The American Journal of Medicine*, 118(11), 1279–1286.
66 Maher, R. (2022). *Do expert credentials or dress enhance credibility and change behavioural intentions in B2B and B2C communications?* Student Disertation Bangor Univeristy.

67 Morales, A. C. (2005). Giving firms an 'E' for effort: Consumer responses to high-effort firms. *Journal of Consumer Research*, 31(4), 806–812.
68 Buell, R. W. & Norton, M. I. (2011). The labor illusion: How operational transparency increases perceived value. *Management Science*, 57(9), 1564–1579.
69 Dolan, P., Hallsworth, M., Halpern, D., King, D., Metcalfe, R., & Vlaev, I. (2012). Influencing behaviour: The mindspace way. *Journal of Economic Psychology*, 33(1), 264–277. https://doi.org/10.1016/j.joep.2011.10.009 (archived at https://perma.cc/W3UA-3RNU)
70 BI Team (2014). EAST: Four simple ways to apply behavioural insights. https://www.bi.team/wp-content/uploads/2014/04/BIT-EAST-handbook.pdf (archived at https://perma.cc/Q99Q-R9JR)
71 Adeyanju, A. (2015, May). Comparative study of social media, television and newspapers' news credibility. In *International Conference on Communication, Media, Technology and Design* (Vol. 2, No. 1, pp. 69–77)
72 Ganzach, Y. & Karsahi, N. (1995). Message framing and buying behavior: A field experiment. *Journal of Business Research*, 32(1), 11–17.
73 Burchell, K., Rettie, R., & Patel, K. (2013). Marketing social norms: Social marketing and the 'social norm approach'. *Journal of Consumer Behaviour*, 12(1), 1–9.
74 Jachimowicz, J. M., Duncan, S., Weber, E. U., & Johnson, E. J. (2019). When and why defaults influence decisions: A meta-analysis of default effects. *Behavioural Public Policy*, 3(2), 159–186.
75 Milosavljevic, M., Navalpakkam, V., Koch, C., & Rangel, A. (2012). Relative visual saliency differences induce sizable bias in consumer choice. *Journal of Consumer Psychology*, 22(1), 6–74.
76 North, A. C. (2012). The effect of background music on the taste of wine. *British Journal of Psychology*, 103(3), 293–301.
77 North, A. C., Hargreaves, D. J., & McKendrick, J. (1999). The influence of in-store music on wine selections. *Journal of Applied Psychology*, 84(2), 271.
78 Morris, W. N. & Schnurr, P. P. (1989). *Mood*. Springer Verlag.
79 Landry, C. E., Lange, A., List, J. A., Price, M. K., & Rupp, N. G. (2006). Toward an understanding of the economics of charity: Evidence from a field experiment. *Quarterly Journal of Economics*, 121(2), 747–782. https://doi.org/10.1162/qjec.2006.121.2.747 (archived at https://perma.cc/5UBJ-N6GP)
80 HMG (2013). Automatic enrolment opt out rates: findings from research with large employers. https://www.gov.uk/government/uploads/system/uploads/attachment_data/file/227039/opt-out-research-large-employers-ad_hoc.pdf (archived at https://perma.cc/C4FL-YGDC)
81 Bettinger, E. P., Long, B. T., Oreopoulos, P., & Sanbonmatsu, L. (2012). The role of application assistance and information in college decisions: Results from the H&R block FAFSA experiment. *The Quarterly Journal of Economics*, 127(3), 1205–1242.
82 Fishbane, A., Ouss, A., & Shah, A. K. (2020). Behavioral nudges reduce failure to appear for court. *Science*, 370(6517), eabb6591. https://doi.org/10.1126/science.abb6591 (archived at https://perma.cc/DXQ9-W3R7)

83 Hakulinen, L., Auvinen, T., & Korhonen, A. (2013, March). Empirical study on the effect of achievement badges in TRAKLA2 online learning environment. In *2013 Learning and Teaching in Computing and Engineering* (pp. 47–54). IEEE.

84 Clement, J., Aastrup, J., & Forsberg, S. C. (2015). Decisive visual saliency and consumers' in-store decisions. *Journal of Retailing and Consumer Services*, 22, 187–194.

85 Dai, H., Milkman, K. L., & Riis, J. (2014). The fresh start effect: Temporal landmarks motivate aspirational behavior. *Management Science*, 60(10), 2563–2582.

86 Rubinstein, A. (2003). 'Economics and psychology'? The case of hyperbolic discounting. *International Economic Review*, 44(4), 1207–1216.

87 O'Sullivan, M., Ryan, C., Downey, D. G., & Hughes, C. M. (2016). A change in behaviour: Getting the balance right for research and policy. *International Journal of Clinical Pharmacy*, 38. https://doi.org/10.1007/s11096-016-0351-0 (archived at https://perma.cc/M3MB-8FKB)

88 Verplanken, B. & Wood, W. (2006). Interventions to break and create consumer habits. *Journal of Public Policy & Marketing*, 25(1), 90–103.

89 McCloskey, K. & Johnson, B. T. (2021). You are what you repeatedly do: Links between personality and habit. *Personality and Individual Differences*, 181, 111000.

90 Machín, L., Curutchet, M. R., Gugliucci, V., Vitola, A., Otterbring, T., de Alcantara, M., & Ares, G. (2020). The habitual nature of food purchases at the supermarket: Implications for policy making. *Appetite*, 155, 104844.

91 Tohidi, A., Eckles, D., & Jadbabaie, A. (2022). *Habits in consumer purchases: Evidence from store closures*. Available at SSRN 4077391.

92 Khatib, R. & Barki, H. (2020). Habits in organizational contexts: Information systems routines, cues, and rewards. *Canadian Journal of Administrative Sciences/Revue Canadienne des Sciences de l'Administration*, 37(4), 528–539

93 Neal, D. T., Wood, W., Labrecque, J. S., & Lally, P. (2012). How do habits guide behavior? Perceived and actual triggers of habits in daily life. *Journal of Experimental Social Psychology*, 48(2), 492–498.

94 Lally, P. Van Jaarsveld, C. H., Potts, H. W., & Wardle, J. (2010). How are habits formed: Modelling habit formation in the real world. *European Journal of Social Psychology*, 40(6), 998–1009.

95 Lally, P. & Gardner, B. (2013). Promoting habit formation. *Health Psychology Review*, 7(sup1), S137–S158.

96 Park, D. C. & Kidder, D. P. (1996). Prospective memory and medication adherence. In Brandimonte, M., Einstein G. O. & McDaniel, M. A. (eds) *Prospective memory: Theory and applications*, Lawrence Earlbaum Associates, 369–390.

97 Lally, P. & Gardner, B. (2013). Promoting habit formation. *Health psychology review*, 7(sup1), S137–S158.

98 Carden, L. & Wood, W. (2018). Habit formation and change. Current opinion in behavioral sciences, 20, 117–122.

99 Dai, H., Milkman, K. L., & Riis, J. (2014). The fresh start effect: Temporal landmarks motivate aspirational behavior. *Management Science*, 60(10), 2563–2582.

100 Johnson, M. & Ghuman, P. (2020). *Blindsight: The (mostly) hidden ways marketing reshapes our brains*. BenBella Books.
101 Stawarz, K., Cox, A. L., & Blandford, A. (2015, April). *Beyond self-tracking and reminders: Designing smartphone apps that support habit formation*. In Proceedings of the 33rd annual ACM conference on human factors in computing systems (pp. 2653–2662).
102 Lally, P. & Gardner, B. (2013). Promoting habit formation. *Health Psychology Review*, 7(sup1), S137–S158.
103 Deci, E. L., Koestner, R., & Ryan, R. M. (1999). A meta-analytic review of experiments examining the effects of extrinsic rewards on intrinsic motivation. *Psychological Bulletin*, 25, 627668.
104 Dickinson, A. (1985). Actions and habits: The development of behavioural autonomy. Philosophical Transactions of the Royal Society B, 308(1135). https://doi.org/10.1098/rstb.1985.0010 (archived at https://perma.cc/6S3N-TFL2).

16 | Market research: A psychological approach

LEARNING OBJECTIVES

- Evaluate the role of market research within consumer psychology.
- Demonstrate the ability to critically assess the generalizability of academic research findings and evaluate the likelihood that they can be replicated in a commercial context.
- Critically analyse the different research approaches used within market research.

Introduction

As a discipline, consumer psychology has come a long way in the last 50 years, and a big part of this is down to the innovative studies psychologists have designed to understand how and why consumers behave as they do. But research methods is a vast subject and to adequately explore it would require its own book. Instead, in this chapter, we are going to focus on the approaches and challenges that are specifically relevant to understanding consumer behaviour, which are usually ignored by most standard research methods books.

What makes a good research project?

Running experiments is nothing new. Allegedly, the first randomized control experiment was designed by Gustav III, the King of Sweden from 1771–1792. At the time, 'stimulating drinks' were banned in Sweden. We're not talking about Red Bull or

Monster, but tea and coffee, which were extremely popular across Europe. King Gustav was convinced that caffeine was bad for his citizens' health but unsurprisingly, there was limited evidence, so the king ordered an experiment, the first randomized control trial(ish).

A pair of identical twins who had been sentenced to death were offered the chance of life in prison if they agreed to participate in an experiment. One twin had to drink three pots of coffee every day and the other twin had to drink three cups of tea every day for the rest of their lives. The twin who drank tea died aged 83, long after the King had died, and nobody knows when the second twin died. The two doctors who were asked to monitor him had died by this point.[1] While this would never meet the definition of credible research today, with its tiny sample size, this created the modern approach to research.

Appreciating the limitations of any research is vital but all too often they are overlooked. Before a marketer makes any decision based on research, they need to ensure that the study is both reliable and valid. At the most basic level, reliability is the concept that if you repeated the study, you would get the same result again, whereas validity is the extent to which you are measuring what you intended to measure. From a market research perspective, this is usually about whether your research will predict how shoppers will behave in an actual retail environment. While there is no black-and-white framework for assessing the validity of research, one of the most useful frameworks is Philip Graves' AFECT criteria. He proposed that when you're reviewing any consumer research, you should ask yourself five questions, as follows.

The AFECT criteria

1 Does the research ANALYSE behavioural data?

Self-report is the easiest and quickest type of data to collect, just asking people how they acted in the past or how they think they will behave in the future, for example, using a questionnaire, focus group or interview. But this comes with one significant drawback: people lie.

This was clearly shown when Rod Humble, a former studio head at Electronic Arts and a key figure behind the development of 'The Sims' computer game series, shared insights from a series of focus groups they conducted in the late 1990s. Unlike most games, in the Sims there wasn't a clear objective, and players created their own challenges, guiding virtual characters through 'life'. In focus groups, when young men were asked what they did in the game, they replied '*Murdered people, starved people, had sex with everybody*'. But when the developers analysed players' actual behaviour, they noticed that the same young men were far more likely to just redecorate the bathroom in their virtual house.[2] So why didn't they admit to this in the focus group? Perhaps they were embarrassed to admit it; researchers call this the *social desirability bias*.

> **KEY TERMS**
>
> Social desirability bias is the idea that in self-report research (e.g. questionnaires, focus groups or interviews) participants answer questions in a way that makes them look more favourable, over-reporting good behaviour and under-reporting undesirable behaviour. For example, if you ask participants if they flush wet wipes down the toilet, something they shouldn't do, people are likely to under-report this behaviour.

But social desirability is not the only potential issue with self-report data. Sometimes people can't remember or aren't aware of their behaviour. This is an artefact of how our memory works. When shopping, we're constantly exposed to lots of different stimuli, but we're only going to remember stimuli that are transferred from short-term to long-term memory. If we ask shoppers who recently bought toothpaste on their last shop, '*which brands of toothpaste did you consider buying on your last supermarket trip?*', the results are likely to be meaningless. Shoppers have no reason to remember which brands of toothpaste they looked at on the shelf, and this information won't be stored in long-term memory. Instead, all they'll tell you is the first brands that come to mind, which may or may not be the ones they looked at.

This is an even bigger issue when collecting data from light users, someone who shops from a category infrequently. A team of researchers from Byron Sharp's Ehrenberg-Bass Institute for Marketing led by Magda Nenycz-Thiel, has shown that when light users are asked to estimate how often they buy a product, their estimates are far more inaccurate than heavy users,[3] with light users giving an inflated estimation of how often they think they bought a product. Consequently, wherever possible, researchers should always try to collect behavioural data and not self-report.

2 Is the participant in the same FRAME OF MIND in the study as they are when they make a purchase decision?

Whenever you ask someone any questions about what products they might buy or what they think of an advert, you should make sure that they're in the same mindset as they would be when they go shopping or see the ad 'in the wild'. If you stop off to do some shopping on your way home from work, you're going to be in a completely different mindset than if you go shopping on a Saturday, and research needs to reflect this. Being stressed changes what we buy.[4]

Again, it's not a case of shoppers deliberately lying to you; often, people deceive themselves about how they are going to act in the future. Take the question '*What movie do you want to watch?*' Reed, Lowenstein and Kalyanaraman have shown that you'll get a very different answer if you ask someone '*What movie do you want to watch tonight or in two weeks' time?'*. When choosing from 24 different films, half of which the researchers classified as 'highbrow' (e.g. *Schindler's List* or Shakespeare's *Henry V*) and half were 'lowbrow' (think Four Weddings and a Funeral), 71% of people opted for a highbrow film when deciding what film they'd like to watch in two weeks' time. But if the question was '*What film do you want to watch tonight?*', now only 44% opted for the highbrow film.[5] Exactly the same pattern is found in food shopping. If people are shopping and they are asked to select what snack they'd like to eat in a week's time, 74% of people opt for something healthy like fruit. But if you're deciding what you'd like to snack on right now, only 30% of shoppers opt for something healthy.[6] If you're launching an altruistic product, just be cautious if shoppers say they'll buy it. They might be deceiving both themselves and you!

3 What ENVIRONMENT is the research conducted in?

Few businesses have access to a 'friendly' store where they can test new ideas. Even if they do, they may be reluctant to test their ideas in a public space where their rivals might see their new concepts. To get around these problems, marketers come up with all sorts of workarounds, such as creating fake research shops, running laboratory studies, or just conducting focus groups. But it doesn't matter how good a job we do, we can never fully recreate the true shopping experience, and that changes behaviour.

As we discussed in Chapter 12, shoppers are influenced by a whole range of external factors, most of which shoppers are not consciously aware of – the width of an aisle, the background music in a shop or even the size of the screen when viewing an online store. Even if we make a perfect recreation of a store, unless it's filled with other customers, has the same background noise and shoppers move around the space in the same way, it will never be a perfect recreation, and shoppers won't behave in exactly the same way.

4 Was it a COVERT study?

It may sound obvious, but people act differently when they know that they are being observed, and this creates a major problem for market research. If we're watching shoppers and they know that they are being watched, it changes how they act and what they buy. Take shopping for bleach. Commercial research conducted by Gareth Harvey in 2012 in a bricks-and-mortar store discovered that typically 70% of shoppers will buy one of the leading national brands, but when it comes to shopping online, even after controlling for socio-economic and income factors, 70% of shoppers bought an own brand product. While there will be population differences between the two groups, a big part of this can be explained by the fact that people are changing what they buy because they know people are watching (and feel like they will be judged for buying an own brand).

This is known as the *Hawthorne Effect* and was first shown in the 1920s and 30s by Elton Mayo, Fritz Roethlisberger and Thomas Whitehead. In the 1920s, companies were starting to switch to electricity to light their factories. However, businesses being businesses, they didn't want to spend more money than they needed to, so they started testing what wattage of lighting had the best impact on productivity, but without increasing their costs. Initially, each time the researchers increased the lighting intensity, the workers became more productive, a great finding for the company. But when the researchers returned the lighting to baseline, the productivity jumped again, which initially the researchers were unable to explain.[7] The final conclusion was that the effect occurred not because of a change in lighting but because the workers felt special about being observed.

Although this is a great story, and it's one academics have believed for nearly a century, it appears not to be true. In 2011, when Steven Levitt & John List from the University of Chicago found the original data and reanalysed it, they found nothing.[8] While the original study may have been flawed, it led to the creation of the human relations movement in organizational behaviour, and we now know that observing people does change behaviour. We now have a century of findings that show that if people think they're being observed, they're more likely to: comply with medical instructions, adopt eco-friendly habits[9] and, of course, change what they buy when shopping, a huge problem for predicting future behaviour.

Potentially, this is an even bigger problem from a marketing perspective than in other disciplines. As soon as shoppers are aware that they're being observed, it triggers a feeling of psychological aversion, a state similar to reactance. The result is that it changes how shoppers decide what to buy and ultimately what goes in their shopping basket. When they know they're being observed, they're far more likely to buy the default option, or even nothing at all.[10] This makes generalizing findings from this research difficult. Of course, not telling people they are being observed and that their behaviour is being recorded creates a range of legal and ethical issues.

5 Was there a TIMEFRAME?

All too often, when researchers conduct research, they ask participants to think carefully about their purchases or to give detailed feedback about a new advert. The only issue is that this isn't how people make purchase decisions or view adverts. When it comes to buying toilet roll, most people buy the same brand they usually buy or grab the first brand that looks like it will do the job. But when researchers stop to ask shoppers to explain their shopping decision, the timeframe is totally different to that split second at the fixture. Focus groups can take an hour, where participants are asked to focus on every small detail. Likewise, a questionnaire prompts shoppers to think about small details that they would never notice in a more naturalistic environment.

How important are the AFECT criteria?

The observant amongst you will have noticed that most studies described in this book wouldn't pass all of these tests. But how much of a problem is this? From a marketing perspective, few studies have systematically attempted to study the results of laboratory vs field trials, however, one of the best was conducted by Pierre Dubois and a team from the Sorbonne.[11] They wanted to understand whether food nutrition labels (see Figure 16.1) have any impact on shoppers' choices in a supermarket. However, they conducted two studies: one in a laboratory and a second conducted across 60 different supermarkets.

In the laboratory study, 691 participants were asked to do their weekly food shop from a paper-based catalogue which contained 290 products. Participants were then asked to unexpectedly do a second food shop, but this time using a different catalogue. The two catalogues were identical except that they contained one of four different nutrition labels (or no label as a control). The field experiment was far more realistic. The four label types were tested in 40 different supermarkets over a 10-week period. That's 60 different supermarkets (20 acted as a control with no labels) and 1.9 million labels were placed on 1,266 different food products. In total, they analysed the purchase behaviour of 1.6 million transactions, a huge undertaking!

Figure 16.1 A recreation of the four different types of labels used in Pierre Dubois' 2021 study

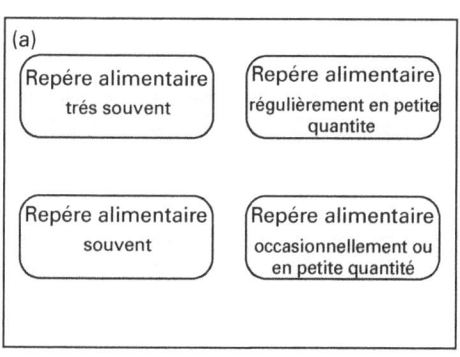

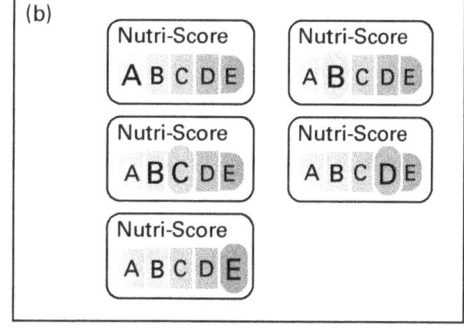

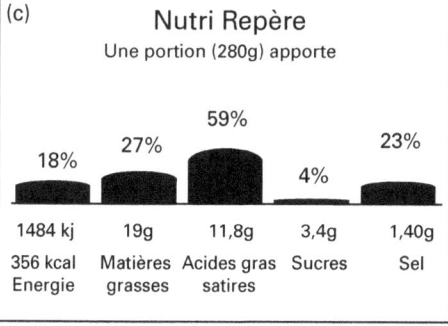

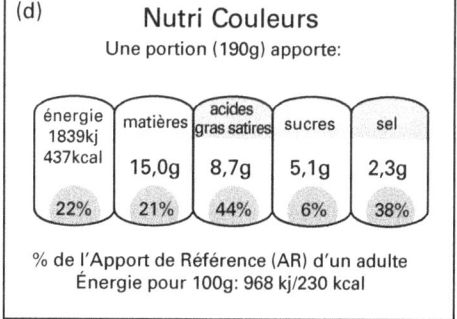

First, the good news: both studies found that the same type of nutritional label was more effective at encouraging customers to purchase healthier products, the Nutri-score label. But here is the worrying news: the difference in effect size between the two studies was massive. The impact of the labels was 17 times smaller in the supermarket than the lab-based study predicted.

From a commercial perspective, this is called a *'voltage drop'*,[12] the idea that the results of experiments often produce smaller effects than expected when rolled out at national level. This voltage drop can occur for a number of reasons, a lot of which can be explained by the AFECT criteria, but sometimes it occurs because both marketers and scientists don't understand how to interpret the results of quantitative research.

Since Ronald Fisher formalized the role of the *p*-values in 1925 and encouraged their use in experimental work, quantitative researchers, and perhaps more importantly, journal articles, have focused on them. Traditionally, if a finding isn't below the .05 criteria, the results were not publishable, although this is now starting to change. This means that researchers fail to consider other important factors, such as the effect size or confidence intervals. In very crude terms, a *p*-value answers the question 'Does the intervention work or not?', whereas an effect size answers the question 'How well does the intervention work?'. With a large enough sample size (an overpowered design), it is possible to achieve a very low *p*-value, but this will not impact the effect size. You would still have a small effect size. When it comes to deciding if a finding from a research project is worth rolling out in the commercial sector, it is more important for marketers to focus on the effect size than the *p*-value.

KEY TERMS

A *p*-value, or probability value, is a number between 0 and 1 that describes how likely it is that your data could have occurred by random chance. The smaller the *p*-value, the less likely that your results could have occurred by chance. Within psychology and business research, normally the *p*-value needs to be lower than .05 to reject the null hypothesis, but other disciplines such as environmental sciences can use a different criterion, such as .1, as their data is noisier.

P-values were never meant to be interpreted in isolation; instead, they should be viewed alongside effect sizes and confidence intervals. To get a better understanding of how to analyse quantitative data without using null hypothesis testing, check out Geoff Cummings' fantastic book *Understanding the new statistics: Effect sizes, confidence intervals, and meta-analysis.*

Secondary data: Letting other people do the work for you

Prepaid databases

When it comes to understanding how shoppers are going to behave, most marketers' first instinct is to collect their own data, referred to as 'primary data'. When you are facing a completely new problem, this is often the only option you have. But most questions that businesses face are not novel, but are exactly the same ones facing their competitors. For example, a frozen pizza manufacturer might want to know: '*What percentage of people complete their grocery shopping online?*', '*What are the best-selling frozen pizza flavours in Switzerland?*' or '*What trends are likely to happen in the marketplace in the next five years?*'.

Despite being highly sector-specific questions, there are companies, such as Statista, Mintel and Euromonitor, that continually collect data and sell it to companies to provide instant answers to questions such as these. Often, the quality of the research is also better than what businesses could conduct themselves. Take Mintel, each month they survey over 1 million consumers across 86 different countries and track 40,000 product launches. Likewise, Statista's database includes statistics and insights for over 80,000 topics from 22,500 sources in 170 industries. This secondary data (data collected by someone else, for a purpose other than the current research project) comes with a cost, but it allows marketers to make decisions quicker.

The internet: What are people searching for?

One of the biggest drawbacks with primary data is having to make sure that people are telling you the truth. However, there is one place where people are far more likely to be honest and that's the internet. If someone has an embarrassing health problem, they are far more likely to search for their symptoms online than go to the doctor (especially if they are male). When we type our symptoms into a search engine, it feels like we're anonymous and we can ask questions we'd be too embarrassed to ask anybody in person. Yet while individuals may feel anonymous, this data is kept and can provide a powerful insight into consumers' desires.

For example, if you own a ski chalet in Crans, Montana, and you're planning on refurbishing it, you could try to ask 500 skiers what facilities they want in their chalet, but this will be an expensive and time-consuming process. But by conducting a key phrase analysis, you can see almost instantly what questions people are searching for. Are more people searching for '*chalets with sauna*' or '*chalets with hot tubs*'? Likewise, are catered chalets more popular than uncatered chalets? Not only will this tell you how many people are searching for each query, but it also allows you to see how the numbers are changing over time, making it easier to spot any trends. You might be interested in how different search terms change over a quarter or an annual basis, but you can also spot changes at a daily or even hourly rate. Take the total solar eclipse that passed over the US in 2024. The number of people searching for phrases such as *'retina damage'*, *'eyes hurt'*, *'can't see'*, *'blind'* and *'eye damage'* all spiked the day after the eclipse.[13] It looks like all of those public awareness campaigns might not have been as effective as people hoped!

> **GIVE IT A GO**
>
> Although there are lots of companies that offer bespoke keyword analysis, Google offers a basic free service, Google Trends (https://trends.google.com/trends/). Choose two competing brands from the same industry and compare them using this tool. What trends emerge for each brand? In which regions are they most searched? What related search terms appear alongside your target keywords? Consider what these insights might mean for your chosen brand.

It is not just the explicit words that customers search for that are revealing. Seth Stephens-Davidowitz has shown that the way people phrase a question is key. In his 2017 book, *Everybody lies*, he describes the 2016 US presidential election between Hillary Clinton and Donald Trump. With Democrats being almost guaranteed to vote for Clinton and Republicans for Trump, it was the 'undecideds' that would determine the election, but their behaviour was the hardest to predict. Often, these members of the electorate were unsure how to vote, and they would ask questions online, such as: *'Should I vote for Trump or Hillary?'* Or *'Will Hillary or Trump make the best president?'*. Both questions seem to be asking the same thing, but the way the question was phrased strongly suggests how someone will vote. If you include both candidates' names in the question, the person you name first is the one you're most likely to vote for.[14] It's not certain why this occurs, but it could just be because that person is more salient to you.

Google (and most other platforms) not only captures the total search data but it allows you to spot patterns based on individuals' location. When you combine these two insights, researchers are able to spot patterns and trends that would otherwise be hidden. Seth Stephens-Davidowitz used this data in his paper 'The cost of racial animus on a black candidate: Evidence using Google search data' to try to answer the question of whether racism impacted the outcome of the 2012 US election between Barack Obama and Mitt Romney. This was the first time a black candidate had won the nomination of one of the major US political parties and was in the running to be president. Commentators were speculating whether racism would play a role in the election and harm Obama's chances. Unfortunately, polls were virtually meaningless in this situation because very few people would openly admit to having racist tendencies. But when Stephens-Davidowitz analysed the Google search data, he found a strong correlation between areas with a high number of racist Google searchers and areas where Obama performed worse, which couldn't be explained by any other factors. Four years later and the same trend could be seen but in reverse. This time, Trump performed far better than expected in constituencies with more racist search questions.[15]

Primary research: Collecting your own data

Quantitative vs qualitative data

Primary data can generally be placed into two categories: quantitative and qualitative. Quantitative data involves collecting data that can be counted or measured in numerical values, whereas qualitative data refers to non-numerical data. While psychologists have traditionally focused on quantitative research, it is important for market researchers not to overlook qualitative data. Qualitative data can provide a richness that quantitative data frequently overlooks, helping marketers understand the nuances, complexities and context that underpins behaviour, generally collected using methods such as focus groups and unstructured interviews.

The objective of qualitative and quantitative research differs significantly. Quantitative research aims to capture numerical data and ensures the results can be generalized to a wider population. Whereas qualitative data aims to acquire a deeper, richer understanding of human behaviour, but the results don't need to generalize. With qualitative data, you are collecting data from a very small sample to ensure that you have the richness. It allows you to test concepts relatively quickly with a small sample. However, to ensure the findings can be generalized to the target population, marketers will develop an idea from the qualitative research (aka, a hypothesis) and test if it applies to a wider population using quantitative research.

Qualitative data is often seen as a simpler approach to collecting data because it doesn't rely on any 'scary' statistics. But this doesn't mean collecting high-quality qualitative data is easy and in many ways it's much harder. With quantitative data, there is a 'right' answer, normally determined by probability and statistics, but with qualitative data, it is more subjective and researchers need to make sure they overcome several psychological challenges.

Qualitative research

Focus groups

Focus groups typically involve bringing together between six and ten people, where a trained moderator will ask a series of open-ended questions to the group. The idea is that one person will say something, and this will trigger other group members to respond, which leads to a more organic discussion. Group members might agree with the first statement, fervently disagree or just add in extra caveats. This can lead researchers to discover far more than if they just interviewed one participant alone. But the role of the moderator shouldn't be overlooked. They don't simply read out the questions from the interview and sit back; they need to make sure that everybody in the group gets a chance to speak. Make sure that nobody dominates the conversation, and that the discussion doesn't go off topic. This means that the moderator is a full-time role, and they can't take notes. Instead, they are normally supported by a note taker who records what is said and by whom, even if the session is recorded.

Yet care needs to be taken when it comes to interpreting the results of focus groups. Individuals might start off with a relatively weak view, but the process of a focus group can give the illusion that their views are far stronger than they are.[16] For example, if you asked a group if they preferred 'logo A' or 'logo B', one participant might prefer the first option, but they don't have a particularly strong view about it, while the rest of the group prefers the second logo. As the group starts to discuss the two logos, the participant who preferred the first option feels like they have to 'defend' their position and it can make them appear to be more entrenched in their viewpoint.

A similar risk is that the moderator can inadvertently lead participants, creating the impression that they have stronger views. As Philip Graves describes, a successful moderator needs to relax participants and encourage them to open up. They do this in both their words and body language. Graves argues that when a moderator asks a question, they typically adopt a bouncy tone (which makes people like them) and raise their voice at the end of a sentence. As a participant answers, they'll make sure they're nodding their head, smile, lean in and make receptive noises. As participants like the moderator, they want to please them and try to tell them what they want to hear, or at least talk more than they intend to, as it pleases the moderator.[17]

From a psychological perspective, focus groups can also be prone to the effects of social conformity. As we've shown in other chapters, these are one of the most powerful tools in a marketer's arsenal. They use phrases such as *'our best-selling product'*, *'join millions who trust Brand X'* or *'see why thousands have switched to Brand X'* to make purchase decisions feel less risky. However, if the first six members of a focus group all express the same opinion, it means that the last two are more likely to claim they agree with the group, even if they don't, just to fit in with the group.

Figure 16.2 Example stimuli used in Solomon Asch's 1956 social conformity experiment

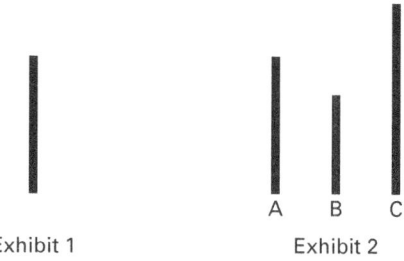

For example, in one focus group, Solomon Asch showed participants three lines of varying length. Next, participants were shown a second line and asked to decide if this line was the same length as line A, B or C (see Figure 16.2). The correct answer was obvious and participants were free to go back and compare. Nobody should get this task wrong. However, the first seven group members were all working with the experimenter and on a number of questions, they all deliberately said the wrong answer. When this happened, the real participant agreed with group's decision 37% of the time. In fact, over the course of the experiment, 75% of participants went against their own eyes at least once and intentionally got a question wrong because that's what everybody else had said.[18]

Interviews

Unlike focus groups, which involve talking to six or eight individuals simultaneously, an interview is a detailed conversation with one person. This means that researchers can avoid the group dynamics associated with a focus group and interviewees may be happier to open up in a one-on-one situation, especially if discussing a sensitive topic. But you don't have to be discussing sensitive topics to benefit from a one-on-one situation. Some people just don't feel confident admitting controversial opinions in a group context. It also means that the researcher is free to ask more in-depth questions and really drill down on a topic that interests them. This is especially useful if the person you are interviewing is an expert in a specific topic and you want to explore their knowledge.

Typically, interviews can be one of three different types. There are structured interviews, where questions are asked without deviating from the script. In many ways, this is no different to someone reading out a questionnaire. There are semi-structured questionnaires, where there is a list of questions to start with, but if the interviewee says something interesting, the interviewer can ask follow-up questions, providing more flexibility. Finally, there are unstructured interviews with a minimal number of questions, more like an informal conversation. This gives a lot more flexibility but can make transcribing and analysing the data much harder (and time consuming), with a one-hour interview typically taking about 6–7 hours to properly transcribe and code.[19]

Quantitative data

Questionnaires

How should participants answer a question? When it comes to collecting quantitative data, perhaps the easiest way to do it is by using a questionnaire. Rather than trying to create your own scale from scratch and having to ensure that it produces both reliable and valid data, it is often easier to use a scale that has already been developed, especially if you are using a standardized metric such as brand personality, purchase intention or customer satisfaction. The Marketing Scales Handbook Vols. 1–12 contain nearly 5,000 of the most popularly used questionnaires.[20]

Although it may seem very easy to throw together a few questions using an online questionnaire platform, how you phrase your questions, and just as importantly, how you get respondents to answer, can dramatically change the answers you get. One of the most popular question types is a Likert Scale. Originally developed by Rensis Likert in 1932,[21] participants are asked a question and they respond on a balanced scale, originally: strongly agree, agree, undecided, disagree and strongly disagree, although there are lots of variations on this theme. But again, researchers disagree on how to use them. Rather than using five-scale options, some opt for seven-, nine- or even eleven-scale options, arguing that the more options you have, the more precise an answer you get. So, what's best?

The fewer options a participant has to choose from, the less precise their answer is, but this is only true up to six options. According to research by Leonard Simms and colleagues, above six options there is no meaningful difference in the way participants respond[22] and to some extent, it may confuse participants. Can they realistically understand a difference between agree, strongly agree and very strongly agree? Even if they can understand the difference, they're more likely to get frustrated completing the questionnaire, so they may give up. This suggests that six (or seven if you want to include a middle option) are an appropriate length. But should you include a middle option? While most marketing scales do, it is probably best not to,[23] although the difference it makes is so small that it probably does not make much difference in reality.[24]

While Likert scales are popular, they're not the only option available. Online platforms such as Gorilla, Qualtrics or SurveyMonkey give you the option of using lots of different formats of questions. If you want to understand how much people will pay for your product, you could ask the question directly, but you then need to decide how people answer. You could use a simple free response box, where participants can type any number they like. A visual analogue scale is another option, where participants are presented with a sliding scale ranging from two numbers and they drag a bar to how much they're willing to pay for the item. Or you could provide them with predetermined options (e.g. CHF 5 – CHF 10, CHF 11 – CHF 25).

If you use a visual analogue scale, this causes people to base their decision on both ends of the scale. They look at the high number and it acts as an anchor, influencing or priming them as to how much they claim they would be willing to spend. However, if you just use a free response box, it causes people to only focus on the lower point. As a result, Tjomas and Kyung have shown that participants estimate that they are willing to spend more when using a sliding scale than versus a textbox.[25] Likewise, if you include option boxes at the top end of the scale that nobody would ever consider paying for your product, just to cover all options, it still has an anchoring effect and inflates the amount participants claim they will pay.

But priming (as described in Chapter 12) is not only likely to happen based on the way participants respond. It is also a risk based on how the question is phrased, or the order in which you ask the questions. If you were writing a questionnaire to measure participants' attitudes towards the building of a new wind farm in their local area, which included the question '*Do you support the building of the new wind farm in your local area?*', participants' responses would differ depending on the questions you ask before it.

For example, if the questionnaire read: (1) Do you appreciate nature?; (2) Do you believe in man-made climate change?; (3) Are you in favour of initiatives that promote sustainability and clean energy solutions?; (4) Do you support the building of the new wind farm in your local area?, participants are far more likely to agree than if you just ask them the last question on its own. This is because each question primes the participant to think about the next question, making it more likely that you'll agree. If you believe in man-made climate change, you will appear to be a hypocrite if you didn't support initiatives that promote sustainability and clean energy. Likewise, if you support initiatives promoting clean energy, then why wouldn't you support the building of a wind farm in your local area?

And if you don't think carefully about how you phrase the question, you can inadvertently influence your participants' responses. For example, research by the UK's Electoral Commission has shown that if a question starts with 'Do you agree', participants are 12% more likely to agree with the statement.[26] The two questions: '*Do you agree that Switzerland has the best skiing in Europe?*' and '*Does Switzerland have the best skiing in Europe?*' are asking for the same information, but based on this research, you are going to get two different answers. The words 'Do you agree' don't contain any useful information, but frame the question, putting it in a positive light, giving the impression that you are meant to agree with it. This is what is known as an acquiescence bias, where participants have a tendency to select the positive response option.

Sampling and sample sizes   In an ideal world, researchers want to know the views of the entire population, from a research perspective, what is referred to as a census, but even for the largest companies in the world, this is neither feasible nor viable. You can't create a questionnaire and get everybody in the country to complete it. For example, the 2021 UK census cost £900 million and even then, a number of people avoided completing it. Instead, companies collect data from a small number of people, known as a sample. Ideally, this sample should be representative of your target population. This means that if your target population is 50% female and 80% of your customers are over 60, your sample should have these characteristics as well, otherwise the results won't represent your target market.

REAL-WORLD EXAMPLE: PSYCH IN ACTION

Interpreting results from a sample that isn't representative can lead to flawed decision-making. Take the first ever US presidential TV debate in 1960 between Nixon and Kennedy. It is widely cited that if you listened to the debate on the radio, you thought that Nixon won the debate, but if you actually watched it on TV, you are more likely to think that Kennedy won the debate. Kennedy looked more relaxed and composed in front of the camera. He knew to wear a small amount of make-up so that the cameras picked up his complexion, and all of this helped to convince voters. And this ushered in a new era of politics, where style is more important than substance; how you look is more important than what you say.

But despite being widely cited, this is more likely down to who listened to the debate vs who watched it. At the time, Republican voters were more likely to be listening on the radio whereas Democrats were watching on TV. Consequently, it's not that style dominated on TV and arguments worked on radio, but that voters thought that their preferred candidate won the debate.[27]

Likewise, consider how the average finishing time for UK ParkRuns has changed over the years. ParkRun is a free 5km fun run that takes place at local parks every Saturday at 9am. The first UK ParkRun happened in 2004 and, by 2005, the average finishing time was 22:17. But by 2023, the average finishing time was over 32 minutes.[28] This doesn't mean that over the course of 19 years the average runner has become nearly 45% slower, it just shows that the sort of people entering ParkRun has changed. In 2005, only serious runners entered ParkRun, whereas today virtually everybody enters – including people who just want to walk it. It just highlights that researchers need to really consider who they are speaking to before making big decisions.

Unfortunately, if you are only speaking to a small sample of the population, there is a risk that their responses are not representative of the target audience, what is known as the sampling error. However, the more people who are sampled, the smaller this error becomes. So, if you have a confidence interval of 95%, and you collect data from 100 people, the margin of error is 10%. In practice, this means that if your research shows that 54% of people prefer product B, you can say that the actual percentage of the total population who prefer the product will be between 44% and 64%, 95 times out of 100. For many marketers, there is just too much variability in this estimate to reach a sensible decision. As such, they need to increase the sample size to reduce the margin of error. A sample size of 1,000 participants gives an error rate of 3% (aka we know the mean is between 51% and 57%), or a sample size of 2,000 gives a mean of 2% (52%–56%) (see Figure 16.3).

Of course, there is always a trade-off with cost. As your sample size increases, your sampling error decreases, but your costs increase. However, this is not a linear relationship, and costs will increase a lot quicker than the sample error will decrease. As a result, most commercial research projects tend to opt for a sample size of between 500–1,000, which offers the best trade-off between cost and accuracy. But it's worth remembering that it doesn't matter how good your sampling method is – if your questionnaire or experiment is poorly designed, then the results will be meaningless. A team of researchers led by Valerie Bradley has shown that a poorly designed survey of 250,000 participants can produce a result that is no more accurate than an estimate from a simple random sample of 10.[29]

A sample size of 500–1,000 participants may sound challenging to recruit, especially for small businesses who are looking to recruit participants from a specific demographic or a representative sample from across a country. In the past, marketers would use specialist recruitment agencies who can virtually recruit any participant group for the right money. If you need to speak to 500 experienced vets, there are agencies that can arrange this, although you may be paying more than £20,000. But in recent years, marketers have more options. New companies such as Amazon's Mechanical Turk (mTurk) and Prolific mean that marketers can recruit participants to complete online studies far cheaper than before. Assuming you want a representative sample from the UK and your questionnaire takes 10 minutes to complete, using Prolific, you will only have to pay about £1.50 per participant, plus a 20% admin fee in 2025. What's more, it is possible to recruit 2,500 participants in just a couple of hours.

List experiments

Questionnaires may be quick and cheap, but it's hard to overcome the fact that participants can and do lie, even if you tell them that their responses will remain anonymous. While you could use an Implicit Association Test or EAST task to measure implicit attitudes (see Chapter 7), both these techniques require specialist software and complex data analysis, which makes them expensive to run. A much cheaper, simpler and easier approach overall is a list experiment.

Figure 16.3 Sampling error estimates for various sample sizes drawn from a population of 70,000,000, calculated using both a 95% and 99% confidence intervals

	Confidence Interval	
Sample Size	95%	99%
10	31%	41%
20	22%	29%
30	18%	24%
50	14%	18%
75	11%	15%
100	10%	13%
200	7%	9%
300	6%	7%
400	5%	6%
500	4%	6%
600	4%	5%
700	4%	5%
800	3%	5%
900	3%	4%
1,000	3%	4%
2,000	2%	3%
3,000	2%	2%
5,000	1%	2%
7,500	1%	1%

A list experiment indirectly measures participants' attitudes, guaranteeing complete privacy as participants are never asked to explicitly share their opinion about any one statement or topic. Instead, they read a list of four statements about four different topics and are asked how many of these statements they agree with. For example, if a sex shop wanted to know how many females had bought a sex toy, participants could be presented with a list of four statements: *(a) I support a football team; (b) I think the government should reinstate the death penalty; (c) Membership of the European Union is a good thing; (d) I have bought a sex toy in the past.*

However, researchers can identify how many people agreed with the last response because they produce two versions of the questionnaire, one which includes the target statement (the veiled response) and one that doesn't. These two questionnaires are completed by different people, and by comparing the average count of items in the direct response condition to the veiled response condition, you can estimate the sensitive behaviour.

It's unsurprising that list experiments are becoming increasingly popular, but there are some drawbacks. Firstly, they require a much larger sample size than a traditional questionnaire.[30] In order to make a comparison between the two conditions, your sample size needs to be big enough that your margin for error for your control questions is relatively small. In other words, you need to ask enough people so that the average response is consistent. This probably means that you need a sample size of 400+ participants to complete each questionnaire, meaning you'll need a sample of 800+ participants.

Experiments

What are experiments? Rather than asking people what they might do in a given situation, it's always better to watch what people really do, and this is where experiments come in. When most people think of an experiment, they think back to chemistry lessons at school. But experiments are at the heart of consumer psychology as they are the only way that allows us to answer the question, 'Does changing an independent variable result in changes to the dependent variable when keeping all other things constant?'. Or, to put it in simple language, if you change one thing (the independent variable) and keep everything else the same, does it affect something else (the dependent variable)?

Experiments are at the heart of both academic and commercial research, although in industry, they are often referred to as A/B testing. Netflix's internal data shows that if a viewer doesn't start watching something within 90 seconds of logging on, they probably won't watch anything. And when it comes down to what we watch, the movie thumbnail is critical. As a result, Netflix wants to make sure that they show viewers the most appealing image. However, each film will supply hundreds of different pictures and they will test which images are the most effective (for each individual viewer). Their data showed some surprising results: generally the most successful film thumbnails were (a) close-up images of faces with a strong emotional expression; (b) photos of the film's villains rather than the heroes; (c) photos that include a smaller number of cast members.[31]

The most successful e-retailers will be running potentially thousands of experiments a year. With potentially tens of thousands of people visiting their website every day, they can constantly make small changes and test what works best to optimize the website. From changing the product's price, to even something as simple as the colour or location of a call-to-action button. And even if you don't have your own website but sell via websites such as Amazon, they have their own experiment facility allowing marketers to test how changes to the (a) main product image, (b) product titles, (c) product description and (d) bullet points have on sales.

If you've decided that you don't want to sell on Amazon or you simply don't have enough traffic to your website to run an online experiment, you may want to create a replica of your online shop using a specialist experimental platform like Gorilla ShopBuilder where you can mimic your shop and test 'wild' ideas without it negatively impacting your customers. However, it is important to note that experiments are not just restricted to e-commerce, but that it is easier (and cheaper) to run experiments online than in store. Just remember the results of what works online will not automatically carry over to a physical store.

Experimental design: Making your experiments work   In practice, there are two main ways you can design your experiment. You can assign participants to different groups where they are exposed to a different intervention, and you then compare their behaviour. For example, you could launch a new packaging design at supermarket A and a different design in supermarket B and see which one sells best, referred to as a '*between-subject design*'. The alternative is a '*within-subject design*', whereby the same participants see both interventions. For example, if a company has developed two new adverts for social media, both versions of the new advert could be posted on the same person's timeline, and you could see which one gets the highest engagement.

Neither is better or worse than the other, it just depends on the situation. Within-subject experiments require you to test fewer people and will reduce the background noise in your data. But it will result in a longer experiment and can be more complex to set up. Sometimes, a within-subject design will not even be feasible. For example, if you wanted to try and persuade someone to buy a new car, is it best to lead with argument A and then B, or should you start with argument B first? This could only be tested using a between-subject design, as once a participant had already heard argument A first, you could never assign them to the second condition as they'd already heard argument A first.

To be a 'true experiment', participants need to be randomly assigned to a condition. While this is easy to achieve in a laboratory-based experiment or on an e-commerce platform, it makes it slightly more difficult in a retail context. If you are launching a new packaging concept at supermarket A and keep the old design at supermarket B, you can't control which store people shop at. Consequently, this is referred to as a '*quasi-experiment*'. Although the results might be slightly weaker as you don't know if you can directly compare your true groups (do more affluent shoppers shop at store A vs store B?), from a business perspective, this is normally good enough.

Conjoint analysis   One of the most frequent briefs market researchers are tasked with is to find out what features customers want and value in a new product. Would a cheaper, more basic product be more attractive or would shoppers prefer a product with more features that costs more? While you could attempt to answer this with a questionnaire, a more sophisticated, precise and accurate method is a conjoint analysis.[32] As such, it has become one of the most popular quantitative techniques used within market research,[33] especially amongst large companies.

A conjoint analysis is a very specific type of experiment which attempts to mimic the trade-offs that shoppers have to make when shopping. For example, if you want to understand how a shopper decides which wine to purchase, you need to first identify the different attributes the shoppers could use to make a decision and then work out what levels there are. For example, you might identify the following features and levels (Table 16.1).

Specialist software (for example, Sawtooth or Conjointly) will create different product combinations and will show participants four different products (with a mix of attributes) and participants are asked to decide which of the four products they would buy, in this case, which wine. Participants will then go through this pro-

Table 16.1   Example of the different attributes that could be used in a conjoint analysis

Colour	Country	Variety	Picture	Price
Red	France	Merlot	No Picture	£5 – £7
White	Switzerland	Chasselas	B&W Picture	£8 – £10
Rosé	Italy	Riesling	Colour Picture	£11 – £14
	Germany	Zinfandel		£15 – 18
	Australia	Malbec		£19 – £22
	US	Barbera		£23 – £25

cess, somewhere between 8 and 20 trials (the more levels, the more trials there will be), with each trial asking participants to make a choice between four different products, with a different mix of features. After this is completed, the software will consider the options chosen (and what was rejected and can calculate which attributes have the biggest impact on participants' purchase decision. So, do shoppers make a purchase by focusing on price and colour most or is the picture on the label more important?

Watching people shop

For security reasons, most large shops will use a CCTV (Closed-Circuit Television) system to deter and help prosecute shoplifters. But like most facets of life, the way CCTV works has changed. It no longer records a video feed of what happens in-store to a video or DVD, but this data is now captured straight onto a hard drive. As this data is now digital, it can be analysed by algorithms to produce heatmaps.

At the most basic levels, these heatmaps produce a map that highlights which areas of the store have the most customers on average. Whereas the more sophisticated systems take this a step further; rather than just producing a static heatmap, they allow you to physically track how shoppers move around the shop. They'll let you know how long shoppers spend in each area of the store, on average, where they go next, and in some cases, even if the shopper is alone or with somebody else.

Whether this is primary or secondary data can get a little blurry. If the CCTV is installed primarily to catch shoplifters, it would be secondary data, but if the system was installed as a dedicated data collection tool, it would be primary data. Yet from a practical perspective, this classification is irrelevant; what is important is the data it captures.

This approach is not only limited to understanding how shoppers move around a complete store, but a variation can be used to understand the effectiveness of specific Point of Sale (PoS) displays. Rather than using CCTV cameras, the PoS or advert will have a small HD webcam built into the display. These cameras can then track: (a) how many people walked past your advert but didn't look at it; (b) the number of people who looked at the advert; and (c) how long they looked at it for. And by combining these metrics, you can easily calculate how effective the ad was at capturing attention, or compare two different campaigns and work out which one was the most effective. The most advanced systems on the market will take this one step further and can even provide some 'basic' demographic data about who is looking at the display. As of 2024, most systems can just detect if an individual is male or female, and whether the viewer is under 18, between 18–65 or over 65.

Businesses might be nervous about using video footage as data captured by CCTV falls under 'personal data' under Article 4 of the General Data Protection Act 2018.[34] However, the data captured by many of these systems gets around this problem as it does not record any video or photographic footage. Instead, the system codes the data and just records data such as: Sex: Male, Age: 18–64, Dwell time: 5,000ms, Viewing time: 2,200ms. Even if a crime occurred directly in front of the camera and the police wanted to see the footage, there would be no footage to view.

Simulated shops

Observational data is exceptionally powerful, but you can only observe people in an environment that is already created. Previously, if a retailer was considering redesigning a section of a store, they would create photos that mock up the section and ask shoppers what they would buy. Now, with new advances in virtual reality, retailers can mock up shops and ask participants to wear VR glasses, and it will provide an immersive shopping experience. Shoppers are transported to an exact replica of an existing shop or a proposed store and they are free to walk around as they please. Cameras and sensors track their movement and what they are looking at, and their view changes instantly, making it feel like they really are in their local supermarket. If a retailer is interested in understanding what impact a new colour scheme or a lower ceiling will have, they just need to change the code and instantly the store looks different. They can then watch how shoppers' behaviour changes. To make the system feel even more realistic, the more advanced systems require participants to wear gloves so that they can pick up virtual products off the shelf and even push a physical trolley around.

While these systems don't perfectly replicate observing shoppers in a real store, they currently provide the best substitute. Research led by Erica van Herpen in 2016 has shown that in these VR shops, shoppers act in a similar way as they would were they in a real store; spending a similar amount of money, buying the same products and the impact of merchandising even acts in the same way[35] (e.g. people are more likely to buy the products at eye level and not on the bottom shelf).

Unfortunately, this does come with a cost. In 2025, the hardware will typically cost over £150,000 and then there are the development costs, with it easily costing over £100,000 to design a virtual store. If you want shoppers to interact with individual products, that's going to cost a minimum of £25,000 per bay. But even if you use the latest system, not everybody will be able to use it, as currently about 10–20% of all participants will experience some form of motion sickness and this experience gets worse the longer the study lasts, especially if you go over the 10-minute mark,[36] which is a big issue for simulated shopping tasks.

If a £200,000+ investment is beyond your budget, an alternative is to use a 'navigation simulator'. Platforms such as Gorilla allow marketers to upload detailed photos of a shop, and it turns it into a platform that participants can explore on a computer, just as if they were walking around a city using Google Street View. While navigation simulators may not provide the same immersive experience as augmented reality, these platforms are designed for running an experiment. If a marketer was thinking of installing a new PoS into a store but was unsure which design to use, they can upload two different concepts into Gorilla and see which PoS captures shoppers' attention the best and leads to higher sales. What's more, there is a huge cost saving when compared to AI. 'Navigation Simulators', such as Gorilla, will cost less than £10,000 a year for a commercial license.

For further details of how this works in practice, view https://gorilla.sc/shop-builder

Eye-tracking

When it comes to developing a new advert, website or product packaging, marketers want to know exactly where shoppers are looking when they make a purchase decision. Shoppers may claim that price is the biggest influence on what they buy, but if we know they don't look at the price at all, how can it be? You can write the most beautiful and engaging copy, but if people aren't reading it, then it's not effective. And this is where eye-tracking comes in.

Eye-tracking can work in one of two ways. It can either be '*stationary eye-tracking*', where participants look at images presented on a computer screen and their eye movement is tracked, or it can be '*mobile*', where participants wear a pair of glasses, walk around freely and the glasses record where they look. From a technical perspective, both approaches work using a similar basic principle but the way it's implemented differs.

When using a static eye-tracker, traditionally, a bar is installed underneath a computer monitor that contains at least two small infrared cameras. A small beam of light shines onto the participants' faces and this light reflects off the participants' pupils back to the camera. Via a process of triangulation, the software can then work out exactly where you are looking on the screen. However, as everybody's eyes are positioned slightly differently, before the experiment starts, participants will have to look at a number of small dots on the edge of the screen to calibrate the algorithm. With mobile eye-tracking, participants wear a pair of glasses that include two cameras, one infrared and one normal. Again, the infrared camera points at a pupil, whereas the other camera records what people are looking at and the software can calculate where a participant is looking.

Regardless of the system used, they both provide similar but not identical output. Within marketing, most clients focus on the heatmap. This is a visual summary of where all participants are looking. The areas where most people look will be a warmer colour and the areas that nobody focuses on will be transparent. This allows marketers to quickly glance at the heatmap and see that although most shoppers are attracted to the brand name, virtually nobody notices the special offer, suggesting that the PoS should be redesigned. However, if you are using a mobile eye-tracker, it is difficult and time-consuming to produce a heatmap. Even if all participants walk around a store following the same route, different shoppers will be looking at different factors, which creates challenges.

To overcome this, marketers define specific areas that they are interested in, what they refer to as '*Areas of Interest*' (AOI). With static eye-tracking, this process is very easy. Researchers simply draw a shape on the screen and define it as the AOI. For example, if researchers wanted to know what features attracted shoppers' attention to a newspaper, the AOI might represent the newspaper headline, the newspaper brand name, the image on the front cover or the price. Researchers don't need to specify just one AOI but all of these areas could be considered different ones. For mobile eye-trackers, the process can be a little trickier. If you are only interested in a relatively small area of a supermarket shelf, some systems allow you to affix infrared sensors around this area. This means that whenever a shopper automatically looks in this area, the system automatically codes it.

When it comes to AOI, marketers are normally interested in four key scores:

- *Eyeball count:* the total number of people who at some point in the study look at least once in the AOI
- *Time to First Fixation (TTFF):* how long it takes from the start of the study for people to first look at the AOI
- *First Fixation Duration (FFD):* how long someone spends looking at the AOI for the first time before looking away
- *Total Fixation Duration (TFD):* how long someone spends looking at the AOI for the whole duration of the study

However, some of the newer systems not only measure where you look but they also measure to what extent your pupils dilate (the extent to which your pupils get bigger or smaller). Most people are aware that your pupils contract in bright light and expand when it's dark, but they also change for two other reasons: cognitive load and arousal. When we are completing a more difficult task and our brains are having to work harder, our pupils dilate[37] (get bigger), and likewise the more aroused we are, the more they dilate.[38] While this sounds like a highly powerful tool, using it in practice is very challenging. Once again, it is almost impossible to use with mobile eye-tracking as minor changes in lighting will cause shoppers' pupils to dilate or contract. And even when it comes to using on-screen eye-tracking, it is only really capable of being used with static images. Just think about when you are on a Zoom call and somebody starts to browse the internet within your network – you can tell by the brightness of the screen changing, and this is enough to cause the size of the user's pupils to change.

Whether you choose to use a static or mobile system will come down to your individual research question, but both have pros and cons. A mobile system is more flexible, allowing researchers to test content in any environment. But this flexibility comes with a cost. A mobile eye-tracking unit typically costs four to five times the price of a desktop approach. Secondly, analysing the data from a mobile eye-tracker is a lot more complex and time-consuming. Consequently, if you just want to test an early-stage concept or a website, a static eye-tracker is perfect. However, if you want to see how your new marketing intervention works in a real retail setting, mobile eye-tracking is the only option.

However, in the last couple of years, marketers have had a third option, AI. Rather than collecting primary data, new computer software simulates where participants will look at a stimuli. This works because psychologists have spent the last 50 years understanding what factors capture attention. Companies such as Neurons have tested 250,000 participants using traditional eye-tracking to create statistical models that 'learn' how people look at adverts, packaging and websites. The result is an algorithm which they believe can predict with 95% accuracy the results of a traditional eye-tracking in a matter of seconds. What's more, the cost of this software is very cheap when compared to any traditional form of eye-tracking. Marketers just need to remember the results are predictions and not actual data, but for many marketing decisions, that is good enough.

Store loyalty cards

Virtually all retailers, whether large or small, will use a stock management system, allowing them to track products and work out what gets sold. While this system lets retailers know how many units are sold on any day, and how many SKUs are bought by each shopper, it doesn't let retailers match up what shoppers bought on different trips. This is essential for retailers as if they can track exactly what people buy, how much they spend and when, retailers can build up highly detailed psychological profiles.[39]

But this all changed in 1995 when Tesco launched the first loyalty card in the UK. For the first time, retailers could track exactly what shoppers were buying over time and spot patterns. They could notice if a shopper bought a bottle of ketchup every three months, and then two months after their last purchase, they could send out a 15% discount on their next bottle of ketchup. It may be a small discount, but it increases the likelihood that a shopper will do their 'big shop' at that supermarket. Likewise, if a supermarket is launching a new upmarket product, they might send an email out to shoppers who buy artisan breads and cheese, premium cuts of meats and expensive wines, as they know the new product will appeal to them. But loyalty card data can spot far more sophisticated patterns.

For example, Target's loyalty card (a leading US hypermarket) 'Pole' was able to identify when a woman realized they were pregnant, but what's more they could calculate the approximate due date. The algorithm identified 25 products that women would either start buying or stop buying, once they discovered the big news. Some of these changes are obvious, such as stopping buying alcohol, but others are more surprising. If a 23-year-old women in March suddenly started buying, cocoa-butter, a handbag big enough to double as a nappy bag, zinc and magnesium supplement and a bright blue rug, Pole would suggest there is an 87% chance she's pregnant.[40]

Most of the time, what we buy is primarily explained by habits rather than any marketing intervention. The only time we change what we buy is if our usual product is out of stock, we change jobs, so we start shopping in a different store, or a major life-changing event, like pregnancy.

How far you take this pattern-marking approach is limited by data, scientists' imagination and new data protection regulation (e.g. GDPR). Rather than trying to identify if a customer is pregnant, the same approach can be used to spot if a shopper has a serious health condition, even before the customer is aware of it. One of the many reasons that it's so deadly is the fact that a lot of people notice the early symptoms but think they're benign and ignore them for months. With ovarian cancer, the early symptoms are: (a) feeling constantly bloated, (b) a swollen tummy, (c) discomfort in your tummy or pelvic area, (d) feeling full quickly when eating, (e) needing to urinate more often than usual. On average, people notice these symptoms and treat them with over-the-counter treatments for four and a half months before they visit a doctor.

But when a team of researchers from Imperial College London led by Hannah Brewer analysed customers' loyalty card data and looked to see when female shoppers started continually purchasing painkillers and indigestion treatments such as antacids, they discovered that they were significantly more likely to be diagnosed with ovarian cancer. The exciting development is that researchers were able to spot these shifts in buying behaviour eight months before they were formally diagnosed with cancer.[41] The challenge is working out how this type of information can be used without unduly worrying shoppers (as the risk of false-positives is high) or breaching data protection laws.

Neuromarketing

As stated in the introduction, 20 years ago, if you asked a marketer what neuromarketing is, it's likely that they would not have had a clue. Today, it is a term that most marketers will have heard, even if they are not certain how to define it. This confusion is understandable as the terms 'neuromarketing', 'consumer neuroscience' and 'consumer psychology' are often used interchangeably, even though originally they each had quite clear definitions.

So, what is neuromarketing? We first need to understand the difference between neuroscience and psychology. At the simplest level, psychology is the study of the mind, whereas neuroscience is the study of the brain. Initially, this appears to be just semantics. After all, colloquially, people frequently use the two terms interchangeably but when you dig a little deeper, the differences become quite important.

Psychology is the study of human behaviour and all the mental and cognitive processes that lead to behaviour, meaning that psychologists study topics such as thoughts, feelings, desires and decision-making. They may not be interested in the brain structures that are activated while people make a decision, but it does not mean the insights are any less powerful.

In contrast, neuroscience focuses on the biological and chemical processes in both our brain and nervous system. Neuroscientists focus less on behaviour and are more interested in understanding how our brain works at a base level. To answer these questions, they rely on tools such as the electroencephalogram (EEG), functional magnetic resonance imaging (fMRI), magnetoencephalography (MEG) and transcranial magnetic stimulation (TMS). Therefore, and as Babiloni defines it, neuromarketing is using techniques from neuroscience to explore how people think, feel and make decisions when they are buying, selling or interacting in a marketplace.[42] This means that neuromarketing studies also depend on EEG, fMRI or other similar tools. If researchers want to avoid explicitly asking shoppers what they think of an experiment, but understand how it impacts them, they will need to use some form of neuromarketing technique.

Measuring arousal: Electrodermal activity or Galvanic Skin Response When it comes to developing a new advert or even a supermarket layout, marketers want to understand how it makes shoppers feel. What emotions does it trigger and how strong are these emotions? Typically, these are measured using Mehrabian and Russell's Pleasure, Arousal, Dominance (PAD) framework. But rather than asking people for their subjective opinions, marketers prefer to objectively measure things, and this is where Electrodermal Activity (EDA) or Galvanic Skin Response (GSR) comes in (both terms mean the same, although EDA tends to be used more than GSR). Although EDA doesn't measure 'pleasure' or 'dominance', it gives us an objective measure of arousal.

Whenever someone sees something that excites them, they start to sweat slightly, especially in the palms of their hands, the soles of their feet and armpits. Hence, if someone is watching a horror movie or if you're scared of heights and you stand next to a big drop, you might notice that you start to get clammy hands. Most of the time, we're completely unaware of these changes as they're too small to notice. Yet our bodies trigger this reaction and an EDA device picks up these changes. These devices look like a small smartwatch that participants typically wear on their wrists or ankles. They contain two small electrodes located about 1cm apart. A very weak current passes between the two electrodes and as water conducts electricity better than our skin, resistance between the two sensors drops.

EDA will give you an objective number, but it is important to remember that these numbers are all relative, meaning you can't compare the EDA scores from one participant to the next. One person might naturally sweat more than someone else, giving them a higher score. Consequently, the more important metric is the relative change from baseline. Likewise, it's also important to remember that if we see something that excites us, it doesn't produce an instant reaction. There is always going to be a delay between a change in the stimulus and the participants' EDA reacting, as much as 1–3 seconds,[43] which can make identifying the cause of any change slightly tricky. Likewise, once someone starts to sweat, this sweat doesn't instantly evaporate. This means that once the sensor has recorded an increase in GSR, there will be a delay in going back to baseline.

This may make it sound like EDA is a flawed measure but it is growing in popularity in commercial research.[44] Firstly, it's one of the cheapest techniques to capture physiological data, with sensors ranging from £30 up to a few thousand. With most neuromarketing approaches costing from £10,000 to over a million for fMRI, EDA looks like a bargain. Next, unlike a questionnaire or any self-report measure, it provides a continual measure of a participant's emotional state, which is vital but hard to get. Finally, as it automatically captures how a participant reacts physiologically, it gets around the issue of participants lying or not even being aware of how they feel.[45]

Some companies have tried to get creative with their EDA sensors. Rather than asking participants to wear a device, they have built the sensor into the handle of shopping trolleys (a little like heart rate monitors in gym machines). While this may sound like a good idea, in practice the results are questionable. These devices are capable of picking up very subtle changes and if someone is walking around the supermarket, that's enough to throw the results off (and that's before someone walks down the fridge or freezer aisle). As a result, EDA tends to be better suited for lab-based studies where you can control the participants' behaviour. Getting a participant to sit down and watch an advert, view a website or even a video of someone completing a shop means that their EDA is not likely to spike for any extraneous reasons.

Electroencephalography (EEG) EEG is currently the most commonly used commercial neuromarketing technique. Whenever we have any thought, neurons in our brain communicate with one another, and the junctions where these neurons meet are called synapses. Most of this information is transferred chemically, but it is also transferred electronically. Participants are asked to wear a cap (a little like a swimming cap) which contains a series of electrodes which act like small voltmeters that can detect when synapses in our brain fire. Depending on the system used, the number of electrodes used will vary between 16 and 256, with the more expensive systems having a higher number of sensors.

As these electrodes are detecting electrical changes, researchers can detect them almost instantaneously, meaning that EEG provides researchers with excellent temporal data, focusing on the timing of changes in the brain.[46] However, as EEG works by measuring changes in electrical activity from the surface of the brain, this means that it can only detect activity from the cortical areas near the surface[47] as anything else is too deep. Also, as the sensors are located on the scalp, it can make it hard to triangulate the precise area the brain activity is coming from, hence EEG has poor spatial resolution. It may only mean the reading is out by a small amount, but with different regions of the brain performing very different functions, small differences make a big difference.

From a marketing perspective, EEG is an exciting tool in the research arsenal as new research suggests that it can implicitly gauge a number of both theoretical and practical measures. From a theoretical perspective, EEG can be used to measure how participants' arousal and engagement levels change when they're thinking or making decisions.[48, 49] Yet some scientists, including Aroa Costa-Feito, argue that EEG can be used to measure constructs such as trust, risk, reward and willingness to buy in real-life situations that have truly excited marketers,[50] although more research still needs to be conducted in this area.

The challenge for marketers is that pure EEG data is highly complicated to analyse, requiring researchers to calculate the event-related potential (ERP) or spontaneous activity. Despite what marketers may think, there is no one region of the brain connected with buying. Neuroscientists need to analyse the output from all the electrodes and interpret the patterns, which is relatively subjective.[51] In response, a number of companies have created commercial units that are mobile, so can be worn as people walk around a shop, but more helpfully, automatically provide standardized outputs such as: excitement, boredom, frustration and immersion. You could ask a participant to watch an advert and instantly see how their excitement or boredom levels change over time.

The challenge is that the algorithms these units use to predict excitement, boredom, frustration and immersion are commercially sensitive. Other scientists are not able to check if they work and peer into the black box. As such, some leading neuroscientists, like Thomas Ramsøy, are sceptical of their reliability and validity.[52] It is also worth noting that most commercial units have between 6–16 electrodes whereas most academic EEG units will be using 64 electrodes or more. No matter how the algorithm works, this will always diminish the spatial resolution of the output. However, as marketers are not trying to publish research, the output just needs to be 'good enough' to give them an advantage over their competition. If the price of these units is right (and they can cost less than £1,000), many companies may think that is good enough for them.

Functional Magnetic Resonance Imaging (fMRI) Currently, fMRI is the most sophisticated and also the most expensive neuromarketing technique that is regularly used. Unlike EEG, which works by measuring changes in electrical activity, fMRI works by measuring changes in blood flow. In simple terms, when an area of the brain is active, it needs more energy in the form of oxygen. An fMRI signal detects these changes in blood flow and commonly records them as a BOLD signal (blood-oxygen-level-dependent). By measuring changes in the BOLD signal, neuroscientists can work out which areas are active, and as scientists know which area of the brain is associated with different functions, they can make inferences about how participants are reacting.

The key distinction between fMRI and EEG is that whereas EEG has excellent temporal resolution and poor spatial resolution, fMRI is the opposite. It can provide researchers with excellent spatial resolution but poor temporal resolution. As neurons become active, they need more oxygen, but the blood doesn't instantly flow to them, known as the '*hemodynamic lag*', which is usually between two and three seconds.[53] To make matters worse, the algorithms used to help clean the data average the data out over a couple of seconds, further worsening the temporal data.

But is fMRI a useful tool for marketers? The answer seems to be yes. When a team of researchers led by Simone Kühn showed participants a series of adverts for chocolate bars, using data collected via fMRI, they were able to predict which bars would sell best in a supermarket far more accurately than explicitly asking participants which advert or bar they liked the most.[54] Similarly, when Gregory Berns and colleagues analysed how participants reacted when they heard new pop songs in an fMRI scanner, they found that the more activity in the nucleus accumbens, the better a song performed in the charts. Once again, this was a better predictor of sales than how much participants claimed they liked the songs.[55]

Unfortunately, fMRI does come with a number of downsides. While EEG units can cost as little as €1,000 and studies cost a few thousand, fMRI machines will typically cost between €1–3 million and the cost of a commercial fMRI study starts from around €30,000 but can easily reach €200,000+. Whether this provides value for money, especially when compared to traditional market research methods, is still up for debate. The ecological validity of an fMRI study is about as poor as it is possible to get. Participants are required to lie perfectly still in a small, claustrophobia-inducing metal tube while a machine is making noises of 100–110dB (about the same noise level as standing 1m away from a speaker in a nightclub. If they move their head, the experiment can potentially be ruined. When Hilke Plassmann asked participants to drink $90 wine via a long plastic straw to see how their brain reacts,[56] it's almost impossible to think of a more artificial environment to drink expensive wine. And as there is no buying region of the brain, interpreting the output of fMRI is even more complicated than analysing EEG data.

Closing thoughts

It is an unfortunate truth that running a business is risky. While it is impossible to eliminate all risk, a well-designed research project can significantly reduce it. However, it is important to understand that market research is not the same as academic research, even if the two are often confused. Academic research is focused on uncovering how the world works and as such, it requires a high level of certainty before any results are published, which explains why it tends to be slow and expensive. In contrast, market research aims to reduce the risk associated with making business decisions. It is not about achieving perfection but delivering a useful answer within the time and budgetary constraints. There is no value in producing a flawless research project that took twelve months to complete if a decision needs to be made in three months.

As a result, a good research project will involve trade-offs. To make the right decision, researchers must understand the strengths and weaknesses of the different approaches and carefully consider how each compromise will affect the quality of the conclusions. Market research may not always be exciting or glamorous, but without it, businesses are far more likely to make costly mistakes, which will give their rivals an opportunity to steal market share.

> **KEY POINTS**
>
> - Where possible, it is usually cheaper and quicker to use secondary data, information collected by someone else, rather than gathering primary data (information that you collect yourself).
> - When choosing secondary data sources, businesses should look beyond traditional databases. Creative options, such as keyword search tools, can reveal valuable insights.
> - Primary data can be classified as either qualitative or quantitative data.
>   - Quantitative data includes information that can be counted or measured numerically.
>   - Qualitative data refers to non-numerical data, often gathered from methods such as focus groups or interviews.
> - The most used primary data collection methods include questionnaires, focus groups and interviews. However, these techniques are vulnerable to social desirability bias.

- To evaluate how well a market research study can be generalized, the AFECT framework is a useful tool for predicting replication success.
    - Does the research ANALYSE behavioural data?
    - Is the participant in the same FRAME OF MIND in the study as they are when they make a purchase decision?
    - What ENVIRONMENT was the research conducted in?
    - Was it a COVERT study?
    - What TIMEFRAME did participants have to make a decision?
- New research techniques such as eye-tracking, facial tracking and in-store surveillance can accurately reveal how people shop, such as what people notice or ignore while shopping. These methods help reduce social desirability bias but are more expensive and are more complex from a legal and ethical perspective.
- To understand which product features consumers value most, researchers often use a conjoint analysis, although this requires specialist software.
- Neuromarketing represents the cutting edge of market research. Three commonly used neuromarketing techniques include:
    - Electrodermal activity (EDA) or Galvanic Skin Response (GSR), which measures changes in participants' arousal levels by detecting changes in how much they sweat.
    - EEG (Electroencephalography), which measures electrical changes in the brain. It provides excellent temporal resolution but poor spatial resolution. By identifying which areas of the brain are active, researchers can then infer what the participant is thinking.
    - fMRI (Functioning magnetic resonance imaging), which measures change in blood flow in the brain. Knowing which areas of the brain require more blood flow provides insight into emotional and cognitive responses.

PUTTING THEORY INTO PRACTICE

1. You are the head of research at a company that designs and manufactures luxury hair products. A member of the marketing team pitches a new product concept. How would you design a research project to evaluate whether there is consumer demand for the proposed product?

2. Find an experiment in one of the latest marketing journals. Do you think the findings would replicate in a commercial context? Justify your choice.
3. When do you think it would make commercial sense for a business to use neuromarketing techniques to tackle research questions?
4. Identify an academic study that meets all of Philip Graves' AFECT criteria. To what extent can studies that do not meet all their criteria still provide value in market research?
5. Marketers often rely on a combination of both qualitative and quantitative research methods. What type of research questions are most effectively addressed using a qualitative research approach?
6. You are working for an advertising agency, and you have been tasked with evaluating a new television advertising campaign. Draft a brief proposal outlining your research design, justifying your choices to the client.
7. You have been tasked with investigating shoppers' brand attitude towards Nescafé, a coffee brand. How would you determine the appropriate sample size for your research project? What are the most important variables you need to consider?
8. While innovative research methods such as conjoint analysis, eye-tracking and neuromarketing often generate excitement amongst marketers, under what conditions might traditional research methods be more suitable, effective or viable?
9. What ethical, legal and moral responsibilities do market researchers have when using data collected from customers' internet search histories, hidden cameras in stores or covert facial tracking technology?

SUGGESTIONS FOR FURTHER READING

Saunders, M., Lewis, P., & Thornhill, A. (2023). *Research methods for business students*. Pearson education.

References

1. Crozier, A., Ashihara, H., & Tomás-Barbéran, F. (2011). *Teas, cocoa and coffee: Plant secondary metabolites and health*. John Wiley & Sons.
2. Wilde, T. (2023, March 27). Former Sims lead says men would lie about how they played during focus groups: 'Actually, what you did is you redecorated that bathroom'. PC Gamer.

https://www.pcgamer.com/former-sims-lead-says-men-would-lie-about-how-they-played-during-focus-groups-actually-what-you-did-is-you-redecorated-that-bathroom/?utm_source=facebook.com&utm_campaign=socialflow&utm_medium=social&fbclid=IwAR0ycqeWTSLZiQ6qIfCntCMdCcDAzYwrFwT_-xZiY6rKEoZOLYfeNQUKVXg (archived at https://perma.cc/MM67-C9HM)

3 Nenycz-Thiel, M., Beal, V., Ludwichowska, G., & Romaniuk, J. (2013). Investigating the accuracy of self-reports of brand usage behavior. *Journal of Business Research*, 66(2), 224–232. https://doi.org/10.1016/j.jbusres.2012.07.016 (archived at https://perma.cc/84GF-8JBA)

4 Albrecht, C. M., Hattula, S., & Lehmann, D. R. (2017). The relationship between consumer shopping stress and purchase abandonment in task-oriented and recreation-oriented consumers. *Journal of the Academy of Marketing Science*, 45, 720–740.

5 Reed, D., Lowenstein, G., & Kalyanaraman, S. (1999). Mixing virtue and vice: Combining the immediacy effect and the diversification heuristic. *Journal of Behavioral Decision Making*, 12(4), 257–273. https://doi.org/10.1002/(SICI)1099-0771(199912)12:43.0.CO;2-6 (archived at https://perma.cc/Z9CE-SY5X)

6 Read, D. & van Leeuwen B. (1998). Predicting hunger: The effects of appetite and delay on choice. *Organizational Behavior and Human Decision Processes*, 76(2), 189–205. https://doi.org/10.1006/obhd.1998.2803 (archived at https://perma.cc/HN8S-2C9W)

7 Roethlisberger, F. J. & Dickson, W. J. (1939). *Management and the worker*. Harvard Univ. Press.

8 Levitt, S. D. & List, J. A. (2011). Was there really a Hawthorne effect at the Hawthorne plant? An analysis of the original illumination experiments. *American Economic Journal: Applied Economics*, 3(1), 224–238.

9 Schwartz, D., Fischhoff, B., Krishnamurti, T., & Sowell, F. (2013). The Hawthorne effect and energy awareness. *Proceedings of the National Academy of Sciences*, 110(38), 15242–15246

10 Zwebner, Y. & Schrift, R. Y. (2020). On my own: The aversion to being observed during the preference-construction stage. *Journal of Consumer Research*, 47(4), 475–499. doi.org/10.1093/jcr/ucab023 (archived at https://perma.cc/W246-5KJ3)

11 Dubois, P., Albuquerque, P., Allais, O., Bonnet, C., Bertail, P., Combris, P., Lahlou, S., Rigal, N., Ruffieux B., & Chandon P. (2021). Effects of front-of-pack labels on the nutritional quality of supermarket food purchases: Evidence from a large-scale randomized controlled trial. *Journal of the Academy of Marketing Science*, 49(1), 119–138.

12 McKay, H. A., Macdonald, H. M., Nettlefold, L., Weatherson, K., Gray, S. M., Bauman, A., ... & Sims Gould, J. (2023). What is the 'voltage drop' when an effective health promoting intervention for older adults—Choose to Move (Phase 3)—Is implemented at broad scale?. *Plos one*, 18(5), e0268164.

13 Cuthbertson, A. (2024, April 9). Solar eclipse 2024: Searches for 'blind' and 'eye damage' surge in US. *Independent*. https://www.independent.co.uk/tech/solar-eclipse-2024-blind-eye-damage-b2525562.html (archived at https://perma.cc/3N7X-W5XK)

14 Stephens-Davidowitz, S. (2017). *Everybody lies: What the internet can tell us about who we really are*. Bloomsbury Publishing.

15 Stephens-Davidowitz, S. (2014). The cost of racial animus on a black candidate: Evidence using Google search data. *Journal of Public Economics*, 118, 26–40.
16 Myers, D. G. & Lamm, H. (1976). The group polarization phenomenon. *Psychological Bulletin*, 83(4), 602.
17 Graves, P. (2013). *Consumerology, new edition: The truth about consumers and the psychology of shopping*. Hachette UK.
18 Asch, S. E. (1956). Studies of independence and conformity. A minority of one against a unanimous majority. *Psychological Monographs*, 70(9), 1–70. https://doi.org/10.1037/h0093718 (archived at https://perma.cc/L9TD-92AC)
19 Halcomb, E. J. & Davidson, P. M. (2006). Is verbatim transcription of interview data always necessary?. *Applied Nursing Research*, 19(1), 38–42.
20 Bruner, G. C., Hensel, P. J., & James, K. E. (2005). *Marketing scales handbook*. Chicago, IL: American Marketing Association.
21 Likert, R. (1932). A technique for the measurement of attitudes. *Archives of Psychology*, 22.
22 Simms, L. J., Zelazny, K., Williams, T. F., & Bernstein, L. (2019). Does the number of response options matter? Psychometric perspectives using personality questionnaire data. *Psychological Assessment*, 31(4), 557.
23 Dalal, D. K., Carter, N. T., & Lake, C. J. (2014). Middle response scale options are inappropriate for ideal point scales. *Journal of Business and Psychology*, 29, 463–478.
24 Simms, L. J., Zelazny, K., Williams, T. F., & Bernstein, L. (2019). Does the number of response options matter? Psychometric perspectives using personality questionnaire data. *Psychological Assessment*, 31(4), 557.
25 Tjomas, M. & Kyung E.J. (2019). Slider scale or text box: How response format shapes responses. *Journal of Consumer Research*, 45 (6), 1274–1293, https://doi.org/10.1093/jcr/ucy057 (archived at https://perma.cc/BC5F-T67J)
26 The Electoral Commission (2013) Referendum on Scottish Independence: Question Testing. https://www.electoralcommission.org.uk/sites/default/files/pdf_file/Ipsos-MORI-Scotland-question-testing-report-24-January-2013.pdf (archived at https://perma.cc/5CQH-JY2U)
27 Bruschke, J. & Divine, L. (2017). Debunking Nixon's radio victory in the 1960 election: Re-analyzing the historical record and considering currently unexamined polling data. *The Social Science Journal*, 54(1), 67–75.
28 Parkrun (2013, September 29). 19 years of parkrun. https://blog.parkrun.com/uk/2023/09/29/19-years-of-parkrun/ (archived at https://perma.cc/4VKZ-GTQM)
29 Bradley, V. C., Kuriwaki, S., Isakov, M., Sejdinovic, D., Meng, X. L., & Flaxman, S. (2021). Unrepresentative big surveys significantly overestimated US vaccine uptake. *Nature*, 600(7890), 695–700. https://doi.org/10.1038/s41586-021-04198-4 (archived at https://perma.cc/H27Z-AEKJ)
30 Glynn, A. N. (2013). What can we learn with statistical truth serum? Design and analysis of the list experiment. *Public Opinion Quarterly*, 77(S1), 159–172.
31 Bolton, D. (2016, May 4). Netflix reveals the shadowy experiments they use to get you to watch their shows. *Independent*. https://www.independent.co.uk/tech/netflix-thumbnails-ab-testing-pictures-experiments-design-watch-a7012966.html (archived at https://perma.cc/KM64-5CVK)

32 Eggers, F., Sattler, H., Teichert, T., & Völckner, F. (2022). Choice-based conjoint analysis. In C. Homburg, M. Klarmann, & A. Vomberg (Eds.), *Handbook of Market Research* (pp. 781–819). Springer. https://doi.org/10.1007/978-3-319-57413-4_23 (archived at https://perma.cc/UWX7-Y39A)

33 Toubia, O. (2018). Conjoint analysis. In *Handbook of Marketing Analytics: Methods and Applications in Marketing Management, Public Policy, and Litigation Support*, 59–75.

34 Data Protection Act 2018, c. 12. https://www.legislation.gov.uk/ukpga/2018/12/contents/enacted (archived at https://perma.cc/S7NW-HYTC)

35 van Herpen, E., van den Broek, E., van Trijp, H. C., & Yu, T. (2016). Can a virtual supermarket bring realism into the lab? Comparing shopping behavior using virtual and pictorial store representations to behavior in a physical store. *Appetite*, 107, 196–207.

36 Chang, E., Kim, H. T., & Yoo, B. (2020). Virtual reality sickness: a review of causes and measurements. *International Journal of Human–Computer Interaction*, 36(17), 1658–1682.

37 van der Wel, P., & Van Steenbergen, H. (2018). Pupil dilation as an index of effort in cognitive control tasks: A review. *Psychonomic Bulletin & Review*, 25, 2005–2015.

38 Bradley, M. M., Miccoli, L., Escrig, M. A., & Lang, P. J. (2008). The pupil as a measure of emotional arousal and autonomic activation. *Psychophysiology*, 45(4), 602–607.

39 Gladstone, J. J., Matz, S. C., & Lemaire, A. (2019). Can psychological traits be inferred from spending? Evidence from transaction data. *Psychological Science*, 30(7), 1087–1096.

40 Hill, K. (2022, August 11). How Target figured out a teen girl was pregnant before her father did. *Forbes*. https://www.forbes.com/sites/kashmirhill/2012/02/16/how-target-figured-out-a-teen-girl-was-pregnant-before-her-father-did/ (archived at https://perma.cc/TWK3-8GSC)

41 Brewer, H. R., Hirst, Y., Chadeau-Hyam, M., Johnson, E., Sundar, S., & Flanagan, J. M. (2023). Association between purchase of over-the-counter medications and ovarian cancer diagnosis in the cancer loyalty card study (CLOCS): Observational case-control study. *JMIR Public Health and Surveillance*, 9(1), e41762. https://doi.org/10.2196/41762 (archived at https://perma.cc/APV5-LQBP)

42 Babiloni, F. (2012). Consumer neuroscience: A new area of study for biomedical engineers. *IEEE Pulse*, 3(3), 21–23. doi:10.1109/MPUL.2012.2189166

43 Dawson, M.E., Schell, A.M. &. Filion D.L. (2017). *The electrodermal system*. Cambridge University Press, New York, NY, US, 217–243.

44 Białowąs, S. & Szyszka, A. (2019). Measurement of electrodermal activity in marketing research. *Managing Economic Innovations–Methods and Instruments*, 73–90.

45 Caruelle, D., Gustafsson, A., Shams, P., & Lervik-Olsen, L. (2019). The use of electrodermal activity (EDA) measurement to understand consumer emotions–A literature review and a call for action. *Journal of Business Research*, 104, 146–160. https://doi.org/10.1016/j.jbusres.2019.06.041 (archived at https://perma.cc/E4NN-H87B)

46 Ramsøy, T. Z. (2015). *Introduction to neuromarketing & consumer neuroscience*. Neurons Inc.

47 Ramsøy, T. Z. (2015). *Introduction to neuromarketing & consumer neuroscience*. Neurons Inc.
48 Bazzani, A., Ravaioli, S., Trieste, L., Faraguna, U., & Turchetti, G. (2020). Is EEG suitable for marketing research? A systematic review. *Front Neuroscience*, 14. https://doi.org/10.3389/fnins.2020.594566 (archived at https://perma.cc/5CF6-ZQQA)
49 Kenning, P. H. & Plassmann, H. (2005). NeuroEconomics: An overview from an economic perspective. *Brain Research Bulletin*, 67(5), 343–354. https://doi.org/10.1016/j.brainresbull.2005.07.006 (archived at https://perma.cc/4V7T-J7ZA)
50 Costa-Feito, A., González-Fernández, A. M., Rodríguez-Santos, C., & Cervantes-Blanco, M. (2023). Electroencephalography in consumer behaviour and marketing: A science mapping approach. *Humanities and Social Sciences Communications*, 10(1), 1–13.
51 Ceylan, B., TÜZÜN, S., & Aydın, A. K. A. N. (2020). Detection of consumer preferences using EEG signals. *International Journal of Applied Mathematics Electronics and Computers*, 8(4), 289–294.
52 Ramsøy T. Z. (2015) *Introduction to neuromarketing & consumer neuroscience*. Neurons, Inc. Rørvig, Denmark.
53 Ramsøy T. Z. (2015) *Introduction to neuromarketing & consumer neuroscience*. Neurons, Inc. Rørvig, Denmark.
54 Kühn, S. Strelow, E., & Gallinat, J. (2016). Multiple 'buy buttons' in the brain: Forecasting chocolate sales at point-of-sale based on functional brain activation using fMRI. *NeuroImage*, 136, 122–128.
55 Berns, G. S. & Moore, S. E. (2012). A neural predictor of cultural popularity. *Journal of Consumer Psychology*, 22(1), 154–160.
56 Plassmann, H., O'Doherty, J., Shiv, B., & Rangel, A. (2008). Marketing actions can modulate neural representations of experienced pleasantness. *Proceedings of the National Academy of Sciences*, 105(3), 1050–1054.

INDEX

Note: Page numbers in *italics* refer to figures or tables.

'28-Day Ab Challenge' 351

A/B testing 379
Aaker, J 136–37
Ackerman Method 345–46
'Active Defence System' 323
Adcock, Philip 162, 261
advertising 3–4
   advertisement imagery 160–63
   behaviour change 36–42, 154–55
   branding and 158–68
   co-branding campaign 159
   expectations and 20
   introduction 153
   print and billboard advertising 159–60
   programmes and adverts 155–58, *156*, *157*
   reactance theory 168–69
   risk of avoidance 170
   rules and limitations 163–68, *164*
AFECT criteria 363–68, *367*
Agnew, Phil 348
AI (Artificial Intelligence) 384–86
Alachua County 209–10
Alaoui, M. D. 257
Alapcin 141
Aldi and Lidl 253
AMA (American Marketing Association) 124
Amazon 13, 133, 293–94, 297, 377
Anderson, James 251
anecdotal evidence 112, 267
Angles 102
Anglo-Saxon 102–03, *102*
Apple 87, 132, 133
'Areas of Interest' (AOI) 385
Areni, Charles 271, 273
Ariely, Dan 203, 213
Aristoff, Mandy 160
Aron, Arthur 270
Asch, Solomon 373
AT&T 134
Atkinson, Richard 78
Atlanta 264
attention 8–13, 22–23
   advertising and 11–12
   bottom-up 10–11, 12
   definition 8
   inattentional blindness 9
   in marketing 10–12
   subliminal advertising 13
   top-down 9–10, 12
   see also perception
attentional blink 143–44
Australia 13, 14, 325
Axe/Lynx 167

B2B 292, 341
   customers 209
B2C
   customers 209
   domain 292
Babiloni, F. 388
Baileys 139
Balthazar 207
Bang & Olufsen 17
Bangor University 118
Bargh, John 272
Baymard Institute 291
BBC 83, 133
BBH Labs 49
behaviour change 36–42, 154–55
   implementation intentions 36–37
   motivation and sustainable behaviour 40–42
behavioural science 5
   vs consumer psychology 5
Behaviourist Manifesto 69
Beichert, Maximilian 186
Bellizzi, Joseph 74
Beltramin, Richard 341
Ben & Jerry's Ice Cream 133
Bernays, Edward 50–51
Berns, Gregory 391
Big Five personality traits 53–55, *57*
bimodal distribution 53
Binet, Les 154–55
Birmingham 115
BMW 141
Boden 237
Body Shop 258
BOLD signal (blood-oxygen-level-dependent) 391
Bordeaux First Growth Mouton Rothschild 207
Bosch 141
bottom-up processing 14–15
Bower, Gordon 110
Bradlow, Eric 250, 254
brand commitment 137
brand management 124, 129
brand manager 126, 129, 138

Brand Personality Scale 136
brand trust 137
branding
    brand myths 138–39
    brand ownership: face of brand 133–34
    brand personality 135–38
    brand ritual 139–40
    creating emotional brands 128–30
    introduction 124
    logo formation 130–33
    product expectations 125–26
    significance of associations 126–27, *127*
    social norms and 140–41
    sonic brands 134–35
    strength measurement 142–45
    unique proposition 127–28
Brenda Soars 266
Brewer, Hannah 387
Briggs, Katherine 52
Bristol, Terry 74
Brown, Haakon 165
Burrows, Lara 272
Burson, K. A. 268
Business Horizons 31
Buy One Get One Free deal (BOGOF) 223–29, *225*, 236–37
    communicating value 232–33

Cacioppo, John 157, 333–34
Cadbury 70–71
Cambridge Analytica 59
Canada 325
Cancer Research UK 164
Capilano Bridge experiment 270–71
Captain Birdseye 317
Caramel chocolate 324
Cartier 139
Cassar, Mario 110
CBSI. *See* Cognitive Brand Strength Index (CBSI)
CCTV (Closed-Circuit Television) 382
Chabris, Christopher 9
Charlotte, Queen 181
ChatGPT 59
Chattopadhyay, A. 157
Chen, Mark 256, 272
Chen, R. 258
CHF 20 303
CHF 25 303
CHF 5 303
Chilean Sea Bass 127
Chintagunta, P. K 304
Chomp 324
Churchill, Winston 103
Clark, Michal 110
classical conditioning 69–71
Claudius (Roman emperor) 102
Claus, Jasper 13

Clinton, Hillary 370
Cobra Effect 38–39
Coca-Cola 70, 81, 88, 127, 128–29, 143
Cognitive Brand Strength Index (CBSI) 144
Colonel Sanders 317
colour psychology 19–20, 24
competence (SDT) 32–33
consumer psychology 3–6
    applications 5–6
    definition 4–5
    vs neuromarketing 4–5
COOP & Migros (Switzerland) 255
COOP.ch 293
copycat packaging strategy 72
copywriting
    abstract vs concrete language 103–06
    apologizing: elements to comprise 115–17
    challenges in finding right words 101–03, *102*
    message framing and healthcare 108–09, *109*
    numbers usage 112–15
    power of story 110–12
    prospect theory 106–07
Cornell University 198
corporate marketing 126
Costa Coffee 131
Costa-Feito, Aroa 390
Cova 257
Covid-19 pandemic 3
Cox, Anthony 71
Craft 128
Crans 369
Cummings, Geoff 368
curiosity and novelty 36–37
customer loyalty 137, 138

'Daily Gainz' 132
De Beers 154
decision-making 4, 14–15, 57–58
decompression zone 252
decoy effect 202–03, *203*
Delboeuf illusion 320
Delhi 39
Democratic Republic of Congo 112–13
Den Bergh, Bram van 263
Denmark 102
'DERMO-EXPERTISE' 323
descriptive norm 140–41
DiCaprio, Leonardo 139
Dichter, Ernest 50, 51
Dijksterhuis, Ap 272
DIN 210–11
Disney World 294
'*Distractor Devaluation Effect*' 12, 170
Dolce & Gabbana 167
Dolega, Les 274
Domino's Pizza 20

Doyen, Stéphane 273
Dresher, Melvin 184
Drew, T. 9
drink-drive campaign 163
Dubois, Pierre 367
Duff, B. R. L. 170
Duolingo 34–35, 77
Dutton, Donald 270

Earl Grey 197
EAST framework 348, 349–50
EAST task 377
Ebbinghaus, Hermann 86, 87
ECG 113
e-commerce platforms 186
Economist, The (magazine) 165, 203
Ekman, Paul 162
Elaboration Likelihood Model 157
Elder, Ryan 161
Electrodermal Activity (EDA) 388–89
electroencephalogram (EEG) 113, 265, 388, 389–90
Elias, Lorin 160
Elmex 128
emotional relationship 129–30, 133
English (language) 102–03, 133
Esso petrol 51
Estes and Streicher 264
EU (European Union) 181, 191, 209, 325
Euromonitor 369
event-related potential (ERP) 390
Everybody lies (Stephens-Davidowitz) 370
Eyeball count 385

Faber, R. J. 170
Facebook 59, 181
facial expressions 162
Fader, Peter 250, 254
Falk, Armin 342
fast-moving consumer goods (FMGCs) 133, 141, 226, 312
fear of missing out (FOMO) 296
FedEx 134
fentanyl 125
Field, Peter 154–55
Financial Times 49
First Fixation Duration (FFD) 385
first-order conditioning 70
Fisher, Ronald 368
Fiverr 132
Flake chocolate 324
Flood, Merrill 184
Florida 209–10
fMRI scanner 206–07
Food Dudes 78
Fortnum & Mason 341
Four Ps 197

France 325
French (language) 133
fresh start effect 38, 351
Freudian marketing 50–52
'Fruit & Veggies' 263
functional magnetic resonance imaging (fMRI) 388, 390–91
FundRazr 181

Galvanic Skin Response (GSR) 265, 388–89
gamification 33–35
    apps and leaderboards 34–35
    intermittent reinforcement 35
    team rewards 34
    see also Self-Determination Theory (SDT)
Gamliel, Eyal 107
Gaviscon 318
General Data Protection Act (2018) 382–83
General Mills 51
George III (King) 181
Georgia 264
Germany 102, 141
Gestalt effect 319
Girard Perregaux 257
Goetz, Ernest 103–04
GoFundMe 181
Gold Blend 202
Goldsmith, Ronald 58
Google 130, 370–71
Google Street View 383
Gorilla 374, 383, 384
Gorilla Experimental Platform 6
'Grab & Go shopper' 260
Graves, Philip 363, 372
Grewal 255
Griskevicius, Vladas 61
'*Gruen Effect*' 252
'*Gruen Transfer*' 252
Gruen, Victor 252
Guinness 139
Gustafsson, A. 252
Gustav III, King of Sweden 362–63

halo effect 322–23
Hargreaves, David 272
Haribo 132
Harrell, Gilbert 251
Harvard Business Review 137
Harvey, Gareth 365
Hawaiian Fashion Guild 154
Hawthorne Effect 366
Heath, Chip 114
Hebb, D. O. 126
Hebb, Donald 82
Heckler, Susan E. 155
'*hemodynamic lag*' 391
Herpen, Erica van 383

Herrington, Duncan 269
Herstein, Ram 107
heuristics 15–16
Hill, Dan 160
'hi-lo' pricing strategy 237–38
Hirsch, Alan 265
Hjortsjö, Carl-Herman 162
Hong Kong University 186
Hui 254, 256
Huixin Deng 190
Human Associative Memory (HAM) 81–82
Humble, Rod 363
Hutchison, Jennifer 160
Hutt, Michael 251

IAT. *See* Implicit-Association Test (IAT)
IBM 134
Ibrahim, Blend 182
Iceland 251
IGT. *See* Iowa Gambling Task (IGT)
Ikea 131
'illusory truth effect' 337
Imperial College London 387
implementation intentions 36–37
Implicit-Association Test (IAT) 142–43, 377
impulse purchases 260–62
inattentional blindness 9
Indiegogo 181
informative campaigns 165
injunctive norm 140–41
'the inoculation effect' 337
Instagram 181, 183, 185, 191
Institute of Practitioners in Advertising 154
insula 197
Intel 135
International Dog Day 191
International Talk Like a Pirate Day 190
intrinsic motivation 32–33, 35, 39, 42
    vs extrinsic motivation 32–33, 35
Iowa Gambling Task (IGT) 144
iPhone 132
Ishango bone 112–13
Ivory Soap, 51
Iyengar, S. S. 253

James-Bond 295
Jiang, Y. 101
Johnson, Dwayne (the Rock) 139
JP Chenet 313–14
Jung, Carl 52
Just Noticeable Difference (JND) 21–22, 223
Jutes 102

Kahneman, Daniel 107
Kalff, Christopher 250
Kalyanaraman, S. 364–65
Karremans, Johan 13

Kellaris, James 71
Kennedy, John F. 376
KickStarter campaigns 140
Kim, David 271, 273
Kit-Kat 139
Kiva 167
Klum, Heidi 139
Knippenberg, Ap 272
Knoferle, Klemens 269
Knoll, Johannes 188
Koenigs, Michael 4
Krishna, Aradhna 161
Krispy Kreme 132
Kühn, Simone 391

L'Oréal 323
Lantz, Lee 127
Larson, Jeffrey 250
Las Vegas Casino 265
Latin 102
Laurent and Vanhuele 205
learning and memory 68–90
    behaviourism 69–76
    classical conditioning 69–71
    cognitive learning 77–78
    creating lasting memories 81–86
    fixed interval schedule 76
    forgetting 86–87, 87
    long-term memory (LTM) 80–81
    operant conditioning 73–75, 74
    reinforce behaviours 75
    repetition 83–84
    retrieval cues and context-dependent memory 87–88
    sensory memory 79
    short-term memory (STM) 79–80, 79
    social learning 77–78
    stimulus generation 71–72
    variable ratio schedule 76
Lehrer, Jonah 80–81
Lepper, M. R. 253
Leung, Fine 186–87
Levenson, Bob 158
Levitt, Steven 366
Leykin, A. 256
Liadeli, Georgia 182
Likert Scale 374
Likert, Rensis 374
Lindisfarne 102
Lindstrom, Martin 263
LinkedIn 181
List, John 366
Liyin Jin 190
Louvre 160
Lowenstein 364–65
loyalty programmes 108
'Lucky Strike' cigarettes 50

Lucozade 132
Lyft 132, 205

MacInnis, Deborah 155
Maeng, A 257
magnetoencephalography (MEG) 388
Malali, Morteza 113
market research
    AFECT criteria 363–68, 367
    quantitative data 374–91, *378*, *381*
    quantitative vs qualitative data 371
    secondary data 369–71
marketing campaign 101, 129, 154
The Marketing Scales Handbook Vols. 1–12 374
Maslow's Hierarchy of Needs 30–32
    levels 30–31
    limitations 31–32
    self-transcendence 31
    see also Self-Determination Theory (SDT)
Mathur, M. 157
Matthes, Jörg 188
Maxwell House 324
Mayo, Elton 366
McDermid, Charles 31
McDonnell, John 266
McGuire, William 337
McKendrick, Jennifer 272
'Meats & Treats' 263
Mechanical Turk (mTurk) 377
Medial Orbotofrontal Cortex 207
Mehrabian, Albert 251, 343
memory. *See* learning and memory
mental availability 138
Mercedes-Benz 141
Meurs, Lex 160
Microsoft 162
midazolam 125
Migros 293
Milk Marketing Board 138
Miller, Geoffrey 60
Milliman, Ronald 269
The Million Pound Drop (TV quiz show) 108
Millward Brown 158
Milosavljevic, Milica 10
MINDSPACE approach 348–49, 350, 353
Minolta SLR camera 203
Mintel 369
mobile phones 110
Monster 363
Mont Blanc 114
Montana 369
Morales 255
morphine 125
Mother's Day 190–91
motivation 29–43
    Cobra Effect 38–39
    definition 29–30

fresh start effect 38
hunger 30
intrinsic vs extrinsic 32–33
novelty 36
Self-Determination Theory 32–33
sustainable behaviour 40–42
Mount Everest 114, 115
mountain biking 40
Myers, Isabel 52
Myers-Briggs Type Indicator (MBTI) 52–53

'Navigation Simulators' 384
Nenycz-Thiel, Magda 364
Nescafé Azera 324
Nespresso 202
Nestlé 202
Netflix 134–35, 379–80
neuromarketing 4–5
neuroscience 128
New Mexico 250
New York 118, 198, 294–95
New York Roll 139
New York World, The 181
Nguyen, Cathy 159
Nguyen, Huy 113
Nivea 131
Nixon, Richard 376
Noble 255
Nordfält 255
normal distribution 53
Norman French 102–03
North America 293
North American shoppers 211
North, Adrian 272
Northumberland 102
novelty and curiosity 36–37

O'Donnell, Michael 272
O'Guinn 257
Obama, Barack 370–71
Ogilvy Consulting 169
Old Norse 102
Old Spice 167
Oliveira, João 183
Olsen, Douglas 11
online shopping 68–69
    customers, conversion of 292–95
    navigating visitors 290–92
    product photography 299–303
    recommendations, testimonials
      and reviews 297–99
    scarcity appeals 295–96
    webpage 287–90
operant conditioning 73–75, *74*
Oral-B 128
'*order 6 x 6-inch Subways and get the 7th
    free*' 231

Oreos 139
Otterbring, T 252

packaging and perception 15–19
    taste 17–19
    touch 16–17
    vision 19–20
packaging, psychology of
    packaging 321–24
    secondary packaging 324–25
    visual salience and customer attention 312–19
Papua New Guinea 162
paracetamol 125
Paris 160
Pavlov, Ivan 69–70, 71
Payne, Collin 250
Peak-End Effect 198
Pepsi 4, 128–29, 131, 143
Pepsi Paradox 128–29
perception 14–21
    bottom-up vs top-down 14–15
    definition 14
    expectations 18–20
    marketers vs psychologists 15
    touch, taste, vision 16–20
    see also attention
Pereira, B. 268
personality
    based messaging into action 56–57
    Big Five model 53–55
    and conspicuous consumption 60–61
    and retail behaviour 57–58
    Freudian marketing 50–52
    in marketing 55–56
    MBTI 52–53
    segmentation 49–50
personalized adverts 56, 59
persuasion, science of 333
    experts in 346–48
    likelihood model 333–35, *334*
    negotiations 342–46
    peripheral routes to 348–52
    rational persuasion 335–42
Petty, Richard 157, 333–34
Philippe, Patek 257
Philips Sonicare 7000 34
physical availability 138
Picnic 324
Pizza Hut 20
placebo 125
Plassmann, Hilke 391
Pleasure, Arousal, Dominance (PAD) framework 388
Point of Sale (PoS) displays 259–60, 382–84
Pokémon GO 77
Ponzo illusion 320

Powerball 114
Presenter's Paradox 226
price perception 20–22
    size reduction vs price increase 21
    Weber–Fechner Law 22
Price-Quality Heuristic 206
pricing
    anchoring 212–14, *214*
    asymmetrical dominance 202–03, *203*
    charm pricing 204–06
    comparative pricing 200–01
    compromise effect 203–04
    customers perception 198–200, *200*
    expectation effects 206–07
    precise pricing 209–11, *211*
    services and price 208–09
the primacy effect 336
Prisoner's Dilemma 184
professional marketers 124
Prolific 377
promotional campaigns 183
Proust Effect 267
psychological principles 180–81
psychological processing 14–15
Pulitzer, Joseph 181
p-value 368

Qian Xu 190
QR code 163
qualitative data 371, 372–73, *373*
Qualtrics 374
quantitative data 371

racism 142–43
the recency effect 336
'red 7' 198
Red Bull 126, 132, 362–63
Reed 364–65
relatedness (SDT) 32–33
'retail therapy' 268
reward schedules 35
RFID (radio frequency identification) chips 250, 264
Richardson, Dan 61
Rick, S. I. 268
Ringler, C. 252
Roberts, P. 259
Rodriguez, Maximo 103–04
Roethlisberger, Fritz 366
Romans 102
Romney, Mitt 370
Rose, Natalie 274
Russel, James 251
Rwandan genocides 267

Saad, Gad 60
Sadoski, Mark 103–04

Sahni N. S. 304
Sainsbury 231
Saxons 102
Schmidtke, K. A. 259
Schmitt, Julien 263
Schwarz, N. 260–61
Seasonal Affective Disorder 273
segmentation 49–50
Self-Determination Theory (SDT) 32–33, 34–35, 42
   application in apps 34–35
   autonomy 32
   competence 32
   intrinsic vs extrinsic motivation 32–33
   relatedness 32
sensation and perception 14
Shapiro, Stewart 155
Shell 132
Shiffrin, Richard 78
shopping environment, psychological influences in
   buying something new 258–59
   contagion effect 255–56
   influence of things 263–64
   music, power of 269–73
   olfactory marketing 265–68
   shelf help 256–58
   shoppers 259–60
   store layout and shopping time 254–55, 255
Shreddies 30
Shultz 155
Siegel, Erika 162
Simons, Daniel 9
Simpsons, The 20
'The Sims' 363
Sirianni, N.J 252
smart TVs 110
social media
   building a following 182–84
   change in rules 191–92
   creating engaging posts 189–90
   influencer marketing 181, 185–89
   right timing of posts 190–91
   role in marketing strategy 180–81
social norms 140
Social Presence Theory 183
Sorbonne 367
special offers 222
   communicating value 232–33
   competitions 239–41
   free gift 229–30
   'hi-lo' pricing strategy 237–38
   long-term implications 235–36
   loyalty schemes and discounts 230–32
   price discounts 223–29, 225
   promotional limits 233–34
   promotions, paradox of choice and 234–35
Stanford University 110

Starbucks 202, 324
Starr, Karla 114
Statista 369
statistical evidence 112
Statue of Liberty 181
'steadily decreasing discount' (SDD) 237
Stella Artois 139
Stephens-Davidowitz, Seth 370–71
stimulus generation 71–72
stock keeping units (SKUs) 253–54, 325, 386
Strava 34
Stroebe, Wolfgang 13
Stroop task 201
Strube, Gerhard 250
subliminal advertising 13–14
SurveyMonkey 374
Sweden 362
Swift, Taylor 185
Swiss Cheese Union 138
Switzerland 138, 181, 209, 301, 325

tachistoscope 160
Take Mintel 369
Tamoxol 112
Tanner 257
Tavassoli 155
Tesco (UK) 231, 255, 270, 386
Tetley 132
Think Tony the Tiger 317
Thomas, Nicole 160
Tian, J. 258
TikTok 181, 183
Tim Hortons 202
Time to First Fixation (TTFF) 385
Tinker, Miles 166
Toblerone 21
top-down processing 14–15, 20
Total Fixation Duration (TFD) 385
Townsend and Kahn 299
Trader Joe's 133
Tranel, Daniel 4
transcranial magnetic stimulation (TMS) 388
Triple-Code Model 200, 201
Trump, Donald 59, 370
Tversky, Amos 107
Twining's 139
Twirl 324
Twitter (X) 181, 183

Uber 105, 116–17
UK ParkRuns 376
Underhill, Paco 252
Understanding the new statistics: Effect sizes, confidence intervals, and meta-analysis (Cummings) 368
Unilever 301
University of Chicago 366

Valentine's Day 190
Valette-Florence 257
ventromedial prefrontal cortex (vmPFC) 128–29
Vicary, James 13
Victoria's Secret 267
Vikings 102
visual guidelines 160
vmPFC. *See* ventromedial prefrontal cortex (vmPFC)
'voltage drop' 368
VR glasses 383

Waitrose 258
Wall Street 207
Wang, P. X. 101
Wang, Y. 101
Warlop, Luk 263
Watson, D. G. 259
Watson, John B. 69

Weber–Fechner Law 22
Wedgwood, Josiah 181
White Activ 323
White Perfect 323
Whitehead, Thomas 366
William the Conquer 102
Williams-Sonoma 204
Windows 95 135
Wispa 324
WPP 169
Wyer Jr, R. S. 260–61

Xu, A. J. 260–61
Xu, X. 258

YouTube 168, 181, 185

Zajonc, Robert 84
Zeigarnik principle 231

Looking for another book?

Explore our award-winning books from global business experts in Marketing and Sales

Scan the code to browse

www.koganpage.com/marketing

More books on Marketing and Sales from Kogan Page

ISBN: 9780749474706

ISBN: 9781398611719

ISBN: 9781398608870

ISBN: 9781398618619

www.koganpage.com

From 4 December 2025 the EU Responsible Person (GPSR) is:
eucomply oÜ, Pärnu mnt. 139b – 14, 11317 Tallinn, Estonia
www.eucompliancepartner.com